CLIENT/SERVER INFORMATION SYSTEMS

A BUSINESS-ORIENTED APPROACH

- JAMES E. GOLDMAN
- PHILLIP T. RAWLES
- JULIE R. MARIGA

Purdue University

JOHN WILEY & SONS, INC

New York • Chichester • Weinheim • Brisbane • Toronto • Singapore

ACQUISITIONS EDITOR	Beth Lang Golub
MARKETING MANAGER	Carlise Paulson
SENIOR PRODUCTION EDITOR	Christine Cervoni
ILLUSTRATION EDITOR	Anna Melhorn
ILLUSTRATOR	Curtis A. Snyder

This book was set in Palatino by Digitype and printed and bound by R.R. Donnelley & Sons. The cover was printed by Lehigh Press.

This book is printed on acid-free paper. ∞

Library of Congress Cataloging-in-Publication Data
Goldman, James E.
    Client/server information systems : a business-oriented approach /
James E. Goldman, Phillip T. Rawles, Julie R. Mariga.

      p.   cm.
   Includes index.

    ISBN 0-471-29654-6 (pbk. : alk. paper)
    1. Client/server computing.   2. Computer network architecture.
  3. Business enterprises—Computer networks.   I. Rawles, Phillip T.
II. Mariga, Julie R.   III. Title.
QA76.9.C55G654   1999.
004'.36—dc21
                                   98-33923
                                   CIP

Printed in the United States of America

10 9 8 7 6 5 4 3 2

James E. Goldman:
To Susan, Eric, and Grant

Phillip T. Rawles:
To Cherí

Julie R. Mariga:
To Lori, Tawni, Maxwell, and Michelle
Also, to my parents for all their love and support

PREFACE

The field of information systems has undergone a major paradigm shift from mainframe-oriented, hierarchical information systems architectures to distributed, client/server information systems architectures. However, this transition is far from complete, as information systems architectures continue to evolve to include seamless integration with World Wide Web and Internet technologies as well as more-transparent interoperability with legacy or mainframe systems. Today's resultant information systems architecture is composed of a complicated array of interacting technologies combining elements of client/server, web-based, Internet, intranet, legacy applications, and database management systems. The drive toward reducing total cost of ownership through such initiatives as network computing, thin clients, and net PCs adds yet another integration challenge to information systems architecture design.

Designing such heterogeneous information systems requires sophisticated business-oriented analysis, design, and problem-solving skills. Furthermore, the collaborative computing and multimedia applications that are likely to be executed on these information systems are highly dependent on properly designed networks for successful delivery of interactive content. The interdependency of application and network development for successful deployment of distributed information systems is all too often overlooked by information systems professionals.

In order to effectively design today's highly integrated, distributed client/server information systems, a comprehensive systems engineering approach that incorporates business analysis, application development, database systems integration, distributed network design, and structured technology analysis is required. Such a business-first, technology-last, top-down model was introduced in *Applied Data Communications: A Business-Oriented Approach* by James E. Goldman of Purdue University. Analyzing and designing the underlying network infrastructure of client/server information systems using such an approach was explored in detail in Goldman's *Local Area Networks: A Client/Server Approach.*

Using this same top-down approach while placing an increased emphasis on the analysis, design, integration, and technology choices involved with deploying effective applications over client/server information systems is the mission of *Client/Server Information Systems: A Business-Oriented Approach.* Unlike many of the currently available books and texts on client/server information systems, which

iv

seem to be either too broadly focused and conceptual or too narrowly focused and technical, this text strikes a balance between the two extremes. It offers the reader a structured approach to client/server information systems analysis and design from initial business considerations through final technology choices.

Business process analysis, systems analysis and design, and application development are discussed in terms of their impact on the choices of hardware and software technology that will be integrated into a cohesive client/server information system. This text is not meant to serve as a substitute for an entire systems analysis and development methods textbook. Rather, this text assumes that students or professionals would have already performed an effective systems analysis and design, and are now ready to perform the research necessary to make intelligent decisions as to which hardware, software, and networking technologies should be chosen to actually build, implement, and manage the client/server information system that will meet previously established business objectives in a secure and reliable manner.

■ DESCRIPTION

Client/Server Information Systems: A Business-Oriented Approach provides a thorough explanation of the analysis, design, integration, and technology choices involved with deploying effective applications over client/server information systems. Thorough coverage of designing the network infrastructure over which such applications will travel, as well as managing and securing these client/server information systems, is also included.

The text is divided into four major sections to maximize flexible use by a wide variety of course orientations:

Part 1: Client/Server Architectures and Infrastructure

Part 2: Client/Server Application Development and Deployment

Part 3: Networking Infrastructure

Part 4: Client/Server Information Systems Administration

Thirteen chapters of manageable length allow instructors to pick and choose chapters as appropriate for course content, focus, length, and intended audience.

Client/Server Information Systems: A Business-Oriented Approach is written in a logical, problem-solving style applauded by both students and faculty from academia and industry. The text material is organized into overall architecture or models. By giving students the "big picture" first, the text assists students in understanding how particular individual topics relate to other topics and to the overall scheme of things. The text stresses analytical questioning and problem-solving skills as being key to successful design of client/server information systems.

This text provides working models that students can use to organize their problem-solving approach. These models are reinforced and used throughout the text. Examples include the following:

Top-Down Model

Client/Server Architecture Model

Client/Server Technology Model

OSI Model

Business cases reprinted from professional periodicals are included in each chapter. Questions guide students toward development of analytical skills and business-oriented client/server information system design capabilities.

The text equips students with real-world skills. Like Professor Goldman's previous texts, *Client/Server Information Systems: A Business-Oriented Approach* teaches students how to design client/server information systems rather than merely telling them about it.

■ APPROACH

The reviews and current level of adoptions of *Applied Data Communications: A Business-Oriented Approach* and *Local Area Networks: A Client/Server Approach* would indicate that the same proven, practical approach should be applied to a text on client/server information systems analysis and design. The text follows the top-down model, examining the many options, standards, interfaces, implications, advantages, and disadvantages in each of the top-down model's five layers:

Business

Application

Data

Network

Technology

Selection of proper client/server hardware and software technology, based on business objectives and applications, is stressed throughout all chapters in the text rather than in isolated chapters on network design. The thinking models that are used throughout the text are introduced in Chapter 1.

Concept roadmaps are located throughout the text, stressing the relationship between chapters, to an overall client/server architecture, and between topics within chapters.

Each chapter begins with an outline of new concepts to be introduced, previous concepts to be reinforced, and the learning objectives for that chapter.

Section and paragraph headings help students organize and identify key concepts introduced in each chapter.

End of chapter material includes chapter summaries, key term listings, abundant review questions, and activities and problems for active student learning.

As previously mentioned, business cases from professional periodicals are reprinted at the close of each chapter, with associated analysis questions to be answered by students or used as the basis for classroom discussion.

A liberal use of clear, concise diagrams adds to the usability of the text and enhances students' understanding of the concepts.

■ TARGET AUDIENCE/COURSES

Owing to the modular nature of this text, a variety of audiences and courses could be well served. Among the courses as potential adoptees of this text are the following:

- An introductory level course on information technology and architectures. The practical nature of the text would be appealing, as well as its broad coverage and architectural orientation. Advanced sections of the text could be easily avoided.

- A survey or conceptual course on client/server applications and architectures. This course could use the text thanks to its client/server architecture organization and orientation. Local area networking chapters could be avoided.

- A junior level course on client/server information systems design and implementation in either a lecture-only or lab/lecture format. Such a course would be part of a concentration in data communications and networking or telecommunications. Such a course may choose to include use of Part III on networking infrastructure.

As client/server information systems have taken on strategic importance to businesses, and local area networks are no longer just departmental computing solutions, the text may also have appeal in those MBA programs offering a concentration in management information systems. The managerial perspective sections and business cases would have particular appeal to this potential audience.

■ SPECIAL FEATURES

Although some of these features have been mentioned previously, they are repeated here to stress the unique nature of this text as a purveyor of practical, business-oriented client/server information systems analysis skills and problem-solving abilities rather than a mere collection of concepts and facts.

- The modular approach allows flexible use of text to fit instructor and course needs.

- Client/server architecture orientation prevents studying information systems design in a vacuum. This ensures that students will conduct client/server information systems analysis and design with both knowledge of and concern for the business impact of these information systems, the nature of the applications that will be deployed, and the underlying local area networks that will be used for transportation.

- Real business case studies stressing the business impact of client/server architectures integrated with web, Internet, and legacy application technologies assist students in sharpening their analysis and problem-solving skills. Directed questions accompanying each case stimulate classroom discussion as well.

- "In Sharper Focus" sections highlight more-detailed, more-advanced, or background information for concepts introduced within a chapter. These sections can be included or excluded at the instructor's discretion.

- "Managerial Perspective" sections take a "bottom-line" approach to client/server information systems analysis and design. The potential impact of management decisions in a variety of situations is highlighted in these sections, which may be of particular interest to MBA audiences.

- The OSI (open systems interconnection) model is used throughout the text as an analysis tool for student problem-solving and design opportunities.

▓ ANCILLARY SUGGESTIONS

The Instructor's Resource Guide will contain thorough answers to all review questions featured at the end of each chapter in the text. In addition, solutions to case study questions will be provided. Finally, an abundant selection of additional questions in a variety of formats will be provided for each chapter.

A CD-ROM with all illustrations in PowerPoint or Windows Metafile format will be provided to adoptees in order to expedite the production of transparencies and class notes to accompany the text.

A web site will be developed to support students and instructors using the text. At a minimum, the web site will include the following for each chapter:

- Bibliographic references sorted by topic to aid in further research

- Technology references with URLs to web sites of vendors of technology pertinent to a given chapter

There are two other possible aspects of the web site:

- Collaboration area for adopting instructors to share ideas and pose questions to the authors

- On-line glossary

ACKNOWLEDGMENTS

We are indebted to a number of people whose efforts were crucial in the development of this book.

For the outstanding quality illustrations that appear in the book, as well as for his unwavering support, we'd like to thank Curt Snyder, our wonderful and talented illustrator.

For their collaborative efforts in turning a manuscript into a professional published book, we'd like to thank the following professionals at John Wiley & Sons:

Beth Golub, Editor; Samantha Alducin, Editorial Assistant; Carlise Paulson, Marketing Manager; Christine Cervoni, Senior Production Editor; Anna Melhorn, Illustration Editor.

▨ REVIEWERS

A special debt of gratitude is owed to the professionals who were kind enough to review the manuscript of this book prior to publication. It is through your effort that an accurate text of high quality can be produced.

Kip Canfield, University of Maryland, Baltimore County
David Gefen, Drexel University
Elena Karahanna, Florida State University
Jahangir Karimi, University of Colorado

ABOUT THE AUTHORS

■ JAMES E. GOLDMAN, PRINCIPAL AUTHOR

James E. Goldman is currently Professor of Computer Information Systems and Assistant Department Head for Telecommunications and Networking in the nationally prominent Department of Computer Technology at Purdue University. An award-winning teacher, Professor Goldman is the only faculty member in the history of the School of Technology to win all three school-level teaching awards: The James G. Dwyer Outstanding Teacher Award, the School of Technology Outstanding Non-Tenured Faculty Award, and the School of Technology Tenured Faculty Award. He has also won the Purdue University Charles B. Murphy Award for Outstanding Undergraduate Teaching.

Professor Goldman is the author of *Applied Data Communications: A Business-Oriented Approach*, now in its second edition, a first-of-its-kind text that took a process-oriented, business-first, problem-solving approach to data communications education. The highly successful follow-up text, *Local Area Networks: A Client/Server Approach*, has been widely adopted in both academia and industry to support courses in client/server information systems as well as local area networking. Professor Goldman maintains an active consulting practice and is a Microsoft Certified Systems Engineer.

■ PHILLIP T. RAWLES, COAUTHOR

Phillip T. Rawles is an Assistant Professor of Computer Information Systems and Technology at Purdue University in West Lafayette, Indiana. Professor Rawles's primary areas of interest are network systems administration, enterprise network management, and network simulation and optimization. In three semesters at Purdue, Professor Rawles has developed or significantly redeveloped courses in local area networking, systems administration, and enterprise network management.

Professor Rawles is a contributing author to *High-Performance Networking Unleashed* (1997, SAMS, IN.) Professor Rawles maintains an active consulting practice and holds Master of Technology and Bachelor of Computer Integrated Manufacturing Technology degrees from Purdue University.

JULIE R. MARIGA, COAUTHOR

Julie R. Mariga is currently an Assistant Professor of Computer Information Systems in the nationally prominent Department of Computer Technology at Purdue University. Professor Mariga's first writing experience was codeveloping the test bank to accompany the fourth edition of *Systems Analysis and Design Methods* by Jeffrey L. Whitten and Lonnie D. Bentley. Professor Mariga's areas of interest include collaborative computing, client/server information systems, and Internet/intranet development. Professor Mariga teaches courses on information technology and architectures, and introductory and advanced courses on collaborative computing.

CONTENTS

PART THREE

NETWORKING INFRASTRUCTURE   355

PART FOUR

CLIENT/SERVER INFORMATION SYSTEMS ADMINISTRATION   509

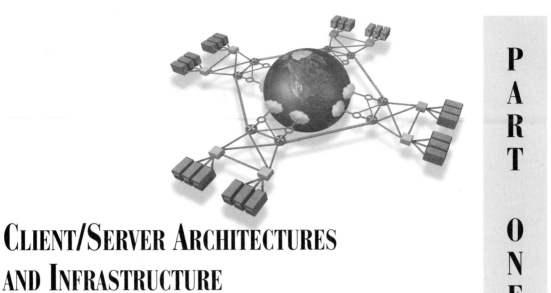

CLIENT/SERVER ARCHITECTURES AND INFRASTRUCTURE

INTRODUCTION

The overall purpose of Part 1 of the text is to introduce the reader to the "big picture" of client/server information systems, including an understanding of the types of hardware and software technology that combine to deliver these distributed information systems. In each case, technology choices, trends, and interactions are discussed from business as well as technical perspectives.

Chapter 1, Introduction to Client/Server Information Systems and Architectures, gives the reader an understanding of the business motivation as well as potential benefits and pitfalls of client/server information systems. In addition, it introduces the client/server architecture as a means of portraying how all of the various component technologies mesh to form a cohesive distributed information system.

Chapter 2, Client Hardware, takes a closer look at a single technological component of the overall client/server information systems architecture. It explores all aspects of client hardware from a systems perspective, noting the interdependencies between the various elements that combine to produce a client workstation. Technological trends of client hardware subsystems are stressed in order to enable the reader to make informed design recommendations and purchasing decisions.

Chapter 3, Client Software, introduces the numerous categories of software that must execute and interoperate compatibly on the client hardware introduced in Chapter 2. This chapter particularly stresses software trends and interoperability dependencies.

Chapter 4, Server Hardware and Software, completes the explanation of the technological infrastructure of client/server information systems by exploring the technological elements comprising the various types of servers that must deliver required services to the client workstations. Interoperability issues and reliability characteristics are stressed in the exploration of server technology.

INTRODUCTION TO CLIENT/SERVER INFORMATION SYSTEMS AND ARCHITECTURES

Concepts Introduced

Client/Server Information Systems	Client/Server Architectures
Client/Server Technology and Tools	Client/Server Analysis
Client/Server Management	Interprocess Communications
Distributed Computing	Distributed Presentation
Database Distribution	Distributed Transaction Processing
Middleware	Transaction-Processing Monitors
Open Systems	Distributed Objects
Top-Down Model	Protocols and Compatibility
OSI Model	

OBJECTIVES

After mastering the material in this chapter, you should understand the following:

1. The business forces motivating the emphasis on information systems downsizing, application rightsizing, and the development of client/server information systems

2. The relationship between client/server architectures and the implementation of distributed computing, application rightsizing, database distribution, and enterprise networking

3. The major hardware and software components of client/server architecture and the role that middleware plays in integrating these components to form a working architecture

4. The additional difficulties and decision making as well as the currently available solutions involved in implementing client/server architectures involving multiple vendors' systems and technology

5. The current state of actual implementation of client/server architectures in industry, the problem areas or limiting factors affecting these implementations, and the outlook for resolution of these limiting factors

6. The unique problems encountered in the management of multivendor, multiplatform client/server architectures and the current state of available distributed enterprise network management systems

■ INTRODUCTION

"Client/server is not just a buzzword. It's two buzzwords. Two buzzwords which, if you seek any future in computing, you cannot afford to ignore."
—Dr. Robert Metcalfe, Ethernet Inventor,
Founder of 3Com and Publisher/CEO of *Infoworld*

This chapter objectively explores why client/server information systems are drawing so much attention, pointing out both potential positive and potential negative outcomes of client/server implementations. Once the business analysis of client/server information systems is complete, the remainder of the chapter introduces much of the remainder of the book. The major purpose of this chapter is to introduce the reader to the overall architectures and technology of client/server information systems. This chapter supplies the proverbial big picture, offering insight into how all the pieces of multivendor client/server information systems fit together.

The intended outcome of this introduction to client/server architectures is an *introductory* understanding of several areas:

- The many interacting hardware and software technology categories that comprise a client/server information system

- Examples of currently available technology within each technology category

- The interfaces between client/server hardware and software categories and how overall compatibility is achieved across these many interfaces

Mastery of the intricacies of client/server technology is not an intended outcome of this chapter. Many topics mentioned only briefly in this chapter are described further in chapters later in the book.

■ BUSINESS ASPECTS OF CLIENT/SERVER INFORMATION SYSTEMS

Business Motivation

As companies sought a competitive advantage in the down-turned economy of the early 1990s, information became increasingly recognized as the corporate asset to be leveraged for that sought-after competitive advantage. More precisely, the timely delivery of the right corporate information, in the right format, to the right decision maker at the right place and time can be the differentiating factor between success and failure in today's business world. It is important to add one additional criterion to the previous sentence: that information must also be delivered at the right price. As profits have dwindled and pressures to decrease expenses have mounted, the cost of maintaining corporate information systems has come under increased scrutiny. The mainframe computer and its associated hierarchical network and maintenance/development budget have been singled out, perhaps unfairly, as the biggest consumer of information systems departments' budgets. As this chapter shows, mainframe computers still have their rightful place in some corporate information systems environments.

Corporate downsizing, not to be confused with **information systems downsizing,** has involved elimination of positions within a corporation through attrition, early retirement, closed operations, or forced lay-offs. The duties of the staff in the eliminated positions are either assumed by remaining employees or deemed dispensable and not assumed by anyone. In many cases, the information systems of these downsized corporations must pick up the slack and deliver better information more efficiently to the remaining employees. "Accomplishing more with less" is one of the aims of the properly "rightsized" application.

Potential Benefits

It is important to understand that information systems downsizing and **application rightsizing** are not merely about saving money. A combination of events, including the following, have combined to produce an entirely new **distributed architecture** for information systems processing and delivery:

- The introduction of reasonably priced, powerful personal workstations

- The emergence of affordable, powerful, "multitasking" server operating systems

- The changing demands on information systems as a result of today's business climate

Information systems constructed according to this distributed architecture paradigm are often referred to as **client/server information systems** because the overall information systems duties are shared between client and server computers. Exactly how these client/server information systems are put together will be explored in the remainder of the chapter. These distributed or rightsized information systems not only save money in many cases, but also deliver better information more flexibly as well as enable quicker business responses to competitive situations.

Although sometimes overshadowed by the more concrete benefits such as performance improvements or budget decreases, the flexibility of design afforded by the distributed nature of the client/server architecture holds the key to the most significant benefits of this new computing paradigm.

Figure 1-1 summarizes the significant benefits of successful client/server information system implementations.

Potential Negatives

Just as there are two sides to every story, there are drawbacks and potential pitfalls to information systems rightsizing efforts. Some of these negative aspects are unique to client/server or rightsizing efforts, whereas others are true for any shift in information systems design or architecture.

Because cost savings are often the key positive attribute of client/server implementation, it seems only fitting that a closer examination of rightsizing efforts sometimes reveals that the cost savings are minimized when **transition costs** are taken into account. If the new client/server system is to replace an existing system, then both systems must be maintained and supported for some period of time. In addition, the cost of writing new software or converting old software should be taken into account, as should the cost for development of new user or management software "tools."

Benefit	Example/Explanation
Reduced costs in comparison to mainframe-based information systems	• Budget reductions of 40–80% are possible, with the potential of significant staff reductions.
Flexibility	• This is cited as a benefit in nearly every case study. Information is more accessible and display formats are more flexible, thanks to the client/server architecture.
Support/respond to business environment changes	• Beyond flexibility, this architecture demonstrates potential for proactive use of information systems in business. Significantly reduced time to develop new applications is a contributing factor.
Improved information accessibility	• Information stored on distributed local area networks (LANs) is more easily accessible to a wider user group than information stored on a mainframe-based hierarchical network.
Faster information	• Distributed processing allows combined power of client PC and server PC to increase processing speed by as much as a factor of 10 over mainframe-based solutions.
Better information	• The "right" information is produced as a result of a combination of faster processing, more flexible formatting, and improved access to a wider array of information.
Open architecture	• The typical PC-based client/server architecture offers unlimited potential for multivendor solutions to information systems opportunities. Mainframe-based, single vendor information systems lock out the competition and, in many cases, innovative solutions.
Empowered users	• Perhaps most significantly, users will play a larger role in information systems design and development as client-based, easy-to-use systems development tools are employed in the client/server architecture.

Figure 1-1 Potential Benefits of Client/Server Information Systems

Other hidden costs have appeared only after the transition to a client/server information system has been completed. Owing to their inherent distributed, multivendor nature, client/server information systems are often more difficult and costly to support and maintain than the single-platform, single-vendor based platforms they replaced.

The lack of existing management tools for the distributed computing architecture is a serious impediment to client/server deployment. Such tools must automat-

ically and transparently cater to system backup, disaster recovery, a
sues such as user login and user access management over the enti
computing network. In short, users expect all of the functionality of th
cated operating systems of stand-alone mainframes on the distributed pla
the client/server architecture.

Because of the increased sophistication and processing power available to
end user at the client workstation, increased user training is a necessity and an a
ditional cost that must be considered by client/server architecture implementation
teams. It follows that these same more-powerful end-user workstations require increased on-going technical support as well.

There can be many negative aspects or potential pitfalls to the shift from traditional information systems architectures to client/server architectures. Although
there seems to be little argument over the fact that the computers used in
client/server information systems are significantly less expensive than the mainframes they replaced, when support, training, management, and maintenance costs
are taken into account, current research indicates that there are no significant cost
savings achieved by transitioning to client/server information systems.

If cost savings are minimal or nonexistent, what is the key benefit to the implementation of client/server information systems? As cited in the Potential Benefits
section, the ability of client/server information systems to deliver better information more flexibly, thereby enabling competitive business advantages and increased
revenue, is really the most significant benefit. Figure 1-2 summarizes some of the
potential negatives of client/server information systems.

Negatives	Example/Explanation
Transition costs	• Often overlooked, these are the "hidden" costs incurred while converting to client/server architectures.
High cost of training, support, maintenance, and management	• Owing primarily to the open, multivendor client/server architecture, training support, maintenance, and management are far more complex and therefore more expensive.
Multivendor architecture	• An open architecture supported by multiple vendors' technology can lead to incompatibility problems and finger pointing.
Lack of management tools for distributed environment	• Although efforts are being made to fill this need, sophisticated management tools capable of managing distributed, multivendor environments are just emerging.
Lack of standards	• This is especially a problem where two competing standards are backed by rival vendors or consortiums.
Technology not ready for mission-critical applications	• Although they are getting more reliable all the time, servers and server operating systems still don't guarantee the reliability and power of mainframes.
Lack of software conversion tools	• Sophisticated tools that can prevent mainframe applications from having to be totally rewritten could reduce transition costs tremendously.

Figure 1-2 Potential Negatives of Client/Server Information Systems

...LLENGES AND SOLUTIONS TO EFFECTIVE CLIENT/SERVER ...ORMATION SYSTEMS ANALYSIS, DESIGN, AND IMPLEMENTATION

...: Information Technology Investment versus Productivity Gains: ...mplemented Technology Meets Business Needs

...e maximize potential benefits and minimize potential negative impact ...ical investments such as client/server information systems? How can ...that implemented technology will meet business needs? This section of ...e chapter introduces the reader to the challenges and solutions of ensuring effective client/server information systems analysis, design, and implementation.

In the past decade, over $1 trillion has been invested by businesses in information technology. Despite this massive investment, carefully conducted research indicates that there has been little if any increase in productivity as a direct result of this investment. This dilemma is known as the **productivity paradox.** Clearly, something is wrong with an analysis and design process that recommends technology implementations that fail to meet strategic business objectives of increased productivity.

What characteristics are required of an analysis and design process with the potential to overcome the productivity paradox?

Solution: The Top-Down Approach

Applied Problem Solving

In order to overcome the productivity paradox, a structured methodology must be followed in order to ensure that the implemented network meets the communications needs of the intended business, organization, or individual.

One such structured methodology is known as the top-down approach. Such an approach can be graphically illustrated in a **top-down model** as shown in Figure 1-3. Using a top-down approach, as illustrated in the top-down model, is relatively straightforward. Insisting that a top-down approach to client/server information system analysis and design is undertaken should ensure that the client/server information system design implemented will meet the business needs and objectives that motivated the design in the first place.

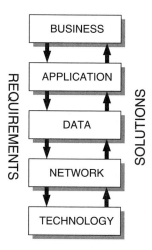

Figure 1-3 The Top-Down Model

This top-down approach requires that network analysts understand business constraints and objectives as well as information systems applications and the data on which those applications run before considering data communications and networking options.

Notice where the network layer occurs in the top-down model. It is no accident that data communications and networking form the foundation of today's sophisticated information systems. A properly designed network supports flexible delivery of data to distributed application programs, allowing businesses to respond quickly to customer needs and rapidly changing market conditions.

The Top-Down Model   How does the proper use of the top-down model ensure effective, business-oriented client/server analysis and design? Figure 1-4 lists the analysis processes associated with each layer of the top-down model.

One must start with the *business*-level objectives. What is the company (organization, individual) trying to accomplish by installing this network? Without a clear understanding of business-level objectives, it is nearly impossible to configure and implement a successful network. In many cases, businesses take this opportunity to critically reexamine their business processes in an analysis methodology known as **business process reengineering** (BPR).

Top-Down Model Layer	Associated Analysis Processes
Business Layer	• Strategic business planning • Business process reengineering • Identification of major business functions • Identification of business processes • Identification of business opportunities
Applications Layer	• Applications development • Systems analysis and design • Identification of information needs • Relation of information needs to business processes and opportunities
Data Layer	• Database analysis and design • Data modeling • Data distribution analysis • Client/server architecture design • Distributed database design • Relation of data collection and distribution to information and business needs
Network Layer	• Network analysis and design • Logical network design (what) • Network implementation planning • Network management and performance monitoring • Relation of logical network design to data collection and distribution design
Technology Layer	• Technology analysis grids • Hardware-software-media technology analysis • Physical network design (how) • Physical network implementation • Relation of physical network design to logical network design

Figure 1-4   Analysis Processes of the Top-Down Model

In what is perhaps the most famous book on BPR, *Reengineering the Corporation: A Manifesto for Business Revolution* by Michael Hammer and James Champy, the authors state that "Business reengineering means starting all over, starting from scratch. Business reengineering means putting aside much of the received wisdom of two hundred years of industrial management. It means forgetting how work was done in the age of the mass market and deciding how it can best be done now. In business reengineering, old job titles and old organizational arrangements—departments, divisions, groups, and so on—cease to matter. They are artifacts of another age."

Once business-level objectives are understood, one must understand the *applications* that will be running on the computer systems attached to these networks. After all, it is the applications that will be generating the traffic that will travel over the implemented network.

Once applications are understood and have been documented, the *data* that those applications generate must be examined. In this case, the term *data* is used in a general sense, as today's networks are likely to transport a variety of payloads including voice, video, image, and fax in addition to true data. Data traffic analysis must determine not only the amount of data to be transported, but also important characteristics of that data.

Once data traffic analysis has been completed, the following should be known:

1. Physical locations of data   (where?)

2. Data characteristics and compatibility issues   (what?)

3. Amount of data generated and transported   (how much?)

With these requirements as determined by the upper layers of the top-down model, the next job is to determine the requirements of the *network* that will possess the capability to deliver this data in a timely, cost-effective manner. These network performance criteria could be referred to as *what* the implemented network must do in order to meet the business objectives outlined at the outset of this top-down analysis. These requirements are also sometimes referred to as the **logical network design.**

The *technology* layer analysis, in contrast, will determine *how* various hardware and software components will be combined to build a functional network that will meet predetermined business objectives. The delineation of required technology is often referred to as the **physical network design.**

Overall, the relationship between the layers of the top-down model could be described as follows: Analysis at upper layers produces requirements that are passed down to lower layers while solutions meeting these requirements are passed back to upper layers. If this relationship among layers holds true throughout the business-oriented client/server information systems analysis, then the implemented technology (bottom layer) should meet the initially outlined business objectives (top layer). Hence the name: the top-down approach.

Challenge: Analysis of Complex LAN Connectivity and Compatibility Issues

Assuming that the proper use of top-down model will ensure that implemented technical solutions will meet stated business requirements, you must address the more technical challenges of client/server information systems analysis and design.

Introduction to Protocols and Compatibility In previous discussions of how client/server information systems are implemented, the term **compatibility** was introduced and explained. Solving incompatibility problems is at the very heart of successful client/server information systems implementation. Compatibility can be thought of as successfully bridging the gap or communicating between two or more technology components, whether hardware or software. This logical gap between components is commonly referred to as an **interface.**

Interfaces may be physical (hardware to hardware) in nature. For example:

- Cables physically connecting to serial ports on a computer
- A network interface card physically plugging into the expansion bus inside a computer

Interfaces may also be logical or software-oriented (software to software) as well. For example:

- Network operating system client software (Windows for Workgroups) communicating with the client PC's operating system (DOS)
- A client-based data query tool (Microsoft Excel) gathering data from a large database management system (Oracle)

Finally, interfaces may cross the hardware-to-software boundary. For example:

- A network operating system–specific piece of software known as a driver, which interfaces to an installed network interface card (NIC)
- A piece of operating system software known as a kernel, which interfaces to a computer's CPU chip

The reason that these various interfaces are able to be bridged successfully, thereby supporting compatibility between components, is the establishment of **protocols.** Protocols are nothing more than rules for how communicating hardware and software components bridge interfaces or talk to one another. Protocols may be proprietary (used exclusively by one or more vendors) or open (used freely by all interested parties). Protocols may be officially sanctioned by international standards–making bodies such as the International Standards Organization (ISO) (de jure protocols), or may be purely market driven (de facto protocols). Figure 1-5 illustrates the relationship between interfaces, protocols, and compatibility.

For every potential hardware-to-hardware, software-to-software, and hardware-to-software interface imaginable, there is likely to be one or more possible protocols supported. The sum of all of the protocols employed in a particular computer is sometimes referred to as that computer's **protocol stack.** Successfully determining which protocols must be supported in which instances for the multitude of interfaces possible in a complicated LAN design is likely to be the difference between success or failure in a client/server information systems implementation.

How can a network analyst possibly keep track of all potential interfaces and their associated protocols between all client/server information systems–attached devices? What is needed is a framework in which to organize the various potential interfaces and protocols in such complicated internetwork designs. More than one such framework, otherwise known as **communications architecture,** exists. Two of the most popular communications architectures are the seven-layer OSI model and the four-layer Internet suite of protocols model.

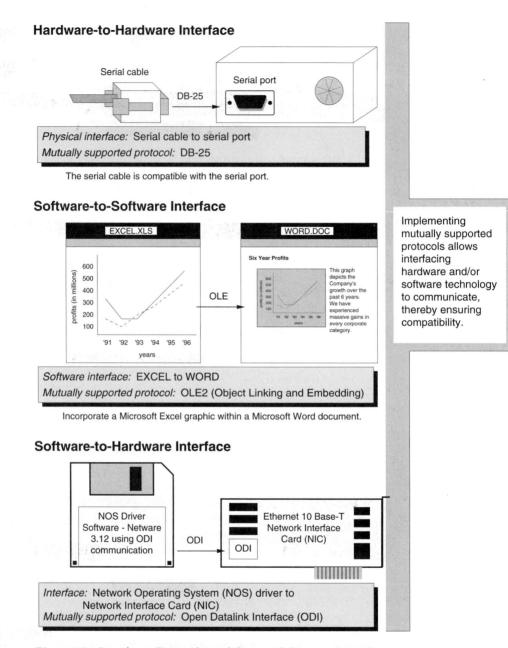

Figure 1-5   Interfaces, Protocols, and Compatibility

Solution: The OSI Model

Determining which technology and protocols to employ to meet the requirements determined in the logical network design, yielded from the network layer of the top-down model, requires a structured methodology of its own. Fortunately, a framework for organizing networking technology and protocol solutions has been developed by the ISO and is known as the open systems interconnection (OSI) model. The **OSI model** is illustrated in Figure 1-6.

OSI Model Layer	Functionality	Automobile Assembly Line Comparison
7 Application	Layer where application programs interact and receive services	Dealer installed options: Options desired by users are added at the dealership.
6 Presentation	Ensures reliable session transmission between applications; takes care of differences in data representation	Painting and finish work: The vehicle is painted and trim is applied.
5 Session	Enables two applications to communicate across the network	Interior: Seats and dashboard are added to passenger compartment.
4 Transport	Ensures reliable transmission from end-to-end, usually across multiple nodes	Electrical: Electrical system and components are added.
3 Network	Sets up the pathways or end-to-end connections, usually across a long distance or multiple nodes	Body: Passenger compartment and fenders are attached to the chassis.
2 Data Link	Puts messages together; attaches proper headers to be sent out or received; ensures messages are delivered between two points	Engine/drive train: Engine and transmission components provide the vehicle with propulsion.
1 Physical	Layer that is concerned with transmitting bits of data over a physical medium	Chassis/frame: Steel is fabricated to form the chassis on which all other components will travel.

Figure 1-6   The OSI Model

The OSI model divides the communication between any two networked computing devices into seven layers, or categories. Network analysts speak in terms of the OSI model. When troubleshooting LAN problems, inevitably the savvy network analyst starts with the physical layer (layer 1) and ensures that protocols and interfaces at each layer are operational before moving up the OSI model. The OSI model allows data communications technology developers as well as standards developers to talk about the interconnection of two networks or computers in common terms without dealing in proprietary vendor jargon.

These common terms are the result of the layered architecture of the seven-layer OSI model. The architecture breaks the task of two computers' communicating with each other into separate but interrelated tasks, each represented by its own layer. As can be seen in Figure 1-6, the top layer (layer 7) represents the services required by the application program running on each computer and is therefore aptly named the application layer. The bottom layer (layer 1) is concerned with the actual physical connection of the two computers or networks and is therefore named the physical layer. The remaining layers (2 through 6) may not be as obvious but nonetheless represent a sufficiently distinct logical group of functions required to connect two computers, unique enough to justify separate layers. As will be seen later in the text, some of the layers are divided into sublayers.

To use the OSI model, a network analyst lists the known protocols for each computing device or network node in the proper layer of its own seven-layer OSI model. The collection of these known protocols in their proper layers in known as the protocol stack of the network node. For example, the physical media employed, such as unshielded twisted pair, coaxial cable, or fiber optic cable, would be entered as a layer 1 protocol, whereas Ethernet or Token Ring network architectures might be entered as a layer 2 protocol.

The OSI model allows network analysts to produce an accurate inventory of the protocols present on any given network node. This protocol profile represents a unique personality of each network node and gives the network analyst some insight into what **protocol conversion,** if any, may be necessary in order to get any two network nodes to communicate successfully. Ultimately, the OSI model provides a structured methodology for determining what hardware and software technology will be required in the physical network design in order to meet the requirements of the logical network design.

Perhaps the best analogy for the OSI reference model, to illustrate its architectural or framework purpose, is that of a blueprint for a large office building or skyscraper. The various subcontractors on the job may be concerned only with the "layer" of the plans that outlines their specific job specifications. However, each specific subcontractor needs to be able to depend on the work of the "lower" layers' subcontractors, just as the subcontractors of the lower layers depend on other, still lower subcontractors to perform their function to specification.

Similarly, each layer of the OSI model operates independently of all other layers, while depending on neighboring layers to perform according to specification while cooperating in the attainment of the overall task of communication between two computers or networks.

The OSI model is neither a protocol nor a group of protocols. It is a standardized, empty framework into which protocols can be listed in order to perform effective client/server information systems analysis and design. As will be seen later in the text, however, the ISO has also produced a set of OSI protocols that correspond to some of the layers of the OSI model. It is important to differentiate between the OSI model and OSI protocols.

The OSI model will be used throughout the remainder of the text as the protocol stacks of various network operating systems are analyzed and in the analysis and design of advanced client/server information system's connectivity alternatives.

Solution: The Internet Suite of Protocols Model

Although the OSI model is perhaps more famous than any OSI protocol, just the opposite could be said for a model and associated protocols known as the **Internet suite of protocols model.** Also known as the TCP/IP protocol suite, or TCP/IP architecture, this communications architecture takes its name from **TCP/IP (transmission control protocol/Internet protocol),** the de facto standard protocols for open systems internetworking. As can be seen in Figure 1-7, TCP and IP are just two of the protocols associated with this model.

Like the OSI model, the TCP/IP model is a layered communications architecture in which upper layers use the functionality offered by the protocols of the lower layers. Each layer's protocols are able to operate independently of the protocols of other layers. For example, protocols on a given layer can be updated or modified without having to change protocols in all other layers. A recent example is the new version of IP known as IPng (IP next generation), which was developed in response to a pending shortage of IP addresses. This proposed change is possible

Layer	OSI	INTERNET	Data Format	Protocols
7	Application	Application	Messages or Streams	TELNET FTP TFTP SMTP SNMP CMOT MIB
6	Presentation			
5	Session			
4	Transport	Transport or Host-Host	Transport Protocol Packets	TCP UDP
3	Network	Internet	IP Diagrams	IP
2	Data Link	Network Access	Frames	
1	Physical			

Figure 1-7   Internet Suite of Protocols versus OSI

without the need to change all other protocols in the TCP/IP communication architecture. TCP/IP and related protocols will be explored in greater depth in Chapter 9, Local Area Network Operating Systems.

Figure 1-7 compares the four-layer Internet suite of protocols model with the seven-layer OSI model. Either communications architecture could be used to analyze and design communications between networks. In the case of the Internet suite of protocols model, the full functionality of internetwork communications is divided into four layers rather than seven. Some network analysts consider the Internet suite of protocols model simpler and more practical than the OSI model.

Solution: The I-P-O Model

Once the protocols are determined for two or more computers or networks that wish to communicate, the next step is to determine the type of technology required to deliver the identified internetworking functionality and protocols.

In order to understand the basic function of any piece of networking equipment, one really need only understand the differences between the characteristics of the data that came *in* and the data that went *out*. Those differences identified were *processed* by the data communications equipment being analyzed.

This input-processing-output, or **I-P-O, model** is another key model used throughout the textbook to analyze a wide variety of networking equipment and opportunities. The I-P-O model provides a framework in which to focus on the difference between the data that came into a particular networked device (I) and the data that came out of that same device (O). By defining this difference, the processing (P) performed by the device is documented.

Although at first glance the I-P-O model may seem too simple, it is another valuable model that can assist network analysts in organizing thoughts, documenting requirements, and articulating needs.

▦ ARCHITECTURES OF CLIENT/SERVER INFORMATION SYSTEMS

Evolution from Mainframe-Based Architectures to Client/Server Information Systems

What is the nature of the process that takes a mainframe-based application and redeploys that application on a distributed client/server platform? The fact is that many possible processes may lead to client/server implementation. Among the commonly used terms used to describe these processes are the following:

- Downsizing

- Rightsizing

- Upsizing

- Smartsizing

These are not really industry-standardized terms, and their use is rather arbitrary. Other terms may be used to describe similar processes. Some people consider these terms nothing more than marketing buzzwords. What is important in this circumstance is an understanding of the variety of possible architectural shifts in the evolution from mainframe-based architectures to client/server information systems, rather than the use or meaning of a particular term.

Downsizing   Downsizing implies that a mainframe-based application has been redeployed to run on a smaller computer platform. That smaller platform may or may not be a distributed client/server information system. Also, the term *downsizing* does not necessarily imply the extent to which the mainframe application was redesigned or reengineered. For example, the original source code could have simply been recompiled and run unaltered on the new, "downsized" platform. Alternatively, the application may have been rewritten in a new language and redeployed. Another possibility is that the programming logic within the program was reexamined, redesigned, and reprogrammed.

Downsizing primarily seeks to take advantage of the increasingly powerful computers available at ever more affordable prices. It does not necessarily involve using that processing power more efficiently or effectively.

Rightsizing   Rightsizing implies that applications are designed for and deployed on the platform, or type and size of computer, that makes the most sense: the "right" size computer. The right computer or platform implies that the choice is based on maximizing the efficiency with which the application runs. The matching of a particular rightsized application with a particular computing platform seeks efficiency not only from a performance standpoint, but also from a cost perspective. The rightsized application is the one that will deliver the most "bang for the buck."

Because efficient execution of the application is at the heart of rightsizing, this process usually implies new or redesigned application development efforts, in contrast to simple downsizing efforts.

Upsizing   Upsizing might be considered as a subset of rightsizing. When applications lack processing power on their existing computing platform, they may be redesigned and redeployed on larger, more powerful platforms. Whether the applications require reengineering before upsizing may vary from case to case.

A possible example of an upsizing need would be when a company has outgrown the capabilities of a multiuser database and must migrate to a more powerful client/server–based relational database management system. Old applications may need to be redesigned and rewritten for the new database system, depending on the efficiency of the old application and the existence of a migration path from the old database system to the newer one.

Smartsizing   Smartsizing implies another level of questioning or reengineering beyond that of rightsizing. Rather than merely reevaluating the application program, smartsizing goes a step further and reevaluates and reengineers the business process that motivated the application in the first place. Once the business process has been thoroughly and objectively reevaluated, then the application programs to support that process are redesigned and rewritten. Finally, the new application is deployed on the right platform to maximize performance and cost efficiency.

Figure 1-8 illustrates the differences between downsizing, rightsizing, upsizing, and smartsizing.

Major Paradigms of the Information Age   Unique combinations of systems architectures and people architectures are often referred to as **paradigms** of the information age. There have been at least two or three major paradigms in information systems prior to the introduction of the client/server model, depending on which information systems philosopher is consulted:

   I.   The age of the mainframe

  II.   The introduction of the personal computer

 III.   The dawn of the client/server architecture and applications rightsizing

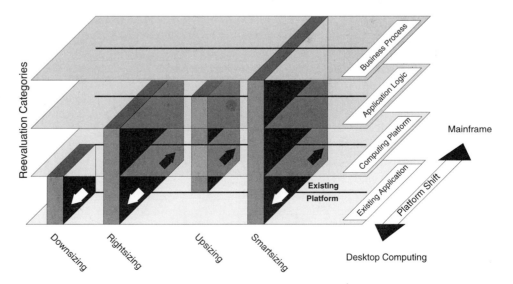

Figure 1-8   Downsizing, Rightsizing, Upsizing, and Smartsizing

The period of time when information systems professionals are madly scrambling to gain competitive advantage for their companies by implementing a "new" paradigm is known as a **paradigm shift.** A paradigm shift is not merely the introduction of new technology. It is much more than that. A paradigm shift occurs when the fundamental underlying processes and environment change to such an extent that significant changes in behavior are required. In short, a completely new way of doing things results from a completely new way of looking at the world of information systems.

Figure 1-9 highlights the major systems and corresponding people architectures of the major paradigms of the information age.

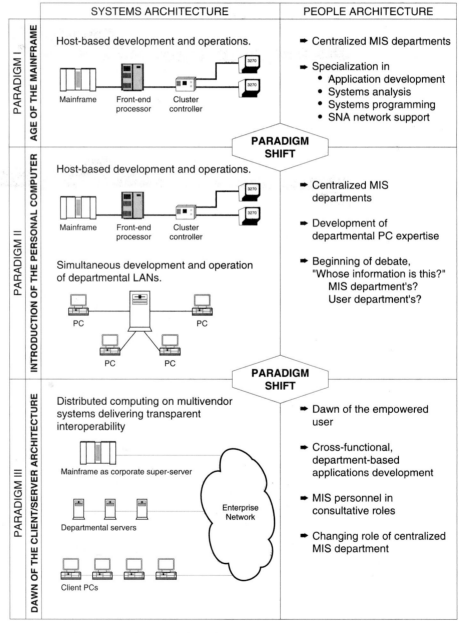

Figure 1-9   Major Paradigms of the Information Age

People Architectures Must Respond to Information Systems Architectures   The key point of paradigm shifts such as those illustrated in Figure 1-9 is the fact that in addition to major technological or systems architecture shifts, there are also correspondingly large shifts in people architectures. Thus, it should not be surprising that the dawn of the client/server age is uncovering a great many people-related issues as the centralized management information systems (MIS) departments of the "old" paradigm are faced with the reality of the distributed systems of the "new" paradigm. Much of the debate in today's evolving people architecture centers around which functions of an MIS department should be distributed to match the systems architecture and which must remain centralized.

There are no easy answers to these questions. The people architecture of the client/server age is still in an evolutionary state. Figure 1-10 summarizes some of the people architecture features and issues of the client/server or applications rightsizing paradigm.

A review of Figure 1-10 should make it obvious that the people architecture changes resulting from the client/server or applications rightsizing paradigm shift are potentially at least as dramatic as the changes in systems architecture. For example, the distribution of processing power, coupled with the distribution of corporate

Feature/Characteristic	Issues/Explanation
The dawn of the empowered user	• Powerful, easy-to-use front-end client-based tools will empower end users to meet many more of their own information needs thanks to easy access to distributed data via the client/server architecture and the enterprise network.
Cross-functional, user department–based application development	• No longer totally centralized, application development will be distributed to end-user departments. • Empowered users of the department, rather than MIS staff, may be project leaders.
MIS personnel in consultative roles	• No longer the sole "owners" of all corporate data and applications development expertise, MIS personnel will work in a more distributed, consultative, or loaned basis for individual end-user department projects for extended periods of time.
Changing role for centralized MIS department	• A smaller, centralized MIS department must still be responsible for certain global information infrastructure concerns such as the following: • Centralized, coordinated user support • Centralized, coordinated user training • Maintenance of the enterprise network • Quality assurance in the areas of database design, applications development, and departmental networking projects • Data administration standards development and enforcement through definition of standard global data definitions for globally used data elements • Standards testing by testing new technology for adherence to corporate standards before allowing organization-wide deployment of that technology.

Figure 1-10   The People Architecture of the Client/Server Paradigm

data and the distribution of application development via a client/server architecture, can raise fundamental issues as to the "ownership" of and responsibility for different aspects of these distributed systems. For instance, are local department personnel responsible for the maintenance, backup, and disaster recovery of local servers, or do these functions remain in the domain of the centralized MIS department? Which organization is responsible for which aspects of the enterprise network?

Managerial Perspective

These people architecture changes will also cause anxiety as people worry about changing job descriptions and long-term security. The development and support of client/server information systems require a new combination of technical skills for long-time information systems professionals. Organizations must find ways to retrain existing personnel or, alternatively, hire new graduates with the required skills. At the same time, current information systems professionals must be willing to retool their skills, and colleges and universities must adjust curricula to offer this new set of required skills. A predictable reaction on the part of many will be to resist the change aggressively. Coping with negativism, and overall effective management of the people side of client/server architecture, is equally as important as coping with rapidly changing technology.

Logical Architectures

Client/Server Information Systems   Simply stated, a **client/server information system** takes advantage of the processing power now available on desktop computers by splitting the job of delivering quality information to end users among multiple computers. Much activity among interacting layers of hardware and software technology goes on behind the scenes in order to accomplish this task. The primary purpose of this section of the chapter is to give readers visual models of client/server information systems in order to give them a better understanding of these previously mentioned interacting layers of technology.

The term *client/server* may be a bit misleading if the reader interprets the phrase as implying a one-to-one ratio between clients and servers. As will be seen throughout the remainder of the text, it is far more common for multiple, specialized servers to be involved with fulfilling the information and communications needs of a single client.

P-A-D Architecture   The most fundamental logical model of client/server information systems takes a closer look at what it takes to deliver quality information to end users. This functional perspective is illustrated in Figure 1-11, the **presentation-application-data,** or **P-A-D Architecture.**

As can be seen in Figure 1-11, the delivery of quality information to end users depends on the interaction of three fundamental processes:

1.   Presentation (also known as user interface)

2.   Application (also known as application logic or processing)

3.   Data (also known as data management or data manipulation)

Some logical models of client/server information systems divide the application layer into the following three sublayers, thereby highlighting the application layer's interfaces with the presentation and data layers:

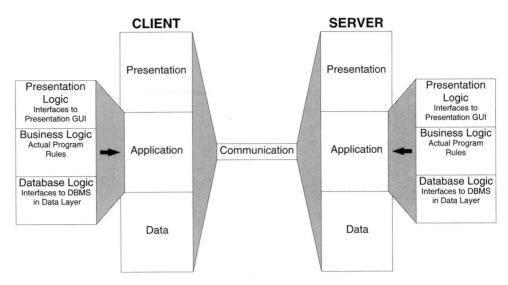

Figure 1-11   Presentation-Application-Data Logical Model

1. Presentation logic: The part of the application program responsible for interfacing to the user interface

2. Business logic: The actual program rules of the application responsible for controlling program execution and enforcing business rules

3. Database logic: The part of the application program responsible for interfacing to the database management system

Presentation, application, and data are nothing new. These three interacting functions are at the heart of the oldest mainframe-based information systems. All client/server information systems introduce to this interaction is the possibility of splitting some or all of these functions across multiple computers. As illustrated in Figure 1-11, this splitting of functions introduces the need for sophisticated communications between cooperating computers. This communication between cooperating computers is supplied by the network, often a LAN. As will be seen later in the text, the network is comprised of both hardware (network interface cards, hubs) and software (network operating systems) technology. The importance of the network to client/server computing should be obvious. Without the network, there is no client/server computing.

In the following sections, each of the elements of the P-A-D model, as well as the interaction between elements of the model, will be explored in more detail.

Categories of Client/Server Information Systems   Figure 1-12 is a matrix of potential categories of client/server information systems based on a variety of combinations of the presentation, application, and data elements of the P-A-D architecture. The new variable introduced in Figure 1-12 is the executing platform for the presentation, application, and data elements. As illustrated, there are three possibilities for how each function or element may be executed:

1. The function is performed totally on the client.

2. The function is cooperatively split between the client and server.

3. The function is performed totally on the server.

Presentation - Application - Data LAYER	Executing Platforms: Client Only	Executing Platforms: Cooperative Client and Server	Executing Platforms: Server Only
Presentation	Client-Based Presentation (Client GUI, Local Presentation, GUI Veneer)	Distributed Presentation (Cooperative Presentation)	Host-Based Presentation (Remote Presentation, Dumb Terminals)
Application	Client-Based Processing	Distributed Computing (Cooperative Computing, Cooperative Processing)	Host-Based Processing
Data	Client-Based Data Management (Local Data Management)	Database Distribution (Distributed Data Management, Distributed Database)	Host-Based Data Management (Remote Data Management)

Figure 1-12 Potential Categories of Elements of Client/Server Information Systems

Because different terms are often used to describe the same processes, synonymous terms are included in parentheses on the matrix.

Practical Advice and Information

Remembering that a client/server information system is made up of a combination of presentation, application, and data functionality, in order to properly categorize a particular client/server information system, a network analyst would need to know the executing platforms of each of these three elements of the P-A-D architecture. However, beware. Often a categorization of one element of the P-A-D architecture implies categorization of the remaining two elements. For example:

- Host-based processing often implies client-based presentation, host-based processing, and host-based data management.
- Client-based processing often implies client-based presentation, client-based processing, and host-based data management.
- Cooperative processing often implies client-based presentation, distributed computing, and distributed data management.

Figure 1-13 graphically illustrates how different variations of presentation, application, and data management elements can be combined to produce different logical client/server information systems architectures.

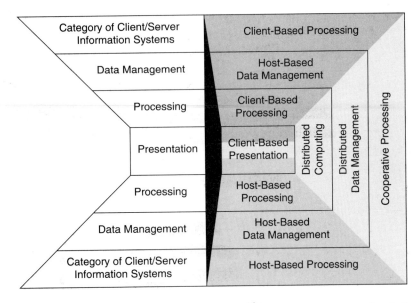

Figure 1-13   Presentation + Processing + Data   Management = Logical Client/Server Architecture

Many other terms are used to describe entire logical architectures of client/server information systems. The important thing for a network analyst to remember is to pay attention to the executing platforms of the constituent presentation, application, and data management elements of the client/server information system rather than to the label or name assigned to the overall logical design.

Client-Based Presentation   All three logical architectures illustrated in Figure 1-13 had only one thing in common: client-based presentation. In order to be considered a client/server information system, the client must handle at least the first element of the P-A-D logical architecture, namely, presentation. Client-based presentation is often handled through familiar **graphical user interfaces (GUI)** such as Windows, OS/2 Presentation Manager, X Windows-based systems such as Motif and Open-Look, or the Macintosh Desktop.

As illustrated in both Figures 1-12 and 1-13, the fact that the presentation is client-based is independent of where the application logic is processed. In client-based–processing client/server information systems, the applications that run on the client must be compatible with the GUI running on that client. If the client uses Windows as its GUI, then the applications on that client must be Windows-compatible. The technical aspects of the interface between GUIs and compliant applications will be studied in detail in Chapter 3, Client Software.

Host-based processing client/server information systems also use client-based presentation software. With the help of a category of software known as **screen scrapers,** or **screen emulation software,** character-based screens that were formerly displayed on dumb terminals are reformatted into GUI format. All that has changed is the client-based presentation. The mainframe, or host-based processing application, remains unchanged. This is often a first step on the road from mainframe-based applications to client/server computing. The GUI interface is more user-friendly than the character-based screens and probably leads to greater worker productivity. However, the key point is that the application is still running unchanged on the expensive mainframe computer.

Distributed Computing Simply stated, achieving **distributed computing,** also known as distributed processing, is nothing more than dividing an application program into two or more pieces and subsequently distributing and processing those **distributed applications** onto two or more computers, either clients or servers. The division of application programs for optimal use by a client/server environment can be a major undertaking and will be explored in greater detail later in the book.

The client portion of the program is often called the **front end,** and it has three primary uses:

- To provide a user interface
- To format requests for data or processing from the server
- To format data received from the server for output to the user

The server portion of the program is often called the **back end,** or **engine,** and it too has three primary uses:

- To retrieve and store data as requested
- To perform computation and application processing
- To provide necessary security and management functions

In summary, the back end does all or most of the processing except the interface and formatting-related tasks performed by the front end. Relatively speaking, this back-end distributed application represents the majority of the total required processing, leading to the term *processing engine.* Figure 1-14 summarizes some of the key characteristics of front-end and back-end distributed applications.

Two of the most important attributes of distributed processing are transparency and scalability. The extent to which each of these attributes is present can vary from one distributed processing installation to another.

Transparency refers to the ability of distributed processing systems to combine clients and servers of different operating systems, network operating systems, and protocols into a cohesive system that processes distributed applications without regard to the aforementioned differences. The true measure of transparency is from the user's perspective. If all of the combinations of multivendor hardware and software do not adversely affect users' ability to get the information they need in order to effectively perform a job, then distributed processing transparency has been delivered. Complete transparency is still a largely unrealized goal of distributed processing. As will be seen when specific distributed processing solutions are explored, limited transparency among a limited number of vendors' equipment, operating systems, and network operating systems is currently possible.

This transparency is achieved via a category of software known as **middleware.** Middleware resides in the middle of the distributed processing system, serving as a transparent insulator surrounding the enterprise network over which the client/server communication actually travels. Middleware will be explored in more detail later in the chapter as well as in Chapter 6.

Characteristic	Front-End	Back-End
Also called . . .	Client-Portion	Engine
Runs on . . .	Client Workstation	Servers
Primary functions	User interface Format requests for data or processing from server Format data received from server	Store and retrieve data Perform computation and application processing Provide security and management functions
Runs . . .	. . . as needed or as activated by user	. . . constantly
Services . . .	. . . individual user at single client workstation	. . . multiple users sending requests for processing/data from multiple client workstations
Examples	E-Mail Systems	
	Receive, read, send personal E-Mail messages as desired	Provide on-going E-Mail delivery service for all attached clients
	Database Systems	
	Format requests for data from data server	Services data requests from multiple clients

Figure 1-14   Distributed Processing: Front-End versus Back-End Distributed Applications

Transparency is closely related to another frequently mentioned characteristic of distributed computing: **portability.** Portability refers to the ability for client/server applications to be developed in one computing environment and deployed in others. **Scalability** refers to the ability of distributed processing systems to add clients and/or servers without decreasing the overall performance of the system. This is possible owing to the fact that as each client is added, the incremental processing power of that client's CPU is added to the overall processing power of the entire distributed processing system.

This distributed processing attribute of scalability should be contrasted with the effect on the mainframe-terminal architecture of the addition of incremental terminals to the mainframe. Because all processing power is concentrated in the mainframe, overall system performance decreases for each terminal added. When overall system performance is seriously degraded, the customary solution in order to increase overall processing power is to buy a bigger mainframe. Obviously, the cost of a bigger mainframe is significantly more than the cost of client workstations. This is not to say that mainframes don't have their rightful place in a distributed computing environment. The changing role of the mainframe will be explored in Chapter 8, Client/Server Application Development and Integration.

It is also worth repeating that the scalability of a distributed processing system is significant only if application programs can be split, or distributed, between clients and servers. This is by no means a trivial task. With this distributed application hurdle overcome, massive amounts of processing power and storage capability can be merged via the enterprise backbone network to effectively form one massively powerful and flexible computer. Figure 1-15 illustrates transparency and scalability, the key attributes of distributed processing systems.

Interprocess Communications After splitting the application logically between the client (front end) and one or more servers (back ends), the next challenge is to make these separate pieces of an application behave as if they were a single application process running on a single computer. Obviously, what is needed is a mechanism that will allow the multiple pieces of the application to communicate with one another. This communication is known as **interprocess communication (IPC)** and is illustrated in Figure 1-16. Interprocess communications protocols are responsible for sending messages and commands between processes and for synchronizing complicated transactions requiring the execution of multiple processes on multiple computers. This interprocess communication can become especially tricky when one considers that the different pieces of the distributed process may be running on computers with totally different combinations of operating systems, network operating systems, and database management systems.

Two of the most popular categories of interprocess communications protocols are known as **remote procedure calls (RPC)** and **message passing** or Message Oriented Middleware (MOM). These IPC protocols are examples of middleware, previously mentioned in relation to distributed computing transparency. More examples and explanations of interprocess communications protocols will be included later in this chapter as well as in Chapter 6, Middleware.

Database Distribution If specially designed distributed applications are split to run as separate client (front end) and server (back end) portions, then database management systems (DBMSs) will have to be somehow specially adapted for the distributed environment as well.

In a distributed environment, data must be able to be stored in multiple physical locations, on different types of server computers, and in a manner that is transparent to the end user. These multiple database servers must be able to communicate with one another, even if they are not running the same DBMS. Specially designed front-end tools perform distributed database inquiry, report generation, and application development. **Distributed database management systems** and their associated front-end tools serve as an additional variable—together with application programs, operating systems and network operating systems—that must interoperate transparently over the enterprise network.

Simply stated, in order to qualify as a true distributed database management system, the product in question must offer **data transparency** to the end-user. Although specific required characteristics will be explored in more detail later in the book, generally speaking, a true distributed database management system should allow a user to access data without regard for the following:

- Front-end tool or distributed application
- Type of server computer (Intel-based, minicomputer, mainframe, and so on)
- Physical location of the server
- Physical details and protocols of the network path to the server

Transparency: Clients and servers cooperatively share processing load *without regard for operating system or protocol differences.*

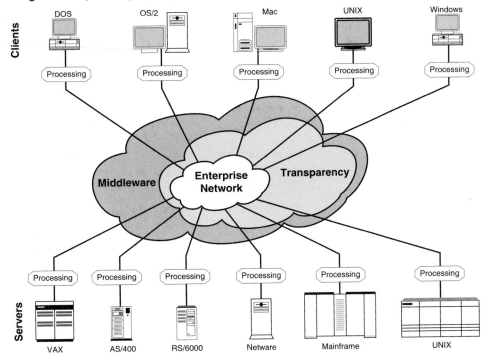

Scalability: Additional clients are added to system with little or no effect on processing load owing to *incremental processing power* added by each client.

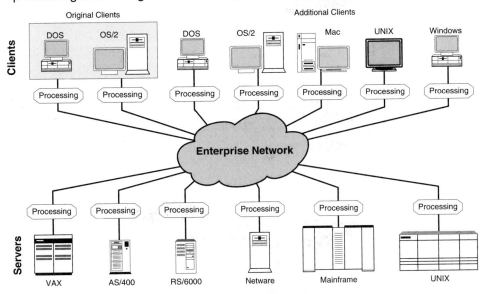

Figure 1-15   Key Attributes of Distributed Processing

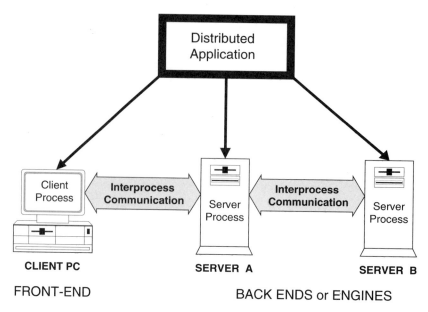

Figure 1-16   Distributed Processing Requires Interprocess Communications

In addition to data transparency, the distribution-related characteristics center largely around the distributed database management system's ability to divide and distribute portions of databases flexibly while maintaining all of the security, integrity, and control functionality of a single site database management system. This last point, the ability to effectively manage distributed databases, is perhaps the single most important issue in the implementation of distributed database management systems. Financial considerations of single-site versus distributed database management systems play a large role in final purchase decisions as well.

Figure 1-17 illustrates the key components of a distributed database environment. Although each of the components illustrated will be explained further either later in this chapter or in Chapter 8, Client/Server Application Development and Integration, the following are brief descriptions:

Database connectivity software is concerned with connecting a variety of front-end tools with a variety of distributed DBMS engines. Key to this required functionality is a standardized database command language known as **SQL (Structured Query Language).** Therefore, database connectivity software must be compatible with a specific database front-end tool or engine on one side, while translating to or from industry standard SQL commands on the other side.

As described fully in Chapter 6, numerous other database connectivity solutions other than SQL exist. ODBC (Open Database Connectivity) and Object-Oriented Middleware such as CORBA (Common Object Request Broker Architecture) and DCOM (Distributed Common Object Model) are two examples of potential object-oriented connectivity solutions.

Rather than offering translation to an industry-standard neutral language such as SQL, **single solution gateways** can actually offer improved performance owing to optimally written code translating between a specific front-end tool and a specific distributed DBMS or between two different database engines. The downside is that single solution gateways offer no flexibility, working only for particular combinations of database technology.

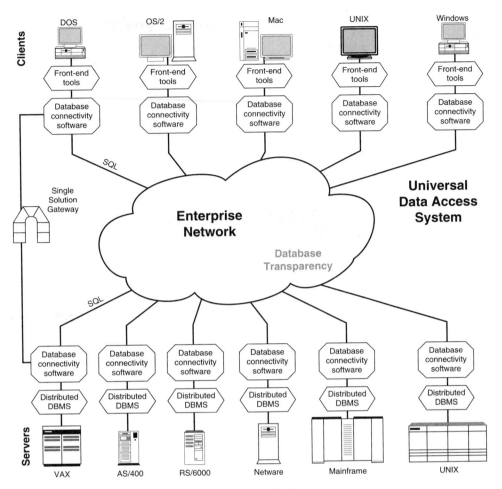

Figure 1-17   Key Components of Database Distribution

Front-end tools for database management systems fall into two major categories:

- Database query and reporting tools
- Multiple-platform client/server application development tools

Tools in each category depend on protocols known as **Application Program Interfaces (APIs)** in order to allow a single application to work with multiple, different database management systems. APIs prevent programmers from having to write specific versions of programs for each unique database management system, network operating system, or operating system combination possible for all servers to whom the front-end tool may ever wish to communicate.

A lack of standardization created by numerous vendor-specific versions of SQL provided a market opportunity for a sort of SQL middleware that could translate transparently between the many versions of SQL implemented on different platforms and databases.

A product known as EDA/SQL (Enterprise Data Access/SQL) from Information Builders, Inc., has taken advantage of that market opportunity. Calling itself a **Universal Data Access System,** EDA/SQL acts as a middleware layer, trapping SQL requests from clients and reformatting them as necessary before transporting them to the appropriate server.

EDA/SQL represents a single-vendor solution to the SQL incompatibility problem. However, any single-vendor solution can be a problem in itself. Single-vendor solutions are generally proprietary solutions, lacking in support of open systems standards and unable to guarantee wide-ranging interoperability.

Distributed Transaction Processing   In business, a transaction is an event such as purchasing a ladder, making a savings deposit, or taking out a loan. In information systems, a **transaction** is the sequence or series of predefined steps or actions taken within an application program in order to properly record that business transaction. Properly recording a business transaction usually implies posting changes to several different files or databases. Transaction processing requires careful monitoring in order to ensure that all, not just some, postings related to a particular business transaction are successfully completed. This monitoring of transaction posting is done by a specialized type of software known as **TP (transaction posting) monitors.** Whereas transaction postings are most often posted to databases, the integrity assured by TP monitors depends on their ability to interact with installed database management systems. Figure 1-18 summarizes the key characteristics of transactions that must be ensured by TP monitors.

In some cases, especially in mainframe-based systems, all of the databases that need to be updated for a given transaction are located on a single large computer. This process is known as local or nondistributed transaction posting and would require a local TP monitor. With the advent of client/server information systems, multiple geographically dispersed computers are linked, allowing transactions to be posted across multiple distributed computers.

Transaction Characteristic	Explanation/Importance
All or nothing	• Also known as atomicity. All of the postings related to a given transaction must be posted successfully, or none must be posted. • Partial postings are not acceptable. • As far as the information system is concerned, the transaction is nonexistent until it is posted completely.
Synchronized lock in progress	• A transaction involving multiple postings is set up to post individual postings in a particular order. • Certain fields of information may need to be locked during these postings to prevent other programs from accessing them. • The TP monitor ensures that postings are posted in the proper order and that fields of information are locked as appropriate for each posting.
Fault tolerant	• Once a transaction had been posted fully, the TP monitor assures that these postings cannot be corrupted by other postings or system failures.

Figure 1-18   Transaction Characteristics Ensured by TP Monitors

This process is known as **distributed transaction processing (DTP)** and requires a distributed TP monitor. DTP is sometimes also known as **Enterprise Transaction Processing,** or **ETP.**

As illustrated in Figure 1-19, DTP monitoring actually requires two levels of TP monitoring. First, the local TP monitor must ensure the integrity of local postings. However, these local postings are just part of a single distributed transaction posting that must be coordinated overall by the **distributed transaction processing monitor (DTPM).** The distributed transaction processing monitor is able to interface to the local transaction processing monitor thanks to a distributed transaction processing application program interface (**DTP API**) protocol supported by both TP monitors.

Business information must be as current as possible. "Accurate as of the start of the business day" is often not sufficient. Information systems that give up-to-the-minute information are sometimes known as **real-time systems.** In order to keep information real-time, business transactions must be posted immediately, rather than in nightly batches, using systems known as **on-line transaction processing (OLTP) systems.**

The Top-Down Model Applied to Client/Server   Figure 1-20 summarizes the logical, or functional, relationships between the elements of distributed information systems by categorizing these functions according to the top-down model. This model

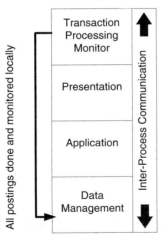

Logical Model of Local or Nondistributed Transaction Processing Monitor

All software installed on same system.

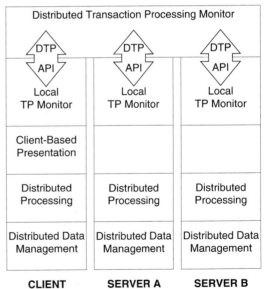

Logical Model of Distributed Transaction Processing Monitor

Local TP monitors ensure integrity of local transaction postings.
Distributed TP monitor ensures integrity of overall distributed postings.
Distributed TP monitor and local TP monitor communicate via DTP API.

Figure 1-19   Local versus Distributed Transaction Process Monitoring

Business	Increased competition on a global scale Corporate downsizing Information systems downsizing Business process redesign/reengineering		
Application	Client presentation Application rightsizing Distributed computing Distribute applications	Distributed Transaction Process Monitors Middleware Interprocess Communication	Client/Server Architecture
Data	Distributed databases		
Network	Enterprise networks Distributed network management		
Technology	To be determined by physical client-server design		

Figure 1-20   The Top-Down Model and Logical Client/Server Architecture

clearly demonstrates *what* a client/server information system must do (logical design). What remains to be seen is *how* these things can be accomplished (physical design).

In order to understand the full impact of client/server architectures, it is necessary to comprehend the physical relationship or technology implementation configuration of the elements of a typical client/server architecture as well. The next section of the chapter introduces the physical/technology architectures of client/server information systems.

Physical/Technology Architectures

Client/Server Architecture versus Mainframe/Terminal Architecture   In order to understand the significant differences between a client/server architecture and a more traditional mainframe/terminal architecture, the location where each of the elements listed in Figure 1-20 is accomplished must be identified. Figure 1-21 illustrates the differences in location of these key information systems elements between client/server and mainframe-based architectures.

The client/server illustration in Figure 1-21 is somewhat of an oversimplification of client/server architectures. First, multiple servers are commonplace in such an architecture. Second, servers are very likely to be distributed geographically. Some servers will be located remotely and linked to geographically dispersed clients via a wide area network (WAN), sometimes referred to as an enterprise network.

The following characteristics of client/server information systems should be evident in Figure 1-21.

- Distributed processing: The processing necessary to produce application program requests for data may take place on either the client workstation or the shared system server.

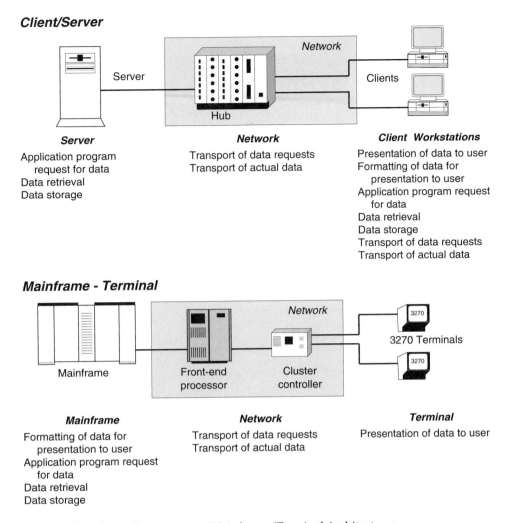

Figure 1-21   Client/Server versus Mainframe/Terminal Architectures

- Database distribution: Data may be stored or retrieved on either the client workstation or the shared system server.

- Enterprise network: The transportation of data requests and actual data for the client/server architecture may be handled with the help of a specialized category of interface software known as middleware.

In contrast, as can be seen in Figure 1-21, the mainframe/terminal environment has limitations:

- It requires all processing of any type to be performed on the mainframe.

- Its terminals act only as "dumb" input/output devices.

Client/Server Technology Architecture   Figure 1-22 illustrates a client/server technology architecture by depicting the categories of software that may be present on client and server computers linked by an enterprise network. This diagram is concerned primarily with software and communications, which is why only a single

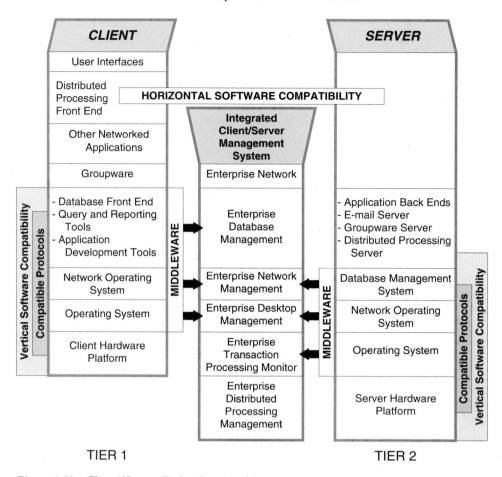

Figure 1-22 Client/Server Technology Architecture

client and server software profiles are illustrated. The fact is, any number of clients or servers may be linked by the enterprise network, but the software compatibility issues illustrated in Figure 1-22 will still remain. Examples of each of the technology categories listed in Figure 1-22 will be reviewed later in this chapter.

The best way to analyze software compatibility is by direction. **Vertical software compatibility** makes sure that all necessary compatible protocols are in place in order for all of the software and hardware within a single client or server to operate harmoniously and transparently. The intricacies of these compatibility issues and the protocols available that support vertical software compatibility will be studied in depth throughout the remainder of the text. The most important thing to remember is that these issues must be analyzed methodically. It is not important to memorize potential compatible protocols. What is important is to use a structured model such as Figure 1-22 in order to uncover any potential incompatibilities before, rather than after, installation. For example:

1. How do I know that a particular version of UNIX (operating system layer) will work on my computer (server hardware platform layer)?

2. If I do get UNIX installed, how do I know which network operating systems and database management systems will be compatible with UNIX and with each other?

Whereas vertical software compatibility is concerned with transparency between *different* layers of software or hardware *within* a particular client or server, **horizontal software compatibility** is concerned with transparency between *similar* software layers *between* different clients and servers.

To elaborate, one of the benefits of a client/server architecture is its ability to incorporate hardware and software technology from multiple vendors into a transparently interoperable information system. The previous statement is easier said than done. Horizontal software compatibility is most often concerned with getting different software of the same category to interoperate transparently between clients, between clients and servers, or between servers. For example:

1. How to I get a NetWare client (Network operating system layer) to interoperate with a Windows NT server (Network Operating system layer)?

2. How do I get an Oracle Database server (database management system layer) to query a Sybase SQL server (database management system layer)?

Horizontal software compatibility between different types of software on different types of computers is a complicated task roughly equivalent to translating between foreign languages. As a result, although vertical software compatibility was achieved by adjacent software layers each supporting a common compatibility protocol, horizontal software compatibility is most often delivered by a category of software known as **middleware.** Middleware is an actual additional installed software program rather than just a set of mutually supported commands and messages. Middleware is often specialized by software layer: database middleware, network operating system middleware, operating systems middleware, or distributed application middleware.

Occasionally, horizontal software compatibility is concerned with transparent interoperability between multiple pieces of software in the same software category layer within a single client or server. For example: How do I get my Excel spreadsheet graph into my Word document?

Practical Advice and Information

Remember, transparency depends on the existence of compatibility protocols or translating middleware. These compatibility protocols and middleware may be proprietary and work only among one or a few vendors' software or may be open, industry-standard protocols. A network analyst must pinpoint where the needs for horizontal or vertical software compatibility are, and what options are available to deliver that compatibility.

The Enterprise Network Connecting the client and server in Figure 1-22 is an entity entitled the **enterprise network.** The enterprise network is the transportation system of the client/server architecture. Together with middleware, it is responsible for the transparent cooperation of distributed processors and databases. In an analogy to a powerful stand-alone mainframe computer, the enterprise network would be analogous to that computer's system bus, linking the processing power of the CPU with the stored data to be processed.

The role of the enterprise network is to deliver the integration and transparent interoperability enabled by the client/server architecture. Further, the enterprise network often also incorporates host-terminal traffic, voice traffic, and videoconferencing traffic in an integrated and well-managed fashion.

What exactly does an enterprise network look like? That depends on what the business enterprise looks like. If the business enterprise is composed of regional

branches or subsidiaries widely dispersed geographically, then the enterprise network will obviously contain WAN links. From a physical standpoint, the enterprise
network is most often the combination of network devices and connections of the
following categories:

- Local area network (LAN)
- LAN-to-LAN or Inter-LAN, also known as internetwork
- Wide area network (WAN)

In addition, the enterprise network plays a key role in managing a client/server
information system. Because of the distributed nature of a client/server information
system comprised of a multitude of widely dispersed processors, the only single location through which all traffic passes is the enterprise network. Therefore, the enterprise network is the only sensible location from which to manage the numerous
shared resources of the client/server information system. A variety of management
hardware and software capable of effectively supporting corporate requirements for
the management of distributed information systems is connected directly to the enterprise network. The enterprise network serves as the backbone of the client/server
information system. Hopefully, this discussion clarifies the truth of the often-heard
statement, "The network *is* the computer."

Whereas Figure 1-22 portrayed a conceptual or logical view of an enterprise
network, Figure 1-23 shows an example of a possible physical topology of a typical
enterprise network. Notice the LAN, LAN-to-LAN, and WAN elements combined
in Figure 1-23 to form the overall enterprise network.

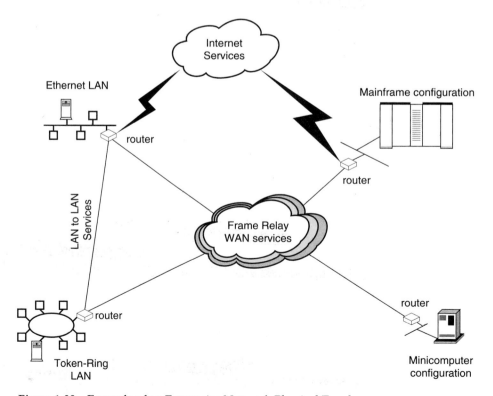

Figure 1-23   Example of an Enterprise Network Physical Topology

Management of Client/Server Information Systems   In order to understand the complexity of a comprehensive management system for a client/server architecture, one needs only to examine the vast array of components within that architecture that can potentially require management.

Most, if not all, of the client/server architecture elements listed in Figure 1-22 are available with some sort of management system or software. The problem is that there is little, if any, similarity or consistency in management system design among vendors, even for elements of similar function. In addition, the multiple layers of management systems listed in Figure 1-22 under the enterprise network component present a management system integration problem of major proportion.

Users do not want "piecemeal" system management caused by the distributed nature of their information systems. They do not wish separate management consoles or systems for database systems, distributed applications, operating systems, network operating systems, and networking hardware. Furthermore, since the client/server architecture can feature multiple client and server operating systems and network operating systems, one could potentially need an entire room just for systems consoles for the management of the various client and server possibilities.

The solution to the management system integration problem comes down to a few key questions about standards:

1. Can management system standards be developed that lend themselves especially well to distributed information systems?

2. More importantly, can and will these standards be adhered to by the manufacturers of the various elements of the client/server architecture?

In fact, open standards for sharing management information have been developed and integrated into several popular **enterprise network management systems.** The following are among the most popular of these systems:

- HP Openview
- IBM NetView
- Sun Sunnet Manager
- Tivoli Management Environment
- Computer Associates Unicenter

However, it is important to distinguish between enterprise network management systems and **integrated client/server management systems.** In addition to managing a multivendor enterprise network, an integrated client/server management system must also be able to supply the following management capabilities:

- Enterprise database management
- Enterprise desktop management
- Enterprise transaction processing management
- Enterprise distributed processing management

Although there are many multivendor enterprise network management systems, most so-called integrated client/server management systems are still in the "vaporware" stage: more theory than reality. Note that enterprise network management is only one component of overall integrated client/server management. Integrated client/server management systems will be discussed in detail in Chapter 12, Client/Server Information Systems Management.

Two-Tiered versus Three-Tiered Client/Server Architectures   Client/server physical architectures are often categorized in terms of tiers. The term *tiers* refers to the relationship between the logical sublayers of the application process of the P-A-D logical architecture (Figure 1-11) and the physical architecture in which those sublayer processes are delivered. In other words, we know we want to implement a distributed processing information system. The question is, how will that processing be distributed? Recall that the application layer of the P-A-D logical model is subdivided into three parts:

- Presentation logic
- Business logic
- Database logic

Two-tiered client/server architectures deliver the presentation logic on the client and the database logic on the server. The business logic may be distributed as follows:

- On the client in a two-tiered architecture known as **fat client**
- On the server in a two-tiered architecture known as **fat server**

Three-tiered client/server architectures, sometimes referred to as **n-tiered client/server architectures,** deliver the presentation logic on the client, the business logic on one or more dedicated servers, and the database logic on one or more superservers or mainframes. Specialized middleware servers are often located on the second (middle) tier as well. Figure 1-24 illustrates two-tiered and three-tiered (n-tiered) client/server architectures.

Which of the two architectures is better? The answer is the classic networking analysis answer: "It depends." Two-tiered architectures are presently far more common and work well for the type of departmental client/server systems that corporations often use as pilot projects to gain experience with downsizing, application rightsizing, and client/server information systems. Development tools and database back ends for two-tiered architectures are widely available and dependable.

Enterprisewide distributed client/server applications require the business-logic processing to be separated from the database logic in order to allow multiple geographically distributed database servers to adhere to the same business logic. In these cases, three-tiered architectures would be preferred. Because three-tiered architectures are newer than two-tiered, predictably there are fewer development tools available and fewer successful installations available as models.

Managerial Perspective

From a network analyst's standpoint, philosophical arguments over the virtues of two-tiered versus three-tiered architectures should be avoided. By adhering to the top-down model, the architecture that most effectively meets the strategic business requirements of the corporation will be evident.

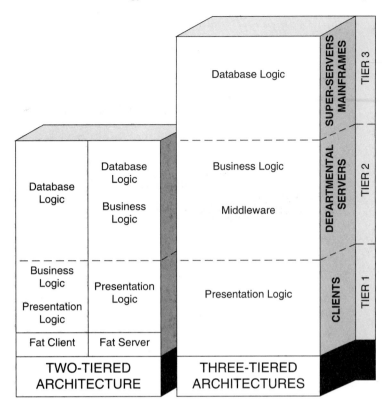

Figure 1-24   Two-Tiered versus Three-Tiered Client/Server Architecture

■ TECHNOLOGY AND TOOLS OF CLIENT/SERVER INFORMATION SYSTEMS

Technology Components and Trends

Client/server information systems require a multitude of hardware and software technology from a variety of vendors to be linked together seamlessly via an enterprise network in order to deliver transparent interoperability to the end user. The term seamlessly implies that all software/software, software/hardware, and hardware/hardware interfaces have been successfully bridged by mutually compatible protocols. This is far from a trivial task.

Figure 1- 22 illustrated the many categories of technology that must successfully interact in a client/server information system. Although many of these technology categories are elaborated on in entire chapters later in the text, the following section will provide some insight into the following areas for each technology category listed:

- Key characteristics and trends

- Current products

SQL and Object-Oriented Databases   As previously mentioned, structured query language is a standard command language supported by database vendors allowing interoperability among multivendor database front ends and database engines. However, the problem with SQL is that individual vendors enhance the language through the implementation of proprietary extensions. As a result, the version of SQL that all database vendors support becomes a least common denominator, or least functional version, of the database interoperability language.

Object-oriented databases and middleware adhering to CORBA or DCOM standards are becoming increasingly popular and well integrated with distributed application programming environments. A variety of databases and middleware technology is described further in Chapters 6 and 8.

TP Monitors   Transaction processing monitors are often considered a category of middleware acting as a supervisor of distributed applications that require postings to numerous distributed databases. TP monitors are currently being adapted for the multivendor, multiplatform client/server world. For example, IBM's CICS (Customer Information Control System) was originally designed for mainframe computers, and Novell's Tuxedo was originally designed for use only on UNIX platforms. Other popular TP monitors include Top End from NCR and Encina from Transarc. TP monitors can work locally in a stand-alone fashion or can work in a distributed environment in coordination with other TP monitors.

Numerous TP monitor standards are evolving, and interoperability among TP monitors from different vendors is by no means guaranteed. All TP monitors perform the following basic tasks:

- Oversee the successful postings of the transaction.

- Route the transaction among multiple clients, servers, or both.

- Load-balance the execution of the transaction.

- Restart the posting of the transaction or handle failed postings predictably.

Groupware   Groupware is a category of software that seeks to take advantage of the fact that workers are networked together electronically in order to maximize worker productivity. If increasing worker productivity is one of the top-layer business needs of the top-down model, then groupware may be of some interest.

Lotus Notes is probably the best known of the currently available groupware offerings. Notes runs on Windows, Windows NT, OS/2, UNIX, and Macintosh platforms and has had numerous third-party add-on products developed for it.

Groupware of any type is heavily dependent on bandwidth intensive applications such as multimedia and videoconferencing. Network analysts should be especially careful in estimating network impact of groupware implementation.

Groupware is a general term that describes all or some of the following software categories:

- Workflow automation

- Interactive work and electronic whiteboards

- Group scheduling

- Document review and management

- Information sharing and desktop conferencing

- Enhanced electronic mail

Groupware is described more fully in Chapter 5, Client/Server Groupware.

Middleware   Middleware is a fairly general category of software. It can be broken down into at least two subcategories based on the nature of the interprocess communication enabled by the middleware.

Remote procedure call middleware works like a locally run application program that activates, or calls, a subroutine stored outside of the application program itself, but usually in a subroutine library on the same computer. However, with the remote procedure call, the call for the execution of a subroutine is made to a remote procedure located on a remote distributed processor via the enterprise network. Where that particular server is located and how the remote procedure call will get transported there are the concern of the RPC middleware rather than the applications programmer.

RPCs are like local subroutines in at least one other characteristic as well. When an application program branches to a subroutine, whether a local or a remote procedure, that application program waits for the local or remote procedure to complete execution and return either data or some type of status message before continuing with its own program execution. This style of interprocess communication could be categorized as **send-and-wait**, or **synchronous**, communication.

Message passing, also known as message delivery, message queuing, or distributed messaging, differs significantly from the previously mentioned middleware subcategories in its ability to establish various types of interprocess communications modes other than the send-and-wait mode of the middleware RPCs.

For instance, distributed applications programs can communicate indirectly with the help of message queues, which are roughly equivalent to post offices. In this scenario, a distributed application could generate a message for another distributed application, forward it to the message queue, and resume its own processing activity. This type of interprocess dialogue is known as **asynchronous** (not to be confused with asynchronous transmission).

Another interprocess dialogue type supported by message delivery middleware is broadcast or multicast dialogues. Broadcast sends messages to all clients or servers on an enterprise network, whereas multicast sends to a selected group.

Message delivery middleware is flexible in the content of interprocess communication messages as well. For instance, message handling middleware can deliver RPC or SQL as its message. Security checking, encryption, data compression, and error recovery can all be supported features of message delivery middleware. Message-handling middleware often has the network savvy to navigate the enterprise network intelligently by responding to changing network conditions.

Middleware is an absolutely crucial component of distributed, multivendor client/server information systems and is described more fully in Chapter 6, Middleware. Without middleware, there can be no transparent interoperability, the key operational characteristic of client/server information systems.

Operating Systems and User Interfaces   In Figure 1-22, the crucial role of both client and server operating systems is immediately evident. The operating system is the first layer of software responsible for communicating with the hardware and delivering the functionality demanded by all of the upper layers of software. Although the technical aspects of present and future operating systems will be reviewed in future chapters, a few key trends are worth mentioning here in nontechnical terms.

First, the major differences between client and server operating systems are disappearing. Because of the demands of distributed processing in the client/server environment, both client and server operating systems must be powerful enough to run multiple applications simultaneously without allowing those applications to interfere with each other. At the same time, these futuristic operating systems should be "backward-compatible," to the greatest extent possible, with users' current hardware and software technology, so that all existing technology continues to function properly.

Although operating systems will continue to be more complicated in order to deliver this increased functionality, they simultaneously need to become more intuitive in their user interfaces. Graphical user interfaces should evolve toward **object-oriented user interfaces (OOUI)** in which users will no longer work by executing a particular application program, but by choosing to accomplish a particular task. The combination of application programs required to complete that task will execute without direct actions from the user.

Server operating systems must be powerful enough to participate in the three-tiered, widely distributed architecture of tomorrow's client/server information systems. These operating systems must be scalable, working equally efficiently on a single processor departmental server and a multiprocessor superserver delivering real-time video and voice conferencing as well as data via a worldwide enterprise network.

Network Operating Systems   Network operating systems (NOSs) play a key role in the overall mission of client/server information systems to deliver transparent interoperability. Network operating systems must serve as an insulating layer, shielding distributed applications that must interoperate transparently from the intricacies of the numerous different operating systems and hardware platforms on which the NOSs execute.

In order to truly deliver this transparent interoperability, current network operating systems must continue to develop in the following areas:

- Global services

- NOS-to-NOS interoperability

- Enterprisewide security

- Middleware incorporation

The term *global services*, sometimes referred to as global naming services or global directory services, refers to a NOS's ability to locate a particular resource, service, or user, regardless of the location of the desired entity. This implies coordination of directory and naming services among the multiple NOSs that comprise an entire enterprise network. Sought resources may be technical, such as printers, processors, data, fax machines, and CD-ROMs, or may be human, such as users, co-workers, or help desk support personnel.

If global naming services are to be successfully delivered across the enterprise, then different network operating systems must develop better interfaces to one another in order to deliver transparent interoperability. Although such a proposal might make perfect sense, it may be difficult to accomplish as competitive pressures and market share percentages exert their influence.

As the enterprise network grows and more mobile users require access to the enterprise network, enterprisewide security becomes a key issue. Traditional user ID or password schemes no longer suffice. Enterprisewide security must be composed of the following distinct processes:

- Authorization

- Authentication

Authorization is the familiar userID or password process that ensures that a certain user is authorized to access a particular enterprise resource. Enhancements to authorization for remote users include call-back security. Once a user has been properly authorized, **authentication** ensures that messages between clients and servers in the distributed processing environment are genuine and have actually been sent from the processor claiming to be the source node on the network. Authentication is usually provided by a dedicated authentication server running specialized software developed specifically for distributed environments.

Figure 1-25 summarizes typical current functionality of operating systems and network operating systems as well as potential future directions for each software category.

Middleware is responsible for allowing a variety of network operating systems, operating systems, and database management systems to interoperate transparently in support of distributed applications. This ability to interoperate transparently in support of distributed applications will become the responsibility of the network operating systems of tomorrow. The functionality supplied today by numerous third-party middleware vendors will be built into tomorrow's NOSs. All network operating systems will be ready to support distributed processing right out of the

	Operating Systems	Network Operating Systems
Current Functionality	• Interface between client hardware and upper layers of client software • Applications programs must be compatible with a particular operating system	• Interfaces between client operating systems and client networking hardware to communicate with network attached resources • NOSs must be compatible with the operating system on the client or server • Some NOSs provide their own operating systems
Future Trends	• Able to perform more than one task simultaneously (multitasking) • Able to split applications across more than one CPU (multiprocessing) • Will include GUI • GUI will evolve to object-oriented interfaces • Will be included within NOS products	• Will include GUI and OS • Will be able to run on a variety of hardware platforms and operating systems • Will be able to seamlessly interoperate with other network operating systems • Will be able to seamlessly interoperate with multiple electronic mail, groupware, and database management systems by including more middleware now purchased from third-party software vendors • Will include increased security

Figure 1-25 Functionality and Trends of Operating Systems and Network Operating Systems

box and will be capable of supporting the protocols necessary to deliver full horizontal software compatibility. Tomorrow's network operating systems will truly be "client/server ready." The best current examples of such truly open network operating systems are DCE (Distributed Computing Environment) from the Open Software Foundation (OSF) and ONC (Open Network Computing) from Sun Microsystems.

Distributed Applications   Many of the previously described technologies represent portions of the infrastructure underlying the real purpose of client/server information systems, namely, the distributed applications. If client/server information systems are to be the absolute information systems architecture of the future, then distributed applications need several improvements:

- They must become easier to develop.

- They should be easier to implement across heterogeneous distributed multi-vendor systems.

- They must become easier to execute.

A key contributing factor toward the achievement of many, if not all, of the aforementioned goals may be the widespread development and adoption of **distributed object technology.** However, the practicality and likelihood of widespread adoption of distributed object technology remains unclear.

As background, an **object** can be thought of as a merger of the business logic and database logic sublayers of the P-A-D model (Figure 1-11) once combined with actual data. Thus, data and the logic and rules to process that data are treated as a single, encapsulated entity that can subsequently interoperate with or encapsulate other objects.

Briefly stated, distributed object technology would enable distributed applications to be more easily developed thanks to the reusability and encapsulation quality of the objects themselves. Furthermore, thanks to an entire Object Management Architecture, objects and interobject communication can be distributed transparently across an enterprise network without requiring application development programmers to know the physical location of required objects. This **object management layer** would reside between the network operating system layer and the distributed application layer in a client/server technology architecture such as Figure 1-22, supposedly offering true application portability. Objects and object management will be discussed further in Chapter 6, Middleware.

Managerial Perspective

With the requirements for vertical software compatibility, it should be obvious that the object management layer, or any other layer for that matter, cannot just be added to the client/server technology architecture and have transparent application portability magically occur. Each layer of software or hardware must support protocols that are understood and supported by adjacent layers in the architecture. In order for the object management layer to be transparently assimilated into the client/server technology architecture, network operating systems and applications layers will need to support protocols defined by the object management layer. This support will be possible only if network operating systems and applications vendors are willing to commit the resources necessary to add this capability to their products. This commitment is by no means a forgone conclusion.

SUMMARY

Although many businesses may begin the exploration of client/server information systems in search of huge financial savings, the key benefit most often derived from their implementation is the flexibility of information delivery due to their distributed nature. Local area networks make up a crucial part of the overall enterprise network infrastructure that serves as the backbone linking the many distributed components of client/server information systems. As companies transition their information systems from mainframe-based to distributed client/server, opportunities exist to reengineer applications and the business processes they support. In order to analyze and design effective client/server information systems, it is essential to understand overall logical and physical architectures that model these distributed systems. The key logical elements that can be deployed across a variety of clients and servers are presentation, processing, business logic, and data management. These conceptual elements are all linked by the enterprise network. Heterogeneous platforms become transparently interoperable thanks to the addition of translating middleware. Designing client/server information systems requires an in-depth understanding of the interfaces between the numerous layers of hardware and software technology that must successfully interoperate. The client/server technology architecture can serve as an effective analysis tool in this regard. If client/server information systems are to become the dominant information systems architecture of the future, then improvements must be made in the ease with which distributed applications can be developed, implemented, maintained, supported, managed, and executed.

KEY TERMS

Application program interface (API)
Application rightsizing
Asynchronous
Authentication
Authorization
Back end
Client/server information system
Corporate downsizing
Database connectivity software
Data transparency
Distributed applications
Distributed architecture
Distributed computing
Distributed database management systems
Distributed object technology
Distributed transaction processing (DTP)
Distributed transaction processing application program interfacing (DTP API)
Distributed transaction processing monitor (DTPM)
Downsizing

Engine
Enterprise network
Enterprise network management system
Enterprise transaction processing (ETP)
Fat client
Fat server
Front end
Front-end tools
Graphical user interfaces (GUI)
Horizontal software compatibility
Information systems downsizing
Integrated client/server management system
Interprocess communication (IPC)
Message passing
Middleware
Object
Object management layer
Object-oriented user interface (OOUI)
On-line transaction processing (OLTP)
Paradigm

Paradigm shift
Portability
Presentation-Application-Data (P-A-D) architecture
Real-time systems
Remote procedure calls (RPC)
Rightsizing
Scalability
Screen scrapers
Send-and-wait
Single solution gateway
Smartsizing
Stored procedures
Structured query language (SQL)
Synchronous
Three-tiered C/S architecture
TP monitors
Transaction
Transition costs
Transparency
Triggers
Two-tiered C/S architecture
Universal data access system
Upsizing
Vertical software compatibility

REVIEW QUESTIONS

1. Describe the fallacy of massive cost savings from implementing client/server information systems.
2. What is the key benefit of client/server information systems in terms of business impact?
3. What are transition costs, and why are they occasionally overlooked?
4. What is the difference and relationship between corporate downsizing and information systems downsizing?
5. What is the productivity paradox?
6. What is the top-down model, and why is it important?
7. What is business process reengineering, and what is its relationship to the top-down model?
8. What is the overall relationship between the layers of the top-down model?
9. If the top-down model is used as intended, what can be assumed about implemented systems?
10. What is the difference between logical and physical network design?
11. Why is it important to allow logical and physical network designs to vary independently?
12. How are the terms *interface, protocols,* and *compatibility* related?
13. What is meant by the term *protocol stack* in terms of its importance to internetwork design?
14. Differentiate between the following protocol-related terms: *open, proprietary, de facto, de jure.*
15. Describe the importance of the OSI model.
16. What is the relationship between the layers of the OSI model?
17. What is the difference between the OSI model and OSI protocols?
18. Compare and contrast the OSI model with the Internet suite of protocols model.
19. Distinguish between the following in terms of effort, costs, and potential impact: *downsizing, rightsizing, upsizing, smartsizing.*
20. What is meant by the term *client/server information system?*
21. What are meant by the terms *paradigm* and *paradigm shift?*
22. Explain some of the impacts of the paradigm shift to client/server information systems.
23. How is a paradigm shift different from the introduction of new technology?
24. What is meant by term *people architecture,* and how is it related to systems architecture?
25. What are some of the major people architecture issues surrounding the transition to client/server information systems?
26. Describe the role of each of the sublayers of the application layer in the P-A-D architecture.
27. Differentiate between the following: client/based processing, host-based processing, cooperative processing.
28. What is a screen scraper, and what role does it play in the transition to client/server information systems?
29. What is the relationship between front ends and back ends in distributed applications?
30. Discuss the importance of each of the following in terms of distributed computing: transparency, scalability, portability.
31. Why is scalability so often mentioned as a business motivation for distributed computing?
32. What is the role of interprocess communications in distributed computing?
33. Why is interprocess communication not an issue in nondistributed computing environments?
34. What are some of the variables that make interprocess communication a complicated technology?
35. What are some of the difficulties that must be overcome when data management functions are distributed?
36. What is SQL, and why is it important?
37. Why is SQL not a perfect solution for database interoperability?
38. What are the advantages and disadvantages of a single solution gateway for database interoperability?
39. What is the outlook for Universal Data Access Systems if SQL standardization becomes more widespread and full-featured?
40. What is a *transaction,* as defined in business terms and in information systems terms?
41. What is the relationship between distributed transaction processing monitors and local transaction processing monitors?
42. What are the compatibility issues surrounding TP monitors and other layers of the client/server architecture?
43. What is a DTP API, and why is it important?
44. What is OLTP, and how does it differ from other TP systems?
45. Compare and contrast mainframe/terminal and client/server architectures.
46. Differentiate between vertical and horizontal software compatibility. How is each achieved?
47. What is middleware, and what is its role in distributed processing systems?
48. What is the role of the enterprise network in client/server information systems?
49. What elements or subnetworks might make up an enterprise network?

50. What types of traffic might an enterprise network carry?
51. Differentiate between enterprise network management systems and integrated client/server management systems.
52. Differentiate between two-tiered and three-tiered client/server architectures in terms of delivered functionality and physical architecture.
53. What is the difference between a fat client and a fat server in terms of functionality?
54. With which client/server architectures are fat clients and fat servers associated?
55. Why are triggers and stored procedures important?
56. What is the difference between a trigger and a stored procedure?
57. What types of functionality do all TP monitors have in common?
58. Why are TP monitors so important in distributed processing systems?
59. What are the major functional differences between RPCs and message passing middleware? Which is more flexible?
60. What is the difference between GUI and OOUI?
61. What are some of the key functional improvements necessary for network operating systems if they are to more effectively support client/server information systems?
62. What is the difference between authentication and authorization?
63. Detail the potential benefits as well as the obstacles facing distributed object technology.
64. What is the function of the object management layer?
65. What changes to distributed applications must occur if client/server information systems are to become more widely adopted?

ACTIVITIES

1. Review trade journals and professional periodicals for information on real-world implementation of client/server information systems. Prepare a chart or presentation summarizing stated benefits and negative impacts of the installations.
2. Find a local business in the midst of a transition from mainframe-based to client/server information systems. Prepare a presentation or chart focusing on the people issues involved with the transition.
3. After reviewing the client/server implementations for activity 1, classify these implementations according to the categories of client/server information systems presented in Figures 2-7 and 2-8. Which is the most common category? Explain your results.
4. Prepare a presentation comparing currently available GUIs. What, if any, are the major differences?
5. Research and prepare a presentation on available front ends and back ends for distributed applications. Focus the presentation on compatibility: which front ends work with which back ends on which types of computing platforms.
6. Research and report on the latest efforts to set SQL standards. How is compliance to any proposed standards ensured?
7. Research and report on database front-end tools.

Prepare a chart illustrating which front-end tools work with which database engines.
8. Research and report on transaction processing monitors. Which TP monitors work on which platforms? Which distributed TP monitors work with which local TP Monitors?
9. Research and report on OLTP applications. What is the systems architecture underlying the OLTP application (distributed or local)? What TP monitors are being used?
10. Prepare a detailed client/server technology architecture for an actual client/server information system. Be sure to highlight protocols and middleware that deliver software compatibility.
11. Research and report on the latest offerings in the enterprise network management and integrated client/server management technology categories. What standards are being used to help ensure multivendor interoperability?
12. Find an example of an OOUI, and demonstrate or report on it. What are the key differences between GUI and OOUI? What is the potential productivity impact of these differences?
13. Research and report on the Kerberos Authentication system. Report on tests to break the system as well as what steps are taken to ensure its security and integrity.

CHAPTER 1

CASE STUDY

CUTTING COSTS, NOT CORNERS

Battling Budgets and Skeptics, a Group of Users Automated a Department's Sales Force and Slashed Costs

Two years ago, National Semiconductor Corp. reorganized leaving Director of Interactive Marketing Phil Gibson with a sales and marketing staff of 17 instead of the 45 he needed. Faced with this problem, Gibson did the last thing you might expect: He took three members of his staff and assigned them the task of creating a sales-force automation system—instead of sending them out to woo customers.

It was an unpopular move. Some of Gibson's colleagues argued that he'd be better off allocating all of his staff to selling, but Gibson figured his department was so understaffed that losing three more people wouldn't make much of a difference.

Today National Semiconductor brags about the Internet-based system, which is helping it slash administrative costs, increase the effectiveness of its sales force, and judiciously allocate production in its factories.

The system uses a public Internet site and a private intranet to tie together customers, resellers, and National employees with a variety of back-end databases and intranet technologies.

On the public site, engineers can browse a database of detailed product specifications and tell the company which of the upcoming chips they plan to buy. Inside the company, National employees get 24-hour updates on the state of the company (what is selling and what is backlogged) so they can focus their attention on the most urgent matters. An automatic communica-

tions system routes and answers E-mail messages from external customers and helps schedule employee meetings and other urgent matters using E-mail alerts on the desktop and U.S. Robotics Access Corp. Palm Pilots.

Gibson, who has a bachelor's degree in electrical engineering and an M.B.A., credits his focus on long-term results and process with getting the job done.

Also crucial were his years of technical, marketing, and sales experience, which helped him see how technology could solve a business problem.

Long-Term Ambitions When he was 10 years old, Gibson's uncle took him along on a sales trip for Xerox Corp. From that moment on, Gibson says, he wanted to go into technical sales. He studied engineering and landed an R & D job at Ford Aerospace creating firmware for real-time systems. Twelve years ago, he moved to National's sales and marketing organization, where he marketed Ethernet chips to Novell Inc. and Apple Computer Inc. before becoming the director of one of National's applications-development groups. InterActive Marketing.

Gibson's background in technology and development dovetails well with National's IS strategy: At National, applications development is handled by business groups, not IS. Instead, IS handles ongoing maintenance and systems.

The project that is now the darling of National began as a joint proposal by Gibson and then-Vice President of Marketing and Communication Anne Wagner, who has since gone on to a similar position at SunSoft Inc. Gibson and Wagner

assembled a small group of people and within three months had a basic infrastructure with data sheets and lots of pretty pictures. But in the first focus session they held with customers, they were told "lose the graphics if you want us to come back," Gibson recounts.

Now the public World Wide Web site is text-rich, with full specifications on about 10,000 devices. Engineers can download data sheets and order sample parts.

The site was created in HTML (HyperText Markup Language) before automated Web tools existed, and now National uses Vignette Corp.'s StoryServer software to automatically update content from its databases. The site gets about 20,000 visitors a day, says Gibson. More important, visitors see about 2.7 screens when they visit, which means they are finding things nearly three times faster than they were before, when visitors stayed for about seven screens, he said.

Once the Web site was in place, Gibson turned his attention to the company's internal communications. About a year ago, his group put together a system that automatically responds to 1,000 E-mail messages a day from customers. Feedback buttons on all the pages of the company's Web site bring up HTML-based E-mail forms with Common Gateway Interface (CGI). These help customers categorize their messages and narrow their queries so that a Lotus Notes–based Feedback Clearinghouse can sort the mail with a series of agents. Notes either mails the message to the manager of the relevant product or sends an automatic reply. A staff member spends about an hour each day responding to the approximately 50 E-mails the system can't categorize, Gibson said.

Last March, the group started developing the National Advisor, a push-based reporting system that gives everyone in the company the latest statistics on product orders and production. The system pulls information from disparate databases throughout the company into a Notes Domino.Broadcast database. This repository, in turn, formats Notes data into the PointCast Inc. channel format. PointCast picks up the data and pushes it out to employee desktops, where it flashes the top company news on a Web-based screensaver. Employees can click on any item to see details on orders and production status.

The National Advisor includes sales-force information; orders from the reseller channel; shipping history; and mainframe-based billing, booking, and backlog data. Having all the information in one place lets employees do triage on the most important products and orders, helping them focus their efforts where they'll be most effective, Gibson says.

"Today [we] can pick any product we have, drill in and find any customer, every part, and its forecasted run rate," Gibson explains. "It allows us to know how important that business is today and down the road." Theoretically, employees could always get this information by running separate queries on different systems, but that was too time-consuming to be practical.

"The difference now is that it's all accumulated in one place and fed to everyone and sorted by point of view," he says. Soon the company will develop algorithms based on history to identify trends and adjust production to meet them.

If it works as planned, this system could give National a huge competitive advantage because the semiconductor business is plagued with sudden increases and sharp falloffs in demand for chips. Because it takes from six months to a year to create a new product, a forecasting mistake can leave a company with too much or too little of a product. To be successful, a company needs to coordinate production and demand—a tricky business that National calls "riding the tsunami." Gibson hopes that the National Advisor will develop into a forecasting system that will let National match supply with demand.

Part of the equation is the new Team Registration application, which lets the company forecast sales through partners (direct sales are forecast on the company's OEM sales-force registration system, a commercial Notes application called OverQuota). The Web-based system lets partners and distributors prepare for sales calls, support any kind of customer request, and track projects and opportunities. The reseller can also use the system to register early interest from a customer in a particular product; in exchange, the reseller gets preferred prices.

According to Gibson, one person wrote the application in Notes Domino in three months, and it went live in July [1997] in the United States. It's being deployed in Southeast Asia, and it will debut in Europe in this month. It's essentially a lighter, simpler version of OverQuota, Gibson said.

With 12,000 employees and customers around the world, performance is an obvious concern. The company runs its own intranet, which consists of Lotus Notes running on Microsoft Windows NT systems. Much of the network relies on Notes, but for heavy-duty data storage and number crunching, the company uses Sybase Inc. products. Its shipping history resides in a Sybase database, and the company's whole mainframe system and data warehouse uses Sybase.

So Gibson brought in Clay Shope, a longtime National employee who had previously installed a private network for North American sales, to oversee operations for the company's external Web site. At first, National planned to build its own mirror sites in Europe and Asia, but Shope quickly discovered that plan to be too complicated and costly. He started looking for an ISP (Internet service provider) with international operations, which is how he found Digital Island Inc., the only network provider with service to Asia.

The company, which is located on an old military base in Honolulu, directly connects to 30 locations in Asia and Europe, providing National's customers with a one-hop connection to National's Web site from any country. When customers dial in, they are connected to a Digital Island virtual server in the nearest city, which in turn is connected directly over private lines to Digital Island in Honolulu, which has a mirrored replica of the National Web site. National has estimated that by contracting with Digital Island, it has saved several million dollars a year.

The project was intended to increase sales, not cut costs—but administrative overhead has decreased. Administrative costs have gone from 18 percent to 11 percent, which has let National change the structure of its regional marketing organization, moving people out of administration and into direct interaction with customers, Gibson said.

Early registration and better forecasting through its direct sales force and reseller program has helped National cut the decision-making cycle of its own design engineers by several months, which in turn cut the one-year design cycle to three months.

The company logs Web clicks and other signs of interest in its products and uses these to decide quickly which products to ramp up or publicly launch. Previously, National interviewed a few select customers before deciding which products to produce.

Gut Instinct Gibson says the idea for the system was as much intuition as anything, but admits that he listened to what the salespeople wanted: A way to get detailed specs on all the company's products while they were face to face with a customer in the customer's office. At the same time, management was demanding more and more reporting from the salespeople in order to forecast sales more accurately.

"The sales force was being buried by requests for project tracking," he says. "If they did nothing but sit in an office and fill out forecasting spreadsheets, they would not have time to sell." He had read about sales-force automation soft-

ware and figured it could solve both problems at once for National.

After estimating the project's cost and getting permission to fund it out of his own budget, Gibson allocated three positions to the project—that was all he could spare. In retrospect, Gibson admits that much of the rationale was gut instinct—he never did a formal cost-benefit study because there was not time and he believed the company had no choice.

"It was automate or die," he says.

His boss Mike Bereziuk, senior

vice president of worldwide sales and marketing, credits Gibson's success to his creativity and perseverance. "Rather than just accept the fact that he could do a partial job with the [limited] resources he had, he set about from day one with the mindset that he needed to excel, that he needed to automate the process," he said. Gibson's combined marketing and technical expertise also helped. It will take more than tools to help National grow its business, but with any luck, National will be able to ride the Internet wave to success.

Source: Cate T. Corcoran, "Cutting Costs, Not Corners" *LAN Times,* vol. 15, no. 2 (January 19, 1998), p. NA-3. Copyright (January 19, 1998), The McGraw-Hill Companies, Inc.

BUSINESS CASE STUDY QUESTIONS

Activities

1. Complete a top-down model for this case by gleaning facts from the case and placing them in the proper layer of the top-down model. After completing the top-down model, analyze and detail those instances where requirements were clearly passed down from upper layers to lower layers of the model and where solutions to those requirements were passed up from lower layers to upper layers of the model.
2. Detail any questions about the case that may occur to you for which answers are not clearly stated in the article.

Business

1. What was the business problem that prompted the creation of the sales force automation system?
2. What were some of the positive business-oriented impacts of the systems implementation?
3. Who are the various constituencies served by the system?
4. How might this system provide competitive advantage?
5. How much was the estimated savings from employing the selected external web site provider?
6. What has been the decrease in administrative overhead percentages as a result of system implementation?

Application

1. How did the sales force automation system meet identified business layer requirements?
2. What type of information is shared between customers and employees?
3. How does the information available through the system allow employees to focus on the most crucial business issues?
4. Which corporate division at National Semiconductor is responsible for application development? Do you think this makes sense? Why or why not?
5. How were responses to customer inquiries automated?
6. What is the purpose of the National Advisor Application?
7. How is the National Advisor application different from how employees would have previously gathered the same information?

Data

1. What type of data is available on the system?
2. What type of information is available on the corporate web site?
3. How many e-mail messages from customers were received per day?
4. What type of information is supplied by the National Advisor application?

Network

1. What combination of networks (public, private, Internet, intranet, extranet) does the system use?
2. What criteria were used in selecting the provider for hosting National's external web services?

Technology

1. What type of technology is linked to the network in order to expedite scheduling of meetings and urgent e-mail alerts?

2. What is the purpose of the Lotus Notes Feedback Clearinghouse?
3. How is push technology incorporated into the system?
4. What combination of technologies comprises the National Advisor application?
5. Which network operating systems and database management systems are employed?

CHAPTER 2

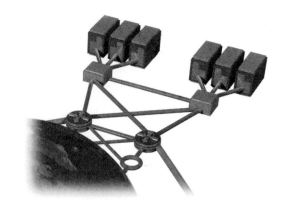

CLIENT HARDWARE

Concepts Reinforced

Client/Server Technology Architecture
OSI Model
Client/Server Technology and Tools

Protocols and Compatibility
Top-Down Model

Concepts Introduced

Comparative Hardware Platforms
PowerPC
Computer Bus Alternatives
Video/Graphics
Computer Storage

CPU Chips
RISC versus CISC
PCMCIA
Computer Memory
Processor Fundamentals

OBJECTIVES

After mastering the material in this chapter you should understand the following:

1. The basic internal functionality and differences among popular CPU chips

2. The impact on overall performance of and interrelationship between the following major computer subsystems:
   - Processor type
   - Memory
   - Disk storage
   - Video

3. The relationship between CPU type, clock speed, and overall performance

4. The differences between and performance impact of a variety of computer bus types

5. The differences between and implication of a variety of computer video standards

■ INTRODUCTION

An examination of the client portion of the client/server technology architecture (Figure 1-22) should make the importance of the client hardware platform immediately evident. The client hardware forms the foundation on which all upper layer software depends. Regardless of how powerful or sophisticated upper layer software such as operating systems, network operating systems, or applications might be, the ultimate limiting factor of overall client performance is the client hardware.

This study of client hardware is not meant to be overly technical. The treatment of the inner workings of client computing platforms in this chapter takes a definite systems-oriented approach. What is most important to information systems and networking professionals is an understanding of how all of the major technological components of a client PC—CPU chip, bus, memory, storage, and video—interact with one another to produce the overall performance characteristics of a given computing platform. The critical outcome of this chapter is the accumulation of sufficient knowledge to ask important analysis questions, rather than rote memorization of technical specifications.

■ THE COMPUTER AS A SYSTEM

Perhaps the most important point to understand about a client computing platform is that it is really a **computer system.** The term *computer system* was very commonly used prior to the introduction of personal computers and is ultimately more descriptive, from a technological perspective, of a computer's true nature.

The following four subsystems contribute to the overall performance characteristics of any computer system:

1. Processor or CPU

2. Memory subsystem

3. Storage subsystem

4. Video or input/output subsystem

A potential fifth subsystem, which ties all of the previously mentioned subsystems together, is known as the bus subsystem. A change in any one of these subsystems can have a profound effect on the overall performance of the computer system as a whole. Each of these subsystems will be studied in detail in the remainder of the chapter.

■ THE CPU

The feature that most uniquely identifies any given computing platform is the processor chip, or **central processing unit (CPU),** in which software instructions are actually executed. Today, there are four predominant families of client computing platforms categorized by their CPU chips:

CPU Chip	Computing Platform
x86 chips, Intel chips	Personal computer (PC)
PowerPC chips (RISC)	PowerPC, PowerMac
Motorola 68000 chips	Macintosh
RISC chips, SPARC	UNIX workstations

Although there are obvious differences among these computing platforms and their installed CPUs, a number of functional similarities exist among different computer chips.

CPU Functionality and Concepts

A generalized view of CPU functionality is important in order to appreciate the comparative advantages and disadvantages of alternative computing platforms and to choose the right client computing platform for the job. An information systems analyst or network analyst must have a basic understanding of CPU functionality in order to appreciate the actual importance of the myriad of technical terminology, technical jargon, and marketing hype encountered in evaluating alternative client hardware.

There is one simple concept to keep in mind in a review of CPU technical functionality:

- Basically only one motivation exists for any technological innovation in a CPU chip: more processing speed.

The need to reliably complete more instructions in a given amount of time is behind most of the technical innovations discussed in this section of the chapter. A network analyst should ask, "How does this innovation help the CPU operate faster and/or more reliably?" Only after answering this question can an analyst perform effective cost/benefit analysis.

The CPU Chip and Clock Speed   One of the first concepts to grasp concerning CPU chips and computing platform performance is **clock speed.** Specialized clock circuitry within the CPU chip is used to keep precise timing of CPU operations. Clock speed is measured in **Megahertz** (MHz), which means millions of cycles per second. A given CPU chip may be incorporated into different computing platforms at different clock speeds. The greater the clock speed, the greater the CPU performance. For example, Intel's Pentium chip is, or has been, available in at least the following clock speed options:

- 60 MHz
- 66 MHz
- 75 MHz
- 90 MHz

- 100 MHz

- 120 MHz

- 133 MHz

- 166 MHz

- 200 MHz

- 233 MHz

Intel Pentium II chips are, or will be, available in clock speeds running from 233 MHz to 450 MHz. For every clock speed cycle (every tick of the clock), the CPU performs one set of operations. What this set of operations consists of and how the CPU optimizes these operations will be elaborated upon shortly. Clock speed alone does not dictate overall performance. It is the combination of the CPU chip design and the clock speed that ultimately determines performance. For example, a 60 MHz Pentium chip may perform on par with a 100 MHz clock speed run on a previous generation of CPU chip such as a 486DX4.

Pipelines, Scalar Architectures, and Superscalar Architectures   Clock speed seeks to improve the overall performance of the CPU by having it work faster. Intuitively, the only other way to increase overall performance would be to find a way to have the CPU perform more than one operation simultaneously for each clock cycle. That is precisely what is achieved in many of today's CPU chips by employing variations of an architectural feature known as **pipelines**. A pipeline is analogous to an assembly line in a manufacturing plant.

In this case, what is being "manufactured" is a completed computer instruction. A pipeline typically divides the overall process of completing a computer instruction into the following five stages or subprocesses:

1. Fetch

2. Decode

3. Operands

4. Execute

5. Write back

The purposes of each of these stages are fairly self-explanatory. The **fetch stage** brings an instruction into the pipeline from a holding area in the CPU known as the **instruction cache.**

With the next tick of the clock, the contents of the fetch stage move to the **decode stage,** and a new instruction is brought into the pipeline by the fetch stage. The decode stage converts the fetched instruction into low-level code understood by the CPU.

With the next tick of the clock, in the **operands stage,** any additional data or numbers otherwise known as the operands, which are required to complete the instruction, are fetched. Meanwhile, the fetch and decode stages work on the next instruction on this same tick of the clock.

With the next tick of the clock, the instruction is executed in the **execute stage** while the fetch, decode, and operands stages work on the next instructions.

Finally, the results of the executed instruction are written out to a memory location or register, usually in a special area called a **data cache** in the **write-back stage.** The role of caches in determining overall CPU performance will be discussed shortly.

A CPU chip with a single pipeline is known as a **scalar** processor. More advanced CPU chips may employ more than one pipeline and are known as **superscalar.** More than one pipeline is analogous to more than one assembly line, with the result that more than one instruction is completed for each clock cycle. A CPU with two pipelines can issue two instructions simultaneously and is often referred to as a **dual-issue,** or two-way, processor; a CPU with four pipelines is called a **quad-issue,** or four-way, processor.

Pipelines can be specialized in other ways to increase overall performance. For example, pipeline execution stages can be especially written to be optimized for certain operations such as handling only the following:

- Floating-point operations

- Integer operations

- Branch logic (if-then-else) operations

These operation-specific options are called **execution units.** Once a pipeline determines which type of operation is required, it forwards data and instructions to the proper execution unit. Execution units represent options for the pipelines execute stage. As a result, CPUs often have a larger variety of execution units than pipelines. CPU chips may have more of some types of execution units than others based on anticipated demand for certain types of instructions.

Some pipelines employ more than five stages to complete a given instruction and are called **superpipelined** architectures, not to be confused with superscalar. For example, floating point pipelines may have more than one execute stage. Intel's Pentium Pro chip has a 14-stage superpipeline.

Figure 2-1 illustrates pipelines, superpipelines, scalar architectures, and superscalar architectures.

CPU Caches   With the manufacturing plant analogy, if the assembly operations have been optimized for efficiency through the use of multiple, properly designed pipelines (assembly lines), what else might have a significant impact on the overall performance of the operations? What if the suppliers couldn't supply these super-efficient assembly lines fast enough? The result would be that the super-efficient assembly lines (pipelines) would be idle some percentage of the time, because the suppliers (main or system memory) were unable to keep the pipelines full.

This scenario is a good example of a principle of data communications in general, and not just CPU design, known as the **principle of shifting bottlenecks.** The principle is really quite simple. As one aspect of a system that had been identified as a bottleneck is optimized, the bottleneck shifts to some other interacting component of the system. In this case, the CPU chip was optimized to the point where the speed of the transfer of data from the system memory into the CPU chip became the new bottleneck.

The solution to the CPU chip to system memory bottleneck is relatively straightforward: Include some high-speed memory directly on the processor chip as a buffer between the slower system memory (random access memory, or RAM) and the fast pipelines. This on-board memory is known as **on-board cache.** On-board cache is also known as on-chip cache, **primary cache,** or **L1 (level 1) cache.** L1 caches are generally only 8 KB to 32 KB.

Scalar (Single Pipeline)

➤ Each pipeline stage processes with each clock cycle.
➤ All instructions travel through a single pipeline

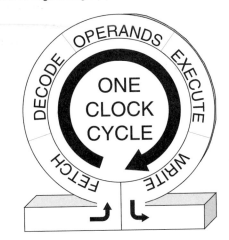

Superscalar (Multiple Pipelines)

➤ Each pipeline stage on every pipeline processes with each clock cycle.
➤ Instructions travel through specialized pipelines dependent on the type of processing required.

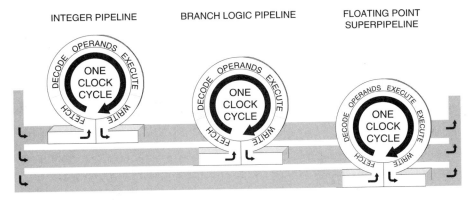

Figure 2-1   Pipelines, Superpipelines, Scalar Architectures, and Superscalar Architectures

Just as pipelines could be specialized in order to increase overall efficiency, primary caches can be specialized. The pipelines must fetch two distinct items: data and instructions. Therefore, it should come as no surprise that some CPU chips include both a **primary instruction cache** and a **primary data cache.**

Primary cache can also be differentiated as to whether the cache is used just as a read-only buffer to hold data or instructions for the fetch stage (stage 1) of the pipeline, or if it can also be used to be written to from the results of the write-back stage (stage 5). Cache that services only the fetch stage is known as **write-through cache,** whereas cache that also services the write-back stage is logically known as **write-back cache.**

The 8 KB to 32 KB generally included in L1 caches is not a great deal of buffer memory, but it is all that can easily be fit on the limited space available on a CPU chip. Once again the bottleneck shifts. What is needed is a high-speed memory cache not directly on, but closely connected to, the CPU chip. This memory is known as off-chip cache, **secondary cache,** or **L2 (level 2) cache.** The L2 cache is connected to the CPU chip through a **memory bus** whose speed is also measured in Megahertz. How many bits of data the CPU can read from and write to the L2 cache for each tick of the memory bus clock is determined by the **data bus width.** This is most often 32 or 64 bits. The amount of installed L2 cache is most often 256 KB or 512 KB, or sometimes as much as 1 MB or 2 MB, and is composed of high-speed SRAM, or static RAM. All of the many variations of types of RAM memory chips available today will be discussed further in the Memory section of this chapter.

Figure 2-2 differentiates between primary (L1) and secondary (L2) caches, and Figure 2-3 differentiates between write-back and write-through caches.

Cache memory is the functional equivalent of a warehouse in the manufacturing analogy. Whereas a warehouse eliminates the dependency of a manufacturing operation on a supplier, by providing a buffer of readily available raw materials, cache memory eliminates the dependency of the pipelines in a superscalar CPU on the relatively slow system memory to deliver data and instructions at a rate fast enough to keep the CPU's pipelines full.

Branch Prediction   Having increased the speed of execution with higher clock speeds and decreased CPU idle time with the incorporation of L1 and L2 caches, what else can we do to improve the performance of the overall process? A fairly accurate answer might be, "Not much."

Many of the advanced CPU design techniques that are beyond the scope of this book have one thing in common. Rather than trying to continue to improve on how *efficiently* data and instructions are moved through the pipelines, they concentrate instead on improving how *intelligently* data and instructions are moved through the

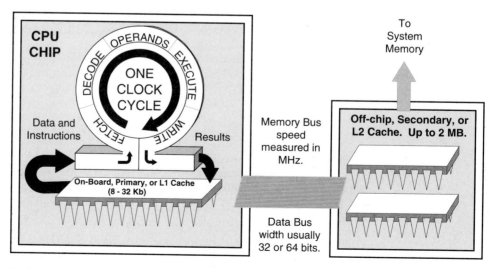

Figure 2-2   Primary versus Secondary Cache

Write-Back Cache

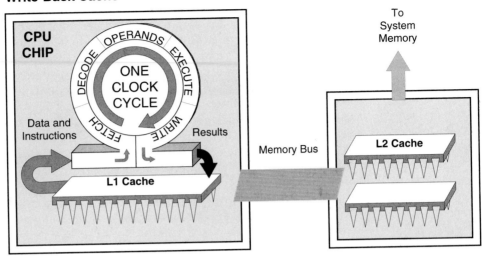

➡ Data and instructions are fetched from L1 cache.
➡ Results are written back to L1 cache.

Write-Through Cache

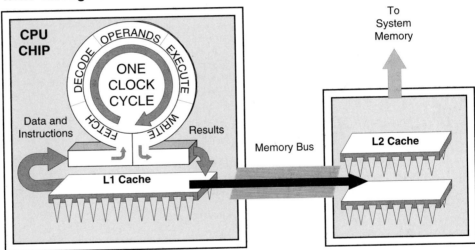

➡ Data and instructions are fetched from L1 cache.
➡ Results are written through L1 cache to L2 cache.

Figure 2-3   Write-Back versus Write-Through Cache

pipelines. This difference is somewhat like the popular phrase, "Work smarter, not harder." The difference between moving data and instructions efficiency and intelligently is subtle but significant. Handling data and instructions efficiently implies improving performance without regard for the content of the data or instructions. Once efficiency has been maximized, the only way to increase performance is to pay attention to the *content* of data and instructions and begin to alter pipeline behavior based on that content according to intelligence built into the CPU chip.

A good and understandable example of this intelligent instruction handling is a technique employed in many CPU chips known as **branch prediction.** A branch is a location or decision in a program's logic represented by an "if-then-else" statement (conditional branch) or a Goto or GoSub statement (unconditional branch). The problem with branches and pipelines is really a matter of timing.

Pipelines allow multiple instructions to be loaded and processed at various pipeline stages simultaneously. However, until the branch statement is evaluated in the execute stage of the pipeline, the CPU doesn't know which condition is true, and consequently, which conditional branch instruction to fetch. The simplest but least efficient way around this problem is to evaluate the branch statement to find out which conditional branch needs to be executed, flush out all of the partially processed instructions in the pipelines, and start over by fetching the proper conditional branch.

A more intelligent way to handle the same situation would be if the CPU could somehow predict which condition of the branch statement will be true and automatically load the associated conditional branch statement. This is exactly what some CPU chips do with branch prediction. Like most forecasting mechanisms, the best way to predict the future is to study the past. Most branch prediction processes employ a **branch target buffer,** or branch target cache that holds the results of as many as the last 256 branches executed in a given program. Using the patterns observed from this past branching behavior contained in the branch target buffer, the chips predict the results of future branches.

In Sharper Focus

BRANCH PREDICTION

Branch prediction is a difficult concept to visualize. The following is a simple example of a branched if-then-else program instruction.

```
READ EXAM_GRADE
If EXAM_GRADE < or = 60
      THEN Print "Slacker"
      ELSE Print "Passing Grade"
END_IF
```

By the time the exam grade has been fetched, gone through the operands stage, and been read into memory in the execute stage, two additional clock cycles would have been able to fetch the next two instructions for processing. The only problem is knowing which instruction should be fetched since the exam grade (the branch decision) has not been evaluated yet.

Without branch prediction, the Print "Slacker" instruction would be ready to execute immediately after the If EXAM_GRADE < or = 60 instruction. But what if the exam grade were greater than 60? We would have the wrong instruction about to execute and would have to flush out all of the partially processed instructions in the fetch and operands stage and proceed down the proper branch by fetching the ELSE Print "Passing Grade" instruction. In so doing, several precious clock cycles of the CPU would have been wasted.

With branch prediction, by keeping track of the results of the If EXAM_GRADE > or = 60 branch decision in branch target buffers, we would gather historical data and find out that, in fact, over 75 percent of the time, EXAM_GRADE is > or = 60. This would lead us to the prediction that 75 percent of the time the branch that should be executed next should be the Print "Passing Grade" instruction. By following this branch prediction technique, we will have the right branch ready to execute immediately after the decision statement the majority of the time leading to a more intelligent use of CPU cycles.

CISC versus RISC Although the debate between the relative merits of **CISC (Complex Instruction Set Computing)** and **RISC (Reduced Instruction Set Computing)** once possessed all the fervor of a religious war, the differences between the two computing architectures have diminished over the years. Periodicals in the information systems field seem to indicate that CISC is becoming more RISC-like and RISC is becoming more CISC-like. Many of the technological features cited in the earlier sections on CPU architecture as being common to most, if not all, modern CPU chips were found only in RISC chips at one time.

In the traditional differences between CISC and RISC, the focus is on the process to transform program instructions into executable code understandable by the CPU chip. In CISC architecture, instructions are interpreted into executable code by microcode, which is itself a small computer software program running on the CPU chip. In effect, CISC required one software program to translate another software program. On the other hand, RISC architectures interpret instructions directly in the CPU chip itself without the added overhead of the executing microcode. As a result of this hardware-based decoding, the processing speed increases.

However, there is a trade-off. Initially, RISC chips worked with a reduced number of only the simplest instructions. In order to accomplish the same tasks that a CISC architecture might do in a single complex instruction, the early RISC architecture would require multiple simple instructions. As a result, so-called second-generation RISC architectures began to increase their instruction set both in number and in complexity.

Key technological innovations credited to the RISC architecture are superscalar and superpipelining CPU chips. As discussed in the previous section of this chapter, both of these features are now included on so-called CISC chips such as the Intel Pentium. The incorporation of floating-point units directly in the CPU chip is another RISC innovation that accounts for RISC chips' traditional superior performance in floating-point operations. The Intel 486DX was the first Intel x86 chip to incorporate a floating-point unit in the CPU chip. Prior to that, x87 math **coprocessors** that included floating-point logic could be purchased separately at the discretion of the computer owner. Some CPU chips, which will be discussed in the next section on CPU technology, take x86-based CISC instructions and translate them into one or more RISC-like instructions.

Although the differences between CISC and RISC chips are diminishing, they have certainly not disappeared. Significant differences remain in terms of compatible operating systems, network operating systems, and applications software. As will be discussed in the following section, purchasing decisions should be made following a structured methodology adhering to the top-down model. They should not be based on a philosophical bias toward one chip architecture.

CPU Technology

This section on CPU technology will examine important characteristics of and key differentiating factors between currently available CPU chips. Emphasis will be on those characteristics or differences that may have a bearing on purchase recommendations of information systems or network analysts.

Intel 486   Although 486 chips are no longer sold, the following information is supplied for historical background. To understand Intel's naming conventions for its CPU chips, one must focus on the three segments that uniquely identify each chip:

1. The chip model number (486)
2. The chip suffix or designator (DX)
3. The clock speed (33 MHz)

Perhaps the most confusing aspect of this naming convention is the designators:

- **SX** implies no built-in math coprocessor (1989)
- **DX** implies a built-in math coprocessor (1989)
- **DX2** implies that the clock speed has been doubled above DX clock speeds (1992)
- **DX4** implies that the clock speed has been *tripled* above DX clock speeds (1994)

As a result, although 486DX4 may be the most popular 486 model currently available, at one time, any or all of these variations were available:

486SX 25 MHz and 33 MHz

486DX 33 MHz and 50 MHz

486DX2 50 MHz and 66 MHz

486DX4 75 MHz, 83 MHz, and 100 MHz

Clock Multiplying   When clock speeds on a given CPU chip are doubled or tripled, the CPU chip works at the higher rate internally only. In other words, instructions are processed in the pipelines at the new, higher rate. However, the many subsystems that interface with the CPU such as memory, bus, disk, and video were all designed to work with the CPU at its original clock speed. As a result, in order to avoid having to redesign all of the CPU's associated subsystems and the associated system board, external clock speeds are not altered.

This fact offers some interesting price/performance ratios. For example, in 1994 a 50 MHz 486DX2 (clock doubled) cost substantially less than a 50 MHz 486DX (no clock doubling) but performed at 90 percent to 95 percent the speed of the more expensive alternative. A 100 MHz 486DX4 cost about $500 more than a 33 MHz 486DX but offered about 2.5 times the performance.

Although it may be obvious that the 2 in DX2 implies a doubling of the DX clock speed, it may not be equally clear that the 4 in DX4 does *not* imply quadrupling clock speeds. In fact, DX4 chips use a variety of clock multiplying factors:

- The 486DX4 75 MHz triples an input clock speed of 25 MHz.

- The 486DX4 83MHz multiplies a 33 MHz input clock speed by a factor of 2.5.

- The 486DX4 100 MHz multiplies either a 50 MHz input clock speed by two or a 33 MHz input clock speed by three.

As can be seen by the 486DX4 83 MHz example, clock multipliers do not have to be whole numbers.

Overdrive Chips   Overdrive chips are replacement CPU chips, manufactured by Intel, that offer clock multiplying capabilities. Among the 486 overdrive chips available at one time were 486DX2 50 MHz overdrive chip designed to double the internal processing speed of a 486SX 25 MHz, and a 486DX4 100 MHz overdrive chip designed to triple the internal processing speed of a 486DX 33 MHz.

These overdrive chips allowed an existing CPU chip to be pulled from a system board and replaced by another CPU running at twice the internal clock speed without requiring any adjustments to any other components. Some system boards come with empty slots for the overdrive chip to be inserted at a later date. It is important to note that after the installation of an overdrive chip, all on-chip (CPU-based) processing runs at the clock-multiplied speed, but as soon as interaction is required with an off-chip component such as external cache (L2) memory, the processing speed slows to the original nonmultiplied system board speed.

Thus, the size of the internal or L1 cache has a lot to do with how much of a performance gain will be realized by purchasing an overdrive chip. 486SX and 486DX models have 8 K, or L1, cache, DX4 models have 16 K. Because of this increased L1 cache size on the DX4, processing is more likely to remain on-chip, at the higher internal clock speed.

Practical Advice and Information

How does a DX4's performance compare with that of a Pentium-based unit? Several references cite that a 100 MHz DX4's performance is roughly equivalent to that of a 60 MHz Pentium-based unit, all other things being equal. With this performance comparison in mind, cost/benefit or price/performance shopping should be fairly straightforward.

Overdrive chips are also available to upgrade certain 486-based computers to Pentium-class machines. However, as shown in the next section, just swapping a 486 chip with a Pentium chip does not make a Pentium computer system. Because of the numerous other changes made to the Pentium system board and surrounding subsystems, tests indicate that 486 computers using the Pentium overdrive chip perform at levels of 60 percent to 70 percent that of a native 90 MHz Pentium computer system. The Pentium overdrive chip runs at a clock speed of 83 MHz in a 33 MHz 486 system and at 63 MHz in a 25 MHz 486 system.

Intel Pentium   The Intel Pentium chip was first shipped in 1993, and millions have been shipped since then. As was illustrated in the Clock Speed section of this chapter, the Pentium chip has been available at no less than ten different clock speeds. However, faster clock speeds is not all that sets the Pentium chip apart.

Among the most significant upgrades from the 486 to the Pentium was the inclusion of a 64-bit on-chip data path as opposed to a 32-bit data path on the 486 chips. This wider data bus allows twice as much information to be fetched with each tick of the CPU clock. The Pentium chip is superscalar, containing two processing pipelines with three execution units to choose from: two integer and one floating point. The Pentium contains the equivalent of 3.3 million transistors and implements branch prediction using a branch target buffer.

Heat buildup was a problem, especially with earlier (60 and 66 MHz) Pentium chips. Large heat sinks and fans were the early answers to this problem. More recently, internal voltages on the chip itself dropped from 5 volts to 3.3 volts, significantly decreasing in generated heat.

The faster processing ability and wide data path offered by the Pentium offer a challenge to systems designers. System boards must be designed to optimize the superior processing power and wide data path of the Pentium chip. Because these system board designs can vary widely, it is easy to see how Pentium computer systems differ. The most important characteristic of a Pentium-based system board is a large (at least 256 KB) L2 external cache connected via a 64-bit data bus to the Pentium's 16 K L1 on-chip cache. The size and speed of the external cache, the size and speed of the main or system memory, and the size and speed of the data path connecting the internal and external memory components are all the responsibility of the system board designers.

Figure 2-4 highlights the differences between Intel's 486 and Pentium CPU chips.

Intel P6, or Pentium Pro   The biggest difference between the P6, or Pentium Pro, and the Pentium chips can be seen with the eye. The Pentium Pro CPU chip itself is just one of two chips mounted in separate cavities in a single die or chip container, sometimes referred to as a package. This second cavity is occupied by a 256 KB SRAM L2, or secondary cache, linked directly to the neighboring Pentium Pro chip through a dedicated 64-bit bus known as the **backside bus.** This directly linked L2 cache is also known as **packaged L2 cache,** and it has major implications for both system design and performance. Systems designers don't need to worry about coming up with their own unique secondary cache designs and links to the CPU. It's already taken care of. With the short distance and dedicated high-speed bus between the L2 cache and the CPU, less time is spent on memory access, and the CPU can be kept busy processing. In terms of performance, the Pentium Pro is one-third faster than a Pentium chip of the same clock speed.

Several functional innovations have also been included in the Pentium Pro:

- **Out of order execution:** A potential problem in scalar or superscalar architectures is known as stalled pipelines. This condition occurs when a pipeline stage, such as an operation or data access, cannot be completed in a single

CPU Type	486DX4	Pentium
Clock Speeds	75, 83, 100 MHz	75, 90, 100, 120, 133, 166, 200, 233 MHz
Transistors	1.6 million	4.5 million
Pipelines	1 (5 stage)	2 (5 stage)
Execution Units	Floating-point unit	3 total: 2 integer and 1 floating point
Level 1 Cache	16K on-board unified cache	32 K total; 16 K instruction, 16 K data
Branch Prediction	No	Yes

Figure 2-4   Intel 486 versus Intel Pentium

clock cycle. Because of a restriction known as in-order execution, *no* pipelines can proceed if *one* is stalled. The Pentium Pro overcomes this restriction by supporting out-of order execution, which allows other pipelines to continue processing if one stalls.

- **Speculative execution:** Speculative execution is really an extension of branch prediction. Whereas branch prediction guesses what the value of a conditional branch will be and predicts which branch will be executed, speculative execution actually begins to execute and store results of these predicted branches. Both speculative execution and out-of-order execution help to keep the powerful Pentium Pro CPU processing as much as possible rather than sitting idle. Because the Pentium Pro is reportedly greater than 90 percent accurate in branch prediction, speculative execution sounds like a fairly safe bet.

- **CISC-to-RISC decoder:** In a process that Intel refers to as **dynamic execution,** the P6 breaks complex CISC instructions down into simpler RISC-like, but not true RISC, instructions known as **micro-ops.** These simpler instructions are then easier to execute in parallel in the multiple pipelines of the superscalar Pentium Pro. The reasoning behind this process is straightforward: Simpler instructions can be processed more quickly and are less likely to cause pipeline stalls.

Figure 2-5 highlights the differences between Intel's Pentium Pro and Pentium CPU chips.

- **Performance:** Comparative performance of Pentium Pro versus Pentium chips depends largely on whether the software being executed is 16 bit or 32 bit. The Pentium Pro outperforms the Pentium when executing 32-bit code, but it actually performs more poorly than the Pentium when executing 16-bit code owing to the additional overhead of running the 16-bit software is emulation mode.

CPU Type	Pentium Pro	Pentium
Clock Speeds	133, 166, 180, 200 MHz	75, 90, 100, 120, 133, 166, 200, 233 MHz
Transistors	5.5 million in CPU, up to 62 million in L2 cache	4.5 million (P55c)
Pipelines	3 (14 stage)	2 (5 stage)
Execution Units	5 total: 2 integer, 1 FPU, 2 address	3 total: 2 integer and 1 floating point
Level 1 Cache	16 K total: 8 K instruction, 8 K data	16 K total: 8 K instruction, 8 K data
Level 2 Cache	256 L to 1 MB packaged	System dependent, external
Out-of-Order Execution	Yes	No
Branch Prediction	Yes, with speculative execution	Yes, without speculative execution

Figure 2-5 Intel Pentium Pro versus Intel Pentium

Intel MMX A common misconception is that **MMX (Multimedia Extensions)** is an entirely new CPU chip. In fact, MMX is a series of 57 additional instructions added to the x86 CISC instruction set. This extended instruction set was then implemented on Pentium CPUs. Specifically, the additional instructions allow multiple mathematical operations to be simultaneously performed on multiple data sets. On an application level, these enhanced mathematical calculation capabilities translate into increased performance on intensive graphics and three-dimensional animation.

Extensions to MMX are under development from Intel as well as from competitors such as AMD, Cyrix, and Centaur. Each Intel competitor is planning to extend MMX in its own manner by adding between 12 and 30 additional instructions. Intel is planning an extension to MMX known as MMX2.

Intel Pentium II The Pentium II CPU runs at 233, 266, 300 MHz, and 400 MHz and adds support for other system improvements such as synchronous DRAM (dynamic RAM) memory, accelerated graphics port (AGP) for enhanced video performance, and faster disk drive access at 33 MBps. In addition, the Pentium II supports the MMX multimedia extensions to the x86 instruction set, runs at 2.8 volts rather than the more common 3.3 volts, and is physically mounted on a 242 pin single-edge connect cartridge (SEC) that plugs into Slot 1 on the motherboard rather than the dual-cavity pin grid array used by the Pentium Pro. Future versions of the Pentium II, code-named Klamath and Deschutes, will have clock speeds to 450 MHz, L2 caches of 2 MB, backside cache bus clock speeds of 450 MHz, system bus clock speeds of 100 MHz, and up to eight-way multiprocessing. Figure 2-6 summarizes some of the key features of the Intel Pentium II CPU chip.

Slots and Sockets All Pentium or P5 CPU-class chips including those manufactured by Intel and others snap into a 296-pin physical interface on the motherboard known as **Socket 7,** otherwise known as a ZIF or zero insertion force socket. The Socket 7 interface was the standard interface for all P5 class chips, regardless of the manufacturer. The 387 pin ZIF physical interface for the dual-cavity Pentium Pro with packaged L2 cache is known as **Socket 8,** and Pentium II chips will snap into 242-pin physical interfaces on the motherboard known as a type **Slot 1** interface. The Pentium II CPUs themselves and L2 cache are now packaged in a sealed daughterboard known as a single-edge contact (SEC) cartridge, rather than the

CPU Type	Pentium II
Clock Speeds	233, 266, 300, 333, 350, 400, 450 MHz
Transistors	7.5 million
Pipelines	3 (14 stage)
Execution Units	5 total: 2 integer, 1 FPU, 2 address
Level 1 Cache	32 KB total: 16 KB data, 16 KB instruction
Level 2 Cache	512 K packaged, up to 2 MB
Out-of-Order Execution	Yes
Branch Prediction	Yes, with speculative execution

Figure 2-6 Intel Pentium II

more familiar flat, black, square or rectangular chip with hundreds of fragile pins sticking out of it. The Slot 1 physical interface and associated bus protocols are patented by Intel and are not available for licensing to their competitors. Slot 1 will probably be used for workstations, and a newer, slightly larger Slot 2 will be used for higher-end servers thanks to its 333 MHz backside bus speed. Intel's competitors are hoping either to come up with their own industry standard interface for P6 processors or to adapt the P5 Socket 7 interface to handle P6 processors.

Intel Clones Competition for Intel in the x86 CPU chip market has come primarily from three companies:

1. Advanced Micro Devices, more popularly known as AMD
2. Cyrix Corporation
3. Centaur, a subsidiary of Integrated Device Technology

In order to compete effectively in this market, Intel's competitors are limited to the following options:

- Offer chips of comparable performance at lower prices than Intel's
- Offer chips of greater performance at similar prices to Intel's

These clone makers cannot afford to alter the guarantee of 100 percent compatibility with Intel's CISC instruction set. Otherwise, programs written to run on Intel chips may not run correctly, or at all, on the clone chips. Although these chips may offer the full CISC instruction set, and therefore look like an Intel chip on the outside, many technical innovations have taken place on the inside of these chips in order to compete with Intel. Figure 2-7 summarizes some of the key features of the currently available Pentium clone chips.

Practical Advice and Information

MMX compatibility can be an especially tricky issue with Intel clone CPUs. Different manufacturers have extended the MMX instruction set in different ways. Some manufacturers have licensing agreements with Intel; others do not. Internally, some CPUs use the normal integer execution units to execute MMX instructions, whereas others use dedicated MMX execution units.

CPU Type	AMD K6	Cyrix 6x86MX	Centaur IDT C6
Pin Compatible	Socket 7	Socket 7	Socket 7
Transistors	8.8 million	6.5 million	5.4 million
Level 1 Cache	64 K total; 32 K code, 32 K data	64 K unified	64 K total; 32 K code, 32 K data
Superscalar MMX	Yes	Yes	Yes
Extended MMX	Yes	Yes	Yes
Speed	233 MHz, 300 MHz	233 MHz	180, 200, 225, 240 MHz

Figure 2-7 Intel Clones

PowerPC/PowerMac   IBM, Motorola, and Apple formed a partnership in 1991 to produce a new family of RISC chips to be incorporated into computing platforms ranging from miniature PDAs (personal digital assistants) to engineering workstations. The partnership has produced a series of chips to date, most recently the PowerPC G3 750, a 450 MHz 64-bit processor.

The PowerPC is a true RISC chip incorporating many of the features discussed previously on Pentium, Pentium Pro, and Intel clone chips. The PowerPC G3 features include the following:

- 64-bit internal data paths

- 100 MHz system bus

- 64 KB of on-chip L1 cache

- Up to 1 MB of L2 cache

- Superscalar architecture with six execution units

- Branch prediction, speculative execution, and out-of-order execution

Like any other CPU chip, the PowerPC chip must be included in a computing platform. IBM, Apple, and other vendors are producing their own computing platforms using the PowerPC chip. IBM has introduced a PowerPC-based RS/6000 workstation, and Apple has produced a series of PowerMacs. Other companies are also producing PowerMac clones.

But the PowerPC is more than just another RISC chip. The PowerPC is also backward compatible with both Macintosh software and Intel x86-based software. Macintosh software is sometimes referred to as 68K or 68000 compatible software, in reference to the Motorola 68000 family of CPUs that powers the Macs. On early versions of the PowerPC chip, this ability to run both Mac and Windows programs was achieved through **software emulation.**

The emulation software required to run native Macintosh applications is included in the PowerMac's operating system, and Mac applications run as well there as on their native platforms. However, running Windows applications on the PowerPC chip is another story. A third-party software emulation package called Soft-Windows is available for Insignia Solutions, but the performance is far from Windows application performance on a high-powered Intel-based machine.

In response to this need, Apple has introduced the DOS card for the PowerMacintosh. This add-on card contains a 486DX2 66 MHz processor and is an example of **hardware emulation.** Windows applications run quite well in this configuration. Not surprisingly, with the RISC nature of the PowerPC chips, when it comes to floating point operations, PowerPC chips significantly outperform Intel-based (CISC) platforms.

People buy computers that will solve business problems. They don't buy architectures or chips and probably don't care about CISC versus RISC. The real issue is: Who is going to buy the PowerMacintosh, and why? Macintosh currently holds about 6 percent market share in the business community, so clearly the demand will not be from corporate America looking for an upgrade. RISC enthusiasts have a variety of vendors to choose from, including Sun, Hewlett-Packard, IBM, and Silicon Graphics, to name a few. Intel-based business applications users have no reason to abandon Intel-based architectures for the PowerPC platform.

That leaves those users who need a computing platform that can run both Windows and Macintosh applications with ease and respectable performance as the most likely prospective purchasers. This market analysis will change significantly if and when applications written specifically for the PowerPC platform become readily available. This is not to say that PowerPC-based computing platforms are not impressive. The PowerMac 9500 (Tsunami) uses a PowerPC 604 chip, runs at either 120 or 132 MHz, and runs 75 percent to 80 percent faster than a 90 MHz Pentium on floating point and integer processing. Figure 2-8 summarizes some key information regarding PowerPC chips.

Future PowerPC 64-bit chip development over the next several years calls for clock speeds ranging from 300 MHz to as high as 1 GHz with 50 to 100 million transistors.

RISC Chips True RISC functionality such as superscalar architectures, superpipelines, branch prediction, speculative execution, and out-of-order execution has been adopted by many of the chips previously discussed. Companies that specialize in pure RISC CPU chips are listed below along with the names of their chip families:

- Digital Equipment Corporation (DEC): Alpha chip
- Sun Microsystems: SPARC chip
- Hewlett-Packard: PA-RISC
- MIPS Technologies: MIPS

	Date of Introduction	Technical Specifications	Applications
PowerPC 601	1993	60 MHz; 32-bit processor	Low-cost, initial PowerPC chip
PowerPC 602	1995	66 MHz; 1 million transistors; 4 KB cache; 4 execution units	Targeted toward PDAs and consumer electronics
PowerPC 603	1993	80 MHz; 1.6 million transistors; 8 KB cache; 5 execution units	Low-power consumption, targeted at notebooks
PowerPC 603e	1997	280, 300 MHz; 2.6 million transistors, 16 KB cache; 5 execution units	High-powered notebooks
PowerPC 604e	1997	200, 225, 300, 350 MHz; 3.6 million transistors; 32 KB cache; 6 execution units	High performance for high-end desktop systems
PowerPC 620	1994	133 MHz; 7 million transistors; 64 KB cache; 6 execution units	Engineering workstations and high-speed servers
X704	1997	466, 500, 533 MHz	PowerPC 604 compatible, Exponential Technology
PowerPC 750	1998	Up to 450 MHz; on board L1 cache; 1 MB L2 cache	

Figure 2-8 Power PC Technical Specifications and Applications

Computing platforms based on these chips are tremendously powerful and are used primarily for engineering workstations running CAD/CAM, two-dimensional modeling, video, or multimedia applications. These chip manufacturers do not have to worry about being backward compatible with x86 or Macintosh architectures because no one in their right mind would buy one of these workstations for that purpose.

CPU Trends

Ever Faster   Users' need for increased computing power seems to be limitless. As more powerful processors are brought to the market, more-demanding applications are able to saturate their power. In summary, there are really only three ways to make faster CPU chips:

1. Increase the CPU's processing capacity by increasing the number of transistors. More transistors means more on-chip capacity for cache memory, specialized execution units, and deeper branch prediction buffers. The down side is that transistors take up space, consume electricity, and generate heat. As a result, current technology is quickly reaching its limit in terms of the density of transistors that can physically be located on a given chip surface.

2. Increase the clock speed. Making the CPU work faster is a reasonable proposal as long as the supporting CPU infrastructure and subsystems can keep up. The main goal is to keep the CPU busy 100 percent of the time. As CPUs become faster and faster, keeping them busy becomes more challenging.

3. Work smarter, not harder. Instead of just increasing the clock speed, concentrate on accomplishing more with each tick of the clock. This is where the efforts to keep the CPU busy 100 percent of the time will be concentrated. Continued evolution in superscalar processes such as speculative execution, out-of-order execution, and branch prediction will be a large part of these efforts.

What cannot change is future chips' support of the complex instructions contained in the x86 CISC instruction set. If this basic "outside" instruction set is changed, every program ever written to run on an Intel chip would have to be rewritten. As a result, although Intel's chips may get more RISC-like on the inside, they will have to stay CISC compatible on the outside.

As CPUs' clock speeds and processing power increases, system bottlenecks shift to those subsystems that must interface with the massively powerful CPUs. Figure 2-9 summarizes some of the key improvements on the horizon for these subsystems.

Merced IA64 — CISC meets RISC   Hewlett-Packard, manufacturer of the PA-RISC chip, and Intel, manufacturer of the x86 CISC chip, have collaborated to produce a next-generation 64-bit chip known as **Merced** or **IA-64 (Intel Architecture-64)** that is supposedly backward compatible with current x86 and PA-RISC software. Initially targeted at high-performance servers and workstations, IA-64's key operational characteristics are summarized in Figure 2- 10.

Subsystem Improvement	Importance/Implication
CPU I/O Bus Speed	Although CPU clock speeds have increased enormously, the I/O buses that interface to them have not. I/O bus speeds will increase from 66 MHz or 75 MHz to 83 MHz or 100 MHz
Faster Memory	In order to keep up with the faster CPU I/O bus speeds, clock-synchronized memory such as SDRAM (synchronous DRAM) will become more prevalent.
Higher-Speed Graphics	In order to improve graphics speed, new accelerated graphics ports (AGPs) will be connected directly to the system chip set rather than through the PCI expansion bus.
Higher-Speed PCI (peripheral component interconnect)	The PCI expansion bus will be upgraded to a 64-bit wide bus running at 66 MHz.
Faster access to L2 cache	Rather than accessing L2 cache through the system CPU I/O bus, L2 cache will be accessed by the CPU through a faster, dedicated backside bus.

Figure 2-9   Overcoming System Bottlenecks

Operational Characteristic	Explanation/Significance
Transistors	The number of transistors will increase from tens of millions to hundreds of millions.
Explicit Parallel Instruction Computing	Fixed-length instructions optimized for execution in a single CPU cycle are grouped in threes into 128-bit long instruction word (LIW) bundles, allowing instructions to be executed in parallel.
Instruction Predication	Beyond speculative execution, instruction predication executes instructions along all branches of an instruction, stores results, and discards unneeded results once the proper branch is determined.
Speculative Loading	In order to have required data ready in the faster cache memory when it is needed, speculative loading will move data from system memory to cache memory before it is needed. Speculative check instructions will verify that required data is in cache memory before instruction is executed.

Figure 2-10   Intel Architecture 64: Key Operational Characteristics

◼ THE BUS

Bus Functionality and Concepts

Internal versus External   The term **bus** refers to a connection between components either within a CPU chip, between a CPU chip and system components, or between system components. For this discussion a bus located strictly within a CPU chip will be referred to as an **internal bus** and a bus located outside of a CPU chip will be referred to as an **external bus.** Internal buses, since they appear within a CPU chip, are most often proprietary and are referred to by a variety of terms. External buses, because of the need to be supported by third-party hardware and software, are more likely to adhere to one of a number of industry standards for buses. In most CPU chip designs, internal buses interface to external buses in a **bus interface unit.**

The following are examples of internal buses that will be explained in more detail in a later section:

- Address bus

- Data bus

Examples of external buses that will be explained in more detail below include the following:

- Main system bus, also known as the processor bus or the frontside bus

- External cache bus, also known as external data bus, memory bus, or backside bus

- Input/output (I/O) bus, also known as the local bus

- Peripheral bus, also known as the expansion bus

Bus Width and Clock Speed   Buses differ primarily according to **bus width,** which is measured in bits and refers to the number of bits that can travel in parallel down a bus. Common bus widths are 8, 16, 32, 64, and 128 bits. Bus width, however, is only one factor contributing to the performance of, or amount of data that travels through, a given bus. The other factor is the clock speed of the bus. The clock speed determines how often a full bus-width of data is loaded onto and transferred down the bus. Bus clock speed in MHz multiplied by the bus-width will yield the bus throughput in bits per second.

The clock speed of a bus may be the full clock speed of the CPU, measured in MHz, or may be one-half, one-third, or one-fourth of the CPU clock speed, which is known as **clock-divided frequency.** External buses frequently run at a fraction of the CPU clock speed. For example, the external buses on a 100 MHz Pentium chip run at 66 MHz, and the external buses on a 90 MHz Pentium chip run at 60 MHz. Part of the bus interface unit's function is to provide a buffer between the higher internal bus speeds and the slower external bus speeds.

A chair lift taking skiers to the top of a mountain serves as an excellent analogy for the relationship between bus width and clock speed. Each chair on one chair lift is identically wide, but chairs on different chair lifts may be of differing widths. Whereas a bus measures its width in bits, a chair lift measures its width in butts. However, the width of the chair alone cannot measure the throughput of the chair lift. The frequency of the chair lift—how often the chairs arrive—needs to be multiplied by the chair width, yielding the throughput of the chair-lift in butts delivered to the top of the mountain in a fixed amount of time.

Figure 2-11 illustrates the relationship between internal and external buses. Terms used in labeling buses are compiled from a number of CPU designs and do not reflect of any particular architecture.

INTERNAL

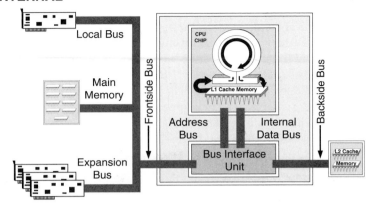

EXTERNAL

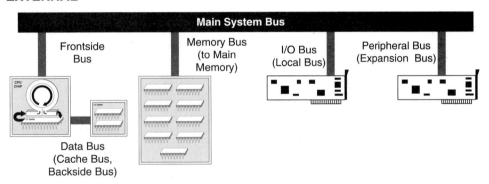

Figure 2-11   Internal versus External Bus Functionality and Concepts

Internal Buses

Address Bus   The width of the address bus controls how much memory a given computer system can access. Just as with street addresses, with longer addresses, more unique addresses are possible. Each memory location to be accessed must have a unique address. If the address bus is 8 bits wide, then 2 to the 8th power, or 256, unique addresses could possibly be transferred down the address bus. Most of the address buses in today's CPUs are 32 bits wide, yielding the ability to address 4 gigabytes of data.

Data Bus   The CPU's internal data bus is responsible for delivering data to and from the L1 cache and processing pipelines. In order to optimize this activity, the internal data cache nearly always runs at the full CPU clock speed. The wider the internal data bus, the more data that can be delivered to the pipelines for processing. Most CPUs have 32-bit- or 64-bit-wide internal data buses.

External Buses

System Bus—Frontside Bus   The system bus should be considered the superhighway of the buses that leave the computer system's CPU. Occasionally, high-speed input-output devices such as disk drives or monitors will hook directly into the system bus, but most often, only other buses such as the local, I/O, and peripheral buses interface directly to the system bus. The memory controller that interfaces to the computer system's main memory is the primary user of the system bus, also known as the processor bus. Most system designs assume that anything that interfaces directly to the system bus must operate at the system bus's clock speed. Slower buses and their devices access the system bus via bus interface units. The standard system bus clock speed for higher–clock speed Pentiums, Pentium Pros, and Pentium IIs has been 66 MHz. Beginning in 1998, Intel will introduce Pentium II processors (code-named: Deschutes) with 100 MHz system bus clock speeds.

Cache Bus—Backside Bus   The external cache bus is responsible for quickly delivering data and instructions between the L2 cache and the CPU. Designs vary widely among systems vendors for the L2 cache bus. The capacity of the L2 cache bus is measured according to the bus width in bits. Most L2 cache buses are 32 or 64 bits wide. Actual throughput of the L2 cache bus can be determined only by also knowing the clock speed, sometimes known as the memory bus speed. This clock speed is usually either the full CPU clock speed or some fraction thereof. For example, Pentium 66 MHz, Pentium 100 MHz, and Pentium 133 MHz CPUs all have L2 cache bus speeds of 66 MHz. The L2 cache bus on the newer Pentium Pro MMX chips will run at one-half the CPU processor speed (133 MHz cache speed on a 266 MHz CPU and 150 MHz cache speed on a 300 MHz chip). Pentium II processors running at 350 MHz to 400 MHz will feature a full-speed L2 cache bus in which the L2 runs at the full speed of the processor.

Local Bus   Strictly speaking, the term *local bus* refers to any bus that interfaces directly to the system bus. The VESA Local Bus (VL) standard is an example of a true local bus architecture. Interfacing directly to the system bus implies that the local bus and its attached devices must operate at the system bus clock speed. As system bus speeds increase, local bus devices must be able to cope with these increased clock speeds. Trying to get local bus devices to operate at faster and faster clock speeds can cause a multitude of problems. An alternative to the local bus architecture is the mezzanine architecture.

Local versus Mezzanine Architecture   A mezzanine architecture takes matters into its own hands and supplies its own clocking signal. **PCI** (peripheral component interconnect) bus, originally developed by Intel, is the best example of a mezzanine architecture. The PCI bus provides its own clocking signal at 33MHz and has a bus width of either 32 or 64 bits. The PCI bus interfaces to the system bus via a PCI bridge, which provides buffering between the two buses. Because of the PCI bus's high capacity, typical PCI devices include high-quality video, CD-ROMs, multimedia devices, high-speed printers, and high-speed networking devices. PCI buses also interface to slower-speed expansion buses. The PCI standard, as well as a variety of expansion bus standards, will be discussed in the Bus Technology section. Figure 2-12 differentiates between local bus architectures and mezzanine architectures.

Expansion Bus   A computer's expansion bus connects add-in cards and peripheral devices such as modems, fax boards, sound cards, additional serial ports, and additional input devices. The expansion bus interfaces to the system bus through a bus interface unit and nearly always runs at a slower clock speed than the CPU clock. The width of the expansion bus in bits differs according to the standard of the expansion bus supported in a particular computer system. Expansion bus standards will be discussed in the Bus Technology and Standards section below.

Local Bus Architecture

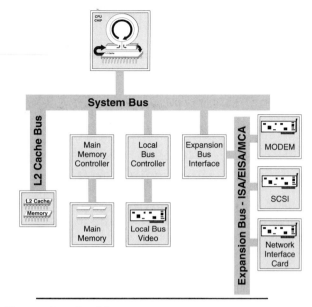

Mezzanine Architecture

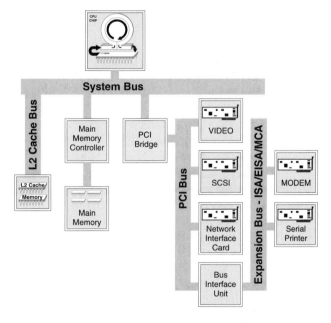

Figure 2-12   Local versus Mezzanine Bus Architecture

Bus Technology and Standards

Expansion Bus Standards: ISA/EISA/MCA   ISA (industry standard architecture), **EISA** (extended industry standard architecture), and **MCA** (micro channel architecture) are all expansion bus standards. EISA is backward compatible with ISA, but MCA is not compatible with either ISA or EISA. When expansion cards such as modems or network interface cards are purchased to be installed in a computer's expansion bus, those cards must be compatible with the computer's expansion bus standard.

Figure 2-13 summarizes the key differences among the three expansion bus standards.

Expansion Bus Standard	Bus Width	Throughput
ISA	16 bit	8 MBps
EISA	32 bit	33 MBps
MCA	32 bit	20 MBps

Figure 2-13   ISA, EISA, and MCA Expansion Bus Standards

PCI, SCSI, and PCI/SCSI   Although PCI was originally developed by Intel, it is, in fact, a processor-independent bus design. RISC system designers such as DEC, Hewlett-Packard, and IBM are able to incorporate PCI buses into their computer systems as well. Recall from Figure 2-12 that all that is required to link a PCI bus to any particular system bus is a compatible PCI bridge. The beauty of PCI is that a PCI device such as a high-capacity disk-drive, tape drive, or CD-ROM will work equally well on a PCI bus installed in a RISC workstation or an Intel-based computer.

PCI specifications are evolving. There are currently two PCI specifications, differing primarily in bus width: 32 bits or 64 bits. The PCI specifications are summarized in Figure 2-14.

Computing the throughput on a PCI bus is straightforward: 32 bits multiplied by 33 MHz divided by 8 bits/byte yields 132 Megabytes per second throughput. Although Figure 2-12 illustrates how expansion buses can be cascaded from a PCI bus, in fact, PCI buses can also be cascaded from other PCI buses. As an example, PCI buses can be put onto a single expansion card allowing the manufacture of four-port PCI Ethernet network interfaces on a single expansion card.

SCSI (small computer system interface) is a specification for an expansion bus that is unique in its ability to daisy-chain up to seven SCSI devices together. SCSI can also be thought of as a truly external bus specification, because these SCSI devices, such as disk drives, tape drives, and CD-ROMs, can be stand-alone models, sitting totally outside of the computer system. SCSI specifications have changed over the years in order to keep up with demands for higher-throughput peripheral devices. Figure 2-15 summarizes the SCSI standards.

By combining PCI and SCSI bus specifications in the form of PCI-based SCSI host adapters, the benefits of both bus architectures can be achieved. As a result, more than one seven-device SCSI chain per computer system can be implemented by simply installing a second PCI/SCSI host adapter card. Although the thought of multiple devices per adapter and multiple adapters per host is indeed appealing, both PCI and SCSI specifications continue to evolve, and compatibility issues can be

PCI Bus Specifications	Bus Width	Clock Speed	Throughput
PCI	32 bits	33 MHz	132 MBps
PCI v2.0	64 bits	33 MHz or 66 MHz	264 or 528 MBps

Figure 2-14   PCI Bus Specifications

SCSI Specifications	Bus Width	Clock Speed	Throughput
SCSI	8 bits	5 MHz	5 MBps
Fast SCSI-2	8 bits	10 MHz	10 MBps
Wide SCSI-2	16 bits	5 MHz	10 MBps
Fast/Wide SCSI-2	16 bits	10 MHz	20 MBps
Ultra SCSI-2	32 bits	10 MHz	40 MBps
PCI 2Ultra SCSI	64 bits	10 MHz	80 MBps
Ultra3			160 MBps

Figure 2-15   SCSI Specifications

a problem. SCSI cards are also available for other expansion bus specifications such as ISA and EISA. However, beware of the lower throughput of ISA and EISA in comparison with PCI.

Figure 2-16 summarizes some of the technical issues to consider when purchasing a PCI/SCSI adapter.

PCI/SCSI Adapter Technical Issue	Explanation/Implication
Which PCI specification is supported?	PCI 2.0 (64 bit) is the current specification, but newer specifications may be forthcoming.
Does the adapter support PCI-to-PCI bridge?	Support for the PCI-to-PCI bridge (PPB) specification is important if PCI buses are to be cascaded.
Which SCSI driver specification is supported?	There are two possible driver specifications for SCSI devices: advanced SCSI programming interface drivers (ASPI) and common access method drivers (CAM).
Which operating system/network operating system drivers are included?	Commonly supported drivers are DOS, OS/2, NetWare, Windows NT, SCO UNIX.
Which data transfer technique from the SCSI card to system memory is used?	Bus mastering is fastest, but programmed I/O is also used on some cards.
Is an on-board basic input/output system (BIOS) included?	This is required in order to simplify booting the card. BIOS is not always included.
Are the SCSI cards Plug-n-Play compatible?	SCSI daisy-chains require termination on the last device in the chain. Plug-n-Play–compatible SCSI devices are self-terminating when they are the last device in the chain.
Which interface connectors are included?	SCSI-1: Centronics 50-pin connector SCSI-2: Micro-50-pin d-connector with thumbclips, also known as MINI 50 or MICRO-DB 50 SCSI-3: Micro-68-pin d-connector with thumbscrews, also known as MINI 68.

Figure 2-16   PCI/SCSI Adapter Technical Issues

Bus Trends

PCMCIA   **PCMCIA,** which actually stands for Personal Computer Memory Card International Association, has been more humorously dissected as People Can't Memorize Computer Industry Acronyms. It has been described as a general peripheral bus, a bus interface, and a bridge bus technology. Originally intentioned solely as a specification for memory cards in notebook computers, PCMCIA represents a tremendous potential for new and innovative technology applications. To most end users, the PCMCIA specification is represented by the PCMCIA slots in notebook computers and the credit-card size cards of a variety of functions that slide into those slots. In addition to the originally intentioned use as memory cards, PCMCIA cards today are used for modems, fax modems, wireless LAN adapters, network interface cards, disk drives, and SCSI ports, to name but a few.

PCMCIA is actually a series of specifications that represent the physical and functional/electrical standards for technology adhering to these specifications. Figure 2-17 summarizes the physical specifications, and Figure 2-18 summarizes the functional/electrical specifications for the PCMCIA standard.

All types must support the standard PCMCIA 68-pin interface and the 85.6 mm by 54 mm credit card–size dimensions. Certain vendors are producing disk drives that are 16 mm thick and calling them PCMCIA Type IV. These standards are strictly proprietary because the PCMCIA Forum has not approved a Type IV specification.

The introduction of PCMCIA technology has not been without its trials and tribulations. Prior to the introduction of the version 2.1 specification, incompatibility problems were very common. The Card Services and Socket Services provided a layer of transparency and compatibility between the notebook computer's hardware, the PCMCIA card, and the notebook computer's operating system software.

PCMCIA Card/Slot Type	Maximum Thickness	Typical Use
Type I	3.3 mm	Memory cards
Type II	5.5 mm	Modems, network interface cards
Type III	10.5 mm	Disk drives

Figure 2-17   PCMCIA Physical Specifications

PCMCIA Specifications

Version	Bus Width	Clock Speed	Comments
1.0	8 bits	Up to 6 MHz	Version 1.0 is used for memory cards. No I/O functions or software drivers are defined.
2.0	8–16 bits	Up to 6 MHz	This version introduced I/O but left software drivers up to card manufacturers.
2.1	8–16 bits	Up to 6 MHz	Version 2.1 introduced Card Services and Socket Services
PC Card (3.0)	32 bits	20–33 MHz	PC Card has up to 80 MBps throughput.

Figure 2-18   PCMCIA Functional/Electrical Specifications

Version 2.1 is currently the most widely supported version of the PCMCIA specification and has minimized, although not eliminated, many of the previous incompatibility problems. Version 2.1 also introduced hot-swappable capabilities, which allow PCMCIA cards to be inserted and removed with the notebook computer powered up.

Version 3.0 actually renames the cards from PCMCIA to simply PC Cards. CardBus has also been mentioned as a replacement name for the much-maligned PCMCIA. More importantly, version 3.0 vastly improves the throughput of the specification by increasing the bus width to 32 bits and the clock speed to as high as 33 MHz. The specification also adds bus-mastering capability in order to increase the efficiency of moving data from the card to the computer's system memory. Finally, version 3.0 defines multifunction capabilities for cards so that a single card might be a fax/modem, an Ethernet network interface card, and 4 MB of cache memory. In the interest of improving battery life on notebook computers, version 3.0 also outlined operations at 3.3 volts rather than 5 volts.

The future looks bright for PC Card. PC Card slots are now being included on desktop computers as well as notebooks in order to allow users to make the most of their investments in peripherals. Vendors are finding new uses, such as dial-in servers, for the PC Card. However, today there is no guarantee that a particular PCMCIA card will work well, if at all, with a particular computer.

Universal Serial Bus   Another peripheral interface that is appearing on computer workstations and servers is the **universal serial bus (USB)** that is able to support daisy-chained USB-compliant devices. Frequently, two USB interfaces are supplied on a given PC. One would be used to daisy-chain a keyboard and mouse, eliminating the need for a variety of proprietary keyboard and mouse interfaces and connectors. The other USB connector could actually support up to 127 daisy-chained peripheral USB devices at throughputs of 12 MBps through the use of cascaded seven-port USB hubs. USB-compliant devices will register with the host system automatically, thereby making them truly "plug-n-play," and will be able to be attached and detached without powering down and rebooting the host system.

▓ MEMORY

Question: What is the impact of memory on CPU performance?

Answer: Research has shown that a 100 MHz Pentium runs at 8 MHz if it has to go outside of L2 cache for data.

Memory Functionality and Concepts

To appreciate recent developments in memory technology, one must first understand the motivation for those developments. The rapid advancement of CPU chip design has produced a discrepancy between how fast the CPU can accept and process data and how fast memory can supply that data. As a result, all of the memory categories to be discussed in the next section have contributed somehow to the same goal:

- Because memory chip speeds have lagged behind CPU chip speeds, future memory chips must deliver not just more information, but more information more quickly.

As background, most of the solutions below start with one of the two major types of **RAM** (random access memory).

- **DRAM,** or **dynamic RAM,** is memory that requires refresh cycles every few milliseconds to preserve its data. DRAM requires address lines for the rows and columns of the memory address to be charged and discharged as a means of selecting particular memory locations. This time delay to allow the lines to stabilize between charges prevents immediate access to memory location contents.

- **SRAM,** or **static RAM,** in contrast, does not require a refresh cycle between accesses and therefore can be accessed much faster than DRAM. SRAM is more expensive than DRAM.

Memory Technology

To meet the challenge of faster delivery of more information, current memory technology developers have taken a variety of approaches. Following is a list of the major approaches to meeting this memory challenge and the names of the memory technology belonging to each category:

- Cached approaches
  - **CDRAM**—Cached DRAM
  - **CVRAM**—Cached VRAM (Video RAM)
  - **EDRAM**—Enhanced DRAM

- RAM to CPU output modifications
  - **FPM**—Fast page mode
  - **EDORAM**—Extended data out RAM
  - **EDOSRAM**—Extended data out SRAM
  - **EDOVRAM**—Extended data out VRAM

- RAM to CPU clock synchronization modifications
  - **SDRAM**—Synchronous DRAM
  - **SVRAM**—Synchronous VRAM
  - **RDRAM**—Rambus DRAM
  - **SLDRAM**—SyncLink DRAM

- Video RAM specific modifications (in addition to those previously listed)
  - **WRAM**—Windows RAM
  - **3DRAM**—three-dimensional RAM

- RAM power needs modifications
  - **Flash RAM**
  - **FRAM**—Ferroelectric RAM

Cached Approaches   Cached approaches add some amount of faster SRAM to DRAM chips. The size of the SRAM cache and the width of the bus between the SRAM and DRAM vary from one manufacturer to another. On typical 4 MB DRAM chips, the SRAM cache could be from 8 Kb to 16 Kb, and the connecting bus width could be from 128 bits to 2048 bits. The SRAM cache fetches data from the slower DRAM and has it ready for quicker delivery to the CPU when requested.

RAM-to-CPU Output Modifications   Another approach to overcoming the problem of having the CPU wait for the memory is to alter the manner in which the memory outputs the data to the CPU. Extended data output (EDO) chips minimize or eliminate the time the CPU has to wait (zero-wait-state) for output from memory by reading the next stored data bit at the same time it is transferring the first requested bit to the CPU.

RAM-to-CPU Clock Synchronization Modifications   Adding clock synchronization to RAM allows memory chips to work at the same clock speed as the CPU. In addition, SDRAM solutions perform a simultaneous fetch operation at the same time they are presenting data to the CPU. As a result, the SDRAM chip is ready to present the next bit of data to the CPU on the next tick of the CPU's clock. SDRAM works with CPU clock speeds greater than 66 MHz, can transfer data at speeds up to 500 Mbps, and has storage capacity of 64 Mb each. Rambus DRAM (RDRAM) offers 500 MHz memory bus throughput by using 8-bit buses and 250 MHz clocks. SyncLink DRAM uses a 16-bit, 200 MHz dual data bus configuration yielding a bandwidth of 800 MBps.

Video RAM Modifications   Because video RAM is designed for a special purpose other than storing and delivering data, modifications specific to optimizing its performance for video delivery can be made. VRAM is a sort of intermediary on a video card, servicing two functions:

- The video controller, which gathers information regarding the image to be created and calculates how to display that image

- The screen drawing or screen refresh function, which actually draws the images on the video monitor

The primary modification made by VRAM is the portion of memory it reserves for servicing the screen refresh function in order to optimize performance for high-resolution graphics. RAM segmented in this manner is sometimes referred to as **dual-ported VRAM.** Other more-advanced VRAM designs add intelligence to the RAM. For instance, in 3DRAM, the depth (z axis) processing is done in RAM, making it up to nine times faster than conventional VRAM for three-dimensional imaging.

RAM Power Needs Modification   Whereas most RAM requires constant voltage in order to maintain its data, nonvolatile RAM does not lose its data if voltage fluctuates. Flash memory, or flash RAM, remembers its data contents until it is flashed by a larger voltage. It is used widely as main memory for portable computers. The bad news is that it wears out after relatively few flashes and is therefore best for jobs that don't require data to be rewritten often. FRAM is a new type of nonvolatile memory currently under development that apparently does not degrade as quickly as conventional flash memory.

Memory Trends

Beyond the previously cited trends in memory development, equally significant trends are occurring in how memory is packaged. Originally, individual **DIP** (dual in-line pin) chips were attached to circuit boards as a means of packaging and selling RAM. More recently, **SIMM (single in-line memory module)** has become the more common method of RAM packaging. SIMMs are small printed circuit boards with attached DRAMs and come in two varieties:

- 30-pin SIMMs composed of 8-bit DRAMs
- 72-pin SIMMs composed of 16-bit or 32-bit DRAMs

An emerging packaging alternative is **DIMMs** (dual in-line memory modules), in which the DRAMs are mounted on both sides of the small circuit board. And yet further into the future, **3D memory modules,** not to be confused with 3DRAM, stack memory chips on top of one another. This packaging process is particularly appealing with the exploding market for portable computers as densities of 2 giga-bytes/cubic inch are being reported using this process.

■ STORAGE

As client operating systems and application programs have grown in size, the disk drives that store these programs have had to grow in capacity as well. CPUs have become faster and faster, so disk drives have had to deliver data faster and faster.

Storage Functionality and Concepts

Basic disk drive functionality has not changed fundamentally in recent years. Although disk drives have gotten larger and faster, the basic technological design remains largely unchanged:

1. Data is stored on disks that are broken up into concentric rings, known as **tracks,** and in portions of those tracks, known as **sectors.**
2. Read/write heads are attached at the ends of mechanical arms that extend and retract over given tracks of the disk.
3. Once the read/write head is positioned over the proper track, the disk platter spins until the proper sector is aligned under the read/write head.
4. Data is read from or written to the appropriate sector of the disk.

In order to properly evaluate disk drive alternatives, one must fully understand the terminology used to categorize and describe disk drive performance. Figure 2-19 lists disk performance terminology, explanations, and implications.

Practical Advice and Information

Disk drive advertisements, like most technology marketing, can be very misleading. Times quoted in advertisements as access times are often actually seek times, which is just a fraction of the true access time.

Storage Technology and Standards

The primary standards of currently available disk drives are **IDE (integrated drive electronics), E-IDE** (extended IDE), and **SCSI** (small computer system interface).

Disk Drive Performance Terminology	Explanation and Implication
Average Seek Time	The time it takes the mechanical arm to extend or retract so that the read/write heads are positioned over the proper track
Average Latency	The time it takes for the disk to spin so that the proper sector is positioned under the read/write heads
Average Access Time	Average seek time + average latency
Data Transfer Rate	The rate at which data is transferred to or from the disk once the read/write heads are over the proper sector
Burst Data Transfer Rate	The rate at which data is read between the disk drive and the buffer memory on board the disk controller (also known as external transfer rate)
Sustained Transfer Rate	The rate at which data is read between the disk drive and main system memory without the use and benefit of the on-board buffer (also known as internal transfer rate)

Figure 2-19   Disk Drive Performance Terminology

The SCSI bus and more recent SCSI-2 standards were previously reviewed in the bus section of this chapter. Figure 2-20 compares these three primary disk standards.

IDE disk drives are distinguished from earlier offerings by the inclusion of the drive controller with the disk drive in a single integrated unit and the use of a bus interface known as **ATA** (AT attachment, Advanced Technology 16-bit PC architecture for x86 processor family). The key limitation of IDE drives is their capacity limitation of 528 MB and ATA's 2MBps to 3MBps data transfer rate. As a result, an improved standard known as extended IDE was proposed by Western Digital, a major disk drive manufacturer. This proposed standard was adapted by the Small Forms Factor (SFF) Committee, an ad hoc standards proposal organization, and forwarded to ANSI (American National Standards Institute) for formal adoption. Officially adopted, it is now known as **ATA-2.**

With the potential throughputs of E-IDE and SCSI drives and the fact that these devices must share the bus to which they are attached with other devices, it should

Disk Drive Standard	IDE	E-IDE	SCSI
Capacity	Up to 528 MB	Up to 8.4 GB	Up to 8.4 GB
Number of Daisy-Chained Devices	2	4	7
Compatibility with Other Device Types	Only other IDE disk drives	ATAPI-compatible CD-ROMS and tape drives	SCSI CD-ROMS and tape drives
Performance	2 to 3 MBps	11.1 MBps	5-20 MBps

Figure 2-20   Comparison of Disk Drive Standards

be obvious why it is preferable to connect these high-capacity disk drives to a local bus rather than to an ISA, EISA, or MCA expansion bus. The actual throughput of the drives as listed on the performance line of Figure 2-20 is controlled by the choice of supported data transfer standards, otherwise known as burst data transfer rates. SCSI disk drives adhere to SCSI transfer rates, as outlined in Figure 2-15. E-IDE data transfer standards fall into two general categories:

- **Processor I/O** (input/output)—Also known as **programmed I/O,** or PIO. This data transfer method relies on a shared memory location in system memory as a transfer point for data between the disk drive and the system or main memory. The CPU is involved with every data transfer between the disk drive and system memory.

- **Direct Memory Access,** or **DMA**—This data transfer allows data to be transferred between the disk drive and system memory without intervention from the CPU. This allows for both faster data transfer and less CPU interruptions.

Figure 2-21 summarizes current burst data transfer standards for E-IDE disk drives.

Another issue that can have a dramatic effect on performance is the use of disk caches. A **hardware cache** is made up of memory chips placed directly on the disk controller, whereas a **software cache** is the use of system memory in the computer reserved for a disk cache. These caches can be used for both read and write operations as follows:

- **Read-through cache** allows data stored in the cache to be forwarded directly to the CPU without performing a physical disk read.

- **Write-back cache** allows disk writes to be stored in the cache right away so that processing can continue rather than waiting for the disk to be idle before doing a physical write to the disk. The danger in using write-back caches is that if power is lost before physical writes are done to the disk, then that data is lost.

Buffers are memory chips located on the disk drive units, which can also be used to improve disk performance. By storing sequential bits of data adjacent to areas just read by the read/write heads in buffers, disk drives anticipate which data blocks the CPU will next request. Transferring data from a memory chip to the CPU

Burst Data Transfer Standard	Burst Data Transfer Rate
Programmed I/O (PIO) Mode 3	11.1 MBps
Programmed I/O (PIO) Mode 4	16.6 MBps
Multiword Mode I DMA	13.3 MBps
Multiword Mode 2 DMA	16.6 MBps

Figure 2-21   E-IDE Burst Data Transfer Standards

is much faster than a data transfer involving a physical read/write. Following are some typical buffer categories:

- **Look-ahead buffer** is the simplest or most generic buffer, implying that a sequence of data blocks beyond that requested by the CPU is stored in anticipation of the next data request.

- **Segmented look-ahead buffers** create multiple smaller buffers in which the next sequential data blocks from several reads can be stored.

- **Adaptive segmented look-ahead buffers** are able to dynamically adjust the number and size of buffers, depending on the situation.

Practical Advice and Information

Which type of disk drive is most appropriate for a client workstation? Disk drives should support local bus architectures such as PCI in order to ensure sufficient throughput. Following are some typical guidelines for capacity:

- Windows users: Not less than 720 MB

- Average user with multiple applications: 1 GB

- Power user with graphics applications or large data files: 1 GB to 2 GB

For the single-user client workstation, E-IDE is a practical choice, although SCSI will also work well. SCSI is preferable in a server computer characterized by multiple users and a multitasking operating system. Server-related disk storage issues such as RAID (redundant array of inexpensive disks) will be reviewed in Chapter 4, Server Hardware and Software.

High-Capacity Removable Storage

As applications have produced larger and larger files, a need for higher-capacity removable storage devices has developed. As an example of the laws of supply and demand, the need for high-capacity removable storage has been met by a variety of products outlined in Figure 2-22.

Storage Trends

Although installation of E-IDE and SCSI disk drives is not as complicated as it once was, it is still far from simple. However, "Plug-n-Play" (PnP) disk drive technology

Device Name	Capacity	Vendor
Zip Drive	100 MB	Iomega
Jaz Drive	1 GB or 2 GB	Iomega
SparQ Drive	1 GB	Syquest
SyJet Drive	1.5 GB	Syquest

Figure 2-22   High-Capacity Removable Storage

may be available in the near future. As will be seen in the next chapter, all hardware requires software in order to operate, and PnP hardware is no exception. Although Windows 95 is supposed to include the necessary software support for PnP technology, compatibility between hardware and software cannot be assumed in all cases. Disk drives or other peripherals must be certified as Windows 95 PnP compatible if the operating system is expected to reliably and automatically detect and configure the peripheral in question.

■ VIDEO

The focus of this section is the video subsystem from the perspective of the average client workstation.

Video Functionality, Concepts, and Technology

The video needs of the average client workstation are fairly straightforward, consisting of the following:

- Monitor

- Graphics accelerator card

- Graphics driver software to link the video hardware with the client workstation's operating system

Figure 2-23 illustrates the conceptual relationship of the various components of a video subsystem.

Many of the components illustrated in Figure 2-23 have been previously discussed. In fact, the only new components are the monitor, the graphics accelerator card, and whatever software may be necessary to bridge various hardware-to-hardware and hardware-to-software interfaces.

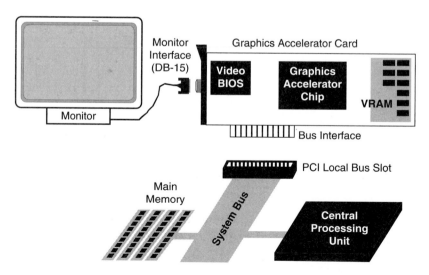

Figure 2-23   Conceptual Relationship of Video Subsystem Components

Monitors   Monitors fall into two major categories based on their technology and use:

- CRT (cathode ray tube)–based monitors for desktop use
- LCD (liquid crystal display)–based monitors for notebook and portable computers

Monitor performance is measured by a variety of criteria. Perhaps most familiar to the average user is the term **resolution.** Resolution refers to the number of **pixels (picture elements)** contained in the viewable area of the monitor screen and is reported as resolution height times resolution width. In simple terms, a greater number of pixels on the screen will produce a sharper image. Following are common resolutions:

- 640 by 480
- 800 by 600
- 1024 by 768 (commonly referred to as Super VGA, or SVGA)
- 1280 by 1024

Another common monitor performance criterion is the **refresh rate,** which refers to the number of times per second a screen image is redrawn, or refreshed. Refresh rate is measured in Hz. The current recommended minimum refresh rate is 72 Hz. At refresh rates of less than 72 Hz, flickering becomes perceptible, not to mention annoying, to the human eye.

Interlacing is a monitor characteristic related to refresh rate. Graphics standards supported by monitors can be either interlaced or noninterlaced. Interlaced monitors update all of the pixels in even-numbered horizontal rows on a screen and then update the pixels in the odd-numbered horizontal rows. Noninterlaced monitors update all rows at the full refresh rate, thereby reducing perceived flicker. A performance criterion that is a direct result of desired resolution and refresh rate is **maximum video bandwidth,** which can be computed with the following formula:

- Required video bandwidth = resolution height × resolution width × refresh rate × 1.5

As a practical example, an NEC Multisync 5FGP offers a maximum video bandwidth of 135 MHz and supports resolutions up to 1280 × 1024, with a refresh rate of 74 Hz. The term **multisync** refers to the monitor's ability to automatically adjust to the installed video card's specifications and to display the desired resolution at the accompanying refresh rate. Clarity and display of greater detail is a function of pitch or dot pitch, which is the size of the dots forming characters and images. Dot pitches of 0.28 mm or less produce excellent clarity.

The number of displayed colors, or **color depth,** is another performance criterion that differentiates monitors. Following are common color depths:

- 16 colors
- 256 colors
- 65,000 colors
- 16.7 million colors

Color depth and resolution have a direct impact on the amount of VRAM required on the graphics accelerator card and will be covered in the section of graphics accelerators.

The widespread use of notebook and portable computers has led to significant development of the monitors for these computers. Although notebook monitors differ in performance level and display techniques, most start with **LCD** (Liquid Crystal Display) technology as a foundation. Simply stated, LCD monitors employ a fluorescent backlight that shines through a "multilayer sandwich" of polarizers, liquid crystals, color filters, and an electrode grid to produce the image on the screen. There are two major categories of LCD monitors:

- **Active matrix displays** employ transistors at each point on the display grid to actively control color and intensity of each "dot" in the display. This technology enables brighter colors, sharper images, and faster response to changing images.

- **Passive Matrix displays** do not employ transistors and therefore do not have individual control over each point in the display grid. As a result, screens are painted and repainted a line at a time in a series. Dual scan passive matrix displays and active addressing passive matrix displays are two technologies that seek to improve on the shortcomings of passive matrix display technology.

Graphics Accelerator Cards   The role of the graphics accelerator card is to provide an interface between the monitor and the application software running in the CPU that is producing the images to be displayed. An important point to understand is the system-oriented nature of the video subsystem. In other words, it won't matter that an expensive monitor supports 1024×768 resolution with 256 colors if the installed graphics accelerator card won't perform at that specification. The performance of a typical graphics accelerator card is dictated by the specifications of the following components:

- Graphics accelerator chip (also known as the graphics accelerator controller chip)
- Video memory
- Bus interface
- Video BIOS

The key performance criterion of a graphics accelerator chip is the width of its data path. In other words, how big a chunk of video information can it process and forward to or from video memory in a single tick of the clock? Most graphics accelerator cards are either 64-bit cards or 32-bit interleaved cards. **Interleaving** is a technique that allows the graphics accelerator controller chip to perform two different operations to adjacent rows of video memory with each tick of the clock. While a 32-bit interleaved chip is forwarding the contents of one row of video memory to the monitor, it is preparing the next row in a step called precharging. With the next tick of the clock, the precharged row is forwarded.

The video memory in the previous paragraph is usually either VRAM or DRAM, as described earlier in the memory section of this chapter. VRAM is more expensive than DRAM and is faster on high-end applications requiring high resolutions, high color depth, and high refresh rates such as two-dimensional imaging.

The amount of VRAM required on a graphics accelerator depends to some extent on the color depth desired. Figure 2-24 outlines some suggested VRAM amounts for given resolutions and color depths.

The data bus width of the bus interface is important to the overall performance of the video subsystem. For this reason, only a local bus architecture such as 32-bit PCI is commonly used for graphics accelerator boards. That is not to say that graphics cards are not also available for ISA, EISA, NuBUS (Macintosh), or VL-BUS, an alternative local bus architecture largely dominated by PCI.

The video BIOS (basic input/output system) is contained on a chip on the graphics accelerator card. Its main function is to identify itself and its operating specifications to the computer's operating system during system startup. The video BIOS provides the interface between the graphics accelerator card (hardware) and the computer system's operating system (software).

Graphics Driver Software   How is it possible for the video BIOS on the graphics accelerator card to speak to the computer system's operating system software? Graphics accelerator cards should ship with specially written software drivers that understand all of the proprietary hardware controls of the particular graphics accelerator card and can also understand the commands of the particular installed operating system. These drivers act as translators between the software and hardware. In addition, most graphics accelerator cards come with specialized drivers for operation with high-powered graphics application software such as AutoCAD. Without the appropriate drivers to bridge the interface between the graphics accelerator card and the operating system, there is no communication and no functional video subsystem.

Video Trends

Plug-n-Play Monitors   An organization known as VESA (Video Electronics Standards Association) has proposed a display data channel specification that will allow a monitor to automatically transfer electronic display identification (EDID) information to the attached graphics accelerator card in order to enable PnP monitor installation.

LCDs to FEDs   Although LCD technology for notebook computer screens continues to develop and improve, **FED (field emission display)** technology may be the next generation of underlying technology for notebook computer displays. Whereas most CRTs and television sets use a single electron gun to shoot electrons across the entire screen, FEDs use individual electron emitters arranged in a flat grid. Each

Resolution	Color Depth	Suggested VRAM
640 by 480	16 colors	150 KB
800 by 600	65,000 colors	960 KB
1024 by 768	16.7 million colors	2.4 MB
1280 by 1024	16.7 million colors	3.93 MB

Figure 2-24   VRAM Requirements as a Product of Resolution and Color Depth

FED is individually addressable and controllable by the video controller. In theory at least, FEDs should produce images as sharp as CRTs, in a package small enough to fit in a notebook computer powered by battery.

Accelerated Graphics Ports   The good news is that PCs equipped with an **accelerated graphics port (AGP)** move graphics traffic from the PCI bus that is shared with other system traffic to a dedicated channel that links directly to the system chip set and subsequently to the system memory. The bad news is that unless applications are written to take advantage of the AGP, no significant improvement in performance will be achieved. AGP-1x promises throughput of 266 MBps. AGP-2x will deliver about 533 MBps, and eventually AGP-4x will deliver throughput of greater than 1 GBps. In terms of interoperability, support for AGP begins in the system chip set and must be supported by the installed operating system. The first chip sets to support AGP were the Pentium II 440LX chip set. Native operating system support is expected in Windows NT 5.0 and Windows 98.

SUMMARY

Client hardware serves as the foundation for the overall processing power delivered to end users. Operating systems, network operating systems, and applications software are totally dependent on client hardware to supply required computing, storage, and input/output capabilities. Client hardware is best described as a computer *system* composed of processing, storage, memory, video, and bus subsystems. A key point of the systems nature of client hardware is the fact that improvements in the technology of one subsystem, such as the CPU, will have a ripple effect through other subsystems. Those other subsystems, such as memory, may or may not be equipped to cope with the advances in CPU technology.

At the heart of the client workstation is the CPU chip, the most distinguishing element of the computer system. The key trend in this area of technology is increasing power. CPU chips continue to become faster and more powerful, and major differences between CISC and RISC architectures are quickly disappearing.

Buses serve as the highway system connecting all of the other systems in the client workstation. PCI buses are gaining in popularity as a method for adding high-speed peripheral devices to a variety of different computing platforms.

Memory is the subsystem that probably has the most development pressure to be able to keep up with the advances in CPU technology. Faster CPU chips are not much use if they're sitting around idle, because memory subsystems are not fast enough to keep the CPU supplied with data.

Bigger, faster disk drives are also required to meet the storage demands of more-powerful CPUs and the larger applications programs and databases that use these advanced CPUs. These same advanced applications programs are putting increased demands on the speed and quality of the video output devices used in today's client workstation. The video subsystem's performance depends on having the right combination of bus width and speed, video memory, and video processing supplied by the graphics accelerator card, in addition to the quality and capabilities of the monitor itself.

A thorough understanding of the technology that underlies the interacting subsystems of the client workstation is essential for information systems analysts and network analysts if they are to perform effective business-oriented systems analysis and design.

KEY TERMS

Accelerated graphics port (AGP)
Active matrix
Adaptive segmented lookahead
  cache
Address bus
ATA
ATA-2
Backside bus
Branch prediction
Branch target buffer
Bus interface
Bus width
Cache bus
CDRAM
Central processing unit
CISC
CISC-to-RISC decoder
Clock-divided frequency
Clock multiplying
Clock speed
Color depth
Coprocessors
CPU
CVRAM
Data bus
Data bus width
Data cache
Decode stage
DIMM
DIP
Direct memory access (DMA)
Dual-issue
Dual-ported VRAM
DX
DX2
DX4
Dynamic execution
Dynamic RAM (DRAM)
EDORAM
EDOSRAM
EDOVRAM
EDRAM
E-IDE
EISA

Execute stage
Execution units
Expansion bus
External bus
Fast SCSI-2
Fast and wide SCSI-2
Fetch stage
Flash RAM
FPM
FRAM
Graphics accelerator chip
Hardware cache
Hardware emulation
IA-64
IDE
Instruction cache
Interleaving
Internal bus
ISA
L1 cache
L2 cache
LCD
Local bus
Look-ahead cache
Maximum video bandwidth
MCA
Memory bus
Merced
MMX
Multisync
On-board cache
Operands stage
Out-of-order execution
Overdrive chips
P6
P7
Packaged L2 cache
Passive matrix
PCI
PCMCIA
Pentium
Pentium II
Pentium Pro
PIO

Pipelines
Pixels
PowerPC
Primary cache
Primary data cache
Primary instruction cache
Principle of shifting bottlenecks
Processor I/O
Quad-issue
RDRAM
Read-through cache
Refresh rate
Resolution
RISC
Scalar
SCSI
SCSI-2
SDRAM
Secondary cache
Sectors
Segmented look-ahead cache
SIMM
Software cache
Software emulation
Speculative execution
Static RAM (SRAM)
Superpipelines
Superscalar
SVRAM
SX
System bus
Three-dimensional memory module
Three-dimensional RAM (3DRAM)
Tracks
Ultra SCSI
Universal serial bus (USB)
Video BIOS
Video memory
Wide SCSI-2
WRAM
Write-back cache
Write-back stage
Write-through cache
Zip drive

REVIEW QUESTIONS

1. Why is a thorough knowledge of client hardware important to network analysts?

2. Name the five subsystems typically included in any computer system.

3. What is the overall role of the bus subsystem in a computer?

4. What is the major development challenge or strategic direction in CPU chip development?

5. What is the relationship behind CPU performance and clock speed?

6. Differentiate among the terms *scalar*, *superscalar*, and *pipelines*.

7. What is the relationship between pipelines and execution units?

8. How do pipelined architectures improve on CPU performance in comparison with nonpipelined architectures?

9. Describe the typical stages found in a pipeline.

10. What is the principle of shifting bottlenecks, and how does it apply to CPU design?

11. Why did L1 cache become necessary?

12. What limits the size of L1 cache?

13. What is the advantage of splitting L1 cache into separate instruction and data caches?

14. Differentiate L1 and L2 cache.

15. What factors can affect L2 cache performance?

16. What is the difference between write-back cache and write-through cache?

17. Which cache-related design issues are the responsibility of the CPU chip designer, and which are the responsibility of the system board designer?

18. What is the relationship between the data bus width and the memory bus clock?

19. How does branch prediction improve the performance of the CPU?

20. From a conceptual or theoretical perspective, what is the major difference between CISC and RISC architectures?

21. What are the practical differences between currently available CISC and RISC chips?

22. Which is better, CISC or RISC?

23. Why can't Intel just abandon the CISC x86 architecture and switch to RISC chips?

24. What is the difference between a coprocessor and an integrated FPU?

25. What is clock multiplying?

26. How does clock multiplying affect internal and external clock speeds?

27. Why are internal and external clock speeds not necessarily the same?

28. Differentiate SX, DX, DX2, and DX4.

29. What are the advantages and disadvantages of employing overdrive chips?

30. What are the significant differences between 486 chips and Pentiums?

31. What was a problem with early Pentium chips, and how was it overcome short term and long term?

32. What are the significant improvements in the P6 chip?

33. How do out-of-order execution and speculative execution improve on CPU performance?

34. What is MMX?

35. Compare and constrast the features of the Pentium, Pentium Pro, and Pentium II CPUs.

36. What are the market realities facing makers of Intel chip clones?

37. What is the PowerPC chip?

38. What advantages does the PowerPC chip possess over the Intel chips? Disadvantages?

39. What is the difference between hardware and software emulation in terms of technology employed and performance?

40. What is likely to be the direction of future CPU chip development?

41. What is a clock-divided frequency, and why is it important?

42. What is the relationship between bus width and clock speed?

43. What is the major difference between the system bus and other buses such as the I/O bus or expansion bus?

44. Why is the PCI bus not a local bus, strictly speaking?

45. How does a local bus architecture differ from a mezzanine architecture?

46. Which types of devices are more appropriate for PCI buses rather than expansion buses?

47. Differentiate ISA, EISA, and MCA.

48. Differentiate the many types of SCSI.

49. What is the relationship between PCI and SCSI?

50. What is PCMCIA, and what is it most often used for?

51. What are the cost and performance differences between DRAM and SRAM?

52. What are the major approaches to improving memory performance?

53. What is the major distinguishing characteristic of flash RAM?

54. What are the major trends in the ways memory is packaged?

55. What is the difference between average seek time and average access time?

56. Differentiate IDE, E-IDE, and SCSI.

57. Differentiate the various terms used to categorize disk performance.

58. What is the difference between PIO and DMA?

59. What is the effect of caches and buffers on disk performance?

60. How do caches differ from buffers?

61. Differentiate the various types of removable storage disks discussed in the text.

62. What are resolution and refresh rate, and what effect do they have on maximum video bandwidth?
63. What are the systems relationships or interdependencies within the video subsystem?
64. What does *multisync* mean?
65. What is color depth, and what effect does it have on VRAM?

66. How is resolution measured?
67. How is refresh rate measured?
68. What is the difference between active matrix and passive matrix displays?
69. What are the four key components of a graphics accelerator card, and what role does each play?
70. What is the role of graphics software drivers, and why are they important?

ACTIVITIES

1. Divide into groups, and assign each group one of the subsystems of a computer system. Each group should research past and present technical developments of its subsystem and prepare a timeline of significant events. Reunite the subsystem groups when timelines are completed. Compare the timing of significant events in each subsystem. Find examples of how significant developments in one subsystem led to technical developments in other subsystems.
2. Research and prepare a presentation on CPU clocks. How are they similar to the technology found in most wrist watches? How are they different?
3. Prepare a presentation on current CPU chip development highlighting pipelining. Stress the differences between the chips in terms of number of pipelines, number and type of execution units, and number of pipeline stages.
4. Find examples of the principle of shifting bottlenecks in areas other than CPU design.
5. Take the logic flowchart from a simple computer program employing if-then-else loops. Using a realistic set of data, perform structured walk-throughs on the program, and save results of conditional branches in a list (branch target buffer). Begin to predict conditional branches based on the previous results contained in your branch target buffer. What percentage of accuracy does your branch target buffer produce? Repeat the experiment with different programs and different data sets.
6. Program the branch prediction logic walked through in Activity 5 in a real program, and execute it with a larger data set. Have the program keep statistics on branch prediction accuracy percentage.
7. Prepare graphs plotting CPU chip performance development over time. Chart items such as number of transistors, clock speed, and MIPS. What do the graphs look like? Has the rate of development been constant, or is it accelerating?
8. Trace the introduction and sales of clones of Intel chips. Analyze the success or failure of these ventures.
9. Trace the sales of computers using the PowerPC chip. Pay particular attention to the types of applications run on these computers. Are they Windows applications? Mac applications? RISC applications? Native PowerPC applications?
10. Use data communications and computer system supply catalogs, and prepare a presentation or bulletin board showing the types of devices that connect to PCI buses versus expansion buses.
11. Collect advertisements and promotional literature on disk drives. Prepare a display highlighting quoted seek times and access times. Can you find examples of when access times quoted are really just seek times?
12. Research the removable storage disk market. Track the rise in storage capacity over time. Plot the price of the disk drives and the price of the removable media over the same time period. Prepare a graphical presentation of your results.
13. Research the differences in the pipeline structure and other internal architectural differences between the Intel Pentium Pro and the Centaur IDT C6 chips. What are the net effects of these differences? How do these architectural differences affect the ability of a new company to enter an established market?
14. Research the PC workstation market and report on the percentage of workstations being shipped with accelerated graphics ports, universal serial buses, or both. Are you able to establish a trend? Present and explain your results.

CHAPTER 2

CASE STUDY

WCB: SLOW AND STEADY WINS THE RACE

As a Major Government-run Insurance Company, the Workers' Compensation Board of British Columbia is a Methodical Organization, Accustomed to Making Careful and Measured Moves

So as other businesses dived in to distributed computing, eagerly installing untested hardware and 1.0 software releases, WCB waited, diligently studying new technologies and learning from the war stories of other companies before launching its first strategic client/server application this year.

As a reselling client, WCB is equally deliberate, to its own advantage as well as that of SHL Systemhouse Ltd. in Ottawa, its reselling partner. SHL Systemhouse is the Canadian arm of Atlanta-based MCI Systemhouse Corp. WCB has slowly expanded its relationship with the systems integrator and VAR in a manner that has paid off handsomely for both: WCB is a savvy customer that purchases services only as it needs them, and SHL Systemhouse has enlarged a key account, broadening its relationship with a valued client.

Within Canada's far-flung boundaries, each of the country's six provinces maintains its own Workers' Compensation Board. The government-run boards serve as employer-funded insurance companies, managing claims from individuals injured in the workplace, conducting site inspections, and running rehabilitation services.

In British Columbia, one of Canada's most populous provinces, with 3.8 million residents, the WCB is a billion-dollar organization that processes tens of thousands of injured workers' claims each year.

From the board's headquarters in Richmond, which is just miles from nearby Vancouver, the 250-person staff of WCB's information services has until recently run a traditional transaction-oriented environment, with an IBM 3270 mainframe and DB2 database crunching through the board's claims operations.

In 1992 WCB's information services began its move to the desktop. As a Big Blue shop, it went into OS/2 and the NetBIOS and TCP/IP protocols for LANs. It also standardized on Microsoft Office. After choosing Powersoft PowerBuilder as its development platform, WCB began the lengthy process of retraining its COBOL and Borland International Inc. dBASE programmers in Microsoft Visual Basic and SQL Server.

While the programmers were honing their new skills on small workgroup applications, WCB worked to better manage its expanding desktop systems. It installed IBM NetView 6000 for network management, New Era Systems Ltd. Harbor for centralized server backup, and Expert Advisor from Software Artistry Inc. for internal help-desk functions.

Progress was slow, but that had its advantages. "By waiting until now to do these systems, we leapfrogged several generations of technology," says Brian Baker, director of technology services. "The focus here is reengineering the business. That's quite a different approach than 10 years ago in the insurance industry," when businesses felt technology alone was the solution to their problems.

Since 1991 WCB had contracted with Computer Innovation Ltd., the technology-services subsidiary of SHL Systemhouse, to provide PC

and server acquisition and installation as well as repairs. As it began contemplating the installation of Microsoft Systems Management Server (SMS) and its planned migration to Microsoft Windows NT, however, WCB realized that the implementation's complexity demanded beefed-up technical reserves.

WCB wanted "an initial implementation service," says Baker. "We were looking for some expertise on TCP/IP to help us through the migration of our architecture. Our thought was, if it worked, we could take it from there."

WCB decided to contract with a systems integrator partly because of the scope of the task and partly because of Vancouver's business realities. To add configuration-management expertise to its team without the expense of extra full-time staff, WCB needed to tap the area's extensive network of independent contractors. With 1.8 million residents, Vancouver is the urban outpost of British Columbia, but its rugged terrain attracts enterpreneurial spirits who favor independent work over full-time employment.

Tried and True SHL Rather than sifting through that intricate network on its own, WCB preferred paying consultants to do it. Its previous, positive relationship with SHL Systemhouse made the company a natural bidder for the SMS-related Request for Proposal (RFP). "SHL was well-connected and could use its network to gather the people to respond to our requirements," says Baker.

SHL's Vancouver office was looking for just such an opportunity. Having recently signed WCB to a further three-year contract to perform all of the board's repair work and to supply its PCs and servers, account executive Nick Skworoda hoped to sell through the integrator's systems-integration and consulting services.

Winning the contract to help WCB acquire and install the SMS software was an important step in that direction, says Skworoda. The project-management services and TCP/IP expertise that SHL Systemhouse supplied "was my first break in the systems-integration and consulting business" in the WCB account, says Skworoda.

But the relationship was about to deepen. The increasing availability and sophistication of client/server software was prompting WCB to consider new uses for the technology as it reengineered its business processes. One of the first functions to be eyed was claims processing, a tedious manual procedure that relied on triplicate paper forms and prodigious faxing from the board's 15 remote sites throughout the province.

Dubbed the Electronic File project, the automation of the claims process still begins with paper forms. The claims forms are faxed from employers to one of WCB's service-delivery locations and then scanned into a PowerBuilder application. When claims can't be resolved by local offices, the form images are transmitted through wide-area links to WCB's home office, where they are stored in an Informix Software Inc. database and are available to anyone who needs to access them. In addition, the Electronic File project connects users to legacy data stored in DB2.

"I knew the Electronic File would drive a lot of change and change the WCB forever," says Skworda. "It had a big effect on the account and [presented] a lot of opportunities."

Indeed, not only was WCB launching the ambitious Electronic File project, but it was also completing its NT migration and converting from a token ring to a switched backbone. It was upgrading its wide-area links from frame relay to ATM and preparing to bring up its 15 remote sites on the WAN. It was also evaluating parallel processing servers to shore up the back end of its distributed environment.

An organization of meticulous planning, WCB knows what it wants. The only function it outsources is the break/fix contract. For all other IS functions, it insists that the experts it hires serve as genuine consultants—not just contractors performing work. "We're committed to our employees and to training, so we look for experts who can also provide coaching skills," says Baker. "They mentor our people. We don't want them to walk out the door without leaving some of their knowledge behind for our staff."

SHL was happy to comply. As a result of the launch of the Electronic File project, it expanded the maintenance contract to include a move/add/changes team and contracted for technical services, including year 2000 impact analysis and architectural assistance in building an NT downloadable module for use with images, among other projects.

Production Momentum Since January [1997] the Electronic File project has gone into production at three of the 11 sites that will use it. It is in use on 500 desktops, with another 500 scheduled to go online by year-end, [1997] which will be the halfway mark.

WCB is using the British Columbia Telephone Company's Ubiquity ATM network to carry the images from the remote locations to the home office. Given the several hundred miles that separate the WCB home office from its rural remote sites, ATM was the most affordable solution, says Pete Munro, manager of network services. "We ruled out T-1 because of the huge distances, and the price was just skyrocketing." Munro says that, although the Ubiquity service provides 10 Mbps Ethernet access from the buildings and into the ATM cloud, 155 Mbps access will be available later this year.

Last month [April 1997] WCB installed the IBM RS/6000 SP parallel server running AIX as the central imaging storehouse, another project to which SHL Systemhouse lent its expertise. Without it, says Baker, "we would have had to buy separate boxes for each service-delivery location." The multiprocessing server devotes one processor each to Electronic File production, development, and data warehousing.

While every WCB division must go out for an RFP, SHL Systemhouse remains the WCB's primary vendor with four contracts under way.

WCB is now devoting the same meticulous care to studying improvements to the front end of its distributed environment. "Now that the Electronic File system will handle a lot of the processing, we need to get more data into the WCB," said Baker. For example, the board recently formed a group for electronic commerce and is piloting a Lotus Domino-based Internet application.

Source: Deborah Asbrand, "WCB: Slow and Steady Wins the Race," *LAN Times* (May 26, 1997). Copyright May 26, 1997, The McGraw-Hill Companies, Inc.

BUSINESS CASE STUDY QUESTIONS

Activities

1. Complete a top-down model for this case by gleaning facts from the case and placing them in the proper layer of the top-down model. After having completed the top-down model, analyze and detail those instances where requirements were clearly passed down from upper layers to lower layers of the model and where solutions to those requirements were passed up from lower layers to upper layers of the model.
2. Detail any questions about the case that may occur to you for which answers are not clearly stated in the article.

Business

1. What is WCB's annual revenue?
2. How many workers' compensation claims are processed annually?
3. What is meant by the statement "The focus here is reengineering the business"?
4. How were people with the required skills for the implementation project contracted?
5. Why was the claims processing business process an ideal candidate for reengineering?
6. How does WCB decide which IS functions it will outsource?
7. What other business processes are candidates for reengineering?

Application

1. In what programming language were the old applications written?
2. What was the new application development environment?
3. What was the Electronic File project?

Data

1. What were the various sources and storage locations for data in the Electronic File project?

Network

1. What were the network requirements to support the Electronic File project?
2. What local area and wide area architectures and services were employed?
3. How many desktops are supported by the Electronic File project?
4. Why was ATM chosen as the preferred WAN service?
5. What are the current and future ATM access speeds?

Technology

1. What was the traditional infrastructure that had supported the WCB's business operations?
2. What technologies were chosen for the transition from a mainframe environment to a client/server-based system?
3. What management technologies were employed?
4. What is the primary server for the Electronic File project? Why was this particular technology chosen?

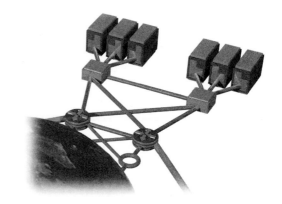

CHAPTER 3

CLIENT SOFTWARE

Concepts Reinforced

Client/Server Technology Architecture   Protocols and Compatibility
Client/Server Technology and Tools   OSI Model
Client Hardware Platforms   Processor Fundamentals

Concepts Introduced

Client Software Architecture   Operating System Architecture
Kernels and Microkernels   Graphical User Interfaces
Client Operating Systems   Client Network Operating Systems
Hardware/Software Compatibility   Platform Independence

OBJECTIVES

After mastering the material in this chapter you should understand the following:

1. The organization and interaction of the various categories of client software from an architectural perspective

2. The concepts and architecture of a typical client operating system

3. The importance of interprocess communications and application program interfaces to client software interoperability

4. The functionality of and major differences between types of currently available client software

■ INTRODUCTION

Having gained an appreciation for both the functionality and variety of client hardware in Chapter 2, the reader must now bridge the functional gap between the client hardware platform and the end user. In order to deliver transparent interoperability to the end user, many different categories of client software must all interact successfully. Understanding the role of each of these client software categories and, perhaps more importantly, how these client software categories communicate with one another to deliver the desired transparent interoperability to the end user is the focus of this chapter.

■ THE CLIENT SOFTWARE ARCHITECTURE

As an introduction to the different categories of client software that will be explored in this chapter, Figure 3-1 illustrates a conceptual view of the interaction of these client software categories.

Several aspects of the client software architecture diagram deserve elaboration. First of all, arrows between conceptual layers indicate the need for a standardized protocol in order to successfully bridge the interface in question. The protocols used for communication between client software categories may vary depending on which particular software technology is being used in each software category. Without agreed upon, mutually supported communications protocols between client software categories, there can be no top-to-bottom communication through the client software architecture. Therefore, in the absence of these protocols, there can be no transparent interoperability delivered from the client hardware to the end user.

The presentation, application, and data management modules of the client software architecture were introduced in Chapter 1 as the key logical elements of distributed computing. The client hardware module that forms the foundation of the entire architecture was covered in Chapter 2. Shifting the application and data management modules into a side-by-side relationship is significant in that within the client software architecture, both of these software categories may need to interact directly with the network operating system as well as with each other.

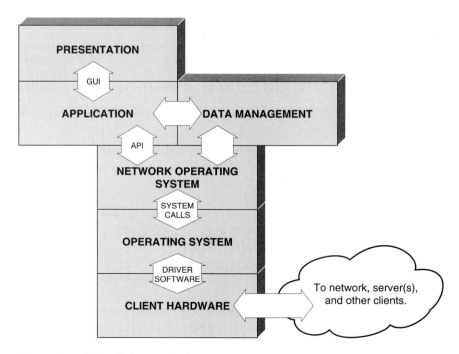

Figure 3-1   Client Software Architecture

Although the presentation, network operating system, and operating system functional models are depicted separately in the client software architecture, currently available software technology may combine these separate functional categories into a single product. Examples of such products will be presented throughout the chapter.

Clients and their associated client software architecture are just part of the overall client/server architecture. As a result, Figure 3-1 depicts how the client software architecture interacts with the network, servers, and other clients via the client hardware layer.

Interacting directly with the client hardware is the function of the operating system module. The functional concepts and current trends in this client software category begin this chapter's discussion of client software architecture. Subsequent sections in this chapter examine client network operating systems software and client presentation software. Client applications software will be examined only in terms of its interaction with presentation, network operating system, and operating system software. Integration of client data management software and client application software in a distributed computing environment will be dealt with later in the text.

CLIENT OPERATING SYSTEMS

Concepts and Functionality

An operating system's primary goal is to allow a user to easily execute applications programs without having to understand the computer hardware on which those applications run. This hardware transparency is extended by the operating system not only to end users, but also to the applications programmers who write the programs. Operating systems allow application programmers to include standard operating system commands or calls in their programs rather than having to write unique lower-level commands for every possible different client hardware combination on which their programs may potentially run.

An operating system can be thought of as a resource manager or resource allocator. The following are among the resources to be managed and allocated among competing applications:

- CPU processing time

- Memory access

- Disk storage/retrieval and file system management

- Input/output resources

An additional key responsibility of operating systems is *secure* management and allocation of the previously mentioned resources. All of the required functions of an operating system could be considered subsystems of the overall operating system. With reference to Figure 3-1, it could be said that an operating system manages and controls hardware resources on behalf of the upper layers of the client software architecture.

Operating System Architecture   The operating system is actually a computer program, at least part of which runs all of the time on any given computer. The operating system program itself is sometimes referred to as a **kernel.** Application programs request computer resources by interfacing to the operating system through mutually supported **system calls.** The kernel then interfaces to the various hardware components and their controllers via small software programs known as **device drivers,** which are specifically written to be compatible with a particular operating system and a particular type of hardware device.

The operating system's ability to allocate system resources to multiple application programs and processes is due to its ability to handle **interrupts** and **exceptions.** An interrupt is, quite literally, an interruption, when the CPU has to stop doing one thing in order to do something else. Key hardware components such as the system bus, the keyboard, the video controller, and serial ports are all assigned interrupt numbers. Higher priority subsystems such as the system bus, keyboard, and video receive lower interrupt numbers than serial port devices such as modems. Application programs can also generate interrupts in order to get the CPU's attention and request services such as disk access or CPU processing time.

Exceptions are error conditions or unexpected events that the operating system must be prepared to handle appropriately. These exceptions are generally related to the operating system's responsibility to effectively manage system resources. For example, an exception that must be properly handled occurs when one application program tries to write into another application program's reserved memory space—an exception condition usually called a general protection fault. Protecting application programs' memory space is a key differentiating factor among operating systems.

Figure 3-2 illustrates the relationship of users, application programs, operating systems, and hardware components in the operating systems architecture.

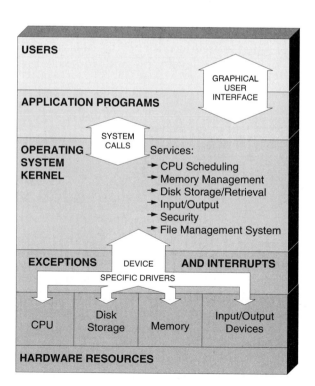

Figure 3-2   Operating System Architecture

Monolithic Architecture Traditionally, operating systems were built according to a **monolithic architecture** model. Required operating system components such as the file management system or the input/output and disk storage subsystem were arranged in a layered architecture, with each layer communicating directly only with the layers immediately above and below it. Maintaining or updating an operating system built with a monolithic architecture, otherwise known as a closed architecture, could be a nightmare. The closed nature of the monolithic architecture implies that all communications between the protocols on the various layers of the architecture were "hard-coded" for the specific corresponding combination of protocols. As a result, alternative protocols could not be substituted on any given layer of the architecture owing to this hard-coded, customized, monolithic architecture. Because all communications from the application program to the device drivers had to pass through all layers of the operating system, a simple change in a single layer could have disastrous and untold consequences in other layers. New subsystems and functionality could not be easily added without rewriting several interacting layers of the operating system.

This difficulty with modification or maintenance is in sharp contrast to systems developed according to open standards architectures such as the OSI model. The key difference between open and closed architectures is that open architectures define the methods or interfaces between layers of the architecture. As a result, any protocol that is able to communicate to a given layer's standardized, open interface specification is able to communicate with the protocols residing in the neighboring layers of the open architecture.

Figure 3-3 is a conceptual representation of a monolithic operating system architecture.

Microkernel Architecture The trend in most of today's client operating systems is movement toward a **microkernel**-based approach. A microkernel is a subset of the overall operating system. A microkernel could be thought of as a tiny, CPU specific operating system. It contains a minimum of hardware-specific instructions written to interact with a particular CPU chip. Although there are no laws as to what should and should not be included in the microkernel, the following CPU-related services, unique to each CPU chip, are typically included:

- CPU processor scheduling
- Interrupt and exception handling
- Multiple processor handling
- System crash recovery
- Interprocess communications management
- Virtual memory management

The microkernel runs in what is known as **privileged mode,** or kernel mode, which implies that it is never swapped out of memory and has highest priority for allocation of CPU cycles. The rest of the operating system is then written in separate add-on modules, or subsystems, that run in **user mode.**

The modular approach afforded by the microkernel architecture contrasts the hierarchical, layered approach offered by the monolithic architecture. Surrounding the CPU-specific microkernel are modules or subsystems that offer the functionality

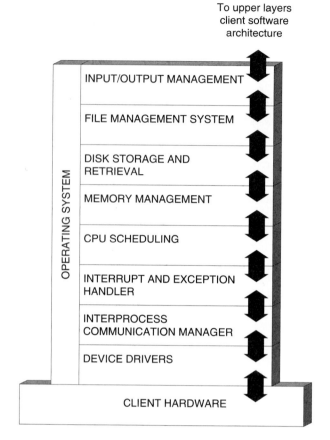

Figure 3-3   Monolithic Operating System Architecture

previously offered by the layers cemented within the monolithic architecture. The operating systems modules converse with one another through the microkernel using mutually understandable message passing and interprocess communication. Figure 3-4 provides a conceptual representation of a microkernel operating system architecture in stark contrast to the monolithic architecture illustrated in Figure 3-3.

The key benefits of a microkernel operating system architecture over a monolithic operating system architecture are as follows:

- More extendible

- More portable

- More reliable

Extendible   As operating systems mature and the demands of information systems change, new features and subsystems are inevitably required to be added to existing operating systems. With the small nucleus of a microkernel and its relatively few microkernel system calls, additional modules can be written with relative ease and integrated with existing operating system modules. This characteristic also

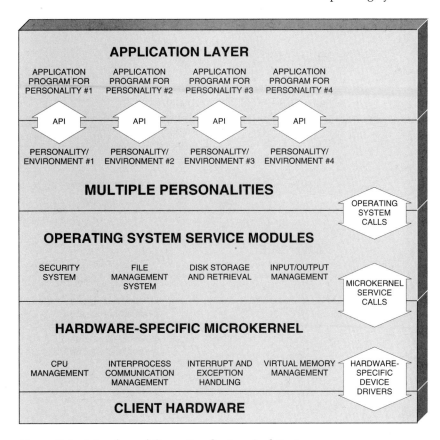

Figure 3-4   Microkernel Operating System Architecture

means that microkernel architectures are more easily customized. Any module or service that users demand can be added so long as that new subsystem communicates with the hardware resources through the microkernel through its minimal set of system calls or commands that enable its available services.

Portable   Because all of the hardware-specific code is restricted to the microkernel, modular operating systems can be ported to any processor that can communicate with their microkernel. From a user's standpoint, this is advantageous because application programs written for a particular operating system could be executed on a variety of hardware platforms. Windows NT is an example of one of these so-called **hardware-independent operating systems** because versions of it are or were able to run on Intel, MIPS, DEC Alpha, and PowerPC CPU chips.

Reliable   Increased reliability is a result of the fact that operating systems programmers need to be concerned with interacting with only the minimal number of microkernel commands. In the monolithic operating system architecture, programmers wrote layers and subsystems that communicated only with the adjacent subsystems and hoped that their programming would not cause unpredictable chain reactions in distant layers.

Figure 3-5 illustrates the key benefits of a microkernel operating system architecture.

RELIABLE

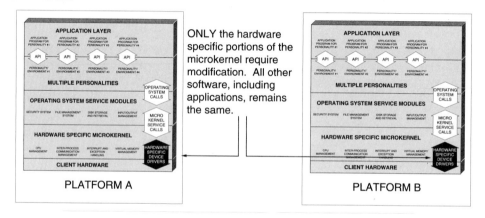

In the
***Monolithic
Architecture***,
programmers
need to be
concerned with
top-to-bottom
communications

In the
***Microkernel
Architecture***,
programmers
need be only
concerned with
interacting
properly with the
minimal number
of microkernel
service calls.

PORTABLE

ONLY the hardware
specific portions of the
microkernel require
modification. All other
software, including
applications, remains
the same.

PLATFORM A

PLATFORM B

EXTENDIBLE

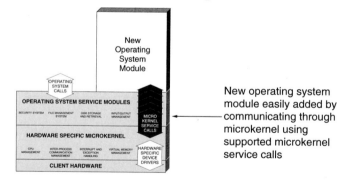

New
Operating
System
Module

New operating system
module easily added by
communicating through
microkernel using
supported microkernel
service calls

Figure 3-5   Key Benefits of Microkernel Operating System Architecture

Multiple Personality Operating Systems   Several current or emerging operating systems have introduced the notion of **multiple personality operating systems,** also known as **multiple workplace environments.** These multiple personality subsystems are further examples of the extendibility of a microkernel-based operating system. As a specific example, Windows NT includes OS/2, 32-bit Windows, 16-bit Windows, and POSIX subsystems that allow applications written for any of those environments to be run on a Windows NT Platform. IBM, Apple, and Novell have all announced plans to produce multiple personality operating systems as well.

Technology and Trends

In Sharper
Focus

COMPARATIVE MICROKERNELS

As illustrated in Figure 3-4, because microkernel-based operating systems can be built in a modular fashion, limited only by the requirement to interface to the microkernel through the minimal number of microkernel system calls, it is possible for different operating systems to be developed from the same microkernel. Two microkernels that have been used as the nucleus for numerous operating systems are the Mach microkernel developed at Carnegie-Mellon University and the Chorus microkernel developed by Chorus Systems, now a division of Sun Microsystems, located in France. Figure 3-6 lists some of the operating systems currently available or under development that are based on the Mach or Chorus microkernels or on their own proprietary microkernels.

Mach Microkernel   The following concepts are essential to an understanding of the Mach microkernel. They also form the basis of an understanding of operating system functionality in general:

- Task
- Thread
- Port

A **task** is the basic addressable unit of program execution. It is sometimes referred to as an execution environment to which resources such as CPU cycles or virtual memory space can be assigned. A task can be accomplished or executed through the work accomplished by one or more **threads.** Threads are the basic unit

Operating System	Mach Microkernel	Chorus Microkernel	Apple Microkernel	NT Microkernel
Windows NT				•
Apple System 9 (Gershwin)			•	
USL UNIX		•		
SVR4				
OSF OSF/1 1.3	•			
DEC	•			
NextStep	•			
Apple Rhapsody	•			
Chorus/MIX		•		

Figure 3-6   Microkernels Used in Various Operating Systems

of execution and are assigned resources only through a given task. Tasks spawn threads in order to accomplish their instructions. The relationship between tasks and threads is sometimes characterized as a parent-child relationship.

As an example of the relationship between tasks and threads, consider a 32-bit application setup program in an operating system such as Windows NT. The setup program is the lone task, acquiring resources such as memory and CPU cycles from the operating system as needed. However, the setup program is actually composed of several independent sub-tasks, or threads, whose execution must be coordinated. The threads of the task must share the assigned CPU cycles and memory space. For example, one thread would be responsible for decompressing all of the required files to install the new application, another thread would be responsible for copying the decompressed files to the proper installation directory on the computer on which the application is being installed, and a third thread would be responsible for modifying any configuration files necessary to ensure that the newly installed application will execute correctly. Although the three threads of execution are independent of each other, their execution must be timed and coordinated correctly by the parent task, the setup program. If we were to display all tasks or processes running in the operating system, we would see the setup program listed, but not its constituent threads.

Threads are essential to distributed computing environments. In a multiple server environment, one or more threads may be required to simultaneously interact with each distributed server in order to accomplish the overall task as dictated by a multithreaded application. Only the parent task interacts directly with the operating system, requesting system resources as necessary to run the multithreaded application. A **port** can be thought of as a queue, or communications pipe, through which computer resources can be assigned to a task.

The structure of the Mach microkernel is not unlike the generic microkernel illustrated in Figure 3-4. The hardware-specific services included in the Mach microkernel are as follows:

- Interprocess communication management

- Virtual memory management

- Task and threads management

- Host and processor sets

- I/O and interrupt support

All other functionality must be offered by the operating systems modules, which are written to interface to the Mach microkernel via microkernel system calls and are free to vary from one operating system to another.

Chorus Microkernel   In a Chorus-based operating system, the microkernel is correctly called the Chorus **nucleus.** The chorus nucleus is functionally organized around the following concepts:

- Actor

- Thread

- Port

- Site

The term **actor** is the functional equivalent of a task in a Mach microkernel or a process in a UNIX environment. **Threads,** as in the Mach environment, do not have their own address space. Threads are able to send messages through **ports.** Ports separate the communication function from the execution function and allow threads to communicate with one another without having to know the other threads' physical locations. A given hardware platform or CPU is considered a **site,** with one nucleus executing at each site.

The Chorus nucleus has built-in support for multiple processors and distributed operating system servers. Embedded within the Chorus nucleus itself are the following services:

- Scheduling

- Memory management

- Real-time events support

- Interprocess communications management

All other functionality is written to operate externally to the nucleus in software modules known as **servers.** Groups of servers are known as **subsystems.** Servers and subsystems interact with the minimized Chorus nucleus (50 to 60KB) via supported nucleus system calls. An entire operating system, such as UNIX V, can be run as a single subsystem as long as interaction with the hardware platform is handled by the Chorus nucleus. Such is the case with the UNIX V implementation included within the Chorus/MiX operating system.

Comparative Client Operating Systems Currently available client operating systems have evolved to include graphical user interfaces and built-in networking software in addition to the traditional operating system functionality. In the following section, a variety of operating systems alternatives will be analyzed from functional and application perspectives.

A few important concepts provide important criteria for operating system comparison:

- **Multiprocessing:** An operating system that supports multiprocessing is able to split the processing demands of applications programs across more than one processor or CPU. The most common type of multiprocessing supported by current operating systems is known as **symmetrical multiprocessing,** or **SMP,** in which processing loads are split evenly among all CPUs.

- **Multiuser:** Multiuser operating systems allow more than one user to log in simultaneously. In addition, multiuser operating systems are able to run the multiple application programs of those multiple users simultaneously.

- **Cooperative multitasking:** Multitasking implies that an operating system can be running more than one program simultaneously. Cooperative multitasking implies that a given application has access to all required system resources until that program relinquishes that control. Misbehaving application programs can monopolize system resources in a cooperative multitasking environment.

- **Preemptive multitasking:** Preemptive multitasking operating systems prevent misbehaving applications from monopolizing system resources by allocating system resources to applications according to priority or timing. When a given application program's time is up, it is "swapped out," or preempted, and another waiting application program is given the system resources it requires.

- **Multithreaded:** Like the relationship between tasks and threads from the section of microkernel functionality, a multithreaded operating system allows multiple threads per task to operate simultaneously. Each thread from a single task is free to communicate individually with other threads throughout the distributed environment. Computing resources for individual threads such as CPU cycles, virtual memory, or message passing are requested through the parent task's port.

Some of these operating system characteristics are likely to be more important on servers supporting multiple users than on single-user client workstations.

Operating System Analysis Questions

Applied Problem Solving

Figure 3-7 summarizes a few general criteria for analysis and comparison of some of today's choices for client operating systems.

Analysis Criteria	Explanation/Implication Follow-Up Questions
Heritage	Was the operating system initially designed with multiuser networks in mind?
Basic Design	How, if at all, does this operating system support multiuser, multiprocessing, multitasking, and multithreaded environments?
Hardware Requirements	Does the operating system require a particular CPU chip? What are the memory and disk requirements for operating system installation?
Networkability	Which networking features are included as part of the operating system? What networking functionality must be added by the network operating system? How available are network operating systems that run over this operating system as clients? As servers? What is the approximate cost per user of network operating systems that run over this operating system?
Interoperability	On how many different vendors' machines will this operating system run? Will this operating system run on Macintoshes, high-powered workstations, and minicomputers or mainframes?
Applications	How available are applications programs that run over this operating system? How easy to develop are applications programs for this operating system? Are applications development tools available for this operating system? Can this operating system run application programs written for other operating systems?

Ease of Use	Consider the ease of use and level of expertise required in the following categories:
	• System installation
	• System configuration
	• System management
	• System use
	• System monitoring
	• System troubleshooting and diagnosis
	Are GUIs (graphical user interfaces) available for this operating system?
Future Potential	What might the future hold for this operating system? Is it in the end or beginning of its product life cycle? Is it the center of controversy among industry giants? Is it governed by domestic or international standards organizations? Is there a definite need for this operating system in the client/server, open systems, distributed-computing world of tomorrow?

Figure 3-7   Operating Systems Analysis Questions

MS-DOS   **MS-DOS,** an acronym for Microsoft Disk Operating System, has gone through an evolution in order to survive in the era of networks. Originally designed to work on stand-alone, single-user PCs, DOS introduced multiuser networking capabilities such as record and file locking with the release of Version 3.1. Network operating systems are able to call these DOS commands transparently to the networking operating system users.

Network operating systems that run over DOS and rely on it for file management and record locking are known as DOS-based LANs. Lantastic by Artisoft and Windows for Workgroups by Microsoft are probably the best-known DOS-based LANs, also known as peer-to-peer LANs. Just because a network operating system is DOS-based does not mean it cannot support many users and offer numerous sophisticated features.

DOS 5.0, which was released in the summer of 1991, added the ability to load programs and files of various types, including device drivers, in the PC's memory above the former 640 KB ceiling. Programs stored in this extended memory are often stored as **TSRs**, or **terminate and stay resident** programs. TSRs do not use any CPU processing time until they are reactivated. Many networking and interoperability software products are stored in expanded memory or extended memory. The categorization of DOS-based memory is summarized in Figure 3-8.

MS-DOS is, strictly speaking, just an operating system Version 6.22 is the latest release. In order to be a fully operational client in a client/server distributed computing environment, a graphical user interface and network operating system functionality must be added. The following were popular options to add this functionality in the past:

- Install Microsoft Windows as the graphical user interface.

- Install Microsoft Windows for Workgroups for both a graphical user interface and networking capabilities.

- Install other DOS-based LANs such as LANtastic for networking capabilities.

DOS Memory Category	Memory Addressed
Conventional (Base)	First 640 KB
Expanded	Between 640 KB and 1 MB
Extended	Above 1 MB

Figure 3-8   DOS Memory Categorization

Microsoft integrated both a graphical user interface and networking software with DOS with the release of Windows 95. It is unclear whether new versions of stand-alone MS-DOS will be forthcoming or whether it will be bundled with networking and GUI software from now on.

Multi-Layer Client Software Products   Windows 95, Windows NT Workstation, and OS/2 Warp Connect all represent top-to-bottom client software products incorporating operating system (OS), network operating system (NOS), and graphical user interface (GUI) functionality. Other products such as Windows for Workgroups and OS/2 Warp also represent more than one layer of the client software architecture. Figure 3-9 illustrates which client software architecture layers are incorporated in a variety of multilayer client software products. Comparative operating system capability of any of these products will be dealt with in this section. Comparative networking capabilities or GUI characteristics will be dealt with in their respective sections.

Windows 95   Among the key operating system–related features incorporated within Windows 95 are the following:

- New graphical user interface
- 32-bit API (applications program interface) in a preemptive multitasking environment
- Plug-n-Play capability

Windows 95 could be considered an all-in-one client software product because it includes graphical user interface, network operating system, and operating system functionality all in a single package. Obtaining all three of these layers of the client software architecture encapsulated in a single product, purchased from a single vendor, goes a long way toward eliminating potential incompatibility issues between client software layers.

	Windows NT	Windows 95	Windows	OS/2 Warp	OS/2 Warp Connect	MS-DOS	Windows for Workgroups	MAC OS	UNIX w/ TCP/IP	Motif or Open-Look
GUI	•	•	•	•	•		•	•		•
NOS	•	•			•		•	•	•	
OS	•	•		•	•	•		•	•	

Figure 3-9   Multilayer Client Software Products

The all-new graphical user interface is designed to be more intuitive and more reflective of the way people work. Users need to know less about which commands are buried beneath which menu selections within which applications. The GUI is organized around a desktop, with various folders containing users' work. The desktop can be customized, and users can "drag and drop" icons of their choice on the desktop. One desktop feature called "the Briefcase" is especially useful for users who take their work home or on the road as well as work in the office. When leaving the office, users can load their "briefcase" of selected files onto their notebook computer. When they get back to the office, they unpack their briefcase, and the file synchronization software automatically updates files on the office computer. The GUI is definitely different from Windows, and even if users find it more intuitive, there are training and transition issues and costs that must be handled honestly.

The 32-bit API is perhaps the most strategically significant feature of Windows 95. However, only applications programmers will actually work with the Win32 API, as it is called. The primary benefits that users will receive from running applications supporting the Win32 API will be increased reliability from two functions:

- Preemptive multitasking
- Memory protection

Preemptive multitasking, explained earlier, prevents ill-behaved programs from monopolizing computer resources. Memory protection grants each application its own memory space and protects that space from other applications trying to write to it. The 16-bit Windows applications run in a shared memory space in a cooperative multitasking environment. The Win32 API is also supported by Windows NT, providing a clear migration path for users who may need more computing power without the need to rewrite application programs.

However, Windows 95 must perform the difficult task of straddling the old world of Windows' cooperative multitasking 16-bit applications and the new world of Windows NT's preemptive multitasking 32-bit applications. Inevitably compromises must be made. As a result, although 32-bit programs run in a preemptive multitasking environment, that environment is really just a subsystem that depends on 16-bit operating system modules retained in order to provide backward compatibility for 16-bit applications. Thus, when a 16-bit application is running in the Windows 95 cooperative multitasking environment, all other 16-bit and 32-bit applications are blocked from obtaining system resources.

The Plug-n-Play capability offered by Windows 95 requires Plug-n-Play components that have been certified as Windows 95 Plug-n-Play compatible. Working with PCMCIA cards, not previously known for their ease of installation, is especially straightforward thanks to the built-in card services and socket services included in Windows 95. Windows 95 is able to automatically detect when PCMCIA cards have been added or removed and whether drivers for those cards are available within Windows 95 or must be loaded from a vendor-supplied diskette.

Windows NT Workstation Windows NT is a top-to-bottom client software product. An alternative, more-expensive version of Windows NT for servers is appropriately named Windows NT Server. Windows NT is a true 32-bit preemptive multitasking operating system. All 32-bit applications execute in protected memory space. As described previously, Windows NT is able to run applications from other platforms such as OS/2 and 16-bit Windows through specially written multiple personality subsystems. These subsystems in which different types of applications are able to execute are sometimes referred to as **virtual machines.**

Windows NT is a microkernel-based operating system with a minimum of hardware-specific code confined to a portion of the microkernel known as HAL, or the hardware abstraction layer. Microkernel philosophy purists argue that Windows NT cannot be considered microkernel-based because certain operating system service managers run in the kernel space in privileged mode. Philosophical arguments aside, the Windows NT architecture, as illustrated in Figure 3-10, clearly illustrates the notion of numerous modular subsystems interacting with a hardware-specific microkernel, in this case referred to as a kernel.

One of the positive attributes of a microkernel-based operating system is that once the minimal amount of hardware-specific code is rewritten, no further operating system modification should be necessary in order for the operating system to execute on a different CPU platform. Windows NT has been arguably more successful at being ported to multiple CPU types than any other microkernel-based operating system. Windows NT currently runs on the following:

- Intel-based chips

- MIPS R4X00 chips

- DEC Alpha AXP chips

Additional ports either planned or underway include the following:

- Power PC chips (Available in Windows NT Version 3.51)

- HP PA-RISC chips

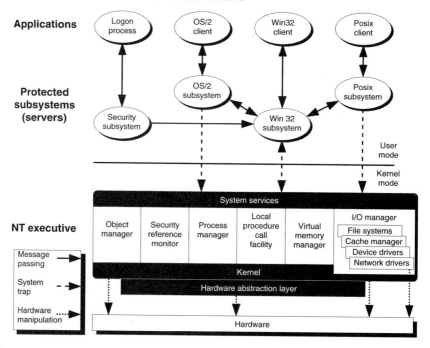

Figure 3-10   Windows NT Architecture

Windows NT is considered extremely reliable and secure. All applications must request services and interact with computer hardware resources through the local procedure call facility, thereby preventing them from interacting directly with hardware and potentially bypassing security or violating another application's memory space. The only negative aspect of this tight security is the fact that some computer games that prefer to interact directly with hardware for performance reasons either operate more slowly or do not at all under Windows NT. Windows NT also has some significant hardware requirements: 12 MB to 16 MB of memory (although 32 MB is even better) and 90 MB to 120 MB of disk space.

Windows 98 and Windows NT 5.0   Overall, Windows 98 seems to be aimed toward the home PC market and businesses that require backward compatibility with 16-bit Windows applications. The following are among the key features introduced in Windows 98:

- Overall compatibility with Windows 95, offering increased performance and reliability

- Inclusion of Microsoft Internet Explorer 4.0, for tighter integration of the web browser and desktop

- Microsoft Outlook Express, which supplies a new e-mail client and desktop information manager

- Microsoft NetMeeting, providing Internet-based audio functions and video-conferencing capabilities

- System File Checker and Windows Tune-up "wizards," which ensure the integrity and currency of system files, thereby leading to increased reliability and decreased management costs

- Several entertainment-oriented features, such as Microsoft NetShow, ability to receive broadcast and enhanced television signals, Active Movie for high-quality video playback, and support for MMX processors

On the other hand, Windows NT 5.0 Workstation seems to be clearly aimed toward business and industry for both the client desktop and server platforms. The following key features were introduced in Windows NT 5.0:

- Overall effort to reduce management complexity and total cost of ownership

- "Intellimirroring"—storing all users' desktop environment settings and preferences on centrally managed network-based servers, eliminating the need for management personnel to maintain such settings individually on users' workstations and making management of roaming or mobile users easier

- A new distributed file system, which allows multiple volumes on multiple platforms to appear as a single logical volume

- Active directory, which creates a hierarchical, scalable enterprisewide directory structure

- Integrated web browser, providing identical user interface to Windows 98

- Increased security, through support of Kerberos and an encrypted file system

- Improved Plug-n-Play and power management, both important features to laptop users

- Enterprise features, such as clustering (Wolfpack), multiuser support (Hydra), and multiprotocol routing (Steelhead), available only on NT Server versions

In the long term, improved migration paths from Windows 95 and 98 to Windows NT support the widely held belief that eventually, 32-bit Windows NT will be the only client platform offered by Microsoft.

Windows CE   Windows CE is a 32-bit, multitasking, multithreaded operating system designed to run on hand-held PCs, the smaller palm PCs, and even the newer speech-enabled automobile PCs. Windows CE supports a subset of the full Win32 API, allowing at least some current Windows applications to be ported to the smaller platforms. A Windows CE Version 2.0 software development kit allows CE-specific applications to be developed as well.

Microsoft is aggressively seeking partnerships that will allow Windows CE to be deployed everywhere. For example:

- A partnership with Motorola will allow Windows CE devices to receive data via one-way and two-way paging systems.

- An agreement with TCI (TeleCommunications Inc.) will embed Windows CE into cable TV set-top boxes in order to enable interactive video and Internet access via television.

WINDOWS 32-BIT API VARIETIES

In Sharper Focus

Windows applications execute over a particular operating system environment by issuing commands understood by both the application program and the operating system. As previously defined, this set of mutually supported commands is known as an API, or application program interface. For 32-bit Windows programs, this API is known as the Win32 API. Variations of the Win32 API have been created in order to allow 32-bit Windows applications to run in a variety of environments. The differences between the following variations of the Win32 API are subtle yet significant.

- **Win32 API:** This is the full-blown 32-bit API that was created for Windows NT.

- **Win32s API:** The *s* stands for *subset*. This API was created for applications that need the processing power of 32-bit applications but must still be able to execute under 16-bit Windows 3.1. The API in Windows 3.1 is commonly referred to as Win16. Simply stated, Win32s is a 32-bit version of Win16 without any of the Win32 API enhancements. The Win32s API is supported by a dynamic link library (DLL), which converts 32-bit API calls to the 16-bit API calls supported by Windows 3.1.

- **Win32c API:** The *c* stands for *compatible*. This is the API included with Windows 95 and 98, and it contains nearly all of the functionality offered by NT's Win32 API while still remaining backward-compatible with 16-bit Windows 3.1 applications.

Operating environments other than Windows, Windows NT, and Windows 95 and 98 can run Windows applications as long as they support the proper Win32 or Win16 API. In the case of OS/2 Warp Connect, the Win32s API is supported, but the full function Win32 API is not. Figure 3-11 illustrates the relationships between the various Win32 APIs and their respective GUI/operating systems.

Figure 3-11   Win32 APIs

OS/2 Warp Connect   From an architectural standpoint, OS/2 Warp Connect is similar to Windows NT in that separate virtual machines are implemented for 16-bit and 32-bit applications. The 16-bit applications can run in a shared environment in which they can potentially write into each other's memory area. In this arrangement, if one 16-bit application crashes, all 16-bit applications crash. Alternatively, each 16-bit application can run in its own protected virtual machine. OS/2 Warp Connect can run 16-bit Windows and DOS applications as well as native OS/2 applications.

OS/2 Warp Version 4.0 supports integrated run-time support for Java applications, allowing these applications to run without a web browser. In addition, OS/2 Warp 4 includes integrated IBM VoiceType technology that integrates the use of voice commands into the user interface. IBM markets OS/2 Warp as a universal client capable of transparently interoperating with any of the following server platforms:

- OS/2 Warp Server
- IBM LAN Server
- Microsoft NT Server
- Novell Netware
- Banyan Vines

Figure 3-12 illustrates OS/2 Warp Connect's architecture, and Figure 3-13 compares operating system characteristics of Windows 95, Windows NT Workstation, and OS/2 Warp Connect.

UNIX   UNIX as a client workstation operating system is limited primarily to implementations in high-powered scientific or engineering workstations. UNIX is much more commonly used as a server operating system, with numerous implementations on minicomputers and mainframes as well. UNIX itself is actually not just a single operating system, but many largely incompatible variations of a single operating system. There are two main versions of UNIX:

- AT&T System V Release 4, commonly written as SVR4: Originally developed by AT&T and later reorganized as USL (UNIX Systems Laboratory), which AT&T subsequently sold to Novell, who subsequently sold it to Santa Cruz Operation (SCO)
- BSD (Berkeley Software Distribution): UNIX from the University of California at Berkeley

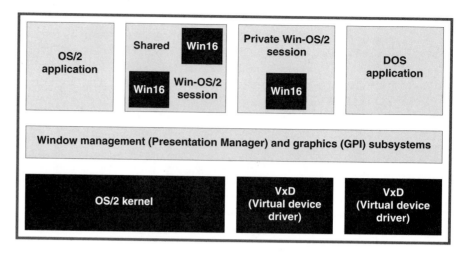

Figure 3-12 OS/2 Warp Connect Architecture

Operating System Characteristic	Windows 95	Windows NT Workstation	OS/2 Warp Connect
Preemptive multitasking—32-bit applications	•	•	•
Preemptive multitasking—16-bit applications		•	•
Supports multithreaded applications	•	•	•
Applications run in protected memory space	32 bit only	•	•
Subsystems run in protected memory space		•	•
Can run Win32s API applications	•	•	•
Can run Win32 API applications	•	•	
Supports symmetric multiprocessing		•	•
Desktop (object-oriented) user interface	•	•	•

Figure 3-13 Comparative Operating System Characteristics: Windows 95, Windows NT Workstation, OS/2 Warp

Many other versions of UNIX are also popular, usually derived from one of these major families. Figure 3-14 summarizes a few of the UNIX variations.

UNIX's heritage of open systems and multiplatform operation has enabled many networking features to be included in the operating system itself, precluding the need to buy an additional networking operating system to run over UNIX. Perhaps best known of these features is the Internet Suite of Protocols, more commonly known as TCP/IP, and associated protocols.

Because UNIX runs not only on PCs, but also on numerous minicomputers and larger platforms, applications written for and installed on larger UNIX machines can be "downsized" to smaller client/server environments. Conversely, applications can be developed on less expensive personal workstations, then installed and executed on larger, more powerful computers. UNIX has become increasingly popular as the operating system of choice for LAN servers. Programs written to run on one of these versions of UNIX will not necessarily run on others.

Company Name	UNIX Variant Name
Hewlett-Packard	HP-UX
Data General	DG/UX
DEC	Ultrix
Sun Microsystems	Solaris
SCO (Santa Cruz Operation)	OpenServer

Figure 3-14   UNIX Variations

Although there are variations between different types of UNIX, it can be fairly safely said that UNIX possesses the following characteristics:

- It is inherently a multiuser operating system.

- It supports symmetrical multiprocessing.

- It supports preemptive multitasking.

- It supports multithreaded applications.

- Its kernel-based operating system insulates hardware from misbehaving applications.

UNIX was developed by and for the scientific community. Objectively, it could be called a cryptic, command-line–oriented operating system. Installation and configuration are anything but straightforward. Of course, these statements are generalizations, and some versions score better than others on the user-friendliness test. Also, these traditional shortcomings of UNIX have not gone unnoticed by major UNIX system vendors. As a result, a universal desktop for UNIX known as CDE, or Common Desktop Environment, has been developed and will be elaborated on in the presentation software section of this chapter. Although often appropriate as a server operating system, UNIX as a client workstation operating system is presently limited largely to high-powered engineering and scientific applications.

Novell DOS   Originally known as DR (Digital Research)-DOS, Novell DOS Version 7 (ND7) is intended as an alternative to MS-DOS 6.22. ND7 is really three products in one:

- DOS

- Universal NetWare Client

- Personal NetWare

The DOS portion of ND7 is distinguished by its ability to run multiple applications simultaneously in a multitasking environment, thanks to a multitasking kernel. ND7 is otherwise compatible with MS-DOS and is able to run either Windows or Windows for Workgroups as the user interface. ND7 also comes with utilities for backup, virus detection, and network management.

The Universal NetWare Client is that portion of the client software stack required to allow a client workstation to access files and services offered by network-attached servers in a client/server environment. The term "NetWare client" implies that this software will allow this client to login to NetWare servers only. The term *universal* refers to the fact that this software allows clients to login to NetWare servers running versions of NetWare from 2.x to 4.x and also allows clients to use a wide variety of network interface cards. The details of client network operating system software will be discussed in the next section.

Personal NetWare is a DOS-based peer-to-peer network operating system that could be considered a competitor to Microsoft's Windows for Workgroups. Peer-to-peer network operating systems allow client workstations to share resources such as disk space and printers. Simple e-mail or chat utilities are usually also included. Clients on the Personal NetWare LAN can use the Universal NetWare client software to reach both Personal NetWare servers and NetWare servers.

Apple's Operating Systems   With the shift in hardware design from the Motorola 680x0 chip series in the Mac to the PowerPC chip in the PowerMacs, it was necessary to design a new operating system which could take maximum advantage of the PowerPC's RISC design. In the meantime, legacy Mac applications had to run on the PowerMacs in emulation mode, with the performance penalty of the additional emulation overhead.

With the release of Version 8.0 of the MacOS, code-named Copland, Apple has produced a totally new, microkernel-based operating system exhibiting the following key characteristics:

- Preemptive multitasking

- Support for multithreaded applications

- Program execution in protected memory space

- Microkernel foundation allowing subsystems to be easily added or modified

- Isolation of hardware-specific code to the hardware abstraction layer portion of the microkernel

Like Windows 95, Version 8.0 required compromises in order to ensure compatibility with older applications. As a result, although preemptive multitasking and memory protection are afforded to newer native applications, older applications written originally to run on the 680x0 series are executed in a shared memory area in a cooperative multitasking environment. Misbehaving applications in this cooperative multitasking area can crash one another but cannot crash the individually protected programs running in the preemptive multitasking environment.

The release of MacOS Version 8.0 achieves at least three important goals for Apple:

- It creates a powerful new microkernel-based operating system.

- It runs legacy applications well.

- It removes hard-coded hardware-to-operating system links to enable Mac Clone hardware vendors and third-party Mac software vendors to fully participate in the PowerMac market.

The latest release of Apple's operating system is known as Rhapsody and is distinctive in its ability to run on PowerPC (604 and 604e) Macintoshes as well as on x86 Pentiums and Pentium II processors. From a software standpoint, Rhapsody is based on Next's OpenStep, which, in turn, is based on the Mach microkernel. Rhapsody supports Java-based applications as well as advanced operating system capabilities such as preemptive multitasking, multithreading, and memory protection. BSD 4.4 Unix is used as a command interface for Rhapsody. Increased emphasis on the Internet and on web development is implemented through support of NFS, increased support of TCP/IP, and an object-oriented development environment that will provide native support for both Windows NT and web-based environments.

Managerial Perspective

Apple's market share as measured by percentage of the client operating system market, has declined from a high of greater than 10 percent in the early 1990s to just over 5 percent by 1997. Because few if any applications are available for Macintoshes that aren't also available for Microsoft systems, it is becoming increasingly difficult for information systems managers to justify the expense in supporting and maintaining a small number of Macintoshes on networks of primarily "Wintel" (Windows and Intel) PCs.

■ CLIENT NETWORK OPERATING SYSTEMS

Concepts and Functionality

Clients are *physically* connected to network-attached resources such as servers via the client hardware layer or, more specifically, network interface cards (Figure 3-1). However, what role does client software play in this connection to network-attached resources? Somewhere in the review of the client software stack, at least two questions must be answered in order to understand how a client workstation is able to access network-attached resources:

1. Is the resource (file, disk drive, printer) requested by the client's application program physically attached to the local client, to a server, or to another client somewhere out on the network?

2. If the resource is network attached, how must the requesting message to that network-attached resource be formatted and delivered?

This section details the general logical process involved in enabling clients to access network-attached resources. More information regarding network communications and network operating systems is available in Chapter 9, Local Area Network Operating Systems.

Client Redirectors For every request for services coming from an application program, a software module known as the **redirector** determines whether those requested resources are locally attached or network attached. Requests for locally attached resources are forwarded to the client's local operating system. Requests for network-attached resources are passed in proper format and properly addressed to the network interface card installed in the client PC for subsequent delivery to the desired network-attached resource.

NetBIOS API A type of software specification known as a network API allows requests for services from application programs to be passed along to the network-attached servers that provide these services. **NetBIOS** (network basic input/output system) is an API that has become the de facto standard of network APIs for PC-based networks.

Technically, NETBIOS or any API is a specification outlining two major elements:

- A particular software interrupt to the client portion of the network operating system, which is executed in order to request network services for transportation of data or messages across the network

- A series of standardized commands, which establish network-based communication sessions, send and receive data, and name network resources

In practice, an API such as NETBIOS allows a person running a word-processing program on a client PC to ask to retrieve a document located on a disk drive that is physically attached to a network-attached server PC. For instance, all the user knows is that the document in located on a drive known as H and that once he or she requests that document, it appears on the screen of the client PC, ready to be edited. The interpretation of requests between the various software layers of the client PC and server PC is of no concern to the user.

A standardized API such as NetBIOS allows applications programs to be written without concern for which network operating system the application may eventually run over as long as that network operating system understands NetBIOS requests. Likewise, a network operating system can run transparently underneath any application program, secure in the knowledge that it will be able to understand any NetBIOS requests for network services.

NetBIOS is, by definition, a system of commands with the following capabilities:

- To interpret requests submitted to it in proper format from the application program

- To pass these requests along to a network communications program

NetBIOS application programs, otherwise known as NetBIOS protocols, that interface with the NetBIOS API have been developed to perform specialized tasks on client and server PCs in order to enable this client/server communication. Two of the most famous of these NetBIOS application protocols are the NetBIOS **Redirector** on the client and the **Server Message Block (SMB) Server** on the server.

Figure 3-15 illustrates the interaction of a word-processing application program, the NetBIOS redirector, NetBIOS API, the SMB server, and the network operating system.

As shown in Figure 3-15, the word-processing program sends out a request for a particular document on a certain disk drive, not knowing whether that disk drive is on the local client PC or on the remote server PC. This request is in an agreed-upon NetBIOS API format or syntax known as **NCB,** or **network control block.** This network control block is received by the NetBIOS redirector and evaluated as to whether the request should be handled by the local PC and passed to the local PC's operating system, or whether it should be sent on to the NetBIOS API for interfacing with the network operating system running on this client PC.

If the requested document is on a remote server, the NetBIOS API tells the network operating system which server the requested document resides on by preparing an SMB for transmission. The network operating system forwards the SMB to the remote server via the local network adapter card and network media of choice.

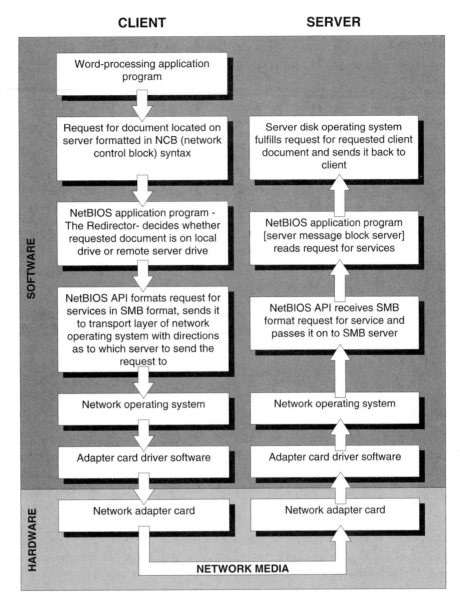

Figure 3-15   NetBIOS, the Redirector, and the SMB Server

Once the SMB is received by the remote server, the NetBIOS API passes it to the SMB server, which passes requests for particular files or documents on to the disk operating system of the server PC. Once the SMB receives the requested document, it sends it back over to the client PC in a similar manner.

Notice how a particular network operating system was not referenced in Figure 3-15. Therein lies the importance of NetBIOS. It is an application program–to–application program communications protocol that is understood by and incorporated into most network operating systems. Different versions of NetBIOS have been developed to run over different network operating systems. These varieties of NetBIOS are summarized in Figure 3-16.

NetBIOS protocol	RFC 1001/1002 (request for comment)	TOP (technical office protocol)	NetBEUI (NetBIOS extended user interface)	NetBIOS/IX
Communications Network Operating Systems	TCP/IP	OSI	LAN Manager LAN Server Windows NT	UNIX

Figure 3-16   NetBIOS Protocol Varieties for Various Network Types

NetBIOS is not the only network communications API ever invented. Several other APIs have been implemented in various network operating systems, as outlined in Figure 3-17. In many cases, these APIs have additional commands and features not found in NetBIOS. However, even in the network operating systems that use non-NetBIOS APIs, such as NetWare or Vines, a NetBIOS emulator is often included to ensure compatibility across varied network operating systems.

NetBIOS or some other network API is at the heart of client/server communication. Without this transparent layer of software keeping track of the location of shared resources and managing the requests for sharing those resources, there can be no client/server computing. To link client and server PCs of various network or disk operating systems, compatibility of the APIs is essential. NetBIOS and its derivatives are the most widely installed and supported API. However, beware—not even all varieties of NetBIOS are fully compatible with each other.

NOS Client Protocol Stacks   NetBIOS or a related network API properly formats messages requesting network-attached resources. However, this message must be successfully transported across the network to the destination server. Successfully transporting messages across networks is the job of the **network operating system (NOS).** More exactly, the successful transport of messages across networks is the job of the **transport layer protocol** of the network operating system.

This transportation of messages across the network must physically start when the local **network interface card (NIC)** interfaces to the network via the network media attached to the NIC. The software/hardware interface between the NOS and the NIC is bridged with a specially written piece of software compatible with both the NOS and the NIC known as NIC **driver** software. Figure 3-18 summarizes the

API (Application Program Interface)	APPC (Advanced Program to Program Communication)	Named Pipes	NCP (Netware Core Protocol)	Streams	Sockets	VIPC (VINES Interprocess Communications Protocol)
Network Operating System	IBM SNA	Microsoft LAN Manager	Novell Netware	AT&T UNIX System V	Berkley UNIX	Banyan VINES

Figure 3-17   Network APIs Other Than NetBIOS and Their Network Operating Systems

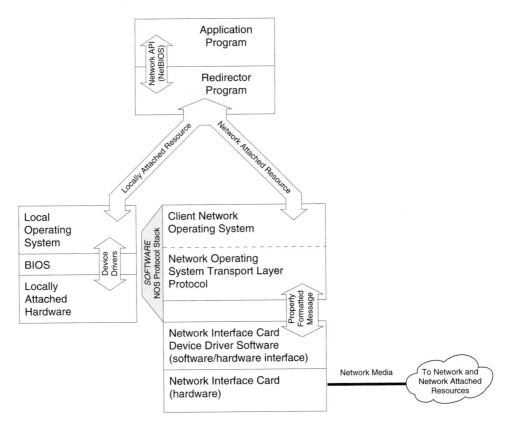

Figure 3-18   Network API, Transport Protocol, and NIC Driver Combined for Network-Based Message Transport

roles of the network API, the transport layer protocol, and the NIC driver in the overall task of successfully transporting messages across networks.

It is important to note the required compatibilities in this process. The Network API, such as NetBIOS, must be supported and understood by the network operating system installed in the client software architecture. The transport protocol of the installed client network operating system must be compatible with the transport protocol of the network operating system installed on the destination server. The client network operating system must support, or talk to, the locally installed NIC. This compatibility is ensured by having the proper driver software installed.

Protocol Stacks and the OSI Model   Every network operating system is made up of layers of protocols that correspond in varying degrees to the seven layers of the OSI model. The transport layer (layer 4) of the OSI model is responsible for ensuring the reliable end-to-end delivery of messages across a local area network. Exactly how the transport layer protocols ensure this reliability and how NOS protocols communicate with one another is detailed in Chapter 9, Local Area Network Operating Systems.

In order for a client and server to communicate successfully, they must both use the same transport layer protocol. Because clients and servers in distributed environments are likely to have different network operating systems installed with different transport layer protocols, some way must be found for them to share a common transport protocol. The following two facts solve most client-to-server transport layer protocol incompatibility problems:

1. Clients and servers are capable of supporting more than one network operating system transport protocol.

2. TCP/IP is seen as a universal protocol stack and is available in versions capable of running on most client and server platforms.

A total explanation of the intricacies and interrelationships of network operating system protocols is beyond the scope of this text. However, what the reader should understand at this point is the role that NOS protocols, such as the transport layer protocol, play in distributed client/server computing environments. In other words, data from applications programs and program requests for network-attached services do not somehow magically get delivered to the proper network-attached server. As will be seen, messages are carefully addressed and "packetized" within standardized NOS protocol "envelopes" in order to ensure proper and reliable delivery. Sometimes these messages are packaged in NetBIOS or NetBEUI (NetBIOS Extended User Interfaces) envelopes, and sometimes they are packaged and addressed in a different type of transport layer protocol envelope such as TCP/IP.

In order for network operating systems to ensure that virtually any client application can talk to any other client or server application regardless of the underlying file system driver, redirector, or transport protocol, flexibility or modularity must be built into the network operating system. For example, Windows NT supports a variety of redirectors and file system drivers that allow it to provide services for a variety of different types of applications. Subsequently, the information from the chosen redirector or file system driver could choose from among several different transport protocols supported by Windows NT. This any-to-any matching between redirectors and transport protocols is possible due to a mutually supported layer of software between the numerous redirectors and transport protocols known as the **transport driver interface (TDI).**

Figure 3-19 introduces network operating system protocols by distributing those protocols into the seven layers of the OSI model. This distribution is not exact because network operating system vendors are free to include whatever functionality they wish in a given protocol. As a result, not all protocols correspond to a particular OSI model layer on a one-to-one basis. Also, Figure 3-19 does not list all of the protocols associated with each NOS. Many additional protocols for specialized tasks such as file management, service naming, internetwork routing management, and e-mail system interoperability are omitted from Figure 3-19 but are covered in later chapters.

Much of the information contained in Figure 3-19 will seem foreign at this point, but the remainder of the text will refer back to it. For a review of the role of the protocols in each of the seven layers of the OSI model, refer back to Figure 1-6.

■ CLIENT PRESENTATION SOFTWARE

Concepts and Functionality

User Interface Trends   User interfaces, like most elements of information systems design, continue to evolve. Following are the three major paradigms, or stages, of computer-to-user interface design:

Figure 3-19 — The OSI Model and Network Operating System Protocols

Network Operating System	Windows NT & Windows '95	Windows for Workgroups 3.11	Other DOS-based LANs	OS/2 Warp Connect	Novell Netware 4.1	Banyan VINES 6.0	Internet Suite of Protocols (TCP/IP)
Layer 7 Application			DOS Redirector		Netware Shell	Redirector	RFS (Remote File Service) / SMB (Server Message Block) / NFS (Network File System)
Layer 6 Presentation	NCP Redirector (Netware Core Protocols (Netware)) / SMB Redirector (Server Message Block (Microsoft))	SMB Redirector (Server Message Block (Microsoft))	DOS Redirector	NCP Redirector (Netware Core Protocols (Netware)) / SMB Redirector (Server Message Block (Microsoft))	NCP Redirector	VINES Remote Procedure Calls / SMB (Server Message Block)	RFS / SMB / NFS
Layer 5 Session			NetBIOS		NetBIOS Emulator	NetBIOS Service	SMTP (Simple Mail Transfer Protocol), FTP (File Transfer Protocol), TELNET (Virtual Terminal Protocol), SNMP (Simple Network Management Protocol)
Layer 4 Transport	SPX (Sequenced Packet Exchange), NetBEUI, TCP (Transmission Control Protocol)	SPX (Sequenced Packet Exchange), NetBEUI, TCP (Transmission Control Protocol)	NetBIOS	SPX (Sequenced Packet Exchange), NetBEUI, TCP (Transmission Control Protocol)	SPX (Sequenced Packet Exchange), TCP (Transmission Control Protocol)	VIPC (VINES Interprocess communications), NetBEUI, TCP (Transmission Control Protocol)	TCP (Transmission Control Protocol), UDP (User Datagram Protocol)
Layer 3 Network	IPX (Internet Packet Exchange), IP (Internet Protocol)	IPX (Internet Packet Exchange), IP (Internet Protocol)		IPX (Internet Packet Exchange), IP (Internet Protocol)	IPX (Internet Packet Exchange), IP (Internet Protocol)	VIP (VINES Internet Protocol), IP (Internet Protocol)	IP (Internet Protocol)
Layer 2 Data Link	Logical Link Control (LLC) sublayer / Media Access Control (MAC) sublayer	Multiple protocol stack NIC driver specifications: ODI, NDIS. — Ethernet - IEEE 802.3, 10BaseT, 10Base2, 10Base5			Fast Ethernet, 100BaseX, 100VG, AnyLAN	Token Ring IEEE 802.5	FDDI	ATM
Layer 1 Physical	NOTE: Protocols listed in layers 1 and 2 will operate with any upper layer protocols as long as compatible network interface card drivers are successfully installed.						

Figure 3-19   The OSI Model and Network Operating System Protocols

- Character-based interfaces
- Graphical user interfaces (GUI)
- Network user interfaces (NUI)

Character-based interfaces are otherwise known as command line interfaces. The DOS command prompt is an example of a character-based interface. GUIs are familiar to most users and have evolved from a Windows-based format, as illustrated by Windows 3.1, to an object-oriented desktop, as illustrated by the Windows 95 and Windows NT presentation formats.

Network user interfaces (NUIs) provide a single browserlike interface for communicating transparently with all resources, whether local or remote. Users will not need to know the physical location (local, corporate network, Internet) or the platform type (mainframe-based, client/server) of a particular resource. The NUI will include embedded search engines for finding required resources regardless of location. Users will be able to display web content and Java applets on their desktop without executing a separate web browser since the user interface itself includes an embedded browser. Furthermore, the customized NUI or desktop will be stored on a network-based server so that users can interact with their familiar desktop regardless of where or on what type of platform they login. NUIs may run on PCs or on thin clients, otherwise known as network computers. Network computing, thin clients, NetPCs, network computers, network user interfaces, and Java will all be explained in more detail in Chapter 8, Client/Server Application Development and Integration.

Event-Driven Presentation for Event-Driven Applications   Event-driven or forms-based applications such as those developed with products like Microsoft's Visual Basic can now be presented in an event-driven format. For example, Computer Associate's interface known as Simply Village will be offered as an add-on interface for Windows 95.

The interface itself is literally a village scene, which hides complex network links to remote servers and on-line services. For example, to perform a banking transaction from home, a user would click on the village bank. Inside the bank would be an on-screen banker that would help the user perform the desired transaction. Such "walk-you-through-it" help characters are commonly referred to as **wizards.** In other operating environments, wizards are known as experts or agents. Other village offerings might include clicking on specialty shops for links to home shopping networks or clicking on the airport or travel agency to purchase airline tickets. Input devices will likely shift from keyboards to voice-recognition technology.

Before the arrival of these fully graphical, revolutionary event-driven interfaces in corporations, interim or evolutionary offerings will likely be introduced. This is where the user interfaces offered by Windows 95 and Apple's Copland are positioned. These systems will contain wizards and advanced help systems that will walk users through solutions. Interim improvements on GUIs will feature **active assistance subsystems** or context-sensitive help systems to which users can describe what they wish to accomplish, such as purchasing an airline ticket or receiving inventory at a loading dock, and the system will lead them through the desired transaction step by step.

Presentation Software for UNIX Environments   Traditionally, graphical user interfaces for the UNIX environment were supplied by software adhering to the **X Windows** environment standards. X Windows itself is not a GUI and should not be confused with Microsoft Windows. X Windows is a standardized system that defines the underlying communication between X server and X client software modules that combine to present a multiwindow graphical user interface on a specially designed X terminal or a client workstation running some type of X terminal emulation.

The closest equivalent to a familiar GUI such as Microsoft Windows in the X Windows environment would be the X manager, which is in charge of managing, sizing, and scaling multiple displays from different UNIX applications or hosts simultaneously. Motif from the Open Software Foundation and OpenLook from Sun Microsystems are the two most popular X Windows Managers and communicate with X server software.

In an architectural setup that may seem opposite of typical client/server relationships, the X server software, which controls display and input, runs on the user's workstation, and the X client that generates the screen-drawing instructions is located on the UNIX applications host. It is important to note that X Windows systems perform strictly presentation functions. Although Microsoft Windows is characterized as a GUI, it actually performs many operating system management-type functions not offered by X Windows. Figure 3-20 illustrates the key components of an X Windows system.

Beyond X Windows UNIX hardware and software vendors Hewlett Packard, Sun, IBM, and Novell (UNIX Systems Laboratory) have joined together to produce a cross-platform window environment for UNIX named the **Common Desktop Environment,** or **CDE.** CDE goes beyond the simple graphical presentation management of X Windows to include the following key cross-platform functionality:

- Desktop management
- Session management
- File management
- Application management
- Productivity tools
- Application development tools

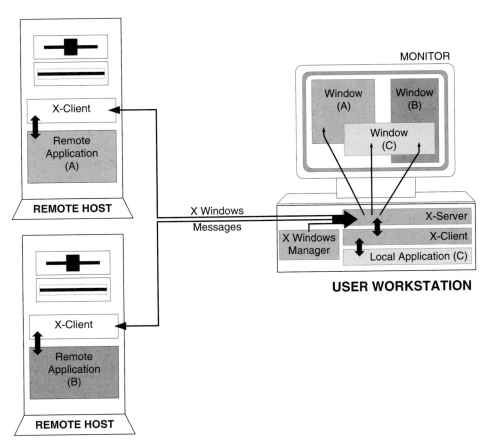

Figure 3-20 X Windows Client, Server, and Manager

The motivation for developing this top-to-bottom cross-platform suite is the inroads Windows NT has made to date and is expected to continue to make in the UNIX server market. CDE will offer a single graphical environment across multiple vendors' UNIX platforms. CDE will run on nearly all versions of UNIX hardware and software and was designed to be constructed from 80 percent of existing "best-of-breed" software and only 20 percent new development. As an example, CDE employs OSF Motif as its X Window Manager. CDE has been targeted at three primary audiences:

- To the end user: CDE offers the multiprocessing, multiuser, multitasking power of UNIX while hiding its complexities.

- To the software developer: CDE offers sets of common services and APIs that will allow developed software to run across a wide variety of CDE-supported platforms.

- To the systems administrator: CDE offers various management tools for handling different platforms with a single suite of management tools.

The only possible bad news in all of this is the fact that the CDE standards are meant to be least common denominators of interoperability among UNIX platforms. UNIX workstation vendors are free to enhance and extend CDE in order to offer product differentiation and maintain profit margins. As a result, although CDE will offer interoperability across multiple vendors' UNIX workstations, it won't necessarily deliver the full functionality offered by all of the attached workstations.

Best of Both Worlds   Multiple Windows applications can be run simultaneously in any environment supporting the Windows API such as Windows 3.1, Windows NT, Windows 95, or OS/2 Warp. Multiple UNIX applications can be run simultaneously in either an X Windows or a CDE environment. But what if an end user has to use a combination of Windows and UNIX applications in order to maximize productivity?

Several solutions exist to give users the best of both worlds. The eXceed 4 Windows NT from Hummingbird Communications, Inc., allows an NT system to act as a PC X server by communicating with X clients, displaying screen updates, and relaying keyboard and mouse input. The UNIX applications would be running on network-attached UNIX hosts such as Sun Sparcstations, IBM RS-6000s, or Cray Supercomputers. To these remote hosts and their installed X client software, the NT workstation looks like just another X server program running on a UNIX workstation. Of course, the NT workstation can still run Windows applications and is able to display these Microsoft Windows applications alongside the X Windows from the UNIX applications.

Whereas the previous solution allowed an NT workstation to act like a UNIX-based X server, Hewlett-Packard offers the HP 500 Windows Application Server that allows Windows applications to be run on UNIX workstations. The product comes either in a hardware/software option including a Pentium server or in a software-only option. Windows applications are converted into X Windows and TCP/IP code and run on a version of UNIX from SCO (Santa Cruz Operation) known as

OpenServer 5.0. Other Windows-on-UNIX implementations are available, including WinDD from Tektronix and WABI (Windows Application Binary Interface) from Sun Microsystems. WABI is the emulation software employed in many PowerPCs and PowerMacs to allow Windows applications to run on the RISC-based PowerPC chips. DESQview/X 2.0 from Quarterdeck allows users to run any combination of DOS, Windows, or UNIX applications in an X Windows preemptive multitasking environment and is installed on a DOS-based PC.

Practical Advice and Information

In comparing Windows-over-UNIX emulation alternatives, analysts must consider both performance and compatibility. All emulation alternatives cannot run all Windows applications. Remember that software emulation is analogous to having one application program run another application program and is most often slower than hardware emulation. These UNIX/Windows integrations should be considered only if a thorough top-down analysis has been conducted and it has been concluded that business objectives can be successfully met only if a combination of UNIX and Windows applications are run from a particular desktop.

SUMMARY

In order to understand how transparent interoperability can be delivered to an end user through a client workstation, the client software architecture and its inherent interprocess communication must be thoroughly understood. Without complete compatibility between all software layers within the client software architecture, client workstations will not be able to communicate transparently with distant networked servers.

The first layer of software that interacts with the client hardware is the operating system. The trend in this area of software development is a movement toward microkernel-based operating systems that offer increased extendibility, portability, and reliability over the more-traditional monolithic-architected operating systems. Many software products offer a graphical user interface, network operating system, and operating system all in a single integrated product. Windows 95 and OS/2 Warp Connect are two such products.

The interface between network operating systems and operating systems is bridged by redirector software conforming to a particular network API such as NetBIOS. These network protocols are responsible for determining whether computer resources requested by applications programs are located on the locally attached computer or on a distant network-attached server. The network API must be compatible with the application program, network operating system, and operating system. The request for network-attached resources is then addressed and packaged in the proper message format according to the transport layer protocol of the particular network operating system installed on the client workstation.

Client presentation software is currently evolving from graphical user interfaces to more intuitive social interfaces characterized by more active help systems that sense when users need help and step users through solutions. UNIX-based client workstations have traditionally used a GUI that supported the X Windows presentation protocol. GUIs now exist that can integrate UNIX and Windows applications in a single presentation environment.

KEY TERMS

Active assistance subsystems
Actor
Applications program interface (API)
AT&T SVR4
BSD UNIX
Chorus microkernel
Client software architecture
Common Desktop Environment (CDE)
Cooperative multitasking
Device drivers
Exceptions
Graphical user interface (GUI)
Hardware abstraction layer (HAL)
Hardware-independent operating systems
Interrupts
Kernel
Mach microkernel
MacOS
Microkernel
Monolithic architecture

Motif
MS-DOS
Multiple personality operating system
Multiple workplace environments
Multiprocessing
Multithreaded
Multiuser
NCB
NCP
NetBEUI
NetBIOS
NetBIOS application program
NetWare core protocol
Network control block
Network operating system (NOS)
Network user interface (NUI)
Novell DOS
Open Look
Operating system architecture
OS/2 Warp Connect
Port

Preemptive multitasking
Privileged mode
Redirector
Server message block (SMB) server
Site
Subsystems
System calls
Task
Thread
TSR
UNIX
User mode
Virtual machines
Win32 API
Win32c API
Win32s API
Windows 95
Windows 98
Windows CE
Windows NT Workstation
X Windows

REVIEW QUESTIONS

1. Explain the importance of compatible protocols to the delivery of transparent interoperability to a client workstation.
2. Describe the role of each layer of the client software architecture.
3. Why do some software products combine presentation, NOS, and OS functionality?
4. What are the primary responsibilities of any client operating system?
5. Describe the role of each component of the operating system architecture.
6. What is the difference between a system call and a device driver?
7. A device driver links which two operating system layers?
8. A system call links which two client software layers?
9. What is the advantage of using separate system calls and device drivers?
10. What is the alternative to using separate system calls and device drivers?
11. What is the difference between an interrupt and an exception?

12. What is the difference between a hardware interrupt and a software interrupt?
13. What are the disadvantages of an operating system that adheres to a monolithic architecture?
14. What is a microkernel?
15. What are the supposed advantages of a microkernel-based operating system?
16. What types of services are typically confined to the microkernel?
17. Why are hardware-specific instructions confined to the microkernel?
18. Why is it important for the microkernel to run in privileged mode?
19. What is the difference between privileged mode and user mode?
20. How can a microkernel architecture enable hardware-independent operating systems?
21. How do microkernel architectures enable multiple personality operating systems?
22. Can an operating system be both hardware independent and multiple personality? Explain.
23. Distinguish between the following: task, thread, port.

24. How can one microkernel be used in different operating systems?
25. How can one microkernel be used on different CPU chips?
26. Differentiate the following: multiuser, multiprocessing, multitasking, multithreading.
27. Differentiate cooperative multitasking and preemptive multitasking.
28. Differentiate conventional, expanded, and extended memory in a DOS environment.
29. What is Windows 95?
30. What are the key advantages and disadvantages of Windows 95?
31. What are the key differences between Windows NT Workstation and Windows 95?
32. Why is a user more likely to choose Windows 95 over Windows NT Workstation?
33. How is Windows 95 both a preemptive multitasking and a cooperative multitasking environment?
34. What are the key new features offered by Windows 98?
35. What are the key new features offered by Windows NT Workstation 5.0?
36. What is Windows CE, and at which computing platforms is this product aimed?
37. What is a virtual machine?
38. Differentiate Win32 API, Win32s API, and Win32c API.
39. Differentiate OS/2 Warp Connect and Windows NT Workstation.
40. What are the key advantages and disadvantages of UNIX as a client operating system?
41. Differentiate between Novell DOS and MS-DOS.
42. What are the key objectives of Apple's MacOS V.8?
43. What are the key features of Apple's Rhapsody?

44. What effect can a requirement to run legacy applications have on operating system design?
45. What is HAL?
46. What is the function of the client redirector?
47. What is the NetBIOS API?
48. What is the difference between the NetBIOS API and a NetBIOS protocol?
49. What is the relationship between the NetBIOS redirector and the server message block server?
50. Why is NetBIOS the default network API for network operating systems?
51. What is the relationship between the network API and the client/server architecture?
52. How can a NOS employ a network API other than NetBIOS, and how is compatibility ensured in such a case?
53. What is meant by the term *NOS protocol stack?*
54. How does the OSI model relate to NOS protocol stacks?
55. What role does the client NOS play in delivering network-attached resources to the client workstation?
56. Describe the user interface evolution.
57. What is a network user interface?
58. What are some of the key functional characteristics of an NUI?
59. What is an active assistance subsystem?
60. What is X Windows?
61. How does X Windows differ from Microsoft Windows?
62. What are Motif and Open Look?
63. What is the CDE, and why is it important?
64. How does CDE differ from X Windows?
65. How can UNIX and Microsoft Windows applications run simultaneously on a single-client workstation?

ACTIVITIES

1. Using the client software architecture, fill in the layers with the names of actual software products, being sure to indicate which mutually supported protocols are used to bridge every software-to-software and software-to-hardware interface.
2. Research which currently available client operating systems are microkernel based. Prepare a presentation on the rationale for this design and how well intended results have been achieved.
3. Research microkernel-based client operating systems under development. Track their progress and delivery schedules. Report on whether all initially promised subsystems are delivered.

4. Research a microkernel-based client operating system for which subsystems have been written by a third-party vendor. Report on what effect the microkernel architecture had on this development effort.
5. Find an operating system adhering to a monolithic architecture. Report on efforts to update or revise the operating system.
6. Find examples of hardware-independent operating systems. Determine the importance and market share of hardware-independent operating systems. Is demand likely to grow?
7. Find examples of multiple personality operating

systems. What percentage of users actually use the multiple personality capability?

8. Collect sales figures and user reviews of Windows 95. Graph the sales figures over time. Calculate market share. What are Windows 95's key competitors?

9. Track the sales of Windows 95 versus OS/2 Warp Connect. Explain your results.

10. Compare market share of MS-DOS and Novell DOS, and prepare a chart or presentation of your results.

11. Collect product information regarding technology available to integrate Windows and UNIX applications on a single-client platform. Draw hardware and software architectures indicating the interaction of the technology for the various alternative solutions. How many distinct approaches are evident?

12. Research the network user interface market. What role has the U.S. Justice Department played in Microsoft's plan to migrate Windows 95 and Windows NT to network user interfaces?

CHAPTER 3

CASE STUDY

CAGERS TEAM UP WITH UNLIKELY PARTNER

The Houston Rockets Won Back-to-Back Championships in 1994 and 1995. But While the Professional Basketball Team Soared to Victory, Its Owner, Rocketball Ltd., was Crawling.

"Our success is measured by how our ticket holders, sponsors, and the public look at us as an organization," says David Jackson, team comptroller. "We want them to be proud to be associated with us."

The problem was, until last spring, Rocket employees at the team's three Houston locations did almost all their work on 286- and 386-based Compaq Computer Corp. PCs, which ran under DOS. One office had a handful of 486-based PCs running DOS, Microsoft Windows 3.0, Windows 3.11, and Novell Net-Ware 3.11, but the LAN they supported was used solely for print sharing.

"We weren't able to portray ourselves as a cutting-edge professional organization," says Jackson. Employees set up meetings and gained CEO approvals for everything from expense reports to car-

pet colors through phone calls, faxes, and the proverbial "sneaker-net." Marketing and sales people couldn't create a simple mailing list of season-ticket holders. And sponsors such as Pepsi received presentations created on a word processor with photocopied images.

When Jackson put the project out for bids, several large system integrators came knocking. But a tiny, three-year-old Houston-based reseller, Micro Support Unlimited, ultimately was handed the ball.

Jackson readily admits that it was MSU's knowledge of the team, as much as its technical capabilities, that won him over. Major Rocketball fans, MSU's employees decorated their office with newspaper articles about the team as well as three autographed basketballs. "That kind of enthusiasm," says Jackson, "is what we were looking for."

MSU is also no slouch when it comes to technical prowess. For the past three years, the 32-employee firm has been raking in mounting sales through month-to-month contracts with customers such as *The Houston Chronicle,* Enron Corp., and

ProEnergy. What's more MSU was a Microsoft Corp. partner, which meant it had the backing of a huge vendor and could offer a turnkey solution. The clincher, however, was that Jackson believed MSU CEO Toni Kaufman and her husband, MSU President Kirvin Kaufman, when they said they'd do whatever it took to make Rocketball better. It was no small order.

The 72-Hour Launch

During a blisteringly hot weekend last May, Jackson prepared to find out whether or not he'd banked on the right reseller team. He timed the launch of the Rockets' new network and systems upgrade to coincide with a move by the team's corporate head office to a new building. That site would be home to 65 new Hewlett-Packard Co. Vectra VL and Pavilion Pentium computers. Jackson wanted all the systems to be up and running flawlessly by Monday morning.

MSU played a critical role in Jackson's weekend mission. The reseller's task was to migrate the team's main 64MB HP Pentium 166 server from Novell 3.11 to Windows NT 3.51, and to make certain that all the old DOS and Windows 3.0 and Windows 3.1 files made it over to the team's new machines. Equipped with 8 MB and 16 MB of RAM, the Pentiums would now run Windows 95 and Microsoft Office 95. Additionally, MSU was responsible for handling user login and logoff procedure documentation, as well as maintaining a network DOS connection to an offsite legacy system.

Jackson knew this was a lot of ground to cover in three days. He'd been fighting an "uphill battle" for two years to get this upgrade. To get the go-ahead, Jackson said he had to promise his higher-ups that this upgrade "would make us better than we'd ever been before."

It was a promise the Kaufmans knew very well. So when the team hit its first snag Friday, it went into overdrive. The independent software vendor hired to set up the remote-access services server according to MSU's carefully diagrammed specifications had installed only Windows NT. That meant MSU had to set up the server with NT server groups, secured directories, shared directories, user IDs, login permissions, standard use configurations, network printers, local printers, and Microsoft Exchange for 62 users—in addition to configuring dozens of desktop computers.

Another glitch was discovered when several of the HP PCs on which MSU had installed Windows 95 would not shut down. What's more, these same machines had a hardware conflict with the NIC that caused them to lock up on the splash screen. "After a good deal of head scratching," recalls Kirvin Kaufman, the reseller was able to track down the problem on Tech-Net, a CD-ROM with Microsoft's knowledge base. As it turned out, several of the HP machines had an older ROM BIOS date that needed to be upgraded.

With those two glitches out of the way, MSU could focus on its original task of desktop configuration. A key objective for the reseller had been to find ways to simplify future upgrades and revisions. To do this, MSU implemented systems policies so users couldn't change things such as the control panel and video. MSU had no time to set up Systems Management Server, part of Microsoft's BackOffice suite, so the reseller installed it on all the workstations and the mail server. All around the MSU team, movers unloaded boxes and arranged office furniture.

The sun shone brightly Monday morning. Jackson and his MSU partners held their collective breath, but not for long. The network was a smashing success, suffering no bugs or crashes that day or during the eight months since then.

How They Did It

How did MSU make what could have been a complicated implementation go as smoothly as a simple upgrade?

The answer is homework. MSU began the process by conducting two months of research during which the reseller spent a half hour with each user in the Rockets' organization, from the CEO on down.

This exercise enabled MSU to model Rocketball's server according to people's actual, rather than perceived, job functions, focusing on the network access they really required.

Robert Fisher maintains the Rockets' statistics and scouting information and assumed he wouldn't need much security. But during an interview, MSU discovered that he also handles highly confidential information about players' salaries and the terms and lengths of their contracts. "He led the way for us to start looking at the mapping of the drives, the security of the workgroups, and the permissions," says Kirvin Kaufman.

The interviews also served as the basis for the 100-plus hours of training that preceded the rollout.

Following the interviews, MSU collected all of the Rocketball employees' forms and made templates that improved workflow. MSU created electronic expense-reimbursement forms, lead-request forms, faxes, memos, and standardized letter templates with an embedded Rocketball logo.

The most significant new application MSU developed was a marketing database incorporating data from a DOS-based TicketMaster database that tracks ticket-sales receipts. But the legacy system could not accommodate anomalies. For example, if a divorced couple wanted to split a pair of season tickets—she getting the first half of the season, he getting the second—the database wouldn't reflect the joint ownership because it allowed only a single field for the owner's name.

The team wanted not only to clean out its database but also to do targeted mailings. To accomplish this, MSU had to sort through all the data, find deviations, and decipher what was going on. This information led to a set of business rules, which MSU used to write procedures in Microsoft Excel that looked for common patterns.

Across the organization, the network has had a major impact. The Rockets game-operations staff now uses the World Wide Web to find game sound effects and to monitor Rockets newsgroups. The team's department of broadcast media relations now uses Excel to create easy-to-read game layouts for radio stations and national broadcasts, and its four remote workers can log in to the network from the road. Media Services people use Microsoft Mail to communicate breaking news to the rest of the staff. Sponsors now receive PowerPoint presentations tailored to their needs. And Rockets salespeople now use multimedia presentations with music, sounds, and game clips.

MSU offers several explanations for the project's success, but chief among them was that they made no assumptions.

As she tells it, Toni Kaufman never assumes she knows her client—even one she's had an eye on for years. It's her modus operandi. And it's been true ever since she taught former president George Bush to use a computer in 1992, and he asked, "OK, Toni, what do I do with this button?"

Source: Natalie Engler, "Cagers Team Up with Unlikely Partner," *LAN Times* (April 28, 1997). Copyright April 28, 1997, The McGraw-Hill Companies, Inc.

BUSINESS CASE STUDY QUESTIONS

Activities

1. Complete a top-down model for this case by gleaning facts from the case and placing them in the proper layer of the top-down model. After having completed the top-down model, analyze and detail those instances where requirements were clearly passed down from upper layers to lower layers of the model and where solutions to those requirements were passed up from lower layers to upper layers of the model.
2. Detail any questions about the case that may occur to you for which answers are not clearly stated in the article.

Business

1. What were some of the business problems caused by the unsophisticated nature of the existing information technology?
2. What was the duration of the system upgrade, and how was the date chosen?
3. Describe how the business analysis of each job function was conducted prior to system implementation.
4. What kinds of information did the business process analysis provide?

Application

1. What types of applications were run to support business processes?

2. What was the most significant new application developed?
3. What benefits did this most significant new application provide?
4. How was data analysis automated?
5. How was workflow improved?

Data

1. What format did most files on the old system use?
2. What format did these files need to be converted to on the new system?
3. What were some of the security issues regarding data?
4. What were some of the problems with the data in the TicketMaster database?
5. How were these problems overcome?

Network

1. What was done to ensure simple upgrades and revisions in the future?
2. How is the World Wide Web now being used?

Technology

1. What types of technology were being employed before the upgrade?
2. What types of hardware and software technologies were employed after the upgrade?
3. What were some of the glitches encountered during the system implementation?

CHAPTER 4

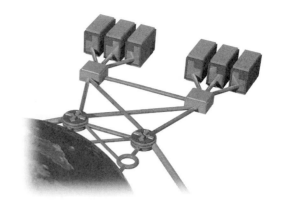

SERVER HARDWARE AND SOFTWARE

Concepts Reinforced

Client/Server Technology Architecture   Protocols and Compatibility
OSI Model   Processor Fundamentals
Hardware/Software Compatibility   Operating Systems Concepts
Network Operating System Concepts   Operating System Architecture

Concepts Introduced

Multiprocessor Hardware   Multiprocessor Operating Systems
Server Storage Alternatives   Fault Tolerance
Server Specialization   Server Hardware Trends

OBJECTIVES

After mastering the material in this chapter, you should understand the following:

1. The difference between client and server hardware technology

2. The significant trends in server hardware development

3. The relationship between server hardware trends and server operating systems trends

▦ INTRODUCTION

Following a thorough explanation of current trends in computing hardware and software in Chapters 2 (Client Hardware) and 3 (Client Software), this chapter will focus on those aspects of computing hardware and software that are unique to servers. In order to afford an appreciation of the unique needs for server functionality, the chapter starts with an overview of the forces that are driving these unique hardware and software requirements. Once the originating forces are clear, specific hardware features and requirements will be elaborated upon.

For example, one of the major jobs unique to servers is the management of massive amounts of storage space. Second, because of the mission-critical role often played by servers, increased hardware reliability and fault tolerance are a must. Server operating systems must respond to these increased demands as well, by offering the ability to work in multiprocessing environments with the reliability often associated with mainframe-based operating systems.

Business Requirements Dictate Server Functionality

As introduced in Chapter 1, the downsizing and rightsizing phenomenon has had a dramatic impact on the performance requirements of servers. The client/server architecture and the enterprise network that provide communications between network-attached resources are being called upon to match or exceed the performance and reliability exhibited by minicomputer and mainframe-based systems. The flexibility offered by properly designed and implemented client/server information systems is an absolute necessity for corporations competing in today's rapidly changing global marketplace. Increased need for access to corporate information—anytime, anywhere—has boosted the needs for powerful remote computing solutions.

Although flexibility and quick response to changing business needs are often associated with server-based information systems, the ability to run enormous, mission-critical, transaction-based applications formerly reserved for mainframes is now expected of servers. The need to have these mainframe-class applications execute in an absolutely secure and reliable environment places additional requirements on server design. Figure 4-1 summarizes some of the business requirements that servers are expected to fulfill, as well as the corresponding functional capabilities offered by servers.

Business Requirement	Server Functionality
It must support downsizing and rightsizing efforts by running mainframe-class applications.	• Faster processors, multiprocessor designs • Faster, wider buses linking server components such as Disk I/O and memory subsystems • Servers optimized for operation with mainframe DBMSs • High-capacity networking components for links to client/server backbone
Performance must be highly available and reliable.	• Redundant components within servers, fault-tolerant design • Redundant storage designs with high-capacity links to servers • Error-correcting memory • Better monitoring and diagnostic systems
Information systems must be easily and effectively managed.	• Open systems designs that support industry standard, multivendor enterprise management systems
It must handle business communication and information systems, which are becoming increasingly mobile and wireless.	• Servers that must be able to communicate with a wide variety of clients over communications links varying in protocol, bandwidth, and quality
Information systems must be able to adjust to the size and scale of the business enterprise.	• Scalable servers, allowing the addition of more processors

Figure 4-1 Business Requirements Dictate Server Functionality

As demonstrated in later sections of the chapter, the business requirements listed in Figure 4-1 also put functional demands on server operating systems, network operating systems, and other aspects of the client/server architecture.

■ SERVER HARDWARE

A server is a computer whose primary function is to offer computing services or manage system resources for client PCs requesting those services. Users do not generally sit at a server and use it as a workstation. Servers have become highly specialized. Although on small information systems, a single server may meet all of the needs of 5 to 25 clients, it is far more common to find multiple servers performing more specific duties. Following are just a few of the types of servers that might be included in distributed information systems:

- Applications servers
- File servers
- Database servers
- Print servers
- Communications servers
- CD-ROM servers
- Fax servers
- Video servers
- Internet servers
- Transaction processing servers

Servers communicate with and deliver services to clients via network connections. Those network connections may be strictly local or may span a very great distance. Although the term *server* can be used generically to mean *any* type of computer, including mainframes, that offers services to client PCs, this chapter refers only to servers employing RISC and CISC chips. Whereas Figure 1-22 (Client/Server Technology Architecture) showed the functional relationship of clients, servers, and networks, Figure 4-2 offers a view of the physical relationship between these key components.

An important point to note about Figure 4-2 is that as applications have left the centralized, self-contained domain of the mainframe and migrated to the distributed architecture of the client/server information system, the network has become responsible for transporting ever-increasing amounts of varying types of traffic. That is not to say, however, that the mainframe has no role in a client/server information system.

THE MAINFRAME AS SERVER

In Sharper Focus

Although the advent of the client/server architecture was predicted to bring about the demise of the mainframe, this has not been the case. The role of the mainframe has changed significantly in the transition from the centralized computing architectural model of yesterday to the distributed computing model of today. Mainframes have become specialized servers, highly valued for their reliable performance and enormous capacity and computing power. When electronic commerce and electronic funds transfer applications demand millions of distributed transactions, it is most often the mainframe computer that acts as the server.

What has changed is how the mainframe interacts with the rest of the elements of the client/server information system. In the days of centralized computing, the mainframe dictated the communications protocols of how peripheral devices were able to communicate with it. Now mainframes have to adapt to more easily communicate with other elements of the distributed client/server information system. For example, a communication protocol known as TCP/IP is the most common communication protocol for client/server information systems. Traditionally, mainframes did not communicate via TCP/IP, although it is estimated that 50% of IBM mainframes will be running TCP/IP by the end of 1998. Mainframes are also being called upon to act as Internet servers and are having Internet security features added to traditional mainframe operating systems such as MVS and OS/390. The traditional communications controllers for mainframes known as front end processors (FEP) have had to change as well to mirror the mainframe's new role as server. New front end processors are now able to communicate via TCP/IP in order to more efficiently integrate with the other elements of the distributed client/server architecture.

The mainframe computer continues to be a vital part of today's modern information system. The ability of mainframe manufacturers to support the evolution of the mainframe's role in tomorrow's information systems will be critical to its long-term viability.

Figure 4-2 illustrates what a server does. Figure 4-3 illustrates how a server might combine a variety of hardware components in order to perform its required duties.

Figure 4-3 is meant to illustrate a generalized view of server hardware components. Depending on a server's assigned specialization, hardware components could differ significantly. Now that the reader has an appreciation for how the various server

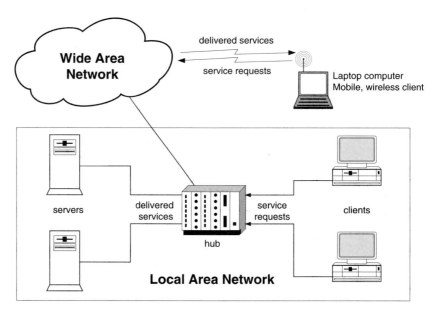

Figure 4-2   Clients, Servers, and Networks

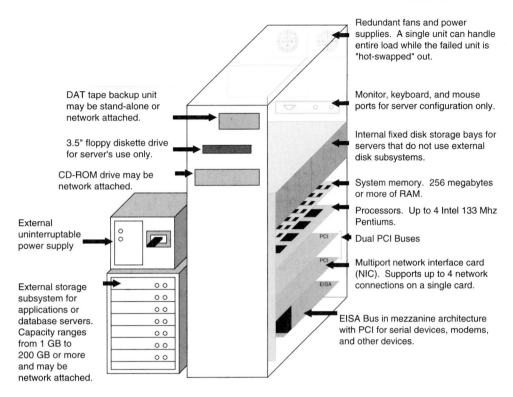

Figure 4-3   Server Hardware Components

hardware components combine to produce overall server performance, individual server hardware components and characteristics are explored in more depth.

**Applied
Problem
Solving**

Server Hardware Component Interaction

It is important to note the interaction of the server hardware components. Each contributes to the overall performance of the server. Remember the principle of shifting bottlenecks! It is important to purchase a server with an effective design featuring components whose capabilities balance, rather than overwhelm, one another.

For example, file and print servers are primarily concerned with transferring large amounts of data among clients, disk drives, and printers. These applications are not particularly CPU-intensive, meaning that the CPU does not typically pose any sort of bottleneck in file and print servers. As a result, bus width and speed, disk drive size and speed, printer speed and buffer size, and the number and speed of network interface cards are more likely to have a dramatic effect on overall performance than increasing the number or performance of CPUs.

On the other hand, applications servers running OLTP (on-line transaction processing) or database servers are more likely to benefit from the increased processing power offered by multiple processors. However, even in these cases, the systems-oriented nature of computer systems must be respected, because merely upgrading CPU capacity without paying attention to memory subsystem design or bus width could yield significant CPU idle time. Figure 4-4 summarizes some practical insight into the interaction of server hardware components.

Server Types	Potential Bottleneck	Solutions/Implications
File or Printer Servers	Input/Output Bound	• Add more drives • Add I/O channels • Change to faster, wider bus • Increase size of printer buffers • Add more NICs • Add faster NICs • Add more RAM for larger cache • Segment the LAN for less LAN traffic

Applications or Database Servers	Compute Bound	• Upgrade to faster CPU
		• Add multiple CPUs
		• Application program, NOS, and operating system must be optimized for use on multiprocessor platforms
		• In order to keep CPU busy, will also need to:
		  • Add cache memory
		  • Add multiple, fast disk arrays

Figure 4-4   Server Hardware Component Interaction

Server Hardware Components

Processors   Although the trends and development of new and more powerful CPUs was thoroughly covered in Chapter 2 (Client Hardware), servers differentiate themselves by the installation and simultaneous use of multiple processors. Although two or four supported processors is a common number for most **multiprocessor servers,** some supercomputer-type multiprocessor servers can employ 128 or more CPUs and cost well over $1 million. Although Intel's Pentium or Pentium II chips at various clock speeds are perhaps the most commonly used CPU chips in multiprocessor servers, several other chips are also employed:

- DEC Alpha chip

- Sun SPARC, SuperSPARC, and HyperSPARC chips

- MIPS R10000 series chips

- Motorola chips

The important hardware/software compatibility issue to remember is that operating systems running on these multiprocessor servers must be compatible with the installed CPU chips.

As shown in Figure 4-4, adding more CPU power is not always the answer to improved server performance. Furthermore, even for compute-intensive applications, continuing to add CPUs will show diminishing incremental performance improvements. This is because of the impact of the various other subsystems that interact with the CPU:

- System architecture

- Buses

- Memory subsystem

- Disk storage subsystem

Equally important to the overall performance of multiprocessor servers are the software components that must interact with the multiprocessor hardware platform:

- Application program

- Operating system

- Network operating system

All of these software components must be specifically written to take advantage of the multiple CPUs in the multiprocessor hardware platform.

System Architecture   System architecture in the case of multiprocessor servers refers to how the multiple CPUs within the multiprocessor server divide the processing tasks. The installed operating system must be specifically written to support the particular system architecture of the multiprocessor server. Systems that support multiple CPUs are generally referred to as **parallel processing** systems because multiple program instructions can be executed simultaneously. The two primary alternative system architectures, or subcategories, of parallel processing are **symmetric multiprocessing** and **asymmetric multiprocessing.**

Symmetric Multiprocessing   Symmetric multiprocessing **(SMP)** is a system architecture in which multiple CPUs are controlled by the SMP operating system and individual threads of application processes are assigned to particular CPUs on a first-available basis. In this manner, all CPUs are kept equally busy in a process known as **load balancing.** In SMP systems, the multiple CPUs generally share system memory and devices such as disk controllers. This is by far the most popular multiprocessor server system architecture, with close to 90 percent of all multiprocessor servers employing this option. Since programs reside in the shared memory area of the multiple CPUs, the application program does not need to worry about keeping track of specific CPUs. The limitation to this type of design is the bus that connects the multiple CPUs to the shared memory space. This bus bottleneck typically limits most SMP designs to between four and eight processors.

Asymmetric Multiprocessing   Asymmetric multiprocessing (**AMP** or **ASMP**) is characterized by assigning entire applications processes, rather than threads, to a particular processor. Processor loads can become unbalanced. In AMP systems, each CPU is generally assigned its own memory and other subsystems. Because of this, AMP systems architectures can extend beyond a single computing platform to include CPU chips from multiple separate machines. Two variations of the asymmetric multiprocessing system architecture take advantage of this horizontal scalability: massively paralllel processing and clustering.

Massively Parallel Processing   **Massively parallel processing (MPP)** systems architectures employ thousands of CPUs, each with its own system memory. Because the CPUs do not share a common pool of memory, they must communicate with one another through message passing over a communications network. These MPP system architectures may be installed in a single machine or may span several machines. MPP machines do not suffer from the bus botttleneck of SMP machines, but they are more difficult to write programs for because each CPU and its associated memory must be specifically loaded with different program segments. These types of computers are best suited for scientific and artificial intelligence applications.

Clustering   **Clustering** implies using the CPU power of multiple CPUs located in separate computing platforms to produce a single, more-powerful virtual computer. Clusters are also sometimes referred to as **virtual parallel machines (VPM).** The concept of clustering is neither new nor unique to PCs. Digital Equipment Corporation (DEC) produced software to link multiple VAX minicomputers together in a VAXcluster during the 1980s. The two primary benefits of clustering are failover and load balancing. Failover usually involves two entire servers working in parallel, with the ability for one server to take over transparently for the other in the case of server failure. Load balancing ensures that critical system resources are being used in a balanced manner in order to avoid having a single overburdened system resource become a bottleneck.

Microsoft has added failover clustering capabilities to Windows NT with a project known as Wolfpack. With Wolfpack, two NT servers that are connected via a dedicated network connection and that share a SCSI disk subsystem are able to exchange status information, known as heartbeat monitoring, and shift processing from the failed server automatically. Wolfpack has been officially released as a Microsoft Cluster Server as part of Windows NT Server, Enterprise Edition. Other features of Windows NT Server, Enterprise Edition include the following:

- 4 gigabyte memory tuning, supposedly offering up to 50 percent more application memory capacity for improved performance

- Support for up to eight CPUs in a single SMP server

- Microsoft Message Queue Server, providing unlimited concurrent users, intelligent routing, and support for third-party gateways

- Support for third-party clustering solutions

Future versions of NetWare will support clustering through a systems architecture that Novell refers to as distributed parallel processing (DPP). Novell plans to offer automatic failover and load balancing for as many as sixteen clustered NetWare servers through a product with working name Orion that will be an add-on to the next generation of NetWare known as Moab.

Practical Advice and Information   Before rushing out and establishing a clustered server environment, be sure to investigate the availability of applications that have been specially written to run in a clustered environment.

Cluster architectures can be categorized by the extent to which resources are shared among the nodes of the cluster. Clusters in which each node has its own memory space and communicates via message passing are known as **shared-nothing** clusters. Such architectures require that applications would need to be rewritten or segmented so that portions of the application can be executed independently on multiple servers comprising the cluster, with each node being able to keep track of which portions of the program are executing on which node. In **shared-memory** clusters, all nodes share the same memory space, thereby precluding the need to rewrite applications. The most popular current clustering architecture is known as **NUMA (nonuni-**

form memory access) and is characterized by multiple SMP computers connected via some sort of intelligent interconnect that allows the entire cluster to appear as a single SMP machine to application programs. Messages need to be passed between the multiple computers that comprise the cluster according to a standard protocol. Among the current message-passing protocols for clusters are the following:

- **PVM: Parallel Virtual Machine**

- **MPI and MPI2: Message Passing Interface**

- **VIA: Virtual Interface Architecture**

Loosely Coupled versus Tightly Coupled Architectures   System architectures can also be categorized according to how system resources are shared by the multiple CPUs. **Tightly coupled** systems architectures, otherwise known as shared memory systems, are characterized by CPUs that share a common pool of system memory as well as other devices and subsystems. Coordination among the multiple CPUs is achieved by system calls to and from the controlling operating system. Most SMP system architectures would be considered tightly coupled.

In **loosely coupled** system architectures, each CPU interacts with its own pool of system memory and devices. Coordination among the loosely coupled CPUs is achieved by some type of messaging mechanism such as interprocess communication between the separate CPUs and their individual copies of the operating system. Most AMP system architectures would be considered loosely coupled.

Figure 4-5 lists the key distinguishing characteristics of various system architectures, and Figure 4-6 graphically depicts the difference between typical SMP and AMP system architectures.

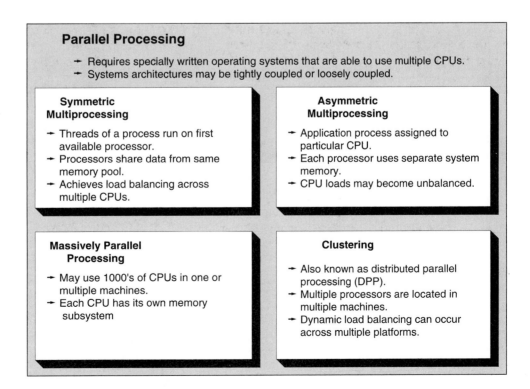

Figure 4-5   Distinguishing Characteristics of Parallel Processing System Architectures

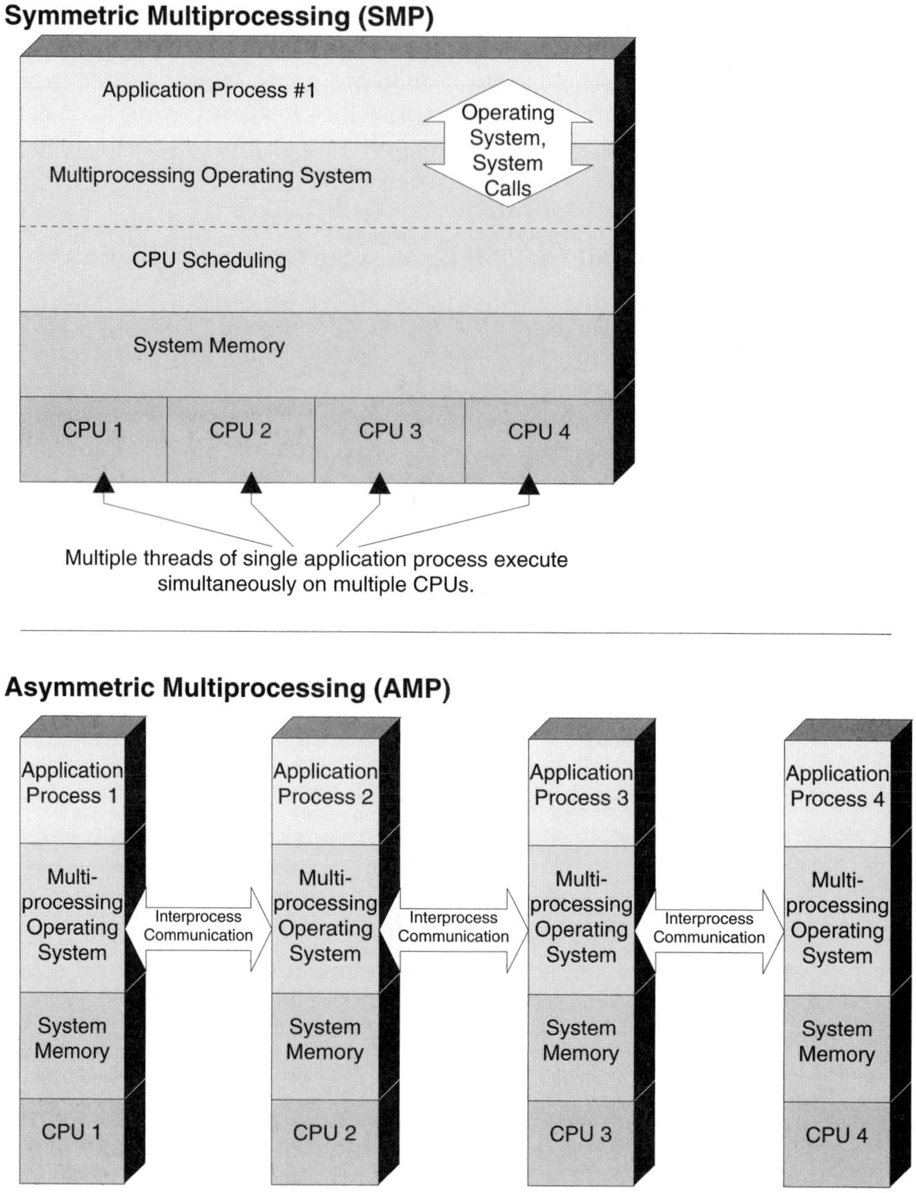
Symmetric Multiprocessing (SMP)
Application Process #1
Operating System, System Calls
Multiprocessing Operating System
CPU Scheduling
System Memory
CPU 1
CPU 2
CPU 3
CPU 4
Multiple threads of single application process execute simultaneously on multiple CPUs.
Asymmetric Multiprocessing (AMP)
Application Process 1
Application Process 2
Application Process 3
Application Process 4
Multi-processing Operating System
Interprocess Communication
System Memory
CPU 1
CPU 2
CPU 3
CPU 4

Figure 4-6 SMP versus AMP System Architectures

Practical Advice and Information

SMP scalability refers to the percentage of increased performance achieved for each additional CPU. For example, 100 percent SMP scalability implies that adding a second CPU will double the original performance or computing power of a computer and that adding a third CPU will triple the original performance of a computer. In reality, owing to the operating system overhead caused by having to coordinate the efforts of multiple CPUs, something less than 100 percent is the highest achievable SMP scalability.

Buses   Multiple high-performance CPUs can obviously process large amounts of data. It is important that the buses connecting computer platform subsystems are both fast and wide enough to handle this large amount of data. Processing power is often measured in **MIP**s (millions of instructions per second). A rule of thumb relating processing power, system memory, and bus capacity is as follows:

Practical Advice and Information

> For each MIP of processing power, 1 MB of memory and 128 KB of I/O bandwidth are required. This ratio is known as Amdahl's Rule, named after Gene Amdahl, founder of Amdahl Computers, a manufacturer of IBM mainframe clone computers.

System buses, sometimes referred to as processor/memory buses or host buses, are usually proprietary and vary from server to server. System buses connect the major subsystems of the server such as CPU, system memory, disk controllers, and the peripheral bus. Peripheral buses are used to connect peripherals such as network interface cards or SCSI disk controllers.

PCI buses seem to be the peripheral bus of choice among servers, although many high-powered multiprocessor servers use proprietary peripheral bus architectures. From a customer's perspective, the danger in purchasing a server with a proprietary bus architecture is that compatible peripheral devices and additional system memory may be available from only a limited numbers of vendors at potentially higher prices.

PCI Version I has the capacity to deliver up to 132 MB per second, whereas PCI Version II boasts a maximum throughput of 264 MB per second. PCI bus architectures also have the ability to expand through cascading to additional PCI buses via a PCI-to-PCI bridge, or to lower speed expansion buses such as EISA.

The **PCI hot plug specification** is a supplement to the PCI specification that will allow PCI cards to be added or replaced without powering down the computer into which they are being installed. The new specification will have to be supported by operating system and server vendors before users will actually be able to start hot-swapping PCI cards. Operating systems will require the addition of the hot plug service software and hot plug system drivers, whereas servers will require the addition of a hot plug controller and PCI slot–specific power controls so that software can power down a certain PCI slot while the remainder of the computer remains operational.

Figure 4-7 illustrates a typical arrangement of buses in a multiprocessor server.

Memory

Memory architectures in tightly coupled multiprocessor servers can be classified as shared, whereas memory architectures in loosely coupled multiprocessor system architectures can be classified as distributed. The memory chips themselves must be fast enough to keep the CPU busy. The relative benefits of SRAM, DRAM, EDO-DRAM, and other types of memory were explained in Chapter 2. Needless to say, multiprocessor servers require fast memory, and plenty of it. System memory RAM capacities into the gigabyte range are not unreasonable.

Error checking and correcting (ECC) memory, also known as error correction code memory, has the ability to detect and correct errors in data stored in and retrieved from RAM memory. It is more expensive than conventional RAM but is worth the added cost in the case of servers.

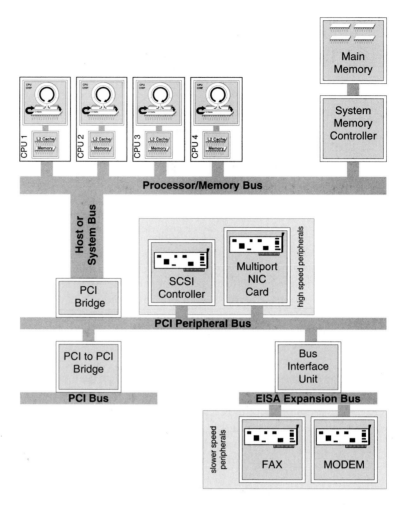

Figure 4-7   Bus Arrangement in a Multiprocessor Server

As discussed in the chapter on client hardware, L2 cache can make a tremendous difference in system performance. This is even more true with multiprocessor servers. The amount of L2 cache included in a given server is usually a design consideration controlled by the system manufacturer and not a user option. In symmetric multiprocessor servers, L2 cache may be dedicated to each CPU or may be shared by all processors.

Intelligent Input/Output—I_2O

Intelligent I/O, or **I_2O,** is a specification that seeks to improve server input/output performance by introducing platform-independent intelligent I/O subsystems that relieve system CPUs from all of the interrupt handling and management of input/output operations. In real terms, I_2O implementations have led to throughput increases of almost 500 percent in test environments. These intelligent I/O subsystems include their own dedicated I/O processors (IOP) and a standardized-platform-independent split driver architecture consisting of operating system specific modules (OSM) that operate in main memory and hardware device modules (HDM) that execute on the I/O controllers' IOPs. In order to implement an I_2O subsystem, a computer's BIOS (basic input/output system) would have to be modified to recognize I_2O devices and build the required message queues to allow the OSM and HDM to communicate. Another benefit of I_2O is that it applies to a wide variety of input/output devices including disk drives, CD-ROMs, network interface cards, and RAID arrays.

CD-ROM

As operating system and networking operating system software continues to gain in sophistication, it also gains in sheer size. As a result, most server operating systems such as Windows NT or NetWare 4.1 are now distributed on CD-ROM rather than on 40 or more 3.5″ diskettes. Not only are the one or two CD-ROMs more convenient, they are also significantly faster to install than loading 40 or more individual diskettes. For this reason, it is important to have a CD-ROM drive on a server for software installation, even if the CD-ROM drive won't be shared with clients as a network-attached device. The required functionality and associated hardware requirement of dedicated, networked CD-ROM servers will be outlined later in this chapter.

Because of the high capacity of a CD-ROM, it is important that the CD-ROM drive be attached to the server via a high-speed bus such as a PCI/SCSI controller, although adapters for IDE, parallel port, EISA, ISA, and MCA are available. Cache memory on the CD-ROM driver itself improves performance: 256KB is a common cache size. The current CD-ROM capacity standard is 680 MB of data per CD, with higher standards in the proposal stages. As with any device added to a computing platform, software drivers that are compatible with both the CD-ROM and the installed operating system are required. If the CD-ROM is to be used only for software installation or for seeking information on a single CD-ROM at a time, then a single slot CD-ROM drive should suffice. CD-ROM "jukeboxes" are more appropriate for specialized, networked CD-ROM servers.

Various standards exist that describe CD-ROM drive performance. Figure 4-8 lists the speed classifications of CD-ROM drives, which provides the most general categorization of CD-ROM driver performance.

CD-ROM Speed Specification	Sustained Average Data Throughput
Single Speed	150 KBps
Double Speed	300 KBps
Triple Speed	450 KBps
Quad Speed (4x)	600 KBps
6x	900 KBps
8x	1200 KBps
12x	1800 KBps
14x	2100 KBps
16x	2400 KBps
24x	3600 KBps

Figure 4-8   CD-ROM Drive Standards

More comprehensive standards are proposed by the Multimedia PC Marketing Council (MPC). MPC Level 1 and 2 standards are summarized in Figure 4-9.

MPC Standard Level	Sustained Transfer Rate	Average Seek Time	Maximum CPU Usage	Minimum Recommended Hardware Configuration
Level 1	150 KBps	1 second maximum	40%	386SX with 2 MB RAM and 30 MB hard drive
Level 2	300 KBps	400 ms maximum	60%	486SX/25 with 4 MB RAM, 16-bit sound and graphics cards, 160 MB hard drive, playback support for XA files

Figure 4-9 MPC Level 1 and 2 Standards

Although many other proprietary CD-ROM standards exist, two additional standards are supported by most CD-ROM Drives:

1. **XA:** Extended Architecture for CD-ROM is Microsoft's Level 2 CD-ROM specification, which supports simultaneous playback of voice, video, image, and text.

2. **Photo CD:** Also known as Kodak Photo CD, this is a standard for displaying photographs proposed by Kodak.

In Sharper Focus

DVD

DVD, known as either **Digital Versatile Disk** or **Digital Video Disk,** is widely believed to be the next-generation successor to CD-ROM for high-capacity storage and distribution. One of the major hurdles standing in the way of widespread adoption of DVD as the medium of choice for PC-based storage is the current array of conflicting standards. On a positive note, DVD is an excellent high-capacity storage medium for audio, video, and data. In many cases, DVD drives allow contents to be rewritten and are also backward-compatible with current CD-ROMs. Figure 4-10 lists some of the characteristics of the current multitude of DVD standards.

DVD Standard	Capacity	Notes
DVD-Video	4.7 GB	Supported by DVD Forum; most widely backed standard
Divx	Flexible	Write once, read for a limited amount of time format for movie rental
DVD-R	4.7 GB	Write once format, primarily for software distribution
DVD-RAM	2.6 GB	Rewritable; incompatible with DVD+RW
DVD+RW	3.0 GB	Rewritable; incompatible with DVD-RAM

Figure 4-10 DVD Standards

Backup

In multiple server networked environments, backup solutions are most often network-based, rather than being done on a individual, server-by-server basis. However, for those cases where a single server requires backup, the following analysis is offered.

The first thing to realize about any backup solution is that it is a combination of hardware and software technology. The backup device itself, the server hardware, the third-party backup software (if applicable), and the server's operating system must all communicate transparently with one another. Figure 4-11 offers a conceptual representation of the compatibility issues involved in a single-server backup solution.

Some of the compatibility requirements identified in Figure 4-11 are supplied by two standards:

1. **Storage Management System (SMS)** defines an API for third-party backup software to interoperate transparently with NetWare servers.

2. **Storage-Independent Data Format (SIDF)** allows portability between tape media and SIDF-compliant backup devices

A variety of backup device choices and accompanying standards is available. Choices differ both in overall capacity and backup throughput speed and in price. Figure 4-12 summarizes the key characteristics of a variety of backup device possibilities.

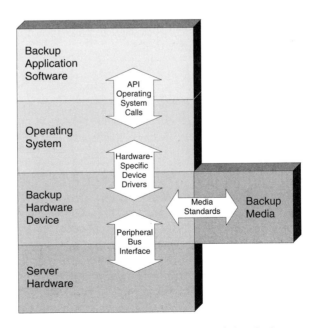

Figure 4-11 Compatibility Issues of Single-Server
Backup Solutions

Media Type	Explanation	Media Capacity	Throughput	Approx. Price
4 mm DAT DDS 1	Digital audio tape, Digital data storage	2 GB	21–23 MB/min	$800–$1700
4 mm DAT DDS 2	Digital audio tape, Digital data storage	4 GB, 8 GB	23–30 MB/min	$1000–$2000
4 mm DAT DDS 3	Digital audio tape, Digital data storage	24 GB	144 MB/min	$1200–$2000
8 mm	8 mm digital magnetic tape	5 GB	15–29 MB/min	$1400–$2500
DLT	Digital linear tape	10 GB	90–150 MB/min	$3100–$25,000
Magneto-Optical	Disk technology uses laser and magnetic read/write	1.3 GB	48–96 MB/min	$850–$1200
QIC	Quarter-inch cartridge magnetic tape	40 MB–25 GB	4–96 MB/min	$1200–$3500

Figure 4-12   Backup Technology Specifications

Applied Problem Solving

Although each backup situation is unique, there are some general rules of thumb for configuring backup solutions. Figure 4-13 summarizes a few possible scenarios and possible solutions.

There are trade-offs to each of the scenarios listed in Figure 4-13. Figure 4-14 shows the physical topology of backup solutions and lists some of the trade-offs inherent to each alternative.

Amount of Data to be Backed Up	Proposed Backup Solution
Less than 2 GB	Attach a backup device to a network-attached client workstation. Install and execute backup software from client workstation.
2 GB–4 GB	Attach a backup device to the server. Install and execute the backup software on the server.
More than 10 GB	Attach multiple backup devices to server. Install and execute backup software on server. *Or* consider a dedicated network-attached backup server.

Figure 4-13   Server Backup Scenarios

Backup Device Installed on a Network Client

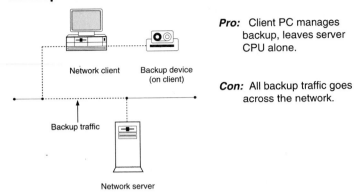

Pro: Client PC manages backup, leaves server CPU alone.

Con: All backup traffic goes across the network.

Backup Device Installed on a Network Server

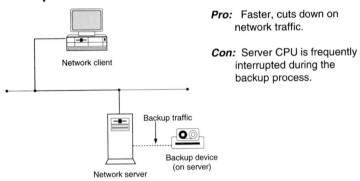

Pro: Faster, cuts down on network traffic.

Con: Server CPU is frequently interrupted during the backup process.

Figure 4-14   Trade-Offs of Alternative Backup Solutions

UPS: Uninterruptable Power Supplies

Uninterruptable power supplies **(UPS)** for server PCs serve two distinct purposes:

1. They provide sufficient backup power in the event of a power failure to allow for a normal system shutdown.

2. They function as a **line conditioner** during normal operation by protecting computer equipment from "dirty" power conditions such as surges, "brownouts," and static spikes.

It is important to protect servers with uninterruptable power because data can be lost and important files can be corrupted due to crashes. In their role as suppliers of uninterruptable power, UPSs must be able to respond quickly enough to a loss of normal power that the server cannot detect the power loss and continues to operate normally as if the flow of power was uninterrupted. Most servers will crash with power losses of 300 milliseconds (3 tenths of a second) or more. Most UPSs are able to supply backup power within 12 milliseconds of the power loss.

UPSs vary in the amount of backup electricity they can supply and how long they can supply it. Remember that UPSs are meant only to provide enough electricity to allow for a normal shutdown, usually about 5 minutes. Some units can offer more power for longer periods of time for a higher price. However, UPSs are not backup generators allowing users to continue to work for hours.

Most UPSs are rated as to capacity in volt-amperes (va), with units offering between 600 and 1500 va being suitable for a single server and two to three workstations. Units in this power range are generally priced between $500 and $1500, depending on amount of power, length of backup period, and number of additional features. Larger UPSs offer backup power in the 3000 to 5000 va range (3 Kva to 57 Kva) and are capable of supporting multiple servers or an entire data center.

Some UPSs also have the ability to link directly to servers, advising them of a loss of power, thereby triggering user notification and an orderly shutdown. This feature is known as **auto-server shutdown,** and it must be compatible with the particular server operating system installed. UPSs communicate with servers through the server's serial port and a specialized serial cable. Another important management feature is the ability of the UPS to transmit status information in a standardized format understandable by enterprise network management platforms. The most common protocol for management information transmission is SNMP (Simple Network Management Protocol), which is a member of the TCP/IP family of protocols.

Expandability

Expandability in a server should be considered in the following categories:

1. *RAM Expandability:* What is the maximum amount of RAM that can be installed in the server? Typical maximum amounts range from 128 MB to several GB. RAM memory is usually added as SIMM or DIMM modules. Therefore, it is important to know both the total number of SIMM/DIMM sockets available and how many are presently occupied.

2. *Expansion and Peripheral Bus Slot Expandability:* As servers demand faster peripherals to keep up with faster CPU performance, PCI is becoming the peripheral bus of choice. Two PCI buses bridged together are better than a single PCI bus. Six to eight empty PCI slots should be considered a desirable number. Expansion bus use will become less important as more and more peripherals shift to the PCI bus. However, for the meantime, four to six available EISA slots are desirable.

3. *Drive Bay Expandability:* Drive bays may be suitable for either 5.25" or 3.5" drives and may be either accessible from the front of the server or totally internal. Obviously CD-ROM drives or diskette drives would need to be accessible, and fixed disk drives can easily be internal. As disk drive capacity continues to increase, the total number of available bays becomes less important. High demands for storage are met by external storage subsystems such as disk arrays, or redundant array of independent disks (RAID), explained in the next section. Typical servers have two 5.25" bays, seven to nine 3.5" bays, and one or two internal bays.

Network Interface Cards

In order to prevent the network interface card from becoming the overall system bottleneck, two important decisions should be made regarding network interface cards for servers:

1. Although the server's network interface card must be compatible with the overall network architecture, that network architecture should be as fast as possible. For instance, if the client/server information system's network is a 10 MBps Ethernet network architecture, then the server must use a 10 MBps Ethernet NIC. However, faster network architectures such as 100 MBps Ethernet do exist. As will be seen in the study of LAN design, servers can be put on faster network segments and bridged to the rest of the network.

2. The second way to prevent the server's NIC from becoming the system bottleneck is to put more than one NIC in the server. Think of the server as a crowded building full of people. In order to get more people out of the building in a shorter amount of time, more doors could be added. The NICs are the exits of the server. In order to get more data out of the server more quickly, more NICs could be added. Second, although the speed of t he interface from the NIC to the network may be fixed (10 MBps Ethernet), the speed that data gets loaded onto the NIC from within the server is variable depending on the bus interface employed. As a result, PCI network interface cards are preferable to ISA or EISA NICs, and multiple PCI NICs are preferable to single PCI NICs. For convenience's sake, four PCI Ethernet NICs can be mounted on a single card that includes a bridged PCI bus.

■ SERVER STORAGE ALTERNATIVES

RAID: Redundant Arrays of Inexpensive Disks

RAID Levels   In an effort to provide large amounts of data storage combined with fault tolerance and redundancy, numerous small disk drives were joined together in arrays and controlled by software that could make these numerous disks appear as one gigantic disk to server operating systems. Exactly how these numerous disks were physically and logically linked was defined according to a series of standards known as **RAID.** *RAID* originally stood for redundant array of inexpensive disks, but now it is often defined as redundant array of independent disks.

RAID is not the first method used to provide fault-tolerant or redundant data storage. Individual network operating systems had previously offered two closely related methods for ensuring data availability for mission-critical applications:

1. **Disk mirroring** involves two disks attached to the same controller acting as mirror images of one another. Everything written to one disk is identically written to the other. In the event that one disk fails, the other disk immediately takes over. The single point of failure in this scheme is the single disk controller that controls the two mirrored disks. If the single controller fails, both disks become unreachable.

2. **Disk duplexing** seeks to overcome the single point of failure inherent in disk mirroring by linking a separate disk controller to each mirrored disk drive.

RAID incorporates disk mirroring and disk duplexing but also goes beyond them to define six different RAID levels. These RAID levels serve as standards for hardware and software vendors wishing to sell RAID technology. RAID standards are maintained by the **RAID Advisory Board (RAB).** Figure 4-15 lists key facts concerning the six RAID levels officially recognized by RAB.

RAID Level	Definition	Comment	Application	Advantages	Disadvantages
Level 1: Disk Mirroring	Disk mirroring, also known as shadowing	Mirroring	System drives, critical files	High reliability	Writing to both mirrored disks degrades write performance; expensive
Level 2: Striped Array Plus Hamming Code	Writes data across multiple disks, adding Hamming code for error detection and correction	Doesn't exist for all practical purposes because it requires a modified disk drive that's too expensive to implement	None	High data transfer rate, high reliability	Not commercially viable
Level 3: Striped Array Plus Parity Disk	Stripes data a byte at a time; Parity is calculated on a byte-by-byte basis and stored on a dedicated parity drive	Parallel access for high read and write rates	Large I/O request applications such as imaging, CAD	Good for large block data transfers	Entire array acts as a single disk and can handle only one I/O request at a time; If parity disk is lost, so is error detection and correction
Level 4: Independent Striped Array Plus Parity Disk	Stripes data in sectors; Parity stored on parity drive. Disks can work independently	Forget it; The write penalty is too high	Not widely available	Good read performance	Poor write performance; If parity disk is lost, so is error detection and correction
Level 5: Independent Striped Array Plus Striped Parity	Stripes data in sectors; Parity is interleaved and striped across multiple disk	Striping across the disks with parity data	High request rate, read-intensive data lookups where write performance is not critical	High data reliability, good read performance	Poor write performance because data has to be striped across multiple disks
Level 6: Independent Striped Array Plus Striped Double Parity	Striped data and parity with two parity drives	Level 5 with data duplication to provide for extra redundancy	High request rate, read-intensive data lookups where write performance is not critical	Highest data reliability, good read performance	Worse write performance than level 5 due to added parity calculation

Figure 4-15   RAID Levels Officially Recognized by RAB

RAID Level	Definition	Application	Advantages	Disadvantages
Level 0: Disk Striping	Stripes data across multiple disks without redundancy	High performance for noncritical data	Fast I/O at low cost	No data redundancy; Not really RAID
Level 10: Levels 1 plus 0	Disk mirroring plus disk striping	Any critical response time application	Excellent I/O performance and data reliability	High hardware cost; Not widely used
Level 7: Independent Striped Array plus Dual Parity Disks	Stripes data in sectors. Parity stored on two parity drives; Disks work independently	High request rate, read-intensive data lookups where write performance is not critical	High data reliability, good read performance	Poor write performance
Level 53: Levels 0 plus 3	Combines disk striping and RAID 3	Large I/O request applications such as imaging, CAD	High performance and high data transfer rates	Poor write performance

Figure 4-16   RAID Levels Not Officially Recognized by RAB

The text included in the comments column in Figure 4-15 is attributed to Joe Molina, the RAID Advisory Board Chairman. These comments are included for insight into the practical, rather than theoretical, significance of the various RAID levels. Other RAID level definitions used by some RAID technology vendors but not officially sanctioned by the RAID Advisory Board are listed in Figure 4-16.

RAID Technology   Nearly all RAID storage subsystems support RAID levels 0, 1, and 5, with fewer RAID technology vendors supporting levels 3, 6, 7, and 10. Figure 4-17 graphically illustrates the categorization of the major types of RAID systems.

The key differentiating factors among the various categories of RAID technology depicted in Figure 4-17 can be summarized by the answers to the following key questions:

1. Where is the RAID software executed?
   - In the CPU of the server (software-based RAID)
   - In a dedicated CPU embedded within the RAID controller board (hardware-based RAID)

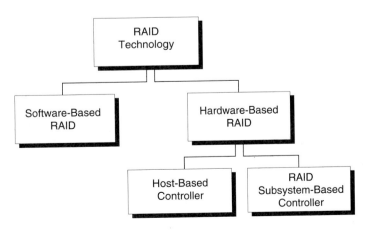

Figure 4-17   RAID Technology Categorization

2. In the case of hardware-based RAID, where is the RAID controller board that contains the dedicated CPU installed?
   - In an available expansion slot in the host system (Host-Controller RAID)
   - In the RAID subsystem cabinet that is linked to the host via a standard SCSI controller (SCSI-to-SCSI RAID)

Software-based RAID uses the CPU of the server to execute the RAID software, which controls the multiple disk drives contained in the redundant array of independent disks. The RAID level implemented is determined by the logic contained within the RAID application software executed on the server. The disadvantage of this approach is that it takes valuable server CPU cycles to control the RAID subsystem, especially in the event of a catastrophic event such as a disk rebuild. Another potential disadvantage is that another ill-behaved application also running on the same server on which the RAID software is executing could interfere with or crash the RAID application, resulting in data corruption. RAID software written as a server application must be written for a particular operating system or network operating system. The advantage of software-based RAID is the fact that it is usually less expensive than hardware-based RAID. Software-based RAID could actually be implemented by purchasing a NLM (NetWare Loadable Module) with RAID functionality and executing that on a NetWare server. NT server includes support for RAID levels 1 and 5. Of course, an array of disk drives would also be required.

Hardware-based RAID is more expensive than software-based RAID, but it is also more reliable and is able to support more operating systems. In the case of **host-controller RAID,** the controller board containing the RAID intelligence is installed in an available expansion slot. This requires bus interface compatibility. Most RAID controllers support ISA, EISA, MCA, and PCI bus interfaces. Several also support NuBus (Apple) and various minicomputer bus interfaces as well. The RAID software contained in firmware on the host-controller RAID card must make system calls to the host's operating system, network operating system, or both, in order to control the disks in the RAID subsystem. Therefore, operating system–specific drivers unique to each host-controller card must be supplied by the host-controller card vendor. Most host-controller cards are available with drivers for the following:

- NetWare (multiple versions)
- Windows NT
- OS/2
- Vines
- Appleshare
- UNIX and its numerous vendor specific varieties

SCSI-to-SCSI RAID keeps all the RAID intelligence in the disk array cabinet. The controller card is installed with the RAID subsystem cabinet and connects to the host server via a standard SCSI controller. SCSI RAID controllers vary as to which SCSI standards are supported (fast, wide, fast and wide, ultra). The advantage to SCSI-to-SCSI RAID is that the RAID portion of the software is operating system independent. Only standard SCSI drivers are required for communication. To the operating system running on the server, the RAID subsystem appears to be one massive SCSI disk drive. SCSI-to-SCSI RAID is ideal for less frequently supported operating systems such as Macintosh or some types of UNIX.

Practical Advice and Information

RAID Technology Analysis   Along with a knowledge of RAID level standards and the broad classifications of RAID technology, a variety of other issues are important to ensure that selected RAID technology will meet the data storage needs of a particular information system. Figure 4-18 summarizes a few of the RAID technology analysis issues that deserve investigation.

RAID Technology Analysis Issue	Questions/Implications
RAID Levels Supported	Look for at least levels 0, 1, and 5. Make sure that you can mix and match RAID levels within the subsystem—that is, support multiple different RAID levels simultaneously.
Subsystem Enclosures	Cabinets should have room for at least seven drives and support hot-swappable components including fans and power supplies. Is there also room for tape drives or optical drives in the cabinet?
Disk Drives	Are disk drives for the subsystem restricted to a particular vendor's drives? Although this may aid compatibility, it may hurt the ability to get the largest, fastest, or least-expensive drives if all drives must come from particular vendor.
Subsystem Capacity	Can the subsystem support more than one controller? How many drives or what size each can be supported? What are the expansion capabilities?
Embedded CPU and BUS	A faster, wider bus such as PCI is preferred. RAID controllers often employ specialized CPUs such as the Intel 1960 RISC chip.
Cache Memory	On-board cache will assist system performance. Write-back cache is acceptable if a method has been devised to save data left in the cache in the event of a power failure.
Management Utilities	Can the RAID subsystem output status information to an enterprise network management system in SNMP format? How easy is it to initiate a drive rebuild? How is the RAID subsystem configured? Is a setup utility included? What platform does the configuration software run on?
Operating System Compatibility	Host-based controllers must be physically compatible with the host server in terms of the peripheral or expansion bus. Controller software must be fully compatible with the operating system/network operating system installed in the host server.
Vendor-Related Issues	What is the vendor's policy on parts replacement? What type of warranty or on-site support is offered at what cost? What is the quality and availability of vendor technical support? What is the cost of technical support? Is an 800 number available? Will this vendor still be in business in five years?

Figure 4-18   RAID Technology Analysis Issues

To standardize the use of the terms used to describe RAID subsystem functionality, the RAID Advisory Board has issued detailed specifications for the following classifications of **Extended Data Availability and Protection (EDAP).** Vendors of RAID products can have their products classified through a RAID Advisory Board program, thereby allowing the vendors to display the "RAB Listed" logo on their products. There are three general classification categories:

- Failure resistant

- Failure tolerant

- Disaster tolerant

Details as to the specific differences between classification categories are available from the RAID Advisory Board at www.raid-advisory.com.

Storage Trends   A combination of increased throughput from SCSI buses and support for increased transmission distances via SCSI and Fibre Channel will allow the development of stand-alone **storage area networks (SANs)** that can be shared by multiple application servers or computing clusters. Fibre Channel is an ANSI X3T9.3 standard for high-speed communications ranging from 100 Mbps to 200 MBps at distances of up to 10 km over fibre optic cable. Figure 4-19 illustrates a possible storage area network implementation.

HSM: Hierarchical Storage Management

Although technologies such as RAID are able to keep tremendous amounts of data on-line and immediately available to users, at some point one needs to ask whether all that data *needs* to be kept on-line and are immediately available. At what point does sales history no longer need to take up valuable disk space? When are other storage media such as optical jukeboxes or tape libraries appropriate?

   Hierarchical Storage Management (HSM) is a technology that seeks to make optimal use of available storage media while minimizing the need for human intervention. HSM starts by looking at information in terms of its urgency or frequency of access

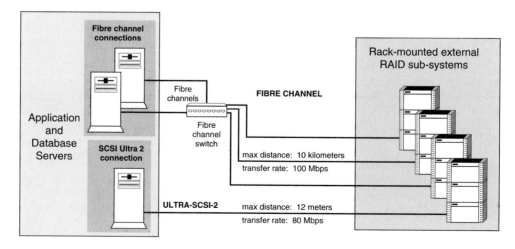

Figure 4-19   Storage Area Networks

and then stores that information on the most cost-effective storage media that meets performance requirements. Levels of access urgency and corresponding storage technologies are organized into a hierarchical model, as illustrated in Figure 4-20.

As illustrated in Figure 4-20, the most frequently accessed data is stored on the fastest on-line media. Information that is less frequently accessed is stored on **nearline,** or near-on-line, devices such as optical jukeboxes, whereas the least frequently accessed data is stored in off-line media such as tape libraries.

HSM software automates the process of migrating data between the various stage storage devices. HSM software does not replace backup/restoral software; rather, it merely manages stored data in an overall organizational scheme so that storage technology is properly utilized. Executing HSM software enables a multi-level system for mass storage characterized by automatic, transparent migration of data between available storage technologies. However, initial setup and configuration of HSM software is time-consuming because numerous thresholds for moving data between storage devices must be set by network managers before the software can take over and run automatically.

LAN-based HSM technology is relatively new, having migrated from the mainframe and minicomputer domains. HSM software must be compatible with a server's operating system and network operating system in order to transparently manage network-attached storage technology. Compatibility with existing backup application software can also be a problem. LAN-based HSM technology is currently available primarily for NetWare LANs. These products differ in the following ways:

- Number of HSM hierarchical tiers supported: Varies from two to unlimited

- Storage media supported: Some support only optical disk or optical disk and 8 mm tape, but others also support 4 mm tape and DLT tape

- Execution mode: Some HSM software runs as an NLM on a NetWare server; other products require a dedicated server

- Price: Price ranges as well as pricing criteria vary widely. Many products charge between $1000 and $10,000 *per server*

Windows NT Server 5.0 will also support HSM.

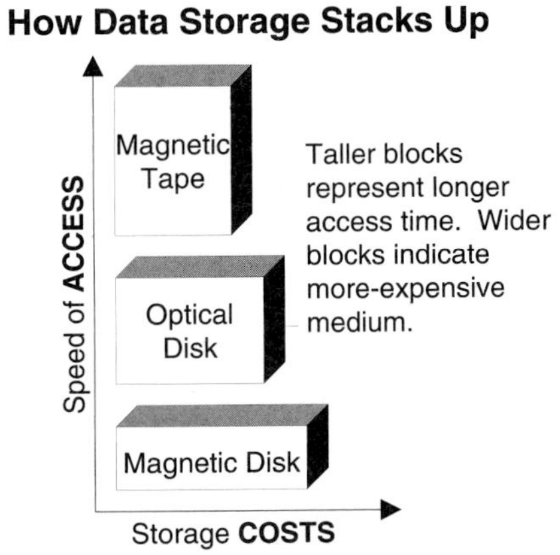

How Data Storage Stacks Up

Figure 4-20 Hierarchical Storage Management Model

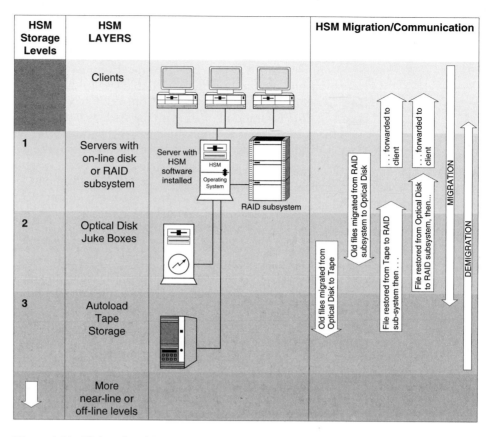

Figure 4-21 Heirarchical Storage Management Technology

Figure 4-21 illustrates the relationship between HSM software, servers, and hierarchical storage technology.

In Sharper Focus

HSM software can vary widely in terms of features and functionality. In order to differentiate between HSM products' management capabilities, a five-layer hierarchy of HSM levels was proposed by a company named Peripheral Strategies and adopted by HSM vendors. It is presented in Figure 4-22. The layers of the hierarchy increase in complexity from 1 through 5, and products supporting higher HSM levels are understandably more expensive.

HSM Level	Required Functionality
1	Simple automatic file migration with transparent retrieval
2	Real-time dynamic load-balancing of disk space based on multiple predefined thresholds. Manages 2 or more levels in the storage hierarchy, such as an optical jukebox and an automated tape library

3	Transparent management of three or more levels in the storage hierarchy. Storage thresholds between different levels in the hierarchy are dynamically balanced and managed. Includes volume management, including media management, job queueing, and device performance optimization. Supports optical and tape devices
4	Policy management and administration at all levels of the hierarchy. Storage management of diverse platforms, from file servers to workstations to application servers. Maintains the ownership, attributes, and location of data thus enabling multiplatform (DOS, Macintosh, OS/2) HSM. Can migrate files based on data type as dictated by policies
5	Object management, including structured or nonstructured records, and nonfile structures. Preserves the relationships of objects at all levels of the hierarchy. Can work with database management systems to migrate portions of a database, rather than the entire file, to and from secondary storage

Figure 4-22   HSM Levels of Functionality

SERVER FUNCTIONALITY AND SPECIALIZATION

Before deciding which particular hardware features are most important to be included in a given server, you must specify the intended use of that server. As LANs have grown and users have demanded more services from those LANs, servers have become increasingly specialized. The overall class of network-attached servers can be subdivided into two major categories:

- Servers that provide access to network-attached resources
- Servers that provide computational services by running back-end applications of one type or another

The difference between the two subcategories of servers is significant because it has major implications for the required hardware and operating systems that must be included in a given server. Servers that provide access to network-attached resources require little in the way of processing power, but servers expected to run back-end engines can use all the processing power they get. Figure 4-23 categorizes many of the specialized servers available today.

In the early days of local area networks, servers functioned primarily as file and printer servers. Novell NetWare gained a large share of the local area network operating system market by doing an excellent job at supplying network-based file and print services. As downsizing and rightsizing efforts have continued, applications servers requiring large amounts of processing power have become more available and affordable, thereby allowing applications formerly deployed on minicomputers and mainframes to execute on multiprocessor LAN-based application servers.

SERVER SOFTWARE

Being able to successfully execute mission-critical, transaction-based, high-end applications on powerful LAN-based multiprocessor servers requires compatible server operating systems that are able to take full advantage of the multiprocessor-powered

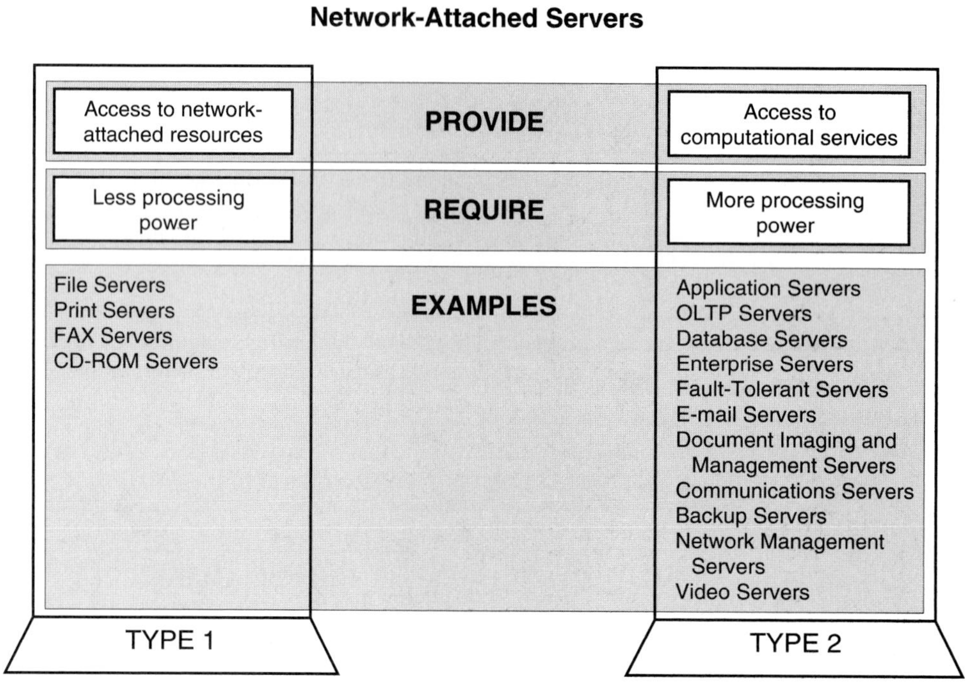

Network-Attached Servers

Access to network-attached resources	**PROVIDE**	Access to computational services
Less processing power	**REQUIRE**	More processing power

File Servers
Print Servers
FAX Servers
CD-ROM Servers
	EXAMPLES	Application Servers
		OLTP Servers
		Database Servers
		Enterprise Servers
		Fault-Tolerant Servers
		E-mail Servers
		Document Imaging and
		    Management Servers
		Communications Servers
		Backup Servers
		Network Management
		    Servers
		Video Servers

TYPE 1		TYPE 2

Figure 4-23   Network-Attached Server Functional Categorization

servers. As LAN-based server hardware has developed and become more powerful and affordable, server operating systems have had to become more powerful as well. The key aspect of this power is the ability to take full advantage of the server's multiple processors and to transparently pass this power along to the application program.

Server Operating Systems

It is difficult to distinguish between server operating systems and server *network* operating systems. Whereas a server must be a LAN-attached device in order to properly service its clients, the server operating system nearly always also includes the required functionality for the server to communicate over the network to which the server is attached. Network operating systems will be discussed in Chapter 9.

Server Operating System Characteristics   The key criteria by which server operating systems can be evaluated are as follows:

- Price

- Performance

- Management

- Security

- Applications integration

Price Price is difficult to compare between server operating systems because pricing schemes vary widely. Some operating systems vendors charge for their software based on the number of processors installed in the multiprocessor server. Others charge in fixed increments based on the number of users. For example, licenses might be available for 5, 25, 50, 100, 250, 1000, or an unlimited number of users. The problem with **fixed-step license pricing** as illustrated in these increments, is that in order to enable 101 users, a 250-user license would need to be purchased. In response to this dilemma, some vendors such as Novell with their NetWare 4.1 software have initiated an alternative pricing mechanism known as **additive license pricing.** With additive license pricing, any combination of license increments may be combined, to allow businesses to buy only the number of user licenses they really need. When computing comparative pricing of operating systems, consider upgrade costs as well as initial costs.

Performance To take advantage of the increased processing powers of multiple processors, server operating systems must be specially written to operate in a symmetrical multiprocessing (SMP) environment. Server operating systems can differ as to the maximum number of processors they can support. Figure 4-24 summarizes the number of processors supported by some currently available server operating systems.

UNIX-based server operating systems such as Solaris and others have been offering SMP capabilities for many more years than operating systems developed in the Intel chip environment. As a result, UNIX-based server operating systems tend to be more stable with servers having more than 16 or 32 processors.

In order to allow greater freedom of choice in matching SMP server hardware with SMP server operating systems, a SMP specification for the hardware/software interface known as **Multiprocessing Specification 1.1 (MPS)** has been proposed by Intel and is widely supported by SMP hardware and software vendors. As stated earlier in the chapter, clustering, now largely confined to minicomputer operating systems and high-powered database engines, will begin to become available for LAN-based servers as more powerful and performance-hungry applications are migrated from the mainframe environment to client/server architectures. By truly distributing applications, on a thread level, as well as associated data over multiple CPUs physically located on multiple machines, clustering-capable operating systems can truly harness all of the available computing power in a client/server environment.

Server Operating System	Vendor	Number of Processors Supported
Windows NT Server	Microsoft	2–32 (up to 8-way SMP with NT 4.0 Enterprise Edition, 32-way with NT 5.0 Enterprise Edition)
OS/2 SMP	IBM	2–16
Solaris	Sun Microsystems	2–64
UnixWare 2	Novell	2–16
OpenServer MPX	SCO (Santa Cruz Operation)	2–30
NetWare 4.1 SMP	Novell	2–32

Figure 4-24 Number of Processors Supported by Server Operating Systems

Practical Advice and Information

When it comes to optimizing performance in a symmetrical multiprocessing environment, remember that the operating system and application program must support not only SMP but also multithreading in order to ensure that the application program runs as efficiently as possible. Applications or operating systems that do not support multithreading may leave some CPUs idle, thereby negating the positive impact of SMP.

Management   As more mission-critical applications are deployed on LAN-attached servers, server operating systems must offer more sophisticated management tools in order to manage those applications effectively. Monitoring ability is essential to determine where potential performance bottlenecks might occur and to react accordingly. Among the server attributes that should be easily monitored in a graphical display are the following:

- Processors
- Network I/O
- Disk I/O
- Memory usage, including L2 cache
- Individual application performance and system impact
- Process and thread performance

The monitor tool should be able to display data in a variety of ways:

- As a graph
- As a report
- As alarms or alerts if preset thresholds are crossed

A strong and flexible alert system is essential to keeping applications running and users happy. Some alert systems have the ability to dial particular pagers for particular alerts and can forward system status information to that pager as well.

A monitoring tool should support multiple open monitoring windows simultaneously so that multiple attributes or applications can be observed. The monitoring or management tool should be open and support industry standard management protocols and APIs so that application-specific management tools can be easily integrated into the overall operating system monitor.

Security   Overall security features fall into three broad categories:

1. Authorization
2. Encryption
3. Authentication

Authorization is concerned with user accounts and passwords. Systems differ as to the level of access allowed before a valid user identification (UserID) and password must be entered. Authorization also controls user access rights to disks and files. User rights assignments can vary widely from system to system. An important security management feature is the level of integration, if any, between applications' security systems and the operating system's security system. For example, does e-mail require a separate UserID and login from the system login? In many cases, the answer is yes. Also, considerable time can be saved if UserIDs can be created or modified using a template or group name instead of having to answer numerous questions for every individual UserID.

Encryption is especially important when passwords are entered. Encrypted passwords are unreadable while being transmitted between a client workstation and the authorizing server.

Authentication involves ensuring that messages received, supposedly from a certain client workstation, really did come from that properly authorized workstation. Authentication security is necessary owing to a process called spoofing, in which bogus network messages that appear to be authentic and properly authorized can be sent to servers requesting data or services. Authentication security is complicated and usually implemented using a dedicated authentication server running the Kerberos authentication system.

In Sharper Focus

Security can be classified by level. Server operating systems often claim to implement **C2-level security.** C2-level security is actually part of a specification known as "Trusted Computer System Evaluation Criteria," which is specified in a Department of Defense document commonly known as "The Orange Book." The book concentrates on seven levels of data confidentiality from D (low) to A1 (high).

In C-level security, users can control the access to their own files. C2-level security more specifically implies that although users can control access to their files, all file access can be monitored and recorded or audited. Furthermore, these file-access audit records are reliable and verifiable and are therefore able to track and prove unauthorized file access. C2-level systems have other capabilities:

- Identification and authentication of users

- Use of hidden passwords

- Resource isolation

- Audit of user activity

Systems claiming to be C2 *compliant* are judged so by the vendor. In systems claiming to be C2 *evaluated* or *certified,* these systems' hardware and software have undergone rigorous testing taking as long as two years.

The Orange Book addressed security concerning only file access and confidentiality of data. The security of networked systems is addressed in another Department of Defense document known as "The Red Book." Encrypting passwords before transmitting them from client to server is a Red Book specification. Some server operating systems also claim "Red Book compliance." Security will be dealt with in more detail in Chapter 13.

Applications Integration   Applications integration refers to the extent to which applications programs are able to integrate or take advantage of the capabilities of the operating system in order to optimize application program performance. Successful applications integration with operating system can increase both convenience and performance.

From a convenience standpoint:

1. Does the application integrate with the operating system's security system, allowing single UserIDs and user accounts, or must two separate security databases be maintained?

2. Does the application integrate with the operating system's monitoring capabilities, allowing it to be monitored from within the operating system?

3. Can the application be configured and maintained from within the operating system's control panel or setup subsystem?

From a performance standpoint:

1. Can the application take advantage of the multithreaded capabilities of the operating system?

2. Can the application automatically detect the presence of multiple processors and respond accordingly?

3. Can the application use the multitasking capabilities of the operating system, or does it supply its own multitasking environment?

4. How easily, and to what extent, can adjustments be made to the operating system in order to optimize the performance of the application?

5. Does the application run as a 32-bit or a 16-bit application?

Managerial Perspective

New versions of server operating systems are released at least annually. When in the market for a server operating system, take a fresh look at all currently available products while bearing in mind current technology investments, business objectives, the characteristics of the application programs to be executed in the proposed server environment, as well as the stability and strategic product development direction of the operating system vendor.

■ SERVER HARDWARE AND SOFTWARE TRENDS

Fault-Tolerant Servers

One of the initial objectives or proposed benefits of client/server information systems was the ability to migrate mainframe-based applications onto rightsized applications servers. An underlying assumption of such a migration is that these applications servers will be able to offer the same levels of performance and reliability as the mainframes.

With the right combination of symmetrical multiprocessing hardware and software, it is now possible to match the performance levels of the mainframe. However, the ability to match the reliability and fault tolerance offered by mainframes is a distinct challenge for today's application servers. This reliability and fault tolerance is required for so-called mission-critical applications. OLTP (on-line transaction processing) systems such as banking systems or airline reservation systems are good examples of mission-critical applications. Control systems involved with military applications or nuclear power plants could also be considered mission-critical applications.

A server that is to be considered fault tolerant and capable of supporting mission-critical applications must exhibit all or most of the following characteristics:

- Fully redundant processors

- Processor auditing to check calculations each clock cycle

- Automatic correction of memory errors up to 8 bits long

- Hot-swappable redundant components such as fans, power supplies

A **redundant processor architecture** goes beyond traditional symmetrical multiprocessing design. In a redundant processor architecture, each primary CPU is shadowed by a secondary identical tandem processor that executes the same instructions. This secondary tandem processor is used only in the event of a primary CPU failure. Third and fourth audit processors perform the same instructions as the primary and secondary CPUs, respectively, and compare the results of every clock cycle for consistency. Thus, in order to deliver two-way (two CPU) SMP in a fault-tolerant redundant processor architecture, a total of eight CPUs (two primary, two secondary, four audits) would be required.

In order to ensure superb performance, additional processors may be dedicated to I/O processing or application processing. Each processor would run its own copy of the server's network operating system and a back-end application program such as an e-mail server. In order to be scalable and cost-effective, the fault-tolerant servers should be able to run standard SMP network operating systems such as Windows NT or NetWare 4.1 SMP. Figure 4-25 illustrates a possible fault-tolerant server layout featuring a redundant processor architecture.

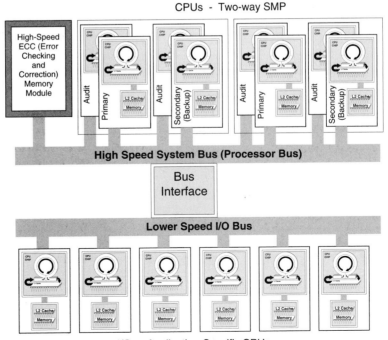

Figure 4-25   Fault-Tolerant Server Architecture

FAULT TOLERANCE VERSUS HIGH AVAILABILITY

As businesses and organizations have come to rely more heavily on their information systems, the constant, uninterrupted availability of those information systems has taken on increased importance. Accordingly, varying levels of availability are possible, depending on the amount of investment a business is willing to make into such systems. In order to differentiate between these varying levels of availability, a somewhat standardized vocabulary has been developed and is summarized in Figure 4-26.

Term	Explanation
Continuous Availability	Highest level of availability. Continuous availability = high availability + continuous operations.
High Availability	High availability = fault tolerance + rapid recovery. Provide availability greater than 99% of time, including unanticipated outages.
Continuous Operations	Avoids planned downtimes such as scheduled maintenance and component (disk drive, CPU) replacement.
Fault Tolerance	Usually provided by hardware solutions with supporting software. Provides 100% availability, zero unexpected downtime with no data loss. Detects, avoids, and corrects faults in order to avoid downtime.
Rapid Recovery	Not quite fault tolerance. Clustering software solutions provide auto-failover capabilities in less than one second. Much more affordable than fault tolerant solutions and good enough for most businesses. Minimizes downtime from unexpected interruptions.

Figure 4-26   Fault Tolerance versus High Availability

Investments in high-availability systems will be justified based on the business's level of dependence on its information systems. With the increase in mobile computing and the explosion of web access for marketing, customer service, or business transactions, it is becoming increasingly important to have information systems available 24 hours per day, 7 days per week. Significant revenue, profit, and productivity losses can be a direct result of system failures. Indirect effects of unavailable systems might include a loss of competitive position and damage to corporate image.

Routing Servers

One of the stated underlying business motivations for client/server information systems was the ability to deliver the right information to the right decision maker at the right place and time for the right cost. One of the dilemmas in achieving this lofty goal is finding a suitable way to deliver full information systems access to users or decision makers in remote branch offices and to mobile computing users in a cost-effective manner.

Although networks can certainly be designed and installed linking every location in an enterprise, one of the great on-going costs in such a network is the cost of training and supporting highly technical networking personnel to be stationed at every remote branch office and location. The fact is that deploying highly paid networking personnel in this manner is simply not cost-effective. As a result, applications servers are being developed that include integrated internetworking capabilities. Microsoft's effort to include routing capability with Windows NT is a project known as Steelhead, due to be released with NT 5.0. NetWare has included multiprotocol routing capabilities with its MPR program.

These hybrid networking/applications servers should be able to transparently link remote branch information systems with corporate headquarters operating systems while simultaneously supporting dial-in access from mobile-computing corporate personnel. Several applications server manufacturers are teaming with internetworking equipment vendors in this effort. A key to this server integration is the caveat that these additional networking duties must not degrade the overall server performance in executing application programs. Second, management of the networking aspects of these servers must be transparently integrated with enterprise network management programs executing at corporate headquarters or centralized network operations control centers.

When easily manageable hybrid servers combining networking and applications server capabilities are widely available and affordable, client/server information systems will have made significant progress toward achieving the overall goal of supplying the right information to the right decision maker at the right place and time for the right cost.

SUMMARY

In order to deliver on the applications rightsizing benefits of client/server information systems, it is essential for servers to be able to deliver high performance in a fault-tolerant, reliable manner if they are to be trusted with mission-critical applications formerly reserved for mainframe computers. High performance expectations require new, scalable system architectures employing parallel processing techniques such as symmetrical multiprocessing. More importantly, no single aspect or subsystem of the server can be allowed to overwhelm or act as a bottleneck for other subsystems. As a result, bus architectures, memory subsystems, CD-ROMs, and backup subsystems must all perform on a par with one another.

Servers must be reliable. In some cases this implies the need for redundant, hot-swappable components such as fans or power supplies.

Reliable electrical power should be ensured with a properly sized uninterruptable power supply.

Server data storage needs must also be met in a high-performance, reliable manner. RAID, redundant array of independent disks, allows a reliable, redundant storage subsystem to be linked to an applications server.

Servers have become more specialized as client/server information systems have matured. Two major subcategories of servers have developed: those which offer access to network-attached resources such as printers, and those which process back-end applications engines such as e-mail servers or database servers.

Server operating systems must complement server hardware architectures by maximizing the effective use of the symmetrical multiprocessing systems architectures in a secure, reliable fashion while integrating fully with applications programs.

KEY TERMS

4 mm DAT DDS 1
4 mm DAT DDS 2
8 mm
Asymmetric multiprocessing (AMP
   or ASMP)
Auto-server shutdown
C2 level security
Clustering
Continuous operations
Disk duplexing
Disk mirroring
Distributed parallel processing
DLT
Double speed
DPP
DVD
ECC memory
Extended data availability and
   protection (EDAP)
Fault tolerance
Hardware-based RAID
Hierarchical storage management
   (HSM)
High availability
Host-controller RAID

Line conditioner
Load balancing
Loosely coupled
Magneto Optical
Massively parallel processing
   (MPP)
Message-passing interface (MPI)
MIP
MPC level 1
MPC level 2
Multiprocessing specification 1.1
Multiprocessor server (MPS)
Near-line
Nonuniform memory access
   (NUMA)
Parallel processing
Parallel virtual machine (PVM)
PCI hot plug specifications
Photo CD
QIC
Quad speed
RAID
RAID Advisory Board (RAB)
RAID level 0

RAID level 1
RAID level 2
RAID level 3
RAID level 4
RAID level 5
RAID level 6
Rapid recovery
Redundant processor architecture
SCSI-to-SCSI RAID
Shared memory
Shared nothing
Single speed
Software-based RAID
Storage-independent data format
   (SIDF)
Storage management system (SMS)
Symmetric multiprocessing (SMP)
Tightly coupled
Triple speed
Uninterruptable power supply
   (UPS)
Virtual interface architecture (VIA)
Virtual parallel machines (VPM)
XA

REVIEW QUESTIONS

1. What are some of the business requirements underlying the importance of client/server information systems?
2. What are some of the server functionalities required to meet the demands of client/server information systems?
3. What are the two major categories of servers?
4. How do the two major categories of servers differ in terms of functionality and potential bottlenecks?
5. Why does a multiprocessor architecture alone not guarantee a high-performance server?
6. Differentiate between the two major subcategories of parallel processing.
7. What is load balancing, and how is it achieved?
8. What are some of the future directions of parallel computing?
9. Which is more efficient: loosely coupled or tightly coupled system architectures. Why?
10. Which bus architecture is preferred in servers, and why?
11. Why is ECC memory important in servers?

12. What is I_2O, and why is it significant?
13. What products must be I_2O compatible in order to support a full implementation?
14. What are the advantages of having a CD-ROM installed in a server?
15. What are some of the acceptable backup media for servers?
16. What are the compatibility issues associated with designing a backup solution for servers?
17. What are the two major functions of a UPS?
18. What are some of the more advanced communication-related features of UPSs?
19. What are the three major categories of expandability to be ensured in a computer, and why are they important?
20. What is the difference between disk mirroring and disk duplexing?
21. Which RAID levels are commercially viable in practical terms?
22. Differentiate between software-based and hardware-based RAID in terms of cost and performance.

23. Differentiate between host-controller RAID and SCSI-to-SCSI RAID in terms of performance and compatibility issues.
24. What are some of the important features to look for when purchasing a RAID subsystem? Why are they important?
25. What is EDAP, and what are the key differences between EDAP classification levels?
26. What is HSM?
27. How is HSM related to RAID, if at all?
28. What is the difference between HSM storage hierarchy levels and HSM functionality levels?
29. What are the major differences between the two major subcategories of server functionality?
30. What are the overall requirements of server software?
31. What are some of the key criteria by which server software can be evaluated? Why are they important?
32. What are some of the different license pricing schemes available today?
33. Why is the prospect of clustering operating systems for client/server architectures so exciting?
34. What are the major areas of security for server operating systems to support?
35. What is C2-level security?
36. What is the difference between C2-compliant and C2-certified?
37. Why is the ease and extent of applications integration important to server operating systems?
38. Why are fault-tolerant servers important to the increased adoption of client/server information systems?
39. What is the difference between fault tolerance and high availability?
40. How can a business justify investments in high-availability or fault-tolerant systems?
41. What are the significant architectural features of a fault-tolerant server?
42. Why are internetworking or routing features being integrated with applications server functionality?

ACTIVITIES

1. Find examples of as many different kinds of mission-critical applications as possible in real business situations. What do all mission-critical applications seem to have in common? How do they differ?
2. What types of computer platforms are the real-word mission-critical applications running on today? Describe any migration plans.
3. What are the requirements or criteria for migrating mission-critical applications from their present platform?
4. Gather product literature and prepare a presentation on SMP versus AMP platforms. Which are more common? More expensive? What types of applications and operating systems are run on each?
5. Investigate and prepare a presentation on some of the future parallel processing platforms such as MPP, VPM, and clustering.
6. Investigate and prepare a presentation on CD-ROM drives. What are the current important standards?
7. Investigate and prepare a presentation on CD-ROM recorders. What are the current important standards?
8. Investigate and prepare a presentation on backup solutions for servers. Pay careful attention to hardware/software compatibility issues.
9. Investigate and prepare a presentation on UPSs. What are the environmental issues, if any, regarding the batteries contained in the UPS? Is special handling or storage required?
10. Investigate available RAID technology, and report on RAID levels supported as well as any other significant technical differences.
11. Investigate the specific differences between the EDAP classification failure resistant, failure tolerant, and diaster tolerant. Perform a market analysis to determine the percentage of RAID technology that is RAB-listed in each EDAP category. Report on and explain your results.
12. Investigate and prepare a presentation about available HSM technology. Pay particular attention to cost, number of hierarchy levels supported, and HSM functionality level supported.
13. Investigate and prepare a presentation on multiprocessor operating systems. Pay particular attention to price, number of processors supported, and number and type of available applications programs. Compare UNIX-based products with non–UNIX-based products.
14. Compare multiprocessor operating systems in terms of their security features. Compare UNIX-based products with non–UNIX-based products.
15. Find examples of fault-tolerant servers. Examine

product literature to determine actual architectural features that deliver fault tolerance. Compare the prices of fault tolerant and "normal" servers.

16. Investigate high-availability solutions and products and compare them in terms of price and functionality to fault-tolerant solutions.

17. Investigate the extent to which I₂O is being supported in hardware and software products.

18. Compare clustering solutions available for NT and Novell servers with the price and capabilities of clustering solutions for Unix servers.

CHAPTER 4

CASE STUDY

RESELLER TEAM RESCUES AMBULANCE ASSOCIATION

Intranet-based Communications Solution

From its offices adjacent to Interstate 80 in Sacramento, Calif., the American Ambulance Association buzzes around the clock with member dispatches and incoming messages. The staff's nine PCs whisk off e-mail and faxes, and two stand-alone fax machines regularly churn out timely messages to as many as 800 members at a time. Voice mail, of course, is indispensable.

Until recently, however, the American Ambulance Association's (AAA's) fleet of technology still fell far short of the integrated communications it needed to effectively monitor pertinent federal and state regulatory and legislative changes for its 800 members.

"Each tool was great but didn't interrelate to any of the others and, in effect, created work rather than reduced it," says Mike Allen, managing partner at Sacramento-based A-K Associates, AAA's paid lobbyist for the last decade.

But in the emerging intranet technologies, Allen spotted a solution to integrating AAA's disparate communications technologies. The lobbyist also saw a new business

opportunity: a separate IT consulting company, Iris Corp., that could help his clients improve their communications infrastructures. In the process of following through on both, Allen uncovered an important object lesson for other resellers: Among the slick intranet technologies that abound, it's often the simple and straightforward ones that clients need most.

Professional membership associations have the unenviable task of motivating a far-flung membership. Their job is to scour regulations and proposed legislation for information that affects their industry and then circulate the pertinent information to members and, more important, inspire them to act on those issues, usually in the form of letters or telephone calls.

But aside from a few high-profile associations such as the American Medical Association and the American Bar Association, most member organizations are small, low-budget operations. In many cases, member alerts still snake their way through the U.S. Postal Service. The speediest communications happen in a flurry of faxing to members, but there's no telling whether individual members will actually see the faxes and act on them.

Allen is a long-time lobbyist who regularly works the halls of

the California state Legislature and Capitol Hill in Washington on his clients' behalf. Sitting in on the 1994 presentation of a BBS to another client, the California Ambulance Association, he immediately envisioned the kind of interconnectivity his clients craved: a secure, members-only system that offered e-mail where key issues could be posted along with ready-made letter templates for members' responses, discussion forums, a reference library, and online transactions such as registration and the ordering of reference materials.

Too many organizations approach communications from a technical point of view, Allen theorized. They diligently study the intricacies of processors, protocols, and packets. "My concept was much simpler: I wanted my clients to look at communications from an operational point of view, look at the basic problems, and then solve them."

It was around this idea that Allen—an early technical adopter himself—opened Iris in 1994. He began working with Botni Inc., a reseller in Sacramento, to develop the new online service. From the start, Allen dismissed the option of an interactive World Wide Web site for two reasons. First, the kind of E-mail functions, discussion forums, file downloads, news, and online ordering he envisioned is still hard to carry on the Web. What's more, a private online service is often easier to use than the often-thorny paths of the Internet—an important factor because many associations are, at best, tentative users of technology, says Allen.

"The Internet has too much information and is too hard to use, regardless of the browser you have," he says. "What's valuable to these organizations is having the information they need on a secure intranet so that they're not flailing around on the Internet."

The resulting system, dubbed Secure Integrated Real-time Information System (SIRIS), is built from off-the-shelf products. SIRIS runs under Microsoft Windows NT 3.51 on any Intel Corp. Pentium-powered PC.

The back-end database is MindWire NT Server 2.03 from Durand Communications Network Inc. The SIRIS development team chose MindWare for its basic, yet complete, set of features—chat, e-mail, online statistics, account information—and for its healthy add-on market. The proliferation of third-party products for everything from scheduling features to source-code tools makes MindWire highly customizable for clients, says Wendell Hubbell, who served on Botni's staff as a SIRIS developer and now consults to Iris.

What's more, MindWire allocates much of the system activity to the client PC—an important consideration, given that many professional membership associations may run desktop PCs with 486 processors and 14.4 Kbps modems. "Waiting for the server to download something every time they need it becomes frustrating at that speed," says Hubbell. Instead, after the initial download, MindWire automatically downloads only what's new to the client PC.

Dial-Up Configuration AAA disperses a wide range of information to members, including health-care guides and state and federal regulations. In late 1995, Allen coaxed longtime client AAA into serving as SIRIS' beta site and first customer.

AAA installed $12,000 in software on its existing hardware. For the rack-mounted server, it presses into service a plain-vanilla Pentium PC; an assortment of 486-based client PCs runs Windows 3.11. Although the SIRIS system can link to the Web, AAA is configured only for dial up. AAA staffers dial in over a T-1 line from Sprint Corp., but most members connect via 28.8 Kbps modems.

For AAA's online transactions, which include ordering text and video materials and registering for seminars, Botni developers used Catalogs Plus, an add-on from Durand. Now, instead of calling the AAA office to order hard copies of state regulations, for example, members make requests through the online ordering system.

The system was installed in July. David Nevins, AAA executive vice president, says that although it's too soon to quantify savings from the SIRIS system, the association is already reaping its benefits: Committee members recently completed their first online edit of a position paper.

From the reseller's point of view, SIRIS and intranet consulting have encountered several obstacles. Local telco support has proven shaky at times. Allen cites a long list of phone-line snags, including improper installation and leaky service boxes. In addition, Iris, which has sold SIRIS to six associations and is now selling it in the general business community, reports that the newness of intranet technology has at times posed the greatest challenge in working with intranet customers.

"The single biggest issue at times is getting the message to the client that they need to commit to using the system," says Allen. "We've taken out the hassle of the system, and we maintain the system and train them in it. Our biggest problem has been teaching people how to use it properly."

That reality check holds valuable lessons for other resellers. "If [clients] want to do leased lines, ISDN, and T-1s, that's all certainly possible," cautions Iris consultant Hubbell. "But for the most part, a direct dial on a 28.8 Kbps modem is as fast as you need because, in our experience, most associations aren't downloading a lot of graphics and videos.

"And no matter what you do," Hubbell adds, "you're at the mercy of the phone company."

Nevins says AAA is "still in the process of learning about the system. It's pretty advanced for us." The same could be said for most of the organization's members. A recent study by AAA indicated that 86 percent of the association's members have the PC technology to use SIRIS, but only 60 percent are expected to use it actively. For a while, at least, AAA's fax machines will continue to whir.

BUSINESS CASE STUDY QUESTIONS ···

Activities

1. Complete a top-down model for this case by gleaning facts from the case and placing them in the proper layer of the top-down model. After having completed the top-down model, analyze and detail those instances where requirements were clearly passed down from upper layers to lower layers of the model and where solutions to those requirements were passed up from lower layers to upper layers of the model.
2. Detail any questions about the case that may occur to you for which answers are not clearly stated in the article.

Business

1. What were the key business processes engaged in by this organization?
2. What was the business impact of the shortcomings of the existing system?
3. What was the new business opportunity that would also overcome the shortcomings of the present system?
4. What types of business processes required on-line transaction processing?
5. What are some of the perceived benefits of the new system?
6. What are some of the difficulties that have been encountered during and since the system implementation?

Application

1. What were the required functionality and characteristics of the application in order to meet business requirements?
2. How was the on-line transaction processing application built?

Data

1. What back-end database was chosen? Why?
2. What kinds of information does AAA disperse to its members?

Network

1. Why were the Internet and World Wide Web dismissed as potential network solutions?
2. Where does most of the processing take place?
3. How were remote sites typically networked to the central site?
4. Is this typical bandwidth sufficient? Why or why not?
5. How was the system designed to accommodate typical download speeds?

Technology

1. What was the technology employed before the upgrade?
2. What technologies were employed to build SIRIS?

CLIENT/SERVER APPLICATION DEVELOPMENT AND DEPLOYMENT

PART TWO

INTRODUCTION

Having gained a basic understanding of client/server architectures and the client and server hardware and software technologies that comprise those architectures, in Part 2 the reader will learn about the information systems and applications that are delivered by the client/server infrastructure. Client/server application development, deployment, communication, and integration are stressed.

Chapter 5, Client/Server Groupware, describes groupware functionality, provides the reader with an understanding of its importance, discusses each component technology of groupware in depth, and explains the current major players in the groupware industry.

In Chapter 6, Middleware, various categories of middleware will be introduced. In addition, the role of middleware in a client/server system will be explored as will middleware categorization and business-oriented selection techniques. As will be seen, middleware is the glue that binds the client and server portions of the applications together.

Chapter 7 is entitled Integration of Internet, Intranet, and Web-Based Technologies within Client/Server Information Systems. After a review of the potential advantages and disadvantages offered by the Internet, intranets, and extranets to business, the chapter will continue with a study of the use of the Internet, intranet, and extranets as a client/server platform. The chapter will stress how companies are integrating these three types of networks to become more productive and more responsive.

In Chapter 8, Client/Server Application Development and Integration, various categories of application development environments and methods of deploying the resulting applications throughout the network will be introduced. While many of the discussed development environments can be used to develop stand-alone applications, emphasis will be placed on the features required to develop and deploy client/server applications. Methods of integrating client/server applications with existing applications will also be covered.

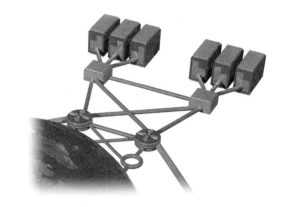

CHAPTER 5

CLIENT/SERVER GROUPWARE

Concepts Reinforced

Top-Down Model   Client/Server Technology Model

Concepts Introduced

Asynchronous Conferencing   Electronic Whiteboards
Calendaring and Scheduling   Groupware
Electronic Mail   Synchronous Conferencing
Electronic Meeting Systems   Workflow

OBJECTIVES

After mastering the material in this chapter you should understand the following:

1. Groupware functionality

2. The benefits and problems with using groupware

3. Electronic mail concepts, issues, and standards

4. Calendaring and scheduling concepts and trends

5. Workflow concepts, standards, technology, and trends

6. Real-time and non–real-time conferencing

7. Electronic meeting systems

8. How groupware and the Internet work together

9. Who the major players are in the groupware market

■ INTRODUCTION

Groupware is a collection of different electronic technologies that supports communication, coordination, and collaboration among two or more people. Groupware seeks to take advantage of the fact that workers are connected together electronically. As client/server architectures have evolved, groupware technologies have matured and expanded. Two of the most commonly used synonyms for groupware are *collaborative computing* and *work group computing*. This chapter describes groupware functionality, gives the reader an understanding of its importance, discusses each component technology of groupware in depth, and explains the current major players in the groupware industry.

■ WHAT IS GROUPWARE?

Groupware can be defined as technologies that allow people to work together electronically to become more productive and increase communication regardless of physical location or time. Groupware products are collaborative products that allow people to work together and share information in a variety of ways.

Managerial Perspective

ENSURING A SUCCESSFUL GROUPWARE IMPLEMENTATION

Groupware technologies have an impact on the way people work, so before a company evaluates and implements any type of groupware technologies, its analysts must ask users for their input. People do not like being told what to do or how to do it. In order to ensure a successful implementation, it is essential to get the users involved. It is important to help users understand the benefits that groupware technology can provide them. It is also important not only to get users' input but also to train them on how to use the new technology effectively so that they will use it and see the benefit firsthand.

There are five fundamental technologies that groupware builds on:

- Electronic mail

- Calendaring and scheduling

- Workflow

- Real-time and non–real-time conferencing

- Electronic meetings

No single groupware product incorporates all of these technologies, but products are becoming more advanced and are incorporating new technologies while improving the technologies already included. These are four main vendors and products in the groupware area:

- Lotus Notes and Domino Server

- Microsoft Exchange Server and NetMeeting

- Netscape Suite Spot and Communicator

- Novell Groupwise

Figure 5-1 shows what a typical application might look like.

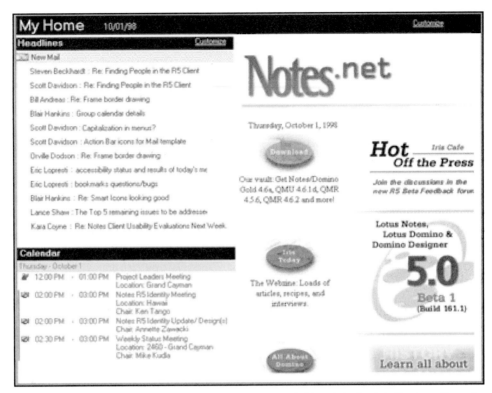

Figure 5-1   Screen Shot of Lotus Notes Calendar

What Are the Benefits of Using Groupware?

There are several benefits to implementing groupware technologies in a company. The benefits outlined in Figure 5-2 can be achieved if the top-down model, introduced in Chapter 1, has been followed to first identify the business objectives and what is to be accomplished with the new technology.

What Are the Problems with Using Groupware?

Along with the benefits of any new technology there are also some problems that can be encountered. Some of the potential problems are outlined in Figure 5-3. These should be remembered when selecting or implementing groupware technology.

Where Should Groupware Be Employed?

Industry analysts are predicting that the groupware market will become a multibillion dollar industry by the end of this century. This leads to two questions: Where should groupware be implemented? Who should implement groupware? The answer is generally the typical IT answer: It depends. Many companies have already

Benefit	Example/Explanation
Increase information access	• Employees can obtain timely information and increase their communication and collaboration efforts with others.
Eliminate redundant information	• By using groupware technology, a company can have one "container" of information.
Improve business processes	• Companies can improve their business processes and in doing so can enhance their customer service, improve communication, and reduce costs.
Automate routine processes	• This can increase productivity by allowing employees to work on other duties instead of doing routine processes over and over.
Improve decision making	• By having one "container" of information, people know where to get the information they need in order to make decisions. This can increase customer service and make a company more flexible and make it easier for them to response to changes and opportunities.
Increase organizational learning	• By allowing employees to have access to the latest company information along with historical data on the company, increased learning and cross-training will develop.

Figure 5-2   Benefits of Using Groupware

started pilot projects, and some have fully implemented groupware technologies in their companies. Some companies have decided to use Lotus Notes and Domino Server as their groupware choice. A few examples follow:

- NYNEX decided to implement Lotus Notes to bring the data warehouse to the desktop. According to Carl Fiore, managing director of NYNEX's Marketing Information Systems division, by providing access to the data, they were able to empower the marketing departments to make faster, better, and easier decisions.

- Another example is Wake Forest University. They have standardized on Notes and Domino and use an intranet to link students to a wealth of on-line information.

- Prudential Insurance Company upgraded its worldwide messaging infrastructure from IBM Mainframe-based PROFS to Notes.

Not all companies select Lotus Notes and Domino Server. For example:

- Nabisco selected Microsoft Exchange Server, and it is providing Nabisco with enterprise e-mail and the added benefits of integrated groupware, public folders, and centralized administration. With Microsoft Exchange's integrated groupware, Nabisco can support a collaborative approach to its sales

Potential Problem	Example/Explanation
Not enough properly trained people	• Since groupware is a relatively new technology, the number of properly trained people in the business community is limited.
Lack of upper management support	• Get support from top-level managers before implementing the groupware technology so that employees can see that managers are not only supporting the idea but also using the technology themselves.
No clear business objective	• Many companies fall into the trap of buying new technology but having no predetermined business need for it. Make sure to use the top-down model to ensure that the implemented technology meets the defined business objectives.
Confusion as to what groupware really is and what it really does	• This goes back to the problem of having very few educated business people who really understand how groupware technology works.
Lack of standards	• This can make a company have to rely on one vendor, and this doesn't sit well with many companies.
Lack of affordability	• Groupware is a client/server technology, and with any new client/server technology there are training and support costs involved, so many small and mid-size companies can't afford groupware.
Less human interaction	• Groupware technologies can lead to reduced human interaction and reduced socialization, which is an important aspect in business. Also, it is much easier to misinterpret electronic communication than it is to misinterpret face-to-face communication.
Resistance to change	• People get used to doing their job one way and don't like it when new technology is introduced that will change the way they work. Plan to reduce resistance to the new technology by having training sessions and discussion forums on how the new technology will be beneficial.

Figure 5-3 Potential Problems with Using Groupware

effort and bring its sales divisions and headquarters into closer contact with one another.

These are just a few examples of companies that have implemented some type of groupware technologies and achieved measurable benefits thanks to careful planning and a clear understanding of how the technology would support business processes.

TIPS FOR SUCCESS WITH GROUPWARE

These are some tips to follow to ensure success in implementing groupware:

1. Use the top-down model to organize requirements, and get top management involved.

2. Implement the groupware technology during a pilot program in one area or department, not the entire organization at once.

3. Get users involved so that they are more willing to accept the change. Remember, users are very resistant to change. Have open communication, and be prepared for resistance.

4. As stated in Chapter 1, realize there will be costs involved with training, maintenance, and support.

5. Results are not always seen immediately.

6. After the pilot program, get feedback from the users, and incorporate their feedback into the next implementation phase.

7. Make sure the groupware technology selected fits with your existing information systems architecture.

■ COMPONENTS OF GROUPWARE

As stated earlier in this chapter, there are five fundamental technologies that groupware builds on:

- Electronic mail

- Calendaring and scheduling

- Workflow

- Real-time and non–real-time conferencing

- Electronic meetings

This section of the chapter is going to look at each component and examine the concepts and functionality associated with that component, as well as the technologies and standards in each component, and finally end with a review of the current trends in that component area. Figure 5-4 illustrates a possible example of the technology that might be required to deliver the previously listed components of groupware.

Electronic Mail

Electronic mail (e-mail) is by far the most popular and most widely used component of groupware. When people hear the term groupware or collaborative computing, the majority of people immediately think of e-mail. It is the easiest of the components to learn how to use. This ease of use has led some people to feel hit with "information overload." The typical information technology worker receives between 20 and 50 e-mail messages per day. A person in upper management can ex-

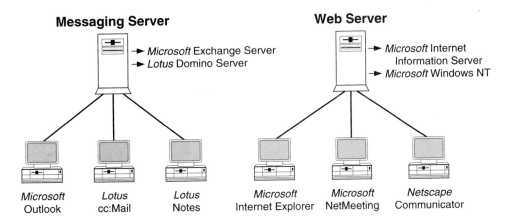

Figure 5-4   Components of Groupware

pect double or triple that number. How can one effectively handle that load and stay on top of the important information? Figure 5-5 provides tips on how to handle excessive e-mail messages.

Another way a company can stay on top of information is to use rules and filters on incoming e-mail messages. Rules and filters can be set up from either the client end or the server end. A company that receives a lot of "spam mail" may want to use some combination of rules and filters. **Spam mail**—unsolicited e-mail usually advertising products—is sent to many mailing lists and newsgroups as well as companies. There is still a lot to be accomplished in the area of setting up rules and filters, but they can be useful to sort out junk e-mail.

Tip	Example/Explanation
Prioritize Messages	• Read the messages from your boss or most important customers first, and read the other messages when time permits.
Delegate Messages	• Have an office assistant scan your mail for you.
Scan Messages	• Review the subject of the message to see if it's important.
Delete Messages	• Don't feel obligated to read every e-mail that is sent to you.
Distribution Lists	• Limit the number of list services that you join. Only join ones that are relevant to your work. Unsubscribe to ones that are no longer useful.
Consolidate Messages	• If you have several e-mail accounts, forward the messages to one account.
Time Management	• Set aside specific time each day to review and respond to your e-mail messages.
Relax	• Don't try to respond to every message as soon as it arrives. Respond when time permits.

Figure 5-5   Ways to Handle Excessive E-Mail Messages

There is an important difference between e-mail and messaging. **E-mail** is the "front-end" application or "client" application that allows users to create and send messages to various people. **Messaging** is the "back end" or "server" upon which e-mail operates. Messaging provides the infrastructure upon which e-mail can reside. E-mail is just one component that uses the messaging infrastructure. The other components of groupware also rely on the messaging infrastructure for delivery of their information.

Electronic Mail Functionality, Concepts, and Technology

E-Mail Environments   Before client/server architectures, e-mail was found mainly on the mainframe system. To get access to the systems, users logged in through a dumb terminal. As technologies have evolved, so have e-mail environments. There are four main e-mail environments in use today. The four environments are listed here along with examples of products that are used in that environment.

- Mainframe-based e-mail: Products include IBM PROFS, Digital ALL-IN-1, and Office Vision by IBM.

- On-line service–based e-mail: Providers include America Online, AT&T Mail, and MCIMail.

- LAN-based e-mail: Products include Microsoft Mail, Microsoft Outlook, and Lotus cc:Mail.

- Internet-based e-mail: An example of a product is Qualcomm Eudora. (This topic is covered in depth in Chapter 7.)

These environments can work independently or work together. The four environments are explored in more depth in the following sections of this chapter.

Mainframe-Based E-Mail   E-mail originated on the mainframe system. Companies are still using these systems for their e-mail needs. Companies are also using the mainframe system in conjunction with newer LAN-based systems. When companies do start making the transition from mainframe-based systems to LAN-based systems, a lot of them continue to use the mainframe for disk and backup services. E-mail gateways are required to link mainframe e-mail systems to LAN-based e-mail systems.

On-line Service–Based E-Mail   This may be a cost-effective choice for residential users or small to midsize companies that want e-mail capabilities but don't want to worry about the messaging infrastructure. The provider handles all of the company accounts, and all messages go through the service provider. There are some benefits to using an on-line service:

- Very little hardware costs other than buying a PC and modem

- E-mail client software, which is sometimes provided by the service provider

- Access to e-mail from remote locations

- Ability to provide other groupware services needed by the company

There are also some negative aspects of using an on-line service:

- Competition among providers: With so many providers, there may be some doubt that the one selected will still be in business in five years.

- Lack of access: This can result as the number of customers increases and the provider is unable to update its infrastructure fast enough to handle the increase. (Remember when America Online went to charging one flat monthly fee and its infrastructure wasn't ready for the customer demand?)

- Lack of control: Subscribing companies have no decision-making power regarding the design or policy of the system.

- Cost: Depending on how the provider charges, this alternative may be more expensive. Make sure to find out how the provider charges—per user, per message, per byte, per hour, etc.

LAN-Based E-Mail   This is the most popular e-mail environment today for businesses. Many companies have moved this way from the mainframe-based environment. The two main factors for moving to a LAN-based environment are the ease of use of the user interface and how much simpler and cost-effective administration is compared with a mainframe-based environment.

Internet-Based E-Mail   Many people are choosing this environment because of how popular the Internet is and how easy it is to use. This environment is used by individuals, companies, academic institutions, and governments as a messaging backbone or gateway to vendors, customers, and others. This environment is covered in more depth in Chapter 7.

The E-Mail Client   Separating the mail functions into client and server roles has allowed for the creation of e-mail clients that are totally independent of mail server engines on the back side. The e-mail client is the software users see and interact with. This software allows users to create, edit, send, and read e-mail messages. There are many different e-mail client front ends that users can use for creating their e-mail messages. Some popular e-mail packages today include cc:Mail from Lotus, Microsoft Mail from Microsoft, Outlook from Microsoft, and Eudora from Qualcomm. There are many other packages available to users. The user interface may vary from package to package, but there are basic features common to each package. Figure 5-6 describes some common features found in most e-mail packages today.

The success of an e-mail package today depends largely on the user interface and how easy it is for users to learn and understand. If users don't understand the user interface, they are less likely to continue to use e-mail. It is important for companies to have good training programs in place so their employees can use the technology to the fullest in order to increase their productivity. Another important reason to have good training programs is to teach users the new features of the latest versions of the software they commonly use.

The Messaging Server   The server is the messaging component of an e-mail system. It provides the infrastructure for delivering e-mail messages. There are three main responsibilities that need to be handled by the messaging server:

- Provide messaging services

- Store messages

- Provide directory services

Messaging Services   This software is responsible for receiving, sorting, and delivering e-mail from one computer to another. The typical user does not see or understand how all the messaging services work. The messaging services part of the

Feature	Example/Explanation
Graphical User Interface (GUI)	• Allows users to easily create, edit, send, and read messages.
Address Books	• Allows users to easily keep track of important contact information.
Reply Button	• Makes it easy for users to reply to messages they have received.
Forward Button	• Makes it easy for users to forward messages to other users.
Attachments	• Makes it easy for users to attach a file with the e-mail message. A user might want to send someone a word-processing or spreadsheet document for review along with the e-mail message.
Folders	• Allows users to easily keep track of their important messages by filing them into folders.
Pointers	• Makes it easy for users to include a World Wide Web address in their e-mail messages.

Figure 5-6 Common Features Found in E-Mail Packages

server also defines the connectivity possibilities and limitations of the overall e-mail system. Many of the necessary messaging services are accomplished through the use of application programming interfaces (APIs). All of the various e-mail APIs are described later in this chapter.

Storing Messages This is where the e-mail messages are stored. The messages are usually stored on the hard drive of the messaging server. Many people refer to the message store as the post office because it is where the users' mailboxes are located. A lot of manipulation occurs at the message store, such as saving messages, deleting messages, navigating through the message store, and searching and forwarding messages. When a message is sent to a post office and the user does not have a mailbox there, then the message is forwarded to the post office containing the user's mailbox. Needless to say, a lot of storing and forwarding occurs on the messaging server.

Directory Services The third major responsibility of the messaging server is to provide directory services. One function of directory services is to keep track of various address books. An address book contains information on recipients and is used to address e-mail messages. Users access the address book from within their client e-mail package. Information contained in an address book can include each recipient's name, business and home address, job title, phone numbers, and e-mail address. Other personal information may be captured in the address book. Users can create their own address books or look up recipients using the company's global directory. The global directory is a part of the overall messaging server and is usually saved in a database. This allows companies to map their other databases to their messaging directory in order to tie company information together. Figure 5-7 illustrates the key elements of e-mail architectures.

Electronic Mail Standards Before selecting e-mail software for a company to run on their clients and servers, spend some time researching and understanding the dif-

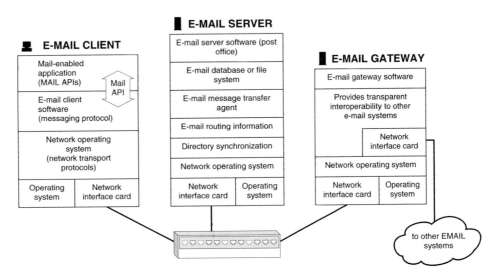

Figure 5-7   Key Elements and Variables of Enterprise E-Mail Architectures

ferent standards, protocols, and APIs involved. Standards cover a broad area and can be defined in different ways. Following are the most important standards related to messaging.

X.400   This standard was defined by the Consultative Committee for International Telephony and Telegraphy (CCITT). This standard was used mainly by large companies that have employees around the globe. The X.400 standard covers the exchange of electronic messages between computer systems. It includes information on all of the three main areas handled by the messaging server. The X.400 standard is losing ground to the increasingly popular SMTP/MIME standard.

X.500   This is also a CCITT standard. The X.500 standard is designed to provide directory information in a global setting. Many people feel as though the X.500 standard is too complex to use.

Lightweight Directory Access Protocol (LDAP)   This protocol is currently the favorite of directory access protocols. It can be used to consolidate personnel information profiles and management of applications, devices, and security. It provides for a single point of administration across multiple directory systems.

Simple Mail Transport Protocol (SMTP)   This messaging protocol is used in TCP/IP networks to exchange e-mail messages. In conjunction with TCP/IP, it is able to establish connections, provide reliable transport of messages, and terminate connections. This protocol will continue to gain support as the Internet and intranets continue to grow. It is used largely by universities, companies, and the government.

Multipurpose Internet Mail Extensions (MIME)   This standard is an extension of SMTP. MIME gives each attachment of an e-mail message its own header. The information included in the header is used to describe the type of information contained in the message and how the message was encoded. MIME is used for standardizing the exchange of files such as word-processing documents or graphics via Internet mail. MIME has helped lead to the increased use of SMTP.

Post Office Protocol (POP-3)   POP-3 is a client-side mail protocol that facilitates off-line operations. Messages are downloaded and manipulated on the client.

Internet Mail Access Protocol (IMAP)   IMAP's features selective downloading, server-side folder hierarchies, shared mail, and mailbox synchronization. IMAP does demand more from the server end than POP, but if the server has the capacity, IMAP can save a lot of work for the users and increase the speed of e-mail communications.

Messaging APIs   There are numerous mail client and server packages to choose from today. How can all of the various clients and servers communicate? The answer is the use of application programming interfaces (APIs). Using APIs makes it easier to mix and match multivendor mail clients and servers. In the messaging area there are three main APIs to choose from, as outlined here:

Common Mail Calls (CMC)   CMC is a cross-platform messaging API. This API was released by the X.400 API Association (XAPIA). This API provides a basic set of services, such as send, receive, and address lookups, through the 12 API calls it supports. This API was established as a result of the war between Microsoft and other vendors regarding messaging APIs. CMC left out advanced functions to promote wide acceptance from vendors. An example of an advanced messaging function not supported by CMC is the ability to attach documents to e-mail messages.

Messaging Application Programming Interface (MAPI)   This is the most popular of the messaging APIs. It was developed by Microsoft and is supported by almost every vendor. MAPI provides a way for applications to access different types of messaging systems. There are two versions of MAPI: simple and extended. Simple MAPI calls provide a way to access various e-mail functions and provide for simple mail, address book, and message-storing services. Extended MAPI provides many more calls and provides interfaces to many mail systems and their address books, message transport, and message store areas.

Vendor-Independent Messaging (VIM)   VIM is an API that is supported by Lotus, Borland, IBM, Apple, Oracle, MCI, Novell, and many other messaging vendors. VIM is a cross-platform interface that allows developers to create mail-enabled applications that work on various platforms. VIM supports address book services as well as message storing and includes services for creating, reading, and sending messages. VIM can link with other messaging APIs, including MAPI. Figure 5-8 illustrates the relationships among numerous e-mail messaging protocols and standards.

Electronic Mail Issues   As messaging technologies continue to grow and gain more popularity, some issues need to be addressed. This section will examine some of the issues and trends related to messaging.

Privacy and Security   Electronic mail is by far the most popular component of the groupware technologies. Millions of people use e-mail for personal and business correspondence. Many of the users of e-mail are concerned about the privacy and security of the messages they send. Once a mail message is sent, it travels through various transfer points, and someone with the proper access at a particular transfer point could read the message.

There are two main competing standards regarding e-mail security. Both of the standards are being proposed to the Internet Engineering Task Force (IETF) for adoption. The first standard is **Secure Multipurpose Internet Mail Extension**

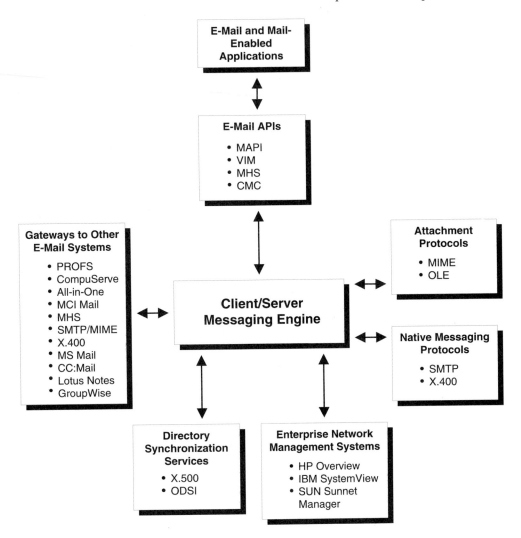

Figure 5-8   E-Mail Messaging Protocols

(S/MIME). S/MIME is a proposed standard for encrypting and digitally signing electronic mail messages. The second standard is PGP/MIME. The proposed standard is based on the **Pretty Good Privacy (PGP)** public key encryption software developed by Phil Zimmerman. PGP gained popularity as shareware on the Internet. Many e-mail vendors have agreed to support S/MIME in their products. If many vendors do support S/MIME in their products it will make S/MIME the number one choice. Companies who go with a different standard face being unable to send or receive secure e-mail. More information on each of these standards can be found in Chapter 13.

Bandwidth   According to recent surveys, the number one way documents are delivered is e-mail. As the number of people who use e-mail continues to grow, this could have an impact on the available network bandwidth and the amount of time it takes to deliver messages. A survey done by Inverse Network Technology from Santa Clara, California, found that the number of Internet e-mail messages delivered in less than five-minutes declined over a five-month period from 92 percent to

81 percent. What will happen to this number as more and more people use e-mail? The point is, it is very important for network analysts to consider the impact of an organization's messaging system on the overall bandwidth availability.

Universal Inbox   *Universal inbox* implies that users can get all of their e-mails, faxes, and voice messages in a single interface. From the universal inbox the users can read, respond to, file, and delete all of their messages. For the most part, the technology is available for users to have a universal inbox. The technology has been maturing over time but still supports only the most basic of features. Although all of this sounds great, we still have some maturing to do in this area. The current technologies need to support more advanced features, and interoperability standards need to be developed. Figure 5-9 illustrates a sample universal inbox. Note the accumulation of e-mail messages, voice mail, and faxes on a single interface.

Calendaring and Scheduling

Calendaring and scheduling make up the second most popular component of groupware technologies. Many organizations use group scheduling technologies to schedule their meetings. Group scheduling generally allows for people to easily schedule meetings with others, share calendars, and keep a task list of items to do. Many of the client scheduling packages today provide a graphical user interface that is easy to learn and understand. The servers take care of sharing data, keeping track of tasks, and setting meetings. Many software packages today combine both e-

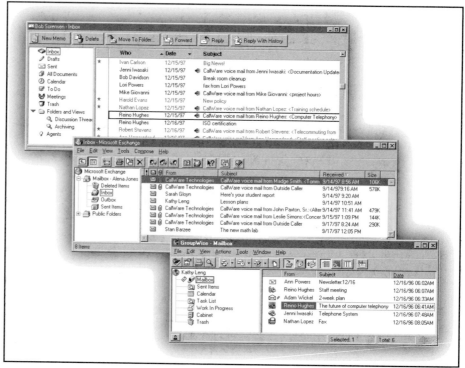

Screen shot reprinted with permission from CallWare Technologies, Inc.

Figure 5-9   Universal Inbox

mail and scheduling functionality into one comprehensive package. Scheduling software not only can schedule meetings but also can be used to allocate resources, such as meeting rooms and equipment. This section of the chapter will discuss the concepts and functionality of calendaring and scheduling and then will take a look at the available technologies and standards. It will then discuss some issues surrounding calendaring and scheduling.

Calendaring and Scheduling Functionality, Concepts, and Technology   **Calendaring** can be defined as the placement and manipulation of data onto a calendar. **Scheduling** can be defined as the communication and negotiation between calendars for the placement of calendar information. Companies are using calendaring and scheduling products because they provide a very cost-effective way of automating processes that people are familiar with and are easy for people to use. When a company first attempts to implement a calendaring and scheduling product, it needs to start with educating and informing the users. Many companies have failed at their first attempt to implement this technology because the users had a lot of fears and anxiety about the new technology. Users typically feel as though they will be bombarded with meeting requests since the technology makes it so easy to schedule meetings. Another common fear users have is that they will lose control of their personal calendar. As pointed out earlier in this chapter, one rule to follow to ensure success is to get the users involved and allow them to voice their concerns. Communicating with the users and training them to use the new technology will dramatically increase the success rate of the project.

Calendaring and scheduling is one of the easiest of the groupware components to cost justify since data can be easily collected on how long it took to coordinate and schedule a meeting without the use of technology and then collect data after the technology is implemented. One company that implemented a scheduling product found it reduced the amount of time needed to schedule a meeting from 20 minutes to 6 minutes. Multiply 14 minutes by the number of meetings held within a company, and you see that an enormous amount of time is saved.

Calendaring and scheduling products can be integrated into software packages that include e-mail and other functions, or they can be stand-alone products. There are tradeoffs with each type of package, so it is important to have the business objectives clearly outlined so the best decision is made regarding the selection of a product. Figure 5-10 shows the meeting planning functionality of a calendaring and scheduling product. Notice how the availability of all the intended meeting participants, meeting room, and required resources is displayed simultaneously.

Classification of Products   Calendaring and scheduling products can be classified into one of three areas: workgroup products, departmental products, and enterprise products. Each of the three product classification areas is discussed in more detail.

Workgroup Products   The products that fall into this area offer the user many features that may not be available in products in the other two areas. The products in this area act as a **personal information manager (PIM)** and are targeted at one person's productivity, not a department's or an enterprise's. They allow for a lot more than just calendaring and scheduling. Products in this area give users a rich amount of functionality and an easy-to-understand user interface. This is the main advantage to using a product from this area. However, if a product from this area is selected, it is at the expense of being able to easily work with others' calendars and other areas of information sharing. The advantages to using a product from this category are personal productivity and minimal administration. The disadvantages to

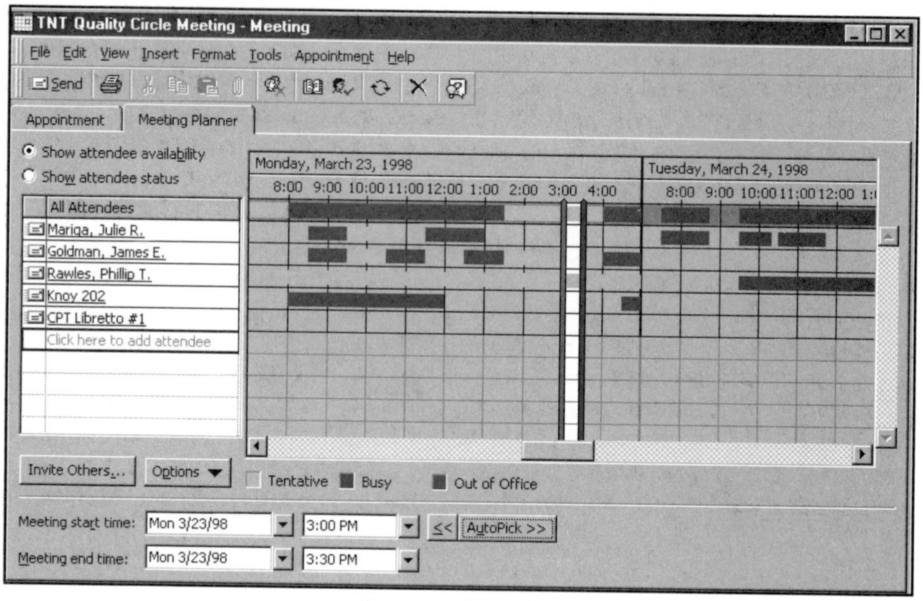

Screen shot reprinted with permission from Microsoft Corporation

Figure 5-10   Calendaring and Scheduling Using Microsoft Outlook

using a product from this category are the limited amount of information sharing it allows and the very little scalability it provides.

Some software-only example products that fall into this category are Lotus Organizer and Pencil Me In. Lotus Organizer integrates a calendar, to-do list, address book, call manager, planner, anniversary reminder, and notepad into a single product. Pencil Me In allows a user to schedule appointments, create action items, set reminders of upcoming events, attach notes to appointments and action items, and manage conflicts. A **personal digital assistant (PDA)** is an electronic device that looks like a palm-top computer. PDAs perform specific tasks such as electronic diary, memo taker, alarm clock, and calculator tasks. These devices are hardware/software combination technologies. Some examples are PalmPilot from 3COM, Newton from Apple, and Windows CE devices available from multiple vendors.

Departmental Products   Many of the products in this area are very popular and used by a variety of companies. When many of these products were first introduced, they were designed to be used by workgroups running LANs. Since these products have matured, many vendors have tried to make their products service larger user groups. The products in this area offer the user a good user interface and advanced functionality, and they can generally support about 500 users. Vendors in this area are starting to feel the squeeze from the workgroup and enterprise vendors.

Some examples of products that fall into this category are Microsoft Outlook by Microsoft Corporation and CaLANdar by Microsystems Software Incorporated. MS Outlook manages e-mail, calendars, tasks, contacts, documents, and to-do lists. Outlook also helps users share information through public folders, forms, and Internet connectivity. CaLANdar allows users to easily schedule meetings and assign tasks. It also supports e-mail integration and provides an IN/OUT pegboard.

Enterprise Products   The products in this area need to be able to support thousands of users and their information-sharing needs in real time. This area of calendaring and scheduling is the most complicated since it deals with the most users and the enterprise architecture. Products in this area do not offer as many features as are found in the workgroup category. Another obstacle in this category is the need for more systems administration. Many companies have mainframe-based calendaring systems because that is where the products began. Companies that do have mainframe-based calendaring systems have started to downsize their products onto company LANs.

Some products that fall into this category include Oracle InterOffice by Oracle Corporation and Calendar Manager by Russell Information Sciences. Oracle InterOffice allows for the following: database messaging, database document management, database workflow, calendaring and scheduling, and custom application development. Calendar Manager allows for scheduling of meetings and resources across local area networks, wide area networks, intranets, and the Internet. It also allows for reminders, automatic conflict resolution, and user-selected personal preferences.

Managerial Perspective

SELECTING A CALENDARING AND SCHEDULING PACKAGE

From which of the three areas of calendaring and scheduling should a company select its products? The answer depends on previously outlined business objectives and needs. The scope of the technology required will be directly proportional to the number and distribution of users whose schedules and calendars must be synchronized by the technology.

Calendaring and Scheduling Standards   The calendaring and scheduling ("calsch") working group of the Internet Engineering Task Force (IETF) is working on developing standards for calendaring and scheduling. The IETF calsch working group is working on three efforts: calendar exchange format, calendar interoperability protocols, and calendar access protocol.

Calendar Exchange Format   The objective of this standard is to define a standard representation for calendaring and scheduling information. This format will allow different calendaring applications to communicate and interchange basic meeting and to-do information. Some work has already been done in this area with vCard, vCalendar, and iCalendar. The vCard and vCalendar were put together by the Internet Mail Consortium and its partners. The vCard is an industry format for describing and displaying information typically found on a business card. The vCalendar is an industry standard format for describing and displaying information about a calendar or schedule. Lotus and Microsoft are codeveloping the iCalendar document, and it is currently in draft format in the IETF calsch working group.

Calendar Interoperability Protocols   These protocols are required so that different calendaring and scheduling products can communicate with one another. The interoperability protocols will allow communication over Internet e-mail and other transports such as hypertext transport protocol (HTTP). Once the protocols are defined by the IETF calsch working group, they will allow users with different calendaring products to send and reply to group meeting requests, search for free times on others' calendars, send and reply to to-do requests, schedule recurring meetings, and schedule meetings in different time zones.

Calendar Access Protocol The objective of this protocol is to allow users to mix and match different calendaring and scheduling clients and servers. An example would be for a cc:Mail client to access a calendar on a Microsoft Exchange Server. This protocol would really allow for companies to have true interoperability. Figure 5-11 illustrates the relationship between these various calendaring and scheduling standards efforts.

Calendaring and Scheduling Trends Companies will continue to integrate their calendaring and scheduling tools with their web tools to give employees an easy way to communicate, coordinate, and collaborate. By combining the two technologies, companies can integrate information access to facilitate information sharing. The calendar and scheduling working group of the Internet Engineering Task Force will continue working on developing calendaring and scheduling standards.

Workflow

Many companies in the early nineties had been through corporate downsizing. The companies still had the same amount of work to do, but with fewer people. Many companies took this as an opportunity to review how they conducted business. That is, they reviewed their business processes and some did some form of business process redesign. Many companies looked at ways to automate routine business processes by implementing technology capable of **workflow automation.**

Workflow Functionality and Concepts If a company is successful at redesigning and automating its business processes by using workflow technology, it can gain a competitive advantage on the competition. There are many more reasons companies are using workflow systems:

- They support ad hoc committee work.

- The cost of buying a package is low.

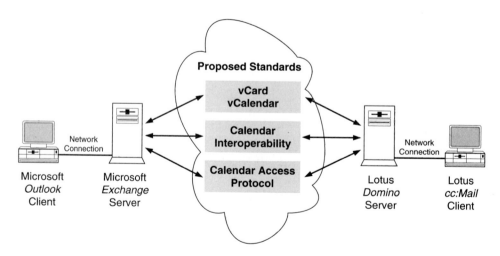

To ensure interoperability between different calendaring and scheduling products, some or all of these proposed standards need to be mutually supported.

Figure 5-11 Calendaring and Scheduling Standards

- The workflow application integrates well with other applications.

- They are easier to program now, with many of them supporting drag and drop functionality.

- They give users tools to track their work in progress.

So the question is, where do we start, or what business process do we look at first? The answer is never an easy one, but there are some guidelines. These guidelines are outlined in Figure 5-12. Implementing some form of workflow automation can decrease personnel costs and resource costs, increase morale among employees, increase the quality of work, and increase revenue for the company.

When looking at automating business processes, one must understand the different types of workflow. There are two main types of workflow. The first type can be considered **ad hoc** because it is generally short lived and is usually only a one-time process. The other type of workflow is **process oriented.** The processes in this area are easy to define and are well-understood business policies and procedures. They can be thought of as the mission-critical business processes. What are the important elements that must be considered when developing workflow applications? Four main elements will be contained in the workflow application.

Guideline	Example/Explanation
Start small by selecting a departmental business process.	• This can allow a company to automate a process on a small scale and learn from the initial implementation. An example might be automating a purchase order.
Select a mission-critical process.	• After automating a departmental process, look at mission-critical processes. Automating these areas can save a company a large amount of money as well as a lot of time.
Involve the users.	• Involving people and getting their input on how to automate the process enables a company to automate the right process. It also makes the users feel important and feel ownership. Don't automate a process that doesn't work.
Select a process that relates to the business goals.	• Understand the business goals and objectives, and try to find a way to automate these processes in order to make the company more profitable or more attractive to potential customers. It doesn't help to automate processes that don't benefit the company.
Educate users.	• Workflow automation changes the way people work, so it is important to educate people on how this can benefit them. People are very resistant to any type of change. Help people understand their new role.
Train users.	• Training is a must if people are going to change their work habits. Teach them how the application works.
Reward users.	• If users are rewarded for using the workflow application, they are more likely to continue using it and more willing to provide feedback.

Figure 5-12   Guidelines to Follow When Automating Business Processes

The first element is some type of **activity** or activities that need to be completed. **People** are the next element in an application, and they perform the activities that need to be accomplished. When people are performing the activities, they follow outlined business conditions or rules. Another important element in a workflow application is the set of **tools** used by the people to perform the activities. The final element of a workflow application is the **data** needed to accomplish the work.

Now that the elements that make up a workflow application are understood, what features do the applications need to include? The workflow software needs to create electronic versions of real-world activities. Because many activities occur in the business world, it is not easy to capture all of them electronically. Analysts should have some idea of the types of business processes that a company wants to automate so that when evaluating different tools, they know if the tool can support all the various situations, rules, and needs. One important item to consider when selecting a tool is how much customization will need to be done. The tool that is selected should support routing, rules, and roles.

Routing is the defined path in which an object travels. An object could be a document, form, message, and so on. Objects should be able to be routed sequentially, one after another or in parallel or in any form the user would need. Objects should also be able to be sent in broadcast mode. An example of broadcast mode is when one person sends out an e-mail message to many people and they all receive it at the same time. Figure 5-13 illustrates a typical example of how a routing workflow diagram can be set up.

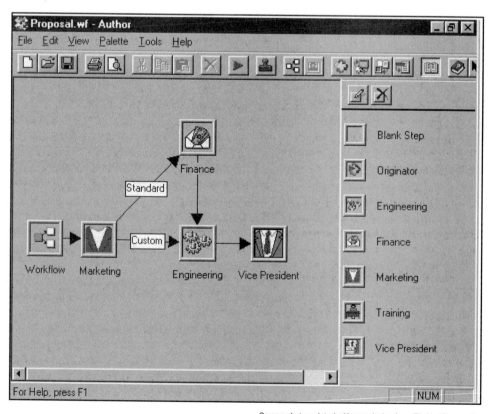

Screen shot reprinted with permission from FileNet Corporation

Figure 5-13   Routing Workflow

Rules can be established when routing objects so that a company can define what information to route and who should get the information. Rules are sometimes referred to as exception handling or conditional routing. Many of the workflow products available today allow for these types of rules. When creating rules for the workflow application, get input from both users and application developers. An example of a rule for a travel approval workflow system might be "If the travel is international, then send the request to the VP, and if the travel is domestic, send the request to the supervisor."

Finally, it is important also to define roles when developing workflow applications. A **role** defines the job functions independently of the people who do that job. This is good because people change jobs frequently, and job responsibilities change as well. By keeping these items independent, the roles can be kept in a role table and can be easily changed if someone's role changes.

WORKFLOW DESIGN

In Sharper Focus

How should a workflow be designed? There are numerous ways. The answer depends on what the workflow is trying to accomplish and depends on the business situation. Listed below are just some of the ways that a workflow can be designed:

- Serial Routing—one activity is completed before the next activity begins
- Parallel Routing—activities can split and be going simultaneously and then come back together into a single route
- Conditional Routing—activities occur based on certain conditions
- Broadcast Routing—the object gets routed to everyone at once
- Ad Hoc Routing—the user determines how the objects should be routed

Where is Workflow Being Implemented?   Workflow is being implemented primarily in four areas within companies today:

- Document management
- Forms processing
- Mail filtering
- Transaction applications

The industries using workflow technologies the most are insurance, banking, manufacturing, and government.

Document Management   Many standard document management products today allow for some type of workflow to occur. Document management products organize and manage electronic files for a company. The ability to use workflow within the document management products depends on the features that are supported within the particular product. Some document management products allow for simple word-processing files to be routed, and other products allow for more high-end, sophisticated routing.

Forms Processing   Most people are very comfortable with forms because there are all types of forms found within companies. In many applications today, the user fills in the form, and then the form is routed based on the information contained within it. Forms processing is one area within workflow that is very popular and can save a company a lot of money.

Mail Filtering   As mentioned earlier in the e-mail section of the chapter, companies are using mail-based rules and filtering as a way to deal with the amount of e-mail received and to deal with information overload. Most mail systems allow for sequential routing and event-based rules.

Transaction Applications   Many workflow applications today allow for transaction workflow. By storing the rules and information on the server, the applications can route transactions to various places based on the programmed rules. For example, when a transaction is posted to the database server, a rule might dictate that the inventory level be automatically checked after each purchase and that when the inventory level reaches a certain reorder point, a purchase order be automatically generated.

Workflow Standards and Technology

Standards   The Workflow Management Coalition (WfMC), established in August 1993, is a body of software vendors, consultants, and user organizations responsible for the development and promotion of workflow standards. Its membership is open to all parties interested or involved in the creation, analysis, or deployment of workflow management systems. The Coalition has proposed a framework for the establishment of workflow standards. This framework includes five categories of interoperability and communication standards that will allow multiple workflow products to coexist and interoperate within a user's environment. The Coalition has four main objectives:

- To develop standard terminology to describe workflow systems and their environment

- To enable interoperability between different workflow systems

- To help users understand workflow through the standard reference model

- To work with other related industry groups to set standards and communicate its work

The Coalition has established various working groups to meet these objectives, and each working group has a specific area of interest. The various working groups and their responsibilities are outlined in Figure 5-14. Figure 5-15 gives a visual representation of the proposed standards using the numbers in parentheses in Figure 5-14. At this time, there are no conformant implementations of the WfMC standards. However, a number of companies and vendors have demonstrated prototypes based on the evolving standards.

Workflow Technology   Workflow technology offerings from different vendors can fall into the following two main categories:

- Products that are created for a LAN

- Products that are created for the World Wide Web (WWW)

Working Group	Responsibilities
Reference Model	• Specify a framework for workflow systems, identifying their characteristics, functions, and interfaces.
Glossary	• Develop standard terminology for workflow.
Process Definition Tools Interface (Interface 1)	• Define a standard interface between the process definition tool and the workflow engines.
Workflow Client Application Interface (Interface 2)	• Define standards for the workflow engine to maintain work items that the workflow client presents to the user.
Invoked Application Interface (Interface 3)	• A standard interface allows the workflow engine to invoke a variety of applications.
Other Workflow Enactment Services Interface (Interface 4)	• Define a variety of interoperability models and the standards applicable to each.
Administration and Monitoring Tools Interface (Interface 5)	• Define monitoring and control functions.

Figure 5-14   Working Groups Established by the Workflow Management Coalition

Examples of workflow products and their vendors are as follows:

Workflow Product	**Vendor**	**Product Platform**
Visual WorkFlo	FileNET	LAN
FileNET Ensemble	FileNET	LAN
FlowMark	IBM	LAN
TeamWARE Flow	TeamWARE	LAN
InConcert	InConcert, Inc.	LAN
Staffware 97	Staffware	LAN
ActionWorks Metro	Action Technologies	LAN and WWW

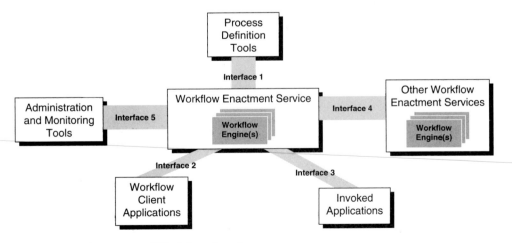

Figure 5-15   Overview of Workflow Interfaces

The key functional areas of workflow products are listed in Figure 5-16. Although it is doubtful that any single workflow product will possess all of these capabilities, those functionalities that are essential to a given business should be identified prior to beginning technology analysis.

**Applied
Problem
Solving**

WORKFLOW PRODUCTS TECHNOLOGY ANALYSIS

Functional Category	Importance/Implication
Authoring Capabilities	• Does it support ad hoc application development? • Does it support structured workflow processes? • Does the product support drag and drop capabilities? • Does it have validity checking built in? • Can a user assign priorities? • Does it support revisions and annotations? • Does it include any sample workflow templates? • Does it archive workflows? • Does it have any form templates? • Can you assign more than one person to a task? • Does it have version control built in? • Can you print workflows? • Can you stop or delete a workflow in progress?
Value-Added Features	• Does the workflow product interface to a document management system or imaging system? • Does it have a check in/out feature? • Does it index document files? • Does it support the use of libraries? • Does it support the ability to create electronic forms? • Does it track work in progress and provide updates? • What type of security does it provide? • What type of voting does it support?
Routing and Attachments	• Does it support sequential routing, conditional routing, and parallel routing? • Does it use recipients and roles for routing? • Does it provide any type of audit tracking? • Can you view the workflow map and response history? • Can you easily attach files and embed objects? • Can you easily create folders? • Does the product allow users to open, delete, or modify attachments?
Architecture	• What server platforms are supported? • What client platforms are supported? • What messaging clients and servers are supported? • What are the memory requirements? • What are the storage requirements? • What network protocols does it support? • Does it support a web browser?

Figure 5-16 Functional Categories of Workflow Systems

Workflow Trends   The Workflow Management Coalition will continue to develop standards. This will allow more interoperability among applications developed with different products. Developing more standards will also allow companies to mix and match different clients and servers with different workflow tools. Many software vendors are now expanding workflow capabilities in their software applications.

Real-Time and Non–Real-Time Conferencing

Client server conferencing can be divided into two main areas:

- Real-time conferencing
- Non–real-time conferencing

This section of the chapter discusses the various options available within each category, discusses the functionality and concepts of each option, reviews the important standards and technologies, and finally discusses trends within each area.

Real-Time and Non-Real Time Functionality and Concepts

Real-Time Conferencing   **Real-time conferencing** can be defined as people working together collaboratively using various technologies in real time. Real-time conferencing is also called **synchronous conferencing.** There are three main categories of real-time conferencing:

- Data conferencing using whiteboards and shared screens
- Group document editing
- Audio and video conferencing

These areas are explored in more depth here. With all of the different options available for conferencing, which one or ones should a company select? The answer is, it depends. Following the top-down model should make the selection of technology very easy.

Data Conferencing   Data conferencing can be very beneficial to companies. **Data conferencing** allows people to share data in real time and combines various collaborative technologies, such as electronic whiteboards and chatting, into one comprehensive product. It can provide a way for employees to communicate and collaborate in real time without a lot of expense. The main advantages to using data conferencing are it is very inexpensive, easy to install and maintain, and most of the time it is the appropriate choice for conferencing. Another advantage is it allows groups the ability to collaborate on documents, make changes, and have discussions all in real time. Many meetings are conducted where it is not necessary to hear or see everyone involved in the meeting. Most data-conferencing software includes a whiteboard and some chat capabilities. Some data-conferencing software products also include true application sharing. A whiteboard can be used to discuss a diagram or document. All the participants can write on the whiteboard and provide their input. Electronic whiteboards are discussed here in more depth. The chat rooms can be used to discuss what is on the whiteboard or can be used for separate discussions that not everyone at the meeting needs to be concerned with. Some available data conferencing software also includes support for audio conferencing. When evaluating different data conferencing software, make sure to know what business situations the software will be used for, and select the software that meets those needs.

Electronic Whiteboards   Whiteboards have been used during meetings for many years. By using an electronic whiteboard, meeting participants are able to share, edit, and save meeting notes. Electronic whiteboards have the capability to transmit the written image or words to remote locations. This is a nice benefit when meeting participants are geographically dispersed. Using software with the electronic whiteboard allows editing, copying, printing, and similar tasks. Electronic whiteboards provide users with a great deal of flexibility and choice in making presentations. An electronic whiteboard can be connected to a variety of sources such as, VCRs, CD-ROM drives, laser discs, or computers. If connected to a computer, the whiteboard could be used to project slide presentations created by the presenter. A nice benefit to using an electronic whiteboard during a meeting is that it can have multiple windows open and can contain information from a variety of sources. Electronic whiteboards can be set up as either point-to-point communication or multipoint communication. The advantage to using a multipoint system is that it allows various groups to gain control of the whiteboard. Electronic whiteboards can be an excellent addition to other collaborative technologies to enhance the overall communication and collaboration efforts. Figure 5-17 illustrates a possible use of electronic whiteboards.

Group Document Editing   Group document editing can be very useful for teams that are collaboratively developing documents. It can also be very useful for teams that are geographically dispersed by allowing them to develop, edit, and revise documents remotely. Group document editing can take place within a word-processing package. For example, in Microsoft Word 97, users can make comments and add revisions as they review a document electronically. If multiple people are making comments and revisions

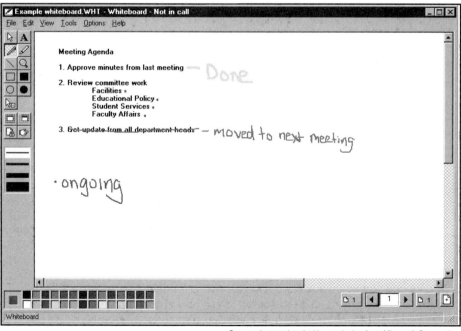

Screen shot reprinted with permission from Microsoft Corporation

Figure 5-17   Microsoft NetMeeting Electronic Whiteboard

to a document, each person's comments show up in a different color in order to make it easy to see who made what revision. When the document owner opens the reviewed document, he or she can easily see the comments made by the various people, and the owner has the option of accepting or rejecting changes. This can save a huge amount of time and effort since it is no longer required to route a hardcopy of the document from person to person. Figure 5-18 illustrates a document that has been group-edited.

Audio and Video Conferencing   Video and audio conferencing systems are becoming more common today thanks to the many advances made in both hardware and software areas. Industry research is predicting that the number of people using videoconferencing will be around 3.2 million by 2001. Many companies still are not using audio and video conferencing for three main reasons:

- Lack of education on how to use and integrate the technology into a company

- Cost

- Sluggish performance of these tools

These negative attributes will change as the technology involved in audio and video conferencing becomes easier to use and implement, less expensive, and better performing. Audio and video conferencing are not new technologies, but combining audio and video capabilities with computers and networks can now provide for a more practical and affordable alternative to group meetings and collaboration.

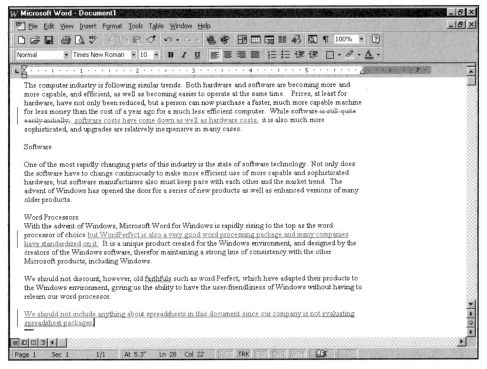

Screen shot reprinted with permission from Microsoft Corporation

Figure 5-18   Example of Group Document Editing

Benefit	Example/Explanation
Builds better relationships	• Using audio and video conferencing technologies allows people to see and hear one another. This can reduce confusion and frustration among employees. • It allows for people in remote areas to communicate more and establish stronger bonds and teamwork. • People feel much more connected when using audio and video conferencing over just data and telephone conferencing.
Reduces travel	• Meeting via audio and video conferencing can greatly reduce the amount of travel involved. This is a benefit to the employees who can accomplish more if they are traveling less, and can benefit a company by significantly reducing its travel expenses.
Increases productivity	• If employees travel less, they can accomplish and finish more work in less time.

Figure 5-19   Benefits to Using Audio and Video Conferencing

There are many benefits to using audio and video conferencing, as outlined in Figure 5-19. Figure 5-20 illustrates a typical network architecture setup for an audio/video conference, and Figure 5-21 illustrates what a multipoint audio/video conference might look like from a user's perspective.

Managerial Perspective

ISSUES IN REAL-TIME CONFERENCING

Several people and technology issues need to be addressed when a company is considering using some type of real-time conferencing. One major issue is the need to get input from various departments on what type of electronic collaboration is needed and potentially beneficial. Once the technology is selected and implemented, it is extremely important to train people on how to properly use the technology, to ensure that they will use it and see the benefit. As discussed earlier in the chapter, groupware changes the way people work. It is important to educate them on how the groupware technol-

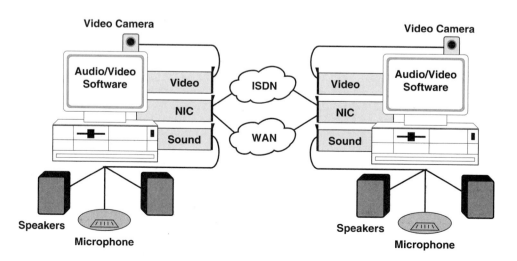

Figure 5-20   Typical Audio/Video Conference Setup

Figure 5-21   Example of a Multipoint Audio/Video Conference

ogy can benefit them and make their jobs easier. Some other issues should be considered when evaluating real-time conferencing tools:

- How does the technology selected allow users to control the whiteboard and chat rooms?

- How many people or groups can the technology support at one time?

- How many people can be involved in the conference for it to be effective?

- Will the selected technology fit into the overall information technology architecture?

- Does the selected technology allow for action items, goals, and meeting outcomes to be stored, communicated, and integrated with other software applications such as project management software?

Non–Real-Time Conferencing   **Non–real-time conferencing** can be defined as people working together collaboratively using various technologies but not in real time. Non–real-time conferencing is also called **asynchronous conferencing.** A benefit to using this type of software is the increase in a company's ability to share information. This is only a benefit if the information that is collected is valuable to others. There are two main categories of non–real-time conferencing:

- Electronic mail (e-mail)

- Bulletin board system (BBS)

Electronic Mail   Electronic mail (e-mail) is the most popular form of non–real-time conferencing. E-mail was thoroughly described earlier in the chapter.

Bulletin Board System   A bulletin board system (BBS) is a computer system that serves as an information center and message-passing center for users who have a connection to the system. The BBS can be accessed through a network connection or through a dial-up connection. Once users are connected to the system, they can read and post messages or upload or download files. A BBS provides an easy way for users who have common interests or work on the same projects to share information electronically. Users read and post information to the BBS when they have time. A BBS can be very beneficial to companies that have a lot of remotely located employees, because it allows users to exchange files and messages regardless of location. When evaluating BBS software, research who is going to use it and how it will be used. The following are some features to look for when considering different BBS software packages:

- How many users can be supported at one time?

- Can users have "real time" conversations?

- Can the BBS share information with other BBSs?

- What type of security does the product offer?

- How does it prevent unauthorized users from gaining access?

- How does it prevent unauthorized access to messages and files?

- What are the system administration requirements?

Real-Time and Non–Real-Time Standards and Technology

Conferencing Standards   The two main "umbrella" standards are T.120 and H.323. The T.120 standard contains a series of communication and application protocols and services that provide support for real-time communications. It was developed by the International Telecommunications Union (ITU) and is a family of open standards. Many key international vendors have committed to implementing T.120-based products and services. The T.120 standard is composed of many components, including T.121 through T.127. There are many benefits to using the T.120 standard, including multipoint data delivery, network and platform independence, network transparency, interoperability, reliable data delivery, multicast-enabled delivery, scalability, ability to coexist with other standards, and support for various topologies.

The H.323 standard provides a foundation for data, audio, and video communications across Internet Protocol (IP) networks. H.323 was recommended by the ITU and is very broad in scope. The standard addresses call control, multimedia management, and bandwidth management for point-to-point or multipoint conferences. The H.323 standard is part of a larger series of communications standards that addresses videoconferencing. The key benefits to H.323 are interoperability; application, platform, and network independence; multipoint support; bandwidth management; compression and depression of video and audio data; and internetwork conferencing. Figure 5-22 summarizes a variety of conferencing standards.

Conferencing Technology   Conferencing technologies from different vendors fall into two main categories:

- Products that are LAN based

- Products that are web based

Videoconferencing Standard	Purpose/Explanation
H.221	• Framing and synchronization specification, which standardizes the CODEC's handshaking and interface to WAN services such as ISDN used for videoconference transmission (CODEC [COder DEcoder] digitizes not only analog video signals but also analog voice signals)
H.230	• Multiplexing specification, which describes how audio and video information should be transmitted over the same digital WAN link
H.231	• Multipoint control unit (MCU) specification, which defines standards for a device to bridge three or more H.320-compliant CODECs together on a single multipoint videoconference
H.233	• Specification for encryption of video and audio information transmitted through H.320-compliant CODECs, also known as H.KEY
H.242	• Specification for call setup and tear-down for videoconference calls
H.261	• Also known as Px64, describes compression and depression algorithms used for videoconferencing. Also defines two screen formats: CIF (common intermediate format), 288 lines $\times$ 352 pixels/line, and QCIF (quarter common intermediate format), 144 **lines** $\times$ 176 pixels/line

Figure 5-22   Conferencing Standards

Examples of conferencing products and their vendors are as follows:

Product	Vendor	Product Platform
Microsoft NetMeeting	Microsoft	Web based
ProShare Conferencing Video System	Inte	LAN based
Concorde 4500	PictureTel	LAN based
CU-SeeMe	White Pine	LAN based

The key functional areas of conferencing products are listed in Figure 5-23.

Applied Problem Solving

CONFERENCING PRODUCTS FUNCTIONALITY ANALYSIS

Functional Category	Importance/Implication
Architecture	• What platforms are supported? • What operating systems are supported?
Standards	• What standards are supported? • What conference transmission protocols are supported? • What image formats are supported?

Figure 5-23   Functional Categories for Conferencing Products

Features	• Is there a shared whiteboard? • Does it support video conferencing? • Does it support audio conferencing? • Does it support application and file sharing? • Does it support chat/messaging/file transfer capabilities? • What type of interactive collaboration is supported?
Price	• How much does the software cost? • How many licenses are included, and what do additional licenses cost? • Are there distinctions between server licenses and client licenses?

Figure 5-23   Continued

Real-Time and Non–Real-Time Trends   As companies continue to look for ways to improve employee productivity and cut costs at the same time, many of them have implemented some form of real-time or non–real-time conferencing systems. Because use of the Internet is growing so rapidly, many companies are using or looking at using a category of software called web conferencing. **Web conferencing** software supports data, document, and audio and video conferencing over the World Wide Web. Web conferencing is quickly evolving to meet the needs of businesses. Many products that were first LAN based are now being moved to the web. Although many companies are taking advantage of IP networks and using it as their infrastructure for collaboration, this does not mean that LAN networks are being replaced. Companies are leveraging both infrastructures to get the functionality they need in order to support the collaborative efforts of their employees.

Electronic Meeting Systems

Electronic meetings are quite common in companies today. An **electronic meeting** is when people meet and exchange ideas and information by using technology that allows for the transmission of information. Why are companies using electronic meeting systems (EMSs)? Companies are looking for ways to make meetings more efficient and effective for their employees. They are also looking for ways to reduce the cost of meetings, especially the travel costs for people from different locations. A great deal can be saved in both time and money if a company can successfully implement an EMS. The following section of the chapter discusses what an electronic meeting system is and how it can benefit a company.

Electronic Meeting Systems Functionality and Concepts   An electronic meeting allows meeting participants to join at any time and from any location. The participants can be working from a desk or from a designated meeting room. The advantages to using an electronic meeting system are outlined in Figure 5-24, and the disadvantages to using an electronic meeting system are outlined in Figure 5-25. Perhaps more important to ensuring success with electronic meetings than the technology that is used is the meeting facilitator. Facilitators play a very important role in electronic meetings. Facilitators first need to understand the objectives and desired outcomes of the meeting. They need to research and gather information relevant to the meeting and prepare an agenda and schedule. They also have to decide who should participate in the meeting and ensure that the technology is in place and working correctly.

Advantage	Example/Explanation
Full participation	• Everyone can participate regardless of physical location. • By allowing everyone to participate, technology increases team morale, and people feel like sharing their ideas.
Time savings	• People at remote locations can participate without having to travel. • This can lead to increased productivity because employees can complete more work if their travel time is reduced or possibly eliminated all together.
Accurate information	• Participants are more willing to be honest when voting and discussing meeting items since they have anonymity. • Data is entered and viewed by everyone so there are fewer misunderstandings.
Better information sharing	• Group meetings tend to have more creative solutions. • People are more willing to share their ideas. • Groups can brainstorm ideas and share information much faster.
Better organization	• These meetings require planning, so the meetings generally stay focused and generate high-quality results. • Generally meetings are run by a trained facilitator.
Meeting output	• All agendas, action items, and discussions are recorded electronically and can be easily reviewed later.

Figure 5-24   Advantages to Using an Electronic Meeting System

During the meeting, the facilitator needs to keep people focused and on track, get everyone involved, resolve any conflicts that arise, and keep track of the meeting information. It is extremely important to train people to become effective facilitators of electronic meetings so that the electronic meetings are effective and successful. Adding technology to a poorly facilitated meeting will only succeed in producing a more technically advanced, poorly facilitated meeting.

Disadvantage	Example/Explanation
Participant resentment	• Participants may feel as though they were unable to contribute fully if the group made a decision that was not supported by everyone.
Unempowered participants	• If a person is used to dominating meetings, he or she cannot in an electronic meeting, because there is anonymity in these types of meetings. • People who like to argue and debate meeting items will not like these types of meetings. • Poor typists may feel left out because it takes them longer to share ideas and respond.
Information overload	• Because it is easy to save things when using an EMS, it can lead to information overload if a group saves everything from every meeting.

Figure 5-25   Disadvantages to Using an Electronic Meeting System

When should an EMS be used for meetings and when should an EMS not be used? Some guidelines follow:

When to use an EMS:

- When companies are trying to reduce travel costs
- When team members are geographically dispersed
- When teams need to share information, ideas, and brainstorm and it can be done in a distributed environment

When not to use an EMS:

- When the purpose of the meeting is for people to get to know one another and it is important for the "social" interactions
- When there is no defined meeting objective
- When it does not make business sense

Figure 5-26 illustrates a possible electronic meeting system scenario.

Electronic Meeting Systems Technology Examples of electronic meeting systems products and their vendors are as follows:

Product	Vendor
Facilitator.com	Facilitate.com, Inc.
GroupSystems	Ventanta

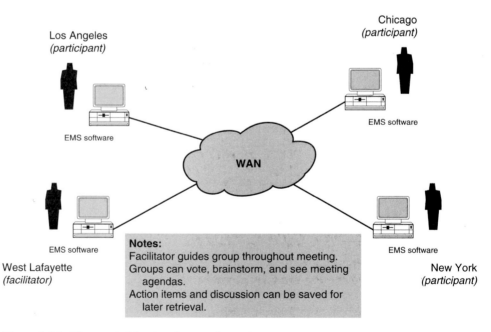

Figure 5-26 Electronic Meeting System Scenario

The key functional areas of electronic meeting system products are listed in Figure 5-27.

ELECTRONIC MEETING SYSTEM TECHNOLOGY ANALYSIS

Functional Category	Importance/Implication
Architecture	• What platforms are supported? • What operating systems are supported? • What are the memory requirements?
Standards	• What standards are supported? • What transmission protocols are supported?
Features	• What features does this product offer? • Does the product support the features your company needs? • Does it support brainstorming? • Does it support surveys? • Does it support action plans? • Does it allow for voting? • Are participants anonymous? • What type of data management does it have? • Does it allow for data to be imported and exported to other applications? • Does it have any type of facilitator training? • Can you attach files for information sharing? • Is it easy to use? • Can you run multiple meetings at one time? • What security features does it have?
Price	• How much does the software cost? • How many licenses are included, and what do additional licenses cost?

Figure 5-27   Functional Categories for Electronic Meeting Systems Products

Electronic Meeting Systems Trends   Companies will continue to adopt technologies that will allow them to have more efficient and effective meetings while reducing costs. An EMS can help companies reach this goal. An EMS can be used in conjunction with other groupware technologies to improve the overall productivity within a company. Just as with other groupware components, it is extremely important to teach users how and why this technology can benefit them. It is also a good idea to train a number of employees to become meeting facilitators so that when EMS technologies are implemented, trained facilitators can help ensure a smooth transition from regular meetings to electronic meetings.

■   THE GROUPWARE MARKET ANALYSIS

This section of the chapter provides an overview of the current major players in the groupware market and provides a technology analysis grid that will compare the products and features supported within each product.

Technology Analysis Grid

An individual working in the information technology industry must always seek out the latest information that the industry has to offer before making recommendations for purchases. An individual must be able to do this successfully in order to ensure a competitive advantage for the company as well as job security for himself or herself. The groupware technology analysis grid shown in Figure 5-28 is an example and a good place to start, but an individual should conduct more research to get the latest information available. The technology analysis grid is divided into the following major categories:

- Administration
- Collaboration
- Server Features
- Security
- Standards Supported
- Web

Groupware System Characteristic		Lotus Domino 5.0	Microsoft Exchange Server 5.5	Netscape SuiteSpot 3.0	Novell Groupwise 5.2
	Server Platforms	Windows NT; IBM OS/2; IBM AIX; HP-UX; NetWare; Solaris	Windows NT	Windows NT; IBM AIX; HP-UX; DEC UNIX; Solaris; SGI	Windows NT; IBM OS/2; NetWare
	Client Platforms	Windows 3x 95, NT; Macintosh; IBM OS/2, AIX; HP-UX; Solaris	Outlook: Windows 3x, 95, NT; Macintosh	Communicator: Windows, Macintosh, UNIX	Windows 3.1, 95, NT; Macintosh; UNIX
Administration	On-line backup	Yes	Yes	Yes	No
	Clustering	Clustering for web browsers	Requires MS cluster server	Third-party vendor	No
	Delegation of distribution lists administration	Yes	Yes	No	Yes
	Hosting of multiple organizations	Yes	Yes	Yes	No
	Network directory synchronization	Windows NT	Windows NT	Windows NT	NetWare NDS
	Real-time server monitoring	Yes	Yes	No	Yes
	One-step mailbox and network creation	Yes	Yes	No	Yes

Collaboration	Support for document libraries	Yes	Yes	No	Yes
	Shared contact list	Yes	Yes	No	Yes
	Forms designer	Yes	Yes	Yes	No
Server Features	Server-side rules	Yes	Yes	Yes	Yes
	Mailbox replication for remote access	Yes	Yes	No	Yes
	LDAP dynamic groups	No	No	Yes	No
	Full text indexing	Yes	Yes	Yes	Yes
	Deleted object recovery	No	Yes	No	No
Security	Digital signatures on e-mail	Yes	Yes	Yes	No
	Key recovery	No	Yes	No	No
	Role-based access control	Yes	Yes	No	Yes
	Interserver-encrypted channels	Yes	Yes	No	Yes
Standards Supported	X.500 hierarchical directory	Yes (X.509)	Yes	No	Yes
	NNTP	Yes	Yes	Yes	No
	LDAP	v3	v3	v2	v2
Web	HTML access to inbox or calendar	Yes	Yes	No	Yes
	HTLM access to custom forms	Yes	Yes	Yes	No

Figure 5-28   Groupware Technology Analysis Grid

Major Players

There are currently four main players in the groupware market:

- Lotus
- Microsoft
- Netscape
- Novell

According to industry research at the end of 1997, Lotus Notes had 15 million users, Novell Groupwise had 8 million, Microsoft Exchange Server had 7 million, and Netscape had 2 million.[1] Industry experts are predicting that by the year 2000, Lotus

---

[1]Stan Augarten, "1.5 Million New Groupware Seats a Month," *Group Computing,* January/February 1998, p. 4.

and Microsoft will have equal market share and that by the end of 1998, Netscape will pass Novell. These market statistics are graphically illustrated in Figure 5-29. The groupware market will continue to change for the next few years. Each of the groupware products is explored in more detail here.

Lotus Notes Lotus Notes is currently the leading client/server groupware product on the market. Lotus Notes is a solution that combines messaging, groupware, and the Internet. The foundation for Notes is the database. The database acts as a repository of information and contains collections of documents that can be viewed and organized in many different ways. Notes databases reside on servers, and users access the databases through the network. A nice feature about Notes is the fact that the databases are not relational. They allow for unstructured information so the user can control what type of information is contained within the database. Previously a proprietary product, Notes version 5 opens Notes up to the Internet. Notes version 5.0 includes the following:

- Browser user interface including forward and backward navigation
- Surfing history of pages
- Single click to launch items
- Enhanced search capabilities
- Push capabilities through Channel Definition Format
- Support of roaming usage model

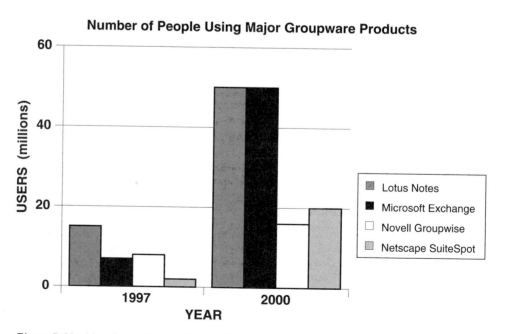

Figure 5-29 Number of People Using Major Groupware Products

Microsoft Exchange Server   Microsoft Exchange Server is a messaging platform. It provides server-based e-mail, fax, and voice integration. The latest version of Exchange Server 5.5 contains the following:

- Exchange 5.5 server
- Outlook 97 client
- MS Mail connector
- Internet Mail service
- cc:Mail connector
- Microsoft Exchange connector
- Connector to Lotus Notes
- Collaboration Data Objects
- Internet News Service
- Microsoft Visual InterDev
- Microsoft Exchange Chat Service

Exchange Server does a good job at providing a solid messaging, calendaring, and scheduling foundation. Exchange Server has public folders where employees can share messages with one another. If a person has access to the public folder, he or she can leave a message in the folder so that everyone can see it. Public folders provide an easy way for people to share ideas and messages. Another nice feature with Exchange Server is the fact that it allows a person to subscribe to a public folder and receive notifications when something has been posted to that particular public folder. If a company needs to do workflow automation, document management, or audio/video conferencing, it will have to buy additional products from Microsoft or choose a different groupware vendor.

Novell Groupwise   Novell Groupwise integrates e-mail, calendaring and scheduling, task management, shared folders, document management, and workflow capabilities into a single product. The latest version of Novell Groupwise is 5.2. This new version allows easy integration for threaded conferencing, remote access, and Internet access, all through the universal mail box. Novell Groupwise provides companies with a broad range of collaboration tools and supports Internet standards. Groupwise expands users' abilities to access different types of information. The following are some of the additional features found in Groupwise 5.2:

- Advanced messaging
- Pager integration
- Imaging
- Web Access
- Web Publisher
- Fax integration
- Intranet access

As described earlier, industry researchers are predicting that Netscape will surpass Novell in groupware market share. One reason is Novell's diminishing market share in the local area network operating system market. As mentioned earlier in this chapter, it is important to investigate the reputation and projected future financial wealth of a vendor before making a purchasing decision.

Netscape SuiteSpot   Netscape SuiteSpot offers a client/server solution for companies looking for ways to improve collaboration among their employees, customers, and suppliers. The current version of Netscape SuiteSpot is 3.5, which provides companies with a comprehensive platform for creating and managing the networked enterprise. Netscape SuiteSpot standard edition includes the following:

- Netscape Communicator standard edition—an open e-mail, groupware, editing, and browsing software

- Netscape Enterprise Server Pro—advanced publishing and information management services

- Netscape Messaging Server—an open messaging system architecture based on Internet standards

- Netscape Calendar Server—open standards-based server software for calendaring and scheduling

- Netscape Collabra Server—a discussion server that makes information sharing among teams easy

- Netscape Directory Server—the central repository for user and group information with SuiteSpot

Netscape SuiteSpot does have a professional edition, which comes with the preceding features plus the following:

- Netscape Communicator Professional Edition—additional features not found in the standard edition

- Netscape Mission Control Desktop—central management of client preferences and software distribution

- Netscape Compass Server—a feature that creates, manages, and updates an on-line catalog of documents and gives users a single point of access to business data

- Netscape Certificate Server—a feature enabling organizations to issue, sign, and manage public-key certificates using secure sockets layer for private communication over intranets and extranets

- Netscape Proxy Server—a feature that replicates and filters web content to improve performance and security, reduces network traffic, and provides a central point to ensure productive use of network resources

■ GROUPWARE TRENDS

Groupware products were first developed for the LAN environment. Many of these products were proprietary. Some of the groupware products that fall into this category are Lotus Notes, Microsoft Exchange Server, Novell Groupwise, and Netscape SuiteSpot. The growth of the Internet and intranets has led many of the vendors of proprietary products to start migrating their products to IP-based networks. As new versions of these products are released, they are starting to incorporate more and more of what the Internet has to offer. The LAN environment will not be replaced by web-based products, but using a common interface, the web browser, makes it easier for collaboration to occur both inside and outside of the company. Again, companies must remember not to merely focus on the technology. They also need to focus on people and their willingness to learn and accept the new technology. The next section will discuss how groupware and Internet technologies are coming together to provide a more flexible information technology architecture for companies.

Groupware and the Internet

The growth of the Internet and intranets has changed the way many companies do business. Companies are looking for ways to improve their information technology architectures and to continue to empower their employees. Companies are turning to groupware technologies, both LAN based and web based, to increase communication, collaboration, and coordination among employees. There are advantages to both architectures and at least for now, both architectures will coexist. The Internet needs groupware for security, interoperability, and strength. Groupware needs the Internet for scalability, openness, and ease of use. The differences between groupware technologies and Internet technologies is shown in Figure 5-30.

Managerial Perspective

GROUPWARE AND THE INTERNET

Which way should a company go? Groupware or Internet technologies? The answer is the typical information technology answer: It depends. If a company is looking for breadth of deployment, then the Internet is the choice. If a company is looking for depth in functionality, then groupware products win. A company should start by using the top-down model and figure out what all of its requirements are. The solutions should flow up the model. Many companies have not adopted a lot of web-based groupware products because the market is immature and the products

Technology	Feature
Groupware	• Robustness through replication and synchronization • Transaction failover, rollback, and tracking • Central object repository • Greater security • Integration with legacy software
Internet	• Universal client access through the browser • Greater scalability • Easier to use and easy to train users • Easier manageability • Open technologies • More application development tools available

Figure 5-30 Groupware Technologies and Internet Technologies

do not offer the same functionality as the LAN-based groupware products. This will change as the web-based products evolve and mature. Companies are also hesitating to implement web-based products because the technology is changing so quickly that it requires continual upgrading. A final reason that companies may be hesitating to implement web-based products is the fact that they want to choose their products from a vendor with a good, established reputation.

How are Internet protocols making their way into groupware products? Figure 5-31 below outlines how Internet protocols are currently being incorporated into groupware products.

Groupware versus Teamware

A new trend in the groupware area is called teamware. **Teamware** is a category of software that enables colleagues, especially geographically dispersed colleagues, to collaborate on projects. Typically, teamware uses the Internet and the World Wide Web to facilitate communication among the team members. The major difference between groupware and teamware is the fact that groupware is traditionally implemented in larger organizations that have the IS staff to help support and centrally manage the groupware applications. Groupware applications also provide for ongoing messaging and discussion tools. Teamware applications focus on short-term, small working groups that are working on a specific project. Teamware applications provide users with a self-service type atmosphere. Teamware applications are less expensive, are easier to use, require less IS support, require less setup time, and provide better performance. A company that looks at teamware applications needs to look at the basic features offered but should also consider how easy the product is to set up and use and see if the product can be customized. Following are some of the features to look for in a teamware product:

- Does it allow for voting?

- Does it have calendaring and scheduling capabilities?

- Does it have a customizable interface?

Internet Protocol	Use in groupware
SMTP, POP-2, IMAP4	High-performance messaging protocols
LDAP	Helps cross-directory lookup and referral
SSL and S/MIME	Allows for secure communications
X.509	Allows for user authentication
HTML	Provides the framework for application presentation
HTTP	A client/server application protocol
Java and ActiveX	Allows for client access universally
JavaScript and VBScript	Used for applications development

Figure 5-31   Internet Protocols Adopted by Groupware

- Does it allow for discussion?

- Does it support any type of real-time conferencing?

- Does it support e-mail?

- Does it provide for document management?

Examples of teamware products and their vendors are as follows:

Product	Vendor
Involv	Changepoint International Corporation
HotOffice Virtual Office Service	HotOffice Technologies Incorporated
AltaVista Forum 98	Digital Equipment Corporation
TeamWARE Office	Fujitsu Software Corporation
Lotus Instant!Teamroom	Lotus Development Corporation
InTandem	IntraACTIVE
WebTop Information Server	Kureo Technology
Netscape Virtual Office by Concentric	Concentric Network and Netscape Communications Corporation
Netopia Virtual Office	Netopia Incorporated
3-2-1 Intranet!	Internet Media Incorporated
eRoom	Instinctive Technology Incorporated

SUMMARY

As client/server architectures have evolved, groupware technologies have become a way for companies to increase communication, collaboration, and coordination among employees, customers, and suppliers.

There are five main components within groupware: electronic mail, calendaring and scheduling, workflow, real-time and non–real-time conferencing, and electronic meeting systems.

Electronic mail is the most common component of groupware. It is the easiest component for users to learn and understand. As e-mail has grown, companies have faced information overload. Also, companies are having to deal with employees' using e-mail for personal reasons.

Calendaring and scheduling has reduced the amount of time required to schedule meetings, thus saving companies time and money. Some calendaring and scheduling packages are also capable of scheduling resources in addition to people and meetings.

Workflow automation can save companies a tremendous amount of time and money. There is a lot involved when companies try to automate business processes. Back in the early 1990s, when companies went through corporate downsizing, many companies used that as an opportunity to do some type of business process reengineering (BPR). Many companies failed at BPR for a number of reasons, but mainly because people don't like to be told what to do or how to do it. When companies look at workflow automation, it is important that they communicate to employees exactly what is going on and how it will benefit them.

Another important area of groupware is conferencing both in real time and in non–real time. The benefits of this type of conferencing can have a huge impact both for the company and for the employee. An area that ties closely to conferencing is electronic meeting systems. Companies are starting to look at alternative ways of conducting both conferences and meetings.

One word of caution when dealing with groupware technologies: They can reduce the amount of face-to-face interaction that occurs within the workplace. The social interaction that occurs within companies is very valuable for building good employee relations and morale. Companies need to be aware that this can happen.

A thorough understanding of the components of the groupware market is essential for information systems analysts and network analysts if they are to perform effective business-oriented systems analysis and design.

KEY TERMS

Activity
Ad hoc workflow
Audio conferencing
Asynchronous conferencing
Bulletin board system
Calendar access protocol
Calendar exchange format
Calendaring
Calendar interoperability protocols
Common mail calls
Data conferencing
Directory services
Document management
Electronic mail
Electronic meeting
Electronic whiteboards
E-mail
Forms processing

Group document editing
Groupware
IMAP
LDAP
Mail filtering
Messaging
Messaging application program-
    ming interface
Messaging services
MIME
Non–real-time conferencing
PDA
PGP
PIM
POP-3
Process-oriented workflow
Real-time conferencing
Role

Routing
Rules
Scheduling
S/MIME
SMTP
Spam mail
Storing messages
Synchronous conferencing
Tools
Transaction applications
Universal inbox
Vendor-independent messaging
    (VIM)
Video conferencing
Web conferencing
Workflow automation
X.400
X.500

REVIEW QUESTIONS

1. What is groupware?
2. What are the major components of groupware?
3. What are the benefits of using groupware?
4. What are some problems companies encounter when using groupware?

5. Why is groupware important?
6. Where should groupware be deployed?
7. What are some tips to follow to ensure success with groupware implementation?
8. What is electronic mail?

9. How are companies dealing with the information overload that has been created with the increased use of e-mail?
10. What are some tips companies can follow to reduce information overload?
11. Distinguish between e-mail on the front end and messaging on the back end.
12. What are the four main e-mail environments in use today?
13. Distinguish between the four main e-mail environments.
14. What are some benefits to using an on-line service provider for e-mail?
15. What are some negatives to using an on-line service provider for e-mail?
16. What are some common features found in many e-mail packages?
17. What are the three main duties of the messaging server?
18. Distinguish between message services, storing messages, and directory services.
19. Distinguish between X.400 and X.500.
20. Distinguish between SMTP, POP, and IMAP.
21. What are the three main messaging APIs?
22. What are some e-mail issues that need to be addressed?
23. What is calendaring?
24. What is scheduling?
25. What are the three product classification areas regarding calendaring and scheduling?
26. What is the calendar exchange format?
27. What is the calendar interoperability protocol?
28. What are some calendaring and scheduling trends?
29. What is workflow?
30. What are some guidelines to follow when automating business processes?
31. Distinguish between ad hoc and process workflow.

32. What are the four main elements that are contained in a workflow application?
33. Where is workflow being implemented?
34. Distinguish between document management and forms processing.
35. Distinguish between mail filtering and transaction applications.
36. What are the four main objectives of the workflow management coalition?
37. What are the working groups within the workflow management coalition?
38. What are some workflow products?
39. What are the key functional areas of workflow products?
40. What is real-time conferencing?
41. What are some examples of real-time conferencing?
42. What is non–real-time conferencing?
43. What is data conferencing?
44. What is an electronic whiteboard?
45. What is group document editing?
46. What is audio conferencing?
47. What is video conferencing?
48. What are the benefits to using audio and video conferencing?
49. What is a bulletin board system?
50. What are some conferencing products?
51. What are the key functional areas of conferencing?
52. What is an electronic meeting system?
53. When should a company use an electronic meeting system?
54. When should a company not use electronic meeting systems?
55. What are some advantages to using an electronic meeting system?
56. What are some disadvantages to using an electronic meeting system?
57. What are some groupware trends?
58. Who are the current major vendors in the groupware market?

ACTIVITIES

1. Research and prepare a presentation on Lotus Notes. What are the advantages to using Notes? What are some disadvantages?
2. Research and prepare a presentation on Microsoft Exchange Server. What are the advantages to using Exchange Server? What are the disadvantages to using it?
3. Research and find where businesses have implemented groupware technologies. Were they successful? Why or why not?
4. Research web-based workflow products, and prepare a report comparing the leading products and their features.
5. Research the latest trends in the groupware market.

6. Collect advertisements and promotional literature on e-mail software packages. Prepare a comparison chart showing the differences between the packages.
7. Research and find any new standards regarding calendaring and scheduling. Prepare a report showing how they will affect calendaring and scheduling products.
8. Research what policies companies have adopted regarding the use of e-mail for personal messages.
9. Research calendaring and scheduling products, and determine which product has the most market share and the best features. Compare prices.
10. Research and report the progress that the workflow management coalition has made.
11. Research desktop videoconferencing software packages, and compare the features and price.
12. Research electronic meeting systems. Prepare a report that compares the functionality, cost, and performance of the products.

CHAPTER 5

CASE STUDY

COLLABORATION MAY BRING HEADACHES TO IS MANAGERS

The Effort Behind Going Global

Looking around his company, Jose Zegarra saw a scattered jigsaw puzzle. At the Mexico City office of ICA Fluor Daniel Corp., an international engineering, procurement, and construction company, Zegarra, an IS manager, examined the pieces: worldwide offices and projects, team members in various time zones, a client here and a task force there. Such is the global workplace.

Like other network managers in international companies, Zegarra wanted to find ways for employees working on the same projects from numerous locations to communicate quickly, efficiently, and cheaply. So he created an intranet based on Netscape Communications Corp. Communicator and SuiteSpot Server and an environment called PROSPERO. The latter is an application that lets project members in different geographical areas transfer files, view engineering drawings simultaneously, highlight vendor data, publish documents throughout the team, and share work in other ways.

"Global data connections let our company hand off projects from office to office around the world, liter-

ally following the sun," Zegarra says. "Although we have interchanged files among offices using our private networks for years, for the first time we have been able to structure a common environment for sharing all sorts of documents and letting each office keep it operating platform intact."

As corporations range worldwide and technology raises businesses' expectations, electronic collaboration promises to go global as well.

In another instance, General Electric Co. is rolling out Microsoft Exchange and Office 97 to 100,000 GE employees worldwide. And ServiceNet, a joint venture between Andersen Consulting and BBN Corp., has launched a program called Managed Collaboration Services, designed to offer businesses an outside option for international collaboration based on Lotus Notes.

"We're at a point now where the technology is primed and ready to be leveraged," says Tom Bailey, service offering manager for Managed Collaboration Services in Herndon, Va.

But despite the apparent interest in international collaboration and the purported importance of doing business on the corporate intranet, not many companies have rolled out large-scale solutions.

According to Jon Johnston, a partner in Creative Business Solutions, a groupware consultancy based in Minneapolis, businesses have only begun looking into global collaboration.

"They're struggling with a lot of [issues]," says Johnston. "The vast majority of companies are nowhere."

Increased interoperability, better encryption and security, and more accepting attitudes in business decision-makers and managers lead the changes necessary before global collaboration catches on, says Johnston.

The problems with security do not necessarily lie in the implementation, but with companies understanding how it works, Johnston says. For example, a company needs to decide how it will scan E-mail and documents downloaded from the World Wide Web for viruses. Then it has to determine who will monitor the management tools that manage the infrastructure, and who will watch the watchers to make sure the security is really secure, Johnston says.

Infrastructure considerations are enough to daunt many businesses considering how to collaborate among their offices. If components of a global groupware system are incompatible with one another, assuring compatibility and smooth functioning can be a complex process, says ServiceNet's Bailey. Once a system is in place, if a business wants to maximize the benefits of collaboration, the system has to be consistently available and stable.

When ICA Fluor built its PROSPERO system, the goal was to use the company's existing operating environment and purchase a minimum of new equipment, Zegarra says. He also wanted to go easy on end users.

"We knew that training the users would not be a problem if we had a browser and a familiar interface to their project activities. Because there are cultural and work-process differences among offices in different countries, we had to decide how to evolve the interface to each office. We even included a double interface, switchable by the click of a mouse, that translates all the buttons and icons in the interface," Zegarra says.

Johnston of CBS says that although the technology exists for companies to initiate global collaboration, the many details of implementing it are hard to digest, and the risk of wasting money, time, and energy may seem too great. He advises companies to start with something simple.

The global collaboration system has worked well for ICA Fluor, saving time and money. Zegarra says that there are plans to make it more extensive, and eventually to add an extranet to do business with partners and customers.

Nevertheless, businesses that want to establish global links will have to look closely at their existing technology, the way they operate, and their goals for global collaboration long before they see its rewards.

Source: Susan L. Thomas, "Collaboration may bring headaches to IS Managers," *LAN Times*, vol. 14, no. 25 (December 8, 1997). Copyright December 8, 1997, The McGraw-Hill Companies, Inc.

BUSINESS CASE STUDY QUESTIONS

Activities

1. Complete a top-down model for this case by gleaning facts from the case and placing them in the proper layer of the top-down model. After having completed the top-down model, analyze and detail those instances where requirements were clearly passed down from upper layers to lower layers of the model and where solutions to those requirements were passed up from lower layers to upper layers of the model.
2. Detail any questions about the case that may occur to you for which answers are not clearly stated in the article.

Business

1. What was the strategy of ICA Fluor Daniel Corporation to improve collaboration?
2. What business reasons led ICA Fluor Daniel to start looking at Netscape Communicator and SuiteSpot Server?
3. Did the implemented technology meet the business objectives that were set forth?
4. What needs to change in the business in order for global collaboration to catch on?
5. What are the key elements a business should look at before establishing a global collaborative environment?

Application

1. Why did ICA Fluor Daniel look at collaborative technologies?
2. What were some of the items the company needed to consider since it was going to be collaborating globally?

Data

1. How is ICA Fluor Daniel Corporation collecting and storing data so employees around the world can retrieve the information they need?

Network

1. What network operating system and communications protocols are being employed?
2. What types of network services are needed in order to deliver the collaboration worldwide?

Technology

1. What technology has been employed to implement ICA Fluor Daniel Corporation's collaboration efforts?
2. What are some other examples of companies implementing collaborative technologies to increase collaboration among their employees?

CHAPTER 6

MIDDLEWARE

Concepts Reinforced

Middleware	Synchronous Communication
Asynchronous Communication	Two-Tier Client/Server Architecture
n-Tier Client/Server Architecture	Application Programming Interfaces

Concepts Introduced

Structured Query Language	ODBC
Universal Data Access	Remote Procedure Calls
Transaction Processing	Message Passing
Message Queuing	DCOM
CORBA	

OBJECTIVES

After mastering the material in this chapter, you should understand the following:

1. The role of middleware in a client/server system

2. Middleware categorization techniques

3. Middleware selection techniques

4. Business requirements for middleware selection

■ INTRODUCTION

Middleware can be considered the "/" in client/server computing: the glue that binds the clients and the servers together into a cohesive system. Middleware is an enabling software layer that provides a transparent means of accessing information between clients and servers. Residing between the business application and the network transport layer on both client and server systems, middleware insulates the business application from the intricacies of the various operating environments upon which the application is running.

In this chapter various categories of middleware will be introduced. Although a fairly detailed technical description of each is presented, the main factor in a middleware decision must be the business implications of each potential solution. Regardless of the perceived technical superiority of a solution, if it does not allow the installed clients and servers to communicate, it is of no value.

◼ THE NEED FOR MIDDLEWARE

To gain a better understanding of the need for middleware, consider the major differentiating factor between client/server applications and traditional applications: In a client/server system, processing takes place on two or more computers connected by some form of communication link rather than on a single computer as in a traditional application. Therefore, both the client and server portions of the distributed application must be able to "talk" to one another over the communication link between them.

Without middleware, both client and server applications would have to be programmed to access the platform-specific communication protocol stack directly. Although it is certainly possible to develop client/server systems in this manner, it adds considerable complexity for the application programmer, who probably does not have significant communication programming experience. This approach requires every client and server application to contain routines to facilitate communication, directly tying the application to the lower-level communication protocols. If a lower-level protocol is changed, the application must be rewritten.

This approach also directly ties a client application to a specific server application. Each client application is written to access a specific server application. If a change is made on either end, a corresponding change may be required at the other end. This direct tie eliminates one of the key advantages of client/server systems: the ability to develop modular systems.

What is needed is a new layer of software that interfaces with the lower-layer communication protocol stack, formats data for transmission between the client and server applications, and provides a standard interface for the application programmer to access. Software that provides these services is known as **middleware.**

◼ MIDDLEWARE ARCHITECTURE

The combined functionality of client and server middleware is to provide a transparent means for the client application to access the services of the server application. In this case, middleware can be thought of as a translator between the language of the client application and that of the server application.

Logical Architecture

Regardless of application or type, all middleware implementations share a common architecture. Aptly named, middleware resides on both clients and servers in the middle of the application stack: between the network operating system and the business application. As shown in Figure 6-1, middleware has a direct interface to

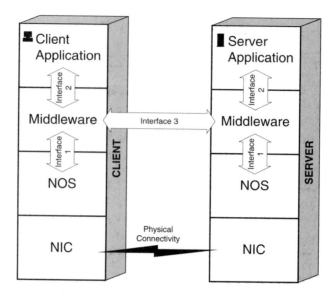

Figure 6-1 Logical Middleware Architecture

the underlying network operating system and the user application and a logical interface to other middleware via the network operating system's communication subsystem.

The interfaces to the network operating system and the application program represent **vertical integration.** Vertical integration refers to integration of components within a single computer. The interface to the network operating system, labeled *Interface 1* in the diagram, is the simplest interface in the middleware architecture. From the perspective of the middleware consumer, *Interface 1* is a binary selection: a middleware solution either will run on a particular network operating system or will not. All subsequent discussion will assume middleware to NOS compatibility.

The other vertical integration interface, labeled *Interface 2* in Figure 6-1, represents integration with the business application. For servers, this interface provides a means for the middleware to communicate with the applications that maintain and serve resources to the clients. For clients, this interface represents the interface used by client applications to access resources on the remote servers.

The interface between middleware and the application is an **Application Programming Interface (API).** An API is a published specification that details the interface to a software component. Through use of the API, an application programmer can write software compatible with the software component in question. The API used between two software components is determined by whichever component is completed first. In the case of client/server computing, server software is usually written before client software. Therefore, the server-side middleware usually is written to conform to the API presented by the existing server application. Client-side middleware is then written to provide an API to the client application developer that provides access to the functionality of the server via the server middleware.

The final interface in a middleware solution, labeled *Interface 3* in Figure 6-1, is a logical interface between the client and server middleware. This is labeled a logical interface because the two software components do not directly communicate with one another. All communication physically takes place on the network interface within their respective network operating systems as accessed by the middleware through Interface 1.

Interface 3 provides **horizontal integration** between the middleware components. The capabilities of the completed client/server solution will depend heavily on the functionality of this interface. Particularly important is the relationship between the API the middleware solution presents to the application developer (*Interface 2*) and the logical communication interface (*Interface 3.*) The functionality represented in *Interface 2* is limited to the capabilities of *Interface 3*.

INTERFACES AS MIDDLEWARE SELECTION CRITERIA

Managerial Perspective

Selection of a middleware solution will depend largely on the standards to which the three interfaces adhere. A middleware solution must be compatible with the target environment for all three interfaces. The best middleware in existence is worthless if it will not run on the desired platform or does not support the desired development environment. A compatibility checklist is shown in Figure 6-2.

Interface	Usage	Example
1—Network Operating System	Client Network Operating System Server NOS	Windows NT Workstation Windows NT Server
2—Business Application	Development Environment (API)	Visual BASIC, C/C++
3—Communication	Middleware Communication Technique	ODBC, RPC, CORBA

Figure 6-2   Middleware Interface Compatibility List

To better understand the flow of data through the middleware architecture, consider a data request from a client application to a database located on a remote server. The client application makes a request via the middleware API to retrieve the desired data. The middleware takes the request and formats it into a message that can be understood by the server application and passes it to the network operating system's communication subsystem for delivery. Upon arriving at the server, the message moves up to the middleware via the server network operating system's communication subsystem. The server middleware then takes the request and reformats it for submission to the server application for processing through the server's application API. The response will return through the same path, in reverse order.

Physical Architecture

As detailed in Chapter 1, client/server applications can be built using either a two-tier or an *n*-tier physical architecture. The choice of physical architecture directly affects the middleware solution. As defined in the middleware logical architecture, each computer in a client/server environment contains middleware. As shown in Figure 6-3, in a two-tier client/server scenario, each client communciates directly to each server.

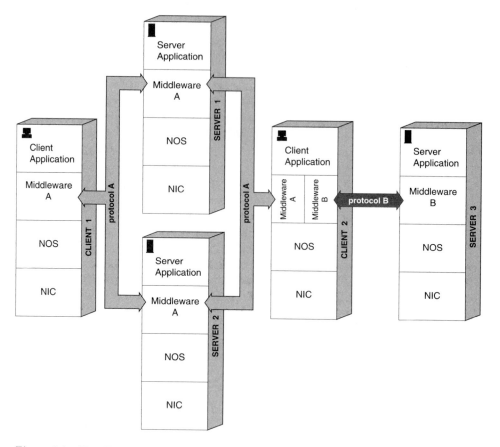

Figure 6-3   Two-Tier Middleware Physical Architecture

Although there are potential issues regarding the number of open connections that are beyond the scope of this chapter, this solution works well as long as each server uses the same middleware solution. As shown in Figure 6-3, Clients 1 and 2 can directly communicate with Server 1 and 2 via the same middleware stack (Middleware A).

However, Client 2 must also communciate with Server 3, which is running a different middleware solution (Middleware B). Therefore, Client 3 must run two different middleware solutions concurrently: one for communication with Servers 1 and 2, and another for communication with Server 3. This solution adds significant complexity to both the installation and maintenance of the client middleware. This is further complicated by the potential assortment of client network operating systems. If an organization needs to support the client application on UNIX, Windows, and the Macintosh platform, two middleware stacks must be installed, tested, and debugged on three different platforms. In some cases, it may not even be possible to run the two middleware solutions concurrently due to base level incompatibilities between the solutions.

An *n*-tier client/server architecture provides a middleware advantage by providing a means to eliminate the need to run multiple middleware solutions on the same client. Figure 6-4 illustrates the clients and servers from the two-tier architecture of Figure 6-3 reorganized into a three-tier solution. In this configuration, each client communicates with an application server that formats the requests for further

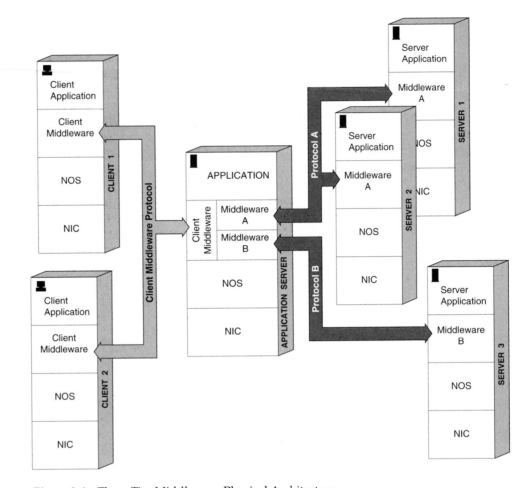

Figure 6-4   The *n*-Tier Middleware Physical Architecture

processing by the resource server. Each application server supports at least two middleware stacks: one for communication to the clients and one for communication to resource servers. This approach provides two major advantages from the middleware perspective:

- The resource server has to communicate with only a few application servers rather than potentially thousands of clients.

- The client has to communicate only with an application server via a single middleware interface rather than multiple resource servers via multiple middleware interfaces.

In this scenario, Client 2 has to have only a single middleware stack loaded to communicate with Servers 1 and 3, even though they are running different middleware solutions. The translation between middleware formats occurs at the application server, greatly simplifying client configuration and maintenance. Another benefit is that there is only one platform required to support multiple middleware formats (the application server) rather than multiple platforms as required in a two-tier architecture.

Synchronous versus Asynchronous Middleware Communication

When a client makes a request to a server, two things can happen: The client can halt all processing while waiting for a reply, or it can continue to perform other processes. If the client application waits for a reply before continuing processing, the middleware communication is said to be synchronous. If other processing can continue while waiting for the reply, the middleware communication is classified as asynchronous.

Synchronous communication is the more common approach taken in middleware solutions. In this scenario, the client application issues a request to the server application. While waiting on a reply to the request, the client is prevented from performing other application tasks. This process is known as **blocking.** A client waiting for a response from a server is referred to as being blocked. While the client application waits for the reply, it will appear to be stalled. In Windows-based applications, an hourglass mouse pointer will commonly appear to indicate that the client is waiting.

In an **asynchronous communication** model, the client application can continue to process other requests while waiting for a reply. In this manner a client application can continue to respond to user input if the next request does not depend on information for which the client is waiting. Asynchronous communication can represent a significant improvement in responsiveness to the user, providing the development environment can take advantage of this capability.

Synchronous communication is most commonly used with structured, procedural programming languages such as COBOL, Pascal, and C. In these single-threaded environments application processing passes linearly through various routines. When a routine makes a call to middleware to process an information request, the application waits until a response is received. Most synchronous communication middleware solutions generate a time-out error if a response from the server is not received within a certain period. Although synchronous communication is easier to program and ensures requests are processed, application responsiveness depends on the speed of the communication link and the server.

Asynchronous communication is most commonly used with event-driven application development environments such as Visual BASIC, Delphi, and Visual C. In these multithreaded environments, each event procedure is free to initiate a communication link to the server.

■ MIDDLEWARE CATEGORIZATION

By its very nature, middleware is complicated to categorize. There are as many different middleware implementations as there are server platforms and development platforms multiplied together. In order to make some sense out of this muddle of middleware, a means of categorizing middleware must be developed.

Middleware categorization is a two-part process based on the applications integrated and the communication methodology used to achieve integration. Categorizing middleware by application type focuses on discriminating between the different types of client and server applications the middleware supports. This categorization strategy focuses on the vertical integration within each host, specifically on the type of business application used with the middleware. Some common application categories of middleware are listed in Figure 6-5.

Category	Application Type	Technology
Database Middleware	Integrates database clients to relational database servers	SQL ODBC
Legacy/Application Middleware	Integrates any type of client to existing applications	TPM
Web Middleware	Integrates WWW clients to any type of resource server	CGI ActiveX Java

Figure 6-5 Application-Based Middleware Categories

Middleware is also categorized by the communication techniques used to integrate the clients and servers. This categorization technique is independent of the applications supported by the middleware. As of this writing there are four major communication-based categories of middleware, although the middleware market is relatively young and consolidation of techniques is likely to reduce the number of commonly used approaches in the future. The four major middleware communication categories are listed in Figure 6-6. Every middleware solution falls into an application-based category and a communication-based category.

◾ APPLICATION-BASED MIDDLEWARE CATEGORIES

Database Middleware

The earliest application of client/server systems was the deployment of distributed database applications. The clients in these systems represent front-end applications accessing data located on remote database servers. These database servers, commonly referred to as database engines, provide a central data repository and ensure that data entered into the system is consistent with the data model as defined in the database schema.

These systems originally were designed and implemented as two-tier architectures, with each client conversing directly with any servers containing required

Category	Application/Development Environment	Example/Standard
Remote Procedure Calls	Procedural Development Languages (COBOL, C, etc.)	DCE
Message-Oriented Middleware	Event-Driven Development Environments (Visual BASIC, etc.)	Message Queuing Message Passing
Transaction Process Monitors	Mainframe Integration High-Reliability Applications	CICS, IMS, ACMSxp
Object-Oriented Middleware	Object-Oriented Development Environments (Smalltalk, etc.)	CORBA DCOM

Figure 6-6 Communication-Based Middleware Categories

data. In such systems, the client processes data entered directly into the system and formats the data for display. The servers represent a repository containing all data required to support client functionality. Middleware for such database systems is limited to providing a means for the application programmer to access and manipulate data located on the remote database servers.

In a database middleware solution, the majority of the business logic (such as data analysis and report generation) takes place at the client. Some business logic can take place on the server through stored procedures, an approach especially useful for queries of large data tables. Rather than transmitting the entire contents of the table across the network for processing by the client, the server can select the subset of data required and transmit only that data. No business logic is performed in the middleware portion of the system.

Structured Query Language Structured Query Language (SQL) is a standard language developed to facilitate querying relational database servers. SQL is a comprehensive relational database language providing a means of performing common database operations such as record additions, updates, and database design modifications in addition to query capabilities. The SQL standard includes methodologies for embedding SQL calls into other programming languages and systems to create client/server applications. The American National Standards Institute (ANSI) has standardized the SQL language. Through the use of ANSI standard SQL syntax, transparent data access between different vendors' database servers can be achieved.

SQL STANDARDIZATION

Practical Advice and Information

Don't be misled by features lists that state an SQL implementation is ANSI compliant, yet list features that are not in the ANSI standard. Although SQL is an ANSI standard, each database vendor has added its own proprietary extensions to the language in an effort to add functionality and create a competitive advantage. This additional functionality works only with products from that specific vendor. The advanced features are not supported when connecting to third-party applications. If true intervendor connectivity is required, base ANSI SQL syntax is usually required.

As shown in Figure 6-7, the application programmer writes an SQL-compliant query and presents it to the client middleware. The client middleware passes the query across the network to the server middleware. The server middleware then executes the query against the database server, which replies with a data set. The data set is then sent back across the network to the client middleware and presented to the client application. From the client application's perspective, the data is located locally.

Most database server vendors provide personal computer network operating system–based client middleware compatible with their database server systems such as SQL*Net from Oracle. This client middleware provides a proprietary API for use by application programmers in the development of client applications. Because of the proprietary nature of the API, the resulting application is in effect linked exclusively to that particular database server. If a decision is made to replace the database server software, the client application may have to be rewritten to support the new database server. A list of proprietary SQL database middleware is listed in Figure 6-8.

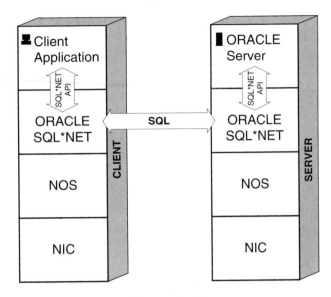

Figure 6-7   SQL Middleware Architecture

Open Database Connectivity   In order to eliminate this direct tie between the client application and the database server, Microsoft developed **Open Database Connectivity (ODBC).** Designed around the relational database/SQL model, ODBC provides a standard means of accessing data residing on a relational database server. As shown in Figure 6-9, ODBC is a dual interface API residing between the user application and the proprietary database middleware on the client workstation. ODBC provides a set of non–vendor-specific APIs that the application programmer can use to create open applications. When a client application needs to access data, it makes an ODBC-compliant request to the ODBC layer. The ODBC layer translates the request to a format compatible with the underlying proprietary client database middleware. ODBC has achieved such market acceptance that most database vendors have suspended further development of their proprietary middleware solutions.

The ODBC architecture consists of two parts: the ODBC driver manager and the actual ODBC driver for the underlying database connectivity layer. The driver manager keeps track of which drivers are connected to which underlying database connectivity software. The ODBC driver makes the actual translation between the standard ODBC APIs and the vendor-specific SQL implementation. ODBC allows

Database Vendor	Database Server	Middleware
Oracle	Oracle	SQL*Net
CA-Ingres	Ingres	Open Ingres
Informix	Dynamic Server	Informix Connect
Sybase	Adaptive Server	Open Client

Figure 6-8   Proprietary SQL Middleware

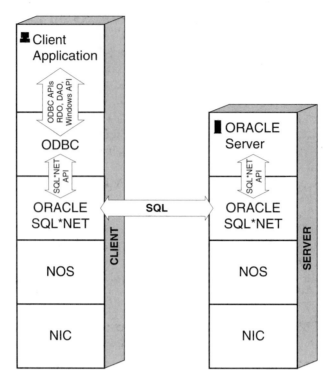

Figure 6-9 ODBC Logical Architecture

each client to access multiple data sources by binding multiple ODBC drivers to the driver manager to create separate ODBC stacks for each data source. However, each client must be individually configured for each data source, creating significant administrative overhead. Combined with increased latency through the various ODBC stacks, this administrative overhead is one of the main problems with ODBC.

Open database connectivity presents three separate APIs to the application programmer. The initial ODBC release was designed as a Windows API, making it accessible only via the Microsoft Jet database engine or to system-level programmers. To provide greater access to the benefits derived from ODBC, the second release added two high-level programming APIs: **Data Access Objects (DAO)** and **Remote Data Objects (RDO).** Data access objects are most commonly used in the Microsoft Access personal computer database platform. Remote data objects are readily accessible via Windows programming languages such as Visual BASIC and Delphi. As long as the application programmer maintains strict adherence to the ODBC API standards, the database server and associated database connectivity software can be changed independently of the application.

Once a Microsoft proprietary protocol, ODBC has now been ratified as an official standard by the **SQL Access Group (SAG).** There are more than 700 ODBC drivers available for most relational database servers from the database vendor, Microsoft, or third-party ODBC driver suppliers. There are also ODBC drivers on the market that include the capability to provide a relational database interface to non-relational database servers. Drivers are available for flat files and most mainframe record and block-based access methods such as **VSAM** and **ISAM.** Although they require significant configuration, by using these drivers, an application programmer can access data from a nonrelational data store through ODBC in the same manner as from a relational database. An applications programmer with ODBC experience can readily create an application that accesses data on database platforms with which the programmer has no practical experience.

Although ODBC greatly increases the portability of client applications, it does not solve all issues related to transparent data access. As shown in Figure 6-10, if a client application needs to access data from two different database engines, two ODBC drivers and transport stacks must be maintained on the client. Maintaining multiple ODBC stacks on each client represents a considerable managerial headache for the systems administrator. In order to eliminate this need, third-party vendors such as Intersolv have developed three-tier ODBC systems that allow for even greater database transparency than the original ODBC specification.

These new proprietary ODBC solutions move the translation to vendor-specific syntax from the client to an application server. As shown in Figure 6-11, this solution removes the need for any client to run multiple ODBC stacks, greatly simplifying client configuration. The client application requests data from the ODBC-compliant middleware interface, which sends the data to the application server as an ODBC request. The ODBC-compliant middleware on the application server then translates the request to vendor-specific syntax, issues the request to the database server, formats the response, and replies to the originating client.

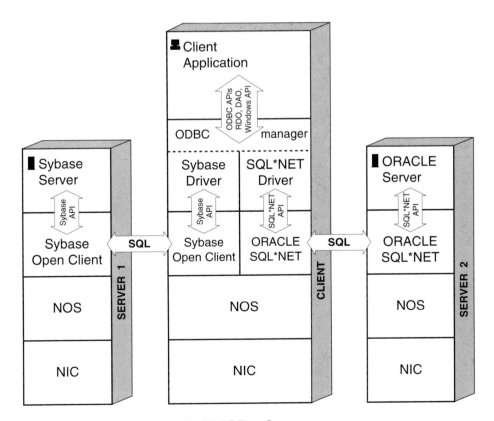

Figure 6-10   Accessing Multiple ODBC Data Sources

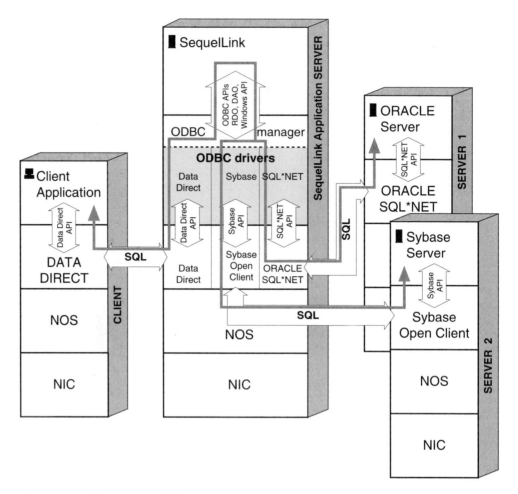

Figure 6-11   Distributed ODBC Architecture

ODBC PORTABILITY

Practical Advice and Information

Third-party vendors are also porting ODBC from the Windows environment to other operating environments such as Mainframes, UNIX, and the Macintosh. Although ODBC is not yet present on all platforms, it is positioned to become the predominant database translation tool across all major platforms, replacing such platform-specific solutions as Apple's DAL on the Macintosh solution.

Universal Data Access   Although ODBC has greatly improved the flexibility and portability of relational database client applications and has some capabilities to access data from nonrelational data sources through specialized ODBC drivers, it is not a complete data access solution. As the importance of accessing data across the enterprise continues to grow, the relational limits of ODBC become evident. Microsoft is in the process of building ODBC into a more feature-rich environment known as **universal data access (UDA).** Universal data access is designed to provide a comprehensive means to access data from both relational and nonrelational data stores.

Universal data access is an umbrella term covering **object layering and embedding database (OLE DB)** services and **active data objects (ADO).** OLE DB defines a collection of interfaces that encapsulate various database management system services. These interfaces enable the creation of software components that enable these services. OLE DB components are categorized as data providers, data consumers, and service components. Figure 6-12 shows a distributed system built using universal data access components.

Data providers are components that store and serve data. Data providers can range from traditional flat files to relational database servers to object-oriented databases. **Data consumers** are components that use the data stored on the data providers. A typical data consumer is a distributed database client application. Service components are those components that process and transport data between data providers and data consumers. To ensure compatibility with existing ODBC technology, the first data provider released was an ODBC provider. Through this provider OLE DB can utilize any data source supported by ODBC.

In order to provide access to nonrelational data, OLE DB replaces the ODBC APIs with a new application layer API known as active data objects (ADO). As illustrated in Figure 6-12, active data objects replace the DAO and RDO APIs used in

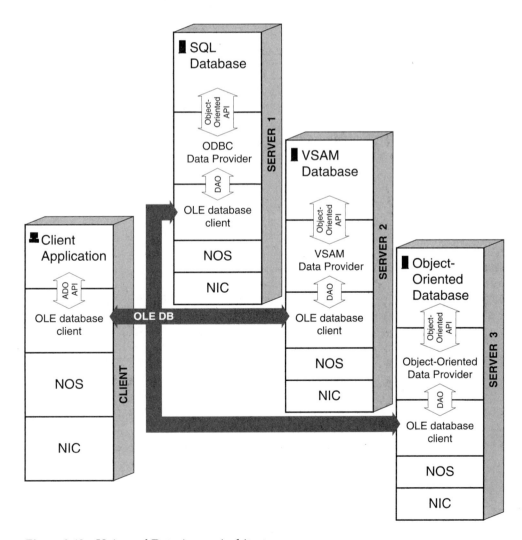

Figure 6-12   Universal Data Access Architecture

ODBC. Active data objects combine the functionality of DAO and RDO along with new functionality to access nonrelational data. The ADO interface also includes functionality designed to ease integration with web browsers. Collectively, the latest versions of ODBC, OLE DB, and ADO are packaged together in a suite called **Microsoft Data Access Components (MDAC).**

Legacy Application Middleware

In addition to building new systems on the client/server model, some companies need to modify existing large-scale monolithic systems to operate in a client/server paradigm. Middleware that helps facilitate this integration is collectively known as legacy application middleware. This modification is accomplished by replacing traditional terminal input screens with client applications. Client applications vary from simply replacing the text-based terminal interface with a similar client-based interface to providing front-end processing of data. In either case, the client application usually sends data to the host application in traditional "screens" of information. Legacy application middleware will be covered in more detail in Chapter 8.

Web Middleware

With the growth explosion of the Internet, many companies are interested in creating a web browser–compatible interface to their existing business systems. Middleware that helps facilitate this integration is collectively known as web middleware. Web middleware varies in scope from simple graphical web clients to applications distributed in real time over the network. Common development environments include **Common Gateway Interface (CGI),** Microsoft **ActiveX,** and **Java.** Web middleware will be covered in more detail in Chapter 7.

■ COMMUNICATION-BASED MIDDLEWARE CATEGORIES

Remote Procedure Calls

The first communication-based middleware category is **remote procedure calls (RPC).** Remote procedure calls evolved from UNIX and are a widely accepted technology for building client/server applications. RPC-based middleware products have been standardized as one of the distributed services of the **distributed computing environment (DCE),** an open standard middleware architecture. DCE is represented by a single source code currently owned and maintained by the Open Group (formerly the Open Software Foundation).

In Sharper Focus

THE DISTRIBUTED COMPUTING ENVIRONMENT

The distributed computing environment architecture is illustrated in Figure 6-13.

DCE is actually a collection of services that are operating system and network operating system independent. These services allow distributed applications to be developed, deployed, and managed in a secure environment. Among the key components of the DCE architecture are the following:

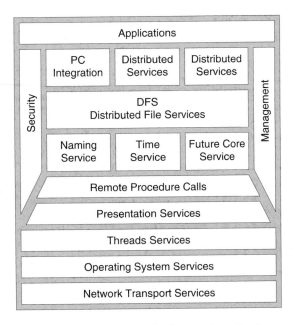

Figure 6-13 Distributed Computing Environment Architecture

Distributed File Services (DFS)   The purpose of DFS is to offer a consistent interface and consistent services for allowing users to access files from any node on the DCE-based enterprise network. DFS acts as a sort of translator between the native file system of the DCE host node and the DCE requesting client by using other DCE services such as the DCE naming service, which guarantees a consistent naming convention for all DFS-accessible files. Likewise, DFS depends on the DCE security services to provide authorization and authentication controls over file access by any DCE client. The RPC messaging subsystem is used to set up point-to-point connections between client and server in order to optimize file transfer efficiency. In order to further improve file transfer efficiency, a DFS cache manager resides on the client workstation to minimize the amount of client-to-server communication. Since the file system is distributed and the possibility exists for more than one client to request access to the same file simultaneously, a token manager is used to ensure that file updates are synchronized to prevent unintentional file corruption.

Naming Service or Directory Service   Just as DCE was responsible for presenting a consistent interface for file access regardless of the native file system of the DCE node, consistent directory services are also required in order for all DCE-compliant clients to quickly and easily access required services. DCE's directory service is not unlike Novell's NDS. Any service or device that can be accessed is referred to as an object, is described by a series of attributes, and is listed as an entry in a directory. Directories themselves are considered objects and can be listed as entries in other directories, thereby supporting a hierarchical directory structure. Through a gateway service known as the global directory agent, local or cell directory services are linked to global directory services such as the X.500 international directory service.

Remote Procedure Calls Service is the interprocess communications mechanism supplied with DCE. In order to ensure consistency and interoperability, the RPC services in DCE are not alterable by users or licensees of DCE. As a result, some proprietary RPC services may offer more sophisticated interprocess communications services. As illustrated in Figure 6-13, RPC provides the basic transport or messaging mechanism for all DCE services as well as for DCE-compliant client applications. RPC provides consistent support for communications via distributed enterprise network connections regardless of the platform or protocol of either the source or the destination node. This transparency means that programmers do not have to worry about platform-specific network communications while developing distributed applications for the DCE environment. RPC works with the DCE security services to provide for secure client/server communications across the enterprise network.

Threads Services are provided to offer multithreaded capabilities to those DCE nodes whose native operating systems are not multithreaded. Threads services are stored as functions that can be called from within a threads library. Although not as efficient as a native multithreaded capability contained within an operating system kernel, the threads service does provide a homogeneous multithreaded environment supported by all DCE nodes. Like most multithreaded environments, DCE threads allow multiple subprocesses of a single application to execute simultaneously. This is particularly useful when RPCs have created a link to a distant server, thereby allowing the local application to continue processing in the interim. Other DCE services such as RPC, security, time, and directory services use the threads service.

Distributed Time Service (DTS) DCE services such as DFS and security services depend on time and date stamps as part of their functionality. It is important, given the distributed, multinode nature of a DCE implementation, that there is a source for an "official" time by which all connected systems can be synchronized. DCE provides three types of time servers in order to coordinate system time across a DCE environment. Local time servers coordinate with other local servers on the same LAN. Global time servers offer similar services across WAN or inter-LAN links. A courier time server is responsible for coordinating with global time servers at regular intervals.

Security Services for DCE are divided into two general categories. *Authorization* grants users access to objects based on the contents of ACLs (access control lists); *authentication* guarantees the identity or authenticity of a user or object. Authentication in DCE is based on the **Kerberos** authentication system, which provides multilevel authentication and encryption services dependent on the level of security required. Authentication can be established only at connection time or can be enforced for every network message that traverses that connection.

RPC Architecture RPCs were designed to work with procedural programming languages such as COBOL or C. From the client perspective, RPCs can be thought of as remote subroutines. The application programmer calls a link to a subroutine or procedure located on a remote server. The local link to the remote procedure is known as a **stub function.** The stub function transfers the calling parameters to the RPC-based middleware on the server and waits until the server responds. Therefore, RPCs are synchronous and blocking by nature. A client application or thread must wait for the server to reply before continuing program execution.

A similar operation takes place on the server. The incoming data request from the client stub goes to a matching server stub. The server stub then calls the actual procedure and waits for the server to complete the task. From the server application's perspective, the request appears as if it were called by a local procedure. The server runs the procedure and replies to the server stub, which sends the result across the network to the client stub. The client stub then sends the reply to the actual calling routine. This process is illustrated in Figure 6-14.

The distributed nature of the RPCs is transparent to the client application. The client application calls the remote procedure in exactly the same manner it would call a local procedure. The application programmer does not need to worry about

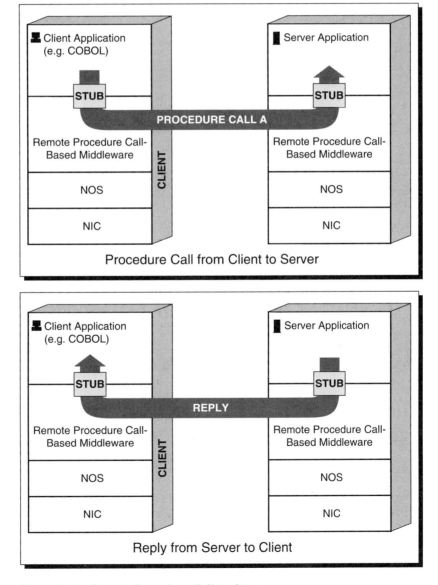

Figure 6-14   Remote Procedure Call Architecture

data synchronization because the client application is blocked until the server application returns a result to the RPC. This make RPCs a very straightforward approach to use with procedural languages like COBOL and C.

Although the server application sees the incoming RPC as if it were being called locally from the server host, the server must perform some housekeeping logic before it can complete the incoming procedure. The server application must register the availability of the service with the directory and authenticate all incoming connections to verify the requesting user and application have authorization to access the desired server resources.

The middleware functionality of RPCs takes place in the stub routines. Located on both the server and the client, stub routines represent a one-to-one direct relationship between client and the server. In order for RPCs to be language independent, a common means of defining the interface between the stubs and a detailed description of all data that needs to be passed between the stubs must be defined.

The responsibility for defining the RPC interface belongs to the server programmer. The interface is composed of definitions for the function name and parameters for the data passed between the stubs, including variable name, type, format, and length. This description of the RPC interface is provided via the **Interface Definition Language (IDL).** IDL is a high-level universal notation language that operates independently of the client and server application programming languages. Once the IDL parameters have been defined, they are input into an IDL compiler for the desired application programming language that creates the actual stub routines. The application programmer merely has to call the RPC and pass parameters via the standard constructs for the chosen application programming language.

Managerial Perspective

RPC ANALYSIS

Although it is straightforward to program, RPC-based middleware provides extremely limited flexibility. Because the client and server stubs have to match one for one, an RPC-based client application is bound to a specific server application. To modify this binding the applications must be modified and recompiled. This problem is exacerbated when a single RPC is potentially called by multiple client applications. Each client application would have to be rewritten and recompiled for the change to take effect. This is a significant drawback to RPC-based middleware compared with other types of middleware that allow linkages between clients and servers to be created and torn down dynamically.

Another drawback to RPC-based middleware solutions is their synchronous blocking nature. Although the blocking behavior of RPCs eliminates many data consistency problems, it adds significant latency to the client application. Rather than continuing to work, the user must wait until each RPC call is completed before moving on. This added latency has a tendency to make RPC-based solutions seem sluggish as compared with other middleware communication methodologies.

Message-Oriented Middleware

Message-oriented Middleware (MOM), or simply **messaging middleware,** refers to middleware solutions that transport information through the network as independent messages. Unfortunately, unlike other middleware categories that are standards based, there are no definitive standards that define message formats. As of this writing there are more than a dozen different messaging middleware products in the marketplace. Each set of server and client applications is free to develop its own specific messaging language. This makes messaging middleware one of the most confusing middleware areas and one of the most difficult to integrate across platforms. Messaging middleware is broken into three basic categories:

- Message passing

- Message queuing

- Publish and subscribe

Messaging Middleware Architecture   Each category of messaging middleware shares a common architecture. Each message consists of a string of bytes that have some meaning to the applications that exchange them. Messages can consist of either data or control parameters designed to store, route, deliver, retrieve, and track the data payload. Messaging is one of the most flexible middleware communication models, with the ability to support both synchronous and asynchronous communication. The ability to support asynchronous communication makes messaging middleware a good fit for event-driven programming environments.

Message Passing   **Message passing** uses a direct program-to-program communication model. Message passing is connection oriented. The client and server applications must maintain a logical connection at all times. Care must be taken to ensure both applications are running before communication is attempted, because a message-passing client immediately initiates a connection to the server upon application launch. If the server is not available, the connection will time out and the application will fail. For this reason, message passing works best with tightly coupled, time-dependent applications.

Message passing middleware architectures support both synchronous (blocking) operation and asynchronous operation. In synchronous mode a message-passing client application will wait for a response from the server before continuing. In asynchronous mode, the client application will send a message to the server, then go about other business while periodically polling the server to see if the request has been completed. When a reply message becomes available, it will be pulled from the server to the client. These processes are illustrated in Figure 6-15.

Message-passing middleware architectures typically support concurrent connections to multiple servers. However, each client and server must support the overhead of maintaining the connection. Message-passing MOM architectures rely on connection-oriented transport protocols such as TCP and SPX. An example of message-passing middleware is PIPES from PeerLogic.

Message Queuing   **Message queuing** replaces the direct connection between applications with a message queue. Each application attaches to a message queue that holds all incoming and outgoing messages until they can be processed. Because the message queue exists independently of the application, this removes the message-passing requirement that both applications be running before communication is attempted.

As shown in Figure 6-16, each application attaches to a message queue on the local host. Each host in turn runs a special process known as a **queue manager,** which manages the message queues and handles delivery of messages. In a message-queuing middleware implementation, all interprocess communication takes place via the message queues. For messages between processes on a single host, the

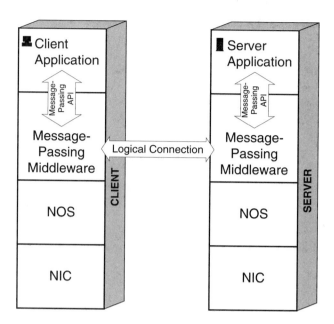

Figure 6-15 Message-Passing Middleware Architecture

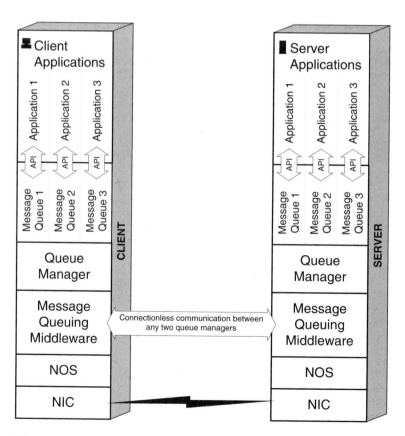

Figure 6-16 Message-Queuing Middleware Architecture

queue manager processes delivery internally. For messages bound for processes on remote hosts, the queue manager manages the communication to a remote message queue attached to the remote process.

The queue manager is the heart of a message-queuing middleware system. In addition to simply processing inbound and outbound messages from the network, they actively control the message delivery process. Queue managers work together to determine the best route through a network and to find backup routes in the event of a partial network failure. Other network services are provided by the queue manager:

- Reliable message delivery—ensures no messages are lost in transit

- Guaranteed message delivery—ensures messages will get to the destination either immediately if the network is available, or eventually if the network is not currently available

- Guaranteed nonduplicate message delivery—ensures messages are delivered only once

Queue managers also add support for different **quality of service** levels. Quality of service refers to the acceptable level of network latency for a particular message. Quality of service can be thought of as a message prioritization scheme whereby time-critical messages are processed prior to non–time-critical messages. Queue managers prioritize messages by quality of service level in both outgoing and incoming message queues.

Queue managers can either be nonpersistent or persistent in nature. **Nonpersistent message queues** are memory based, and messages are lost in the event of queue manager failure or host shutdown. **Persistent message queues** are disk based and remain intact when the queue manager is not running. As soon as the queue manager is restarted, it will begin to process the messages remaining in the queue. In general, nonpersistent queues impart better performance than persistent queues, but persistent queues are more reliable. Deciding which queue type to use depends on the application requirements. A banking application is an example of an application that requires a persistent queue: You wouldn't want the bank to forget that you deposited your paycheck because of a queue manager failure.

Because message queuing relies on queues rather than on direct communication between clients, it is connectionless. The remote process does not even have to be running in order to receive a message. The message will arrive at the remote host and be put into the process's incoming message queue for processing. Some message-queuing implementations support **triggers** that will "awaken" a process that is not running and alert it that a message has arrived for processing. In this manner, unused processes can be unloaded from memory to conserve system resources, yet still remain available when needed.

Most message-queuing products support **network message concentration.** With this technique a single connection is established between queue managers regardless of the number of message queues each supports. As illustrated in Figure 6-17, network message concentration allows a queue manager to concentrate the communication requirements from multiple applications. This approach greatly reduces communication overhead, resulting in lowered network bandwidth requirements and communication costs compared with the direct connection requirements of message passing.

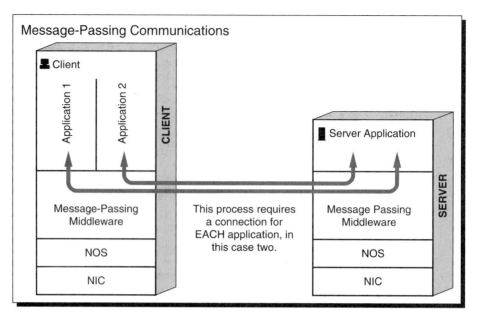

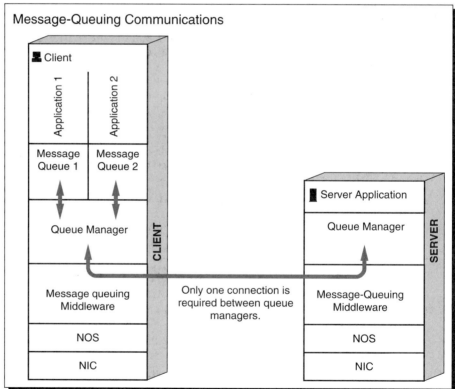

Figure 6-17   Network Message Concentration

Message-queuing middleware presents a highly flexible, relatively simple API to the client application developer. Because of its connectionless nature, message-queuing middleware is an ideal solution for event-driven applications. An event in one application can cause a message to be sent to a second application, leading to a specific result in the second application.

Message-queuing middleware is rapidly outdistancing message-passing middleware in most applications. The advantages of a looser coupling between applications and the reliability advantages of persistent queues combine to make message-queuing middleware more flexible for most applications. Example message-queuing middleware solutions include BEA Systems DECmessageQ, IBM's MQSeries, and Microsoft Message Queue (previously known as Falcon).

Publish and Subscribe   **Publish and subscribe** middleware relies on a distribution model similar to that of a newspaper. In a publish and subscribe messaging system, there are no servers or clients in the traditional sense. Each host on the network is a potential source and consumer of messages. As shown in Figure 6-18, each host connects to a **logical message bus.** When a host has a piece of information potentially of interest to other hosts, it broadcasts (publishes) it to the message bus. Any host that subscribes (listens) to the message bus receives the message and passes it to an application for further analysis and subsequent action.

Publish and subscribe systems have the ability to rapidly propagate a message through a system with minimal messaging overhead. Publishers and subscribers do not even need to know of each other's existence, making it possible to dynamically reconfigure the network. Although publish and subscribe is a relatively new category of messaging middleware, it has great potential as a technique to integrate a new generation of loosely coupled, flexible business systems. For example, it can distribute pricing information to automated stock trading systems. An example publish and subscribe middleware solution is Tibco's Software Rendezvous (formerly Teknekron Information Bus).

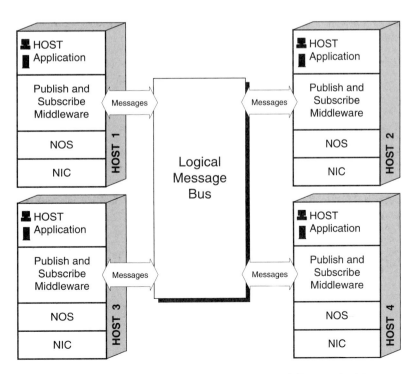

Figure 6-18   Publish and Subscribe Messaging Middleware Architecture

Managerial Perspective

MESSAGE-ORIENTED MIDDLEWARE ANALYSIS

The message orientation of MOM makes it especially flexible. Messages can be defined on a per-application basis, enabling messaging to solve many complex middleware problems. However, this flexibility makes message-oriented middleware difficult to integrate varying applications because there are no definitive messaging standards. Message-oriented middleware supports both synchronous and asynchronous communication modes. This makes it an especially good solution for event-driven application development environments such as Visual BASIC. As shown in Figure 6-19, each of the three basic types of messaging middleware has specific strengths and weaknesses.

	Synchronous Communication	Asynchronous Communication	Procedural Languages	Event-Driven Languages	Message Concentration	Security	Fast Broadcasts
Message Passing	●		●	●		●	
Message Queuing		●		●	●	●	
Publish and Subscribe		●		●	●		●

Figure 6-19   Message-Oriented Middleware Technology Analysis Grid

Message passing is the most basic messaging middleware type and provides basic middleware functionality. The requirement that all applications that need to share data via message passing be available at all times makes message passing less flexible and more system resource intensive than other messaging middleware solutions. Message-passing solutions also tend to be more bandwidth intensive than the other choices.

Message queuing provides the most flexibility and reliability of the messaging middleware categories. The ability to utilize persistent queues allows the application of message-queuing systems to applications requiring high reliability, such as financial applications. Under most circumstances, message-queuing middleware provides the best mix of flexibility and functionality.

Although publish and subscribe represents a niche in the overall middleware marketplace, it provides a unique solution to applications where data security is not as important as quick, efficient distribution of information. Final messaging middleware selection criteria will depend on achieving the balance of flexibility, reliability, and efficiency required by the distributed application.

Transaction Process Monitors

Transaction Process Monitors (TPM) are a mature technology with roots in mainframe-based monolithic applications and UNIX database applications. Transaction process monitors are used with database systems to oversee (monitor) the database transactions between clients and servers. One of the key features of transaction process monitors is their ability to ensure secure database transactions across heterogeneous database servers. In order to provide this integration capability, all current transaction process monitors conform to the X/Open standard for **Distributed Transaction Processing (DTP).**

In Sharper Focus

TRANSACTION PROCESSING

Transaction processing refers to series of operations that take place in response to a business transaction. For example, let's consider the case of a customer entering a furniture store and purchasing a couch on the store's in-house credit plan. This single business transaction will result in postings to several information systems. The inventory control system must be updated to reflect the sale of the item. A pick slip must be sent to the warehouse to indicate the couch is to be brought to the dock for pick-up. The accounts receivable system must be updated to reflect the credit purchase. Collectively these operations make up a single transaction.

As their name would suggest, TP monitors monitor the processing of database transactions. The transaction process monitor's main purpose is to ensure that the transaction is processed completely. If any aspect of the transaction cannot be completed, the entire transaction process must be reversed or "rolled back." In this manner the TP monitor ensures data integrity throughout the system.

Transaction roll-back is made possible through a two-phase commit process. In a two-phase commit, the transaction is sent to the affected database servers. The transaction process monitor then issues a "pre-commit" command to each server. Upon receipt of the "pre-commit" command, the database servers test to see if the commit can be completed and report the result to the TP monitor. If every database server can complete the commit, the TP monitor then issues a "commit" command and the database servers permanently make the changes. If any server responds negatively to the "pre-commit" command, the entire transaction is rolled back from all of the servers.

Database Requests versus Transaction Management   Every database transaction must conform to a set of rules or traits to ensure the transaction is completed successfully. These rules ensure that data integrity is maintained when a transaction updates multiple databases. Commonly referred to as the **ACID test,** these rules collectively constitute transaction management:

- **Atomicity:** A database transaction is considered to be single unit of work that must be wholly completed. If any portion of the transaction fails, the entire system must be **rolled back** (restored) to its state before the transaction attempt began.

- **Consistency:** At the end of a transaction, all resources that participated in the processing of the transaction should be left in a consistent state.

- **Isolation:** Each transaction should be isolated from all other transactions. Concurrent access to shared resources should be coordinated to ensure independence.

- **Durability:** All updates to resources that have been performed within the scope of a transaction will be persistent or durable.

In all other middleware categories, transaction process management is performed by the database engines themselves. The function of the middleware is limited to providing a means of transporting the request to the database engine for transaction processing. Transaction process monitors perform transaction process management as a function of middleware. In addition to reducing the processing requirements of the database server, transaction process monitors provide a means to manage transactions across heterogeneous database servers. Transaction process monitors can also ensure transaction processing rules are met for record-oriented files and queues as well as relational databases.

Transaction Process Monitor Architecture   The DTP standard defines a standard transaction process monitor architecture. As shown in Figure 6-20, transaction process monitors are usually implemented as a three-tier middleware solution. The client application accesses TPM middleware through the **Standard Transaction Definition Language (STDL).** STDL provides a vendor-independent transaction definition language. STDL is analogous to SQL in a relational database environment.

The TPM middleware processes the STDL request and makes a request to the transaction process monitor through the TX protocol. The transaction process monitor takes the incoming TX requests from each client and groups them into logical units of work to be performed by server applications or by the database servers themselves. The TPM then forwards the requests to the database servers. The TPM can connect to database servers directly via the XA protocol or to a server applica-

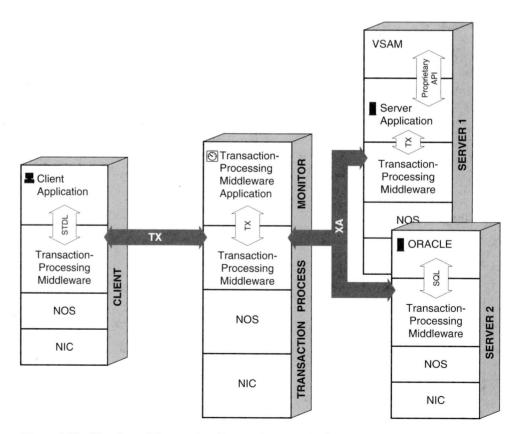

Figure 6-20   Distributed Transaction Process Monitor Architecture

tion via the TX protocol. Each of these scenarios is illustrated in Figure 6-20, with the Oracle connection being direct and the VSAM data connection going through a back-end server application.

The ability of a TPM to consolidate database requests is one of the key features of the technology. The TPM maintains connections to each client and concentrates the requests for each database server into a single database server connection, freeing the database server from the overhead of maintaining the connections itself. This three-tier architecture also allows the TPM to manage transactions across heterogeneous database servers and technologies.

Applied Problem Solving

CHARACTERISTICS OF TRANSACTION PROCESS MONITOR SYSTEMS

Figure 6-21 lays out the functional characteristics of translation process monitors.

Transaction Process Monitor Functional Characteristic	Importance/Implication
Communication Models	• The transaction monitor must communicate with all servers in the system. • What protocols and models does the TPM support?
Resource Managers	• The TPM must support the application interfaces of the resource servers. • Most transaction process monitors will support the XA standard, but what about record-oriented file systems, journal-based files, and RDBMS systems?
Client Platforms	• The TPM must include client support for all clients that need to post transactions. • Most will currently support Windows NT and Windows 95, but what about DOS, Macintosh, UNIX, web clients?
Network and Systems Management	• Distributed transaction process monitor systems can be complex to manage and administrate. • Does the TPM support Simple Network Management Protocol (SNMP)? • Is there a means to automatically update all clients with newer versions of the client software?
Security	• Does the TPM support encryption?
Server Development Characteristics	• What server-side development environments does the TPM support (C/CC++, COBOL, Java)?

Figure 6-21   Transaction Process Monitor Functional Characteristics

Managerial Perspective

TRANSACTION PROCESS MONITOR ANALYSIS

Transaction process monitors off-load transaction processing from the database server to a separate task. This allows for transactions to occur between heterogeneous database server environments ranging from list-based files to relational databases. This capability is especially important when a client application needs to access and update data controlled by monolithic mainframe-based applications.

Implementation of transaction process monitor–based middleware has several additional benefits. Transaction process monitors serve as a network connection concentrator to reduce the number of incoming connections to a server application, resulting in increased server capacity and responsiveness. The ability to dynamically start additional transaction process management processes allows a system to automatically scale to meet demand. As is the case with other middleware categories, the key compatibility issue is the requirement that the transaction process monitor be compatible with the platform operating environment.

One of the first TP monitors widely deployed was IBM's Customer Information Control System (CICS). Originally developed to monitor transactions for mainframe applications, CICS has been ported to the AS/400, OS/2, and UNIX platforms. In addition to its role as a TP monitor, CICS also provides mainframe programmers with a method to develop screen displays without detailed knowledge of the terminals being used.

In addition to CICS, there are many other TP monitors available in the marketplace. Current generation products are designed to be implemented as a middle tier in *n*-tier client/server systems. These products include Tuxedo from BEA Systems, IBM Transaction Server, and NCR Top End.

Object-Oriented Middleware

Remote procedure calls, messaging middleware, and transaction process monitors provide excellent middleware functionality, but they are all designed to work with procedural or event-driven programming environments. Many software developers are in the process of transitioning to object-oriented (OO) programming environments. These OO programming environments represent a significantly different development environment. Object-oriented programming environments require a middleware solution that provides a high level of abstraction. Such middleware is referred to as **object-oriented middleware.**

Object-Oriented Middleware Architecture   There are two major object-oriented middleware solutions currently available in the marketplace: CORBA and DCOM.

CORBA   The **common object request broker architecture (CORBA)** is a set of object-oriented middleware specifications published by the Object Management Group (OMG). The CORBA specifications define the way objects are defined, created, dispatched, and invoked and how they communicate with one another.

There are four main service components in a CORBA system: object services, common facilities, domain interfaces, and application interfaces. The key difference between these services is the level at which they are available. Services can exist within an application, within a domain of related applications such as manufacturing or telecommunications, or at the global inter-domain level.

Object services are domain-independent interfaces used by distributed object programs to locate available objects and services. Example object services include the naming service, which allows clients to find objects based on names, and the trading service, which allows clients to find objects based on their properties.

Common facilities are also domain-independent interfaces. However, common facilities provide interfaces directed toward end-user applications rather than the underlying objects. An example common facility is the distributed document component facility (DDCF). DDCF provides a method of linking multiple objects together into a single compound object. For example, a spreadsheet may be linked into a word processing document.

Domain interfaces fill roles similar to object services and common facilities at the domain level. These services are tailored for specific industries. One of the first domain interfaces standardized by the OMG was the product data management enabler for the manufacturing domain. Any object that conforms to the manufacturing domain standards can access data through this service.

Application interfaces are interfaces developed specifically for a given application. Because they are application specific, they are not standardized by the OMG. However, if certain broadly useful services emerge within an application domain, they may be integrated into the domain standard and become domain interfaces.

The key communications component in the CORBA architecture is an **object request broker,** or **ORB.** An ORB is a distributed software component that provides an interface through which objects make requests and receive responses. An ORB is installed on each host to provide services to the OO-based applications running on that host. Depending on the solution, ORBs are either included in the network operating system or supplied by third-party vendors.

As shown in Figure 6-22, the distributed ORB middleware represents a logical ORB bus connecting all objects in the system. All communication between objects is accomplished via the ORBs, allowing the location of the destination object to be masked from the programmer. From the perspective of the source object, both local and remote objects are accessed in the same manner.

Objects can be accessed via static interfaces or dynamic interfaces. Static interfacing implies that the object's interfaces do not change over time. This is the most commonly implemented CORBA interface technique. It takes place via the **static i nvocation interface (SII).** The static invocation interface works much like remote procedure calls do in a procedural programming environment. The interface

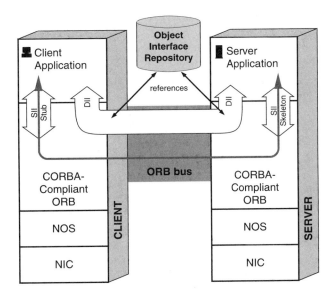

Figure 6-22   ORB Architecture

characteristics for an object are defined using the **Object Management Group interface description language (OMG IDL).** OMG IDL is a derivative of the IDL language used in DCE standard RPCs. As in an RPC implementation, the IDL code describes the interfaces of the object.

The IDL code is input into an IDL compiler, which creates a stub object that is implemented on the client and a skeleton object that is implemented on the server. The IDL code is also stored in an object interface repository. Just as in RPC-based middleware, the application development environments supported are determined by the IDL compiler. Currently, CORBA-compliant IDL compilers exist for C, C++, Smalltalk, and Java. Mappings for COBOL and ADA 95 are under development.

As illustrated in Figure 6-22, a client using the SII accesses a remote object via the stub object. The information sent to the stub is sent to the actual remote object by the ORB through the server skeleton object. As with RPCs, SII supports only synchronous communication. The client application is blocked until the server application responds to a request.

CORBA also supports dynamic interfacing of objects via the **dynamic invocation interface (DII).** DII-based applications support both synchronous and asynchronous communication. Using the DII a client looks up the IDL code for the destination object in the object interface repository to determine the destination object's interface capabilities. In this manner a client application can be built with a generic interface that automatically adapts to changes in the server application. Although DII has tremendous potential for the development of intelligent, self-configuring information systems, the high complexity of building the multitude of CORBA calls required to traverse the object interface repository practically limits the feasibility of this approach.

As object-oriented applications continue to expand, developing a means of communicating between ORBs from different vendors increases in importance. The second version of the CORBA standard focuses on such ORB interoperability. As shown in Figure 6-23, an SII invocation from a client of ORB 1 passes through its IDL stub into the ORB. The ORB examines the object reference and looks up the location of the destination object in the object implementation repository. If the implementation is local to ORB 1, it passes the invocation through the appropriate skeleton for processing by the destination object. If the implementation is remote, ORB 1 passes the invocation across the communication pathway to ORB 2, which routes it to the appropriate skeleton for processing.

This implies that a mechanism exists through which the two ORBs communicate. There are two such mechanisms that enable inter-ORB communication: ensuring each ORB supports the same protocol or installing bridges to translate between protocols. CORBA 2.0 addresses both of these issues. All CORBA 2.0–compliant ORB implementations must support the **Internet Inter-ORB Protocol (IIOP),** an implementation of the general inter-ORB protocol (GIOP) that runs on TCP/IP based networks. The general inter-ORB protocol consists of three specifications:

- Common data representation (CDR)—defines representation of all OMG IDL data types

- GIOP message formats—defines seven specific message formats used to carry the invocation

- GIOP message transport requirements—requires a connection-oriented transport protocol that supports reliable communication

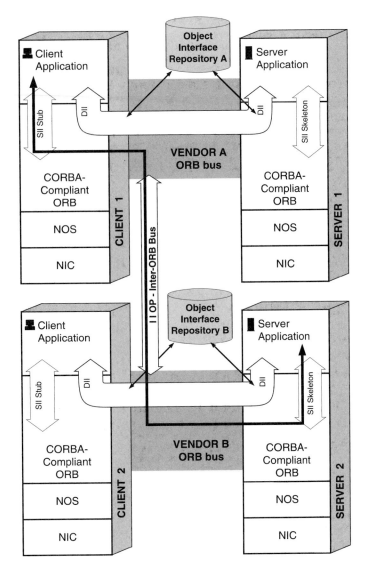

Figure 6-23   Inter-ORB Communication

CORBA SERVICES

In addition to the core CORBA specification, the OMG has specified additional middleware services that can be implemented. These services, collectively known as CORBA services, provide additional functionality to ease the development of distributed object-oriented applications:

- Naming—binds names to objects

- Events—provides event channels for asynchronous communication

- Transactions—provides transactional capabilities for communication between objects

- Concurrency control—enables multiple clients to coordinate their shared object access

- Relationships—provides the capability to represent entities and relationships

- Externalization—defines protocols for externalizing and internalizing objects

- Life cycle—defines conventions for creating, deleting, copying, and moving objects

- Persistence—provides a means of storing the state of objects

- Object trader—supports routing of client requests to servers based on rules

- Security—defines the security interfaces required for distributed client/server applications

DCOM   The **Distributed Common Object Model (DCOM)** is a Microsoft proprietary solution for building distributed object-oriented applications. Providing similar functionality to CORBA-based solutions, DCOM allows objects to be defined, created, dispatched, and invoked and to communicate with one another. However, rather than being a set of specifications like CORBA, DCOM is a software product. Because DCOM is a product rather than a set of specifications, it provides binary compatibility between objects that have been built using varying programming environments allowing a software developer to purchase software objects from multiple vendors and integrate them into a custom application with certainty that they will interoperate successfully.

At the center of the DCOM architecture is the **Component Object Model,** or **COM.** As illustrated in Figure 6-24, the component object model consists of a library of objects, a service control manager, a proxy manager, and a stub manager. Similar to an ORB in CORBA-based solutions, the service control manager (SCM) manages all communication between objects.

Like CORBA, object invocations can be either static or dynamic. In the case of a static invocation, the client issues a request for an object. The SCM on the client determines if a server containing the desired object is currently running. If not, it will search the registry for the location of a server containing the object. Once the destination server location is identified, the client SCM establishes an RPC connection with the

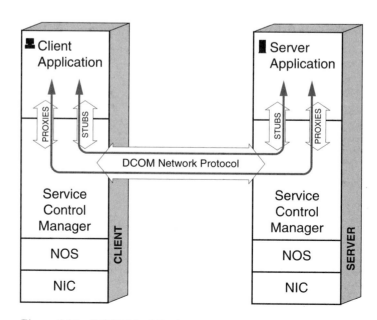

Figure 6-24   DCOM Architecture

server SCM. The SCM on the client and server then load specific proxy stubs into the client and server processes via the proxy and stub managers on each node. Just as in CORBA SII, static invocations in DCOM rely on a version of IDL to define an object's interfaces. Microsoft's IDL implementation supports the COM notation that an interface is defined as a family of logically related operations or methods.

Dynamic object invocations occur through object layering and embedding automation (OLE Automation). OLE automation allows a client to dynamically build a request and issue it against a remote object. As with CORBA, the client can retrieve all of the required interface information from a repository. However, OLE automation also provides a means to interrogate an object at runtime about the interfaces it supports. In this manner, client applications can discover new server objects and ask them about their interfaces dynamically without updating the client's object information store.

Managerial Perspective

OBJECT-ORIENTED MIDDLEWARE ANALYSIS

Object-oriented middleware solutions provide a means of integrating middleware functionality into object-oriented development environments. If an object-oriented development environment such as C++ or Smalltalk is used, the middleware solution of choice is either CORBA or DCOM. These two middleware solutions share many features, but there are several significant differences.

Applied Problem Solving

CORBA VERSUS DCOM TECHNICAL ANALYSIS

Although they provide similar functionality, CORBA is a standard set of specifications, and DCOM is a proprietary product. DCOM supports binary compatibility between all objects, enabling complete program language independence. A C++ client can use an object written in Smalltalk transparently. CORBA's binary compatibility is on a product-by-product basis: Objects written in the same language are binary compatible providing the development environment supports binary compatibility. Otherwise, platform independence is achieved through communication between ORBs using the IIOP protocol.

DCOM does not support multiple implementation inheritance; only interface definitions can be inherited. However, DCOM supports multiple interface definitions per object. This can be of significant use for upward compatibility. When a revised server object is implemented, it will continue to support its old set of interfaces in addition to any new interfaces changed or added in the upgrade. Existing client applications can continue to use the old interfaces until they are upgraded. This greatly simplifies version control in a distributed application environment.

DCOM is currently limited to the Microsoft Windows NT network operating system. However, third parties are currently porting DCOM to non-Windows platforms. CORBA solutions are available for all major operating environments. DCOM is bundled in the NT network operating system at no additional cost, but CORBA-based solutions must be purchased separately. It remains to be seen what the pricing strategy will be for non-Windows implementations of DCOM. However, Microsoft has indicated that it will work with the third-party developers to keep costs low to ensure the technology becomes pervasive. Most CORBA products charge a fee per development module, and in most cases they require a run-time license for all hosts using the product.

DCOM supports late binding through OLE automation that eliminates the need to write IDL code and bind stubs into applications. Although similar capabilities exist in CORBA via DII, it is substantially more complex to develop DII compliant applications. Therefore, most CORBA implementations rely on SII static binding through stubs written in IDL.

**Managerial
Perspective**

MIDDLEWARE SELECTION

Middleware is a relatively immature software category. Competing standards and varying technologies combine to make middleware selection a complicated decision. In order to clear up the technology muddle, the relationship between the middleware and applications must be examined.

The first question that must be addressed is the types of applications the middleware solution must support. Are you working on a distributed relational database project, or does the middleware need to provide access to data on nonrelational servers such as VSAM and ISAM data?

The second question to address is the application development environment. Is the client going to be written in a traditional procedural language such as COBOL, an event-driven language like Visual BASIC, or an object-oriented environment such as C++? Figure 6-25 illustrates the relationship between application types, application development environments, and middleware communication categories.

	Remote Procedure Calls	Messaging Middleware	Transaction Process Monitors	Object-Oriented Middleware
Application Type				
• Database	X	X	X	X
• Web	X	X	X	X
• Legacy Application	X	X	X	
Development Environments				
• Procedural (COBOL, C, Pascal)	X	X	X	
• Event-Driven (Visual BASIC, Delphi)	X	X	X	
• Object-Oriented (C++, Smalltalk)				X
Middleware Services				
• Multiple Communications Protocols	X	X		
• Consistent Cross-Platform API	X	X	X	X
• Security System	X		X	
• Synchronous Communications	X	X	X	X

• **Asynchronous Communications**		X	X	
• **Publish and Subscribe**		X		
• **Network Session Concentration**		X		X
• **Dynamic Binding**		X	X	X
• **Load Balancing**			X	
• **Broadcasting/Multicasting**		X		
• **Naming Services**	X		X	
• **Quality of Service**		X		
• **Triggering**		X		X
• **Fault Tolerance**			X	
• **Message Prioritization**		X	X	

Figure 6-25   Application Development Environment to Middleware Mapping

SUMMARY

Middleware can be thought of as the "/" in client/server computing—the glue that holds the clients and servers together. Middleware is classified in two different ways: by application type and by communications methodology.

There are three basic middleware application types: database, web, and legacy application middleware. Database middleware is the predominant application in most systems, with web middleware rapidly gaining in importance.

Database middleware relies heavily on SQL to provide a means of communication between clients and servers. In order to isolate the client application from specific database server implementations, ODBC was developed. ODBC is a vendor-independent programming interface accessible from most application programming environments. Recently ODBC has been superceded by universal data access, a superset of ODBC that includes methodologies to access nonrelational data.

There are four basic middleware communications types: remote procedure calls, messaging middleware, transaction process monitors, and object-oriented middleware. Each

middleware technology implementation can be categorized as being from one application category and from one communications category. For instance, a middleware solution can be referred to as database–transaction process monitor middleware.

Remote procedure calls are a blocking, synchronous communications method best suited for procedural programming environments such as COBOL and C.

Messaging middleware relies on communicating computers to exchange data via a series of messages. Messaging middleware is further divided into three subcategories: message passing, message queuing, and publish and subscribe.

Transaction process monitors are a specialized middleware solution designed to ensure that database transactions are posted across distributed database servers in a reliable manner.

Object-oriented middleware is used with object-oriented programming environments such as C++ and Smalltalk. There are two categories of object-oriented middleware: CORBA-compliant solutions and Microsoft DCOM.

CORBA-compliant object-oriented middleware solutions are based on a standard from the object management group. Compliance to the CORBA standard allows middleware solutions from different vendors to interoperate. CORBA-compliant middleware can use many different communications protocols, but each solution must comply to the IIOP protocol that runs over TCP/IP.

DCOM is a series of products released by Microsoft for the Windows environment. DCOM utilized the common object model to provide binary compatibility between objects and object programming environments. In this manner, a programmer can purchase objects and know they will work with whatever programming language they wish to use. DCOM is currently only supported on the Windows platform, although third-party vendors are in the process of porting it to other operating environments such as UNIX.

Regardless of the specific middleware technology used, the key concept in middleware is to select a solution that allows the required applications to communicate in a manner consistent with the overall needs of the system.

KEY TERMS

ACID test
ActiveX
ADO
Application programming interface
Asynchronous communications
Blocking
CGI
COM
CORBA
DAO
Data consumers
Data providers
DCE
DCOM
DII
Distributed transaction processing
Horizontal integration

IDL
IIOP
ISAM
Java
Kerberos
MDAC
Message queuing
Messaging middleware
Middleware
Network message concentration
Nonpersistent queues
ODBC
OLE
OLE DB
ORB
Persistent queues
Quality of service

Queue manager
RDO
Roll-back
RPC
SAG
SCM
SII
SQL
STDL
Stub function
Synchronous communications
Transaction process monitor
Triggers
Universal data access
Vertical integration
VSAM

REVIEW QUESTIONS

1. Compare and contrast vertical and horizontal middleware integration.
2. Differentiate between synchronous and asynchronous communications.
3. What programming environments are best suited for synchronous communications?
4. What programming environments are best suited for asynchronous communications?

5. What are the three basic middleware application categories?
6. What are the four basic middleware communications categories?
7. What language is most commonly used to query relational database systems?
8. Are all SQL implementations compatible? Why or why not?

9. What is the primary benefit to ODBC?
10. What are the two APIs associated with ODBC?
11. Can ODBC be implemented as a three-tier solution? How?
12. What are the components of universal data access?
13. What APIs are associated with universal data access?
14. What development environments are associated with web middleware?
15. What is the relationship between DCE and RPCs?
16. In terms of RPCs, what is a stub?
17. What is the purpose of IDL?
18. Are RPCs synchronous or asynchronous?
19. Explain the concept of blocking.
20. What are the three categories of message-passing middleware?
21. Which category of message-passing middleware supports QOS?
22. Compare and contrast message-passing and message queuing.
23. Differentiate persistent and nonpersistent message queues. For what types of applications are each best suited?
24. Explain network message concentration.
25. In terms of middleware, what is a trigger?
26. What types of applications are best suited for publish and subscribe middleware solutions?
27. What does transaction processing mean?
28. Explain the ACID test of database transaction management.
29. What is STDL?
30. What are the X/Open standard interfaces for portable transaction monitors?
31. What programming environments are best suited for object-oriented middleware?
32. What is an ORB?
33. In terms of CORBA-compliant middleware, differentiate SII and DII.
34. What is IIOP used for?
35. What functions do CORBA services provide?
36. Does DCOM support dynamic binding of objects? If so, how?
37. What is IDL used for in DCOM?
38. Is DCOM a standard?
39. Differentiate DCOM and CORBA.
40. Explain the middleware selection process.

ACTIVITIES

1. Investigate VSAM and ISAM data files, and report on their usage.
2. Research the ANSI SQL standard. Prepare a report on how closely individual SQL implementations follow the standard.
3. Prepare a report on SQL functional areas and the basic statements used in each area.
4. Prepare a chart outlining the middleware interface model. As new middleware solutions are encountered, map them to the model.
5. Research ODBC implementation. What platforms currently support ODBC?
6. After completing the previous activity, research universal data access implementation. Have universal data access implementations significantly eroded the ODBC market share?
7. Prepare a report on DCE. Is DCE gaining or losing market share?
8. Research RPC-based communications. Which middleware solutions rely on RPC communications techniques?
9. Research message-oriented middleware solutions. Create a chart of the available solutions, and categorize each solution as message passing, message queuing, or publish and subscribe.
10. Prepare a report on the X/Open transaction processing standard.
11. Research transaction process monitors. Create a chart describing the available solutions and the data types they support.
12. Create a chart of the CORBA model. Research CORBA-compliant middleware solutions, and map them onto the chart.
13. Prepare a report on the DCOM architecture. What are the underlying technologies used?
14. Report on the current state of CORBA and DCOM implementations. Has either solution increased its market share in the last twelve months?
15. Create a series of questions that can be used as a middleware selection tool. Contact a representative of your company or school, and work through the selection process with him or her to select the best middleware solution currently available.

CHAPTER 6

CASE STUDY

THREE TIERS OF INFORMATION

Using Object-Oriented Technology, Penn State Links Students to Mainframe Through the Web

As visionary developers begin building a new generation of Internet-savvy client/server applications, the true potential of the World Wide Web as a vehicle for information exchange is coming into focus. Most first-generation Web applications were designed as standalone systems, but user organizations are now looking to the Web to leverage their other application assets and data stores.

"Accommodating the Web is meaningless if you can't preserve existing application and database investments," says Peter deVries, director of advanced technology for Pennsylvania State University in University Park, Pa.

Since last March, deVries has been entrenched in a massive Internet development project designed to give students and staff members direct access to a wealth of institutional information. The Secure Web Instruction Management System (SWIMS) provides a custom search engine, a hypertext listing of suggested academic and advising references, open access to student information systems, an artificial-intelligence–based advising service, and a variety of support services for faculty and staff.

Creating the new system and integrating it with the existing application assets has not been an easy matter. PSU has an enormous legacy of mainframe databases and transaction-processing environments, many of them based on Software AG's ADABAS database and Natural forth-generation language. PSU is a statewide system of 22

campuses and 76,000 students, plus faculty and administration. All the data for the entire university system—including student, faculty, and administrative records, and financial and academic information—is centralized on IBM mainframe systems running the MVS OS.

"We've been building mainframe systems for 20 years," deVries says. "As we create client/server and intranet applications, our philosophy is to transition and improve the capabilities of those mainframe systems, not replace them."

Establishing the architecture initially, staff members in the university's Office of Administrative Systems (OAS) decided to implement a two-tier client/server system. Personal computers would handle all processing requirements for the presentation layer, allowing the mainframe to focus on data access and processing tasks. Unfortunately, the mainframe was quickly becoming overburdened by this combination of new and old systems, to the point where key business applications came to a grinding halt during periods of particularly heavy usage.

Seeking Strategies   Realizing they needed to offload most of the processing requirements from the legacy system, deVries and his colleagues considered several data-access strategies. "Much of the data [being sought] was information the students were requesting on their own behalf, such as course information, grades, and transcripts," says Ken Blythe, senior director of administrative systems. "If the university could set up a system that would let the students help themselves to this information in a secure

fashion, it would save on administrative expenses, speed information response, and take a tremendous load off the university staff."

At this point the framework of a three-tier system began to take shape. The mainframe would remain as the data server. Web servers would host the primary application logic. And the presentation layer would be a combination of traditional desktop clients and thin clients running Web browsers.

"The biggest challenges from a development standpoint were twofold," Blythe says. "The system would have to support 80,000 student users, with peak access rates of 20,000 hits per hour. And it would have to be ready by the next academic year."

Achieving these ambitious development goals meant finding a software-development system that was robust, supported multiple client platforms, and could tie the new tier of web servers seamlessly with existing legacy systems. The university eventually opted for VisualWave from ParcPlace-Digitalk Inc., a development environment based on object-oriented (OO) technology.

Objects are suited to the Web's distributed makeup. Rather than storing data and business functions separately, as most business applications do, objects are composed of both procedures and data so that they can be combined more flexibly and shared among applications.

"An OO architecture enabled rapid development and provided us with the opportunity to continually expand the system through component reuse," says deVries.

"This was our first major OO project, so the real learning curve came with understanding Smalltalk and the fundamentals of object-oriented development," deVries adds. "Several developers took a training class from ParcPlace that helped us get up to speed."

Once PSU developers had created the business logic, they could expand and modify the interface connections without having to significantly alter the core system. They rapidly built a complete client/server Web system, enabling both Web access and access through traditional client systems such as Apple Computer Inc. Macintosh and Microsoft Windows personal computers. They also linked to their legacy system for data access and implemented a security system based on the Kerberos protocols for password protection and authentication.

On the client side, VisualWave streamlined the creation of the user interface and the Web-to-database access mechanisms. "VisualWave automatically generates the HTML [HyperText Markup Language] and the CGI [Common Gateway Interface] scripts necessary to execute a client/server application as a Web application," deVries explains. "It allowed us to create an application in one complete graphical environment which is automatically deployable on the Web."

Scaling the System DeVries makes a distinction between two-tier, client-oriented development tools and three-tier environments such as VisualWave and Forte Software Inc.'s Forte Application Development Environment.

Two-tier tools pack all the code for the user interface, application logic, and business rules into the client, relying on a database server to retrieve data for processing.

In contrast, three-tier architectures add an intermediate tier of servers to support application logic and distributed computing services. Many applications can share these middle-tier services. Instead of writing the same function or service in every new application, developers can write the function once and place it on a server accessible by all applications. This improves the scaleability and reuseability of client/server environments.

"Three-tier applications are easier to adapt to the Web's distributed makeup because of their distinct separation between business logic, presentation, and data," deVries says. "This simplifies the translation into HTML files. Client browsers present the application, while Web servers funnel queries and transactions to an intermediate tier of database and application servers."

Many Web sites run into bottlenecks that can be traced to a single point of threading between the Web server and the mainframe. Visual-Wave supplies a multi-threaded CGI, which is used whenever a browser needs to call a service that is external to the Web server. Visual-Wave sessions manage application states for each user, enabling a true two-way dialog between the user and the application.

"Many Web applications show their limitations as traffic increases," deVries says. "We're planning to use Smalltalk to scale the middle tier as the system becomes more popular. We can add Web servers as necessary and distribute the application logic among them."

Other SWIMS enhancements will involve replacing much of the HTML interface logic with Java applets. "Java will allow more processing and more active participation on the client side," deVries says. "For example, instead of querying a student schedule on the server, the schedule could be downloaded to the client as a Java applet."

By allowing students and faculty to have direct access to administrative records and services, the SWIMS system has streamlined the university's administrative processes, thereby reducing expenses.

"We have been able to create a complete client/server Web system from the ground up," Blythe says. "The end product has significantly eased processing requirements for the university's existing legacy system while preserving a substantial investment in mainframe technology."

Source: David Baum, "Three Tiers of Information," *LAN Times,* vol. 14, no. 21 (October 13, 1997), p. 33. Copyright October 13, 1997, The McGraw-Hill Companies, Inc.

BUSINESS CASE STUDY QUESTIONS

Activities

1. Complete a top-down model for this case by gleaning facts from the case and placing them in the proper layer of the top-down model. After having completed the top-down model, analyze and detail those instances where requirements were clearly passed down from upper layers to lower layers of the model and where solutions to those requirements were passed up from lower layers to upper layers of the model.

2. Detail any questions about the case that may occur to you for which answers are not clearly stated in the article.

Business

1. What were the key business activities of the business described in this case?
2. What were the problems that led to the development of the new systems?
3. What was the key business justification for a new system?

Application

1. What applications were supported on the existing mainframe system?
2. Which of these applications were moved to the new client/server system?

Data

1. What was the scope of the data stored on the existing mainframe system?

2. What type of data was most commonly being accessed?

Network

1. What client/server architecture was chosen? Why?
2. Were there any problems with the implementation of the new system?
3. Are there any plans to move toward a more distributed environment? If so, what are they?

Technology

1. What interface is used to access data?
2. How are mainframe bottlenecks being addressed?
3. Were there any scaleability issues encountered? If so, how were they resolved?
4. Compare the technologies employed in the old system and the new system. Highlight the changes.
5. What middleware technologies are used to interface clients and servers?

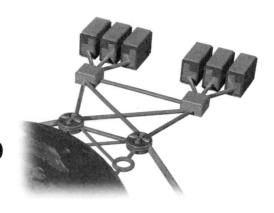

CHAPTER 7

INTEGRATION OF INTERNET, INTRANET, AND WEB-BASED TECHNOLOGIES WITHIN CLIENT/SERVER INFORMATION SYSTEMS

Concepts Reinforced

Client/Server Technology Architecture
OSI Model
Top-Down Model

Protocols and Compatibility
Hardware/Software Compatibility
Server Hardware Fundamentals

Concepts Introduced

Intranet Connectivity Services
Internet Connectivity Services
Internet/Intranet Web Client Software
Internet/Intranet Web Server Hardware
Internet/Intranet/Extranet Business
   Considerations

Internet/Web Server Software
Internet Client/Server Design
Integrating Internet/Intranet/Extranet
   Technologies

OBJECTIVES

After mastering the material in this chapter, you should understand the following:

1. How Internet clients and servers are able to connect to the Internet

2. How intranets and extranets are set up and how they connect to the Internet

3. Available hardware and software technology for building client/server connections to the Internet/intranet/extranet and the World Wide Web

4. The business implications of Internet/intranet/extranet use

5. The security implications of using the Internet/intranet/extranet

6. How Internet/intranet/extranet access technology integrates with a corporation's overall client/server information system

◼ INTRODUCTION

The **Internet** is a wide area network linking millions of host computers. Originally developed as a means for the research, education, and scientific communities to share information, the Internet has been opened up in recent years to more commercial uses as well as to access by individuals. The purpose of this chapter is to explore the use of the Internet, intranets, and extranets from a business perspective. It will also explore how companies are integrating the Internet with their intranets and extranets.

This chapter will not deal with how to "surf the 'net" or "navigate the web." Many books have been written on the best ways to travel through cyberspace on the Internet. Rather, this chapter will offer business-oriented network analysts and management a top-down approach to objectively evaluating the merits of connecting to the Internet, establishing an intranet and extranet, and developing the logical and physical network designs to do so.

More specifically, after a review of the potential business advantages and disadvantages offered by the Internet, intranets, and extranets, the chapter will continue with a study of the use of the Internet, intranet, and extranets as a client/server platform. The chapter will stress how companies are integrating these three types of networks to become more productive and more responsive.

◼ BUSINESS PERSPECTIVE ON THE INTERNET

Why Connect to the Internet?

From a business perspective, the Internet is currently being used primarily as a marketing tool rather than a sales tool. With a few notable exceptions, millions of dollars in potential sales transactions are not presently taking place on the Internet. Most companies currently using the Internet for marketing purposes are doing so to build image rather than to directly increase profits. This is changing as the Internet becomes more secure, as more and more people use the Internet, and as new products are developed for the Internet.

A recent survey of businesses currently using the Internet for marketing purposes produced the following results:

- 72% of companies surveyed said the purpose of their Internet usage was to enhance their company's image

- 22% said their Internet usage was financially rewarding

- 40% didn't expect financial rewards for 12 to 24 months

- Fewer than 6% of companies conduct credit card transactions over the Internet

From the potential customer perspective, four to five times more people use the Internet for browsing than buying.

What Are the Available Services and Resources?

The Internet is currently in a state of major transition from a government-funded entity designed for a research and education audience to a privately funded entity catering increasingly to commercial concerns. The Internet offers four major service categories:

1. The World Wide Web

2. Information servers
   - FTP servers
   - Gopher servers
   - WAIS servers
   - UseNet servers

3. Global e-mail

4. Internet chat rooms

The World Wide Web   The **World Wide Web (WWW)** is a collection of servers accessed through the Internet that offer graphical or multimedia (audio, video, image) presentations about a company's products, personnel, or services. WWW servers are accessed via client-based front-end software tools commonly referred to as **web browsers**. Companies wishing to use the World Wide Web as a marketing tool establish a **web site** on the Internet and publicize the address of that web site. Web presentations can be interactive, inviting visitors to the web site to register their visit, complete marketing surveys, watch product demonstrations, download available software, and a variety of other multimedia activities. The web site and web server presentation design, implementation, and management can be done in-house or can be contracted out to professional web site development and management services.

Information Servers   Text-based information stored in Internet-connected servers can be accessed by remote users logging into these servers via a TCP/IP protocol known as **Telnet.** Once they are successfully logged into an Internet-based information server using either previously assigned user accounts and passwords or general access "anonymous" user accounts, users are able to execute programs on the remote computer as if they were locally attached.

In order to download, or transfer, information back to their client PCs, users would access another TCP/IP protocol known as **FTP** (file transfer protocol). Servers that support such activity are often called **FTP servers** or anonymous FTP servers. Users can access FTP servers directly or through Telnet sessions. The difficulty with searching for information in this manner is that a user must know the Internet address of the specific information server (Telnet or FTP) they wish to access.

A menu-based client/server system that features search engines that comb through all of the information in all of these information servers is referred to as the **Gopher** system, named after the mascot of the University of Minnesota, where the system was developed. The key difference between Gopher and the World Wide Web is that Gopher's information is text-based, whereas the World Wide Web is largely graphical. Also, Web sites tend to be more interactive. The Gopher subsystem is analogous to searching for information in a library and then extracting or checking out that desired information. Gopher client software is most often installed on a client PC and interacts with software running on a particular **Gopher server,** which transparently searches multiple FTP sites for requested information and delivers that information to the Gopher client. Gopher users do not need to know the exact Internet address of the information servers they wish to access.

A third type of information server offers a text-searching service known as **WAIS,** or **Wide Area Information Services.** WAIS indexers generate multiple indexes for all types of files that organizations or individuals wish to offer access to via the Internet. **WAIS servers** offer these multiple indexes to other Internet-attached WAIS servers.

WAIS servers also serve as search engines. They can search for particular words or text strings in the indexes located across multiple Internet-attached information servers of various types.

UseNet servers or news group servers share text-based news items over the Internet. Over 10,000 news groups covering selected topics are available. UseNet servers update one another regularly with news items that are pertinent to the news groups housed on a particular server. UseNet servers transfer news items back and forth using a specialized transfer protocol known as **NNTP (network news transport protocol)** and are also known as NNTP servers. Users wishing to access NNTP servers and their news groups must have NNTP client software loaded on their client PCs.

Global E-Mail   Millions of users are connected worldwide to the Internet via the **global e-mail** subsystem. From a business perspective, Internet e-mail offers one method of sending intercompany e-mail. Most companies have private networks that support e-mail transport to fellow employees but not necessarily to employees of other companies. By adding Internet e-mail gateways to a company's private network, e-mail can potentially be sent to users all over the world. However, Internet e-mail gateways are a double-edged sword. Unauthorized access from the Internet into a company's private network is also possible unless proper security precautions are taken. Such security issues as firewall servers will be discussed later in the chapter.

Global e-mail users can subscribe to e-mail mailing lists of their choice on various topics of interest. Companies can easily e-mail to targeted audiences by sending a single e-mail message to a list server and allowing the list server to forward that e-mail message to all subscribed users. Targeted list servers provide the best commercial use of global e-mail for marketing or sales. Global e-mail also affords access to specifically targeted electronic magazines (**e-zines**) and topical discussion groups (often referred to as "frequently asked question" groups or **FAQ groups**). FAQ groups are similar to ListServe groups that users can subscribe to via e-mail.

Internet Chat Rooms   **Internet relay chat (IRC)** has become very popular as more people get connected to the Internet because it enables people connected anywhere on the Internet to join in live discussions. Unlike older chat systems, IRC is not limited to just two participants. To join an IRC discussion, you need an IRC client and Internet access. The IRC client is a program that runs on your computer and sends and receives messages to and from an IRC server. The IRC server, in turn, is responsible for making sure that all messages are broadcast to everyone participating in a discussion. There can be many discussions going on at once.

What Are the Potential Advantages?

In order to gain the maximum benefit from Internet connectivity, a company would probably wish to avail itself of the services of all four of the previously mentioned Internet subsystems rather than choosing just one. By combining the benefits offered by the World Wide Web, Gopher, global e-mail, and Internet chat rooms, a company could have access to highly focused marketing campaigns, almost limitless research data, and access to peers, partners, and customers throughout the world. More-specific examples of benefits or trends supporting increased Internet

Benefit or Supporting Trend	Implication/Explanation
More readily accessible Internet access	Local, regional, and national Internet access providers are now plentiful, leading to competitive pricing. AT&T, Sprint, and MCI as well as most RBOCs (regional Bell operating companies) offer Internet access services of some type.
Realistic bandwidth	Mere access to the Internet is not enough. The "pipe" (bandwidth) into the Internet must be wide enough to accommodate desired traffic. Graphical traffic from the WWW is especially bandwidth intensive. Advances in modern technology support 56 KBps over dial-up lines, whereas ISDN (Integrated Services Digital Network) offers up to 144 KBps and is becoming more widely available.
Improved front-end tools	Improved front-end tools or browsers mean that even novices have a reasonable chance of finding what they're looking for on the Internet. Many of these tools will be integrated into more familiar products such as word processors and presentation graphics packages.
Improved server tools	Internet access gateways and Internet server software will be increasingly integrated into mainstream server operating systems from companies such as IBM, Novell, and Microsoft. This will make the software easier to use, more tightly integrated, and more reliable.
Improved information services	The types of information and services that can be accessed on the Internet continue to improve and broaden in scope. Airline reservations, stock trading and quotations, weather forecasts, publishers, government agencies, and high-tech companies are but a few of the types of information and services available.

Figure 7-1   Benefits or Supporting Trends of Internet Access for Business

access by business are highlighted in Figure 7-1 and will be elaborated upon in the chapter.

What Are the Potential Disadvantages?

From a business perspective, the current major concern of widespread business use of the Internet is probably a perceived lack of adequate security. As will be seen later in the chapter, several alternate methods have been proposed to deal with this perception. If the Internet is to succeed as a viable commercial communications link for business, then financial transactions of any magnitude must be able to be conducted in an absolutely secure and confidential manner. Figure 7-2 summarizes some of the other potential disadvantages or obstacles to widespread use of the Internet by business.

Disadvantage/Obstacle	Implication/Explanation
Bandwidth availability	Although ISDN is becoming more widely available, it is still not universally available. Bandwidth must be reasonably priced as well. Also, local providers of Internet access bandwidth vary in their financial backing and commitment to provide adequate bandwidth as user traffic demands grow.
Search abilities	The information on the Internet is rather loosely organized. If it is to be commercially viable, information must be organized and cataloged such that it is easier to find. Busy business people do not have a lot of time to "surf" for information. Sophisticated search agents and global search engines would suggest best or nearest sources of desired information. Although front-end tools are improving, they are still new and largely unproven.
Internet ownership	The management and funding of the Internet is transitioning from government to the private sector. Questions remain as to who is (and will be) responsible for network maintenance, upgrades, management, and policy development and enforcement.
Internet regulation	The Internet is unregulated. Questions are being raised in the U.S. Congress as to what represents acceptable use of and behavior on the Internet. It is uncertain whether the Internet will remain unregulated. Some information available on the Internet may be considered offensive to certain people. The Internet is accessed by millions of users, most of them "surfers," not buyers.

Figure 7-2   Disadvantages and Obstacles to Widespread Use of the Internet by Business

■ WHAT IS AN INTRANET?

An **intranet** is a private network based on TCP/IP protocols. It belongs to an organization and is accessible only by the organization's members, employees, or others with authorization. An intranet's web site looks and acts just like any other Web site, but the firewall surrounding an intranet fends off unauthorized access. Like the Internet itself, intranets are used to share information. Secure intranets are now the fastest-growing segment of the Internet because they are much less expensive to build and manage than private networks based on proprietary protocols. Figure 7-3 illustrates the relationship of intranets, firewalls, and the Internet. In order to prevent unauthorized access from the Internet into a company's confidential data, specialized software known as a **firewall** is often deployed. Firewalls are discussed later in the chapter but are covered in more depth in Chapter 13, Client/Server Information Systems Security.

What Are the Potential Advantages?

To gain the maximum benefit from an intranet, a company should start small in scope and then extend the company intranet as employees become comfortable using it. More-specific examples of benefits or trends supporting increased intranet development and access are highlighted in Figure 7-4.

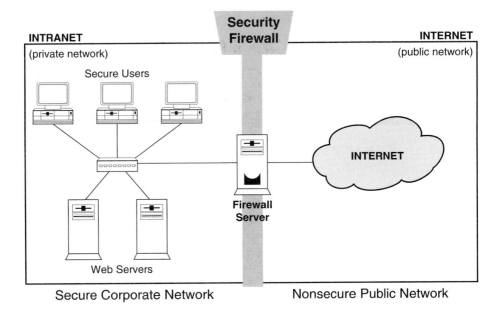

Figure 7-3 Intranets, Firewalls, and the Internet

Benefit or Supporting Trend	Implication/Explanation
Access to information	Companies are finding the web is an excellent way to distribute information.
Platform independence	Browsers are available for most platforms, so developers no longer need to worry about cross-platform development.
Allowance for multiple data types	It allows developers to provide access to various data types as well as textual information.
Access to data	Companies are integrating their data warehouses, data marts, databases, and legacy systems for access to corporate data worldwide.
Similar interface	Users will use the same interface regardless of the source of the data.
Return on investment	Companies are saving money by having the company information available to employees on-line and by reducing their paper costs.
Increased productivity	Employees can find the information they need much faster now, which leads to increased productivity.
Increased information sharing	By having a common interface and integrating applications and data, employees are able to share their ideas, brainstorm, and share their overall knowledge, which is a key to being a successful company.
Bottom-up approach	Most intranets are a result of employee interest and enthusiasm. This is one major reason why users eagerly embrace the technology.

Figure 7-4 Benefits or Supporting Trends of Intranet Development and Access

What Are the Potential Disadvantages?

From a business perspective, the current major concern of widespread business use of intranets is probably deciding where to start and what tools to use. Figure 7-5 summarizes some of the other potential disadvantages or obstacles to widespread use of intranets by business.

Disadvantage/Challenges	Implication/Explanation
Number of users	Companies need to try to estimate the number of users who will be using the intranet so they can set up an appropriate infrastructure.
Infrastructure	The number of internal servers may grow, the number of documents stored may grow, and the need for additional clients may grow as well. The growth could be hard to keep up with if the intranet is a huge success with employees.
Continuous growth and change	The type of information contained on the intranet is information that is continuously changing and growing.
Security	This may be an issue depending on the size of the company and how the infrastructure is set up.
Bandwidth	What type of impact is the intranet going to have on the available network bandwidth? Companies need to try to anticipate the size and type of information that is going to be stored and accessed on the intranet.
Scalability	Can the intranet expand without a negative impact on users?
Manageability	How easy will it be to manage the intranet?
Loss of skilled webmasters and designers	More and more companies are designing and implementing intranets to increase employee productivity by giving employees the information and resources they need to do their jobs. There is a demand for people who have skills at developing materials for both the Internet and intranets.
On-going maintenance	In order to have a successful intranet, the information must be relevant and timely. This requires continuous maintenance of the information and is one of the difficulties companies face when implementing an intranet.

Figure 7-5   Disadvantages and Challenges to Widespread Use of Intranets by Business

Issues in Designing and Implementing an Intranet

As companies start to think about designing and implementing an intranet, some issues should be addressed:

- Understand clearly the intended business objectives.

- Design around business goals, not the technology. Follow the top-down model.

- How much is it going to cost? Include costs for hardware and software purchases.

- How much will it cost to support? Include upgrades to servers and other hardware, management tools that may be needed later, labor cost, software upgrades, and licensing issues.

- Is it manageable? As the intranet grows and expands, can the company keep it manageable?

- How does it fit in with the existing systems? Will it be easy to integrate with legacy systems?

- What type of training will users need? What type of training will developers need?

- Should a company outsource the development and maintenance of the company intranet?

- What impact will it have on productivity?

- How secure is the intranet? Are policies in place?

There are many issues to consider before designing and implementing an intranet. Companies that take the time up front to address these issues and get input from people throughout the organization are going to have a higher success rate with their intranet implementations.

What Are Some Intranet Applications?

Companies are using and developing intranet applications to do a variety of jobs. The following are some examples of common types of Intranet applications:

- Discussion forums

- On-line polls

- Organizational directories

- Company policies and procedures

- Company forms

Remember, the key difference between these intranet-based applications and the collaborative applications discussed in Chapter 5 is the web-based interface and protocols of intranet applications.

Discussion Forums This can be a very powerful tool that employees within a company can use to share information and ideas. It also allows for discussions to take place on various issues that affect the company and how it operates. Users interact with each through their web browser. The discussion forum software should include the following features:

- The ability of users to post messages that contain a subject, e-mail attachments, documents, URLs, and just plain text messages

- The ability of users to read messages in various orders (i.e., by author, by date, by subject)

- The ability for users to follow up on posted messages

- Administration features such as backing up messages, deleting messages, and setting up user authorization

- The ability for users to search through all posted messages based on keywords

On-line Polls Polls can give groups and departments or the entire organization an easy way to conduct surveys or questionnaires and get a much higher return rate than the traditional paper-based approach. It also is easy for users to fill out these surveys because users are on-line and can use their web browser to answer the questions. Another nice feature of on-line polls is the fact that they may allow users to see the results of the surveys or questionnaires and see how other employees answered.

Organizational Directories Many companies start with directories when developing an intranet. The traditional form of organizational directories was paper based. Moving the company directory on-line can save an enormous amount of money and time. Updates can be made very easily and are seen immediately by employees, whereas with the traditional approach it could be months or even a year before updates were published, owing to the high cost of publishing the materials. Much information can be included in the on-line directory: employee name, department, job title, mailing address, phone number, fax number, e-mail address, web address, picture, birthday, and so on. This can give employees the ability to easily contact another employee and get the information they need and it can also help employees collaborate. Another nice feature of having an on-line directory is the fact that it can be searched based on keywords.

Company Policies and Procedures Providing employees with the company policies and procedures on-line can save a lot of time, money, and paper. Instead of asking another employee for an answer to a question about the company's policy regarding a particular issue, an employee can look on-line for the information. Employees can also search for information based on keywords. They can also keep up-to-date on the latest policies and procedures by going on-line. Access can be limited to sensitive information by assigning a user identification and password to the information.

Company Forms Forms are at the heart of most business processes. If a company can successfully implement some or all of the company forms on the intranet, it can save a huge amount of time and money by having the forms filled out electronically and possibly automatically routed to the proper employee for approval or storage.

Companies That Have Implemented an Intranet

Many companies have already implemented a pilot intranet with great initial success and are now looking at moving some mission-critical applications to the intranet. Other companies are still designing and developing smaller intranet applications. Below are some real-world examples of how companies are using an intranet to distribute company information and improve customer service:

- Federal Express has taken tracking data from its mainframe and has developed a software interface to query the mainframe via a web browser interface. Users can connect to the Federal Express tracking application via the Internet. When first developed, this intranet application was for internal use, but now Federal Express has allowed the public to use it. This is an excellent example of how companies can use their existing infrastructure and expand it to allow for better customer service.

- Hewlett Packard has over 200 internal web servers that can be accessed by their employees. The employees use the intranet to coordinate projects among geographically dispersed team members. They also use it to schedule meetings, get software configurations, request equipment, and generate reports.

- IBM Corporation has implemented an intranet with a virtual meeting place for employees as well as a place where they can get company information. For example, employees can get travel information and download software.

- Sun Microsystems has implemented an intranet that provides valuable company information to its employees. Employees have access to the company's organizational chart, product information, product catalog, and human resources information. Sun has been so successful with its implementation of the intranet that it also has a place on the intranet where employees can use applications to improve their productivity.

WHAT IS AN EXTRANET?

An **extranet** is a network that uses Internet technology to link businesses with their partners, customers, suppliers, and other businesses that share common goals. The extranet is a derivative of both an intranet and the Internet. It requires both an internal network (intranet) to provide the content and an external network (Internet) to provide the connectivity. The purpose of an extranet is to give both internal and external environments access to computer-based information. Figure 7-6 illustrates a high-level architectural view of an extranet implementation.

What Are the Potential Advantages?

To gain the maximum benefits from an extranet, a company should first identify the business partners, suppliers, and others it wants to include in the extranet. Then it should identify and discuss how the extranet will be set up and also discuss what data will be accessible. Planning for the development and implementation of an extranet can help a company in many ways. More-specific examples of benefits or trends supporting increased extranet development and access are highlighted in Figure 7-7.

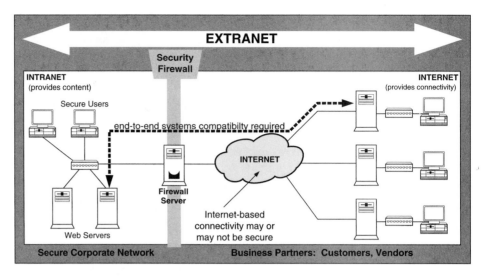

Figure 7-6 High-Level Architectural View of Extranets

What Are the Potential Disadvantages?

From a business perspective, the current major concern of widespread business use of extranets is probably operational: deciding where to start and what tools to use. Figure 7-8 summarizes some of the other potential disadvantages or obstacles to widespread use of intranets by business.

Benefit or Supporting Trend	Implication/Explanation
Streamlined business processes	By allowing electronic communication to occur with suppliers and business partners, all the parties involved can get more accomplished in less time.
Flexibility and scalability	Companies can easily add new business partners to the extranet without having to make a huge investment.
Reduced traditional barriers	By developing and implementing a successful extranet, companies can reduce the barriers that exist between them and start to work together more cooperatively.
Decreased costs	By improving business processes, companies can reduce cost and achieve high return on investment.
Ease of use and maintenance	If the architecture is set up correctly, it should be easy for users to use the extranet and easy for information technology professionals to maintain it.
Versatility	Companies can exchange documents and forms, have on-line discussions, and share information much faster.
Cost and return on investment	To develop, implement, and maintain an extranet, the cost is quite low. It can be easy to cost justify, and according to industry research, the payback period can be as short as 15 weeks.

Figure 7-7 Benefits or Supporting Trends of Extranet Development and Access

Disadvantage/Challenges	Implication/Explanation
No support from top management	In order for an extranet to be successful, top managers from all companies need to outline the business objectives and goals for the extranet. It is important to get input from everyone in all organizations.
Maintenance of information	If the companies included within the extranet do not keep their information current and up to date, their business partners could be making decisions with incorrect information. This could cause companies to dissolve their relationships.
Lack of training	If people don't understand the benefits or are not trained on how to use the extranet, then it will be unsuccessful.
Information overload	Employees may feel overwhelmed with the amount of information available on the extranet. Also, the web administrators may feel stress at having to maintain and update all the information.
Waste of productivity	If it isn't valuable to the company and employees, then it is a waste of time to design and develop.
Security	Companies need to have cooperation and good communication about what type of information is going to be exchanged. Once that is determined, it is extremely important to decide how security issues will be handled.

Figure 7-8   Disadvantages and Challenges to Widespread Use of Extranets by Business

Issues in Designing and Implementing an Extranet

As companies start to think about designing and implementing an extranet, they should address some issues:

- Security. This is the number one issue that must be addressed so that only the companies with permission have access to the information. As information leaves one company and is being delivered to the other company, it needs to be delivered securely. The architecture must be secure so that companies will use and expand the extranet in the future. One way companies are securing their extranets is by using virtual private networks (VPN). In order to provide virtual private networking capabilities using the Internet as an enterprise network backbone, specialized tunneling protocols needed to be developed that could establish private, secure channels between connected systems. Virtual private networks are discussed more in Chapter 13, Client/Server Information Systems Security.

- Compatibility. When companies are linking their systems together, they must make sure of the proper level of compatibility.

- Flexibility and adaptability. As relationships are created and ended, the extranet needs to be flexible and adapt to new business situations.

- Scaleability. As a company grows, the need for the extranet to grow heightens. When designing the extranet, consider scaleability. As business environments change, the business extranet must be able to change with the business.

- Who should be included as members of the extranet?

- What are the business objectives and goals?

- How will the extranet be coordinated and controlled?

- What business gain is there by making a given company a member of the extranet?

- How much does the company want to spend on this investment?

- How is the company going to measure its return on investment?

- What applications can be developed and deployed on the extranet?

There are many issues to consider before designing and implementing an extranet. Companies need to commit the time to address these issues and answer the questions. It is also important to get input from employees within the company as well as from business partners, suppliers, and customers.

What Are Some Extranet Applications?

Companies are using and developing extranet applications to do a variety of jobs. Here are some examples of extranet applications:

- Private news groups and collaborative projects

- Common business materials

- Electronic commerce

- Improved customer service and sales

Private News Groups   Private news groups can be set up between business partners, suppliers, and others to share information and brainstorm solutions. This can help increase the number of ideas and allow employees at various companies to collaborate with one another and get to trust one another. Another use of news groups can be the sharing of valuable experiences and information on customers. Members of the extranet can also collaborate in developing applications that are beneficial to everyone involved.

Common Business Materials   An extranet can allow different companies to develop applications jointly that benefit all parties involved. This can be beneficial in that the development of an application can benefit multiple companies and save companies money by working on the project collaboratively instead of individually. Companies can also share other business materials such as training materials and other educational materials.

Electronic Commerce   Many companies have either already developed and implemented electronic commerce or are researching how they can buy and sell their products electronically. This area of extranets is growing the fastest because many companies believe that in order to be competitive, they must be able to reach their customers in new ways before their competitors beat them to it.

There is a difference between electronic commerce (e-commerce) and electronic data interchange (EDI). **EDI** involves the transfer of business documents by electronic means rather than traditional means. EDI is generally text-based, whereas electronic commerce can be text-based and can also contain other data types. EDI existed long before electronic commerce was around. **Electronic commerce** can be defined as conducting business on-line, which includes buying and selling products with digital cash. As the popularity of the Internet and WWW increases, the number of companies looking to conduct business via electronic commerce is increasing. Secure Electronic Transactions (SET) are discussed in Chapter 13, Client/Server Information Systems Security.

Some companies that are using electronic commerce to reach their customers are Southwest Airlines and Federal Express. For example, customers can track the status of their package through the Federal Express extranet. This can lead to improved customer service since it is one more service offered by the company to their customers.

Improved Customer Service and Sales   Customers can get increased service by being able to track, find, and compare information and make the best purchasing decision for themselves or for their companies. Extranets can also help companies sell more of their products by providing customer service representatives and employees with the most up-to-date information. The information could include the latest marketing brochures, company forms, templates, product catalogs, or customer information.

Companies That Have Implemented an Extranet

Many companies have already successfully implemented an extranet and are now looking at expanding it. Other companies are still designing and developing extranet applications. Here are some examples of how companies are using an extranet to distribute company information, improve business relationships, and improve customer service:

- Fruit of the Loom has implemented an extranet and has already seen an increase in the number of sales and an increase in market share. The extranet links Fruit of the Loom with its distributors, and it lets distributors sell its competitors' tee-shirts along with the Fruit of the Loom brand. The distributor must make a two-year commitment to sell products from the Fruit of the Loom extranet. Distributors that use the extranet can order and check inventory online.

- Countrywide Home Loans has implemented an extranet. It allows banks and mortgage brokers select access to financial information contained in the company intranet. By allowing its business partners access to the financial information, Countrywide can move mortgage applications through the approval process much faster.

- The Chicago Title Insurance Company, the nation's largest real estate title insurer, has implemented an extranet that has already paid for itself by allowing the company to reduce the number of paralegals needed to complete business transactions. The extranet lets lawyers search court records to make sure there are no liens on the property they are selling. The extranet contains all the forms and property information needed to complete a commercial real estate transaction and purchase title insurance. The lawyers can easily access the extranet by using a web browser. In order to use the extranet for free, the lawyers must purchase the title insurance from Chicago Title Insurance Company. The implementation of this extranet has been so successful that the company is looking at expanding it in other geographical locations.

A CLIENT/SERVER APPROACH TO INTERNET CONNECTIVITY

Before deciding which combination of technology and network services must be employed in order to provide the desired Internet access, businesses must first determine what the nature of that Internet access will be. When it comes to Internet access, companies can be either **information consumers, information providers,** or a combination of the two. Depending on the nature of the desired access to the Internet, technology requirements can vary dramatically.

Overall Client/Server Architecture for Internet Connectivity

Figure 7-9 illustrates an overall view of some of the ways in which businesses can access Internet services as either information consumers or providers. Elements of the overall architecture are explained below, and more-specific alternative connectivity options for World Wide Web, information servers, and global e-mail access follow.

As will be explained further in the section on Internet connectivity services, a company should be able to purchase as much or as little Internet connectivity assistance as it deems appropriate. Although there are no firm rules, Internet service providers are often categorized as follows:

- **Internet Access Providers (IAPs).** Also known as Internet connectivity providers (ICPs), these are primarily concerned with getting a subscriber company physically hooked up to the Internet. The IAP may provide for additional hardware acquisition and maintenance, but it is unlikely to provide programming services. IAPs may be the local or long distance phone company or may be a business entirely independent of established phone companies. IAPs are most concerned with the infrastructure required to provide Internet access for subscriber companies.

- **Internet Presence Providers (IPPs).** These providers are primarily concerned with designing, developing, implementing, managing, and maintaining a subscriber company's presence on the Internet. IPPs may depend on IAPs for the actual physical access to the Internet. If a company wanted a web page on the World Wide Web but did not want to invest in the required hardware and personnel to launch such a venture in-house, that company would be likely to contract with an IPP.

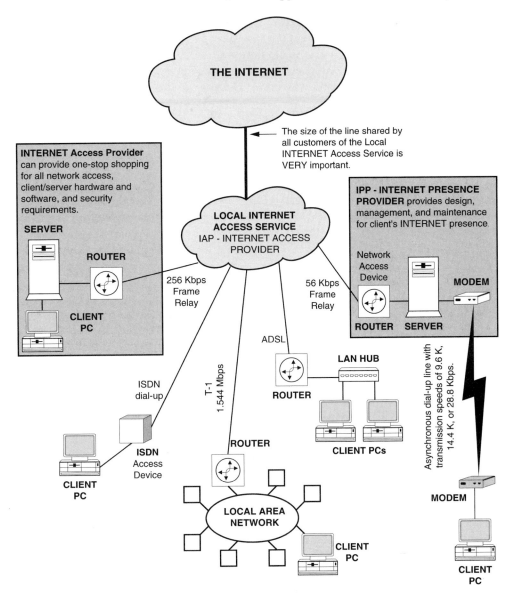

Figure 7-9   Overall Client/Server Architecture for Internet Connectivity

Clients, servers, and local area networks are connected to the Internet via a **network access device** such as a modem, an ISDN network access device, or a router. Which particular network access device is required in each case is a function of the type and bandwidth of the access line and the characteristics of the client or server to which the network access device must interface.

Those companies that wish to be only Internet information consumers require only a properly configured client PC to be connected to the Internet. Companies wishing to be only information providers on the Internet require a properly configured server to be connected to the Internet. Companies wishing to both consume and provide Internet information must have both clients and servers properly attached.

Service-Specific Client/Server Architectures for Internet Connectivity

Configurations of client and server hardware and software will vary, depending on which Internet services a company wishes to access. Alternative configurations for each major category of Internet services are explained in the following section.

World Wide Web Connectivity Alternatives   Internet information consumers wishing to access the World Wide Web will require a client PC configured with a front-end software tool or web browser such as **Internet Explorer** or **Netscape.** Several connectivity alternatives exist for those companies that wish to establish a presence or web site on the World Wide Web. The characteristics of these alternatives are detailed in Figure 7-10 . Each connectivity option listed in Figure 7-10 is broken down into the major processes involved in establishing and maintaining a web site. Depending on the connectivity alternative chosen, these processes may be the responsibility of the company (C) wishing to establish the web presence or of the vendor (V) providing the web connectivity service. Approximate costs are also included for each connectivity alternative.

Managerial Perspective

Each of the alternatives for establishing a web site outlined in Figure 7-10 has its advantages and disadvantages. There is no single best way for all businesses to establish a World Wide Web presence. A company must first understand the business objectives of establishing such a presence:

- Improved customer service to existing customers

- Increased or more focused marketing opportunities toward potential customers

- Response to competitive pressures

- Need for profitability of web presence

While the first alternative listed in Figure 7-10, "Post Customer-Designed Page on Access Provider's Server," is relatively inexpensive, the sophistication of the web presentation will not match that of the more-expensive web connectivity alternatives. For example, it is less likely that such web pages would be highly interactive and possess the ability to prompt and store customer responses.

Hiring a web service provider to perform all aspects of establishing and managing a web site is certainly a quicker and more certain way to get on the web, but obviously this option can run up a substantial financial investment. The experience offered by at least some of these providers enables the production of professional quality presentations, which can then be incorporated into **cybermalls** with other professional-quality web pages adhering to the standards established by the cybermall management.

Hiring, training, and keeping an in-house staff to maintain a company's web site is a distinct third alternative. Hiring experienced web site developers can be costly, but waiting out the learning curve of new hires will delay the establishment of a web site. Operation costs for maintaining the web server and access to the Internet also need to be considered, as does the security concerns of anonymous access to corporate network facilities.

Finally, a mix of the previous three approaches is also possible. Perhaps a web service provider could be hired on a fixed length contract to quickly establish a quality web site. Depending on customer response and potential profitability of the web site, in-house staff could be hired and trained as management of the web site is gradually transitioned to them.

Connectivity Alternative	Design, Develop, and Maintain Web Page	Establish and Maintain Internet Node	Establish, Maintain, and Manage Network Access	Configure and Maintain the Web Server	Approximate Cost, Both Recurring (RC) and Nonrecurring (NRC)
Post Customer-Designed Page on Access Provider's Server	C	V	V	V	$20–$40/month (RC)
Hire Web Service Provider	V	V	V	V	$100–$1000 (NRC) $25–$10,000/ month (RC)
In-House Development and Deployment	C	C	C	C	$1,000s/month (RC)—Depends on number of staff assigned

Figure 7-10   Web Server Connectivity Alternatives

Information Server Connectivity Alternatives   Information servers such as FTP/Telnet, Gopher, UseNet, and WAIS are not mutually exclusive of one another or of web servers. A company does not need to make a strategic decision to implement one of the four types of information servers. They all share a common goal to present primarily text-based information to Internet users. They differ in the manner in which that information is organized and accessed. In some cases, one type of information service can be integrated within another. Figure 7-11 illustrates the complementary nature of the various types of information servers.

The diagrams in Figure 7-11 represent logical or functional design alternatives. How each of these logical designs are physically implemented is elaborated upon in the section "Client/Server Technology for Internet Connectivity."

Global E-Mail Connectivity Alternatives   An abundance of alternatives exist for how a company can connect to the Internet for global e-mail services. As with other Internet service connectivity alternatives already reviewed, options vary primarily in cost, available functionality, ease of use, and security. Figure 7-12 summarizes some of the functional features of selected global e-mail connectivity alternatives, and Figure 7-13 compares the physical connectivity of each of these global e-mail connectivity alternatives.

Internet Transport Protocols   TCP/IP (Transmission Control Protocol/Internet Protocol) is the transport protocol used within the Internet, which allows different types of computers and network access devices to exchange messages and deliver data and e-mail. In Figure 7-13, the network access devices, most often routers, that connect to Internet services package their messages according to the Internet-standard TCP/IP protocols. The phone lines connecting the network access devices to the Internet are direct or leased lines that are constantly connected. In this way, it is as if the remote network access device is directly connected to the devices on the Internet and therefore can converse with the Internet-attached computers (nodes, hosts) using the native transport protocol, TCP/IP.

Nonintegrated

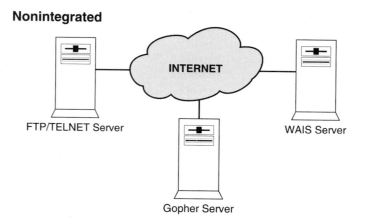

Two-Layer Integration

Three-Layer Integration

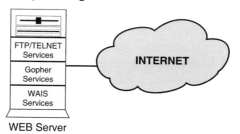

Figure 7-11 Information Server Connectivity Alternatives

However, it is not cost effective for individual client PCs to have expensive leased-line connections to Internet access providers. Instead, these stand-alone PCs, which need only occasional access to the Internet, use dial-up circuits of one type or another. Transport protocols belonging to the TCP/IP family of protocols, more properly known as the Internet Suite of Protocols, that support communication over serial or dial-up lines are **SLIP (serial line Internet protocol)** and the more recently released and more functional **PPP (point-to-point protocol).**

■ CLIENT/SERVER TECHNOLOGY FOR INTERNET CONNECTIVITY

Web browser software, otherwise known as web client software, is executed on client hardware for the purpose of accessing previously developed web pages available on Internet-attached web servers. These web servers run specialized web server software that supports **HTTP (HyperText Transport Protocol)** in order to

Global E-Mail Connectivity Alternative	Required Technology	Company Responsibilities	Approximate Cost
E-Mail Client Front-End	Internet e-mail front-end software, modem, dial-up line, Internet connection. Single user at a time solution.	Supply all required technology for each client to be connected to global e-mail. Maintain network connections.	Software: $50–$200 Modem: $150–$250 Connection: $30–$50/month plus phone charges.
E-Mail Server Gateway	Can use existing LAN server hardware. E-mail gateway software often included with either e-mail software or network operating system. Need a network access device such as a router that will allow for more than one LAN user to access e-mail services simultaneously.	Maintain gateway software and authorization for access to/from gateways. Gateways are two-way devices. They allow users into a company's LAN as well as allowing company employees to access global e-mail. Security may be an issue. Make sure size of network access line is sufficient to support required number of simultaneous users.	Software: E-mail gateway probably included. Hardware: $5000–$15,000 for server if existing one is not available, plus $3000–$5000 for router, plus network connection.
E-Mail Commercial Service	Allows individuals to connect via front-end software and modems, or corporations to connect via gateways. Software is usually supplied by the service, but many e-mail packages, network operating systems, and communications software already contain software to link to specific commercial services.	Commercial e-mail service is responsible for maintaining network connections and may also offer hardware and software support at user or corporate sites. Commercial services often offer value-added services beyond simple e-mail such as news and information services, fax, or full Internet connection to WWW.	Monthly fees of $30 to several hundred dollars per month depending on number of users and level of usage.

Figure 7-12   Functionality of Global E-Mail Connectivity Alternative

manage the multiple web client requests for web pages. These web pages are collections of text, graphics, sound, and video elements and are programmed using web publishing software that may run on either client or server platforms. The web pages are programmed using text formatted with **HTML (HyperText Markup Language).** Because HTML is text-based, any text editor could be used to generate the HTML code, which would then be interpreted by the HTTP server software.

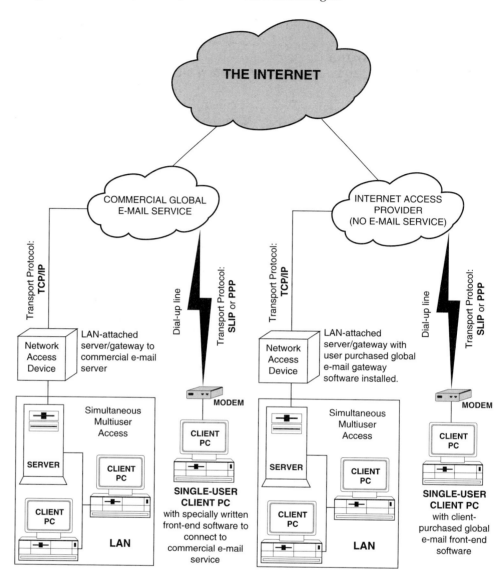

Figure 7-13 Physical Connectivity of Global E-Mail Alternatives

When a web client running web browser software requests a web page or constituent element from a web server by clicking on a hyperlink, a TCP/IP message is sent to the web server identified in the **URL (Uniform Resource Locator).** Included in this message is the identity of the requested web page file noted with an HTML extension, and a version indicator identifying which version of HTML the requesting client understands. In response, the web server retrieves the requested file and transfers it to the web client. Figure 7-14 distinguishes between web browsers, web servers, and web publishers.

Web Clients

Web Browsers Web browsers are a client-based category of software that is undergoing tremendous development owing to the vast interest in the World Wide Web.

WEB PAGE PUBLISHING

➡ Web page is published using Web publishing software running on either a client or a server.

➡ Web page is formatted using HTML (Hypertext Markup Language).

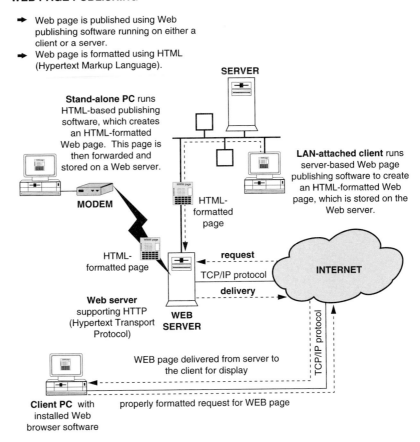

Figure 7-14 Web Clients, Web Servers, and Web Publishers

The scope of web browser software is expanding horizontally to include access not only to Internet-attached resources but also to other resources:

- Local client-attached resources

- Local area network–attached resources

- Enterprise or corporate network–attached resources

The latest web browser products display all reachable resources, from the local PC to the worldwide Internet, on a single hierarchical file tree display. The scope of web browser software is also expanding vertically by including access to all Internet-attached resources and services and not merely to the World Wide Web. By combining navigation features of traditional web browsers and search features of information server front ends, the latest web browsers include many resources:

- Global e-mail

- Search agents

- FTP

- Gopher

- WAIS and other index and search engines

- UseNet news groups

Web browsers' transition to managing locally attached hardware resources means that they must now be more closely integrated with client operating systems. Whereas in the past, web browsers were just another application program executing over a particular operating system via APIs and operating system calls, they are now more like a single integrated piece of software with a particular client operating system embedded within the web browser software. This is an interesting phenomenon to observe, as web browser software vendors such as Netscape and Wollongong attempt to embed operating systems within their web browsers and traditional operating systems vendors such as Microsoft, IBM, and Novell attempt to embed web browsers within their operating systems. For example, Windows 95 features an add-on known as the Internet Explorer Browser, and OS/2 Warp includes the Web Explorer.

Many high-quality web browsers can be downloaded from the Internet and are available at little or no charge. In general, all web browsers offer transparency to users from the following concerns and compatibility issues:

- Geography—users do not need to know the web address or physical location of the destination web server

- Storage file format—users do not need to know the file format of the target web page feature regardless of whether the web page feature is text, sound, video, or image

- Hardware characteristics and operating system of the destination web server

- Type of network or transport protocol involved with the destination web server

Figure 7-15 summarizes the key comparative criteria to consider when evaluating web browser software.

One thing to bear in mind about web browsers and their ability to search the World Wide Web for a particular web page or topic is that web browsers still require a master web index service or home page. The Lycos home page at Carnegie-Mellon University is an example of such a master web indexing service. Indexed web pages located throughout the Internet are accessible through Lycos via hot-clickable links known as **URLs,** or **uniform resource locators.**

URLs are also used within a given web page to allow **hypertext** links to other related web pages, documents, or services such as e-mail. The term *hypertext* merely refers to documents that have the ability to link to other documents. In web pages, hypertext is usually highlighted in a different color and hot-clickable for instant access to the linked document.

Pull technology is to request data from another program or computer. The opposite of pull is **push,** where data is sent without a request being made. The terms *push* and *pull* are used frequently to describe data sent over the Internet. The World Wide Web is based on pull technologies, where a page isn't delivered until a browser requests it. Increasingly, however, information services are using the Internet to broadcast information using push technologies. A prime example is the Point-Cast Network.

Web Browser Characteristic	Explanation/Implication
Vertical Integration	• Does the web browser software supply access to all Internet-attached resources, including global e-mail?
Ease of Set-Up and Use	• How easy is the software to install and configure? • Is technical support available and helpful? • Can the web browser handle dial-up connections using SLIP/PPP as well as LAN-attached connections using TCP/IP?
Performance	• Can multiple sessions be executed simultaneously? • Can the web browser be easily customized with user bookmarks, which remember paths to particular Internet resources? • Can graphics be partially displayed while they are still being downloaded? • Can the web browser link easily to other programs such as word-processing, spreadsheet, or presentation graphics programs? • Can downloaded material be easily transferred into other applications programs? • Can the web browser support a variety of sound and video compression and storage formats? • Can URLs (uniform resource locators) for new resources be added easily? • Can hot lists (local lists of bookmarks for favorite web pages) be annotated with user notes? • Which versions of HTML does the browser support?
Horizontal Integration	• Does the web browser organize access to only Internet-attached resources, or are locally and network-attached resources also accessible through the browser?

Figure 7-15   Web Browsers Differentiating Criteria

Applied Problem Solving

WEB BROWSER TECHNOLOGY ANALYSIS

An individual working in the information technology industry must always seek out the latest information that the industry has to offer before making recommendations for purchases. An individual must be able to do this successfully to ensure that the company can gain a competitive advantage as well as to ensure his or her own job security. The web browser technology analysis grid shown in Figure 7-16 is an example and provides a good place to start, but an individual should conduct more research to get the latest information available. The technology analysis grid is divided into the following major categories:

- Browsers
- Push/Off-line Browsing/Web Desktops
- Collaboration
- News and Mail
- HTML Authoring

Web Browser Characteristic		Questions or Issues to Address
Browser	Page rendering	• How fast does the browser render pages? • How does it handle Java script?
	Search tools	• Is it easy to use search tools? • Are the major search engines listed in one of the toolbars?
	File uploading and downloading	• How quickly does it upload or download pages?
	Customizable toolbars	• Does it allow you to change the typeface and size? • Does it allow you to select which e-mail reader or news reader you want to use?
	Interface	• Does it allow you to customize your interface? • Is the interface easy to use and understand?
	Toolbars	• Is it easy to see search results, recently visited sites, or favorites? • Does it allow for customizing of toolbars?
	Bookmarks	• Does the browser allow for users to have a window open showing their bookmarks in addition to the main window?
	Printing	• Does it allow the user to print individual frames? • Does it allows a user to print a page of links?
Push/Off-Line Browsing/ Web Desktops	Channel availability	• What channels are supported by the browser? • Does it allow the user to control how much information is downloaded from a channel? • Does it allow the user to control how much information is downloaded from a channel?
	Web integration	• Can users make their desktop look like the web browser interface? • Does it provide the user with the choice of having an active desktop?
	Off-line browsing	• How does the browser cache browser and channel content? Together, separately, not at all?
Collaboration	Options	• Does the browser offer audio, video, whiteboarding, chatting, application sharing, or other collaborative features? • Does it support multiple party collaborating? More than two people at a time? • Does it allow for collaborative browsing? • Does it allow for personal or group scheduling? • Does it support cross-platform collaboration?

News and Mail	Customizable interface	• Does the browser support e-mail and news? • Can the user customize the interface? • Are the e-mail and news reader interfaces easy to use and understand?
	Inbox rules and filters	• Does it support the use of rules and filters?
	Off-line support	• Can you consolidate messages from a variety of different accounts?
HTML Authoring	WYSIWYG (what you see is what you get) editing	• Does the browser come with a basic web page editor? • How powerful is the editor? • How easy is it to use?
	Options	• Does it include a spell checker? • Does it come with any wizards?
	Preview in browser	• Does it allow the user to preview the web page in the browser automatically?
	Uploading to web site	• Does it have built-in file transfer tools to transfer the web pages to the web site?

Figure 7-16   Web Browser Technology Analysis

Internet E-Mail Front Ends   Although Internet or global e-mail front-end functionality may be included in web browser software, the unique nature of the protocols and functionality involved with Internet e-mail front ends warrants a separate discussion. Figure 7-17 illustrates the relationship between mail clients, mail servers, Internet post-offices and associated protocols.

A key feature of Internet e-mail front ends in their ability to allow attached documents of various types such as reports, spreadsheets, or presentations to be attached to the Internet e-mail. The e-mail recipient on the destination client is able to unattach the previously attached documents from the received e-mail message. A protocol known as **MIME (Multipurpose Internet Mail Extension)** allows documents to be attached to e-mail regardless of the source application program, operating system, or network operating system. Figure 7-18 highlights some of the key comparative criteria to consider when evaluating Internet e-mail front ends. Depending on the operating system or network operating system installed on a client PC, a separate Internet e-mail front end may not be required. For example, Microsoft Mail client is included with Windows NT, Windows for Workgroups, Windows 95, and the Microsoft Office application suite.

Mail server management protocols may be either **POP (Post Office Protocol)** or **IMAP (Internet Mail Access Protocol)**. IMAP is a more recent standard and possesses features added in response to increased remote connectivity and mobile computing. In order to minimize the amount of time and bandwidth required to download one's e-mail for review, a stand-alone Internet e-mail client connected via a dial-up line to an Internet e-mail server can download just the headers of received e-mail, stating the e-mail sender, date, subject, and hopefully file size. Remotely connected e-mail users can then selectively download only those e-mail messages that they wish to see immediately.

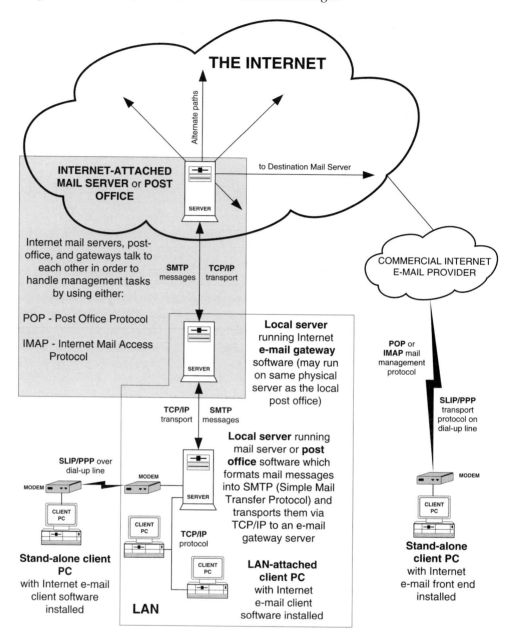

Figure 7-17   Internet E-Mail Clients, Servers, Post Offices, and Protocols

Internet/Web Gateways

Internet E-Mail Gateways   LAN-based mail servers act as post offices, delivering mail to intended LAN-attached recipients and forwarding nonlocal destination mail onto other distant mail servers (post offices) for eventual delivery to clients. Mail servers run a particular type of mail server software such as Microsoft Mail or cc:Mail. When clients on the LANs to which these mail servers are attached run the same type of e-mail client software, no translation between mail systems is neces-

Internet E-Mail Client Characteristic	Explanation/Implication
Setup and Installation	• How easy is it to set up this Internet e-mail client? • What are the memory and disk requirements? • What client operating systems is this e-mail software compatible with?
Mail Creation and Editing	• How flexible is the address book creation? • How easy is it to copy or send to multiple recipients? • Is the mail creation editor nearly as powerful as a word processor? • Is spell checking available? • Can different types of documents be attached to e-mail? • Is MIME supported?
Mail Handling and Management	• Can mail be routed as well as sent to multiple recipients? • How easy is it to reply to, forward, or print mail? • Can just e-mail headers be downloaded from remote locations? • How many ways can incoming or sent mail be sorted? • Can private folders in which to sort mail be created? • Can the folders be arranged hierarchically? • How easy is it to create and maintain public and private address lists, including groups? • What levels of security are provided? Passwords? Encryption? • Can other applications that correspond to attached documents be launched from within the e-mail client software?

Figure 7-18   Internet E-Mail Clients Differentiating Criteria

sary. However, when a Microsoft Mail client wants to send e-mail via the Internet to a cc:Mail client, translation is required. This translation is supplied by an **Internet e-mail gateway.** The Internet e-mail gateway acts as a translator, speaking a LAN-specific e-mail software protocol on one side and speaking the Internet's **SMTP (Simple Mail Transport Protocol)** on the other. Depending on the transport protocol used by the local area network, the Internet e-mail gateway may also have to translate between transport protocols since the Internet uses strictly TCP/IP.

Figure 7-19 illustrates the relationship between LAN-based mail servers, Internet e-mail gateways, and the Internet.

A key differentiating factor among Internet e-mail gateway products is their ability to support document attachment through support of protocols such as MIME. Some e-mail gateways also limit the number of attachments per e-mail message. Whether or not the Internet e-mail gateway software can be monitored by the local area network's system monitoring or performance monitoring is also important. Gateways are a likely location for system bottlenecks owing to the amount of processing involved with translating between mail protocols, especially at high traffic levels.

The Internet e-mail gateway product itself is actually strictly software. It is installed like any other application over a particular operating system, most often DOS or OS/2. The required power of the hardware on which the gateway software must execute is a product of the amount of Internet e-mail that must be translated by the gateway. In some cases, the gateway software may be physically installed on

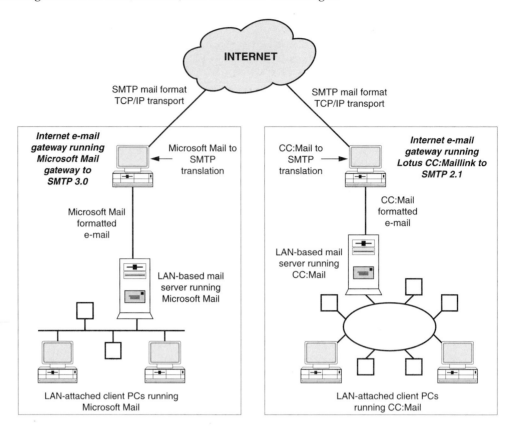

Figure 7-19   LAN-Based Mail Servers, Internet E-Mail Gateways, and the Internet

the same server as the LAN-based e-mail server software. In other cases, increased Internet-bound e-mail traffic warrants a dedicated server.

Internet Gateways versus Internet Servers   While Internet e-mail gateways offer translation strictly between different LAN-based e-mail packages, **Internet Gateways** offer a LAN-attached link for client PCs to access a multitude of Internet-attached resources including e-mail, FTP/Telnet, news groups, Gopher, and the World Wide Web. An Internet gateway is a software product that includes multiuser versions of the client front-ends for each supported Internet-attached resource. The Internet gateway also translates between the local area network's transport protocol and TCP/IP. An Internet gateway is an *access*-oriented product.

An Internet gateway offers no Internet-attached services for users from distant corners of the Internet. An Internet gateway is strictly an on-ramp into the Internet. LAN-attached client PCs accessing the Internet through the Internet gateway must seek the Internet services they desire from an **Internet server.** An Internet server runs a server application and offers e-mail services, Gopher services, news group services, or World Wide Web services to all Internet-attached users.

As an alternative to an Internet gateway, LAN-attached client PCs can also set up individual links to Internet servers via a shared router. Each client PC must be loaded with TCP/IP software and Internet client software for whatever Internet services the user wishes to access. Figure 7-20 distinguishes between the connectivity of Internet gateways, Internet servers, and Internet-enabled clients. Figure 7-21 highlights the advantages and disadvantages of Internet gateways versus Internet-enabled clients.

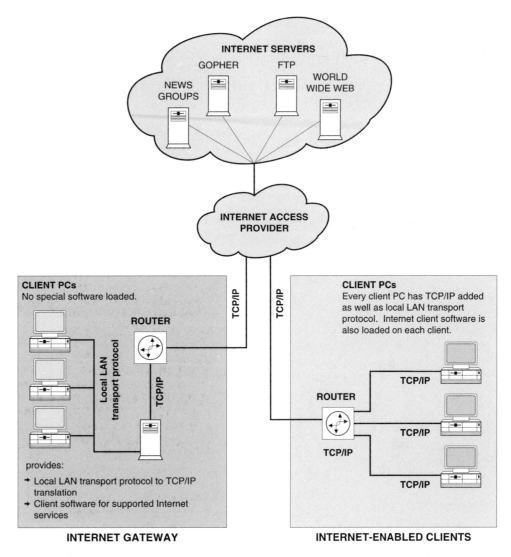

Figure 7-20   Internet Gateways, Internet Servers, and Internet-Enabled Clients

	Internet Gateway	Internet-Enabled Clients
Advantages	• Single location of TCP/IP and client front ends easier to implement and manage than multiple client locations.	• Eliminates gateway as potential bottleneck.
Disadvantages	• Gateway can become a bottleneck with a large number of users.	• Every client requires its own TCP/IP software and Internet client front ends. • Each client PC must be individually configured and managed. • Client PCs also need to be able to use local LAN transport protocol.

Figure 7-21   Internet Gateways versus Internet-Enabled Clients

Internet/Web Servers

An **Internet server** requires a combination of hardware and software to offer these services:

- Web services
- Global e-mail
- FTP/Telnet services
- UseNet news group services

A **web server** combines hardware and software components to offer primarily web services, but increasingly web servers are also offering links to Gopher, FTP, and news services, making the terms *web server* and *Internet server* more and more synonymous. Web servers may also contain software to develop or program web pages and web applications.

Server Hardware/Software Analysis   Any Internet or web server implementation requires four basic components:

1. A link to the Internet via an appropriately sized (sufficient bandwidth) access transmission line

2. An IP address that uniquely identifies the intended server among all Internet-attached servers

3. The server hardware that will connect to the Internet and fulfill client requests

4. The server software that will run on the server hardware; in the case of a web server, this server software is usually based on the HTTP (HyperText Transfer Protocol) server from NCSA (National Center for Supercomputing Applications)

The link to the Internet would be purchased from a local telecommunications company and would be terminated at a chosen Internet Access Provider (IAP). In some cases, the IAP will make the arrangements for the access line with the local telecommunications vendor. The IP address to uniquely identify an Internet or Web server could be provided by either the IAP or the InterNIC, which is the sole official authority in charge of issuing Internet IP addresses.

In order to understand the types of hardware and software required to successfully implement an Internet or web server, one must first examine intended objectives of the server, focusing especially on the server's intended audience and what services will be offered to that audience. The server may strictly offer access to web pages or may also offer gateway services to file transfer and search resources such as FTP, Gopher, UseNet, and WAIS.

For example, a company that wishes to offer only product information could suffice with a web server, but a gateway to file transfer and search engines would be required for a company wishing to offer on-line technical support as well. Because proposals for implementing security protocols to ensure the confidentiality of financial transactions over the Internet are pending, companies should be wary of implementing widespread financial dealings via the Internet. Web security will be discussed shortly in the section on Internet/web application development. Some companies may wish only to display product information on web pages, that others may want customer input for demographic or product development purposes. The ability to handle customer input forms is a web server software capability that cannot be assumed.

Server Software   Internet/web server software differs in its ability to deliver any or all of the following capabilities:

- Web page display and management

- Gateway to Internet file transfer and search engines such as FTP, Gopher, UseNet, and WAIS

- Level of security supported

- Ability to develop and manage customer input forms

- Ability to monitor and report on web page or Internet resource usage (This feature is important in order to be able to cost justify the investment in server hardware and software. Is the intended customer audience responding in the intended fashion?)

- Ability to integrate management functions with the enterprise management system of the server's operating system

Besides just displaying web pages, web servers may also possess the ability to execute interactive web applications such as the previously mentioned customer input forms. Some servers offer a standardized API known as **CGI** or **common gateway interface,** which allows web applications to be written and potentially executed on multiple different web servers.

Some web server software supports **proxy servers,** which act as holding bins or repositories for previously requested web pages from distant Internet servers. If a request from a local client is received for a previously requested web page still in the local proxy server, that web page can be delivered quickly to the local client without the normal delay associated with downloading the web page again in its entirety across the Internet. The term *proxy server* is also used to refer to an application-level firewall, explained further in Chapter 13, Client/Server Information Systems Security.

Perhaps most significant among the differentiating characteristics of server software is the supporting operating system. Owing to the high processing demands of a web server, UNIX in its many variations has been the standard operating system, although Windows NT-based web server software is now available. For lower-end applications, web server software is also available for Macintosh computers.

Server Hardware   Retrieving and transmitting the highly graphical web pages with a good response time to multiple users simultaneously calls for high-performance server hardware. In order to know a recommended hardware configuration, a web server manager (webmaster) must really know how many inquiries per day are anticipated on the web server. In general, the following minimum recommendations are generally agreed upon for web server hardware configuration:

- CPU: The 120 MHz (or faster) Pentium is acceptable, but higher-speed RISC chips such as the DEC Alpha or Mips R4600 will be required for high-performance servers.

- Storage : Graphical images, digitized voice, and video take up a lot of space, so provision should be made for numerous drive bays or attachment to a RAID subsystem.

- Bus: PCI bus for fast internal transfer of images is needed.

- Memory: 128 MB installed is not unusual for web servers, with desirable potential capacities up to 1024 MB.

- Network Interface Cards: 100 MBps Ethernet or multiple 10 MBps Ethernet cards should be sufficient. Remember, Internet-attached users will be accessing this server via telecommunications lines of various bandwidths. These transmission lines are most often the least bandwidth of the entire system.

As demands for server performance increase to 250,000 or more inquiries per day, high-end UNIX workstations with over 128 MB RAM and 1 GB of disk are recommended.

Server Trends   The web server software market is very young and changing rapidly. Although many of the original web server software offerings were shareware or offered by third-party vendors, mainstream software vendors such as IBM, Microsoft, and Novell are aggressively pursuing this market. The advantage of web server software produced by the leaders in software development will be increased integration with that vendor's enterprise management system and application suites.

Applied Problem Solving

Internet Connectivity Services

A Top-Down Approach to Internet Connectivity Needs Analysis

Internet service providers vary widely in their levels of provided services and in the fees they charge for services. In order to ensure that purchased Internet services meet the business objectives of a given company, a top-down approach to Internet connectivity needs analysis should be executed. By starting with business objectives and detailing, in writing, all of the performance requirements associated with each layer of the top-down model, the network analyst will possess detailed documentation that can serve as the basis for negotiations with Internet service providers. In this manner, there is no doubt what is expected of the Internet service provider and that provided Internet services will meet stated business objectives. Figure 7-22 divides the numerous issues surrounding Internet connectivity needs analysis into their respective top-down model layers.

As is always true of top-down analysis, if the business objectives of Internet connectivity are clearly stated and verified by senior management, and each successive layer of the top-down model successfully meets the requirements of the preceding layer, then the physical network design produced on the technology layer will produce an Internet connectivity network capable of meeting initial business objectives.

Top-Down Model Layer	Internet Connectivity Needs Analysis Issues

Business	• What are the business objectives for Internet connectivity?
	   • Increased market exposure
	   • Improved customer service
	   • Response to competitive pressures
	   • Increase market share
	   • New market entry
	   • Improved market research capabilities
	   • Improved intra- and intercompany communications
	• What are the budgetary limitations of this connectivity, if any?
	• Does senior management have a preference between outsourcing or in-house development, support, management?
	• What are the availability requirements? (24hrs/day?)
	• What are the reliability requirements? (length of acceptance down-time?)
	• What are the security requirements regarding this Internet connection?
	• What are the acceptable uses of the Internet by employees?

Application	• What applications are required to support identified business objectives?
	   • Global e-mail
	   • World Wide Web
	   • Information/news services
	   • FTP/Telnet
	   • Gopher
	• Will the company be offering Internet services (web pages) for Internet users or strictly accessing Internet services?
	• How many users will be offered access to which services?
	• What is an acceptable response time for the various required Internet services? Remember, there are millions of users sharing the same network on the Internet.

Data	• Depending on the applications required, how much data (in KB) is likely to be required? • Graphical applications (WWW) have much higher bandwidth demands than text-based services.

Network	• Complete a logical network design, outlining the required functionality of the network that will successfully support the data, application, and business layer requirements of the top-down model.
	• For the amount of data required to be transferred and the acceptable response time, what is the minimum required size (KBps or MBps) of the access line to the Internet services provider?
	• What is the anticipated growth of bandwidth demand for Internet connectivity access?
	• What will be the Internet connectivity network configuration?
	   • Internet (TCP/IP) enabled clients
	   • Internet gateway
	   • Dial-up links into Internet service provider's Internet server
	• Reliability issues:
	   • What kind of redundant circuits are required?
	   • What kind of redundant or hot-swappable networking hardware is required?

Figure 7-22   Internet Connectivity Needs Analysis

Technology
- Produce a physical network design that will support the logical network design completed in the network layer of the top-down model.
- Depending on the choice of Internet connectivity services provider, any or all of these technology issues may be handled by that provider.
  - Installation, management, troubleshooting of access line
  - Size of access line between Internet provider and the Internet
  - Choice of Internet front ends, web browsers
  - Choice of web page development software
  - Choice of web/Internet server software
  - Use of proxy servers and/or local domain name servers
  - Choice of network access devices, routers
  - Development of firewalls and other security capabilities
- Who is responsible for ensuring integration and compatibility of all of the hardware and software technology?
- Who is responsible for ensuring a reasonable migration and upgradability path for acquired technology?
- What types of data transmission services are available from local telecommunications providers at each corporate site? (ISDN?, T-1?, T-3?, ATM?)
- What are the local telecommunications providers' plans for deploying high-speed data services?

Figure 7-22   *Continued*

Differences Between Internet Connectivity Service Providers   Once the Internet connectivity needs analysis has been completed and documented using the top-down model, the next step is to find the Internet connectivity service provider that best matches the business objectives and technological needs of the company. Although the range of services offered by potential Internet service providers is constantly changing, there are basically three categories of vendors involved in this market:

- Internet presence providers
- Internet access providers
- Telecommunications companies

Internet presence providers are full-service organizations offering everything from web page setup to 24-hour monitoring of Internet links. Examples of such high-end providers are the following:

- BBN Planet
- InternetMCI
- IBM Global Network

AT&T has combined its worldwide networking expertise with the Internet experience of BBN Planet in order to become a major player in the Internet presence provider arena.

Numerous local and regional Internet access providers have emerged since the recent explosion of interest in the Internet in general and the World Wide Web in particular. It is important to evaluate the financial stability of Internet service providers. Many such newly formed operations may not be sufficiently capitalized to be able to afford necessary upgrades to maintain satisfactory service levels. Especially important is the bandwidth of the access line between the Internet access provider and the Internet itself. That access line is shared by all subscribers of a particular Internet access provider. If the access line between the Internet access provider and the Internet becomes a bottleneck, then the size of a company's access line to the Internet access provider is irrelevant. Such companies may lack sufficient technical expertise to diagnose or troubleshoot compatibility or technology integration issues. It is important to have written agreements on the division of user and Internet service provider responsibilities in terms of technology integration.

If the development, installation, and management of Internet access and services is to be handled in-house, then arranging the installation of a data line for Internet access with the local telecommunications vendor may be the only interaction with outside vendors required. Outside of large metropolitan areas, the availability of data transmission services from local telecommunications vendors can vary widely. Increased deregulation of the local access market may have a dramatic effect on the availability of local data transmission services. Some local and regional telecommunications companies have developed Internet presence provider and Internet access provider services in addition to their basic data transmission services. Ameritech and PacTel are two of the more aggressive RBOCs (regional Bell operating companies) in the Internet presence provider market.

Figure 7-23 lists the typical types of activities required in order to complete a connection to the Internet and which of those activities are typically provided by Internet presence providers, Internet access providers, and local telecommunications vendors. The term *local telecommunications provider* in this case refers to companies or divisions that offer only basic data transmission services, without any Internet-related value-added services.

Beyond Internet Connectivity   Connectivity to the Internet does not necessarily meet all the wide area communications needs of a global enterprise. Another category of services commonly known as **business communications services** goes beyond Internet connectivity to include additional services:

- Video conferencing

- Simultaneous document sharing

- Electronic data interchange (EDI)

- Global fax service

- Electronic document distribution

- Paging

- E-mail

- News and information services

Internet Connectivity Activity	Internet Presence Provider	Internet Access Provider	Local Telecommunications Provider
Provide local access line for Internet connectivity	•	•	•
Monitor and manage local access	•	•	
Provide terminating equipment for local access	•	•	•
Offer security services	•		
Design and develop web page	•		
Manage and monitor web/ Internet activity	•		
Guarantee sufficient bandwidth/growth pain	•		
Provide web server hardware	•		
Provide web server software	•		
Provide client front-end software	•		
Provide Internet (IP) address	•	•	
Resolve incompatibility issues	•		
Manage global e-mail addressing issues	•		

Figure 7-23 Internet Connectivity Activities and Providers

These additional services enable globally dispersed enterprises to function as if all network-attached users were physically located in the same building. In other words, anything coworkers in the same building can accomplish ought to be possible for distant coworkers with the business communications services network. Linking people in this way is sometimes referred to as a **virtual corporation. Business communications services** can differ widely in exact services offered, but some examples include the following:

- AT&T Easylink Services
- GE Information Services Business Network
- networkMCI Business
- Sprint Mail

Some of these business communications services include access to global e-mail via the Internet. These business communications services will likely be integrated with Internet presence provider services offered by the same vendor at some time in the future.

▉ INTEGRATING THE INTERNET, INTRANETS, AND EXTRANETS

Now that we have distinguished between the Internet, an intranet, and an extranet, the remaining question is, how are companies integrating these technologies? Companies that have found a way to successfully integrate the Internet with their intranets and extranets have gained a tremendous competitive advantage over their competitors. This section of the chapter focuses on specific products and standards that companies are using to successfully integrate the Internet, intranets, and extranets.

Intranet Development Tools

Deciding what technology to use to develop both an internal intranet and an external extranet is extremely important. The first place developers want to start is with the business goals and objectives that the intranet and extranet are to meet. After determining the business goals and objectives, developers should spend some time talking to users from various areas of the company to see what their needs are and to understand how the companywide intranet can benefit everyone. After the business needs are known, then developers can use those needs as guidelines when evaluating different development products. The tools available to help people develop an intranet have grown from basic tools to more advanced tools. Here are some of the advanced features to look for:

- Does it allow for connectivity to a database?

- Does it have a visual-form designer?

- Does it generate reports?

- Does it support dynamic HTML?

- Does it support version control?

It's important to look at the various features a product has to offer, but it's also important to keep in mind the following more-general issues:

- How easy is it to use, both for developers and end users?

- Is it easy to extend?

- Is it easy to manage? Does it have built-in management tools?

- What type of performance does it have?

- What hardware platforms does it run on?

- What network operating systems and operating systems does it work with?

These are just a few examples of features to look for when evaluating development tools for the company intranet, but again, start with the business needs and use those as a guide. The intranet tool development market is still very young, so there will be many changes in this market over time.

This section of the chapter reviews and compares four intranet development tools:

- Visual InterDev from Microsoft Corporation

- Visual Café for Java from Symantec Corporation

- IntraBuilder from Borland International

- Sapphire/Web from Bluestone Software

These tools are classified as intranet development tools. Lower-level application development languages such as Java, ActiveX, XML, and VRML will be discussed in Chapter 8.

Visual InterDev   Visual InterDev is a product that was developed by Microsoft Corporation. Some of the nice features of this tool are good site management tools, good database access, full scripting, and numerous wizards. Two other features distinguish this tool from the others: Design Time ActiveX controls and support for Active Server Pages (ASP).

Design Time ActiveX controls will generate both client and server side scripts that are platform independent and will work with any browser. Active server pages are based on server-side scripts that dynamically create HTML pages. This tool used in conjunction with Microsoft Internet Information Server (IIS) provides developers with an easy way to develop active server pages.

There are a few disadvantages to using this tool. One of them is the fact that the tool is designed for developers using Windows 95 or Windows NT 4.0. Another big disadvantage of this tool compared with the others is that a developer has to manually code the design. As mentioned earlier, this tool comes with many different wizards, but industry reports show that they are not easy and straightforward to use. What type of company should use such a tool? A company that has experienced programmers and an infrastructure dominated by Microsoft products. If a company is looking for easy programming and wants to use Java, explained further in Chapter 8, this is not the tool to select. Microsoft also develops Microsoft FrontPage which is a web authoring tool. Visual InterDev is a much more developed and sophisticated web development tool than FrontPage.

Visual Café   Visual Café is a good tool to select if a company is starting an intranet from scratch. Visual Café provides a company with all the tools necessary to design and implement an intranet. Visual Café comes in different editions. A company can purchase the Web Development Edition, the Database Development Edition, or the Professional Development Edition. The Database Edition of Visual Café comes with everything a company would need in order to create and implement an intranet:

- Symantec Visual Page HTML editor

- Support for Sun Microsystems' Java Developer's Kit 1.1

- Symantec dbANYWHERE database server

- Sybase SQL Anywhere relational database

- FastTrack web server

- Netscape Communicator

Visual Café is considered a Rapid Application Development (RAD) tool and works with Windows 95 or Windows NT 4.0. Visual Café gives developers a nice, easy-to-use interface. This is one of the features that separates Visual Café from the other tools listed here. Visual Café comes with various wizards to help developers and is a great tool for programmers. Visual Café allows programmers to visually create applications using forms while the Java code is automatically written behind the form. This is a nice advantage if a company has experienced programmers who are not necessarily familiar with Java. This can be an easy way for those programmers to learn Java. A lot of the programming can be done visually, which can help reduce the amount of time needed to create a program and in turn reduce the overall cost. A company that doesn't have a lot of experienced Java programmers or that wants to interface with the corporate database a lot should consider this tool as an option.

IntraBuilder   IntraBuilder is a very robust intranet development tool. It comes in three different editions: Client/Server Edition, Standard Edition, and the Professional Edition. This tool can run on Windows 95 and Windows NT 3.51/4.0 platforms. A nice feature about this tool is its ability to interact with numerous web servers such as Microsoft Internet Information Server, Netscape FastTrack Enterprise Server, and others. This is helpful for companies that have various internet server platforms throughout the company. Developers like using this tool because it gives them an extremely powerful visual interface and easy-to-develop applications. This tool also comes with numerous wizards that developers can use, or developers can create their own forms and use more-advanced features. This tool should also be considered if a company wants different developers with different experience levels to create applications. This tool can create enterprisewide applications and also highly scalable applications. This tool is more expensive than Visual Café and Visual InterDev, but if a company is looking to do serious intranet application development at the enterprise level, then it should seriously consider the client/server edition of this tool.

Sapphire/Web   Sapphire/Web is an intranet application development tool that gives developers an easy-to-use interface and a wide variety of features. Because of the cost and complexity of the product, Sapphire/Web is a tool that should be used by companies that are going to do a lot of intranet application development. This tool is by far the most expensive of the ones discussed in this chapter. Bluestone Software, the vendor of this product, recommends that any company that chooses to use Sapphire/Web should send a programmer through a three-day training class so that the programmer can learn about all of the advanced features offered in the product. Sapphire/Web can run on Windows 95, Windows NT, and UNIX platforms. A nice feature of Sapphire/Web is the way it allows a developer to import existing HTML pages and use them. This can be a huge advantage if a company already has a lot of existing HTML pages because this product will allow for reuse of those pages. The product has a good on-line help system and includes both templates and tutorials. A company looking at doing major intranet development should consider this product, which can save developers a lot of time and money.

INTRANET DEVELOPMENT TOOLS TECHNOLOGY ANALYSIS

Figure 7-24 charts the features of four intranet development tools.

Intranet Development Total Characteristic		Visual InterDev	Visual Café	IntraBuilder	Sapphire/Web
Development Platforms	Windows NT	4.0	4.0	3.51, 4.0	3.51, 4.0
	Windows 95	Yes	Yes	Yes	Yes
	UNIX	No	No	No	Yes
Database Support	ODBC support	Yes	Yes	Yes	Yes
	JDBC support	No	Yes	No	Yes
	Platform support	Access, DB2, Informix, Oracle, SQL Server, Sybase, Visual FoxPro	Sybase, SQL Server, Oracle, Informix	Sybase, SQL Server, Oracle, Informix, Paradox, DB2, dBase	Sybase, SQL Server, DB2, Oracle, Informix
	Middleware support	DCOM	N/A	COM, DCE, OLE, RPC	RMI, IIOP, IDL
Features	Wizards	Yes	Yes	Yes	Yes
	Templates	Yes	Yes	Yes	Yes
	Java beans	No	Yes	No	Yes
	Java applets	Yes	Yes	No	Yes
	JavaScript	No	No	Yes	Yes
	VB script	Yes	No	No	Yes
	ActiveX controls	Yes	No	Yes	Yes
	Database browser	Yes	Yes	Yes	Yes
	Site management	Yes	No	No	No
	Automatic visual documentation	No	Yes	No	Yes
	Java code creation	No	Yes	No	Yes
Price		$500	$500	$2000	$5000

Figure 7-24   Intranet Development Tools Technology Analysis

Managerial Perspective

SELECTING THE APPROPRIATE INTRANET DEVELOPMENT TOOL

Keep in mind that all of these tools are in the infancy stage of development, so always check out professional magazines or the web sites of these vendors to get the latest information on the products. A company that has experienced programmers and already has an infrastructure dominated by Microsoft products should select Visual InterDev as the tool. A company that doesn't have a lot of experienced Java programmers or that wants to interface with the corporate database a lot should consider Visual Café as the tool. If a company is looking to do serious intranet application development at the enterprise level, then the client/server edition of IntraBuilder should seriously be considered. A company looking at doing major intranet development should consider Sapphire/Web because it can save developers a lot of time and money.

Standards

Companies that have developed an intranet and are looking to expand into the extranet area need to consider what standards they will use to allow interoperability between their systems and the systems of their partners. Most companies that have extended their intranet into an extranet have done so by using open application standards instead of proprietary standards. The key open application standards are outlined in Figure 7-25.

Security

The other major prerequisite for widespread use of the Internet for commercial transactions is the development and deployment of increased security for those transactions. Security of Internet transmissions actually involves multiple processes, such as the following:

- **Encryption** renders data indecipherable to any unauthorized users that might be able to examine packets of data traffic. Encryption is especially important when transmitting credit card numbers or other confidential information.

- **Authorization** screens users according to userIDs and passwords and determines by examining **Access Control Lists (ACLs)** whether a given user is authorized to access requested files or system resources.

- **Authentication** uses **digital signatures** attached to transmitted documents to ensure both the authenticity of the author and the document's **message integrity,** which verifies that the document has not been tampered with.

Each of these issues will be discussed in more detail in Chapter 13, Client/Server Information Systems Security.

Firewalls

When a company links to the Internet, a two-way access point out of as well as *into* that company's confidential information systems is created. In order to prevent

Standard	Explanation/Benefit
TCP/IP	This stands for transmission control protocol/Internet protocol. This protocol is the basis for the Internet, and it controls the reliable transmission of data from place to place.
HTML and HTTP	These support platform-independent content creation and publishing.
SMTP	This stands for simple mail transfer protocol. This messaging protocol is used in TCP/IP networks to exchange e-mail messages. In conjunction with TCP/IP, it is able to establish connections, provide reliable transport of messages, and terminate connections.
IMAP	This stands for Internet message access protocol. IMAP's features include selective downloading, server-side folder hierarchies, shared mail, and mailbox synchronization.
MIME	This stands for multipurpose Internet mail extensions. This standard is an extension of SMTP. MIME gives each attachment of an e-mail message its own header.
NNTP	This stands for network news transport protocol. UseNet servers transfer news items using this specialized transfer protocol.
LDAP intelligent directory services	This protocol will store and deliver contact information, registration data, certificates, configuration data, and server information. These intelligent services provide support for a strong authentication and secure logins.
X.509 v3 digital certificates	This standard provides for a secure container of validated and digitally signed information. Digital certificates eliminate the process of login and password dialog boxes when connecting to secure resources.
S/MIME	This stands for secure MIME. This standard uses certificate-based authentication and encryption to transmit messages between users and applications.
vCard	The vCard is an industry format for describing and displaying information typically found on a business card.
Signed objects	These allow for trusted distribution and execution of software applications and applets as part of an extranet.
EDI INT	This protocol gives a set of guidelines that combine the existing EDI standards for transmission of transaction data with the Internet protocol suite.

Figure 7-25 Open Application Standards

unauthorized access from the Internet into a company's confidential data, specialized software known as a **firewall** is often deployed. Firewall software usually runs on a dedicated server that is connected to but outside of the corporate network. All network packets entering the firewall are filtered, or examined, to determine whether those users have authority to access requested files or services.

Filtering

Every packet of data on the Internet is uniquely identified by the source address of the computer that issued the message and the destination address of the Internet server to which the message is bound. These addresses are included in a portion of the packet called the header.

A **filter** is a program that examines the source address and destination address of every incoming packet to the firewall server. Network access devices known as routers are also capable of filtering data packets. **Filter tables** are lists of addresses whose data packets and embedded messages are either allowed to proceed or prohibited from proceeding through the firewall server and into the corporate network. Filter tables can also limit the access of certain IP addresses to certain directories. This is how anonymous FTP users are restricted to only certain information resources. It obviously takes time for a firewall server to examine the addresses of each packet and compare those addresses to filter table entries. This filtering time introduces **latency** to the overall transmission time. A filtering program that examines only source and destination addresses and determines access based on the entries in a filter table is known as a **port-level filter** or **network-level filter.**

Application-level filters, otherwise known as **assured pipelines,** go beyond port-level filters in their attempts to prevent unauthorized access to corporate data. Whereas port-level filters determine the legitimacy of the party asking for information, application-level filters ensure the validity of what they are asking for. Application-level filters examine the entire request for data, rather than just the source and destination addresses. Secure files can be marked as such, and application-level filters will not allow those files to be transferred, even to users authorized by port-level filters. Understandably, assured pipelines are more complicated to configure and manage, and they introduce increased latency compared with port-level filtering.

Encryption

Encryption involves the changing of data into an indecipherable form prior to transmission. In this way, even if the transmitted data is somehow intercepted, it cannot be interpreted. The changed, unmeaningful data is known as **ciphertext.** Encryption must be accompanied by decryption, or changing the unreadable text back into its original form.

The decrypting device must use the same algorithm or method to decode or "decrypt" the data as the encrypting device used to encrypt the data. Although proprietary standards do exist, a standard known as **DES (data encryption standard),** originally approved by the National Institute of Standards and Technology (NIST) in 1977, is often used, allowing encryption devices manufactured by different manufacturers to interoperate successfully. The **DES** encryption standard actually has two parts to offer greater overall security. In addition to the standard algorithm or method of encrypting data 64 bits at a time, the DES standard also uses a 64-bit key.

The encryption key customizes the commonly known algorithm to prevent anyone without this **private key** from possibly decrypting the document. This private key must be known by both the sending and the receiving encryption devices and allows so many unique combinations (nearly 2 to the 64th power), that unauthorized decryption is nearly impossible. The safe and reliable distribution of these private keys among numerous encryption devices can be difficult. If this private key is somehow intercepted, the integrity of the encryption system is compromised.

As an alternative to the DES private key standard, **public key encryption** can be utilized. Public key encryption could perhaps more accurately be named public/private key encryption because the process actually combines usage of both public and private keys. In public key encryption, the sending encryption device encrypts a document using the intended recipient's public key. This public key is readily available in a public directory or is sent by the intended recipient to the message sender. However, in order to decrypt the document, the receiving encryption/decryption device must be programmed with the recipient's private key. In this method, only the receiving party needs to know the private key and the need for transmission of private keys between sending and receiving parties is eliminated.

As an added security measure, **digital signature encryption** uses this public key encryption methodology in reverse as an electronic means of guaranteeing authenticity of the sending party and assurance that encrypted documents have not been tampered with during transmission. The digital signature has been compared with the wax seals of old, which (supposedly) guaranteed tamper-evident delivery of documents.

With Digital Signature Encryption, a document digital signature is created by the sender using a private key and the encrypted document. To validate the authenticity of the received document, the recipient uses a public key associated with the apparent sender to regenerate a digital signature from the received encrypted document. The transmitted digital signature is then compared by the recipient to the regenerated digital signature produced by using the public key and the received document. If the two digital signatures match, the document is authentic and has not been tampered with.

**In Sharper
Focus**

Two primary standards exist for encrypting traffic on the World Wide Web:

- S-HTTP: Secure Hypertext Transport Protocol
- SSL : Secure Sockets Layer

Secure HTTP is a secure version of HTTP that requires both client and server S-HTTP versions to be installed for secure end-to-end encrypted transmission. S-HTTP is described as providing security at the document level because it works with the actual HTTP applications to secure documents and messages. S-HTTP uses digital signature encryption to ensure that the document possesses both authenticity and message integrity.

SSL is described as wrapping an encrypted envelope around HTTP transmissions. Whereas S-HTTP can be used only to encrypt Web documents, SSL can be wrapped around other Internet service transmissions such as FTP and Gopher as well as HTTP. SSL is a connection-level encryption method providing security to the network link itself.

SSL and S-HTTP are not competing or conflicting standards, although they are sometimes viewed that way. In an analogy to a postal service scenario, SSL provides the locked postal delivery vehicle, and S-HTTP provides the sealed, tamper-evident envelope that allows only the intended recipient to view the confidential document contained within.

Another Internet security protocol directed specifically toward securing and authenticating commercial financial transactions is known as **Secure Courier** and is offered by the market leader in web software, Netscape. Secure Courier is based on SSL and allows users to create a secure digital envelope for transmission of financial transactions over the Internet. Secure Courier also provides consumer authentication for the cybermerchants inhabiting the commercial Internet.

An Internet e-mail specific encryption standard that also uses digital signature encryption to guarantee the authenticity, security, and message integrity of received e-mail is known as **PGP,** which stands for **pretty good privacy**. PGP overcomes inherent security loopholes with public/private key security schemes by implementing a web of trust, in which e-mail users electronically sign one another's public keys to create an interconnected group of public key users. PGP as well as other network-related security issues are discussed in more detail in Chapter 13, Client/Server Information Systems Security.

SUMMARY

The Internet is a wide area network linking many host computers. Originally developed as a means for the research, education, and scientific communities to share information, the Internet has been opened up in recent years to more commercial uses as well as to access by individuals. Before investing in the required technology to link to the Internet, a business should first have a thorough understanding of the types of services available on the Internet and what business objectives are to be achieved by such a link.

The World Wide Web is a fully graphical Internet service that has generated a great deal of interest recently. Other Internet services include global e-mail, FTP servers, Gopher servers, and UseNet groups. Depending on how much support is required, a company may choose to enlist the services of either an Internet presence provider or an Internet access provider. These Internet connectivity services differ dramatically in the level of services offered and in some cases, level of technical expertise and financial stability.

Intranets are the fastest-growing area of the Internet. An intranet is a private network based on TCP/IP protocols belonging to an organization, accessible only by the organization's members, employees, or others with authorization. Companies are developing and implementing intranets to offer the following items: discussion forums, on-line polls, organizational directories, company policies and procedures, and company forms.

Another area that is gaining popularity is the use of extranets. An extranet is a network that uses Internet technology to link businesses with their partners, customers, suppliers, and other businesses that share common goals. The extranet is a derivative of both the intranet and the Internet. It requires both an internal network (intranet) to provide the content and the external network (Internet) to provide the connectivity. Companies are using and developing extranet applications to do a variety of jobs. Some examples include private news groups, collaborative projects, common business materials, electronic commerce, and improved customer service and sales.

With the Internet itself acting like a global LAN, an Internet-based client/server architecture would require specialized client hardware and software and server hardware and software. The particular software required depends on which Internet service a company wishes to access or offer. Clients are Internet services consumers, and servers are Internet services providers.

In order to develop a presence on the Internet, a company needs four basic elements: an access transmission line of sufficient bandwidth, an IP Internet address, server hardware, and appropriate server software designed for a particular Internet service.

Deciding what technology to use to develop both an internal intranet and an external extranet is extremely important. Companies should start by determining their business goals and objectives and then following the top-down model to determine the appropriate technology. Some example intranet development tools are Visual InterDev, Visual Café, IntraBuilder, and Sapphire/Web.

If the Internet is ever to become a viable medium for widespread commercial financial transactions, then security issues must be addressed. Security on the Internet goes beyond just encrypting credit card numbers. When a company links to the Internet, it is opening up its own corporate network to any of the estimated 10 to 20 million Internet users, unless proper procedures are implemented to prevent such access. A thorough security program should address all three major security areas: encryption, authorization, and authentication. The digital signature encryption standard and its derivations are among the most popular today. Security solutions for the Internet continue to evolve. Given the enormous potential for commercial use of the Internet for financial transactions, security issues will likely be dealt with in a manner satisfactory to both the consumers and the merchants of the Internet's cybermalls.

KEY TERMS

Access control list (ACL)
Application-level filter
Assured pipeline
Authentication
Authorization
Business communications services
Ciphertext
Common Gateway Interface (CGI)
Cybermalls
Digital Encryption Standard (DES)
Digital signature
Digital signature encryption
E-commerce
Electronic commerce
Electronic Data Interchange (EDI)
Encryption
Extranet
E-zines
FAQ groups
Filter
Filter tables
Firewall
FTP
FTP servers
Global e-mail
Gopher

Gopher server
Hypertext link
HyperText Markup Language (HTML)
HyperText Transport Protocol (HTTP)
Information consumers
Information providers
Internet
Internet Access Providers (IAP)
Internet E-Mail Gateway
Internet Explorer
Internet Gateway
Internet Mail Access Protocol (IMAP)
Internet Presence Providers (IPP)
Internet Relay Chat (IRC)
Internet Server
Intranet
Latency
Message integrity
Multipurpose Internet Main Extension (MIME)
NetScape Communicator
Network access device
Network level filter

Network news transfer protocol (NNTP)
Point-to-point protocol (PPP)
Port-level filter
Post office protocol (POP)
Pretty good privacy (PGP)
Proxy server
Public key encryption
Secure Courier
Secure HyperText Transport Protocol (S-HTTP)
Secure sockets layer (SSL)
Serial line Internet protocol (SLIP)
Simple mail transfer protocol (SMTP)
Telnet
Uniform Resource Locator (URL)
UseNet servers
Virtual corporation
WAIS servers
Web browsers
Web server
Web site
Wide Area Information Services (WAIS)
World Wide Web (WWW)

REVIEW QUESTIONS

1. Why might a business be interested in connecting to the Internet?
2. What are some bad reasons for a company to connect to the Internet?
3. Distinguish between the available Internet services in terms of information available, ease of access, and most probable uses/users.
4. What is the World Wide Web?
5. How does the World Wide Web differ from other Internet services in terms of information offered and hardware/software requirements?
6. Distinguish between the major types of information servers available on the Internet.
7. What are the business advantages of global e-mail?
8. What trends have combined to produce this increased interest in corporate access to the Internet?
9. What are some of the potential pitfalls of corporate access to the Internet?
10. Differentiate IAP and IPP.
11. Differentiate WWW connectivity alternatives.
12. What is a cybermall?
13. Differentiate global e-mail connectivity alternatives.
14. When are transport protocols such as SLIP or PPP used?
15. What is the difference between HTTP and HTML?
16. What is a web browser?
17. Name two popular web browsers.
18. Distinguish between web client, web browser, web page, web server.
19. Describe and differentiate hypertext links and URLs.
20. What is the importance of MIME to global e-mail?
21. Differentiate POP and IMAP.
22. Differentiate Internet gateways and Internet e-mail gateways.
23. What are the advantages and disadvantages of an Internet gateway?
24. Distinguish between accessing Internet services via an Internet gateway and using Internet-enabled clients.
25. Differentiate an Internet server and a web server.
26. What are the most likely sources for web browser and web server software?
27. What is the potential value of CGI?
28. What is the impact of proxy servers on network performance?
29. Differentiate between Internet presence providers, Internet access providers, and local telecommunications providers in terms of services offered.
30. How do business communications services differ from Internet services?
31. What is a virtual corporation, and how is it related to business communications services?
32. Differentiate between encryption, authorization, and authentication.
33. What two assurances does authentication offer?
34. What is a firewall, and what function does it serve?
35. What is filtering?
36. Differentiate between port-level filters and application-level filters in terms of function, effectiveness, and introduced latency.
37. Differentiate between public key encryption schemes and private key encryption schemes.
38. Explain how digital signature encryption works and what security guarantees it delivers.
39. Differentiate the two primary WWW encryption methods.
40. Why could SSL be considered a more-flexible encryption method?
41. Are SSL and S-HTTP competing standards? Why or why not?
42. What features does Secure Courier offer beyond SSL?
43. Which market is Secure Courier aimed at?
44. What is an intranet?
45. What are some advantages to developing an intranet?
46. What are some disadvantages to developing an intranet?
47. What are some issues to address when implementing an intranet?
48. What are some examples of intranet applications?
49. What is an extranet?
50. What are some advantages to developing an extranet?
51. What are some disadvantages to developing an extranet?
52. What are some issues to address when implementing an extranet?
53. What are some examples of extranet applications?
54. Name four intranet development tools.

ACTIVITIES

1. Prepare a position paper or organize a debate on any or all of the following questions:
   - What should a company's policy be regarding employee use of corporate Internet accounts after business hours?
   - Should employees have to distinguish, disclaim, or otherwise identify personal opinions and messages posted to the Internet from corporate accounts?
   - Should an official company spokesperson be designated to represent a company's on-line position and image?
   - Should employees be able to upload or download software of their choice to and from the Internet via corporate Internet accounts?
   - Should "cyberporn" sites be declared off-limits or restricted from corporate Internet accounts regardless of time of day?
   - Should the federal government regulate the use of the Internet?
2. Gather statistics and prepare a graph, chart, or presentation regarding the growth of the Internet in general and the WWW in particular.
3. Try to access the following WWW home pages or others of your choice:
   - For general information regarding the WWW: http://akebono.stanford.edu/yahoo/bin/menu?95,7
   - For information about the Internet in general: http://www.cc.gatech.edu/gvu/stats/NSF/merit.html
   - For information about web server security: http://www.commerce.net/software/Shttpd/Docs/manual.html
   - For information about building a home page: http://www.ncsa.uiuc.edu/demoweb/html-primer.html
   - For information about building a web server: http://info.cern.ch/hypertext/WWW/Daemon/JanetandJohn.html
   - For an index of available home pages: http://www.biotech.washington.edu/WebCrawler/WebQuery.html
   - For information about web browsers and clients: http://www.ncsa.uiuc.edu/SDG/Software/Mosaic/NCSAMosaicHome.html
   - For information about getting an Internet IP address: http://www.internic.net/
4. Gather statistics on the number of companies that have implemented an intranet and prepare a presentation on your findings.
5. Interview a MIS professional who has developed an intranet site for a company.
6. Gather statistics on the number of companies implementing extranets.
7. Prepare a report on intranets and extranets. Include example products and issues to consider, and then create a presentation.

CHAPTER 7

CASE STUDY

SPIKE: HEAD OF THE CLASS

Homegrown Desktop Environment Teaches IS New Lesson

Kendall Whitehouse, associate director of computing at the Wharton School of Business at the University of Pennsylvania in Philadelphia, likes to give users the Spike.

Despite the often tense relationship between users and IS departments, it's not as bad as it sounds.

Whitehouse is talking about distributing the Wharton IS department's software brainchild, an intranet interface called Spike 3, which he delivers to every incoming class of MBA students.

Whitehouse lives in Spike, and he likes it. There are Spike graphics adorning his wall. There are piles of disks loaded with old versions of Spike stacked in the corner of his office. And nearly all of the MBA students at Wharton are greeted with the Spike interface on their desktop computers, regardless of whether they're using Apple Computer Inc. Macintoshes, PCs, or Unix workstations.

When he explains Spike, you could mistake Whitehouse for a marketing manager at a Silicon Valley startup. He peppers his description with allusions to open World Wide Web standards, push technology, and cross-platform availability. But although Spike is based on technology from some of the leading Web-technology vendors, most notably Netscape Communications Corp., Whitehouse stresses that vendor products are customized to give users what they want and help them get a handle on information overload. "These Web technologies are growing like wildfire," says Whitehouse. "It's great that each department runs its own Web site, but it presents an information problem for the students. The idea is to manage that information."

User-Driven Design The school's IS group, Wharton Computing and Information Technology (WCIT), decided that the explosion of Web technologies and the creation of a campus intranet meant they needed to determine the students' information needs and deliver a one-stop resource in a customized "Webtop" product. After all, what would be the point of building the technology framework for an intranet if people didn't know what was available on it?

Whitehouse and others in his department, under the direction of Wharton CIO Gerry McCartney, had started down the path of managing web information long before the Internet became an information superhighway. According to Whitehouse, his team started playing around with Web technology in 1993. Whitehouse knew they were on to something because the idea for Spike came out at about the same time that the National Center for Supercomputing Applications was first getting attention with a Web browser called Mosaic.

"It was clear that the Web was something special," says Whitehouse, "Particularly when Mosaic became available for both [Microsoft] Windows and Macintosh. We liked the open architecture, but we saw ways of adding functionality. So by adding a customized front end we thought we could provide the functionality of a proprietary information service while maintaining an open-standards architecture."

Spike isn't an acronym, and the name doesn't have any kind of hidden meaning. Originally offered as a working title during the development cycle, no one could come up with anything more interesting when the product was finished. So the name stuck, says Whitehouse. "It's just Spike."

The first version of the desktop, Spike 1, was introduced in 1995, giving users basic access to E-mail and Internet services. But as Web technology exploded, it became clear that the product couldn't sit still, and Spike became WCIT's major preoccupation. WCIT saw that software was moving toward Web-like interfaces and that additional functionality and standardization was paramount. Given the fervor and precision with which Whitehouse explains the benefits of open messaging standards such as Internet Mail Access Protocol 4 (IMAP4), push technology, and server-side scripting, one might even say that it's become an obsession.

Taking a Leap This passion appears to have paid off. Spike's distinct look and feel have since become the identity of WCIT, providing a jumping-off point to nearly everything a student needs to do on Wharton's network.

"We decided to do it ourselves because it's provided a definition of our services," says McCartney. "It really tells people what we do. That's a problem for many IS departments. People don't know what they do."

This strong identity, which has evolved into this year's release, Spike 3, originated from WCIT's strong connection with the products' users. WCIT worked with a student group to establish the requirements for Spike so that students would no longer have to go around gathering Internet resources on their own. Spike was to provide one simple interface for them to get everything they needed—E-mail, course descrip-

tions and catalogs, Web access, and discussion groups.

McCartney said the department was eager to develop its own solution because vendors didn't fully understand the problems their products created on Wharton's network. "We're not going to re-engineer our network to make it fit a vendor's new product," he says.

McCartney is also critical of products that are too hard to use. "We didn't want something that would take a long time to train users. On one hand, the students need our services, but you have to be able to train them in three minutes."

Spike 3 takes steps to update the interface with the latest Web technology. Tightly integrated with Netscape Navigator, Spike 3 uses push technology and Netscape's JavaScript to provide custom channels and dynamically generated web pages that point to intranet content. For example, when students open Spike 3, they are greeted with a daily update of school news, along with a calendar that is linked to student events—all in graphical, hyperlinked format.

Users can change and add specific Web and intranet links to the Spike 3 interface. And they can use the server's scripting techniques to build their own home pages in a matter of minutes. The flexibility gives users control over what they see, but IS can still manage the desktop.

The focus on Spike has led the WCIT team to set up what looks like a miniature software factory. When *LAN Times* visited the Wharton IS department recently, the group was closing in on the production deadline for Spike 3, which had to be ready in time for the fall semester. There were sheets of labels being printed to put on the disks, which would carry the code and documentation to help new students get started.

Whitehouse has done most of the coding for Spike himself. Colleague Beverley Coulson, an information-management specialist who helped oversee the project, became the graphics visionary behind Spike. She designed the icons for the interface and developed labels for the disks that would be distributed to the students set to arrive in late July. The rest of the department helped with administration and development of the servers and network access needed for Spike.

"I have a new appreciation for the people who do software graphics," says Coulson. "It's really hard to fit it into such little spaces. But it's a lot of fun."

For Whitehouse, Spike was a way to make distributing software and training students easier. The initial versions of Spike, versions 1 and 2, required interface software on each of the students' computers. Spike 3 still requires that software be distributed—each student is provided with a customized version of Netscape Navigator—but Spike itself is downloaded from the server automatically. This gives Whitehouse and his staff explicit control over Spike and ensures that every user has the most current version.

For this reason, Whitehouse decided to write the new Spike 3 interface in JavaScript, a development language from Netscape that is delivered from the server. This lets the Wharton IS staff update the software application on Web servers without touching the individual desktops. Every day students log on to the Spike server, and the server generates a dynamic interface.

"We get the benefits of the thin-client architecture in that most of it is done on the server side and it's cross-platform," said Whitehouse.

In addition to providing a cross-platform interface, Whitehouse says that Spike also let WCIT provide better performance than would accompany a typical browser-and-server system. For example, rather than requiring a browser to run scripts on the server every time a user wants to access the School's databases, WCIT developed a system in which the Spike server periodically accesses the databases on its own.

When the users access the Web server, the database information has already been updated, so time-consuming database calls are avoided. This feature is a component of the school's Spike Broadcast Server, which was written by WCIT employee Chris Maguire.

Whitehouse has no intention of stopping with Spike 3. In fact, WCIT is branching out into offshoots of Spike to implement push technology. Another recent addition is the integration of Spike capabilities with PointCast Inc. server technology, letting school data be pushed across to users' screensavers when their computers are inactive. WCIT is also planning to implement Microsoft Corp.'s proposed Channel Definition Format (CDF) for pushing Spike data to Windows desktops and PointCast 2.0 clients.

Future projects are even more ambitious. For example, to alleviate the overwhelming demand to see one professor's daily market analysis, WCIT is looking at ways to integrate streaming video into the Spike framework, to give students the ability to observe lectures from their computer desktops.

WCIT's McCartney says the Spike project has shown that IS departments can use the cross-platform advantages of intranet technology to more easily keep up with the demands of users.

"I really feel like this is a golden age of computing," says McCartney. "A lot of things are coming together."

Source: R. Scott Raynovich, "Spike: Head of the Class," *LAN Times*, vol. 14, no. 18 (September 1, 1997), p. 25–28. Copyright September 1, 1997, The McGraw-Hill Companies, Inc.

BUSINESS CASE STUDY QUESTIONS

Activities

1. Complete a top-down model for this case by gleaning facts from the case and placing them in the proper layer of the top-down model. After having completed the top-down model, analyze and detail those instances where requirements were clearly passed down from upper layers to lower layers of the model and where solutions to those requirements were passed up from lower layers to upper layers of the model.
2. Detail any questions about the case that may occur to you for which answers are not clearly stated in the article.

Business

1. What are the school's strategies to attract more students and provide better information to them?

Application

1. What applications did Spike 1 involve?
2. What applications did Spike 2 involve?
3. What applications did Spike 3 involve?

Data

1. What type of data is accessed from Spike?
2. What type of data might be accessed from Spike in the future?
3. How is the data updated and kept current?

Network

1. How many PCs are involved in the school?
2. How many users are there in the school?
3. Is everything accessed locally or is wide area transmission involved?

Technology

1. What were the three levels of technology Spike went through?
2. What were the major technology components used by the school?

CHAPTER 8

CLIENT/SERVER APPLICATION DEVELOPMENT AND INTEGRATION

Concepts Reinforced

Middleware   ODBC
HTML   Web Development

Concepts Introduced

Procedural Programming   Event-Driven Programming
Object-Oriented Programming   Application Distribution
Java   ActiveX
Network Computing   Legacy Application Integration
SNA/LAN Integration

OBJECTIVES

After mastering the material in this chapter, you should understand the following:

1. Structured programming

2. Event-driven programming

3. Object-oriented programming

4. Application deployment techniques

5. Network computing techniques

6. The pros and cons of legacy application integration techniques

7. SNA/LAN integration

■ INTRODUCTION

By definition, client/server systems consist of two applications joined together by middleware. In this chapter various categories of application development environments and methods of deploying the resulting applications throughout the network will be introduced. Although many of the discussed development environments can be used to develop stand-alone applications, emphasis will be placed on the features required to develop and deploy client/server applications. Methods of integrating client/server applications with existing applications will also be covered.

APPLICATION DEVELOPMENT ENVIRONMENTS

Client/server applications (or programs) consist of a specialized list of instructions. Applications can be thought of as recipes for business functions. When the application is executed, these instructions cause the computer to complete a predetermined task. Through the use of statements and variables, the application performs a business task. Regardless of the sophistication of the computer system, it is only as useful as the application it's executing. Business applications are developed using computer languages. There are two types of computer languages: low level and high level.

Low-Level Languages

Low-level languages are languages close to the actual code the computer executes. **Machine language** is the most basic language. Machine language is the only language a computer can natively understand. Machine language code consists of binary instructions for the computer's central processing unit (CPU). Each CPU has a different machine language. Although easily understood by the CPU, machine language is almost impossible for human programmers to develop because it consists entirely of binary numbers. In order to ease the development of business applications, a means of abstracting machine language CPU instructions into something more meaningful to humans is required.

The next level of language abstraction is assembly language. **Assembly language** is similar to machine language in that it uses the same basic instructions as machine language. However, assembly language uses names for instructions rather than numbers, making assembly language much easier for human programmers to understand. Before it can be executed, assembly language code must be converted to machine language code by a specialized program called an assembler.

Assembly language is significantly easier for programmers to use than machine language, but it is still very abstract. Using the assembler, the programmer must manually manipulate the CPU's data stack. It can take multiple lines of assembly language code to perform even the simplest of operations such as adding two numbers together. Although assembly language is difficult to write, it has the advantage of creating very small, efficient code. Assembly language is also very powerful because it allows the programmer to manipulate the CPU at the most basic levels. Some tasks can be performed only in assembly language.

Assembly language is an alphanumeric abstraction of a particular CPU's machine language. As shown in Figure 8-1, each machine language instruction is represented by a short mnemonic code, thus making assembly language easier for humans to understand. However, there is a one-to-one mapping between assembly language codes and machine language instructions, so assembly language is also CPU dependent. Because they are difficult to program and are CPU dependent, low-level languages are typically used only to write operating systems and specialized programs that convert higher-level languages into machine language.

Instruction	Comment
mov sign,0	;initialize sign
mov di,buf	;set first character of buffer to dummy
mov byte ptr [di],'*'	;value to guarantee first character not null
mov bx,control	;get address of control string
inc bx	;skip over initial %
cmp byte ptr [bx],'c'	;is it a character?
je character	;if so, output character
cmp byte ptr [bx],'h'	;is it a short int?
je short_int	;if so, output short int
cmp byte ptr [bx],'d'	;is it an int?
je norm_int	;if so, output integer
cmp byte ptr [bx],'l'	;is it a long int?
jne next	
jmp long_int	;if so, output long int
next: cmp byte ptr [bx],'s'	;is it a string?
je string	;if so, output string

Figure 8-1   Sample Assembly Language Program

High-Level Languages

The complexity and CPU-dependent nature of low-level languages make them a poor choice for writing business applications. What is needed are languages that provide a higher level of abstraction from the CPU. Such **high-level languages** are significantly closer to human language, making them much easier for programmers to use. High-level languages have a larger and more powerful set of commands than low-level languages, easing the programmer's job. When converted to machine language, each high-level language command requires multiple lines of machine code to implement.

High-level languages are also CPU independent, allowing a programmer to write programs that can run on multiple types of computers. The high-level language written by the programmer is called source code. Because a computer cannot natively understand high-level language, the source code must be converted into machine language before it can be executed. There are two tools that can make this conversion: interpreters and compilers.

An **interpreter** is a special program that runs whenever the high-level language program is executed. As its name implies, an interpreter converts the high-level language commands into machine language commands in real time. However, just as there is a delay when a human language interpreter is used to allow two people who speak different languages to communicate, there is an inherent latency associated with high-level language interpreters. The interpreter must convert each high-level command into machine language every time the command runs. For code segments that are run repeatedly, this conversion must occur during each iteration.

A **compiler** is a specialized program that converts the entire high-level language program into a machine language "executable." Given high-level language source code, the compiler creates a machine language executable. Because a compiler must convert the whole program into machine language before program execution can begin, it takes longer for program execution to begin than in an interpreted environment. However, because the whole program is already converted into machine language, the resulting executable normally runs much faster than the same code would run using an interpreter.

INTERPRETERS VERSUS COMPILERS

Practical Advice and Information

All things being otherwise equal, a compiled application will always deliver better performance than an interpreted environment. Some development environments allow for the use of an interpreter for application development and debugging, then provide a compiler for the creation of the application executable.

COMPILER SELECTION

Managerial Perspective

Because compilers translate high-level languages into a CPU-dependent machine language, a separate compiler is required for each high-level language/CPU combination. For example, there is a C compiler for Intel-based personal computers, another for Apple Macintosh computers, and yet another for UNIX computers. To make compiler selection more interesting, the compiler industry is quite competitive. There are actually many compilers for each language on each type of computer. For instance, more than a dozen companies develop and sell C compilers for the Intel x86 platform.

There are many different high-level programming languages and environments available for use in building client/server applications. A recently published list included over 120 different high-level programming languages from Ada to ZPL. Each of these languages has specific strengths and weaknesses, making them better for some types of development than others. To better understand the differences between programming languages, they can be broken into three major categories: procedural languages, event-driven environments, and object-oriented environments.

Procedural Languages

Procedural languages (also known as imperative languages) were the first application development environments to be developed. Originally developed for single-tasking, single-threaded operating environments, these languages allow the programmer to maintain total control over the execution of the code. As the name would imply, procedural languages follow a specific set of instructions exactly in order.

In a **procedural language** the programmer determines the sequence of instructions (the procedure) a program will execute at design time. The user can affect operation of the program only when the program requests input. This complete control over the program's execution is the key differentiating factor between procedural languages and other application development environments.

If software developed in a procedural language contains more than one feature, a methodology for users to select the feature they wish to utilize must be included in the program. The most common method used to allow such selections is a menu. However, even when a menu is used, the programmer is still in control of the process. The programmer determines when the user can select a choice from the menu and what code will run when any given menu item is selected.

Structured Programming

When developing applications using procedural languages, programmers use structured programming techniques. **Structured programming** is a method of organizing a computer program as a series of hierarchical modules, each having a single entry and exit point. Processing within a module takes place step by step without unconditional branches (such as GOTO statements) to higher levels within the module.

Program flow within a module is based on three basic structures: sequence, iteration, and test. If a line of code requires no decision, program execution continues with the next line of code in the sequence. If a line of code is to execute multiple times, a structure such as For-Next is used to control iteration. Without the ability to test conditions and take action based on the outcome of such a test, computers would be worthless. If a code structure involves a test, it must contain instructions for the computer to take for all possible outcomes of the test. The *if* command is used to trigger test structures in most high-level computer languages.

Within a structured program, a main routine is automatically entered when the program is executed. From within this main routine, control is passed to the various modules of the program. Modules within a structured program interact with other modules by the passing of **parameters.** When a module calls another module, it passes control and parameters containing any information the called module needs to execute.

There are two basic types of structured program modules: functions and subroutines. **Functions** are modules that return a single result based on the parameters passed to them. An example of a function would be a module that determines a monthly car payment. When the function is called, the calling module passes the following parameters: cost of the vehicle, the amount of any down payment, the length of the term, and the annual interest rate. Based on these parameters, the function determines the monthly payment.

The second type of structured program module is the subroutine. **Subroutines** are code modules that perform general processing. Unlike functions, subroutines can return any number of items to the calling module, including none. Subroutines can be nested so that one subroutine calls another subroutine. By dividing frequently used code segments into subroutines, a programmer can greatly reduce code repetition within a structured program. An example of a subroutine would be a module that creates a message box to display information and asks for input from the user. The information displayed by the message box can be passed to the subroutine and the resulting user input can be passed back to the calling routine. In this manner, this one subroutine can process all requests for information from the user, regardless of topic.

The use of structured programming techniques allows a programmer to develop an application that includes minimal code repetition. Such code can be interpreted or compiled into efficient machine language code. Structured programming also makes it easier for programmers to understand one another's work. This is especially important if more than one programmer is working on a single application development project. Structured programming techniques originated with procedural languages, but the basic concepts are used in all programming environments.

Common Procedural Languages

There are many procedural languages currently used to develop client/server applications. The following is brief list of the more common languages and the type of applications for which they are most commonly used.

COBOL COBOL (COmmon Business-Oriented Language) is the second oldest high-level programming language in use today (FORTRAN is the oldest). Developed in the late 1950s, COBOL has traditionally been the language of choice for business-oriented mainframe applications. In fact, COBOL is inextricably linked to text-based mainframe applications. Compared with other high-level languages, COBOL is a verbose language. While this wordiness makes COBOL code easier to understand, it reduces the efficiency of programs written in the language. Due to the size and limited efficiency of COBOL, it has typically not been used on the personal computer platform. In terms of client/server computing, COBOL is most commonly used as a development environment for mainframe-based server applications.

COBOL AND THE YEAR 2000

Managerial Perspective

Although COBOL is rarely used to develop new applications today, the vast majority of existing business applications were written in COBOL. As long as these systems remain in production, there will be a demand for COBOL programmers to update and maintain these systems. In fact, in the late 1990s the demand for COBOL programmers increased significantly as businesses tried to solve the "year 2000" glitch.

In the 1960s and 1970s, many business applications written in COBOL were designed to represent dates as two-digit numbers in order to save disk space, which was costly at the time. However, the approach of the year 2000 represents a significant problem for applications written in such a manner. Many applications perform operations such as subtracting a person's two-digit birth year from a two-digit representation of the current year. When the two digit representation of the current year is 00, such calculations return negative numbers—creating a host of other problems. While the so-called "year 2000" problem is not the direct result of the use of COBOL, most of the affected business systems were written in COBOL.

Pascal Named after Blaise Pascal, a seventeenth-century French mathematician who constructed one of the first mechanical adding machines, the Pascal programming language was created in the late 1960s. **Pascal** requires programmers to design programs that conform to the concepts of structured programming, so it is a very popular teaching language. Although Pascal itself has had limited use in the development of business applications, many popular business programming languages (such as C) have their roots in Pascal. Recently, Pascal has reemerged as a business programming language as the structured language used in Borland's Delphi event-driven programming environment.

C C was developed at Bell labs in the 1970s during the development of the UNIX operating system. C was originally designed as a systems programming language used to write operating systems and systems programs. Although it is a high-level language, C is much closer to assembly language than most other high-level languages. This allows C to create very compact, efficient code that requires fewer system resources than do most other high-level languages. Because of this efficiency, C has gained considerable use as a business application language on the personal computer and UNIX platforms.

BASIC BASIC (Beginners All-purpose Symbolic Instruction Code) was developed at Dartmouth College in the 1960s. One of the first high-level languages, BASIC is also one of the simplest languages for a beginner to understand and is therefore commonly used as an introductory teaching language. BASIC was extensively used during the 1970s and early 1980s as a programming language for business applications, but it was largely supplanted in the market by C until the release of Microsoft Visual BASIC, an event-driven programming environment.

Event-Driven Languages

Procedural languages work well with text-based operating environments, but they are limited in their ability to work with graphical user interface (GUI) environments. Graphical user interface environments are typically object-based applications consisting of multiple objects, such as text boxes and buttons. The user manipulates these objects in no specific order. The programmer is no longer in control of program execution.

Unlike procedural languages, an event-driven application does not ask for input from the user. The user provides input to the application, then initiates an **event** that triggers an event handler (or procedure) within the application to process the input. Each **event handler** is effectively a separate program that should follow structured programming rules. The **window manager,** part of the GUI operating system, monitors the application for events. When an event occurs, the window manager starts a process to complete the code associated with the event handler for the triggered event. In effect the user controls execution of the program.

Just about anything the user does triggers an event. Such user events include clicking the mouse, pressing a key, moving the scroll bar, moving the mouse pointer, and changing windows. In addition to user events, there are also many system events triggered automatically by the window manager when certain system functions occur. System events include clock ticks and system shutdown. By using the system shutdown event, an application can automatically ask users if they wish to save their changes when the shutdown command is issued.

Event-driven programming languages are mainly used for the development of client applications for GUI-based operating systems such as the Apple Macintosh, X-Windows, and Microsoft Windows. An example event handler and the screen from which it is called are shown in Figure 8-2.

*The following code is a portion of the event handler for a change in the **Exhibitor Name** control:*

```
Private Sub txtExhibitorName_Change()
    'declare variables
    Dim I As Integer
    I = 0

    'clear lstnamelookup list box
    lstNameLookup.Clear
    'check for 'in box - trap if there
    If Right$(txtExhibitorName, 1) = "'" Then
        txtExhibitorName = Left$(txtExhibitorName, (Len(txtexhibitornmame) − 1))
    End If

    'find the first match in the rsExhibitorName recordset
    rsName.FindFirst SearchFieldName & " like '" & txtExhibitorName & "*'"
    If Not rsName.NoMatch Then
        'there was at least one match
    :
    :
```

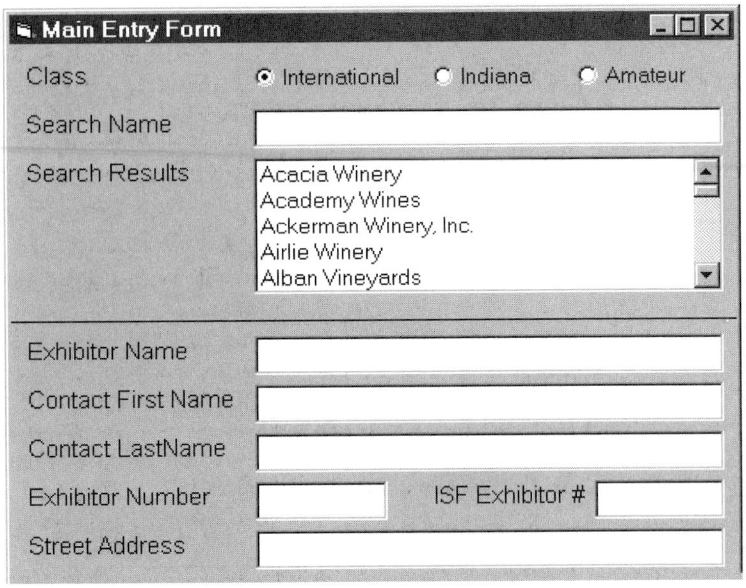

Figure 8-2   Example Event Handler Code and Screen

Common Event-Driven Languages

There are many event-driven languages currently in use for the development of client/server applications. The following are some of the more common languages and the applications for which they are typically used.

Visual BASIC   **Visual BASIC** is one of the most popular event-driven languages for the development of business applications. Designed for the Microsoft Windows family of operating environments, Visual BASIC provides a powerful development platform, yet it is easy to program. As the name would suggest, Visual BASIC utilizes the BASIC language for the development of event handlers.

Although Visual BASIC is not a true object-oriented programming language, it is an object-based programming environment. By using objects, Visual BASIC can provide additional capabilities. In addition to the base objects that ship with Visual BASIC such as text boxes, buttons, lists, and labels, Visual BASIC has the ability to use third-party objects. These third-party objects are packaged as **OCXes** (object layering and embedding custom controls, or simply custom controls.) Custom controls provide a means of modularizing code within Visual BASIC. As shown in Figure 8-3, multiple applications can include a custom control and make use of its functionality.

Developers can create custom controls that provide specific services and package them separately from an application. Many different software developers are currently developing custom controls that range from user interface extensions to special input/output objects that manage connections to remote devices. The ability to use this large selection of third-party software objects is one of the attractions of Visual BASIC.

Visual BASIC integrates with database server applications through the use of Open Database Connectivity (ODBC). As described in Chapter 6, ODBC is a database-independent API that allows a client application programmer to develop database

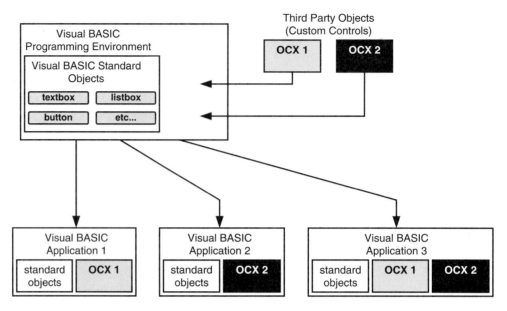

Figure 8-3 OCX Packaging

applications that will work with any database engine that implements the relational database design. Combined with ease of development, adherence to the ODBC standard is one of the main reasons Visual BASIC has enjoyed significant market success. The sample event-driven code shown in Figure 8-2 was developed in Visual BASIC.

VISUAL BASIC EXECUTION

Practical Advice and Information

Visual BASIC currently operates in an interpreted manner. Therefore, Visual BASIC is better suited for the development of business applications rather than the development of general purpose Windows programs such as word processors and spreadsheets. Although newer versions of Visual BASIC have significantly increased execution speed by converting the BASIC code to native code, a quasi-compiled mid-tier language, Visual BASIC application execution speed remains slower than compiled environments.

Delphi **Delphi** is an event-driven language from Borland designed for the Windows family of operating systems. Delphi event handlers, written in a derivative of the Pascal language, are compiled directly into machine language for faster execution.

Delphi also supports OCXes as a means of including third-party objects into the operating system. Delphi is also well equipped for use as a database client. In addition to ODBC, a series of native SQL database drivers for most major relational database management systems are presented to the programmer. Although use of the native database drivers limits flexibility to easily move to nonsupported database servers, they can result in significant performance gains compared with using ODBC.

Object-Oriented Languages

One of main problems facing the developers of business applications is decreasing application development time while increasing the ability of the resulting code to be easily maintained. As mentioned in the preceding section, one method of accomplishing these goals is to package code into reusable objects that can then be used in multiple applications. Although object-based event-driven languages provide significantly more modularity and potential for code reuse than procedural languages, code reuse is still somewhat limited.

One of the chief limitations with event-driven languages is the fact that there is no way to dynamically create objects at run time, forcing the programmer to create all objects at design time. **Object-oriented** programming environments address this shortcoming by including a mechanism to dynamically create objects at run time. For instance, an object called *car* that provides a framework for information about a car can be used to create new cars. By entering values for the information defined in the car object, a user can create a new object called Mustang that describes a specific type of car.

Properly implemented, object-oriented programming environments can provide faster development, increased quality, easier maintenance and understandability, and enhanced modifiability compared with procedural languages or event-driven languages. However, object-oriented programming environments are still developing. As such, the features and mechanisms supported by object-oriented programming environments are still being developed. New techniques, concepts, and executions will continue to be developed as the paradigm continues to evolve.

Object-oriented programming depends on the concept of abstract entities called software objects. Software objects, just objects for short, range from items on a screen such as text boxes and buttons to more-advanced items such as stacks and queues. Objects typically have **state,** or parameters that describe the current condition of the object (such as whether it is selected). An external force to change state must act for most objects to change their state, but some objects are capable of changing state independently of any such external manipulation. Such objects are referred to as **active objects** or actors. An example of an active object is a timer. When the duration of the timer has expired, the state of the timer will automatically change.

There are two major categories of objects: classes and instances. A **class** is an object that contains information on the structure and capabilities of another object along with a mechanism for creating objects based on these instructions. Classes create objects based on these rules. The objects created by a class are **instances** of the class. The process of creating an instance is sometimes referred to as **instantiation.** For example, consider an application that controls a CD jukebox. An object-oriented programmer could create a class called *CD* that describes the required information for a CD button. The CD button for each CD installed in the jukebox based on the CD class would be considered an instance of CD.

Through the use of classes, an object-oriented programmer can allow the application to create new objects during program execution. In this manner, the application can automatically adapt to any changing requirements placed upon it. In the preceding example, when a new CD is inserted into the system, the application can automatically create a new instance of CD and add the button to the screen for selection by the user.

All objects have a well-defined set of commands. These commands are referred to as the **methods** of the object. An object's methods determine what the object is capable of doing and how it will behave within a system of objects. Objects interact with one another by passing messages to each other to invoke methods, much in the same manner subroutines pass parameters among one another in a structured programming environment. Objects can pass messages within a program on a single computer or between distributed applications across a network. For instance, when a CD button from the previous example is pressed, it can send a message to load the CD to the object that controls the CD changer. After the changer has placed the appropriate CD in the player, it can send a message to the CD player to begin playing the disc.

One of the key concepts in maintaining software modularity is **encapsulation.** Encapsulation is the process of packaging an object so that only the details that affect the object's use are accessible. An object should be a self-contained entity with only state and methods available. The underlying implementation details should not be accessible to the object programmer. An object can be thought of as the proverbial black box—an item that performs a task through some unknown process. A programmer using the object to perform a task cannot alter the object. In this manner object independence and reusability can be maintained.

Objects interact with one another through **interfaces.** Every object has a public interface that is accessible by all other objects. By accessing an object's public interface, the state of the object can be altered or the methods of the object can be invoked. A second interface exists on classes for use exclusively by instances of the class to gain access to information about the class. This interface is known as the **inheritance interface.** As its name suggests, the inheritance interface provides a means for instances to automatically gain information from their parent class. Through inheritance a change in a class can quickly proliferate through all its child instances. The interaction between objects through their interfaces is illustrated in Figure 8-4.

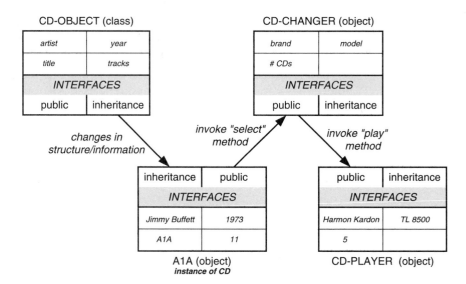

Figure 8-4 Object Interfaces

Object-oriented applications are built by assembling a group of objects into a system. Such an object system allows each object to interact with the other objects within the system to modify state and invoke methods.

Common Object-Oriented Languages

Object-oriented programming techniques are less mature than either procedural languages or event-driven languages. Therefore, there are fewer object-oriented languages available. The two object-oriented languages most commonly used to develop client/server applications are Smalltalk and C++.

Smalltalk   **Smalltalk** was developed in the late 1960s at the Xerox Palo Alto Research Center (PARC), the same facility that has developed many other important information technologies such as Ethernet. As the first object-oriented programming language, many people still believe Smalltalk to be the only true object-oriented development language. Smalltalk was written from the ground up as an object-oriented programming language rather than having object extensions added after the fact, so it provides the most complete object implementation of any object-oriented programming language.

After getting little use for the greater part of 30 years, Smalltalk has emerged as the most commonly used object-oriented programming environment for business applications. With interest in object technologies at an all-time high, many MIS shops are converting from COBOL to Smalltalk as their predominant application development environment. Based both on technical merit and its ability to handle large projects, Smalltalk is an excellent fit for business application development.

There are many different versions of Smalltalk commercially available. As of early 1998, VisualWorks from ParcPlace is the most commonly used version for business application development. Built on top of VisualWorks is Distributed Smalltalk, a version that adds CORBA (see Chapter 6) compliant object distribution. For applications intended for the Microsoft Windows environment, IBM's VisualAge provides a good balance of functionality, speed, and Windows integration. Another Smalltalk implementation optimized for speed on Microsoft Windows platforms is VisualSmalltalk, also from ParcPlace.

C++   Originally developed in the mid 1980s, **C++** adds object orientation to the C procedural programming language. Because of this relationship, C++ programs were originally "precompiled" into standard C source code, then compiled using any C compiler. Modern compilers have eliminated this precompilation by integrating it into the C compiler itself.

As this relationship would indicate, C++ is a superset of C. This allows C programmers to begin using C++ by simply including C++ statements in their code. Compared with Smalltalk, C++ has a weaker object model and is more difficult to program. Although some business application development is occurring in C++, it is most commonly used for applications that have traditionally been developed in C, such as operating systems and system applications.

Many different versions of C++ are currently available in the marketplace. Most versions of UNIX include C++ capability in their C compilers. Borland and Microsoft both market C++ compilers for personal computer environments. Microsoft Visual C++ combines many advantages of event-driven languages with true object orientation.

DEVELOPMENT ENVIRONMENT SELECTION

Rarely are application development environment questions a black and white issue. Many factors, including personal bias, combine to make development environment selection more of an art than a science. However, the process of selecting an application development environment can be eased by asking a few key questions:

1. Upon what platform will the final program execute?

2. What are the characteristics of the application?

3. Are programmers available with knowledge of the environment?

The first question is inherently obvious: The development environment selected must be capable of producing machine language code for the platform upon which the application will execute. If the target platform is a mainframe, Visual BASIC can automatically be removed from consideration because it doesn't run in a mainframe environment.

The second question takes the characteristics of the application into account. As discussed in the preceding section, different languages have different strengths and weaknesses. Visual BASIC, Delphi, or COBOL would not be good choices to write a system-level application or operating system. Conversely, C++ is more difficult to develop a simple database application with than any of the above choices. Another key issue to address is the maintainability of the final application. It is certainly possible to write a business application in assembly language, but it would be exceptionally difficult and expensive to maintain.

The final question focuses on human resource issues. If there is no one available to write the application in a particular language, it might make sense to select an alternate language for which developers are available. However, if the reasons to use a particular language are compelling, it might make sense either to train an existing developer on the new system or to hire a new developer who already has the required skills.

CASE Tools

Each of the programming environments discussed so far requires a human programmer to develop the business application. Originally **CASE** (computer-aided software engineering) tools were specialized computer applications designed to assist the application programmer in the development of business applications. These earlier CASE tools focused on the development of mainframe applications, most commonly using the COBOL procedural programming language.

Newer CASE implementations have become more specialized and support specific parts of the overall software development process. The various levels of CASE are illustrated in Figure 8-5. A few CASE tools continue to automate the entire systems development process, but the trend is for specialized tools that focus on specific sections. Such systems are commonly referred to as upper CASE, middle CASE, or lower CASE tools. This new approach has resulted in a change in the meaning of the CASE acronym to computer-aided *systems* engineering. Although the focus and acronym may have changed, the goal of CASE tools remains to help increase the productivity of application developers.

Computer-Aided Systems Engineering

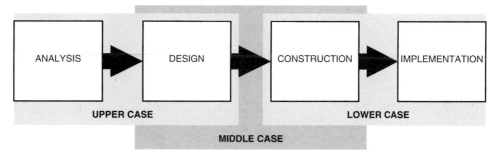

Figure 8-5   CASE Classification

Managerial Perspective

THE NEED FOR CASE

The development of business applications is arduous and time intensive. Programmers must determine the requirements of the application, create a logical application design that fulfills these requirements, and then create the code to implement the finished solution. This process has changed little throughout the duration of the modern computer era.

As organizations become more dependent upon their information technology systems, the need for reliable business applications that can be easily maintained and upgraded has increased dramatically. According to a report by the National Research Council, computer software is now in excess of a $1 trillion a year business, with an annual growth rate in excess of 8 percent. This tremendous growth has led to a shortage of qualified computer programmers. In order to meet the needs of this rapidly expanding market, a means of increasing the accuracy and productivity of software developers must be developed. CASE tools are a means of helping achieve this quality and productivity increase.

Before determining exactly what a CASE tool is, programmers must understand what a CASE tool is not. CASE is not a means of eliminating or replacing application programmers with computer programs that write other computer programs. CASE is an advanced tool kit to assist an application developer throughout the application development life cycle—from analysis through code development. CASE tools provide many different capabilities to the application developer. Common CASE functionality includes the following:

- Summarizing initial requirements
- Developing flow diagrams
- Scheduling development tasks
- Preparing documentation
- Controlling software versions
- Developing program code

KEEPING CASE IN PERSPECTIVE

Although many CASE tools are marketed as a panacea for the software industry with promises to increase productivity while increasing quality, in reality they are just another tool in the application developer's arsenal. Recent research has found that the highest levels of quality and efficiency are reached by using a combination of CASE and manual development. It has also been determined that CASE techniques work best on large projects. Projects with fewer than four developers rarely, if ever, see a benefit from the use of CASE technologies. Contrary to the implications of some trade publications, CASE tools do not represent a silver bullet to solve the shortage of labor power the software industry currently faces. Instead, CASE tools should be thought of as specialized project management platforms for software development.

There are literally hundreds of different CASE tools in the marketplace, making the selection of a tool a difficult task. It is impossible to determine a single best CASE tool because different applications types and development environments lend themselves to different requirements and hence different tools. When a development project is determined to be a candidate for CASE, a careful selection process should be used to determine the tool best suited for the application type, development language, development environment, and personnel involved.

◼ APPLICATION DEPLOYMENT

Regardless of the development environment used, both client and server applications must be deployed throughout the network. Server applications are typically easier to deploy because they are relatively few and are often centralized. Client applications, in contrast, can be very difficult to deploy as they are spread throughout the network. The deployment of client applications is further complicated by the fact that there can be many different client applications running on many different platforms connected to the same server application.

Server Application Deployment

Server applications usually support multiple instances of a client application. It is not uncommon for a single server application to process data for thousands of clients. In order to meet the demands for such large numbers of clients, server applications are implemented on large hardware platforms ranging in scale from uniprocessor PC-based servers that sit under a desk to mainframes that can take up hundreds of square feet of space.

Because of the size and operational requirements of server applications and their hardware, they are commonly deployed in a few centralized locations. By consolidating server applications, the overhead required to maintain these large systems can be spread across multiple applications. This is particularly important because each location not only needs to have physical space and adequate power to install the server, but also must provide operations staff to maintain the hardware and software.

Server applications can run on many different operating system platforms ranging from Windows NT to UNIX to full-scale mainframe operating systems such as IBM's MVS. Many commercially available server applications, such as relational database management systems, are supported on multiple hardware platforms, depending on the number of clients that need to attach. In this manner a server application can be scaled up to meet the needs of the users as demand increases.

The main purpose of a server application is to store and process data while exchanging it with multiple client applications. Server applications are optimized to interact with client applications rather than humans. Therefore, the chief development parameter for most server applications is processing speed. User interface is a secondary consideration. The application programmer focuses his or her attention on the client interface (through middleware) and the physical interface with the server hardware. Because of this focus, most server applications are written in efficient languages such as C or C++.

The server application must maintain the system's data integrity and perform transaction processing for items that cross the boundaries between user applications. As illustrated in Figure 8-6, a user in the shipping department might enter that a particular item was shipped. At that time, the server application would perform many postings, such as removing the item from inventory, adding the value of the sale to accounts receivable, and generating an invoice for the customer. All of this processing takes place at the server without the knowledge of the shipping clerk, who has shifted focus to preparing the next item for shipping.

TRANSACTION PROCESSING

In Sharper Focus

Transaction processing refers to a series of operations that take place in response to a business transaction. For example, let's consider the case of a customer entering a furniture store and purchasing a couch on the store's in-house credit plan. This single business transaction will result in postings to several information systems: The inventory control system must be updated to reflect the sale of the item; a pick slip must be sent to the warehouse to indicate the couch is to be brought to the dock for pick-up; the accounts receivable system must be updated to reflect the credit purchase. Collectively these operations make up a single transaction. Please refer to Chapter 6 for further discussion on transaction processing.

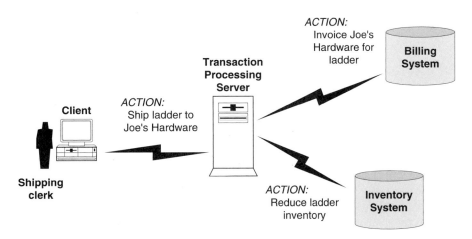

Figure 8-6 Transaction Processing Nature of Server Applications

Client Application Deployment

Many different client applications may access a common server application. In our shipping example from Figure 8-6, the shipping clerk is working on an application specifically designed to assist in shipping product. It may include the ability to print shipping labels and automatically notify the transportation company that there is a package ready to ship. At the same time, someone in the accounting department is using a different client application tied to the same server application to determine who is currently behind in paying for goods shipped. If an invoice exceeds a certain age, the accounting user can deny credit to the customer, effectively changing the behavior of the shipping clerk's client system.

Not only can multiple client applications access a single server application, but each client application can be written in a different language and run on a different hardware platform. In the previous example, the shipping clerk could be using an application written in C on a UNIX terminal while the accountant is using a Windows NT application written in Smalltalk on an Intel-based personal computer. Collectively, this ability to mix and match software components is what gives client/server systems their flexibility. It also makes distribution and maintenance of client/server systems difficult.

In sharp contrast to server applications that are optimized for processing, client applications are primarily concerned with providing user access to the underlying data. As such, the user interface for such systems is critical to the usability and the final success or failure of the system. Users of client applications want simple systems that are easy to operate and provide a means of entering data into the server applications. Although speed is certainly a factor in client application design, it is secondary to user interface issues in importance. If a user cannot understand how to use a client application effectively, it is irrelevant if the application can perform a transaction in under a tenth of a second.

Client application programmers typically utilize development environments that take advantage of the graphical user interfaces common to most modern client operating systems. Visual BASIC, Visual C++, and Smalltalk are all commonly used to develop client applications for windowed application environments. Procedural languages are currently rarely used for the development of client applications.

In addition to custom-developed applications, standard productivity software can be programmed to serve as a rudimentary client. For instance, the Microsoft Office productivity suite for Windows and Macintosh clients provides an advanced macro development environment. A subset of Visual BASIC called VBA (Visual BASIC Application edition) can be programmed to access data from many server applications. For relational database servers supported by ODBC (see Chapter 6 for more detail), a tool called Microsoft Query can be used to retrieve and update data records for processing within spreadsheets and word-processing documents. In many cases, it is possible to rapidly create applications in this manner to either solve a pressing need or prototype a more robust, full-featured solution based on a more-traditional development environment.

Client Software Distribution   No matter what application development environment is used, the resulting application must be distributed to all of the client systems that will execute it. Managing the distribution of such client-based applications throughout a large network is a daunting task. Traditionally, an administrator would have to physically visit every client to install and test each application, creating considerable expense. The cost of maintaining client/server systems has been estimated as being up to three times the cost of purchasing the enabling hardware and software. In fact, the cost of maintaining client/server systems in this manner can easily surpass the cost of maintaining mainframe-based systems.

In order to reduce this cost, many organizations have opted to run applications from file server systems rather than installing them directly on each client. In a file server–based system, the actual client application code is kept on a file server, and each client accesses it through the network. This approach also allows for increased application security. If a user does not have adequate authorization, the file server will not allow the user to execute the client application.

CLIENT-BASED APPLICATIONS VERSUS SERVER-BASED APPLICATIONS

In Sharper Focus

In a client-based application environment, the executable application is stored on the client's local hard drive. When the application is executed, it is loaded directly from the hard drive. Only data is sent across the network. Client-based solutions minimize network usage requirements, but they require that each client be individually maintained.

In a server-based application environment, the executable application is stored on a file server. When the application is executed, it is pulled from the file server to the client. Both the application and data are sent across the network. Server-based applications reduce the cost and time required to maintain the clients, but they require additional network resources to transport the application to the clients.

The architectural differences between client-based applications and server-based applications are illustrated in Figure 8-7.

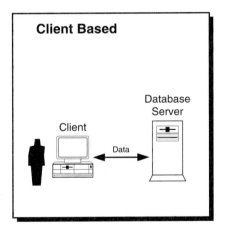
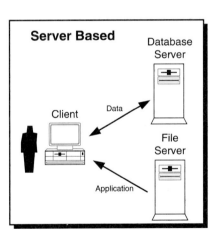

Figure 8-7   Client-Based Applications versus Server-Based Applications

File server systems do not completely eliminate client configuration issues. What is needed is a means of automatically distributing software to client workstations. Several products are now in the marketplace that perform automatic software distribution. These products, such as Microsoft System Management Server, have the ability to "push" software from a distribution server to the client. Use of these products effectively eliminates the requirement that an administrator physically visit each client.

Although automatic software distribution reduces the labor cost of maintaining client based software, it utilizes significant network capacity. For this reason, most automatic software distribution tools allow client updates to be scheduled at times when the network is not heavily loaded. Updates can be scheduled to take place after hours or on weekends to minimize the network impact on business applications.

REQUIREMENTS FOR AUTOMATIC SOFTWARE DISTRIBUTION

Practical Advice and Information

Automatic software distribution represents a tremendous time savings if properly implemented, but several items must be taken into account for it to reach its potential.

- A relatively large number of stations must exist. It takes considerable time to develop an error-resistant software distribution package. For networks of fewer than 100 clients, automatic software distribution rarely delivers a reduction in either time or effort unless the clients are widely distributed. If physically going to each of five clients would require five flights to five different cities, it might make sense to use an automatic distribution system despite the low number of clients.

- The distribution environment should be as homogeneous as possible. Each different configuration must be fully tested prior to distribution. If a large population of clients is composed of several groups of different system types, the time spent developing distribution packages for each system type could once again surpass the time it would take to distribute the software manually. For some environments, it might make sense to use automatic software distribution for some client types and manually distribute software for others.

Web Applications   Another method to solve the software distribution problem is to use Internet technologies to provide client services. In addition to web surfing, World Wide Web browsers have the capability to serve as client application environments. However, the web paradigm convolutes the separation between clients and servers somewhat, as the web itself is a client/server system.

Web-based solutions are categorized based on the location of the web in the business system client/server architecture. If the business application client resides at the WWW server, the implementation is considered a server-side solution. Conversely, in client-side solutions, the business application client distributes directly to the end user's computer through the web.

Server-side solutions are similar in concept to traditional terminal-based mainframe applications. The business client resides on the web server and connects to the business server in the same manner as any other client. The difference is that interaction with the user requires the business client to send and receive data through the web server to the user's web browser. The server-side web application architecture is illustrated in Figure 8-8.

The most common method of implementing server-side solutions is through the **Common Gateway Interface (CGI)** specification. The CGI specification allows a web page designer to create a web page that represents the client application's data. The business client running on the web server, referred to as a CGI application, dynamically interfaces with the fields on the end user's web browser at run time. In addition to connecting to the business server, CGI applications must run on the web server platform and conform to the CGI specification. CGI applications can be written in any high-level programming language.

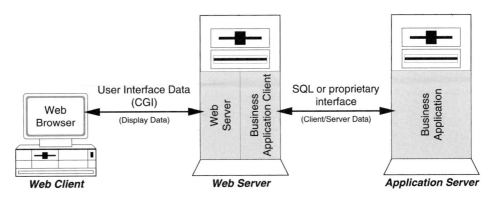

Figure 8-8   Server-Side Web Application Architecture

In contrast to server-side solutions, client-side solutions do not introduce the web paradigm into the overall client/server architecture. In this model, the web server acts as a distribution server to distribute a copy of the business client to the user's computer through the web. The client application then runs locally on the web client just as in a traditional client/server environment. The client-side web application architecture is illustrated in Figure 8-9.

There are currently two main technologies used to develop web-distributed applications: Java and ActiveX.

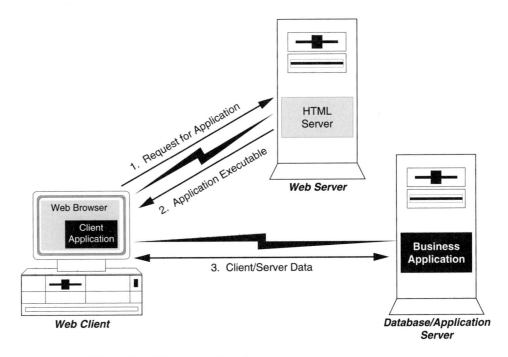

Figure 8-9   Client-Side Web Application Architecture

Java   Originally developed by Sun Microsystems in the mid 1990s as a programming language for hand-held devices, **Java** is a general purpose, object-oriented, high-level programming language. Roughly based on C++ in terms of syntax and command structure, Java has a simplified command structure designed to ease application development and reduce many common programming errors.

The major difference between Java and other high-level programming languages is the manner in which the completed application is executed on the client. Java is an interpreted language. Rather than being directly compiled into an executable, Java applications are compiled into **bytecode,** an intermediate format capable of running on any platform that supports a Java interpreter, or **virtual machine.** Figure 8-10 illustrates the Java run-time environment.

By using Java, a programmer can write a single client application that can be run on any client regardless of hardware or software platform, providing the client supports a Java virtual machine. As virtual machines are included in the latest versions of all major web browsers, a user merely has to click on an item on a web page and the application is automatically downloaded to the computer and executed. With Java almost all client distribution issues can be eliminated. The downloaded Java executable is often referred to as a Java applet. An **applet** is a small application that runs inside of another application. In this case, the Java applet is running on the virtual machine inside of the web browser.

Although the ability to configure a client to automatically download a portable application and execute it directly on the client greatly simplifies software distribution, it creates the potential for serious security problems. Because the applet is running directly on the client computer, the potential exists for it to damage or steal data from the client's storage system. Such applets are referred to as malicious or hostile applets and will be discussed in more detail in Chapter 13, Client/Server Information Systems Security. Java addresses these issues by limiting the client system resources a Java applet can address. In a Java virtual machine, a limited environment called the **sandbox** is created for the exclusive use of the applet. The applet cannot access any system resources beyond the domain of the sandbox.

Java represents an architecturally efficient method of creating web-enabled client applications, but it is currently somewhat of a limited programming environment. Because of its hardware independence and the limitations of the sandbox, mechanisms to write to local disk or access a local printer are highly limited. In order to accomplish these functions, the Java programmer must often make calls directly to the underlying operating system. However, such action leads to the application being tied directly to a specific hardware/software platform, effectively

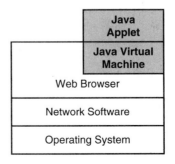

Figure 8-10   Java Run-Time Environment

removing one of the chief advantages of Java. If these issues can be resolved, the write-once-run-anywhere nature of Java, combined with the ease of web-based software distribution, could combine to make Java a serious contender for business client application development.

JAVASCRIPT

JavaScript is the name of a scripting language, originally named LiveScript, developed by Netscape Communications. After Java gained popularity, Sun and Netscape renamed LiveScript to JavaScript to capitalize on the market appeal of the Java name. In fact, Java and JavaScript have little in common other than the name *Java* and their ability to run on multiple operating systems.

JavaScript is an interpreted scripting language. The main function of JavaScript is to allow multiple parts of a web page to work together to form a cohesive whole. Using JavaScript, parameters can be sent to a Java application based on the result of other web page activity.

ActiveX   An alternative web application development environment is **ActiveX** from Microsoft. Although the term *ActiveX* actually refers to a wide variety of distributed software technologies, including the Component Object Model (COM) and the Distributed Component Object Model (DCOM), the key ActiveX technologies for building web-based applications are ActiveX controls.

An extension of object layering and embedding (OLE) custom controls, ActiveX controls are precompiled software objects that can be embedded into other applications. ActiveX controls can be written in a variety of programming languages including C, C++, Visual BASIC, and Java. They can be embedded into any application that supports DCOM, including web browsers, productivity applications, and high-level programming environments such as Visual BASIC or Smalltalk. By using ActiveX controls, a web designer can add local functionality to a web page, making it look and feel more like an application running on the user's local computer.

Distribution of ActiveX controls depends on the application within which they are embedded. For high-level programming environments such as Visual BASIC, the control is distributed with the executable. For web-based applications, the web page designer references the control from within the web page. Upon loading the web page, the web browser will check if the control is present on the client. If so, it is executed. If not, the browser downloads a copy of the control to the client, then executes the control.

In sharp contrast to Java applets that play in a specific sandbox, ActiveX controls are designed to interface directly with the operating system. They are therefore operating system dependent rather than platform independent. This ability allows ActiveX controls to perform tasks that require direct system interaction such as printing and disk access, but it also constitutes a potential security exposure. A hostile ActiveX control could be written that erases all of the data from the client's disk drive. This exposure is relatively low for high-level programming environments, because all of the required ActiveX controls are distributed with the application. However, the risk is substantially higher for web pages that download controls through the network.

To minimize the risk of downloading a hostile control, ActiveX uses a security model known as **trust.** Before a web browser downloads an ActiveX control, it displays a digitally signed certificate that acts as an authentication tool by stating who developed the control and its function. The user then has the option of downloading and installing the application or deciding not to execute the object. From a practical perspective, a user can trust that ActiveX controls coming from a known server (such as www.microsoft.com) are safe. Java applets are also beginning to make use of trust security as the need to access system resources increases.

To build web-based applications using ActiveX controls, a web page designer creates a basic web page layout and adds references to the required ActiveX controls using HTML. The various controls and other elements of the page are then tied together into a cohesive application through the use of VBScript, a scripting language based on Visual BASIC. Web-based applications built using these technologies offer exceptional integration between components; however, they will only run on Microsoft Windows operating systems.

XML   Regardless of whether CGI, Java, or ActiveX is used to develop a web-based application, some type of markup language must be used to define the basic structure of the page. As discussed in Chapter 7, the HyperText Markup Language (**HTML**) is currently the standard markup language for the web.

HTML was originally designed to provide a means of structuring document content and controlling document presentation. Implemented as a compromise between these two functions, HTML currently has limited capabilities in both areas. In response to the shortcomings of HTML in the presentation area, browser vendors expanded HTML to include presentation management functionality. Elements that control the font type of the text and various layout elements were added to the language. Despite these changes, HTML remains a very limited language in terms of controlling document presentation.

In response to these shortcomings, browser vendors have adopted a new mechanism to separate content structure and document presentation. To separate presentation and content, document presentation is controlled by cascading style sheets while document structure is defined by HTML. By separating presentation and content, it becomes significantly easier to update either aspect of a web page. The roles of content generation can be divided among several people with assurances that the resulting web pages will have a consistent look and feel.

Although the use of style sheets can greatly improve HTML's presentation management ability, HTML also has shortcomings in the area of document structuring. One of the issues is the fact that HTML is not extensible: There is no means of creating user-defined elements, thus limiting a web page designer's ability to cleanly structure data. If a web page designer is developing content about cars, he or she must manually manage and format all of the information about each aspect of every car.

If a means of creating user-defined elements is provided, the web page designer could define data **tags** for body styles, engines, transmissions, and other aspects of a car. The information within the web page could then be structured (and ultimately formatted) based on these tags. Upon opening the web page, the browser would download the tag description, enabling it to properly process the page content.

The **eXtensible Markup Language (XML)** solves these issues by adding extensibility to web page design. Rooted in the Standard Generalized Markup Language (SGML), the same language that originally spawned HTML, XML has the potential of easing the creation and structuring of data on the web while maintaining the same basic feel as HTML. XML also eases the task of building web-based applications that share data between multiple applications. As long as the applications agree on a common set of user-defined tags, the structured XML data can be used as an intermediate file format to transfer complex data structures between applications across the web. However, XML is not a direct replacement for HTML. In most applications XML would contain the document content and HTML would retain control over document presentation.

Despite the technical advantages associated with XML, it remains to be seen if the language will ever gain widespread adoption. The sheer volume of existing HTML code and the number of designers who are familiar with HTML development ensure HTML's short-term market dominance. With new features consistently being added to HTML, HTML may evolve into an extensible markup language in its own right. However, if that is the case, the odds are high that it would share much with XML.

Network Computers   One of the key issues associated with the application, administration, and maintenance of client/server computing technologies has been cost. While client/server computing technologies have certainly allowed systems to be created that have had a significant positive impact on business operations, operating cost has almost universally exceeded estimates.

Three major expense categories are associated with the deployment of distributed client applications platforms: initial implementation costs, user training costs, and administration and maintenance costs. Collectively these costs are referred to as **total cost of ownership.** In order to make the client/server computing model more affordable, each aspect of total cost of ownership must be addressed.

Traditionally, initial implementation costs were considered the largest expense associated with the deployment of distributed systems. This category includes the cost of computer hardware, operating systems, application software, and required network infrastructure. Easy to quantify and cost justify, initial implementation costs are commonly used as the economic model upon which client/server decisions are made.

Unfortunately, initial implementation costs are just the tip of the iceberg in terms of total cost of ownership. Over the life of the client, system administration and maintenance costs have been proven to reach up to four times the initial implementation cost. The high cost of administration and maintenance is the result of the high labor quotient of these tasks. At a time when the demand for people with such training is outpacing supply, the overall cost of administration and maintenance is consistently trending upward.

Many factors combine to make client system administration and maintenance such a labor-intensive, significant expense. The personal computer technology typically used for network clients is inherently difficult to configure and troubleshoot. The operating system must be installed locally, and the network interfaces must be properly configured before the client can participate on the network. To make matters worse, configuration files are typically stored locally on the machine, where any user can alter them either intentionally or by attempting to install additional software.

After the client system is initially configured, application software must be installed before it can be deployed into the field. Although there are now methods to automate this process, as mentioned in a previous section, a systems administrator must test and debug each installation procedure prior to releasing it to the network. Then whenever a change is made to any deployed application, each client system must be upgraded, often all at one time to ensure data integrity.

Another issue with traditional client/server computing is the fact that clients require a personal computer. For users who only need to run a few basic programs, the power of a complete personal computer platform, with the configuration and administrative costs associated with it, is often overkill. Rather than deploying a personal computer for such applications, a specialized computer designed to run a few applications over the network would suffice. This new paradigm is known as **network computing.**

There are many different opinions as to what constitutes network computing. At the low end are computer platforms that have minimal memory, no disk storage, and an operating system specifically designed to run software downloaded at application run time. Such systems, known as **NCs,** or network computers, include a Java-based OS designed to run Java applications. As illustrated in Figure 8-11, in NC environments, all configuration information and applications are kept in a centralized location and sent across the network as required, eliminating almost all client configuration and software distribution issues. A consortium of companies including Sun Microsystems, Oracle, Apple, IBM, Netscape, and Acorn are currently supporting the development of NCs built around the Java model.

Although Java applications fit the NC model well, they are unable to run existing Windows applications. Users who have an investment in existing Windows applications could alternatively investigate **Windows terminals.** Windows terminals are similar to Java-based NCs in that they also contain a minimal amount of hardware and software. However, instead of running the application locally, Windows terminals act as a graphical terminal for Windows applications running on a remote host. As shown in Figure 8-12, this approach is conceptually very similar to mainframe-style processing. Terminals display the output of client applications running on a remote host and serve as input devices to the remote client application.

WINDOWS TERMINAL SERVER CONFIGURATION

Practical Advice and Information

Windows terminal servers or hosts are typically Windows NT servers running special software such as Citrix Win-Frame or Microsoft Terminal Server, previously known as Hydra. Because the server must execute the applications for all of the attached Windows terminals, a Windows terminal server can support far fewer clients than a typical Windows file server. The exact number of clients a server can support will depend on the nature of the applications executed, but most Windows terminal manufacturers recommend that no more than 50 clients be attached to a single server, with 15 clients per server as the practical limit for most early installations.

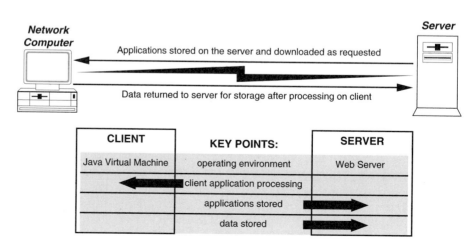

Figure 8-11   Network Computer Architecture

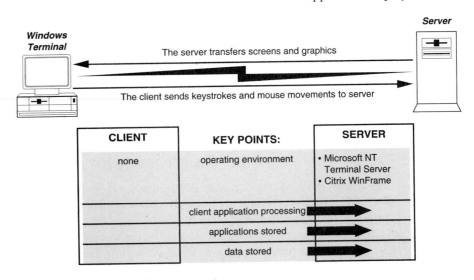

Figure 8-12 Windows Terminal Architecture

When configuring servers for use in supporting Windows terminals, provide adequate processor speed and memory. A server configured to support 50 concurrent clients running Office 97 would require a multiprocessor server with approximately one gigabyte of memory.

At the opposite end of the network computing spectrum are **Net PCs.** Net PCs are low-end personal computers optimized to run applications from a network file server. Similar in concept to diskless workstations, these platforms are designed to run existing Windows applications directly on the distributed platform. The main difference between net PC clients and full-featured PC clients is the fact that net PCs are designed from the ground up to be centrally administered. Like NCs and Windows terminals, they boot across the network and rely on the server to maintain their configuration information. The net PC architecture is illustrated in Figure 8-13.

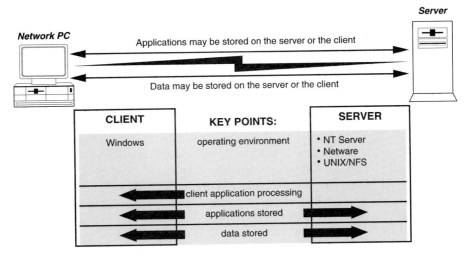

Figure 8-13 Net PC Architecture

NCs, Windows terminals, and net PCs are all designed for deployment in areas where a few basic applications are required. General applications such as word processing and web browsing, along with specific applications such as a bank teller application or customer service application, are excellent candidates for these technologies. For larger applications such as computer-aided design or environments that require a large number of supported applications, traditional PC clients will continue to the platform of choice.

Managerial Perspective

DOES NETWORK COMPUTING REPRESENT THE END OF THE PC?

None of these network computing technologies are going to make personal computers obsolete anytime soon, but they have resulted in the development of many new technologies designed to make distributed personal computer systems easier to administer and maintain. Microsoft has announced the Zero Administration Windows effort, and Novell has responded with Zero Effort Networking. Each of these initiatives includes multiple utilities designed to reduce the effort and cost associated with supporting distributed PC systems. These initiatives to reduce the total cost of ownership of client/server systems will be the legacy of network computing systems regardless of the final level of network computing technology adoption.

Practical Advice and Information

NETWORK IMPACT OF NETWORK COMPUTING

Although network computing techniques can greatly reduce administration and maintenance expenses for small homogeneous environments, they do so at the cost of increased network traffic. At a bare minimum, these devices boot and transfer configuration information and applications across the network. In the case of Windows terminals, whenever the user enters data or updates the screen, data is sent between the terminal and the host. Special care must be exercised in the design and implementation of data networks that will support these technologies.

■ INTEGRATION WITH EXISTING APPLICATIONS

Third-Party Software

Rather than develop extensive client/server-based business applications in-house, many companies are purchasing complete systems from external vendors. Although these systems represent a significant investment, they are typically less of an expense than hiring a team of programmers to design, develop, test, and debug a custom application suite. Another major reason for purchasing business systems is implementation time. A third-party application can be selected and installed in less time than most development efforts can define system objectives and modules.

There are many different third-party business application suites available in the marketplace, but three applications represent the majority of the packaged business software market: BAAN, Peoplesoft, and SAP R/3. A brief description of each of these products is shown in Figure 8-14.

Although third-party software has the potential to significantly reduce development and implementation expenses, potential drawbacks must be considered before making a purchase decision. One of the key issues with purchased software is configuration and extensibility. Most third-party application suites support modularized modification through the use of scripting languages. In this manner, modifica-

Vendor	Major Project	Application Areas
BAAN	BAAN	• Manufacturing • Finance • Project • Distribution/Transportation • Service
Peoplesoft	Peoplesoft	• Human Resource • Financials • Distribution • Materials Management • Manufacturing • Supply Chain Management • Student Administration
SAP	R/3	• Accounting and Controlling • Production and Materials Management • Quality Management and Plant Maintenance • Sales and Distribution • Human Resources Management • Project Management

Figure 8-14 Major Third-Party Applications

tions can be made within the structure of the application without modifying the application's source code. Such modifications can typically be carried forward into new versions of the software without causing compatibility issues.

If a customer needs to add functionality that exceeds the capability of the configuration and scripting capabilities of the application, the IS staff may need to write a separate application. Such a custom application would access the underlying data structures of the purchased application. The purchased application is left unmodified, allowing an easy upgrade path, and the customer is able to add the required functionality into the system.

With this approach it is typically better to write the custom application to access data through a vendor-defined API. All major application suite vendors support such an API through which a customer can access data from custom applications. By using the customer API, the custom application developer is assured that data integrity will remain intact.

If the needs of the custom application exceed the ability of the API to deliver data or if the customer wishes to create an application that will run independently of the purchased application, the programmers can write the custom application to directly access and potentially modify the purchased application's database. This approach requires extensive knowledge of the data structures and operation of the purchased application. The application programmer must be careful to properly lock any data resources opened for write access and minimize the duration that any such resources are locked, as the main application is expecting to control access to the data store.

Writing custom applications to interface with purchased applications either through the application's API or directly through the application's data store requires significant knowledge of the purchased application. Because such in-depth knowledge is usually beyond a new customer, consulting firms who specialize in the development of such custom solutions have entered the marketplace. In fact, many companies who implement purchased solutions contract the implementation and operation of the systems to such consulting firms, thus eliminating the need to train operations personnel to maintain the application.

Although purchased solutions are gaining in popularity, most organizations continue to maintain their own proprietary business solutions. This is particularly evident in niche industries where the marketplace is too small for the major application developers to see an adequate return on their investment.

Legacy Applications

Before the advent of client/server computing, most business applications ran on **mainframe** systems. Unlike client/server systems that distribute processing among multiple computers, mainframe systems centralize all processing on a large central computer. This computer is responsible for maintaining the data and running applications to access and modify the data for each user. Users connect to the mainframe from terminals through specialized communications networks designed and optimized for terminal traffic. Mainframe applications are commonly referred to as **legacy applications** because they predate client/server development efforts.

Legacy applications represent the majority of the business systems at most companies. Typically written in COBOL, many of these applications are decades old and have been extensively modified through the years. Although they are sometimes patched together, these systems are typically very effective at performing the business functions of the company. Rather than replacing these venerable workhorses, companies are looking for ways to develop client applications that access the data-processing capabilities and existing data stores of their mainframes.

Managerial Perspective

MAINFRAMES AREN'T DEAD YET

It has been estimated that as of December 1997, more than 80 percent of corporate data remains on mainframes. Client/server computing continues to gain popularity, but mainframe applications will remain significant for the foreseeable future.

The process of taking a legacy application and making its functionality and data accessible in a client/server environment is known as **wrapping** the application. A new software envelope that hides the actual implementation details from the end user is developed to surround the legacy application. Wrapping can be considered the process of developing new user interfaces for existing legacy applications. There are many applications for wrapping:

- Making legacy applications available in client/server environments

- Enabling client applications to access existing mainframe data

- Creating a single application from a group of related legacy applications

- Eliminating access to parts of a host application

- Making legacy systems amenable to new productivity tool technologies such as business process reengineering and workflow management

There are four main methods of wrapping legacy systems into client/server environments:

- Database wrapping

- API wrapping

- Scripting

- Screen scrapers

Database wrapping is the process of developing a new client application that integrates with the legacy system directly through the legacy application's data store. When accessing a mainframe data store, ensure data integrity because most legacy systems do not use relational database technologies. Data is kept in indexed files, and resource locking and data integrity are the responsibility of the legacy application itself. For this reason database wrapping typically only allows read only access to the legacy data. Database wrapping is illustrated in Figure 8-15.

The ability to read legacy data can still be extremely useful. Applications can be built that periodically pull data from the legacy application into relational database structures that can be queried by multiple client applications. Customer service applications can be written that allow a customer service representative to easily see all pertinent data about a customer's account on a single screen, regardless of the legacy systems that maintain each data point. This process can be extended to allow a customer to connect via a touch-tone phone or via the web to access account data.

Many legacy applications have their own APIs designed to allow other legacy applications to exchange information. For these applications, an **API wrapper** can be built to convert between client application calls and legacy application functions. From the perspective of the legacy application, the wrapper is viewed as another mainframe application and the wrapper application is viewed as an application server from the perspective of the distributed client. As shown in Figure 8-16, the application acts as a gateway, converting between requests from the client and API calls for the legacy application.

Although API wrapping allows significant flexibility in the creation of client/server systems, there are several issues to consider. Because each invocation of a legacy application typically serves one user, supporting multiple client applications through an API wrapper can create data consistency problems. When an error occurs in the legacy application, it must be properly handled to preserve data integrity and inform the final client application of the severity and result of the error condition.

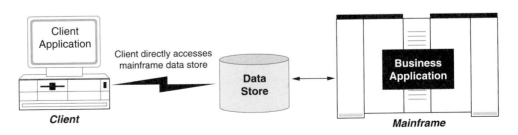

Figure 8-15   Database Wrapping

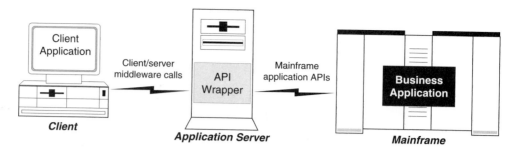

Figure 8-16   API Wrapping

Some legacy applications do not have an API. Such applications, typically smaller in scope, have multiple command line options that can be specified when the application is executed. Depending on the option given, the application performs different tasks. As illustrated in Figure 8-17, **script wrapper** can be used to interface to these types of legacy applications. Similar to an API wrapper, a script wrapper executes the legacy application for each potential command line flag. This can lead to difficulties with the handling of varying complex I/O and potential performance problems on both the application server and the legacy system.

For legacy applications that cannot be accessed in any other way, a screen-driven interface can be developed to execute the legacy application and exchange data fields between the terminal screen and the client application. A **screen scraper** is a piece of software used to provide interaction between a legacy application and a client through the terminal screen interface originally designed for human use of the legacy system. As shown in Figure 8-18, the screen scraper presents an API to the application programmer and emulates a user terminal session to the business application. From the perspective of the mainframe application, the screen scraper appears as a human operator.

The screen scraper converts between API calls for the client application and data screens for the mainframe application. Depending on the characteristics of the mainframe applications being accessed, the screen scraper may have maintain multiple virtual terminal sessions with the mainframes. Due to the significant overhead associated with screen scraping, it should be used only as a last resort when no other methods of wrapping a legacy application are available.

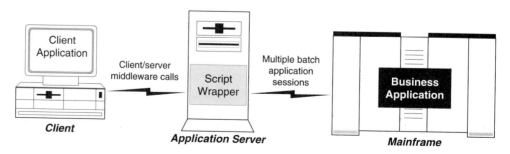

Figure 8-17   Script Wrapping

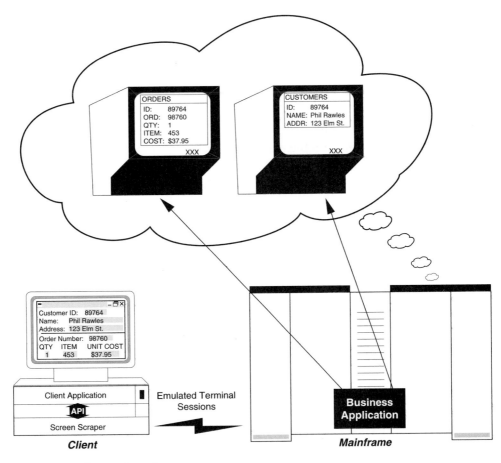

Figure 8-18   Screen Scraping

SUMMARY

There are many different ways to write and deploy client/server applications. Traditional client and server applications can be developed using procedural languages, event-driven languages, or object-oriented languages. Regardless of the development method used, client applications must be distributed throughout the network in some manner. Although there are some techniques available to reduce the labor-intensive nature of delivering and maintaining distributed applications, labor still represents a considerable portion of the total cost of ownership of client/server systems.

In an effort to ease software distribution and reduce the cost of maintenance, some companies have turned to web technologies. The web can be used as either a "terminal" to a client application running on the web server or as a means of distributing the client application through the network. These technologies have been further extended to create a new class of network computing devices that function only as network-based clients. Although these devices can function well for specific applications, they are not going to replace personal computers in the near term, if ever.

Mainframes still maintain the majority of corporate data. There are several methods of creating client applications that access this data ranging from directly attaching to the mainframe's data store to creating applications that work with a terminal emulator to interact with existing mainframe applications. Before a client can interact with a mainframe, a means of physically communicating with the mainframe must be in place. As most mainframe systems in the marketplace run IBM's SNA network, this means a technique to convert between SNA and LAN protocols must be installed.

With all of these choices for developing and deploying client/server applications, it might appear difficult to make a development decision. However, the best development method is usually easily distinguishable as long as the developer remembers that the method chosen should be based on the requirements of the application in question.

KEY TERMS

Activex
API wrapper
Applet
APPN
Assembly language
BASIC
Broadcast Filtering
Bytecode
C
C++
CASE
Central directory server
CGI
Channel-attached gateways
COBOL
Compiler
Data Link Switching
Database wrapping
Delphi
DLUR/S
Encapsulation
End nodes
Event
Event handler
Functions

Gateway
High-level languages
HTML
IBM 3270
Inheritance interface
Instances
Instantiation
Interfaces
Interpreter
Java
Legacy applications
Low-level languages
Machine language
Mainframe
Methods
Micro-mainframe connectivity
NC
Net PC
Network computing
Network nodes
Object oriented
OCX
Parameters
Pascal

Peer-to-Peer internetworking
Poll spoofing
Procedural language
Protocol conversion
Proxy polling
Sandbox
Screen scraper
Script wrapper
SDLC conversion
Smalltalk
State
Structured programming
Subroutines
Tags
TCP/IP encapsulation
Total cost of ownership
Trust
Virtual machine
Visual BASIC
Window manager
Windows terminal
Wrapping
XML

REVIEW QUESTIONS

1. What is a low-level language?
2. List two types of low-level languages.
3. What is a compiler?
4. What is an interpreter?

5. Which provides faster application execution, an interpreter or a compiler?
6. What are the characteristics of a procedural language?

7. What is structured programming?
8. Compare and contrast a function and a subroutine.
9. List procedural languages and the applications for which they are best suited.
10. Who controls program execution in an event-driven application environment?
11. What is an event handler?
12. What is the function of the window manager?
13. List two event-driven languages.
14. What is the difference between an object-based programming language and an object-oriented programming language?
15. What is the difference between classes and instances?
16. What is inheritance?
17. Which object-oriented programming language has the best object model?
18. Which object-oriented programming language is used to require a precompiler?
19. What is a CASE tool?
20. Will CASE tools replace programmers?
21. What development languages are most commonly used to develop server applications?
22. How are server applications most commonly distributed?
23. What development languages are most commonly used to develop client applications?
24. List two problems associated with the distribution of client applications.
25. For automatic distribution of client applications to be cost effective, what conditions must be met?
26. How is CGI implemented in a client/server environment?

27. Compare and contrast server-side and client-side web-based solutions.
28. What is a Java virtual machine?
29. What is the main appeal of Java?
30. How closely are Java and JavaScript related?
31. What is the security model used with ActiveX?
32. Compare and contrast Java and ActiveX.
33. In terms of markup languages, what does the term *extensibility* mean?
34. Will XML replace HTML? Why or why not?
35. Explain total cost of ownership.
36. What are the three main categories of network computing?
37. Under what circumstances do network computers make sense?
38. Where does a client application run in a Windows terminal environment?
39. Compare and contrast NCs and net PCs.
40. What is the impact on the network of network computing technologies?
41. List two methods of integrating with third-party applications.
42. What is a legacy application?
43. Explain database wrapping.
44. Explain API wrapping.
45. Explain script wrapping.
46. What is a screen scraper? How is it used?
47. What is SNA?
48. What does the term *3270 emulation* mean?
49. Which is less expensive: front-end processors or channel-attached gateways?
50. List four solutions to integrate SNA and local area networks.

ACTIVITIES

1. Research and report on assembly language.
2. Research structured programming techniques, and prepare a guide to structured programming.
3. Investigate COBOL usage. Is COBOL truly going away?
4. Contact business application developers at your company or school, and research the application development languages they're currently using.
5. Prepare a paper on object-oriented programming technologies.
6. Research CASE tools. Prepare a chart listing the major tools and their key features.
7. Visit the machine room at your company or school. Draw a map of the various servers and their purposes.
8. Research client software distribution strategies. What products currently on the market help automate this process?
9. Research total cost of ownership for distributed systems. Draw a pie chart that breaks total cost of ownership into categories.
10. Connect to a web site that uses CGI. Download the source HTML code and identify the embedded CGI commands.
11. Research Java. Prepare a report on the state of Java related to business application development.

12. Research ActiveX. What operating system environments currently support ActiveX?
13. Research SGML, the parent of both HTML and XML. Why is SGML not used for web page design?
14. Research third-party business software. Create a chart that describes the major third-party business software vendors and their products.

15. Research legacy application wrappers. What techniques are currently in use? Which products have the largest market share?
16. Contact the data center at your company or school. What techniques are they using to connect their LANs to their mainframes?

CHAPTER 8

CASE STUDY

BIG-IRON DINOSAURS DO DOUBLE DUTY

For its sprawling $10.5 billion transportation empire, CSX Corp. had a simple goal.

"It wanted interaction with the company to be so simple and easy that customers wouldn't want to go anywhere else," says Alex Zoghlin, president and founder of Neoglyphics Media Corp., a World Wide Web developer in Chicago.

Using Sun Microsystems Inc. Java technology, Neoglyphics created a contemporary, Web-enabled front end for CSX's big-iron databases and opened their contents to customers such as Ford Motor Co., Westvaco Corp., and General Electric Co. that rely on CSX for freight transportation through its railroad, trucking, and shipping lines.

Neoglyphics has made a specialty of performing legacy database integration for Fortune 500 companies. It's a lucrative niche that simplifies one of the stickiest challenges facing large corporations: piping the contents of behemoth legacy databases through new relational databases and out to customers via the Web.

"Legacy links are all about putting a 1990s interface on applications and then giving them to a new audience," says Zoghlin. "That gets

companies out of the rut they have been in of building a new COBOL application for every problem. The idea is to let your end customer work with as many as 14 or 15 back ends—without ever knowing it."

At first glance, Neoglyphics and CSX—like many of the companies Neoglyphics works with—couldn't appear more different. CSX is a multibillion-dollar corporation that traces its roots to 19th-century railroad and shipping companies.

Neoglyphics is a hip, 2-year-old company that plies its trade in intranet/extranet design from a converted loft just north of downtown Chicago. It works extensively with Java and is considered one of the largest developers of the cross-platform applications-development language. It has already formed strategic partnerships with Netscape Communications Corp., Sun, and Oracle Corp.

The first meeting of Neoglyphics and CSX was serendipitous. In Jacksonville, Fla., to meet a client, Neoglyphics representatives were introduced by the local Sun salesperson to CSX Technology, the IT subsidiary of CSX.

When CSX demonstrated a Java-based tracking application it had commissioned, Zoghlin cringed. "It was the worst Java app I ever saw," he says. Bulging at 200KB, the ap-

plication could easily have run at a slim 40KB or 50KB. "It wasn't useable at all," says Zoghlin.

The two companies immediately struck a deal, and Neoglyphics went to work on the project the next day. In addition to Neoglyphics, CSX had contracted with Sun Professional Services, which did the platform work, and with consultants from Oracle. CSX's staff did the data replication.

CSX's existing customer-service application was a 10-year-old, DOS-based dial-up system that tapped in to the company's mainframe in Jackonsville. Over 1500 customers had used the system to retrieve information from Information Management Systems and IBM DB2 mainframe databases crammed with terabytes of freight data, such as shipping routes and estimated times of arrival.

Considering "what was available for transportation customers at the time, it was one of the best systems," says Donna Hohlfelder, director of global logistics management at CSX in Richmond, Va. But the system was slow, and enhancements were rare because of the distribution headaches associated with client-resident software. And in the era of splashy graphics, customers expected much more than a character-based display.

Replacing the outmoded system with a secure, Internet-based private network would make it easier for CSX customers to eye their shipments' progress. There would be no need to set up communications parameters on the modem, no proprietary dial-up system to wrestle with, and many fewer calls to CSX for technical support.

The resulting extranet, called Transportation Workstation (TWSNet), would be one of the most-aggressive Java applications to date. Other companies undertaking ambitious customer-focused Java programs include Black & Veatch, a multibillion-dollar engineering-consulting company that built a platform-independent, on-line performance-monitoring utility that runs in real time, and R.R. Donnelley & Sons Inc., a publishing conglomerate in Chicago that has an application in the works that will allow customers to reformat Oracle-based publishing content.

Within six weeks of their start, Neoglyphics' staff had produced a prototype of the user interface for TWSNet. The application works with any Java-based browser. To enable CSX to support more-sophisticated queries from the Internet and more speedily access the Oracle database, Neoglyphics developers created what they call lightweight middleware, says Nathan Schrenk, director of software development at Neoglyphics.

"It can improve response time for CGI [Common Gateway Interface]-type applications, where requests are part of a stateless protocol like HTTP [HyperText Transport Protocol]," explains Schrenk. "So instead of opening a connection to the database every time [a query is made], you connect to the middleware, which already has an open connection." To draw data from the mainframe, the TWSNet application uses remote procedural calls.

Among TSWNet's most innovative features is the use of a graphical tracking map. Customers can click on any geographical area and bring up information on shipments in that locale. Encryption and firewalls provide system security.

With the success of TWSNet, CSX hired Neoglyphics again, this time to begin work on Global Logistics Module (GLM), an expanded version of TWSNet designed specifically for automaker Nissan Motor Corp. GLM tracks all CSX freight operations, including trucks, intermodal shipment, and barges. In addition, it tracks data from Sea-Land Service Incorporated, CSX's container-shipping unit and the world's largest ocean transporation and distribution-services company.

For GLM, Neoglyphics supplied the user interface, the database connectivity, and the logic to read the database. The GLM team eventually grew to five developers, all doing Java programming.

To generate the user interface and to retrieve the data it needs, the GLM application connects to the Oracle database, using server-side as well as client-side Java. CSX sped the application's query-response time by installing a layer of middleware that moved batches of data from the mainframe to the Oracle database. Data stored on the mainframe is copied to the Oracle database at regular intervals.

The project posed several programming challenges. Security was an issue. CSX "wanted to provide a solution to their clients that would let the information travel in a secure manner," says Dave Claussen, a software engineer at Neoglyphics. Instead of using conventional sockets, which would have required Neoglyphics to write extra security code, the developers used HTTP. As a result, all the communication is done via encoded URLs.

From a software programmer's point of view, Web development is interesting for a lot of reasons. "It's cross-platform, portable, and a nice front end to a system that's easy to use and doesn't take long to develop," says Claussen.

But GLM is a particularly intriguing application because it uses server- and client-side code in concert. Each piece uses the advantages of each platform: The client platform lets users edit and do things on the fly; the server piece uses the server's capability of processing a lot of information.

The GLM application's beefy size—3MB including source code, including a 124KB applet—was also a challenge. "With a large Java applet, you have a lot of issues that haven't been solved before because there aren't a lot of large-scale Java applets out there."

As befits a leading-edge Internet company, Neoglyphics interacts with customers over the password-protected areas of its own Web site. Because much of the development for GLM was done at Neoglyphics' offices—in quarters that once housed an adding-machine factory—posting finished work to the Web site gave CSX a way of following Neoglyphics' progress from afar.

"We're Web-centric," says Claussen. "We'd post estimated completion dates and Gantt charts. So, day to day, CSX could see our progress—or lack thereof."

The resulting application provides a finer level of detail than TWSNet does. It displays the train, the cars on the train, and the place where each product is stored on the cars. GLM can also search shipments for items with particular characteristics. For example, Nissan can search for cars by color or type of engine, getting as specific as requesting information on all 1997 Altimas that are blue and en route to Detroit. Information is available in text-report or map form.

With GLM now in pilot, CSX's simple goal is becoming more of a reality.

So is Neoglyphics' vision of creating programs from generalized objects. The company asks its clients to share code ownership, with each party agreeing not to reuse code for resale or for competing organizations. "That gives us a cache of useable code," says Zoghlin. "So we can go to the next customer with 80 percent of the project done."

For a demonstration of three Java applets Neoglyphics has created, visit http://www.neog.com/sundemos.

Source: Deborah Asbrand, "Big-Iron Dinosaurs Do Double Duty," *LAN Times,* vol. 14, no. 5 (March 3, 1997). Copyright March 3, 1997, The McGraw-Hill Companies, Inc.

BUSINESS CASE STUDY QUESTIONS

Activities

1. Complete a top-down model for this case by gleaning facts from the case and placing them in the proper layer of the top-down model. After having completed the top-down model, analyze and detail those instances where requirements were clearly passed down from upper layers to lower layers of the model and where solutions to those requirements were passed up from lower layers to upper layers of the model.
2. Detail any questions about the case that may occur to you for which answers are not clearly stated in the article.

Business

1. What was CSX Corporation's simple goal?
2. What is the business purpose for CSX Corporation's extranet?

Application

1. What applications are included in the tracking system?
2. Compare and contrast TWSNet and GLM.

Data

1. What data does the system maintain?
2. What database environment originally stored the data?
3. What database environment stores the data after the conversion?

Network

1. What was the network infrastructure for the existing tracking system?
2. What was the network infrastructure for the new tracking system?
3. What client/server architecture is used in the new solutions?

Technology

1. Compare the existing system with the replacement system. Highlight the major changes.
2. What development environment was used to develop the new systems?
3. What middleware is used to interface between the clients and the servers?
4. How is security addressed in the new systems?

NETWORKING INFRASTRUCTURE

INTRODUCTION

The distributed nature of client/server information systems implies a strong dependence on a distributed networking infrastructure to physically link the clients and servers and provide a dependable mechanism for the delivery of collaborative computing power. The data highway linking these clients and servers may be local or may span the globe. As users are increasingly on the road rather than in the office, these networks may well employ a variety of wireless or remote access solutions.

The purpose of Part 3 is to provide the user with an overview of the issues surrounding the analysis and choice of those networking technologies that can be combined to build network infrastructures for client/server information systems. This section of the text cannot provide sufficient information to qualify the reader to single-handedly design network infrastuctures. Rather, the aim is to give the reader an overall understanding of the categories of technology that combine to form a network, the technology choices within each of these categories, and the issues and implications of those choices.

Chapter 9, Local Area Network Operating Systems, describes the software layer that provides network-based services to the distributed applications deployed on the client/server information system. For more detailed information on particular network operating systems, local area network architectures, and local area network hardware and media, the reader may want to refer to *Local Area Networks: A Client/Server Approach*, James E. Goldman (John Wiley & Sons, New York, 1997).

In Chapter 10, Wide Area Networking Concepts, Architectures, and Services, the reader is introduced to a broad foundation of information concerning wide area networking. This information is critical to an appreciation of the issues involved with linking local area networks over long distances.

In Chapter 11, Remote Access and Wireless Networking, the analysis of remote access solutions based on a thorough understanding of user needs, network architecture alternatives, available technology, and available WAN services is studied with significant emphasis on the increasingly important field of wireless data communications.

CHAPTER 9

LOCAL AREA NETWORK OPERATING SYSTEMS

Concepts Reinforced

OSI Model
Protocols and Standards
Network Architectures

Top-Down Model
Hardware/Software Compatibility

Concepts Introduced

Network Operating System
   Functionality
Peer-to-Peer Network Operating
   Systems
Network Technology Analysis
Client Network Operating System
LAN Software Architecture

Functional Network Analysis
Client/Server Network Operating
   Systems
Network Operating Systems
   Architectures
Server Network Operating Systems
Client/Server Technology Model

OBJECTIVES

After mastering the material in this chapter you should understand the following:

1. The role that network operating systems play in an overall client/server information system architecture

2. The compatibility issues involved with implementing local area network operating systems

3. The basics of network operating system functionality

4. The important differences between peer-to-peer and client/server network operating systems architectures

5. The emerging role of the client network operating system and the universal client

6. How to analyze functional networking requirements and match those requirements to available technology

▦ INTRODUCTION

Network operating systems, like most other aspects of data communications, are undergoing tremendous change. As a result, before examining the operational characteristics of a particular network operating system, one must gain an overall perspective of network operating systems. In particular, network operating systems architectures are in a state of transition from closed environments in which only clients and servers running the same network operating system could interact, to open environments in which universal clients are able to interoperate with servers running any network operating system.

Network operating system functionality is examined for both client and server network operating systems. The functionality examined is representative of current network operating systems in general, rather than any particular product. Network operating systems comprise a key layer in a client/server architecture. They are responsible for serving as the delivery mechanism required by distributed applications by interacting successfully with a wide variety of local area networks, wide area networks, and internet hardware and network services.

▦ WHERE DO NETWORK OPERATING SYSTEMS FIT?

The network operating systems that enable communication between networked client and server computers across enterprise networks are but one type of software required to implement a secure and fully functional client/server information system. Several different categories of LAN software must be able to interoperate successfully in order for transparent, productive access to information to be delivered to end users.

Client/Server Software Architecture

In order to organize and illustrate the interrelationships between the various categories of client/server software, a **Client/Server Software Architecture** can be constructed. As illustrated in Figure 9-1, client/server software is divided into two major categories:

1. Network operating systems

2. Application software

The **network operating systems** are concerned with providing an interface between LAN hardware, such as network interface cards, and the application software installed on a particular client or server. The network operating system's job is to provide transparent interoperability between client and server portions of a given application program.

Applications software in a client/server information system is divided into **client front ends** and **server back ends** or **engines** and is concerned with accomplishment of a specific type of task or transaction. Applications software can be divided into two major subcategories:

1. Productivity software

2. Resource management software

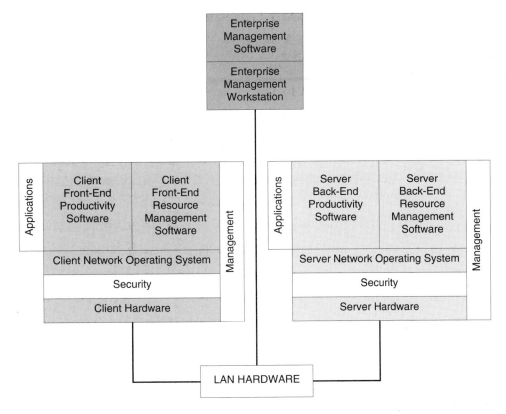

Figure 9-1   Client/Server Software Architecture

Productivity software is application software that contributes directly to the productivity of its users. In other words, this is the software that people use not only to get their work done, but more importantly, to get their work done more quickly, effectively, accurately, or at a lower cost than if they did not have the benefit of this software. Examples include e-mail, scheduling software, and groupware. Groupware and other types of collaborative computing productivity software were explored further in Chapter 5.

Resource management software is more concerned with providing access to shared network resources and services. Examples of such shared network-attached resources include printers, fax machines, CD-ROMs, modems, and a variety of other devices and services.

Two overlying elements are required in any client/server software configuration:

1. Security

2. Management

Security is especially important in networked, client/server software environments because logged-in users can be physically dispersed over large areas. Increased deployment of remote workers has led to increased need for remote access to corporate information resources. As important corporate data is transferred over network links, precautions must be taken to prevent unauthorized access to transmitted data, as well as to corporate networks and computer systems.

Finally, **management software** must be incorporated in order to provide a single, consolidated view of all networked resources, both hardware and software. From a single location, all of the distributed elements that comprise today's client/server information systems must be able to be effectively monitored and managed. This single enterprise management platform must be able to integrate management information from not just networking components, but also application programs, database management systems, and client and server hardware.

A more detailed view of where network operating systems fit in terms of their compatibility and interoperability with a wide variety of hardware and software technologies was illustrated in Figure 1-22. The client/server technology architecture is reprinted here as Figure 9-2.

NETWORK OPERATING SYSTEMS ARCHITECTURES

Having gained an appreciation of where networking operating systems fit in an overall client/server architecture as well as how compatibility issues between network operating systems and various software and hardware components must be dealt with, the reader will find that the remainder of the chapter focuses on the ar-

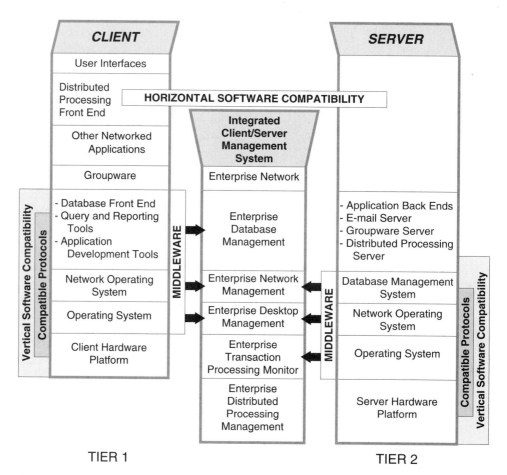

Figure 9-2   Client/Server Technology Architecture

chitecture, functionality, and technology analysis of the client and server network operating systems themselves.

Traditional Differentiation: Peer-to-Peer versus Client/Server

Traditionally, there were two major product categories of network operating systems:

- **Peer-to-peer network operating systems,** also known as DOS-based LANs or low-cost LANs, offered easy to install and use file and print services for workgroup and departmental networking needs.

- **Client/server network operating systems** offered more powerful capabilities, including the ability to support hundreds of users and the ability to interact with other network operating systems via gateways. These client/server network operating systems were both considerably more expensive and considerably more complicated to install and administer than peer-to-peer network operating systems.

Peer-to-Peer   One of the early appeals of peer-to-peer network operating systems was their relatively minimal hardware requirements in terms of memory and disk space. In addition, the fact that they ran as a background application over the DOS operating system made them considerably less complicated to install and administer than client/server network operating systems. When printer sharing and file sharing for less than 50 users represented the major functional requirements of a network operating system, peer-to-peer network operating systems such as Artisoft's LANtastic and Performance Technology's PowerLAN were popular choices in this technology category.

In most peer-to-peer LANs, individual workstations can be configured as a service requester (client), a service provider (server), or a combination of the two. The terms *client* and *server* in this case describe the workstation's functional role in the network. The installed network operating system is still a peer-to-peer network operating system, because all workstations in the network are loaded with the same networking software. Most peer-to-peer network operating systems lacked the ability to access servers of client/server network operating systems and suffered from diminished performance as large numbers (greater than 50) of users were added to the system. As a result, traditional peer-to-peer network operating systems were characterized as lacking interoperability and scalability.

Client/Server   In contrast, traditional client/server network operating systems require two distinct software products to be loaded onto client and server computers. The specialized client software required less memory, needed less disk space, and was less expensive than the more-complicated, more-expensive server software. NetWare 3.12 and Microsoft LANManager are examples of traditional client/server network operating systems. The client software was made to interact only with the corresponding server software. As a result, although traditional client/server network operating systems overcame the scalability limitation of peer-to-peer network operating systems, they did not necessarily overcome the interoperability limitation. Functionally, client/server network operating systems offered faster, more-reliable performance than peer-to-peer LANs as well as improved administration and security capabilities. Figure 9-3 illustrates the key differences between traditional peer-to-peer and client/server network operating systems.

Current Differentiation: Client NOS versus Server NOS

Functional Requirements of Today's Network Operating Systems   Although traditional peer-to-peer and client/server network operating systems successfully met the functional requirements for workgroup and departmental computing, as these departmental LANs needed to be integrated into a single, cohesive, interoperable, enterprisewide information system, the limitations of these traditional NOS (network operating system) architectures became evident.

To understand the architectural specifications of today's network operating systems, it is first necessary to understand the functional requirements that these network operating systems must deliver. In taking a top-down approach to network

Peer-to-Peer

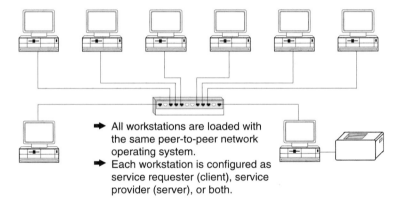

➡ All workstations are loaded with the same peer-to-peer network operating system.
➡ Each workstation is configured as service requester (client), service provider (server), or both.

Client/Server

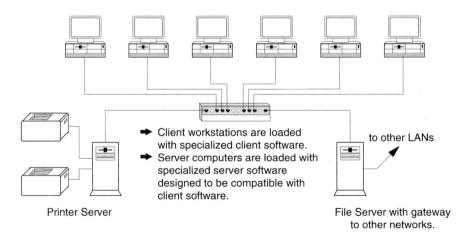

➡ Client workstations are loaded with specialized client software.
➡ Server computers are loaded with specialized server software designed to be compatible with client software.

to other LANs

Printer Server

File Server with gateway to other networks.

Figure 9-3   Peer-to-Peer versus Client/Server Network Operating Systems

operating system requirements analysis, one might ask, "What are users of an enterprisewide information system demanding of a network operating system in terms of services?" The answer to this question lies in the application layer of the top-down model. Given that it is distributed, multitier, client/server applications that will enable enterprisewide productivity and decision making, the underlying network operating systems must support these distributed applications by supplying the message services and global directory services required to execute these applications in an enterprisewide, multiple server environment.

Figure 9-4 illustrates these functional requirements and contrasts them with the requirements traditionally demanded of client/server and peer-to-peer network operating systems.

As illustrated in Figure 9-4, new or emerging demands are being put on network operating systems:

- **Application services**

- **Directory services**

- **Integration/migration services**

Key points about each of these emerging required services are listed in Figure 9-4. These same key areas of functionality will be used as a basis of comparison among currently available network operating system products later in the chapter. In order to successfully meet these functional requirements, network operating system architectures have shifted from integrated, single-vendor client/server network operating systems, as illustrated in Figure 9-3, to independent, distinct, multivendor, client and server network operating systems. The functional characteristics of these distinct client and server network operating systems are described in detail later in this chapter. Figure 9-5 illustrates this architectural shift in network operating system development.

Client Network Operating Systems: The Universal Client   Client network operating systems, as illustrated in Figure 9-5, integrate traditional operating system functionality with advanced network operating system features to enable communication

Traditional Requirements		Emerging Requirements		
		All services delivered seamlessly across multiple server platforms regardless of installed network operating system		
FILE SERVICES	PRINTER SERVICES	APPLICATION SERVICES	DIRECTORY SERVICES	INTEGRATION/MIGRATION SERVICES
		➤ Database back-end engines ➤ Messaging/communication back-end engines SUPPORT FOR: ➤ 32-bit symmetrical multiprocessing ➤ Preemptive multitasking ➤ Applications run in protected memory mode ➤ Multithreading	➤ Global directory or naming services ➤ All network objects defined in single location and shared by all applications ➤ Directory information is stored in replicated, distributed databases for reliability, redundancy, fault tolerance	➤ Allow multiple different client network operating systems to transparently interoperate with multiple different server network operating systems ➤ Provide easy-to-implement paths for upgrades to more-recent versions or migration to different network operating systems

Figure 9-4   Required Services of Network Operating Systems: Traditional versus Emerging

Client/Server Network Operating System

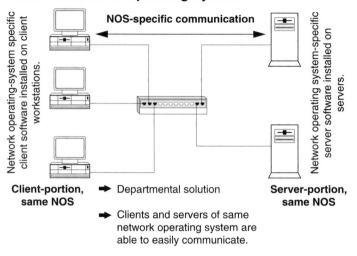

**Client Network Operating System
and
Server Network Operating System**

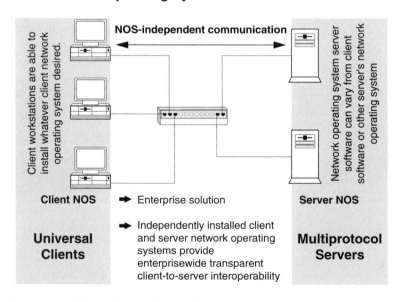

Figure 9-5   Client/Server Network Operating Systems versus Client *and* Server Network Operating Systems

with a variety of different types of network operating system servers. This client workstation's ability to interoperate transparently with a number of different network operating system servers without the need for additional products or configurations is described as a **universal client** capability.

Server Network Operating Systems   **Server network operating systems** may be chosen and installed based on their performance characteristics for a given required functionality. For example, NetWare servers are often employed as file and print servers, whereas Windows NT, OS/2, or UNIX servers are more likely to be employed as application servers, database servers, or transaction-processing servers. Because of the universal client's ability to communicate with any server, and the server network operating system's ability to communicate with a variety of different client network operating systems, the choice of server network operating system can be based more on optimizing functional performance than on delivering required communication protocols.

Small Business Network Operating Systems   Traditional peer-to-peer network operating systems have undergone both functional and architectural transitions in response to new functional requirements. Peer-to-peer networking functionality—such as file sharing, printer sharing, chat, and e-mail—is now included in most client network operating systems. As a result, traditional peer-to-peer network operating systems products such as LANtastic and PowerLAN had to differentiate themselves somehow from emerging client network operating systems such as Windows 95 and IBM OS/2 Warp Connect.

Architecturally, rather than remaining as closed, identically configured, peer-to-peer environments, today's small business network operating systems offer interoperability with server network operating systems via universal client capabilities. In addition, they offer their own 32-bit server software to offer greater performance than the 16-bit peer software merely configured as a server.

One important characteristic of the latest **small business network operating systems** is that they continue to exhibit all of the positive attributes of the peer-to-peer network operating systems from which they evolved:

- DOS-based, low memory and disk requirements

- Easy installation, configuration, and management

- High-quality file and print services

Additionally, small business network operating systems have had to differentiate themselves from client network operating systems by offering more-advanced features:

- Dedicated 32-bit server software

- Bundled workgroup software

- Easy migration path to server-based network operating systems

Small business network operating systems seem to be getting squeezed between the client and server network operating systems and are functionally situated to offer a migration path between the two markets. Figure 9-6 illustrates the architectural transition from traditional peer-to-peer network operating systems to today's small business network operating system.

Peer-to-Peer Network Operating System

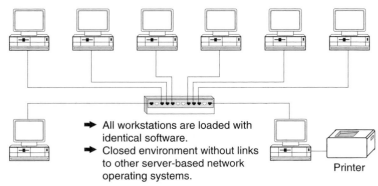

➡ All workstations are loaded with identical software.
➡ Closed environment without links to other server-based network operating systems.

Printer

Small Business Network Operating System

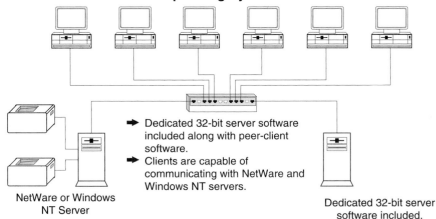

➡ Dedicated 32-bit server software included along with peer-client software.
➡ Clients are capable of communicating with NetWare and Windows NT servers.

NetWare or Windows NT Server

Dedicated 32-bit server software included.

Figure 9-6   Architectural Transition from Peer-to-Peer to Small Business Network Operating Systems

Applied Problem Solving

SMALL BUSINESS NETWORK OPERATING SYSTEM ANALYSIS

Figure 9-7 summarizes some of the key functional characteristics and analysis questions to consider before purchasing a small business network operating system.

Small Business NOS Functional Category	Importance/Implication
Platform Issues	• How much memory is required for client functionality? Server functionality? Both? • Are standard network interface cards supported, or are proprietary NICs required? • Are multiprotocol specifications such as NDIS and ODI supported? • Which network architectures are supported? Ethernet, Token Ring, Arcnet, LocalTalk?
Interoperability	• Is NetWare client software included? • Is Windows client software included? • Is remote access software to enable remote clients included?

Workgroup Software	• Is e-mail software included?
	• Is group scheduling software included?
	• Is fax gateway software included?
	• Is CD-ROM sharing software included?
File Sharing	• What is the extent of security available?
	• Can files be hidden?
	• Can users share (mount) multiple remote disks?
	• Can applications be executed on remote shared clients?
Printer Sharing	• How many printers can be attached to a given computer?
	• How many printers can be managed overall?
	• What is the extent of management capabilities available to the administrator?
	• How much printer management can users do on their own?
	• Can printers be assigned to classes based on performance characteristics with jobs queued to printer classes rather than to specific printers?
	• Are printer usage statistics available by user?
Scalability	• Is a 32-bit compatible server program available?
	• Are any client changes necessary to interoperate with the 32-bit server?
	• Is there a maximum number of client nodes supported?
Management	• Is a centralized management facility available?
	• What is the management platform? DOS, Windows?
	• Does the management facility keep a log of all network events?
	• Is an SNMP agent available to link to enterprise management systems?
	• How much information is available about active users and processes?
	• Can login time restrictions or password expiration dates be set?

Figure 9-7   Small Business Network Operating Systems Functional Characteristics

CLIENT NETWORK OPERATING SYSTEMS FUNCTIONALITY

The previous section explained the new architectural arrangement of network operating systems consisting of distinct, interoperable, multivendor, client and server network operating systems (see Figure 9-5). This section details the functional aspects of client network operating systems categories, and the next major section outlines server network operating systems. Overall functionality of a variety of client network operating systems was initially introduced in Chapter 3, Client Software. More-detailed emphasis on the network operating systems functionality of these products will be the primary focus in this chapter.

Client network operating systems such as Windows 95, OS/2 Warp Connect, and Windows NT Workstation offer three major categories of functionality:

- Operating system capabilities

- Peer-to-peer networking capabilities

- Client software for communicating with a variety of different server network operating systems

The logical relationship of these three distinct yet complementary categories of functionality is illustrated in Figure 9-8. Figure 9-8 also points out potential areas for compatibility and protocol consideration where the various software and hardware layers interface.

In the following sections, each of these major categories of functionality of client network operating systems is reviewed from the perspective of the network analyst. The importance of each functional category to the overall network operating system is explained, as are key differences in the implementation among available technology of any given functionality. From such a review of network operating system functionality, the network analyst should be able to construct a logical network design listing the functionality required to meet business objectives.

This logical network design would then be used as an evaluation mechanism for comparison with the delivered functionality of currently available technology. Logical network design functionality can be compared with available technology's delivered functionality in a technology analysis grid such as Figure 9-15 (Client Network Operating System Technology Analysis Grid). Employing a technology analysis grid in such an endeavor ensures that purchase decisions or recommendations are made based on previously identified, objective functional requirements rather than creative packaging or effective marketing.

Operating System Capabilities

The following desirable operating systems characteristics are listed and briefly explained here in terms of their importance to overall network operating system performance. Most of these concepts were originally explained in Chapter 3, Client Software.

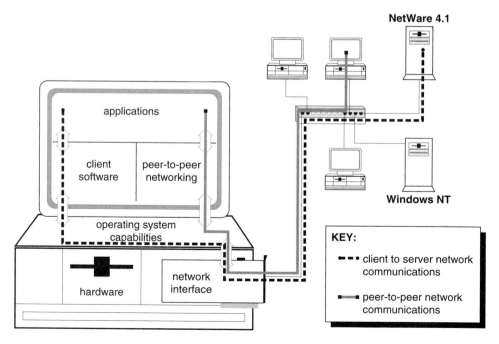

Figure 9-8   Logical Relationship of Client Network Operating System Functional Categories

- A **32-bit operating system** will allow more sophisticated and higher performance 32-bit applications to execute more quickly.

- **Preemptive multitasking** prevents misbehaving programs from monopolizing systems resources at the expense of the performance of other applications.

- **Protected memory space** prevents application programs from accidentally writing into one another's or the operating system's memory space, thereby preventing general protection faults, system crashes, or both.

- **Support for symmetrical multiprocessing** (SMP) is especially important for server network operating systems owing to the processing load imposed by multiple simultaneous requests for services from clients. Some high-powered client applications such as three-dimensional modeling or simulation software may warrant SMP support on client platforms as well.

- **Multithreading** allows multithreaded applications to achieve performance increases because a multithreaded operating system allows more than one subprocess to execute simultaneously.

User Interface **Object-oriented user interfaces** present the user with a graphical desktop on which objects such as files, directories, folders, disk drives, programs, or devices can be arranged according to the user's whim. More importantly, as objects are moved around the desktop, they retain their characteristic properties. As a result, when a desktop object is clicked on, only legitimate actions presented in context-sensitive menus appropriate for that class of objects can be executed.

Unlike object-oriented user interfaces, Windows-based user interfaces, although graphical, do not allow icons representing directories, files, disk drives, and so on to be broken out of their particular window and placed directly on the desktop. Figure 9-9 contrasts Windows-based user interfaces and object-oriented user interfaces.

Application Program Support A very important aspect of any migration plan to a new client network operating system is the extent of support for **backward compatibility** in terms of application support, also known as **legacy application** support. Most companies cannot afford to replace or rewrite all of their application software in order to upgrade to a new client network operating system.

Although it was stated previously that 32-bit client network operating systems are desirable, the vast majority of network-based applications are still 16-bit applications. In addition, many of these 16-bit application programs, commercially produced as well as "home-grown," bypass supported API calls and commands in favor of conversing directly with or controlling hardware devices. This type of programming was done initially in the interest of increased performance in most cases. Programs or subroutines that write directly to computer hardware are sometimes referred to as employing **real-mode device drivers.**

Many 32-bit network operating systems do not allow application programs to address or control hardware directly in the interest of security and protecting applications from using one another's assigned memory spaces and causing system crashes. Instead, these more secure 32-bit operating systems control access to hardware and certain system services via **virtual device drivers,** otherwise known as **VxDs.** Windows NT is perhaps the best example of a 32-bit network operating system that prevents direct hardware addressing. As a result, many 16-bit applications, particularly highly graphical computer games, will not execute over the Windows

Windows-Based User Interface (Windows 3.1)

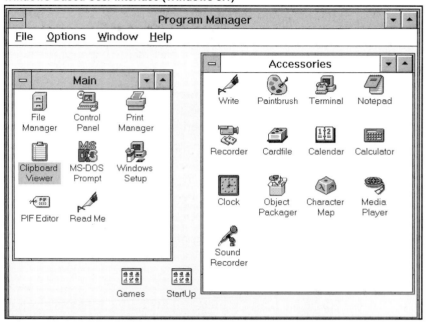

Object-Oriented User Interface (Windows '95)

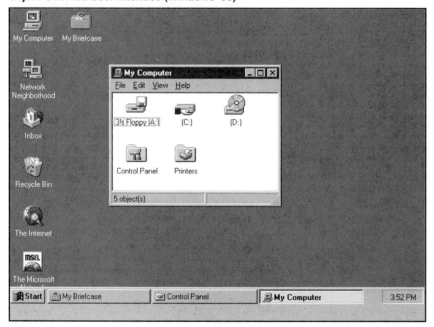

Screen shot(s) reprinted with permission from Microsoft Corporation

Figure 9-9   Windows-Based User Interfaces versus Object-Oriented User Interfaces

NT network operating system. On the other hand, Windows NT is extremely stable.

Another issue concerning the execution of 16-bit applications is whether those applications execute in a shared memory address space, sometimes referred to as a

16-bit subsystem. If this is the case, then a single misbehaving 16-bit application can crash the 16-bit subsystem and all other executing 16-bit applications. Some 32-bit operating systems allow each 16-bit application to execute in its own protected memory execution area.

When it comes to 32-bit applications, client network operating systems may execute these applications in their own address space, otherwise known as **protected memory mode.** However, all of these protected mode 32-bit applications may execute over a single 32-bit subsystem, in which case a single misbehaving 32-bit application can crash the entire 32-bit subsystem and all other associated 32-bit applications.

Whether an application is executable over a particular network operating system depends on whether that application issues commands and requests for network-based services in a predetermined format defined by the network operating system's **application program interface (API).** Each network operating system has its own unique API or variation. For example, Windows, Windows NT, and Windows 95 all support variations of the Win32 API.

Some client network operating systems, such as Windows NT, have the ability to support multiple APIs and multiple different operating system subsystems, sometimes known as **virtual machines.** This feature allows applications written for a variety of operating systems such as OS/2, DOS, or POSIX to all execute over a single client network operating system.

Figure 9-10 illustrates some of the concepts of application program support by client network operating systems.

Plug-n-Play Features   **Plug-n-play (PnP)** features are included in varying degrees in most client network operating systems. The goal of plug-n-play is to free users from having to understand and worry about such things as IRQs (interrupt requests), DMA (direct memory access) channels, memory addresses, COM ports, and editing CONFIG.SYS whenever they want to add a device to their computer. Although that goal has not been fully realized, definite progress has been made toward that goal. Ideally PnP functionality will achieve the following:

- automatically detect the addition or removal of PnP devices
- set all of the previously mentioned settings so that they do not conflict with other devices
- automatically load necessary drivers to enable the particular device

PnP standards also include support for **dynamic reconfiguration,** which will enable several functions:

- PCMCIA cards being inserted into and removed from computers without a need to reboot
- "Hot docking" (powering up) of laptop computers into docking bays or stations
- Dynamic reconfiguration-aware applications software, which could automatically respond to changes in system configuration

Eventually, PnP devices will include not just network interface cards but also controllers of many types, SCSI devices, monitors, printers, and a variety of

Real Mode Drivers versus API and VXD

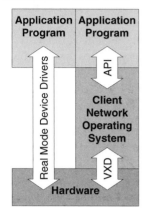

Shared 16-bit Subsystems versus Individual 16-bit Address Spaces

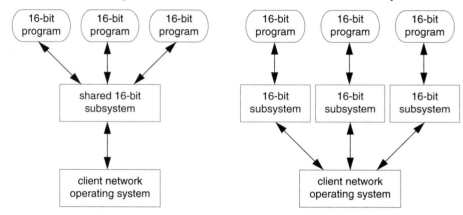

A single misbehaving program can crash the entire subsystem.

A single misbehaving program crashes only its own 16-bit subsystem.

Figure 9-10 Application Program Support by Client Network Operating Systems

input/output devices. SCSI controllers will be configured according to a PnP standard known as **SCAM,** or **SCSI Configured Automatically.** PnP-compliant monitors will be controlled and configured according to the PnP **DDC,** or **Data Display Channel** standard.

Compatibility issues are important to the achievement of full PnP functionality. To be specific, three distinct elements must all support PnP standards:

1. A **PnP BIOS** (Basic Input/Output System) is required to interface directly to both PnP and non-PnP compliant hardware.

2. PnP capabilities must be supported by the client network operating system through interaction with the PnP BIOS. Windows 95 possesses the most PnP capability among currently available client network operating systems.

3. The devices that are to be installed must be PnP compliant. This means that the manufacturers of these devices must add some additional software and

processing power so that these devices can converse transparently with the PnP operating system and BIOS. In some cases, PnP-compliant device drivers may also need to be supplied.

In order to cater to the vast majority of legacy (non–PnP-compliant) devices, many PnP-compliant client network operating systems also assist in easing configuration hassles with these non–PnP-compliant devices. Using a variety of detection techniques, the client operating system detects non-PnP devices, then executes an assistant agent program, sometimes referred to as a hardware wizard, which attempts to walk the user through the configuration routine. Such programs are often capable of detecting and displaying IRQs and DMA addresses used by other devices, allowing users to often accept supplied default answers in this semiautomatic configuration scenario.

Peer-to-Peer Networking Capabilities

Many of the same functional capabilities discussed previously in the section on the evolution of the small business network operating system are included as part of the peer-to-peer capabilities of client network operating systems. In fact, it is this inclusion of workgroup application software in client network operating systems that forced the vendors of traditional peer-to-peer network operating systems such as LANtastic and PowerLAN to add new, more advanced features to their offerings.

File and Printer Sharing   Perhaps the most basic of peer-to-peer network functions is file and printer sharing. In many cases, other resources such as CD-ROM drives can also be shared. Network operating systems supporting peer-to-peer networking can vary widely in their ability to limit access to certain drives, directories, or files. How finely access can be controlled (by disk, directory, or file level) is sometimes referred to as the **granularity** of the access control scheme. In addition, access to drives, directories, or files must be able to be controlled by user groups or individual users. Sophistication of the printer management facility can also vary from one client network operating system to another.

Not all client network operating systems include peer-to-peer networking capabilities. For example, Windows 3.1 gains its peer-to-peer networking from the Windows for Workgroups 3.11 upgrade. IBM OS/2 Warp Connect, rather than OS/2 Warp, is the only version that offers peer-to-peer networking. As client network operating systems have grown in sophistication, file and printer sharing services are now available to client platforms other than those configured with identical client network operating systems. Figure 9-11 illustrates some of the cross-platform peer-to-peer file and printer sharing capabilities of Windows 95.

Practical Advice and Information

One very important point must be made regarding the type of cross-platform interoperability illustrated in Figure 9-11.

Interoperability solutions cannot be assumed to be two-way or reversible. For example, as illustrated in Figure 9-11, although NetWare clients are able to connect to a Windows 95 client running file and print services for NetWare, the converse is not true. Windows 95 or NT clients are not able to log into, or share the disks and files of, the NetWare clients. An additional piece of software from NetWare known as the Client32 (or IntraNetWare Client for NT), available with NetWare 4.11, is required in order to link a Windows 95 or NT workstation with a NetWare server.

Windows '95, Windows NT, and Windows for Workgroups Clients

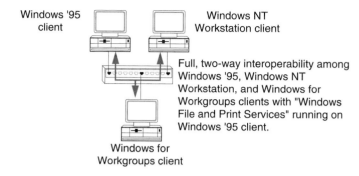

Windows '95 client

Windows NT Workstation client

Full, two-way interoperability among Windows '95, Windows NT Workstation, and Windows for Workgroups clients with "Windows File and Print Services" running on Windows '95 client.

Windows for Workgroups client

Windows '95 and NetWare Clients

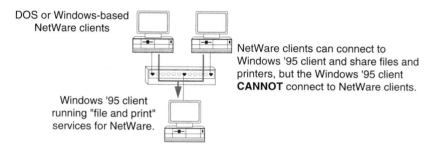

DOS or Windows-based NetWare clients

NetWare clients can connect to Windows '95 client and share files and printers, but the Windows '95 client **CANNOT** connect to NetWare clients.

Windows '95 client running "file and print" services for NetWare.

Figure 9-11   Cross-Platform File and Printer Sharing

Workgroup Applications   Ever striving to find new ways to differentiate their products from the competition, computer companies are offering client network operating systems bundled with such workgroup application software as the following:

- Terminal emulation
- Calculator
- Clock
- Games
- Paintbrush
- Sound recorder
- Remote access software
- CD player
- Backup
- Chat
- Phone dialer
- Performance and network monitors
- Diagnostic software
- Screen savers

- Web browsers

- Fax access software

Managerial Perspective

The client network operating systems that offers the greatest number of workgroup applications is not necessarily the best or most appropriate choice. Although free application software is nice, priority should be given to client network operating systems characteristics such as the following:

- Application program support and operating system characteristics

- Peer-to-peer networking capabilities

- Flexibility and ease of installation and use in acting as a client to a variety of server network operating systems

Client network operating systems that are able to connect to a great many different server operating systems are sometimes referred to as a universal client. In support of multivendor, multiplatform, distributed information systems, this is perhaps the most important evaluation criteria of all when selecting a client network operating system.

Client Networking Capabilities

As illustrated architecturally in Figure 9-12, three distinct elements of networking functionality, in addition to the previously mentioned application support capabilities, must be included in a client network operating system. In some cases, more than one alternative is offered for each of the following elements:

- Client software and network drivers that allow a particular client to communicate with a compatible server. These are MAC (Media Access Control) protocol specifications such as NDIS and ODI.

- Network transport protocols that package and transport messages between clients and servers. These protocols correspond to the network and transport layers of the OSI model.

- Network redirectors that trap API (application program interface) calls and process them appropriately. Redirectors are concerned with providing file system–related services in support of application programs.

As previously stated, more than one alternative protocol may be provided in a given client network operating system for each of the three network protocol categories. Figure 9-13 displays the protocol stacks for the following four client network operating systems:

- Windows for Workgroups

- Windows NT Workstation

- Windows 95

- OS/2 Warp Connect

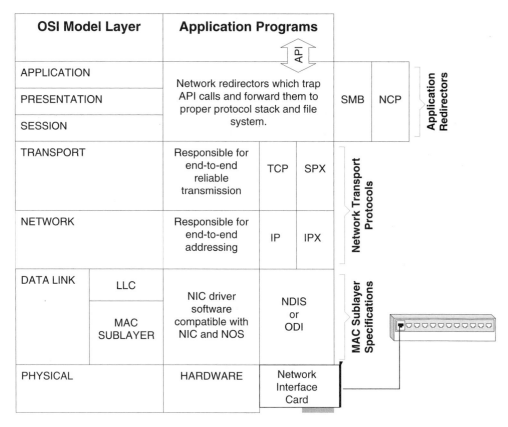

Figure 9-12   Client Networking Functionality

Rather than organize protocols in an OSI model architecture, Figure 9-13 divides the protocols into layers according to networking functionality.

Network Client to Multiple Servers   In most client network operating systems, the combination of these three elements of network functionality—MAC protocols, network transport protocols, and network redirectors—combine to allow client platforms to automatically find and connect to reachable, compatible servers. For example, a properly configured Windows NT client will be able to automatically display network connections and connect to Windows NT and NetWare servers that are physically reachable and to which the client has been assigned access privileges. The client software does not have to be preconfigured with any information about these servers. The server discovery and access is all handled transparently by the client network operating system.

In addition to offering network operating system client software such as Net-Ware 3.x and 4.x clients, client network operating systems often also included specialized application-oriented client software. For example:

- FTP (File transfer protocol) client software

- E-mail client software

- Scheduling systems client software

- Web browsers and Gopher clients

	Windows for Workgroups		Windows NT Workstation			IBM OS/2 Warp Connect			
Application Support	WIN16 API 16-bit Windows applications supported		WIN32 API 32-bit and some 16-bit Windows applications supported		WIN32 API 32-bit and most 16-bit Windows applications supported	Supports DOS applications, 16-bit Windows applications, and native OS/2 applications				
Application Redirectors and File Systems	SMB — Server Message Block Redirector (Microsoft)	FAT — File Allocation Table File System (DOS/Windows)	NCP — Netware Core Protocol Redirector (Novell) / SMB — Server Message Block Redirector (Microsoft) / FAT — File Allocation Table File System (DOS/Windows) / NTFS — NT File System		NCP — Netware Core Protocol Redirector (Novell) / SMB — Server Message Block Redirector (Microsoft) / FAT — File Allocation Table File System (DOS/Windows)	NCP — Netware Core Protocol Redirector (Novell) / SMB — Server Message Block Redirector (Microsoft) / NFS — Network File System (UNIX) / HPFS — High Performance File System (OS/2)				
Network Transport Protocols	IPX/SPX / NETBEUI — NetBIOS Extended User Interface (Microsoft) / TCP/IP		IPX/SPX / NETBEUI — NetBIOS Extended User Interface (Microsoft) / TCP/IP / Apple-Talk		IPX/SPX / NETBEUI — NetBIOS Extended User Interface (Microsoft) / TCP/IP	IPX/SPX / NETBEUI — NetBIOS Extended User Interface (Microsoft) / TCP/IP				
MAC Sublayer Specifications	NDIS — Network Data-Link Interface Specification (Microsoft/3Com) / ODI — Open Data-Link Interface (Novell)		NDIS — Network Data-Link Interface Specification (Microsoft/3Com)		NDIS — Network Data-Link Interface Specification (Microsoft/3Com) / ODI — Open Data-Link Interface (Novell)	NDIS — Network Data-Link Interface Specification (Microsoft/3Com) / ODI — Open Data-Link Interface (Novell)				

Figure 9-13   Client Network Operating Systems Protocol Stacks of Networking Functionality

In the case of the e-mail and scheduling clients, compatible e-mail and scheduling application servers must be available. The client portion is merely the front-end to a back-end application engine executing in some other network-accessible location.

Remote Access   Specialized client software written to allow remote access to network operating systems servers is included with or available for most client network operating systems. These remote access clients must access a specialized portion of the server network operating system specifically designed to handle incoming remote access clients. Following are the most popular server-based remote access software to which client portions are generally available:

- **Windows NT Remote Access Server (RAS)**

- **NetWare Connect**

Both of these products would execute on a typical server platform, either as a dedicated communications server or in conjunction with applications' server duties. An alternative to server-based remote access software is a stand-alone device alternatively known as a **dial-up server** or **remote node server.** Such a self-contained unit includes modems, communications software, and NOS-specific remote access server software in a turnkey system. Shiva is perhaps the best known vendor of dial-up servers. As a result, some client operating systems include remote access client software written especially to interface to Shiva dial-up servers.

Some client network operating systems include not only remote access client software but also remote access server software. With this capability, other remote access clients can dial in to each other for file sharing, e-mail exchange, schedule synchronization, and so on. Windows NT Workstation extends this scenario by offering limited local server capability as well as remote access server capability. Figure 9-14 illustrates the relationship between remote access client and remote access server software as well as the architectural differences between applications server–based and remote-node server–based remote access.

Laptop Synchronization   Mobile computing on laptop and notebook computers has grown exponentially, so a need to synchronize versions of files on laptops and desktop workstations has quickly become apparent. Such **file synchronization software** was initially available as a stand-alone product or included as a feature on remote access or file transfer packages. Also known as **version control software** or **directory synchronization software,** this valuable software is now often included as a standard or optional feature in client network operating systems.

Laptops may be linked to their related desktop system in a number of different ways:

- The laptop and desktop computer systems may be locally linked directly via serial or parallel cables.

- The laptop and desktop computer systems may be remotely linked via modems and a dial-up line.

- The laptop and desktop computer system may be remotely linked via a local area network running a network operating system such as NetWare, Windows for Workgroups, or Windows NT.

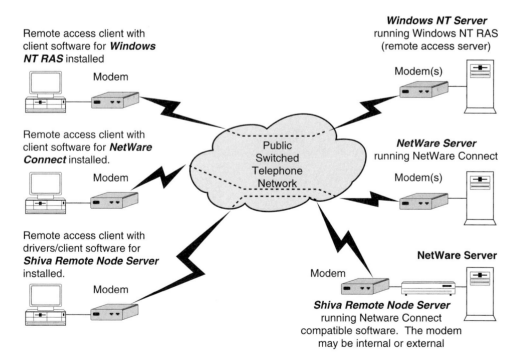

Figure 9-14   Remote Access Client Software

Client network operating systems should support laptop synchronization in all of the aforementioned connectivity options, especially LAN-based alternatives. Laptop synchronization should happen automatically when the laptop computer is docked in its docking station. E-mail clients and scheduling system client software should automatically synchronize with the LAN-attached e-mail and scheduling application servers.

Some of the important functional characteristics or differences among laptop synchronization software are the following:

- Copy by date option, in which files and directories can be selectively synchronized by selected data range

- Bidirectional option, in which file synchronization can occur from laptop to desktop, desktop to laptop, or both (bidirectional)

- Cloning option, guaranteeing that the contents of a directory on one system exactly match the contents of the same directory on another system

- Refresh option, copying only newer versions of files that are already located on both systems from one system to another

- Delta file synchronization, which transfers only the changes to a file

Delta file synchronization is perhaps the most significant file synchronization option in terms of its potential impact on reducing required bandwidth and file transfer time to accomplish the synchronization. Rather than sending entire files across the dial-up or LAN link, delta file synchronization transfers only the changes to those files.

Applied Problem Solving

CLIENT NETWORK OPERATING SYSTEM TECHNOLOGY ANALYSIS

Figure 9-15 is a technology analysis grid comparing key architectural and functional characteristics of the following client network operating systems:

- Windows for Workgroups
- Windows NT Workstation
- Windows 95
- OS/2 Warp Connect

This grid is included as an example of how technology analysis grids can be used to effectively and objectively map networking functional requirements to available technology solutions. This technology analysis grid is not meant to be absolutely authoritative or all-inclusive. Its primary purpose is to provide a concrete example of the type of analysis tool used in a professional top-down network analysis and design methodology. Network analysts should create new technology analysis grids for each networking analysis opportunity based on their own networking functional requirements and the latest technology specifications available from buyer's guides or product reviews.

The client network operating system technology analysis grid is divided into the following major sections:

- Hardware/Platform-Related Characteristics
- Operating System Capabilities
- Peer-to-Peer Networking Capabilities
- Client Networking Capabilities

Client Network Operating System Category	Windows for Workgroups	Windows NT Workstation 4.0	Windows 95	OS/2 Warp Connect
Hardware and Platform				
Required/ Recommended Memory	4 MB/8 MB	16 MB/32 MB	8 MB/16 MB	8 MB/16 MB
16 or 32 bit	16 bit	32 bit	32 bit	32 bit
User Interface	Windows	Object-oriented desktop	Object-oriented desktop	Object-oriented desktop
Operating System Capabilities				
Preemptive Multitasking	No	Yes	Yes	Yes
Supports SMP	No	Yes	No	Yes
Protected Memory Program Execution	No	Yes	Yes	Yes
Multithreading	No	Yes	Yes	Yes
Runs 32-bit Applications	No	Yes	Yes	Yes, but not Windows 95 or Windows NT 32-bit applications
Runs 16-bit Applications	Yes	Some. Won't support real-mode drivers	Yes	Some; won't support real-mode drivers
Peer-to-Peer Networking				
File and Printer Sharing	Yes	Yes	Yes	Yes
Workgroup Applications	Yes	Yes	Yes	Yes

**Client
Networking**

Network Clients	Windows NT, Microsoft Mail & Schedule	NetWare, FTP, Internet	Windows NT, NetWare, Microsoft Exchange	NetWare, Internet, Gopher LAN Server, LAN Manager
Network Transport Protocols	NetBEUI	NetBEUI, TCP/IP, IPX/SPX, Appletalk	NetBEUI, TCP/IP, IPX/SPX	TCP/IP, OS/2 NetBIOS
Remote Access	Yes	Yes	Yes	Yes
Laptop Synchronization	No	No	Yes	No

Figure 9-15   Client Network Operating System Technology Analysis Grid

SERVER NETWORK OPERATING SYSTEM FUNCTIONALITY

Changing Role of the Server Network Operating System

Traditionally, file and printer sharing services were the primary required functionality of server-based network operating systems. However, as client/server information systems have boomed in popularity, **application services** have become the criteria by which server network operating systems are judged. The distributed applications of the client/server model require distinct client and server portions of a given application to interact in order to execute that application as efficiently as possible. It is the server network operating system that is responsible for not only executing the back-end engine portion of the application, but also supplying the messaging and communications services to enable interoperability between distributed clients and servers. Other servers must offer database services, directory synchronization services, and transaction process monitoring services for the multiple pieces of the overall distributed application. Figure 9-16 illustrates the evolving role of the server network operating system from an architectural perspective.

    The examination of server network operating system functionality in the remainder of the chapter will focus on those aspects of functionality that are most important to the support of distributed applications and their associated distributed clients and users. As illustrated earlier in Figure 9-4, beyond traditional file and print services, the next-generation network operating systems must also offer application services, directory services, and integration/migration services at the very least.

    Although various types of UNIX are often still employed on mission-critical application servers, two other current server network operating systems are popular:

- NetWare 4.11 (IntraNetWare)

- Windows NT Server 4.0

However, the market for the so-called "next-generation" network operating systems featuring a wider variety of services demanded by today's client/server information systems is fairly competitive. Among the emerging choices for server network operating systems are the following:

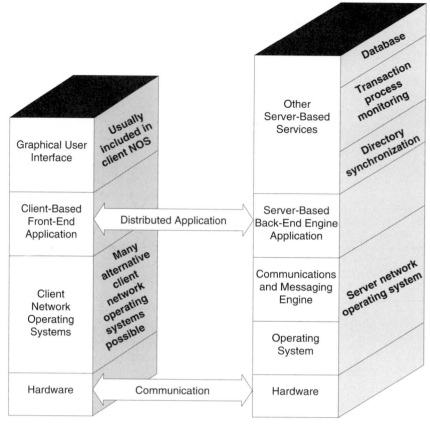

A server network operating system must be
capable of communicating transparently with
many different client network operating system
platforms.

Figure 9-16 Role of Server Network Operating Systems in Distributed Applications

Network Operating System	Vendor
NetWare 5 (Moab)	Novell
Windows NT 5.0	Microsoft
UnixWare 7	SCO (Santa Cruz Operation)
Solaris 2.6	Sunsoft
HP-UX 11.0	Hewlett-Packard

After a brief introduction to UNIX and TCP/IP issues in general, many of these potential next-generation network operating systems will be explored in more detail.

UNIX, TCP/IP, and NFS as a Network Operating System

Various types of UNIX combined with TCP/IP as a network protocol and NFS as a network-aware file system have been, and continue to be, popular as an applications server platform. However, this combination of operating system, network protocols, and file system is not as fully integrated or feature-rich as NetWare 4.11 or Windows NT Server 4.0 and probably does not deserve the label of "next-generation" NOS.

Nonetheless, UNIX servers are still prevalent on enterprise networks, especially as applications servers and enterprise network management servers. Although it is not distributed as a ready-to-run single product, UNIX as an operating system, combined with the TCP/IP family of protocols for network communications and NFS for a network-aware file system, is a very common combination of elements that offers all the functionality of commercially available single-product network operating systems.

Figure 9-17 conceptually illustrates how UNIX, the Internet suite of protocols (TCP/IP), and NFS can be combined to offer full network operating system functionality to network-attached clients and servers.

UNIX   UNIX is, in fact, a large family of related operating systems that all descended from work initially done by Ken Thompson and Dennis Ritchie at Bell Laboratories in the late 1960s and early 1970s. The name UNIX was derived as a play on words from another Bell Labs/Massachusetts Institute of Technology project of the same era, which produced a mainframe computer utility known as Multics. Although many innovations have been introduced in different UNIX implementations as the UNIX evolution has continued, all variations still share much of the original UNIX architecture and its resultant functionality.

UNIX Architecture   Figure 9-18 illustrates the basic components of the UNIX operating system architecture. UNIX is an operating system consisting of two layers:

- **UNIX systems programs**

- **UNIX system kernel**

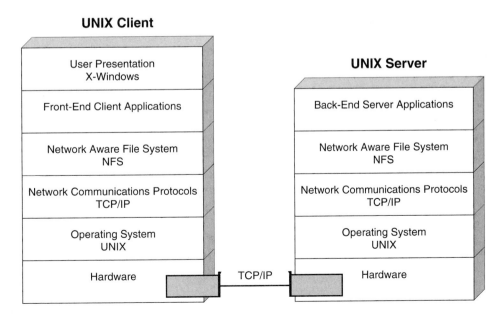

Figure 9-17   Unix, TCP/IP, and NFS as a Network Operating System

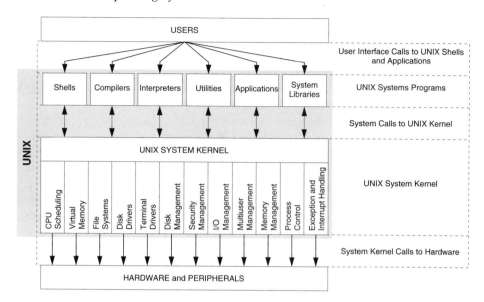

Figure 9-18   UNIX Operating System Architecture

Most UNIX system programs and kernels are written in C, allowing for easy portability to any hardware platform with a compatible C compiler. UNIX system programs and utilities deliver requested functionality to users by issuing system calls to the UNIX system kernel. The kernel then fulfills these requests by interacting with the hardware layer and returning requested functionality to the system programs and utilities. In this layered architecture, only the UNIX system kernel needs to be concerned with the particular hardware devices with which it must interact. Even within the kernel, most hardware-specific code is confined to device drivers. UNIX system programs, utilities, and end-user applications are hardware-independent and are required only to be able to issue standardized system calls to the UNIX kernel.

Most of the functionality of the UNIX kernel is concerned with managing either files or devices of some type. In order to simplify and standardize system calls, devices are treated just as a special type of file in UNIX.

Perhaps the most significant characteristic of the UNIX operating system is the availability of the source code, allowing individual programmers to enhance and modify UNIX over the years. The ability to enhance and modify UNIX as desired or required is due to the layered modular design, as illustrated in Figure 9-18. New utilities or systems programs could be added as long as they issued standard system calls to the kernel. Modifications could be made to the kernel as long as they were compatible with the locally installed hardware including the local C compiler.

The UNIX operating system's two chief positive attributes can be concluded from the previous discussion of the major architectural characteristics of UNIX:

- Portability: Portability is a characteristic of UNIX on two distinct levels. First, UNIX itself is portable across numerous hardware platforms as long as the CPU-specific kernel has been developed. Second, application programs written for UNIX are also inherently portable across all UNIX platforms as long as these platforms have compatible C compilers so that application source code can be successfully recompiled.

- Modularity: UNIX is a viable, dynamic operating system to which functionality can be added in the form of new system utilities or system programs. Even modifications to the UNIX kernel itself are possible.

UNIX Shells   In UNIX, the command interpreter, which is the user's interface to the system, is a specialized user process known as a **shell.** Popular UNIX shells include the following:

- Bourne shell

- C shell

- TC shell

- Korn shell (combines features of Bourne and C shells)

Each of the aforementioned shells has its own associated shell scripts. Users are also able to write their own shells.

Cross-shell, cross-platform scripts and programs can be developed using either of the following languages:

- Perl

- Rexx

The **Perl language** adds the following functionality to that offered by the Korn and Bourne shells:

- List processing

- Associative arrays

- Modern subroutines and functions

- More control statements

- Better I/O

- Full function library

In addition, Perl is free via download from the Internet. On the negative side, Perl is similar in syntax and commands to the more-cryptic UNIX shells it sought to improve on. As a result, Perl may still not be the answer for UNIX novices.

The **Rexx** scripting language alternative is easier to learn and use. Rexx supports structured programming techniques such as modularity while still offering access to shell commands.

UNIX File System   UNIX implements a hierarchical, multilevel tree file system starting with the root directory, as illustrated in Figure 9-19. In fact, UNIX is able to support multiple file systems simultaneously on a single disk. Each disk is divided into multiple **slices,** each of which can be used to accommodate a file system, a swap area, or a raw data area. A UNIX slice is equivalent to a partition in DOS. Each disk has one and only one root file system, and each file system has one and only one root directory.

In UNIX, files are treated by the kernel as just a sequence of bytes. In other words, although application programs may require files of a particular structure, the kernel merely stores files as sequenced bytes and organizes them in directories.

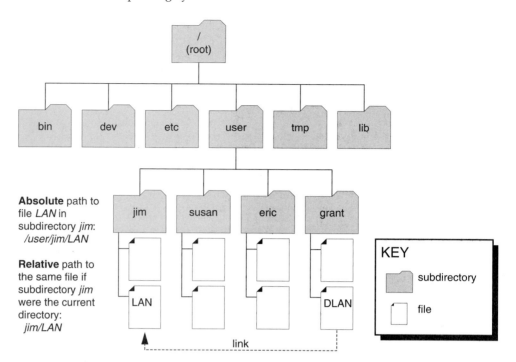

Absolute path to file *LAN* in subdirectory *jim*: */user/jim/LAN*

Relative path to the same file if subdirectory *jim* were the current directory: *jim/LAN*

Figure 9-19   UNIX File System

In the UNIX file system, directories are treated as specially formatted files and contain information as to the location of listed files. The basic job of the file system in UNIX is to offer file services as a consistent interface without requiring user application programs to worry about the particulars of the physical storage hardware used.

Path names are used in UNIX to identify the specific path through the hierarchical file structure to a particular destination file. **Absolute path names** start at the root directory in the listing of the path to the destination directory, and **relative path names** start at the current directory. The difference between absolute and relative path names is also illustrated in Figure 9-19.

Links are another unique aspect of the UNIX file system that allow a given file to be known and accessed by more than one name. A link is nothing more than an entry in a directory that points to a file stored in another directory, or another whole directory. Links are also illustrated in Figure 9-19.

TCP/IP   **TCP/IP (transmission control protocol/Internet protocol)** is the term generally used to refer to an entire suite of protocols used to provide communication on a variety of layers between widely distributed different types of computers. Strictly speaking, TCP and IP are just two of the protocols contained within the family of protocols more properly known as the **Internet suite of protocols.** TCP/IP was developed during the 1970s and widely deployed during the 1980s under the auspices of **DARPA,** or Defense Advanced Research Projects Agency, in order to meet the Department of Defense's need to have a wide variety of computers be able to interoperate and communicate. TCP/IP became widely available to universities and research agencies and has become the de facto standard for communication between heterogeneous networked computers.

Overall Architecture   TCP/IP and the entire family of related protocols are organized into a protocol model. Although not identical to the OSI seven-layer model, the **TCP/IP model** is no less effective at organizing protocols required to establish and maintain communications between different computers. Figure 9-20 illustrates the TCP/IP model, its constituent protocols, and its relationship to the seven-layer OSI model.

As can be seen in Figure 9-20, the OSI model and TCP/IP model are functionally equivalent, although not identical, up through the transport layer. While the OSI model continues on with the session, presentation, and applications layers, the TCP/IP model has only the application layer remaining, with utilities such as Telnet (terminal emulation) and FTP (file transfer protocol) as examples of application layer protocols. As illustrated in Figure 9-20, the functionality equivalent to the OSI model's session, presentation, and application layers is added to the TCP/IP model by combining it with the network file system (NFS) distributed by Sun Microsystems. As a result, in order to offer equivalent functionality to that represented by the full OSI seven-layer model, the TCP/IP family of protocols must be combined with NFS, sometimes known as the open network computing (ONC) environment.

NFS   **NFS**, or **network file system,** was originally developed by Sun Microsystems as part of its open network computing (ONC) environment. NFS allows multiple different computing platforms to share files. To all of the heterogeneous computers that support NFS, the NFS file system appears as a transparent extension to their local operating system or file system by making remote disk drives appear to be local. Print jobs can also be redirected from local workstations to NFS servers. Although originally developed for the UNIX operating system and TCP/IP transport protocols, NFS is now supported on a variety of platforms, including PCs. This fact has allowed network operating systems such as NetWare and Windows NT to transparently support NFS as well, thereby offering transparent interoperability with UNIX workstations, minicomputers, and mainframes. Using NFS as an interoperability solution for multiplatform file systems requires a platform-specific version of NFS to be installed on any computer wishing to use NFS in this manner. NFS becomes a neutral file services language that is able to communicate with all of the native platform-specific file systems.

Although NFS is often considered functionally equivalent to the file systems of fully integrated network operating systems such as NetWare or Windows NT, in

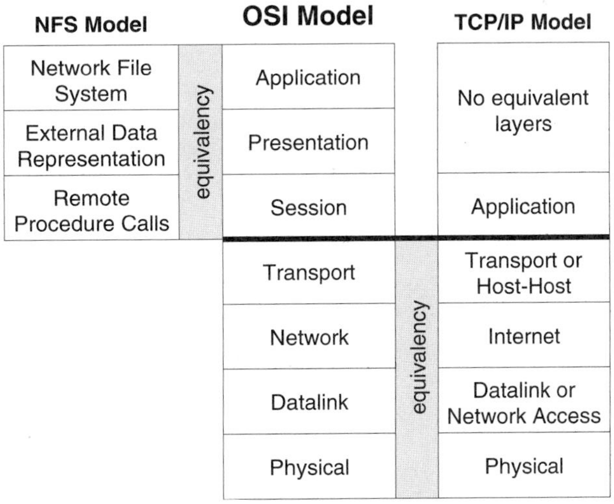

NFS Model		OSI Model	TCP/IP Model
Network File System	equivalency	Application	No equivalent layers
External Data Representation		Presentation	
Remote Procedure Calls		Session	Application
		Transport	Transport or Host-Host
	equivalency	Network	Internet
		Datalink	Datalink or Network Access
		Physical	Physical

Figure 9-20   The TCP/IP Model

fact, NFS derives much of its functionality from the native operating system of the platform on which it is installed. Additionally, although NFS is capable of supporting file sharing between different computing platforms, more advanced file management features such as user and group access rights, file and record locking, and conversion between different file types may not be universally supported. In other words, in some cases, NFS is able to implement only those features common to all linked file systems and computing platforms as opposed to the most-advanced file management functionality of any particular computing platform.

In Sharper Focus

SAMBA AS AN ALTERNATIVE TO NFS

As an alternative to installing NFS on all computers that wish to share file services, **SAMBA** allows UNIX hosts and their files and printers to be instantly and transparently accessible by any Windows for Workgroups, Windows 95, Windows NT, or OS/2 computer. SAMBA is an implementation for UNIX servers of the **Server Message Block (SMB)** NetBIOS protocol that is native to all Microsoft and numerous other operating systems. SMB provides a platform-independent command language offering such services as file and printer sharing, user authentication, and interprocess communications. (Refer back to Figure 9-13 to see SMB support among various client network operating systems.) SAMBA is transport protocol independent, working equally well over TCP/IP, IPX/SPX, or NetBEUI. Installing SAMBA on the UNIX host allows interoperability with all SMB-compliant computers, without any modifications to the SMB-compliant computers. The SAMBA server for UNIX hosts is available as VisionFS from SCO (Santa Cruz Operation). The shareware version is available from http://samba.canberra.edu.au/pub/samba.

NFS Architecture The term *NFS* is generally used to refer to a collection or suite of three major protocols:

- **NFS**, or network file system

- **XDR**, or external data representation

- **RPC**, or remote procedure call

Strictly speaking, NFS is only the API portion of a collection of programs and utilities that offer the transparent file management interoperability typically associated with the NFS suite of protocols. Transparency is a key point because the client application requesting files does not know that the NFS client software will be used to communicate with a remote NFS server in order to deliver the requested files. Each NFS client protocol stack interacts with the native operating system and file system of the computing platform on which it is installed and translates requests and responses for NFS services into standardized NFS protocols for communication with similarly configured NFS servers. NFS could be considered an example of an OSI layer 7 protocol.

XDR is a presentation layer protocol responsible for formatting data in a consistent manner so that all NFS clients and servers can process it, regardless of the computing platform or operating system on which the NFS suite may be executing.

RPC is a session layer protocol responsible for establishing, maintaining, and terminating communications sessions between distributed applications in an NFS environment. NFS protocols may use either UDP or TCP for transport layer services. The architectural relationship between the NFS suite of protocols and the TCP/IP suite of protocols is illustrated in Figure 9-21.

Comparative Network Operating System Functionality

The emerging network operating systems of today that will be expected to support widely distributed applications across a variety of computing platforms require advanced functionality in the following major areas:

- Directory services

- Application services

- File services

- Networking and connectivity services

- Management and administration services

- Integration/migration services

- Security services

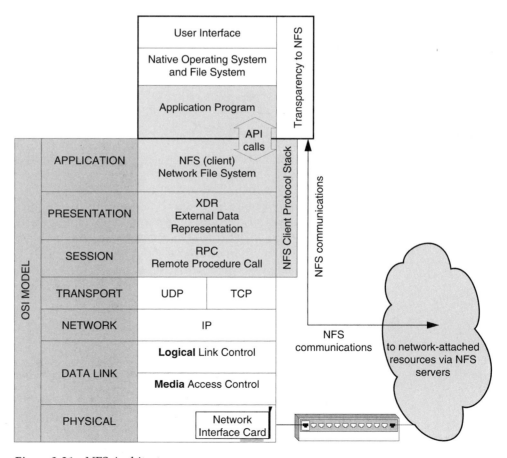

Figure 9-21   NFS Architecture

In the following section, a brief review of the extent to which these services are delivered by today's "next-generation network operating systems" will be provided. Some of the topics presented briefly in this review will be explored in more depth in later chapters.

Directory Services   Network operating systems have always depended on some sort of naming service or directory in which to store information about users as well as systems resources such as disks, servers, and printers. NetWare 3.x servers stored this type of information in a **bindery.** NetWare 4.1 employs a **global directory service** known as **NDS,** or **NetWare Directory Services,** and Windows NT 4.0 uses a **domain directory service.** NT 5.0 uses introduces an enterprise-oriented directory service known as **ADS,** or **Active Directory Service.**

Global Directory Services versus Domain Directory Services   Global and domain directory services differ primarily in the organization of information concerning network users and resources. Global directory services organize all network user and resource data into a single hierarchical database, providing a single point of user and resource management. The hierarchical database is based on an organizational hierarchical tree structure of the network that must first be designed. All servers that are part of this global hierarchical network can see all other parts of the hierarchical network. In this sense, the hierarchical directory database is merely a reflection of the hierarchical network itself.

This global directory database may well be **distributed,** implying that different portions of the data are physically stored on multiple distributed servers linked via the network. In addition, this global directory database may be **replicated,** implying that multiple copies of identical data may also be stored on multiple servers for redundancy and fault tolerance purposes. In terms of a logical view of the network, global directory services provide a view of a single, enterprise network.

In contrast, domain directory services see the network as a series of linked subdivisions known as **domains.** Domain directory services associate network users and resources with a primary server known as a **PDC,** or **Primary domain controller.** Each domain's directory must be individually established and maintained. Domains can be individually maintained and controlled in terms of how much of other domains can be seen.

Directory services can also vary in what types of information are stored in the directory services database. In some cases, all users and network resources are considered **network objects,** with information concerning them stored in a single database, arranged by object type. Object attributes can be modified, and new network objects can be defined. In other cases, network users and network resources are kept in separate databases. Frequently, separate databases are maintained for network user account information and e-mail user account information.

**In Sharper
Focus**

DIRECTORY SERVICES COMMUNICATION

In a global directory service such as NetWare 4.1's NDS, when a user wants to access resources on a remote or foreign server, that server performs a lookup in the NDS database to authenticate the user's right to the requested service. This NDS database lookup is repeated for every request for service from remote users. The NDS database is distributed, so the physical location of the server containing the rights information of the requesting user may be located anywhere in the hierarchical distributed network.

In the case of a domain directory service such as Windows NT 3.51 or 4.0, the remote or foreign server receives the user authentication from the user's primary domain controller (local server) in a process known as **interdomain trust (IT).** By having servers act on behalf of their local users when verifying authenticity with remote and foreign servers, every user ID does not have to be entered and maintained in every domain's directory service. In addition, once the interdomain trust has been established for a particular user, the remote domain server does not repeat the request for authentication.

As enterprise networks become more heterogeneous, comprising network operating systems from a variety of different vendors, the need will arise for different network operating systems to share one another's directory services information. This is especially true for user information and e-mail addresses from various e-mail systems. A directory services specification known as **X.500** offers the potential for this directory services interoperability. NetWare 4.1's NDS is based on X.500 with proprietary extensions.

Another potential protocol for directory interoperability is known as **lightweight directory access protocol (LDAP).** LDAP is basically a simplification of X.500's directory access protocol. It allows computers executing LDAP client software to manage a hierarchical directory database using TCP/IP as a transport protocol. LDAP is not a directory service, but a protocol for exchanging information between different vendors' directory systems. Companies such as NetScape, Banyan, Novell, IBM, Microsoft, and Lotus have expressed support for LDAP. LDAP version 3 is either currently supported or will be supported by Microsoft's Active Directory Service as well as by Novell's NDS and NetScape. Microsoft is also promoting its own directory interoperability standard known as **open directory services interface (ODSI).** Still another possibility for open directory standards is DCE (distributed computing environment) cell directory services, which has been included in the latest release of OS/2 Warp Server. The importance of enterprise directory interoperability standards such as X.500, ODSI, DCE, and LDAP are explored further in Chapter 6, Middleware.

NOS-Independent Enterprise Directory Services   One way to provide common directory services across multiple network operating system platforms is to isolate the directory services layer from the rest of the network operating system, allowing a third-party directory service to work over a variety of network operating systems. An early motivator for this product market was the lack of a native enterprisewide directory service for NT 3.51 and NT 4.0. Figure 9-22 lists some of these enterprise directory services and their key characteristics.

Applications Services   If the primary objective of the next-generation server NOS is to provide high-performance application services, the most important enabling NOS characteristic delivering that objective is the NOS's ability to support symmetrical multiprocessing. As numbers of users and sophistication of application programs continue to increase, the only real solution is for the application to be able to use more processing power simultaneously. Not all server network operating systems support symmetrical multiprocessing, and those that do may vary in the maximum number of processors supported. Other server network operating system characteristics are essential to optimization of application program performance:

- Preemptive multitasking

- 32-bit execution

- Multithreaded application support

- Program execution in protected memory space

As applications become mission-critical, network operating systems must provide fault tolerance and high availability. Clustering with failover, rapid recovery, fault tolerance, high availability, and continuous operations, as introduced in Chapter 4, must be supported by network operating systems as well as by computing hardware platforms in order to support implementation.

File Services Applications programs are stored in a particular file system format. In addition, when these application programs execute, they may request additional services from the resident file system via API calls. Server network operating systems vary in the types and number of supported file systems. Some network operating systems, such as Windows NT, can have multiple partitions on a disk drive, with one partition supporting FAT (File Allocation Table) file system and another partition supporting the NTFS (NT file system) file system. Figure 9-23 lists some possible file systems supported by server network operating systems.

Other file services offered by some server network operating systems include file compression utilities and **data migration** utilities, which manage the migration of data among different types of storage devices as part of a comprehensive hierarchical storage management (HSM) program. Finally, just as client network operating systems were either bundling or offering optional workgroup software as part of their package, server network operating systems are offering a variety bundled back-end engines as part of their offerings. For example, as an option or add-on to Windows NT Server, a bundled product known as Microsoft Back-Office offers the following suite of server applications:

Enterprise Directory Services	Vendor	Functionality
StreetTalk for Windows NT	Banyan Systems	TCP/IP-based version of Vines StreetTalk that identifies enterprise network objects by unique names, stored in a distributed database
NetScape Directory Server	NetScape Communications Corporation	Uses LDAP to let users and administrators browse and manage LDAP-compliant directories
Synchronicity for NT	NetVision Incorporated	Enables NT domains to be controlled exclusively by NDS administration utility (NWADMIN)
NDS for NT	Novell	Full NDS port to Windows NT; also available on SCO UNIX, HP-UX, RS-6000 AIX, S/390 mainframes, and Unisys

Figure 9-22 NOS-Independent Enterprise Directory Services

File System Name	Associated Network Operating System
FAT—File Allocation Table	Windows NT Server
HPFS—High Performance File System	OS/2 LAN Server
NetWare File System	NetWare 3.12 and 4.1
NFS	UNIX (native); most other NOS, optional
NSS	Novell Storage System. New file system for NetWare 5
NTFS—NT File System	Windows NT Server
Vines File System	Banyan Vines 5.54

Figure 9-23   File Systems and Associated Server Network Operating Systems

- System management server
- SQL server
- Mail and schedule (exchange) server
- SNA gateway to IBM mainframe networks

Networking and Connectivity Services

Network Clients Supported   In addition to the client network operating systems previously reviewed, server network operating systems may also have to communicate with client platforms with only the following operating systems installed:

- DOS
- Windows
- Macintosh
- OS/2
- UNIX (implies support for NFS file system)

In these cases, because the previously listed operating systems possess no native networking functionality, the server network operating system must possess the ability to generate diskettes with the necessary operating system–specific network communications capabilities. These diskettes are then loaded on the intended networking client, and the required network communication capabilities are merged with the native operating system.

Network Protocols Supported   The key question concerning network protocols and server network operating systems is not just how many different network protocols are supported, but more importantly, how many network protocols can be supported simultaneously? In these days of heterogeneous multivendor enterprise networks, it is essential that server network operating systems possess the ability to support multiple network protocols simultaneously in order to maximize not only the different types of clients, but also the number and type of other servers with which a given server can communicate. The ease with which multiple network protocols can be supported, or whether multiple network protocols can be supported at all, can vary among different server network operating systems.

Related to the ability of a server network operating system to simultaneously support multiple protocols is the ability of a server network operating system to support multiple network interface cards. If a single NIC is the bottleneck to network communications, additional NICs can be added so long as multiple NICs can be supported by the computer's bus, and they can communicate with the server network operating system. As PCI buses and PCI-based NICs have increased in popularity, PCI cards containing up to four NICs are being produced. Unless the server network operating system has the ability to communicate with four NICs simultaneously, this four NIC PCI card would be of little use.

Multiprotocol Routing   Underlying a server network operating system's ability to process multiple protocols simultaneously is the presence of **multiprotocol routing** software. This multiprotocol routing software may be either included, optional, or not available, depending on the server network operating system in question. Multiprotocol routing provides the functionality necessary to actually process and understand multiple network protocols as well as translate between them. Without multiprotocol routing software, clients speaking multiple different network protocols cannot be supported. Figure 9-24 illustrates the relationship between multiple network protocols, multiple network interface cards per server, and multiprotocol routing software.

Remote Access and Gateway Services   Remote access communication requires compatible remote access software to be installed on both client and server computers. This remote access software may or may not be supplied with the client or server network operating system. It is important that these remote access servers are well integrated with the server network operating system in order to assure remote users of both reliable performance and the full functionality offered to locally connected users. Windows NT RAS (Remote Access Server) is integrated with Windows NT Server 3.51 and 4.0, and NetWare Connect is the remote access server that integrates with NetWare 4.1.

In some cases, it may be necessary for either clients or servers to access IBM mainframe computers or AS/400s linked on IBM's proprietary network architecture, known as **SNA (Systems Network Architecture).** In such cases, it makes more sense for the translation software necessary to access the SNA network to reside on

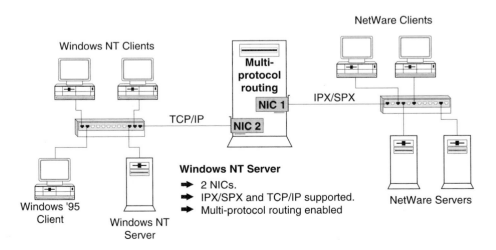

Figure 9-24   Multiple Network Protocols and Server Network Operating Systems

a single server than on multiple clients. In this scenario, the server with the SNA translation software installed becomes a **gateway** to the SNA network. Windows NT's product for IBM mainframe access is called SNA Gateway. NetWare's is called NetWare for SAA (Systems Application Architecture).

Management and Administration Services

Installation, Configuration, and Administration   Recent reviews of server network operating systems consistently list **autodetection and configuration** of installed controllers, interface cards, and peripherals as the most important installation-related feature. The ability of a server network operating system to automatically configure a controller, adapter, or peripheral depends on the network operating system's possessing a compatible driver for that device. The greater the number of drivers supported by a given network operating system, the greater the probability that autoconfiguration will be successful.

Another hardware compatibility issue related to installation is the number of different CPUs on which a given server network operating system can operate. For example, although NetWare 4.1 can only operate on Intel chips, Windows NT server can operate on Intel chips and DEC Alpha chips. At one time NT also ran on PowerPC chips and MIPs RISC chips, but this support has been dropped. Most next-generation network operating systems will likely need to be able to run on the next-generation 64-bit CPU chip from Intel and Hewlett Packard known as IA-64 or Merced.

In order to appreciate the differences in ease of administration offered by server network operating systems, it is important to scale the vision of the network to be administered to a multiserver enterprise network serving hundreds if not thousands of users. With this scenario in mind, the network analyst might ask some pertinent questions:

- How many steps are involved in creating a new user account?

- What is involved in giving a user access to remote servers?

- How easily can a user profile be copied and used as a template to automatically generate other user profiles? This feature is particularly important in academic settings where user profiles must be constantly generated in large numbers.

- What tools are available to assist in managing multiple servers simultaneously?

Server network operating systems can vary widely in the sophistication of the **performance monitoring** software included or available as an add-on. Ideally, the monitoring software should offer the ability to set thresholds for multiple system performance parameters. If these thresholds are exceeded, alerts or alarms should notify network management personnel of the problem and offer advice on possible diagnoses or solutions. Event logging and audit trails are often included as part of the performance monitoring package.

In multiple-server environments, it is particularly important that all servers can be monitored and managed from a single management console. Desktop and server management software offers capabilities beyond the monitoring software included in server network operating systems. For example, performance statistics are often gathered and stored in databases known as **MIBs (Management Information**

Bases). In addition, this performance management information can be communicated to enterprise management systems such as HP OpenView or IBM SystemView in the proper **SNMP (simple network management protocol)** format. Microsoft's desktop and server management product is known as SMS, or System Management Server, and Novell's is known as ManageWise.

Integration and Migration   Integration and migration features of next-generation network operating systems are clearly aimed at one audience: the high number of servers running NetWare 3.12 (more than 60 percent of servers as of October 1997). **Integration** refers to that transition time in the migration process when both network operating systems must be running simultaneously and interacting to some degree. **Migration** features are aimed at easing the transition from NetWare 3.12 to either NetWare 4.1 or Windows NT. Key among the migration concerns is the conversion of the directory services information stored in the NetWare 3.12 bindery into either NetWare 4.1 NDS or Windows NT domain directory services. Utilities are available from third-party software vendors as well as from Novell and Microsoft to at least partially automate the bindery conversion.

Following are among the most important incompatibilities between NetWare and NT that must be overcome:

- Interoperability issues will differ depending on which version of NetWare is involved. For example, NetWare's VLMs are not interoperable with NT.

- Communications protocols incompatibilities are fairly easily solved thanks to Windows NT's ability to run IPX/SPX as its native communications protocol.

- File systems and directory services incompatibilities must be overcome.

Figure 9-25 summarizes some of the NetWare/NT interoperability solutions currently available. In evaluating any interoperability solution, network analysts should ask several key questions:

1.   What level of interoperability is offered?

2.   Is this service included in the NOS, or is it a separately purchased product?

3.   Is the product installed on every client or just on servers?

4.   How difficult is the product to install, configure, and manage?

5.   Is the product designed to offer interoperability, or is it actually designed to provide a transition or migration path from one product or platform to another?

Managerial Perspective

Although interoperability with NetWare is certainly achievable with the array of products available from Microsoft, the fact remains that their primary purpose is to form a suite of products that make the transition from NetWare to NT as painless as possible.

Security   Several important security enhancements have been added to NetWare 4.1. Owing to a well-publicized security hole in NetWare 3.x, which allowed impostors to gain supervisory privileges, **authentication** is perhaps the most important of

Product Name	Functionality/Explanation
NWLink	Windows NT's IPX/SPX protocol stack is NDIS compliant and allows Windows NT servers and clients on which it is installed to access NetWare servers without requiring any additional hardware or software. NWLink only allows NT clients and servers to execute applications on the NetWare server. It does not provide direct access to files and printers.
Client Service for NetWare	This service allows a Windows NT client to access file and print services from a NetWare server. Clients can access NetWare 4.1 servers only in bindery emulation mode.
Migration Tool for NetWare	Available from Microsoft, this product migrates the user and group accounts of a NetWare 3.x bindery to NT server.
Gateway Service for NetWare	This service allows a Windows NT server to access file and print services from NetWare servers and also offer these NetWare services to attached NT clients that are not running their own Client Service for NetWare software. NT servers can access NetWare 4.1 servers only in bindery emulation mode.
NetWare Requestor for Windows NT	Available from Novell, this product allows NT clients to access NetWare servers. This product allows NT clients to access NetWare 4.1 NDS databases through NT's File Manager utility. Allows NT clients to login to NetWare 4.1 servers as NetWare users.
Directory Service Manager for NetWare	Available from Microsoft, this product is intended for networks transitioning from NetWare 3.x to NT rather than ongoing network interoperability. It requires Gateway Service for NetWare. This product is able to import NetWare bindery files and transform them into databases on NT primary and backup domain controllers. From that point forward, all of the former bindery information can be maintained from Windows NT.
File and Printer Service for NetWare	Available from Microsoft, this service allows a Windows NT server to offer file and print services to NetWare clients. The NetWare clients are unmodified and think that they are interacting with a native NetWare server. Such a product is aimed at allowing NetWare users who wish to use NT as an application server to also use NT for file and print services as well.
BW-Multiconnect for Windows NT	Available from Beame & Whiteside, a traditional TCP/IP client developer, this product offers similar functionality to Microsoft's File and Print Service for NetWare. It has slightly less functionality than the Microsoft product, such as a lack of support for NetWare login scripts and client print utilities.

Figure 9-25   NT/NetWare Interoperability Alternatives

the security innovations. Using a combination of private encryption keys and passwords, the VLM requester security agent on the client workstation and NDS file server combine to ensure that users are properly authenticated before being logged in. Should even higher security be required, every packet transmitted from a particular client workstation can have a unique, encrypted digital signature attached to it that can be authenticated only by the server in a process known as **packet signing.** However, a performance price of 5 percent to 7 percent is paid for the increased security as valuable CPU cycles are spent encrypting and decrypting digital signatures.

While authentication and packet signing ensure that only valid users are accessing system resources, an extensive **auditing system** monitors and reports on what those valid users are doing. The auditor acts independently of the supervisor in an effort to ensure a proper system of checks and balances in which no single person could remain undetected while performing potentially harmful acts. The auditing system separately monitors activity on both the file system as defined by volumes and the NetWare Directory Services database as defined by container units. Figure 9-26 illustrates the organization and capabilities of the NetWare Auditing System.

Security is an integral part of the Windows NT operating system rather than a shell or subsystem. As a result, security in Windows NT offers not only user authorization services typically associated with network operating system security, but also an assurance that the programs and processes launched by those authorized users will only access system resources to which they have the appropriate level of permission. In Windows NT, no interprocess communication takes place without the knowledge and approval of the Windows NT security system.

The overall security system is organized around the concept of objects, not unlike NetWare 4.1's view of the NetWare Directory Services object-oriented database. In Windows NT, examples of objects are files, directories, print queues, and other networked resources. All objects are assigned permission levels, which are then associated with individual users or user groups. Examples of permission levels are as follows:

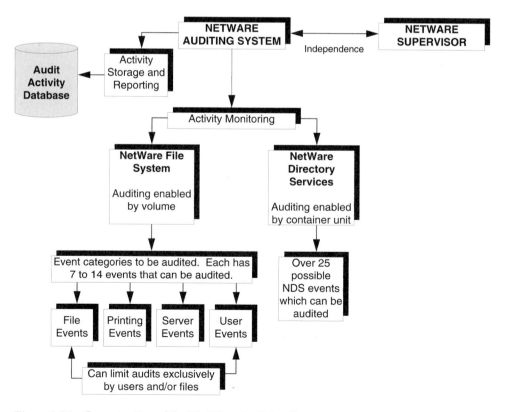

Figure 9-26 Organization of the NetWare Auditing System

- Read

- Delete

- Write

- Change permission level

- Execute

- Take ownership

- No access

By monitoring permission levels, NT security can monitor and control who accesses which objects as well as how those objects are accessed. In addition to monitoring and control, NT security can also audit and report on these same object accesses by users according to permission level. The components of the Windows NT security model are illustrated in Figure 9-27.

A logical start for introducing the interacting components of the Windows NT security model might be the **logon process,** which is responsible for the interaction with the user on whatever computer platform they may wish to log in on. This is really a client presentation layer function, identified as a separate component in order to allow login processes for a variety of different computer platforms to all interact with the Windows NT security model in a standardized manner.

The platform-specific login process interacts with the **local security authority,** which actually provides the user authentication services. Specifically, the local secu-

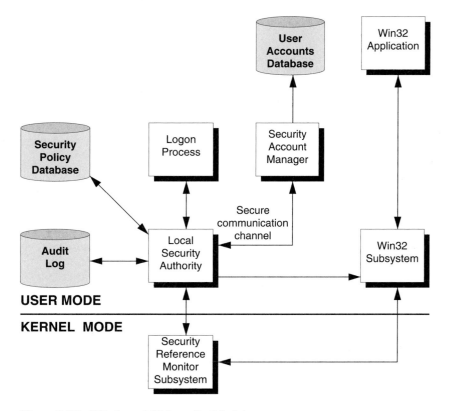

Figure 9-27 Windows NT Security Model

rity authority generates a **security access token** for authorized users, which contains **security IDs (SIDs)** for this user and all of the user groups to which this user belongs. This security access token accompanies every process or program launched by this user and is used as a means to reference whether or not this user and the spawned processes have sufficient permissions to perform requested services or access requested resources. The local security authority also controls the security model's audit policy and generates audit messages, which are stored in the audit log.

All of the user and user group ID and permission level information is stored in and maintained by the **security account manager,** which interacts with the local security authority to verify user IDs and permission levels. The **user accounts database** is physically stored on the primary domain controller except when an individual workstation may have a need to verify specific user IDs for remote access to that workstation. The links between components of the NT security model involved in the logon process are designed as secure communication channels to ensure that traffic that is supposedly received from a given workstation or computer actually does come from that computer. This authentication is accomplished in Windows NT by a process very similar to the challenge handshake authentication protocol (CHAP) employed in NetWare 4.1 for a similar purpose. Passwords are encrypted before being transmitted during the logon process.

The only kernel mode portion of the NT security model is the **security reference monitor (SRM),** which really serves as the security engine or back-end application for all of the previously mentioned security client applications. It is the security reference model that has the ultimate responsibility for ensuring that users have the proper authority to access requested network resources. The SRM is able to meet this responsibility by comparing the requested object's security description as documented in **access control lists (ACL)** with the requesting user's security information as documented on the security access token. Besides access validation, the SRM is also responsible for audit checking and audit message generation.

**Applied
Problem
Solving**

SERVER NETWORK OPERATING SYSTEM TECHNOLOGY ANALYSIS

A network analyst's job is to always seek out the latest information the industry has to offer before making recommendations for purchases that could have a significant bearing on both the company's prosperity and the analyst's job security. The following server networking operating system technology analysis grid (Figure 9-28) is given as an example but is not meant to be either authoritative or all-inclusive. The technology analysis grid is divided into the following major categories:

- Hardware/Platform Characteristics

- Installation and Configuration

- Networking and Connectivity

- Management and Administration

Server NetWork Operating System Characteristic	Windows NT Server 4.0	NetWare 4.1
Hardware/Platform		
Min/Max Memory	16 MB/4 GB	16 MB/4 GB

Min/Max Disk Space	90 MB/1700 TB	75 MB/32 TB
CPUs	Intel, DEC Alpha, MIPs, RISC, Power PC	Intel
Symmetrical Multiprocessing	Yes	Yes
Preemptive multitasking	Yes	Yes
Multithreading	Yes	Yes
Protected Memory Application Execution	Yes	Yes, but not with NLMs
Installation and Configuration		
Automatic Detection and Configuration of Adapters and Peripherals	Yes	No
Requires a Separate Administrator Console	No	Yes
Number of included NIC Drivers	98	68
Networking and Connectivity		
Clients Supported	DOS, Windows, Windows for Workgroups, OS/2, Windows NT, Windows 95, Mac, UNIX	DOS, Windows, Windows for Workgroups, Windows 95, UNIX, OS/2, Windows NT, Mac
Network Protocols Supported	TCP/IP, IPX, NetBEUI, Appletalk, TCP/IP encapsulated	TCP/IP, IPX, Appletalk, TCP/IP encapsulated IPX, IPX encapsulated NetBIOS
Routing Supporting	TCP/IP, IPX	TCP/IP, IPX, Appletalk
Supports DHCP, WINS, and DNS Integration	Yes	No
Multiprotocol Routing Software Included	Yes	Yes
Remote Access Services	Windows NT RAS included	NetWare Connect optional
E-Mail Gateways	Mail server optional	MHS included
Clients Able to Access Remote Resources	Yes	Yes
Web Browser and Server Included	Yes	Yes
Messaging Services	Requires Exchange Server	Requires GroupWise
Management and Administration		
Can Act as SNMP Agent for Enterprise Management System	Yes	Optional

Can Set Performance Thresholds and Alerts	Yes	Yes with ManageWise (optional)
Central Management of Multiple Servers	Yes	Yes
Audit Trails and Event Logs	Yes	Yes
Security Level Supported	C2	C2
RAID Levels Supported	0, 1, 5	0, 1

Figure 9-28   Server Network Operating System Technology Analysis Grid

Key functional features of several next-generation network operating systems are summarized in Figure 9-29.

NetWork Operating System	Vendor	Key Functional Characteristics
Windows NT 5.0	Microsoft	• Enterprisewide active directory services; replaces WINS with DNS • Clustering (Wolfpack) two-node cluster • Transaction server • Index server • Message queueing server • Enhanced remote management capabilities; Microsoft Management Console • Zero Administration Windows—electronic software distribution to lower total cost of ownership
NetWare 5 (Moab)	Novell	• Native support of Java Software Developer's Kit and JVM (Java Virtual Machine) • Native TCP/IP support • Unified OS kernel better supports SMP, virtual memory, preemptive multitasking • NSS—Novell Storage System; improved file system • NDS now available on numerous platforms • Clustering (Orion) 16-node cluster • Supports I_2O—Intelligent Input Output
Solaris 2.6	SunSoft	• Includes Internet Server Extension 1.0 • Supports up to 64 CPUs SMP • Supports up to 64 GB of RAM • Four node clusters • Includes IMAP4 server, HTTP server • Supports SMB, NCP and AppleShare for transparent client support • NFS included
UnixWare 7	SCO	• Combines UnixWare with SCO OpenServer
HP-UX 11	Hewlett Packard	• 64-bit operating system • Supports up to 16 GB of RAM • Eight node clusters

Figure 9-29   Key Functional Characteristics of Next Generation Network Operating Systems

NT VERSUS NETWARE

Network managers, analysts, and consultants are constantly asked, "Which is the better network operating system, NT or NetWare?" No single network operating system is best in all cases. The best network operating system in any given situation depends on a variety of factors including business needs and objectives, current and planned applications, and current and planned network infrastructure.

Windows NT is being installed in corporations for use as web servers, database servers, applications servers, SNA servers that act as gateways to mainframe computers, DHCP servers that lease IP addresses to attached workstations, messaging servers that support Microsoft Exchange, and workstations or server operating systems. In general, NT's greatest strength is as a back-end or application engine platform.

NetWare has always been known as a good file and print services system. With the release of NetWare 4, Novell introduced NetWare Directory Services (NDS). NDS can be managed either centrally or in a distributed fashion and has the ability to allow all network resources (printers, users, groups, servers) to be viewed as a single entity. NDS is very scalable with its ability to effectively manage hundreds of thousands of network resource objects. NDS has been around for several years now and is a stable enterprisewide directory service. Microsoft will be launching its initial try at enterprise directory services with ADS (active directory services) in NT 5.0. Regardless of how much testing and debugging ADS undergoes, it will not be initially as stable as a product such as NDS, which has been on the market for several years and has undergone several fixes and upgrades.

NetWare and Windows NT each have unique strengths. Which is the better network operating system? Whichever one provides the required functionality as defined in a thorough top-down analysis for the best price.

SUMMARY

Network operating systems have traditionally provided shared file and print services among networked clients. With the increase in client/server architectures and the associated increase in distributed applications, network operating systems are being called on to provide application services, directory services, and messaging and communications services in support of these distributed applications.

Network operating systems were once categorized as either peer-to-peer or client/server. The network operating system evolution shows peer-to-peer network operating systems evolving to small business network operating systems and client/server network operating systems evolving to distinct, independent, client and server network operating systems.

Client network operating systems functionality can be categorized into operating systems capabilities, peer-to-peer networking capabilities, and client networking capabilities. Client networking capabilities are largely measured by the number of different server network operating systems with which the client can transparently interoperate. Remote access capability is also important.

Server network operating systems are now primarily concerned with high performance application services for back-end application programs. Enterprisewide directory services must also be provided. The two major approaches to enterprise directory services are global directory services and domain directory services. In order to communicate with numerous client platforms, server network operating systems must support a variety of different network clients as well as a variety of different network transport protocols. Multiprotocol routing and remote access services are also essential to deliver transparent interoperability to the greatest number of client platforms. In the multiple server environments of the enterprise network, monitoring, management, and administration tools play a critical role.

KEY TERMS

16-bit sub-system
Absolute path names
Access control list (ACL)
Active directory service (ADS)
Application program interface
Application services
Applications software
Auditing system
Authentication
Autodetection and configuration
Automatic failover
Backward compatibility
Bindery
Client front ends
Client network operating systems
Client/server network operating systems
DARPA
Data display channel (DDC)
Data migration
Delta file synchronization
Dial-up server
Directory services
Directory synchronization software
Distributed parallel processing (DPP)
Domain directory services
Domains
Dynamic reconfiguration
Dynamic scalability
Engine
Enterprise network
Enterprise network management system
File synchronization software
Global directory services
Granularity
Integrated client/server management system
Integration
Integration/migration services

Interdomain trust (IT)
Internet suite of protocols
LAN productivity software
LAN resource management software
LAN software architecture
Legacy applications
Lightweight directory access protocol (LDAP)
Links
Load balancing
Local security authority
Logon process
Management information base (MIB)
Management software
Middleware
Migration
Mirrored server link
Multiprotocol routing
NDS
NetWare 4.1 SFT III
NetWare 4.1 SMP
NetWare Connect
NetWare Directory Services
Network file system (NFS)
Network objects
Network operating systems
Object-oriented user interfaces
Packet signing
Path names
PDC
Peer-to-peer network operating systems
Performance monitoring
Perl language
Plug-n-Play (PnP)
PnP BIOS
Primary domain controller
Protected memory mode
RAS

Real-mode device drivers
Relative path names
Remote node server
Rexx
RPC
SAMBA
SCAM
SCSI configured automatically
Security
Security account manager
Security ID (SID)
Security reference monitor (SRM)
Server back end
Server duplexing
Server message block (SMB)
Server network operating systems
Shell
Simple network management protocol (SNMP)
Small business network operating systems
SMP kernel
SMP scalability
Symmetric multiprocessing (SMP)
Systems network architecture (SNA)
TCP/IP model
Transmission control Protocol/ Internet protocol (TCP/IP)
Universal client
UNIX system kernel
UNIX systems programs
User accounts database
Version control software
Virtual device drivers (VxDs)
Virtual machines
Virtual parallel machines (VPM)
XDR
X.500

REVIEW QUESTIONS

1. What effect has the adoption of client/server architectures and distributed applications had on network operating systems architectures?
2. Differentiate peer-to-peer network operating systems and client/server network operating systems.
3. Distinguish between today's client network operating system and the client portion of client/server network operating systems.
4. How does the combination of today's client and server network operating systems differ from a client/server network operating system implementation?
5. What is a universal client?
6. Why is a universal client important to enterprise computing?
7. What new demands for services are being put on today's server network operating systems?
8. Describe the importance of the following service categories: directory services, applications services, integration/migration services.
9. Differentiate peer-to-peer NOS and small business NOS.
10. What forces have caused the transition from peer-to-peer to small business NOS?
11. Describe the major categories of functionality of client network operating systems.
12. What are the major differences between an object-oriented user interface and a graphical user interface?
13. Explain the difficulty in supporting legacy applications while offering protected memory mode execution.
14. What are real mode device drivers, and how do they differ from applications that interact with the operating system via APIs?
15. Why do many computer games use real mode device drivers?
16. Why don't some client and server network operating systems support real mode device drivers?
17. Describe how 16-bit or 32-bit applications running in their own protected memory space can still cause system crashes.
18. What is the objective of PnP standards?
19. Describe the components required to deliver a PnP solution and the relationship of these components.
20. Which client network operating system is most PNP compliant?
21. What is meant by the statement, "Interoperability is not two-way."
22. Describe the three elements of networking functionality belonging to client network operating systems, paying particular attention to the relationship between the elements.
23. Why is it important for a client network operating system to be able to support more than one network transport protocol?
24. Describe the importance of laptop synchronization as a client network operating system feature.
25. Describe the major differences between global directory services and domain directory services in terms of architecture and functionality.
26. What is accomplished by having directory services databases be both distributed and replicated? Differentiate between the two techniques.
27. What is interdomain trust?
28. How does interdomain trust save on network administration activity?
29. What is X.500?
30. What is LDAP, and how does it differ from X.500?
31. What is relationship between file systems, APIs and application services?
32. Why might it be important for a network operating system to support more than one file system?
33. What is the role of NCP and SMB redirectors in offering application services?
34. What is the difference in terms of functionality and communication between a client running only an operating system such as Windows and a client running a network operating system such as Windows 95?
35. What is the role of multiprotocol routing in a server network operating system?
36. What is the role of gateway services such as SNA server?
37. What are some important functional characteristics of server network operating systems related to installation and configuration?
38. What are some important functional characteristics of server network operating systems related to integration and migration?

ACTIVITIES

1. Using back issues of a publication such as *PC Magazine,* prepare a presentation tracing the functionality of peer-to-peer LANs from 1992 to the present. Prepare a graph detailing price, number of supported users, and required memory over the research period.

2. Using back issues of a publication such as *PC Magazine,* prepare a presentation tracing the functionality of client/server LANs from 1992 to the present. Prepare a graph detailing price, number of supported users, and required memory over the research period.

3. Gather current market share statistics for the following market segments and prepare a presentation: peer-to-peer NOS, small business NOS, client NOS, server NOS.

4. Analyze the results of the previous activity. Which products are gaining market share, and which are losing market share? Relate the market shifts to product functionality. Present your results in a top-down model format.

5. Prepare a presentation on the comparative functionality of Windows 95 versus OS/2 Warp Connect. Compare marketing campaigns and current market share.

6. Conduct a survey of users of object-oriented user interfaces (Windows 95, OS/2 Warp) and graphical user interfaces (Windows). What are users' impressions of the two? Does one really make users more productive than the other? Is this increase in productivity measurable?

7. Review advertisements and catalogs for devices that support the PnP standard. Prepare a list detailing which types of devices have the most PnP offerings. Which network operating system (if any) do devices claim to be compatible with?

8. Prepare a product review of dial-up or remote node servers, paying special attention to the source and compatibility of client software. Are most dial-up servers NOS specific? Why or why not?

9. Research and prepare a presentation on X.500. What software categories supported X.500 specifications originally? Currently? What key vendor groups or standards bodies (if any) support X.500? What is your prediction as to the widespread adoption of X.500?

10. Compare the performance monitoring capabilities of various server network operating systems. Which are best at monitoring a single server? Multiple servers? Which are best at setting thresholds and alerts? Which are best at linking to enterprise management systems such as HP OpenView or IBM NetView?

11. Compare the functionality of Microsoft Systems Management Server and Novell Managewise. Contrast these programs with enterprise management systems such as HP OpenView and IBM SystemView in terms of functionality and price.

12. Investigate and compare the structures of NetWare 3.12 bindery and NetWare 4.1 NDS database.

13. Prepare a product review of software tools designed to automate the migration from the 3.12 bindery to the 4.1 NDS database.

14. Research and prepare a presentation on the evolution of and industry support for LDAP.

15. Research and prepare a presentation on market acceptance of the following client or server network operating systems: Windows 98, Windows NT 5.0, NetWare 5.0.

16. Research the percentages of servers running some type of UNIX versus those running NT or NetWare. Explain your results.

CHAPTER 9

CASE STUDY

21ST CENTURY CALLS COLLEGE

Infrastructure Upgrade Ensures Support for Multimedia and Distance Learning as Well as Internet Access

When Alan Gelhar arrived at Cerri-tos College in August 1996, the new director of computing had a clear mandate: Create a network infra-structure that would carry the Southern California community col-lege into the 21st century. This net-work of the future would need to provide high-speed network access for university students, faculty, and staff—onsite and off campus—to a new generation of IT-driven re-sources such as multimedia curricula and applications to facilitate distance learning.

The ultimate goal, according to Gelhar, was for Cerritos to be able to "train students anywhere in the country—anywhere in the world—because faculty can work with students outside the classrooms in a virtual environment that lets them share desktop applications with video and voice support."

Network expansion of any kind would prove to be no small feat at Cerritos, where a heady vision stood in stark contrast to sobering reality. The college's shared, 10Mbps Ethernet network was already filled to capacity with campus and Internet traffic. The technical challenge was compounded by political, budgetary, and staffing considerations that made Gelhar's self-imposed two-year deadline look impossible to the college's faculty and staff.

"Initially, even my own staff thought it would never happen," says Gelhar. So, it's not without some relish that Gelhar delivers a glowing implementation status report 16 months into the job: "This thing is going without a hitch."

Not a hitch? On a $4 million project that migrated the college infrastructure from shared Ethernet to a fully meshed ATM backbone with switched 10 Mbps Ethernet to the desktops, completely recabled the entire 30-building campus, and upgraded 800 network nodes and added 2,700 more? "Well, we're about two weeks behind," says Gelhar, "but for a $4 million project that covers 30 buildings, that's not bad." Not bad, indeed.

To deliver the network on time and on budget, Gelhar had to hit the ground running. He made the decision to focus the project first on the campus network and then, when it was up and running, to move beyond the firewall.

His strategy started to gel before setting foot on the Cerritos campus in his official role. One of the first things to consider was the network backbone, which would wind up handling voice, video, and data traffic. The amount of traffic, as well as the need to prioritize time-sensitive voice and video, made ATM the logical choice. Gigabit Ethernet was deemed an immature technology. "Gigabit Ethernet is a long ways away—the standards aren't set," says Gelhar, "[ATM] seemed the best for us, our growth, and the things we wanted to do here with distance education and multimedia and all."

The next step was to secure the help of a systems integrator that would act as the general contractor for the job. Although Gelhar's three-person network staff included cabling, network, and technology experts, nobody had ATM expertise. Moreover, the staff of three was responsible for day-to-day operations of the college's network. Saddling them with the upgrade task was out of the question, so Gelhar turned to Anixter Inc. for help with network design and implementation, project management, and vendor and subcontractor management. Anixter had proven its integration services prowess to both Gelhar and Cerritos in previous jobs, and the integrator was an approved contractor under the California Multiple Awards Schedule.

Listening to Offers With Anixter's help, Cerritos solicited and evaluated equipment bids from 3Com Corp., Bay Networks Inc., and Cisco Systems Inc. as well as cabling contractors.

Simultaneously, Gelhar worked to secure the support of the skeptical college departments, divisions, and the board of trustees. Here Gelhar would find his biggest challenge to the project—convincing his peers and superiors that the network was worth its $4 million price tag. "To muster that kind of money generally means that you've got to take it from other sources, other areas," says Gelhar. "So we had to convince everybody that they'd benefit immensely from this kind of an infrastructure, and that it's an investment for, minimally, the next 15 to 25 years."

Backbone to the Edge Manageability of the Microsoft Windows NT-based network was critical to design decisions. "That's one of the reasons 3Com was chosen," says Chris Barwick, south bay territory manager for Anixter's Networking Division in Los Angeles. "Cerritos wanted to manage all of the platforms from a single, NT-based management application, and they felt 3Com was the only vendor with an enterprise, NT-based application."

To support the new high-bandwidth environment, the campus needed to be rewired. Cabling contractors, supervised by Anixter's Structured Cabling Group, ran single-mode and multimode fiber optics between buildings and inside the data center. Every edge building with more than 45 users would have multiple 155 Mbps OC-3 connections to the data center for both fault tolerance and future growth. Category 5, level 6 copper-wire cable was used to connect desktops in the 30 edge buildings.

"Our emphasis was really the right backbone and the right cabling infrastructure," says Gelhar. "We wanted to guarantee 2.5[Mpbs] to 5Mbps to the desktop in a complete switched network today, and level 6 will get us up to 155Mbps transmission across the copper for the future."

With deployment dependent on the cabling upgrade, the network is being rolled out in stages. The backbone is handled first, then edge buildings as they are upgraded are rewired. The data center backbone is made up of seven 3Com CoreBuilder 7000 high-density ATM switches loaded with approximately 130 OC-3 ATM connections. AST Research Inc., Compaq Computer Corp., and Digital Equipment Corp. servers feed edge buildings connected to the backbone through

3Com CoreBuilder 5000 and Super-Stack II Switch 1000 workgroup switches, providing switched 10Mbps Ethernet connections to campus desktops.

Gelhar determined that networked campus desktop PCs needed at least an Intel Corp. 486-based processor and 32MB of RAM to run Windows NT 4.0 and Microsoft's Internet Explorer, Outlook Express, Office 97, and Net Meeting. Apple Computer Inc. Macintoshes needed to run Mac OS 7.5 or later to run a similar application suite.

As of January [1998], the fiber cabling between buildings was approximately 75 percent complete, and contractors were starting to wire the inside of the buildings. Barwick predicts that the job will be wrapped up by summer, well within Gelhar's deadline: "We've probably got another six months before everything is complete, and the entire campus is recabled and all the networking pieces are done."

Keys to the Rollout One of the keys to smooth implementation has been Anixter's staging facility in Memphis, Tenn. There, the company sets up the Cerritos network, preconfigures it, and runs applications over it before shipping to Cerritos. The staging strategy gives Anixter engineers the opportunity to put all the network gear in one room and do a lot of the preconfiguration and tweaking that would be far more difficult if the network were spread over 30 buildings.

For example, before implementing the backbone at Cerritos, Anixter engineers were able to burn in each product for 48 hours, test all the ports, load IP addresses, put in virtual LAN (vLAN) configuration information, and verify the same revision levels between the equipment.

"When we shipped all the [backbone] equipment to Cerritos, we had an average of three to four systems engineers out there for about a week to implement the backbone. That included removing the old equipment, moving ports over, getting it tested and running, and familiarizing Cerritos with the equipment," says Anixter's Barwick. "By staging the backbone in Memphis, we probably cut the implementation time by three to four weeks."

Another key that has helped make the Cerritos implementation a success for the college and its reseller partner has been Gelhar's methodological planning. To make sure everything ran precisely, Gelhar made graphical drawings of all of the buildings and identified where all of the workstations were to be located. These blueprints were turned over to the contractors. Gelhar also relied heavily on Gantt charts, which detailed tasks and task dependencies.

With his Gantt charts, Gelhar can see what is not getting done and why. Weekly progress is then reviewed every Friday morning in a meeting with Gelhar, Barwick, and representatives from 3Com and the cabling contractors.

"I think the planning was well worth the effort," says Gelhar. "There's less anxiety because the plans are there, so it's allowed us to control the details and control the budget pretty well."

By proving he can bring the job in on time and on budget, Gelhar is setting himself up for an easier approval process when he focuses the next phase of the college's infrastructure—Internet connectivity. "Right now we've got T-1 lines connected to the Internet," says Gelhar. "We know that once this infrastructure rollout is completed, the T-1 lines aren't going to be fast enough. We're going to [need to have] higher bandwidth to connect to the world."

With that connection to the outside world, the Cerritos College vision will be complete—an infrastructure capable of delivering voice, video, and data applications to students across campus or across the world. The fiber and copper cabling deployed in the campus infrastructure can deliver up to 155Mbps to the networked desktops at Cerritos. The ATM backbone itself can scale to gigabit-per-second speeds to support the increased demands for applications and services that the college anticipates from local and remote students.

"Cerritos's goal was to design a network that would support the student body with virtual classroom environments that need high-speed access to data and multimedia applications," says Barwick. "The solution we're helping them implement will do exactly that, making them one of the premier technical colleges in Southern California."

Source: Brent Dorshkind, "21st Century Calls College," *LAN Times* (March 2, 1998), Copyright March 2, 1998, The McGraw-Hill Companies, Inc.

BUSINESS CASE STUDY QUESTIONS

Activities

1. Complete a top-down model for this case by gleaning facts from the case and placing them in the proper layer of the top-down model. After having completed the top-down model, analyze and detail those instances where requirements were clearly passed down from upper layers to lower layers of the model and where solutions to those requirements were passed up from lower layers to upper layers of the model.
2. Detail any questions about the case that may occur to you for which answers are not clearly stated in the article.

Business

1. What was the ultimate business goal that would need to be met by application and network solutions?
2. How much did the network upgrade cost, and how long did it take?
3. What was the biggest obstacle to the implementation?
4. How did staging affect the implementation process?

Application

1. What desktop application software is typically installed?

Data

1. What types of traffic would the network have to carry?
2. What were the characteristics of this traffic that would have a bearing on the backbone network selected?

Network

1. What were the network requirements as dictated by the business and application requirements?
2. What was the network configuration prior to the upgrade?
3. What was the network configuration after the upgrade?
4. Why was ATM chosen as the backbone technology?
5. What were the management requirements of the network?
6. What is the current bandwidth for Internet connectivity?
7. What is the bandwidth potential to the desktop? On the backbone?

Technology

1. Which networking technology was chosen, and why?
2. What cabling was used between buildings and to the desktop? Why?
3. What desktop technology was chosen, and why?

CHAPTER 10

WIDE AREA NETWORKING CONCEPTS, ARCHITECTURES, AND SERVICES

Concepts Reinforced

OSI Model   Internet Suite of Protocols Model
Top-Down Model

Concepts Introduced

Wide Area Network Architecture   Switching Architectures
Transmission Architectures   Multiplexing
Packetization   Local Loop Transmission Alternatives
Broadband Transmission   Wide Area Network Services

OBJECTIVES

After mastering the material in this chapter, you should understand the following:

1. The concept of multiplexing in general as well as several multiplexing techniques and related technology and applications in particular

2. The relationship between business motivation, available technology, and carrier services in creating wide area networking solutions

3. The advantages, limitations, and technology of current and forthcoming packet switching networks

4. The importance of standards applied to wide area networking

5. The interrelationships and dependencies between the components of any wide area network architecture

6. The impact of the evolution in switching methodologies as it applies specifically to frame relay and cell relay

■ INTRODUCTION

When client/server applications must be distributed over widely dispersed geographic areas, analysts must have an understanding of the wide area networks on which such distribution depends. One of the most significant differences between wide area networks and the local area networks that were studied in the previous chapter is the dependency, in most cases, on third-party carriers to provide wide area transmission services. The ability to understand the transmission and switching architecture that underlies and enables the variety of wide area transmission services offered by these carriers is of critical importance to successful wide area network managers.

In order to understand wide area switching and transmission architectures, one must first understand some basic principles of wide area networking such as multiplexing, packet switching, and circuit switching. Once switching and transmission architectures are understood, the wide area network services, both wireless and wireline, that are enabled by these architectures can be more effectively understood.

■ BASIC PRINCIPLES OF WIDE AREA NETWORKING

Underlying Business Issues

To understand the basic technical principles of wide area networking, start by looking at the basic business principles of wide area networking. In wide area networking, as in most areas of business, the desire to maximize the impact of any investment in technology is a central focus. Figure 10-1 illustrates the underlying business motivation of wide area networking principles. Given five systems (including LANs, computers, and terminals to mainframes) that need to be linked over long distances, there are basically two choices of physical configurations. A dedicated wide area link can be provided for each system-to-system connection, or somehow both the principles and technology necessary to share a single wide area link among all five system-to-system connections can be found. The basic principles, architectures, and services involved in establishing, maintaining, and terminating multiple wide area system-to-system connections constitute the topics covered in the remainder of the chapter.

Underlying Technical Concepts

The two most basic principles involved in sharing a single data link among multiple sessions, as illustrated in Figure 10-1, are packetizing and multiplexing. **Packetizing** is the segmenting of data transmissions between devices into structured blocks or packets of data that contain enough "overhead" or management information, in addition to the transmitted data itself, to ensure delivery of the packet of data to its intended destination. **Multiplexing** then takes this packetized data and sends it over a shared wide area connection along with other packetized data from other sources. At the far end of the single wide area network link, this stream of multiple source, multiplexed data packets are demultiplexed and sent to their respective destination addresses. A long-distance parcel shipping analogy may clarify the underlying technical concepts of packetizing and multiplexing. Figure 10-2 illustrates this analogy.

As can be seen in Figure 10-2, multiple packages of several presents each are transported over a long distance through a single transport mechanism and subsequently delivered to their individual destinations. The equivalent wide area data transmission events are listed along the top of Figure 10-2, illustrating several packets of data from multiple sources being transmitted over a single, shared wide area

A. Dedicated Multiple Wide Area System-to-System Connections

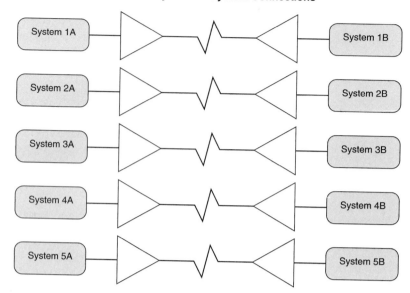

B. Single Wide Area Link Shared to Provide Multiple System-to-System Connections

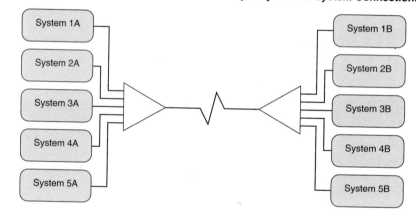

Figure 10-1   WAN Technical Principles Motivated by Business Principles

communications link and subsequently demultiplexed and delivered to their individual destination addresses.

Packetizing

A **packet** is a group of data bits organized in a predetermined, structured manner, to which overhead or management information is added in order to ensure error-free transmission of the actual data to its intended destination. These generalized packets may be alternatively known as frames, cells, blocks, data units, or several other names. The predetermined, structured nature of a packet should not be overlooked. Recall that all of the raw data as well as any address information or error control information is nothing more than bits of data, 1's and 0's, that will be processed by some type of programmed, computerized communications device.

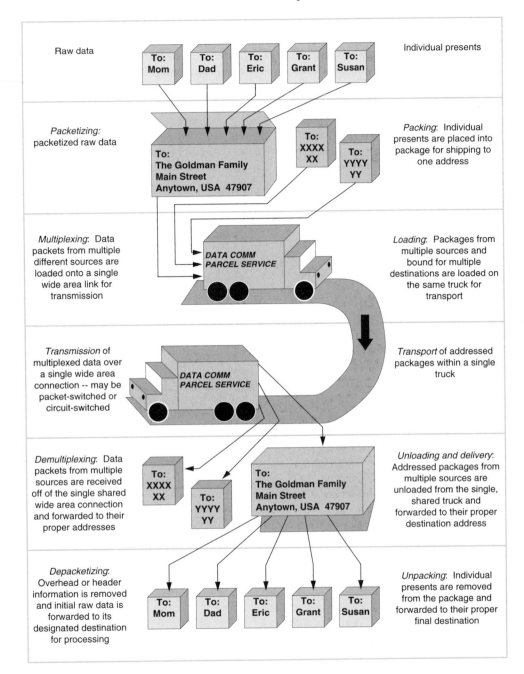

Figure 10-2   Packetizing and Multiplexing: A Parcel Shipping Analogy

This programmed data communications device must be able to depend on exactly where certain pieces of key information, such as destination address and error check numbers, are located within a packet containing both raw data as well as overhead information.

By knowing exactly which bits within a packet represent a destination address and which bits represent data to be forwarded, the data communications device can process incoming data packets more quickly and efficiently. See Figure 10-24 as an example of a WAN-based packet format.

The parcel shipping analogy also illustrates the need for predetermined, structured packets. When shipping a parcel with nearly any parcel shipping company, one must fill out the company's standardized "structured" shipping forms, putting all data in the properly marked spaces. By doing so, the wide area transport mechanism, the parcel shipping company, can process packages more quickly and efficiently by reading only one type of form and knowing where specific data is located on that form. Regulations pertaining to maximum and minimum package size as well as packaging techniques also serve to allow the parcel shipping company to perform more efficiently. As will be seen, maximum and minimum packet lengths in wide area data transmission are important to overall transmission efficiency as well.

Multiplexing

Two basic techniques are employed in multiplexing digitized traffic:

- **Frequency Division Multiplexing**
- **Time Division Multiplexing**

A variation of TDM known as **statistical time division multiplexing (STDM)** is also commonly employed for digital data.

The previous three multiplexing techniques are limited to digitized traffic in which bits of data are transmitted as discrete voltages of electricity. In the optical transmission world, in which bits of data are represented by bursts of light energy of varying wavelengths, a relatively new multiplexing technique known as **wavelength division multiplexing (WDM)** has been developed. WDM technology is deployed primarily by telecommunications carriers with extensive long-distance fiber optic networks in order to increase transmission capacity up to 10-fold without the need to install additional fiber.

Frequency Division Multiplexing In frequency division multiplexing, multiple input signals are modulated to different frequencies within the available output bandwidth of a single composite circuit, often a 3000 Hz dial-up line, and subsequently demodulated back into individual signals on the output end of the composite circuit. Sufficient space in between these separate frequency channels is reserved in **guardbands** in order to prevent interference between the two or more input signals that are sharing the single circuit. Figure 10-3 illustrates a simple frequency division multiplexing configuration.

The communications device that employs frequency division multiplexing is known as a frequency division multiplexer, or FDM. At one time, FDMs were employed to transmit data from multiple low-speed (less than 1200 bps) terminals over dial-up or leased lines. As the speed of frequency division multiplexed terminals increases, the guardband width between channels in the shared composite circuit must increase also. As terminal speeds and demand for more bandwidth per terminal have risen, frequency division multiplexing is no longer the most practical multiplexing method employed.

Although FDM is seldom if ever still used to multiplex data from multiple terminals, it is still employed in devices known as **Data Over Voice** units, or DOV units. DOV units are most often employed where data transmission is desired to a location that is currently wired for phones but which cannot be easily or affordably

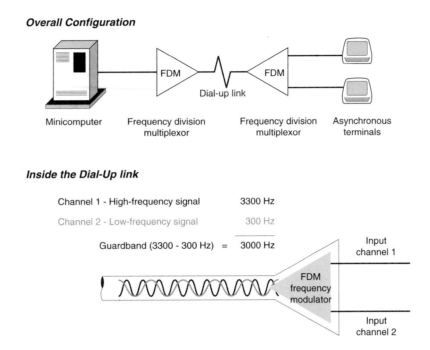

Overall Configuration

Minicomputer   Frequency division   Frequency division   Asynchronous
                  multiplexor   multiplexor   terminals

Inside the Dial-Up link

Channel 1 - High-frequency signal   3300 Hz

Channel 2 - Low-frequency signal   300 Hz

Guardband (3300 - 300 Hz) =   3000 Hz

Figure 10-3   Frequency Division Multiplexing

also be rewired for data. In these cases, both the data and the voice transmission are simultaneously transmitted over the existing phone wiring. What's more, the data and voice transmissions are independent of one another. A person can be talking to someone else across the country while being on-line with a data transmission to the local computing center. It is important to point out that DOV units cannot be used over the PSTN (public switched telephone network). They must be used in environments that are served by a local PBX (private branch exchange). College campuses are probably the most popular environment for DOV unit usage.

In FDM, the total bandwidth of the composite channel is divided into multiple subchannels by frequency. With FDM, from a connected terminal's point of view, a portion of the total bandwidth is available 100 percent of the time, yielding the appearance of a dedicated circuit. As a result the timing of signals between a connected terminal or device and the centralized processor is not affected.

Time Division Multiplexing   In time division multiplexing, just the opposite is true. With this setup, from a connected terminal's point of view, 100 percent of the bandwidth is available for a portion of the time. The portion of time available to each connected input device is constant and controlled by the time division multiplexer (TDM). A key point to understand about time slots in a TDM environment is that a fixed portion of time, measured in milliseconds, is reserved for each attached input device whether the device is active or not. As a result, efficiency is sacrificed for the sake of simplicity.

There are times in a TDM environment when a terminal with nothing to say is given its full time allotment while other busy terminals are waiting to transmit. A TDM is really a fairly simple device employing many familiar elements such as buffer memory and flow control. Figure 10-4 illustrates simple time division multiplexing.

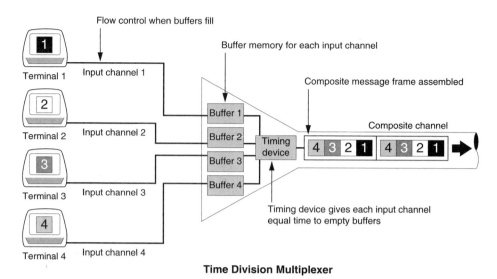

Figure 10-4 Time Division Multiplexing

As can be seen in Figure 10-4, each input channel has a fixed amount of buffer memory into which it can load data. Flow control, either XON/XOFF or CTS/RTS, tells the terminal to stop transmitting to the buffer memory when the buffer memory fills. A **central clock** or timing device in the TDM gives each input device its allotted time to empty its buffer into an area of the TDM, where the combined data from all of the polled input devices is conglomerated into a single message frame for transmission over the composite circuit. This process of checking on each connected terminal in order to see if any data is ready to be sent is known as **polling.**

If a terminal was inactive and had nothing in its input buffer to contribute to the consolidated message frame, that input terminal's allotted space in the **composite message frame** is filled with blanks. The insertion of blanks, or null characters, into composite message links is the basis of TDMs' inefficient use of the shared composite circuit connecting the two TDMs. Although the data from the various input terminals is combined into a single message frame, each individual terminal's data is still identifiable by position within that composite message frame. This fact is important because once the composite message frame has finished its journey down the transmission link, it must be resegmented back into the individual terminal's original data format.

Statistical Time Division Multiplexing Statistical time division multiplexing (STDM) seeks to offer more efficient use of the composite bandwidth than simple TDM by employing increased monitoring and manipulation of input devices to accomplish two major goals:

1. Eliminate "idle time" allocations to inactive terminals

2. Eliminate padded blanks or null characters in the composite message blocks

In a "stat mux," allocation time is dynamically allocated to input devices. As terminals become more active, they get more time to send data directly to the stat mux. As terminals become less active or inactive, the stat mux polls them for input less frequently. This dynamic time slot allocation takes both processing power and additional memory. Statistics are kept as to terminal activity over time and hence the name: statistical time division multiplexers. Specially programmed microprocessors and additional buffer memory are key upgrades to STDMs and contribute to their increased costs over the simpler TDMs.

To increase the efficiency of use of the composite link, padded blanks and null characters are not inserted into message frames for inactive terminals. Remember the purpose of the blanks: to occupy the space in the composite message frame assigned to that particular device. In an STDM, rather than assign space to input devices in the composite message frame by position regardless of activity, the STDM adds control information to each terminal's data within the composite message frame that indicates the source terminal and how many bytes of data came from that terminal. Figure 10-5 illustrates composite message block construction in STDMs.

Practical Advice and Information

A few important points about stat muxes:

- The time allocation protocols and composite message frame building protocols are proprietary and vary by manufacturer. As a result, multiplexors from different manufacturers are not interoperable.

- The dynamic allocation of time afforded to individual terminals or devices by the STDM can interfere with any timing that might have been previously set up between the remote device and the central processor. This is particularly important in manufacturing or process control operations.

STDM COST/BENEFIT ANALYSIS

Managerial Perspective

From a business standpoint, what does a cost/benefit analysis of an STDM reveal? The STDM's increased costs are due to increased buffer memory, more sophisticated programming, and an integral microprocessor. On the benefits side of the equation, STDMs produce increased efficiency in time slot allocation and composite bandwidth usage. Some STDMs also include proprietary data compression techniques. These increased efficiencies in STDMs seem to produce "something for nothing."

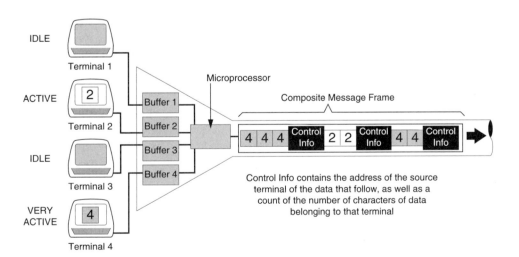

Figure 10-5   STDMs Make Efficient Use of Composite Bandwidth

For example, it is not unheard of for STDMs to seemingly transmit data at four or even eight times the speed of the composite link. For instance, I have installed 16-port STDMs with four printers running at 2400 bps and 12 asynchronous terminals running at 4800 bps for an apparent bandwidth requirement of 67.2 Kbps (2400 × 4 plus 4800 × 12). The fact is, these 16 devices ran just fine over a 9600 bps leased line! This apparent discrepancy is due largely to the "statistical" nature of data transmission from terminals which demonstrates the likelihood that only a relatively small percentage of terminals will be transmitting data at any split second in time. It is the STDM's sophisticated dynamic time slot allocation capabilities that take advantage of this relatively large "idle time." Figure 10-6 illustrates the STDM's apparent ability to offer something for nothing.

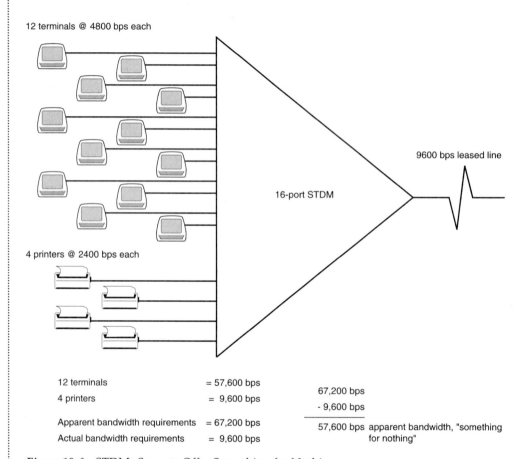

Figure 10-6   STDMs Seem to Offer Something for Nothing

Wide Area Network Architecture

In order to better demonstrate how packetizing, multiplexing, and other wide area networking principles combine to create all of the current and emerging wide area networking technologies and services, Figure 10-7 provides a simple model defining the major segments and interrelationships of an overall wide area network architecture.

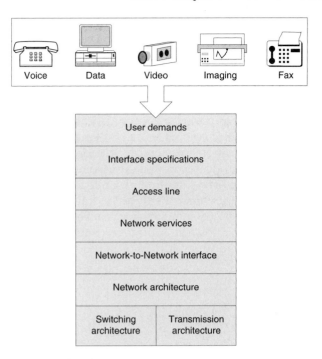

Figure 10-7 Major Components of a Wide Area Network Architecture

As shown in Figure 10-7, **user demands** are the driving force behind the current and emerging wide area **network services** that are offered to business and residential customers. Companies offering these services are in business to generate profits by implementing the underlying architectures that will enable them to offer the wide area networking services that users are demanding at the lowest possible cost.

In order for users to take advantage of network services, standardized **interface specifications** must be developed to ensure interoperability among different manufacturers' end-user equipment. As an example, the X.25 interface specification ensures that users can purchase packet assemblers/disassemblers from any manufacturer and be able to successfully interface to a packet switched network service. Having packetized user payloads according to standard interface specifications, the equipment must access carrier network services via an appropriately sized **access line** running from the user's residence or business to the entry or gateway to the carrier's network service.

To ensure transparent delivery of network services to users regardless of location, several carriers may need to cooperatively hand off user payloads to one another. The transparent interoperability of network services from different carriers requires predefined **network-to-network interfaces.**

Network services cannot be offered unless the underlying infrastructure of the carriers and companies wishing to offer these services is technically capable of doing so. The combination of sophisticated switches **(switching architecture)** and transmission facilities **(transmission architecture)** comprising this infrastructure is known as the **network architecture.** Switching architectures or methods, such as circuit switching or packet switching, ensure the proper routing of information (data, voice, video) from the data's source to its destination. Transmission architectures or methods are the circuits or data highways over which the information is actually delivered.

To return to the parcel shipping analogy, switching is the activity that takes place inside depots and warehouses, and transmission takes place in the trucks on the highways and in the planes in the air. By adjusting depot organization, labor resources, floor space, or equipment, a parcel shipping company could adjust its switching capacity or sophistication. By utilizing varying numbers of planes or trucks, or changing truck or plane routes, the same parcel shipping company could adjust its transmission capacity or sophistication.

In the case of wide area or packet-switched networks, the copper, fiber, microwave, and satellite links and the protocols that control access to and monitoring of these circuits constitute the transmission architecture of wide area networks. The central office switches and packet switches that build connections from source to destination utilizing these transmission circuits constitute the switching architecture of the wide area or packet switched network. The importance of the relationship between the two architectures is well illustrated by the parcel shipping company analogy. If the parcel shipping company were to increase switching capacity and sophistication by building several new depots, but did not upgrade its transmission capacity by increasing numbers of trucks and planes, the result would be less than optimal. Similarly, providers of wide area network services are in the process of upgrading both their switching and transmission facilities in order to be able to meet future user demands for sophisticated and reasonably priced wide area network services.

■ WIDE AREA NETWORKING SWITCHING

Switching of some type or another is necessary in wide area network architectures because the alternative is unthinkable. To explain: Without some type of switching mechanism or architecture, every possible source of data in the world would have to be directly connected to every possible destination of data in the world—not a very likely prospect. Switching allows temporary connections to be established, maintained, and terminated between message sources and message destinations, sometimes called **sinks** in data communications. There are two primary switching techniques employed in switching architectures:

- **Packet switching**
- **Circuit switching**

In packet-switched networks, users' packetized data is transported across circuits between packet switches along with the data of other users of the same packet switched network. In contrast, in circuit-switched networks, users get dedicated bandwidth on circuits created solely for their use.

Packet Switching

In a **packet-switched network,** packets of data travel one at a time from the message source to the message destination. A packet-switched network, otherwise known as a **public data network (PDN),** is represented in network diagrams by a symbol that resembles a cloud. Figure 10-8 illustrates such a symbol as well as the

Circuit Switching

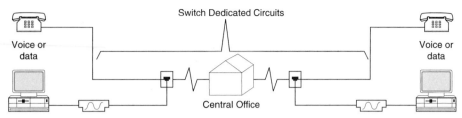

All data or voice travel from source to destination over the *same* physical path

Packet Switching

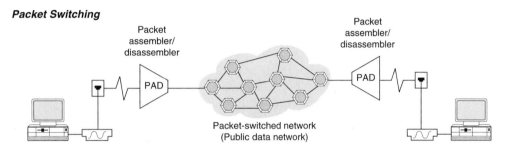

Data enter the packet-switched network one packet at a time;
Packets may take *different* physical paths within packet-switched networks.

Figure 10-8   Circuit Switching versus Packet Switching

difference between circuit switching and packet switching. The cloud is an appropriate symbol for a packet-switched network because all that is known is that the packet of data goes in one side of the PDN and comes out the other. The physical path a packet takes may be different than that of other packets and in any case is unknown to the end users. What is beneath the cloud in a packet-switched network is a large number of **packet switches** that pass packets among themselves as the packets are routed from source to destination.

Remember that packets are specially structured groups of data that include control and address information in addition to the data itself. These packets must be assembled (control and address information added to data) somewhere before entry into the packet-switched network and must be subsequently disassembled before delivery of the data to the message destination. This packet assembly and disassembly is done by a device known as a **PAD,** or **packet assembler/disassembler.** PADs may be stand-alone devices or may be integrated into specially built modems or multiplexers. These PADs may be located at an end-user location or may be located at the entry point to the packet-switched data network. Figure 10-8 illustrates the latter scenario, in which the end users employ regular modems to dial up to the packet-switched network that provides the PADs to properly assemble the packets prior to transmission. This setup is often more convenient for end users, who can still employ their modem for other dial-up applications as well.

The packet switches illustrated inside the PDN cloud in Figure 10-8 are generically known as **DSEs,** data-switching exchanges, or **PSEs,** packet-switching exchanges. DSE is the packet-switching equivalent of the DCE and DTE categorization that were first encountered in the study of modems and dial-up transmission.

Another way in which packet switching differs from circuit switching is that as demand for transmission of data increases on a packet-switched network, additional users are not denied access. Overall performance of the network may suffer, errors and retransmission may occur, or packets of data may be lost, but all users experience the same degradation of service. This happens because, in the case of a packet-switched network, data travels through the network one packet at a time, traveling over any available path within the network rather than waiting for a switched dedicated path as in the case of the circuit switched network.

Connectionless versus Connection-Oriented Packet-Switched Services   For any packet switch to process any packet of data bound for anywhere, packet address information must be included on each packet. Each packet switch then reads and processes each packet by making routing and forwarding decisions based upon the packet's destination address and current network conditions. The full destination address uniquely identifying the ultimate destination of each packet is known as the **global address.**

Because an overall data message is broken up into numerous pieces by the packet assembler, these message pieces may actually arrive out of order at the message destination owing to the speed and condition of the alternate paths within the packet-switched network over which these message pieces (packets) traveled. The data message must be pieced back together in proper order by the destination PAD before final transmission to the destination address. These self-sufficient packets containing full source and destination address information, plus a message segment, are known as **datagrams.** Figure 10-9 illustrates this packet-switched network phenomenon.

A switching methodology in which each datagram is handled and routed to its ultimate destination on an individual basis, permitting packets to travel over a variety of physical paths on the way to their destination, is known as a **connectionless** packet network. It is called connectionless because packets do not follow one another, in order, down a particular path through the network.

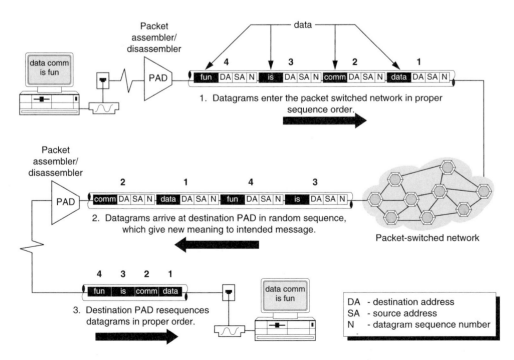

Figure 10-9   Datagram Delivery on a Packet-Switched Network

There are no error-detection or flow-control techniques applied by a datagram-based or connectionless packet-switched network. Such a network would depend on end-user devices (PCs, modems, communication software) to provide adequate error-control and flow control. Because datagrams are sent along multiple possible paths to the destination address, there is no guarantee of their safe arrival. This lack of inherent error-detection or flow-control abilities is the basis for connectionless packet networks' other name: **unreliable** packet networks.

Virtual Circuits   In contrast to the connectionless packet networks, **connection-oriented** or **reliable** packet networks establish **virtual circuits,** enabling message packets to follow one another, in sequence, down the same connection or physical circuit. This connection from source to destination is set up by special packets known as **call setup packets.** Once the call setup packets have determined the best path from the source to the destination and established the virtual circuit, the message-bearing packets follow one another in sequence along the virtual circuit from source to destination. Unlike a connectionless service, because of the establishment of the virtual circuit, a connection-oriented service can offer checksum error-detection with ACK/NAK (ACKnowledgment/Negative AcKnowledgment) retransmission control and flow control, thereby ensuring increased reliability. These services can be offered by the packet network itself rather than depending on the end-user devices. Because connection-oriented packets all follow the same path, or **logical channel,** from source to destination, they do not require the full global addressing on each packet as the connectionless datagram network packets do. Instead, connection-oriented network packets have an abbreviated **logical channel number,** or **LCN,** included with each packet. The details that relate the LCN to a physical circuit consisting of an actual series of specific packet switches within the packet-switched network are stored in a **virtual circuit table.**

Connection-oriented packet-switching networks actually define two types of virtual circuits: **switched virtual circuits (SVC)** and **permanent virtual circuits (PVC).** The switched virtual circuit connection is terminated when the complete message has been sent and a special **clear request packet** causes all switched virtual circuit table entries related to this connection to be erased. The virtual circuit table of the permanent virtual circuit is not erased, making the PVC the equivalent of a "virtual" circuit-switched leased line.

While the use of LCNs as opposed to full global addressing reduces overhead in connection-oriented packet networks, the following elements add to that overhead:

1. Connection setup

2. Network-based, point-to-point error detection and flow control

Figure 10-10 contrasts the overhead as well as several other key differentiating criteria of connectionless versus connection-oriented packet-switched networks.

Practical Advice and Information

The truth is, unless a company plans to set up its own packet-switched network, decisions regarding the relative merits of connectionless versus connection-oriented packet-switched networks will not have to be considered. It is more likely that a company will access a major commercial packet-switched network service. In that case, what goes on "inside the cloud" is invisible to the users of that packet-switched network. In such a case, an end user's only concern is how to interface to "the cloud."

	Overhead	Greatest Strength	Call Setup	Addressing	Also Known As...	Virtual Circuit	Error Correction	Flow Control
Connectionless	Less	Ability to dynamically reroute data	None	Global	Datagram unreliable	None	Left to end-user devices	Left to end-user devices
Connection-oriented	More	Reliability	Yes	Local logical channel number	Reliable virtual circuit	Created for each call; virtual circuit table established	By virtual circuit	By virtual circuit

Figure 10-10   Connection-Oriented versus Connectionless Packet-Switched Networks

Circuit Switching

In a **circuit-switched network,** a switched dedicated circuit is created to connect the two or more parties, eliminating the need for source and destination address information such as that provided by packetizing techniques. The switched dedicated circuit established on circuit-switched networks makes it appear to the user of the circuit as if a wire has been run directly between the phones of the calling parties. The physical resources required to create this temporary connection are dedicated to that particular circuit for the duration of the connection. If system usage should increase to the point where insufficient resources are available to create additional connections, users would not get a dial tone.

Managerial Perspective

A BUSINESS PERSPECTIVE ON CIRCUIT SWITCHING VERSUS PACKET SWITCHING

If the top-down model were applied to an analysis of possible switching methodologies, circuit switching and packet switching could be properly placed on either the network or the technology layers. In either case, in order to make the proper switching methodology decision, the top-down model layer directly above the network layer—namely, the data layer—must be thoroughly examined. One data layer question is key:

- What is the nature of the data to be transmitted, and which switching methodology best supports those data characteristics?

The first data-related criterion to examine is the data source.

- What is the nature of the application program (application layer) that will produce this data?

- Is it a transaction-oriented program or more of a batch update or file-oriented program?

A transaction-oriented program, producing what is sometimes called interactive data, is characterized by short bursts of data followed by variable length pauses as users read screen prompts or pause between transactions. This "bursty" transaction-oriented traffic, best categorized by banking transactions at an automatic teller machine, must be delivered as quickly and reliably as the network can possibly perform. In addition to data burstiness, time pressures and reliability constraints are other important data characteristics that will assist in switching methodology decision making.

Applications programs more oriented to large file transfers or batch updates have different data characteristics than transaction-oriented programs. Overnight updates from regional offices to corporate headquarters or from local stores to regional offices are typical examples. Rather than occurring in bursts, the data in these types of applications is usually large and flowing steadily. These transfers are important, but not often urgent. If file transfers fail, error detection and correction protocols such as those examined in the study of communications software can retransmit bad data or even restart file transfers at the point of failure.

From a business perspective, the two switching techniques vary as well. Both circuit-switched and packet-switched services usually charge a flat monthly fee for access, but the basis for usage charges differs. In general, circuit-switched connections are billed according to time connected to the circuit. Leased lines are billed with a flat monthly fee that varies according to circuit mileage. Packet-switched networks usually charge according to packet transfer volume.

To analyze further, if a company gets charged for connection time to the circuit-switched circuit whether it uses the circuit or not, it had better be sure that while it is connected, the data is steady and takes full advantage of available bandwidth.

One other switching difference is worth noting before some conclusions are drawn. In terms of the need to deliver bursty, transaction-oriented data quickly and reliably, call setup time can be critical. With circuit-switched applications, dial tone must be waited for and the number must be dialed and switched through the network. With connection-oriented packet-switched networks, call setup packets must explore the network and build virtual circuit tables before the first bit of data is transferred. Datagrams don't require call setup but offer no guarantee of safe delivery.

By first carefully examining the characteristics of the data traffic to be transported, a network analyst can more reliably narrow the choices of possible network services to consider.

■ WIDE AREA NETWORKING TRANSMISSION

WAN transmission technologies and services fall into two overall categories. This categorization is based largely on WAN services as they are organized by and purchased from carriers.

- **Local loop transmission** provides bandwidth to users' residences and businesses, generally offering connectivity between these end points and the carrier network service of choice. Strictly speaking, the term *local loop* is a geographic designation.

- **Broadband transmission** usually refers to transmission services offering greater than 1.544 Mbps transmission rates that offer connectivity between network switches or between different carriers' network services. Large consumers of bandwidth may require broadband transmission services to their various corporate locations as access lines.

Local Loop Transmission Alternatives

Local loop transmission, sometimes referred to as "the last mile," provides a means for users' residences or businesses to connect to the voice or data services of their choice. As indicated in the wide area network architecture diagram (Figure 10-7), local loop services must be properly sized in order to provide sufficient bandwidth to deliver user payloads efficiently and cost effectively. Although a wide variety of local loop transmission services are possible, among the most popular current or emerging local loop technologies are the following:

- POTS (plain old telephone service)

- ISDN (integrated services digital network)

- ADSL (asymmetric digital subscriber line)

- Cable TV

POTS   POTS (plain old telephone service) is what most readers are familiar with as the default local loop technology. Users employ V.34 (28.8 Kbps) or V.34+ (33.6 Kbps) modems for transmitting data over the analog POTS network. Owing to line impairments and interference on analog transmission lines, research indicates that optimal transmission rates are seldom achieved and rarely maintained.

ISDN   ISDN is somewhat of a phenomenon in the telecommunications industry. A constant topic of discussion, some consider a revolutionary breakthrough; others are absolutely convinced that it won't ever materialize. ISDN has brought more humor to telecommunications than nearly any other topic, with the various interpretations of the ISDN acronym. Examples are It Still Does Nothing, and I Still Don't Need it. ISDN has been described as a solution in search of an application. The need for dial-up access to Internet services at transmission rates greater than those available via POTS has significantly increased the interest in ISDN as a local loop transmission alternative.

Architecture   ISDN, sometimes known as **Narrowband ISDN,** is a switched digital network service offering both voice and nonvoice connectivity to other ISDN end users. Voice, video, and data are all transportable over a single ISDN connection. Depending on bandwidth requirements, voice, video, and data may even be transported simultaneously over a single network connection. The fact that ISDN is a switched service allows temporary connections to be constructed and terminated dynamically among a variety of ISDN sites, unlike other digital services of similar bandwidth that are available only as static point-to-point circuits. Figure 10-11 illustrates a high-level view of possible ISDN use.

Narrowband ISDN is deliverable in two different service levels or interfaces. **basic rate interface,** or **BRI,** is also referred to as **2B+D**. This 2B+D label refers to the channel configuration of the BRI service in which two bearer channels (64 Kbps each) and one delta or data channel (16 Kbps) are combined into a 144 Kbps interface. The **bearer channels** are intended to "bear" or carry services such as voice, video, or data transport. The **D channel** is intended for network management data for call setup and teardown, calling number identification, and other ISDN-specific network signals. In some cases, 9.6 Kbps of the D channel may be used for additional X.25 packet-based transmissions, in a service known as ISDN D Channel Packet service.

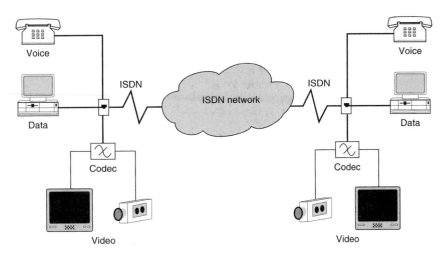

Figure 10-11   ISDN Architecture

The use of this side D channel "for carrying signal data is known as **out-of-band signaling** and is one of the key features of ISDN. The "out of band" refers to the fact that the signal control information does not have to be intermingled with the user data, thereby maximizing the available bandwidth for user data. Prior to ISDN, control information was passed over the network within the user channels in a technique known as **in-band signaling.** This is why many so-called ISDN services such as **automatic number identification** can be offered without ISDN.

A second ISDN service level known as **PRI (primary rate interface),** also known as **23B+D,** is composed of twenty-three 64 Kbps bearer channels and one 64 Kbps data channel for a combined bandwidth of 1.536 Mbps. With a small amount of additional overhead, PRI maps nicely onto the 1.544 Mbps **T-1** circuit. In Europe, ISDN is offered in a **30B+D** configuration yielding 1.984 Mbps. Additional overhead in this case maps nicely to the **E-1** (European Digital Signal Level 1) of 2.048 Mbps. Figure 10-12 summarizes the narrowband ISDN architectural information.

In some cases, users may want variable amounts of bandwidth depending on specific applications and circumstances. In such cases, **multirate ISDN** may be employed. Multirate ISDN uses a technique known as **inverse multiplexing,** in which a collection of 64 Kbps B channels are dialed up and combined together into a single logical channel of sufficient bandwidth to meet application needs such as videoconferencing. In order to ensure interoperability among inverse multiplexing devices, a standard known as **BONDING (bandwidth on demand interoperability group)** is supported by most ISDN inverse multiplexers.

Services   Earlier in its history, ISDN was widely criticized for spotty deployment leading to "islands of isolation" for those ISDN pioneers that decided to adopt the service. The ISDN coverage situation has improved significantly. In 1996 in the United States, roughly 75 percent of RBOC (Regional Bell Operating Company) customers were able to access ISDN services, with a goal of 100 percent accessibility set for 1997. This goal had still not been reached in late 1998. However, technical issues may keep this goal from fruition. Signaling requirements limit ISDN installations to residences and businesses within 18,000 feet, about 3.4 miles, from the ISDN switch. Another often overlooked service-related issue of ISDN is that ISDN customer premises equipment requires external AC power, unlike today's analog phones.

Services	Video freeze-frame Voice Data	LAN Interconnect Full motion video Voice Data
Transport category	BRI (Basic Rate Interface)	PRI (Primary Rate Interface)
Transport capacity	2 B + D 2 x 64 Kbps 128 Kbps + 16 Kbps 16 Kbps 144 Kbps	23 B + D 23 x 64 Kbps B channels + 64 Kbps D channels 1.536 Mbps
Transport architecture	2-wire Dial-up	T-1
Inter-switch protocol and switching architecture	Signaling System 7 (SS7)	

Figure 10-12   Narrowband ISDN Architectural Information

Whereas today's POTS customers have grown accustomed to having phone service even during power failures, this would not be the case with ISDN-based phone service. Charges for ISDN vary from carrier to carrier, although most charge a flat monthly rate plus a per-minute usage charge.

The heart of an ISDN network is the **ISDN switch.** Prior to 1992, two competing ISDN switches, **AT&T 5ESS Switch** and **Northern Telecom's DMS100 switch,** had slightly different specifications as to interfaces with **customer premises equipment (CPE).** Customer premises equipment that supported the AT&T specification would not operate on Northern Telecom switches and vice versa. In 1992, the Corporation for Open Systems International and the North American ISDN Users Forum launched an effort entitled Transcontinental ISDN Project 1992 (TRIP 92) to define necessary specifications to eliminate incompatibilities between ISDN networks. The interoperability specification is known as **NISDN-1 (National ISDN-1),** which defines a national standard for ISDN switches as well as inter-switch communication.

Managerial Perspective

Although deployment and technology incompatibility difficulties may have been overcome, ISDN ordering and implementation is neither easy nor foolproof. In order to properly interface an end user's ISDN equipment to a carrier's ISDN services, desired ISDN features must be specified. In some cases, end user equipment such as remote access servers must be programmed with **service profile identifier numbers (SPIDs)** in order to properly identify the carrier's equipment with which the user equipment must interface. Depending on what combinations of voice, video, or data traffic a user wishes to transmit over ISDN, up to 20 or more **ISDN Ordering Codes (IOCs)** are possible. To try to further simplify this process, an alternative ordering code scheme known as **EZ-ISDN** has been proposed by the National ISDN Users Forum. However, some of the EZ codes duplicate IOC codes and others do not correspond to existing IOC codes, leaving network administrators to do their best to work with carrier personnel to see that required ISDN features are implemented.

Technology   Uses of ISDN fall into two broad categories of connectivity:

- Single user connectivity to office or Internet
- Office-to-office connectivity

Applications for single user connectivity to office or Internet include telecommuting, Internet services access, simultaneous voice and data technical support, and collaborative computing. Applications for office-to-office connectivity include remote office routing, LAN-to-LAN connectivity, and disaster recovery through the use of ISDN lines as a backup to failed leased lines.

In order to get voice or data onto the ISDN network, the equivalent of an ISDN modem known as an **ISDN Terminal Adapter** must be employed. A terminal adapter is a type of ISDN CPE (customer premises equipment) that allows analog devices such as phones and fax machines to interface to the all-digital ISDN network. Without the terminal adapter, special digital ISDN phones would have to be purchased to interface directly to the ISDN service. These ISDN terminal adapters are available both as PC cards for installation into a PC's expansion bus, as stand-alone units, or integrated into ISDN data/voice modems.

Practical Advice and Information

Software compatibility issues should not be overlooked. Just as asynchronous modems required compatible communications software with appropriate modem setup strings, in order to have ISDN terminal adapters automatically dialing up switched ISDN connections, compatible software and drivers must also be available. This software and drivers must be compatible with installed network operating systems as well as with the purchased terminal adapter. Most often this software complies with NDIS and ODI driver specifications and is supplied by the terminal adapter vendor.

A **network termination unit-1 (NTU-1)** or **(NT-1)** is required to physically connect the ISDN line to a user's ISDN CPE. Most integrated ISDN equipment includes built-in NT-1s, although stand-alone models are available.

In order to support office-to-office connectivity needs, ISDN terminal adapters and NT-1s are often integrated with internetworking technology such as routers and access servers. It is important at this point to understand why ISDN is well suited to such applications. For occasional communications between offices for LAN-to-LAN connectivity or database updates, ISDN routers can be much more cost effective than leased line routers. Although rates may vary according to location, a general rule of thumb is that ISDN access for office-to-office connectivity is cheaper than leased lines of equivalent bandwidth when connectivity needs are four hours per day or less. Figure 10-13 illustrates the installation and interaction of a variety of ISDN technology.

ADSL   An alternative digital local loop transmission technology is known as **asymmetric digital subscriber line,** or **ADSL.** Unlike ISDN, ADSL works along with POTS for traditional voice services. In fact, ADSL works over POTS, at higher frequencies, on the same copper pair that currently carries voice transmission. Unlike using a modem on a voice line, ADSL does not interfere with voice services. That is to say, one could be connected to the Internet via ADSL and still make and receive voice phone calls on the same line.

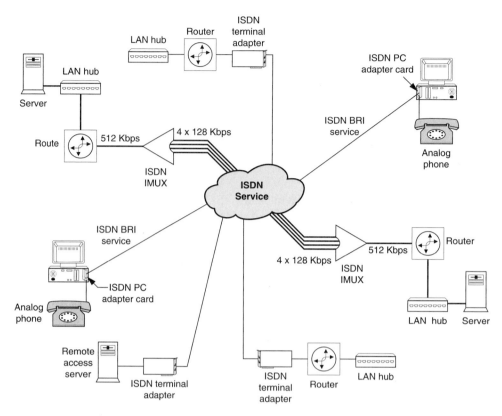

Figure 10-13   ISDN Technology

Architecture   The term *asymmetric* in ADSL refers to the service's differing upstream (away from the user) and downstream (toward the user) bandwidths. The bandwidths and associated distance limitations from the carrier's central office of two of the most common ADSL implementations are listed in Figure 10-14. Other transmission speeds and distance limitations are possible.

In order to transmit high-bandwidth data simultaneously with circuit-switched voice conversation, ADSL employs frequency division multiplexing as described earlier in this chapter. While POTS occupies the lowest frequencies from 0 KHz to 4 KHz, upstream data uses from about 25 KHz to 200 KHz, and downstream data uses from about 250 KHz to 1.1 MHz.

There are currently two competing standards for how ADSL units manage bandwidth for data transmission:

ADSL Upstream	ADSL Downstream	Distance Limitation
150 Kbps–640 Kbps	1.5 Mbps	18,000 ft
640 Kbps	6.0 Mbps	12,000 ft
640 Kbps	9.0 Mbps	9,000 ft

Figure 10-14   ADSL Bandwidth Comparison

- **Carrierless Amplitude and Phase (CAP)** treats the frequency range as a single channel and uses a technique similar to quadrature amplitude modulation to build constellations and avoid interference. CAP is a de facto standard, deployed in many trial ADSL units, and was developed by AT&T Paradyne.

- **Discrete Multitone (DMT)** divides the 1 MHz of usable bandwidth in 4 KHz channels and adjusts the usage of any of the 4 KHz channels in order to minimize interference and noise. DMT has been approved as an ADSL standard (ANSI Standard T1.413) by the ANSI T1E1.4 working group.

At least three other DSL solutions are currently in various stages of development. All DSL solutions support simultaneous POTS service:

- **VDSL (very high speed DSL)** provides 52 Mbps downstream and between 1.6 Mbps and 2.3 Mbps upstream over distances of up to only 1,000 feet. It is being explored primarily as a means to bring video-on-demand services to the home.

- **RADSL (rate adaptive DSL)** is able to adapt its data rate to the level of noise and interference on a given line. Currently, however, it is unable to support this adaptive rate on a dynamic basis.

- **SDSL (Symmetric DSL)** differs from ADSL in that it offers upstream and downstream channels of equal bandwidth.

Technology   ADSL is an attractive alternative from a carrier perspective because it does not require carriers to upgrade switching technology. Separate ADSL units, about the size of a modem, are deployed at customer sites and at the central office, where voice frequencies are stripped off and passed to existing voice-switching equipment and data frequencies are separated off and forwarded to an Internet service provider. The ADSL units provide an ethernet 10BaseT interface for data that may be connected to the 10BaseT interface in the user's PC, to a shared 10BaseT hub, or to a 10BaseT router.

Carriers may need to recondition or replace some lines within the 18,000-foot distance limitation in order to provide ADSL services. ADSL equipment cannot work through bridge taps and loading coils that carriers have installed over the years to boost voice signals to residences beyond 18,000 feet from the closest central office. Figure 10-15 illustrates a typical installation of ADSL technology.

Practical Advice and Information

The author participated in an ADSL trial with GTE in West Lafayette, Indiana, from November 1996 through August 1998. ADSL works very well. Downstream rates from the Internet were consistently at the expected 1.5 Mbps level, and the data transmission had no effect on existing voice services.

Cable TV as a WAN Service   At first glance, it might seem that cable television providers have ample bandwidth available for wide area data and voice transmission. When all of the facts are known however, cable TV as a WAN service may not have such a distinct advantage over carrier-based services such as ADSL.

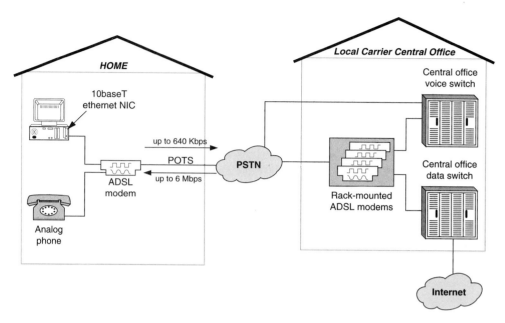

Figure 10-15 ADSL Technology Implementation

Architecture Most cable TV systems were built for one-way broadcast transmission, downstream from the cable head end to the users' residences. In order to provide the necessary upstream bandwidth, cable providers have two basic options:

- Provide upstream bandwidth over POTS while providing downstream bandwidth in a coordinated fashion over the installed cable plant. This architecture does not deliver simultaneous voice capability as in ADSL architectures.

- Modify cable architecture to support simultaneous upstream and downstream transmission. Current implementations of such as architecture provides up to 30 Mbps downstream and 768 Kbps upstream.

However, providing upstream bandwidth is only one of the architectural obstacles that cable providers must overcome. Whereas phone carriers provide voice service via a switched media architecture (circuit switching), cable companies provide cable service via a shared media architecture in which an entire neighborhood may be served by the same shared coaxial cable. Therefore, although 30 Mbps downstream bandwidth may sound impressive, one needs to know the number of users sharing that 30 Mbps. The access methodologies for sharing cable bandwidth are being standardized as **IEEE 802.14** cable network specifications.

Cable companies, like voice-service carriers, must either develop their own Internet access services or buy these services from an existing Internet service provider in order to provide transparent Internet access to their customers.

Technology Cable modems will be provided by cable companies and will connect to standard RG-59 coaxial cable for the network connection while offering a 10BaseT ethernet connection for users' local data access. Figure 10-16 illustrates a typical cable modem network implementation.

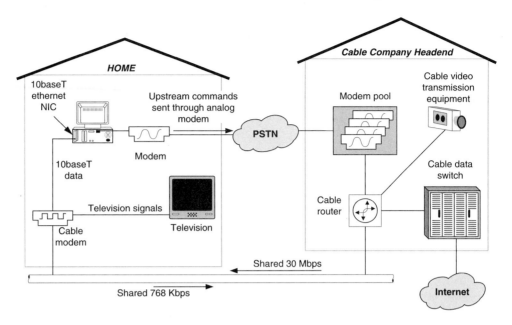

Figure 10-16   Cable Modem Installation

Broadband Transmission

T-1   In order to effectively establish and manage long-distance telecommunications links between end user locations as well as between multiple vendors, standards were required to outline both the size and the organization of high-capacity digital communications links between carriers. The standard high-capacity digital transmission circuit in North America is known as a **T-1,** with a bandwidth of 1.544 Mbps. In other parts of the world, the standard high-capacity digital circuit is known as an **E-1,** with a bandwidth of 2.048 Mbps.

T-1 Framing   The T-1 circuit is divided into twenty-four 64 Kbps channels in order to allow more flexible use of the 1.544 Mbps of bandwidth. In this manner, some of the 24 channels can be used for voice and others are used for data. Differentiating between channels is accomplished through a technique known as **framing,** which is really an adaptation of the TDM (time division multiplexing) techniques explored earlier in the chapter.

With a voice digitization technique known as **pulse code modulation (PCM),** eight bits are required in order to transmit the PCM sampled amplitude of an analog signal. Since 8,000 samples per second are required to ensure quality transmission of digitized voice and each sample requires eight bits to represent that sampled bandwidth in binary (1's and 0's) notation, 64,000 bits per second is the required bandwidth for transmission of voice digitized via PCM. A DS-0 circuit has a transmission capacity of exactly 64 Kbps. Twenty-four DS-0's are combined to form a T-1, yielding the fact that a T-1 can carry 24 simultaneous voice conversations digitized via PCM. However, any or all of these 64 Kbps channels could just as easily carry data traffic or any other type of digitized traffic.

In a technique known as **periodic framing** or **synchronous TDM,** twenty-four channels of eight bits each (192 bits total) are arranged in a **frame.** Each group of eight bits represents one sampling of voice or data traffic to be transmitted on its associated channel. Each group of eight bits is known as a **time slot.** Twenty-four time slots are grouped into a frame, sometimes also known as a **D-4** frame. Each frame is terminated with a **framing bit** in the 193rd position. Such a frame is illustrated in Figure 10-17.

Rather than just using the 193rd bit as a simple frame marker, techniques have been developed to combine the values of sequential framing bits into meaningful arrangements that provide management and error control capabilities for the T-1 transmission service. A group of 12 frames is known as a **superframe,** and a group of 24 frames is known as an **ESF,** or **Extended Superframe.** Superframes and extended superframes are illustrated in Figure 10-18.

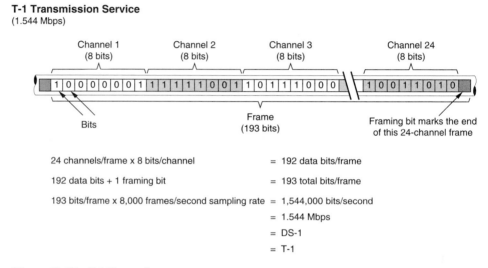

T-1 Transmission Service
(1.544 Mbps)

24 channels/frame x 8 bits/channel	= 192 data bits/frame
192 data bits + 1 framing bit	= 193 total bits/frame
193 bits/frame x 8,000 frames/second sampling rate	= 1,544,000 bits/second
	= 1.544 Mbps
	= DS-1
	= T-1

Figure 10-17   T-1 Frame Layout

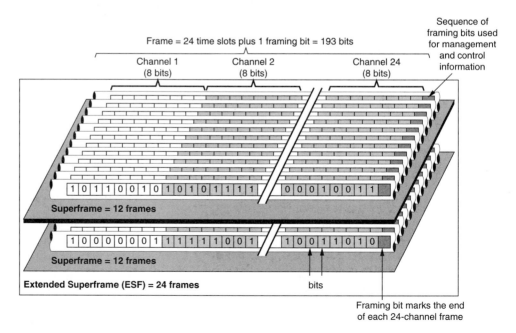

Figure 10-18   Superframes and Extended Superframes

Digital Service Hierarchy   The 1.544 Mbps standard is part of a hierarchy of standards known as the **digital service hierarchy** or **DS** standards. These standards are independent of the transmission services that may deliver the required bandwidth of one of the standards. For instance, technically speaking DS-1 is not the same as T-1, but the two terms are very often used interchangeably. To be exact, a **T-1** transmission service delivers **DS-1** equivalent bandwidth. Figure 10-19 summarizes the digital service hierarchy for North America as well as the CCITT standards for international digital service. Although numerous transmission service designators may be listed, T-1 and T-3 are by far the most common service levels delivered. T-1 service is most often delivered via four copper wires (two twisted pairs). T-3 service is most commonly delivered via optical fiber media.

T-1 Architecture   T-1 lines are examples of leased or private lines, also known as dedicated lines, and they differ from circuit-switched line usage in several ways.

With leased lines there is no dial tone. The circuit is always open and available. The end user is billed for the circuit, 24 hours per day, seven days per week. With leased lines, it is even more imperative than with circuit-switched lines to ensure sufficient data traffic to utilize as close to 100 percent capacity as possible 100 percent of the time in order to cost-justify circuit costs. Higher bandwidth leased lines cost more per month than lower bandwidth leased lines.

Before the advent of high-speed packet services and high-speed modems that worked over dial-up (circuit-switched) lines, leased lines were the only available means of high-speed data transfer over a wide area network. Network managers did their best to get the most out of these relatively expensive leased lines through the use of STDMs, explained earlier in the chapter.

Digital service (DS) hierarchy

Digital Service Level	Number of Voice Channels	Transmission Rate		Corresponding Transmission Service
DS-0	1	64	Kbps	DS-0 or switched 64K
DS-1	24	1.544	Mbps	T-1 or switched T-1
DS-1C	48	3.152	Mbps	T-1C
DS-2	96	6.312	Mbps	T-2
DS-3	672	44.736	Mbps	T-3
DS-4	4032	274.176	Mbps	T-4

CCITT digital hierarchy

Digital Service Level	Number of Voice Channels	Transmission Rate		Corresponding Transmission Service
1	30	2.048	Mbps	E-1
2	120	8.448	Mbps	E-2
3	480	34.368	Mbps	E-3
4	1920	139.264	Mbps	E-4
5	7680	565.148	Mbps	E-5

Figure 10-19   Digital Service Hierarchy and CCITT Standards

Leased lines do not get set up in a matter of seconds in a manner such as circuit switched lines. In most cases, a four- to six-week lead time is required for the installation of a leased line. Leased lines are constructed to circumvent central office switch facilities so as not to monopolize limited circuit-switching capacity.

In some cases the multiple 64 K channels within a T-1 transport circuit can be manipulated or utilized on an individual basis. A service that offers such capability is known as **Fractional T-1, or FT-1.** The fact of the matter is that the full T-1 circuit must be physically delivered to the customer premises, but only a given number of 64 K channels within the T-1 are enabled. Fractional T-1 is really just a creative marketing practice on the part of the carriers as a means of increasing sales of digital transmission services.

T-1 Technology In order to access T-1 service offered by carriers, users may use a variety of T-1 technology. The most basic piece of T-1 technology is the **T-1 CSU/DSU** (channel service unit/data service unit) that interfaces directly to the carrier's termination of the T-1 service on the customer premises. Physically, a T-1 is delivered as a four-wire service (two for transmit, two for receive) most often terminated in a **RJ48c** jack. Most T-1 CSU/DSUs have a corresponding RJ48c jack to connect to the carrier's RJ48c jack. The CSU/DSU will transfer the 1.544 Mbps of T-1 bandwidth to local devices such as routers, PBXs, or channel banks via V.35, RS-530, or RS-449 high-speed serial connectors or RJ-45 connectors for direct connection to 10BaseT or 100BaseT ethernet networks. Because these T-1 CSU/DSUs-play such an important role in a corporation's wide area network, they are often able to communicate status and alarm information to enterprise network management systems via SNMP (simple network management protocol).

T-1 multiplexers are able to aggregate several lower speed data or voice channels into a single composite T-1 link. T-1 "muxes" often have CSU/DSUs built in and require all data input channels to be in digital format, adhering to such transmission standards as RS-232, RS-449, or V.35. Voice input to T-1 muxes must already be digitized in a digital voice PBX and output in a transmission format known as DSX-1. **Fractional T-1 multiplexers** are able to use less than the full 1.544 Mbps of composite T-1 output bandwidth. Obviously, FT-1 multiplexers make good business sense if less than 1.544 Mbps of composite bandwidth is sufficient, thereby saving on monthly carrier charges. A **T-1 IMUX** or **inverse multiplexer** is able to combine multiple T-1 output lines to provide high bandwidth requirements for such applications as LAN-to-LAN communication via routers or high-quality videoconferencing.

A **T-1 Channel Bank** is similar to but more flexible than a T-1 mux. A T-1 channel bank is an open chassis-based piece of equipment with a built-in CSU/DSU to which a variety of data and voice input channel cards can be flexibly added. Input data channels may be synchronous or asynchronous at a variety of different speeds and serial transmission protocols. Voice channels may accept analog voice traffic to be digitized by a variety of voice digitization techniques. Output of a T-1 channel bank is typically just a single T-1. Finally, **T-1 switches** can be employed by companies wishing to build their own private wide area networks. T-1 switches are able to switch entire T-1s or particular DS0s among other T-1 switches in order to flexibly deliver voice and data to a variety of corporate locations. Figure 10-20 illustrates the implementation of a variety of T-1 technology.

SONET SONET (**Synchronous Optical Network**) is an optical transmission service delivering multiple channels of data from various sources thanks to periodic framing or TDM, much like T-1 transmission service. The differences between T-1 and

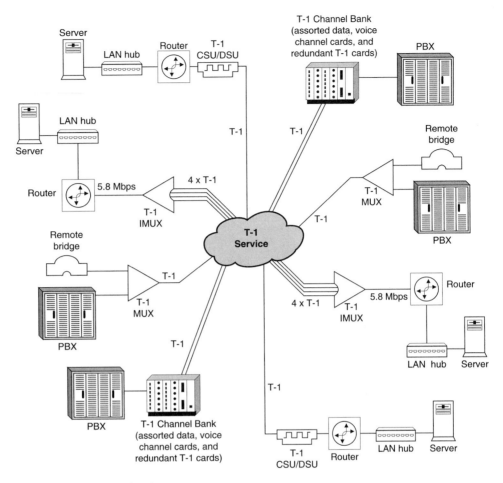

Figure 10-20   T-1 Technology

SONET transmission services lie chiefly in the higher transmission capacity of SONET owing to its fiber optic media and the slightly different framing techniques used to channelize this higher transmission capacity.

Just as the digital service hierarchy defined levels of service for traditional digital service, optical transmission has its own hierarchy of service levels. Rather than being designated as DS levels, optical transmission is categorized by **OC** or **Optical Carrier** levels and illustrated in Figure 10-21. Because SONET will eventually carry voice, video, and image as well as data, the basic unit of measure is referred to as an **octet** of eight bits rather than a byte of eight bits. *Byte* usually refers to data only and is often synonymous with a character.

SONET Framing   In many ways, SONET framing is the same as T-1 framing. The basic purpose of each is to establish markers with which to identify individual channels. Because of the higher bandwidth of SONET (51.84 OC-1 versus 1.544 Mbps T-1) and its potential for sophisticated mixed-media services, more overhead is reserved surrounding each frame than the single bit reserved every 193rd character in a T-1 frame.

Rather than fitting 24 channels per frame delineated by a single framing bit, a single SONET frame or **row** is delineated by three octets of overhead for control

SONET's OC (Optical Carrier) standards

Digital Service Level	Transmission Rate	
OC-1	51.84	Mbps
OC-3	155.52	Mbps
OC-9	466.56	Mbps
OC-12	622.08	Mbps
OC-18	933.12	Mbps
OC-24	1.244	Gbps
OC-36	1.866	Gbps
OC-48	2.488	Gbps

Figure 10-21   Optical Carrier Levels

information followed by 87 octets of **payload.** Nine of these 90 octet rows are grouped together to form a **SONET superframe.** The 87 octets of payload per row in each of the time rows or the superframe is known as the **synchronous payload envelope,** or **SPE.** The electrical equivalent of the **OC-1,** the optical SONET super-frame standard is known as the **STS-1,** or synchronous transport signal. The SONET frame structure is illustrated in Figure 10-22.

Virtual Tributaries in SONET   Unlike the T-1 frame with its 24 predefined eight-bit channels, SONET is flexible in its definition of the use of its payload area. It can map DS-0 (64 Kbps) channels into the payload area just as easily as it can map an entire T-1 (1.544 Mbps). These flexibly defined channels within the payload area are known as **virtual tributaries,** or **VTs.**

For instance, a T-1 would be mapped into a virtual tributary standard known as **VT-1.5,** with a bandwidth of 1.728 Mbps. The difference between that figure and the 1.544 Mbps T-1 is accounted for by the additional SONET overhead.

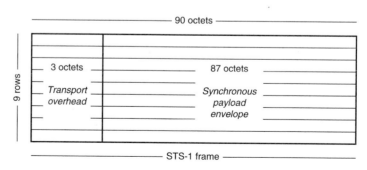

90 octets/row x 8 bits/octet = 720 bits/row

720 bits/row x 9 rows/frame = 6,480 bits/frame

6,480 bits/frame x 8,000 frames/second (sampling rate) = 51,840,000 bits/second

Transfer Rate of 51.84 Mbits/second

Figure 10-22   SONET Framing

The virtual tributaries of SONET are equivalent to circuit-switched transmission services. In addition to the three octets per row of transport overhead in OC-1, there is also a variable amount of path overhead imbedded within the SPE to keep track of which virtual tributaries start where within the SPE payload boxcar. This path overhead brings the total overhead to about 4 percent before any additional overhead embedded within the SPE payload boxcar is considered.

SONET Deployment SONET services are currently available within many major metropolitan areas. Accessing such services requires the local carrier to bring the fiber-based ring directly to a corporate location and to assign dedicated bandwidth to each SONET customer. Because of the limited geographic scope of most SONET services, it is most appropriate for those organizations with very high bandwidth needs (OC-1 to OC-48) between multiple locations within the limited SONET service area. Such companies would typically be employing multiple T-3s and looking at SONET as an attractive upgrade path.

Add-drop multiplexers, sometimes referred to as broadband bandwidth managers, are the customary type of hardware used to access SONET services. Such devices are often capable of adding several T-1 or T-3 digital signals together and converting those combined signals into a single channelized optical SONET signal. In some cases, ATM switches are equipped with SONET interfaces for direct access to either a local SONET ring or commercial SONET services.

Another key advantage of SONET is the fault tolerance and reliability afforded by its fiber-based architecture. In the event of a network failure, traffic can be rerouted. There are two principal architectures for SONET deployment:

- Unidirectional path-switched rings (UPSR), in which all users share transmission capacity around the ring rather than using dedicated segments

- Bidirectional line-switched rings (BLSR), in which each user's traffic is specifically rerouted in the case of a fiber failure

Conclusion: So What Is SONET? SONET is a service-independent transport function that can carry the services of the future such as B-ISDN (broadband ISDN) or HDTV (high-definition television) as easily as it can carry the circuit-switched traffic of today such as DS-1 and DS-3. It has extensive performance monitoring and fault location capabilities. For instance, if SONET senses a transmission problem, it can switch traffic to an alternate path in as little as 50 msec (1000ths of a second). This network survivability is due to SONET's redundant or dual ring physical architecture. Based on the OC hierarchy of standard optical interfaces, SONET has the potential to deliver multigigabyte bandwidth transmission capabilities to end users.

Managerial Perspective

SONET availability is currently limited to large metropolitan areas in most cases. SONET availability implies that a high-capacity, dual ring, fiber optic cable-based transmission service is available between the customer premises and the carrier central office. SONET services cost about 20 percent more than conventional digital services of identical bandwidth. The benefit of the 20 percent premium is the network survivability offered by SONET's dual ring architecture. Unless a corporation has identified mission-critical network transmissions requiring fault-tolerant circuits, SONET's benefits may not be worth the added expense.

◼ WIDE AREA NETWORK SERVICES

As illustrated in Figure 10-7 (Major Components of a Wide Area Network Architecture), the foundation of any wide area network architecture depends on the particular switching and transmission architectures employed therein. Wide area network services that are offered to consumers depend on these underlying transmission and switching architectures. Switching architectures and transmission architectures have already been reviewed in this chapter. In this section, different wide area network services will be reviewed along with the business aspects of these services, the underlying switching and transmission architectures required, and the technology employed to interface to such services.

X.25

X.25 is an international CCITT standard that defines the interface between terminal equipment (DTE) and any packet-switched network (the cloud). It is important to note that X.25 does *not* define standards for what goes on *inside* the cloud. One of the most common misconceptions is that the X.25 standard defines the specifications for a packet-switching network. On the contrary, X.25 ensures only that an end user can depend on how to get information into and out of the packet-switched network by defining how information must be packetized before entering such a network.

X.25 is a three-layer protocol stack corresponding to the first three layers of the OSI model. The total effect of the three-layer X.25 protocol stack is to produce packets in a standard format acceptable by any X.25-compliant public packet-switched network. X.25 offers network transparency to the upper layers of the OSI protocol stack. Figure 10-23 illustrates the relationship of the X.25 protocol stack to the OSI model.

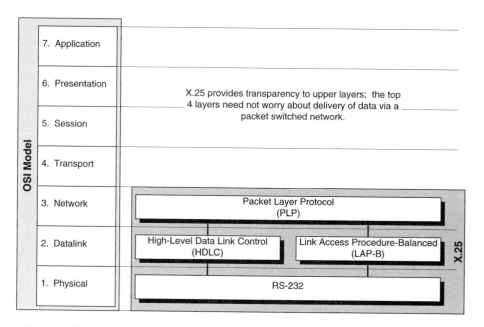

Figure 10-23   X.25 and the OSI Model

Architecture The X.25 standard consists of a three-layer protocol that ensures transparent network access to OSI layers 4 through 7. In other words, applications running on one computer that wish to talk to another computer do not need to be concerned with anything having to do with the packet-switched network connecting the two computers. In this way, the X.25-compliant packet-switched network is nothing more than a transparent delivery service between computers.

The physical layer (layer 1) protocol of the X.25 standard is most often RS-232 or some other serial transmission standard. The data-link layer (layer 2) protocol is known as **HDLC,** or **high-level data link control.** HDLC is very similar to IBM's SDLC in structure. Functionally, HDLC accomplishes the same things as any other data-link layer protocol, such as ethernet or token ring:

- It organizes data into structured frames that may contain more than one packet.

- It ensures reliable delivery of data via error checking.

- It provides point-to-point data delivery between adjacent nodes.

Figure 10-24 illustrates an HDLC frame. In the case of HDLC and X.25, error checking is achieved via a 16-bit frame check sequence. The control field transports important management information such as frame sequence numbers and requests for retransmission. Newer implementations of X.25 use **LAP-B,** or **Link Access Procedure–Balanced,** a subset and functional equivalent of the full HDLC frame, as a data link layer protocol. The network layer (layer 3) X.25 protocol is known as **PLP** or **packet layer protocol.** Because the job of any OSI layer 3 (network layer) protocol is the establishment, maintenance, and termination of end-to-end connections, PLP's main job is to establish, maintain, and terminate virtual circuits within a connection-oriented packet-switched network.

Figure 10-25 lists important standards related to X.25 and a brief explanation of their importance.

Technology X.25 requires data to be properly packetized by the time it reaches the cloud. Terminals and computers that do not possess the X.25 protocol stack internally to produce properly formatted packets employ a **PAD,** or **packet assembler/ disassembler,** to packetize their output data into X.25 format for entry into the cloud. Such devices usually have several (4 to 16) RS-232 serial ports for input from PCs, terminals, or host computer ports that wish to transmit traffic via a carrier's X.25 service. These input ports are typically asynchronous. The single composite output port is synchronous and is most often limited to 2 Mbps, although most X.25 carrier services are limited to about 9.6 Kbps. This seemingly excess composite output capacity is due to the fact that many X.25 PADs are also capable of accessing higher speed packet-switched network services such as frame relay (explained in the next section). Inside the carrier's X.25 cloud, X.25 switches are connected together in a mesh topology and are most often connected to one another via high

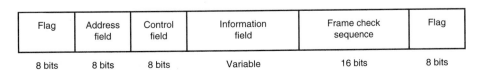

Flag	Address field	Control field	Information field	Frame check sequence	Flag
8 bits	8 bits	8 bits	Variable	16 bits	8 bits

Figure 10-24 X.25 Data Link Layer Protocol: HDLC

Standard	Explanation/Importance
X.121—Global Addressing Scheme	As packet-switching networks have become global in nature, a global addressing scheme was necessary to allow transparent global access to these networks. X.121 defines zone codes, country codes, and PSN codes within countries. This four-digit global addressing prefix is followed by up to ten digits to uniquely identify the destination address node.
X.28 and X.32—Dial-Up Access Directly into PADs	X.28 (asynchronous) and X.32 (synchronous) define standards that allow users to dial up a PAD and subsequently place a call over the packet-switched network.
X.75—Internetworking Packet Switched Networks	X.25 defined the interface from the end user device into the packet-switched network cloud. A standard was required to define a standardized interface between different packet-switched networks. X.75 is that standard and has been referred to as the packet-switched network gateway protocol.

Figure 10-25   X.25-Related Standards

speed digital transmission services such as T-1. Figure 10-26 illustrates X.25 technology implementation.

Frame Relay

Figure 10-27 illustrates the relationship between a packet-switched network service such as X.25 and other packet-switched and circuit-switched network services. The

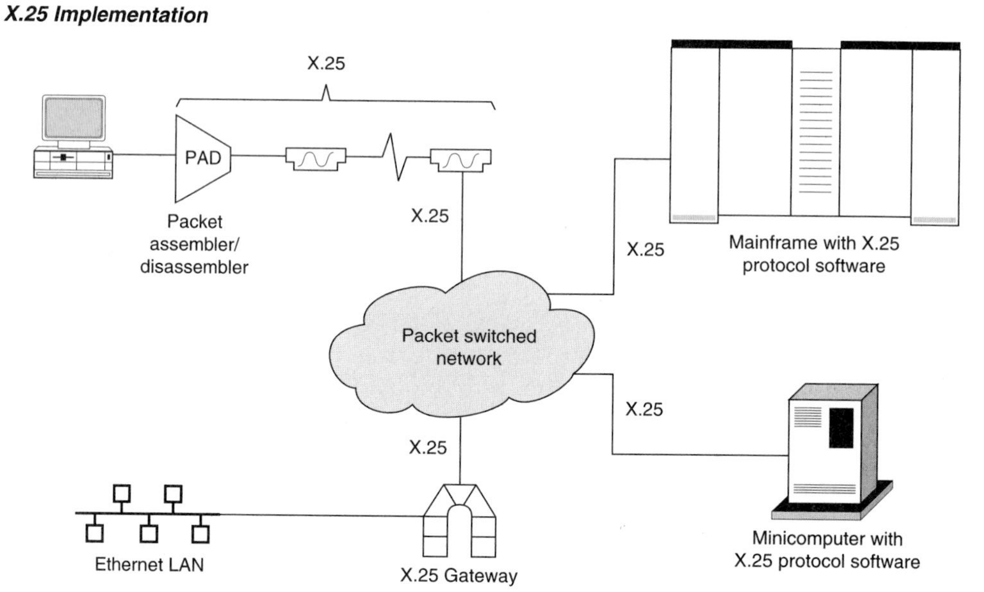

Figure 10-26   X.25 Technology Implementation

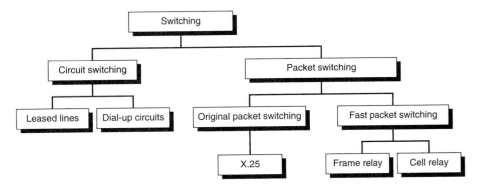

Figure 10-27   Switched Network Services Hierarchy

differences between circuit switching and packet switching have already been explained. The differences among the various packet-switched network services are based largely on transmission speed and overhead.

In order to understand how these packet services could be made faster, examine the source of the overhead or slowness of the existing X.25 packet-switching networks. Recall from the previous discussion of connection-oriented packet-switched networks that error-checking and retransmission requests were done on a point-to-point basis between adjacent packet switches. This point-to-point–oriented error checking is sometimes also called hop-by-hop error checking.

At the time X.25 was first introduced about 20 years ago, the long-distance circuits connecting the X.25 packet switches were not nearly as error free as they are today. Transmission errors are measured by **bit error rate (BER).** As a result, in order to guarantee end-to-end error free delivery, it was necessary to check for errors and request retransmissions on a point-to-point or hop-by-hop basis at every X.25 packet switch in the network. Although it was necessary, this constant error checking and correction added significant overhead, and therefore delay, to the X.25 packet transmission process.

Today's long-distance digital transmission systems are largely fiber based and are far less error prone than those of 20 years ago. As a result, new packet-switching methodologies such as **frame relay** were introduced that sought to take advantage of the decreased bit error rate on today's transmission systems. The basic design philosophy is simple: With the quality of the transmission system, stop all point-to-point error correction and flow control within the network itself and let the end nodes worry about it!

The end nodes, such as PCs, servers, and mainframes, would use higher-level (layers 4 to 7) protocols to perform their own error checking. In the case of a PC, this would likely be a sliding window file transfer protocol. This philosophy works fine as long as the basic assumption, the low bit error rate of today's transmission system, holds true. If not, then retransmissions are end-to-end spanning the entire network, rather than point-to-point between adjacent packet switches.

Architecture

Error Detection and Correction   It is important to distinguish between **error detection** and **error correction.** Both frame relay and X.25 perform point-to-point error detection by comparing generated **CRCs (cyclic redundancy checks)** with transmitted CRCs, also known as **FCSs (frame check sequences).** The difference and resultant processing time savings for frame relay occurs in the action taken upon detection of an error.

An X.25 switch will always send either a positive ACK or a negative NAK acknowledgment upon the receipt of each packet and will not forward additional packets until it receives an ACK or NAK. If a NAK is received, the packet received in error will be retransmitted. Packets are stored in X.25 switches in case a NAK is received, necessitating retransmission. This is why X.25 packet switching is sometimes called a **store-and-forward** switching methodology.

On the other hand, if a frame relay switch detects an error when it compares the computed versus transmitted FCSs, the bad frame is simply discarded. The correction and request for retransmission of bad frames is left to the end node devices: PCs, modems, computers, and their error correction protocols. Technically speaking, in frame relay, there is point-to-point error detection, but only end-to-end error correction. While X.25 networks were typically limited to 9.6 Kbps, frame relay networks typically offer transmission speeds of T-1 (1.544 Mbps) and occasionally T-3 (44.736 Mbps). Figure 10-28 illustrates point-to-point versus end-to-end error correction.

In terms of the OSI model, the difference between X.25 packet switching and frame relay is simple. Frame relay is a two-layer protocol stack (physical and data link); X.25 is a three-layer protocol stack (physical, data link, and network). There is no network layer processing in frame relay, accounting for the decreased processing time and increased throughput rate.

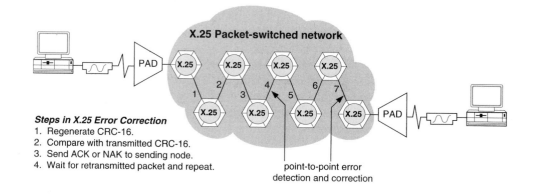

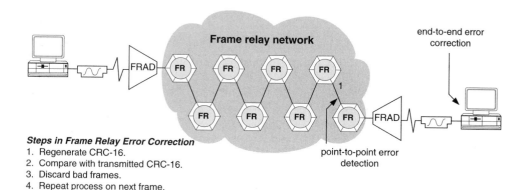

Figure 10-28   Point-to-Point versus End-to-End Error Correction

Flow Control   Although end node devices such as PCs and modems can handle the error detection and correction duties shed by the frame relay network with relative ease, **flow control** is another matter. End nodes can only manage flow control between themselves and whatever frame relay network access device they are linked to. There is no way for end nodes to either monitor or manage flow control within the frame relay network itself. Some frame relay switch vendors have implemented their own flow control methodologies, which is sufficient if only that vendor's switches are being used.

In the frame relay frame structure diagram in Figure 10-29, there are three bits in the frame definition known as **BECN, FECN,** and **DE,** which stand for **backward explicit congestion notification, forward explicit congestion notification,** and **discard eligibility,** respectively. BECN is sent back to the original source user to tell the frame relay access device to throttle back its transmission onto the frame relay network. FECN warns the destination recipient of this frame of the congested network conditions. If the discard eligible field is set, then the carrier managing the frame relay network is granted permission to discard such frames in order to relieve network congestion. These bits are the elements of a scheme to allow frame relay devices to dynamically adjust flow control. Some frame relay devices even have the ability to read or write to these fields.

Practical Advice and Information

The only problem is, what action should be taken by a given device in the event that any of these bits indicate a flow control problem has not necessarily been agreed upon or uniformly implemented by frame relay technology manufacturers? Unless you were responsible for setting up your own frame relay network, you might not think much of this problem. On the other hand, it demonstrates the need to have a healthy dose of cynicism when shopping for data communications devices, even when those devices "support all applicable standards." If standards are not uniformly implemented by technology manufacturers, they are of little use.

In a similar manner to X.25 packet formation, frame relay frames are formatted within the FRAD, or in computers or PCs that have frame relay protocol software loaded to build frame relay frames directly. The **frames** that a frame relay network forwards are variable in length, with the maximum frame transporting nearly 8000 characters at once. Combining these potentially large, variable-length frames with the low overhead and faster processing of the frame relay switching delivers a key characteristic of the frame relay network: high throughput with low delay.

Figure 10-29 illustrates the frame definition for frame relay networks. This frame definition is said to be a subset of the LAP-D protocol. **LAP-D** stands for **link access procedure–D channel,** where the *D channel* refers to the 16 Kbps delta channel in BRI (basic rate interface) ISDN (integrated services digital network).

The variable length frames illustrated in Figure 10-29 can also be a shortcoming. Because there is no guarantee of the length of a frame, there can be no guarantee of how quickly a given frame can be forwarded through the network and delivered to its destination. With data, this lack of guaranteed timed delivery or maximum delay is of little consequence.

However, in the case of more time-sensitive information such as voice or video, it could be a real issue. Digitized voice or video can be packetized or put into frames like any other data. The problem arises when framed voice and video do not arrive in a predictable timed fashion for conversion back to understandable voice

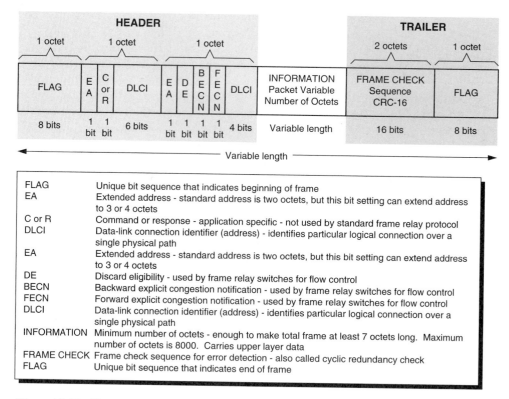

Figure 10-29   Frame Relay Frame Layout

and video. As a result, frame relay is often described as a data-only service. That's not exactly true. Options do exist to transport digitized, compressed voice transmissions via a frame relay network. However, most voice over frame relay technology is proprietary, requiring all FRADs and switches that support voice over frame relay to be purchased from the same vendor.

Virtual Circuits   Frame relay networks most often employ **PVCs (permanent virtual circuits)** to forward frames from source to destination through the frame relay cloud. **SVC (Switched Virtual Circuit)** standards have been defined but are not as readily available from all carriers. An SVC is like a dial-up call, so in order to transport data over an SVC-based frame relay network, a LAN NOS such as Netware or Windows NT would have to communicate call setup protocol information to the frame relay network before sending a data request or transaction update to a remote server.

Frame relay transmission rates are commonly as high as 1.544 Mbps and occasionally as high as 44.736 Mbps. Because multiple PVCs can exist within the frame relay network cloud, another key advantage of frame relay over circuit-switched options such as leased lines is the ability to have multiple PVCs supported from only one access line. From a cost justification standpoint, this would allow a frame relay user to replace multiple leased line connections with a single access line to a frame relay network. Remember also that frame relay network charges are based on usage, whereas circuit-switched leased lines charges are based on flat monthly fees whether they are used or not. Figure 10-30 illustrates the concept of multiple PVCs per single access line.

Before: Circuit switched

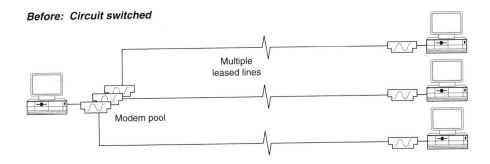

After: Frame relay, single access line, multiple PVCs

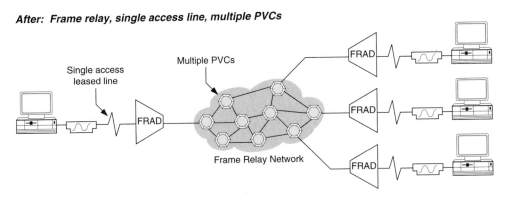

Figure 10-30   Multiple PVCs per Access Line

Dynamic Bandwidth Allocation   Another important characteristic afforded by the many transmission options available with the mesh network of the frame relay cloud is the ability to allocate bandwidth dynamically. In other words, up to the transmission limit of the access line and the circuits between the frame relay switches, the frame relay network will handle bursts of data by simply assembling and forwarding more frames per second onto the frame relay network, over multiple PVCs if required.

This ability to handle traffic in bursts is especially appealing for LAN interconnection. Inter-LAN communication tends to come in bursts, with intermittent requests for data and file transfers. Remembering that this inter-LAN communication should be as transparent as possible, frame relay's ability to handle bursts of traffic by dynamic bandwidth allocation is especially appealing. In the case of frame relay network access for LAN interconnection, the internetwork bridge or router is often integrated with a frame relay assembler/disassembler or frame relay protocol software.

A word of caution, however: "Bursty" traffic is not easy to define. How large a burst, in terms of maximum bandwidth demand, and of what duration is the frame relay network expected to be able to handle? An attempt has been made to structure the discussion with the following two terms:

- **CIR,** or **committed information rate,** refers to the minimum bandwidth guaranteed to users for "normal" transmission

- **CBS,** or **committed burst size,** defines the extent to which a user can exceed its CIR over a period of time. If a user exceeds the CBS, the frame relay network reserves the right to discard frames in order to deliver guaranteed CIRs to other users.

Protocol Independence and Network-to-Network Interface   Another frame relay feature that is appealing for LAN interconnection is the fact that frame relay merely encapsulates user data into frames and forwards it to the destination. Frame relay is merely a delivery service. It does not process user data and is therefore protocol independent, or protocol transparent. It can forward SNA/SDLC traffic just as easily as it can forward TCP/IP or Novell IPX traffic.

An issue hindering widespread global use of frame relay is the need for better coordination among the different frame relay network vendors in order to offer transparent access between them in a manner similar to the standard interfaces developed by phone companies for voice traffic. A conceptual standard known as **NNI,** or **network-to-network interface,** would be the functional equivalent of the X.75 internetwork standard for X.25 packet-switched networks.

Technology   As can be seen in Figure 10-28, the technology configuration for the X.25 packet-switched network and the frame relay network are amazingly similar. In the case of the frame relay network, the access device is known as a **FRAD** or **FAD** (frame relay or frame assembler/disassembler) rather than a PAD, and the switching device is known as a **frame relay switch,** rather than a packet or X.25 switch. FRADs are also known as **frame relay access devices.** FRADs and frame relay switches are available in numerous configurations and integrated with numerous other internetworking devices such as bridges, routers, multiplexers, and concentrators.

Conclusion: What Is Frame Relay?   First and foremost, frame relay is an interface specification. The LAP-D data link layer protocol defines a frame structure that contains destination address, error checking, control information, and user data all in a single protocol layer frame. It is this interface specification that allows faster processing to take place within the frame relay network.

Second, frame relay is also a network service, offered by several regional and long-distance phone companies primarily for the purpose of LAN interconnection. Frame relay's ability to dynamically allocate bandwidth over a single access line to the frame relay network makes it particularly well-suited for the intermittent nature of inter-LAN traffic. Private frame relay networks can be established as well.

Finally, frame relay could also be considered a switching architecture. What goes on inside the frame relay network cloud is unimportant to end users, as long as the interface specification causes frame relay frames to enter the cloud and frame relay frames to exit the cloud. However, there are true frame relay switches designed specifically to forward frame relay frames at an optimal rate. A mesh network composed of these "native" frame relay switches could legitimately be considered a switching architecture.

SMDS

SMDS, switched multimegabit data service, is a connectionless network service delivering switched LAN internetworking and data dial tone in a metropolitan area network deployment. It adheres to the IEEE 802.6 and DQDB (Distributed Queue Dual Bus) protocols by delivering fixed length cells of data to their destinations via a SONET transmission system at speeds up to T-3 (45 Mbps). Architecturally, it differs from frame relay primarily in the fact that it is a connectionless service and does not support virtual circuits.

Managerial Perspective

Practically speaking, SMDS is losing the WAN services battle to frame relay. In 1996 27 percent of WAN services customers purchased frame relay services; only 1 percent purchased SMDS. Projections for 1999 call for frame relay usage to increase to 47 percent and SMDS usage to increase to only 6 percent of WAN services customers. Some studies predict no SMDS market growth whatsoever. Part of the reason for the small market share has to do with a lack of support from carriers. Among the local service providers, only Ameritech, Bell Atlantic, Bell South, PacTel, GTE, and Southwestern Bell offer SMDS services. MCI is the only long distance carrier offering SMDS.

The service advantage that SMDS possesses over frame relay due to its connectionless architecture is its ability to broadcast to multiple sites by sending data only once to the SMDS service provider. SMDS is best suited for highly interconnected or meshed networks carrying high-capacity data traffic. SMDS advocates have submitted proposals to the ATM Forum proposing protocols that will allow SMDS to be transmitted over ATM networks. In this manner, SMDS popularity may stand a better chance of improvement by piggybacking on the increasing popularity of ATM.

Cell Relay — ATM

Architecture   As seen in Figure 10-27 (Switched Network Services Hierarchy), **cell relay** is another "fast packet" switching methodology and a key part of future network architectures. **ATM** or **asynchronous transfer mode,** is the widely accepted standardized cell relay transmission service. The key physical difference between cell relay and frame relay is that, unlike the variable length frame relay frames, all cells in ATM networks are of a fixed length, 53 octets long. (An octet is 8 bits.) Forty-eight of the octets per cell are reserved for user data or information from higher-layer protocols, plus a five-octet header.

ATM Protocol Model   Because of the constant-length cells, cell relay switches can perform much faster than frame relay switches. By being able to depend on constant cell length, cell relay switches can include more instructions for processing in firmware and hardware. The constant-sized cells also lead to a predictable and dependable processing rate and forwarding or delivery rate. The lack of a predictable maximum delivery delay is a key weakness in frame relay.

This predictable delivery time of every cell makes cell relay a better choice for transmission of voice or video applications as well as data. Cell relay switching can provide switching capability on a similar scale to the highest-capacity transmission alternatives such T-3s (45 Mbps) and fiber optic transmission circuits with capacity of up to 2.4 gigabytes per second.

ATM is presently defined by two different cell formats. One is called the **UNI (User-Network Interface)** and carries information between the user and the ATM network. The second cell standard is known as **NNI (Network-Network Interface)** and carries information between ATM switches. Figure 10-31 depicts the ATM UNI protocol model, which conceptually illustrates how inputs of data, voice, or video can all be processed and transmitted as homogeneous ATM cells. Figure 10-32 relates the layers of the ATM model to the layers of the OSI Model.

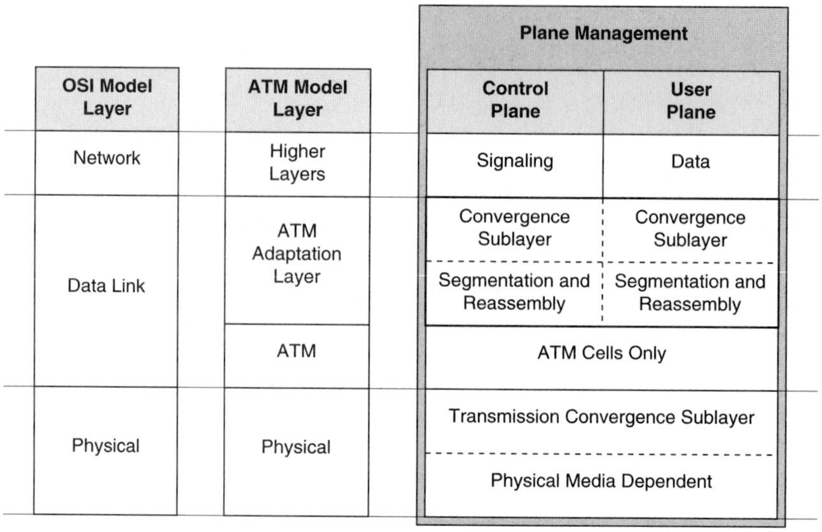

OSI Model Layer	ATM Model Layer	Plane Management	
		Control Plane	**User Plane**
Network	Higher Layers	Signaling	Data
Data Link	ATM Adaptation Layer	Convergence Sublayer	Convergence Sublayer
		Segmentation and Reassembly	Segmentation and Reassembly
	ATM	ATM Cells Only	
Physical	Physical	Transmission Convergence Sublayer	
		Physical Media Dependent	

Figure 10-31   ATM UNI Protocol Model

OSI Layer	ATM Layer	Explanation
Network	Signaling	Fault management, performance management, connection management
	Data	User data, voice, video input that must be adapted into ATM cells
Data Link	AAL (ATM Adaptation Layer)	Divided further into CS (convergence sublayer) and SAR (segmentation and reassembly) sublayers. Converts input data, video, and voice into ATM cells
	ATM (Asynchronous Transfer Mode)	ATM cell processing layer. Flow control. Address assignment and translation
Physical	TCS (Transmission Convergence Sublayer)	Cell delineation, header error check, path overhead signals, multiplexing
	PMD (Physical Medium Dependent)	Physical transport and connectivity, framing, bit timing, line coding, loopback testing

Figure 10-32   ATM Model versus OSI Model

ATM Cell Structures   User inputs of data, video, or voice must be processed into fixed-length ATM cells before they can be forwarded and delivered by ATM switches. This processing is done on the **AAL,** or **ATM adaptation layer.** Depending on the type of input (voice, video, or data), a different type of adaptation process may apply, and different types of delivery requirements or priorities can be assigned within the ATM network. After emerging from the ATM adaptation layer, all cells are in an identical format, as illustrated and explained in Figure 10-33.

ATM Cell Field Name	Explanation
GFC: Generic Flow Control	Multiple devices of various types (voice, video, data) can gain access to an ATM network through a single access circuit. These different devices may require different flow control signaling.
VPI: Virtual Path Identifier	The virtual path identifier uniquely identifies the connection between two end nodes and is equivalent to the virtual circuits of X.25 or frame relay networks. A VPI consists of several VCIs.
VCI: Virtual Channel Identifier	Because ATM can carry multiple types of information (voice, video, data), several channels of information could be traveling along the same end-to-end connection simultaneously. The VCI uniquely identifies a particular channel of information within the virtual path.
PT: Payload Type	The PT indicates whether cell contains user information or network control information.
CLP: Cell Loss Priority	If an ATM transmission exceeds its allotted bandwidth, including concessions for intermittent bursts of data, a cell can be marked by the ATM network in a process known as policing. If congestion occurs on the network, these marked cells are the first to be discarded.
HEC: Header Error Control	HEC ensures that header information contains no errors. The biggest concern is that the VPI and VCI are correct.

Figure 10-33   ATM Cell Structure

AAL Protocols   ATM adaptation layer protocols are designed to optimize the delivery of a wide variety of possible types of user inputs or traffic. However, all of these different types of traffic vary in just a few ways:

- Delay sensitivity: Can the traffic tolerate variable delay, or must end-to-end timing be preserved?

- Cell loss sensitivity: Can the traffic tolerate the occasional cell loss associated with connectionless transmission services, or must connection-oriented transmission services be employed in order to avoid cell loss?

- Guaranteed bandwidth: Must the traffic receive a constant amount of guaranteed bandwidth, or can it tolerate variable amounts of bandwidth?

- Additional overhead required: In addition to the five octets of overhead in the ATM cell header, some AAL protocols require additional overhead to manage payloads properly. This additional overhead is taken from the 48-octet payload. This can raise overhead percentages to as high as 13 percent.

To date, four different types of ATM adaptation protocols have been defined and are summarized in Figure 10-34.

ATM Bandwidth Management   As illustrated in Figure 10-34, the type of bandwidth required for a given type of traffic varies according to which AAL protocol was employed. There are currently three different categories of bit rates or bandwidth management schemes supported by ATM standards:

ATM AAL Protocol	Timing	Cell Loss	Bandwidth	Payload	Application/Notes
AAL-1	Preserved end-to-end	Connection oriented	Constant bit rate	47 octets	Used for mapping TDM services such as T-1, T-3
AAL-2	Preserved end-to-end	Connection oriented	Variable bit rate	45–47 octets	Variable rate compressed video
AAL-3/4	Variable delay acceptance	Connection-less	Variable bit rate	44 octets	Compatible with connectionless WAN data services such as SMDS
AAL-5	Variable delay acceptance	Connection oriented	Variable bit rate	48 octets	Currently most popular AAL protocol. Also known as SEAL (Simple and Efficient Adaptation Layer)

Figure 10-34   AAL Products

- **CBR,** or **constant bit rate,** provides a guaranteed amount of bandwidth to a given virtual path, thereby producing the equivalent of leased T-1 or T-3 line. On the negative side of CBR, if this guaranteed amount of bandwidth is not required 100 percent of the time, no other applications can use the unused bandwidth.

- **VBR,** or **variable bit rate,** provides a guaranteed minimum threshold amount of constant bandwidth, below which the available bandwidth will not drop. However, as intermittent traffic requires more bandwidth than this constant minimum, that required bandwidth will be provided.

- **ABR,** or **available bit rate,** provides leftover bandwidth whenever it is not required by the variable bit rate traffic. Figure 10-35 illustrates the relationship between CBR, VBR, and ABR.

Technology   The key benefits that the ATM architecture affords actual implementations of ATM technology are as follows:

- Constant cell length allows faster, predictable delivery times.

- Constant cell length and predictable delivery times allow voice, video, and data to all be transported effectively via ATM.

- ATM protocols are supported from the LAN to the WAN, from network interface cards to ATM WAN switches, thereby removing the necessity for multiple protocol conversions from the desktop across enterprise networks.

ATM on the LAN   ATM network interface cards are currently available at speeds from 25 Mbps to 155 Mbps. Workstations equipped with ATM NICs would be linked to one another via an ATM hub that would usually have a higher-speed ATM uplink to a higher-speed ATM enterprise switch. Workstations with Ethernet or Token Ring NICs do not have to have those NICs replaced in order to access ATM enterprise networks. **ATM gateway switches,** otherwise known as **ATM access switches,** can provide switched access for an entire legacy shared media LAN to an

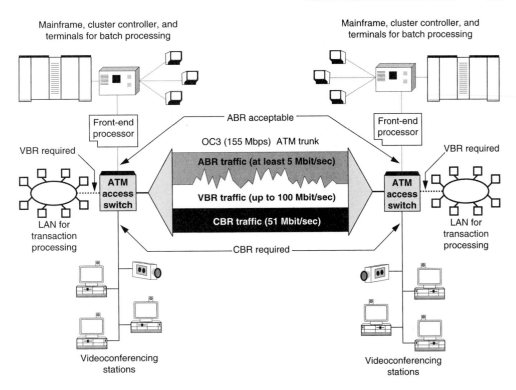

Figure 10-35   CBR, VBR, and ABR Bandwidth Management for ATM

ATM enterprise network. Ethernet switches with ATM uplinks are a common example of an ATM gateway switch.

A virtual LAN refers to a group of workstations that appear to be all locally connected to one another but that, in fact, are geographically dispersed. Virtual LANs can be created across an enterprisewide ATM network among geographically distributed workstations through an ATM capability known as **ATM LAN emulation.** In ATM LAN emulation, LAN MAC layer addresses are converted to ATM network addresses and forwarded via switched ATM connections across the enterprise network to their destination workstation. This capability allows workstations and legacy LANs to take advantage of ATM's speed without having to make any hardware or software modifications to the LAN workstations themselves.

ATM Across the WAN   An implementation of an ATM-based enterprise network would consist of ATM access devices as well as a "cloud" of ATM switches. The ATM access devices would take user information in the form of variable-length data frames from a LAN or workstation, digitized voice from a PBX, or digitized video from a video codec and format all of these various types of information into fixed-length ATM cells. The local ATM switch could route information to other locally connected ATM devices as well as to the wide area ATM network.

In a sense, the general makeup of the ATM network is not unlike the X.25 or frame relay networks. Access devices ensure that data is properly formatted before entering "the cloud," where the data is forwarded by switches specially designed to handle that particular type of properly formatted data. However, the functionality an ATM network can offer far exceeds that of either the X.25 or frame relay networks. Figure 10-36 illustrates a possible implementation of a variety of ATM technology.

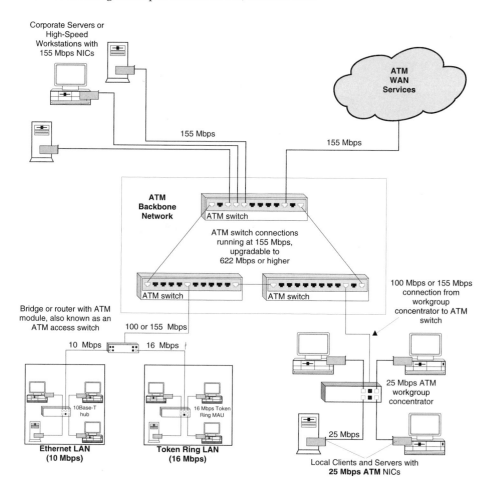

Figure 10-36   Implementation of ATM Technology

Broadband ISDN

SONET is the optical transmission interface and mechanism that will deliver **broad-band ISDN** services. ATM is the switching architecture ensuring that video, voice, data, and image packets delivered by **B-ISDN** services are delivered to the proper destination. Together, ATM and SONET form the underlying network architecture of the B-ISDN of the future. ATM provides the cell relay switching fabric providing bandwidth on demand for intermittent data from any source (voice, video, etc.) while SONET's Synchronous Payload Envelope provides empty boxcars for ATM's cargo. Simply stated, SONET possesses the flexibility to carry multiple types of data cargo (voice, video, and so on) simultaneously, and ATM has the ability to switch multiple types of data simultaneously. The fact that the complementary nature of the two architectures produce a network service known as B-ISDN should come as no surprise.

Much of the excitement concerning B-ISDN is due to its ability to support existing services (T-1, T-3), emerging services (SMDS, frame relay), future services (HDTV, medical imaging), and services as yet undiscovered. B-ISDN should be the service that finally delivers true bandwidth on demand in a uncomplicated, transparent, and hopefully affordable manner.

SUMMARY

In order to understand the basic technical principles of wide area networking, one must start by looking at the basic business principles of wide area networking. In wide area networking, as in most areas of business, the desire to maximize the impact of any investment in technology is a central focus.

The two most basic principles involved in sharing a single data link among multiple sessions are packetizing and multiplexing. Packetizing is the segmenting of data transmissions between devices into structured blocks or packets of data that contain enough "overhead" or management information in addition to the transmitted data itself, to ensure delivery of the packet of data to its intended destination. Multiplexing then takes this packetized data and sends it over a shared wide area connection along with other packetized data from other sources.

An overall wide area network architecture is a simple model defining how packetizing, multiplexing, and other wide area networking principles combine to create all of the current and emerging wide area networking technologies and services. Switching architectures and transmission architectures combine to enable network services.

Packet switching and circuit switching are the two major categories of switching architectures. Transmission architectures include local loop transmission alternatives such as POTS, ISDN, ADSL, and cable. Broadband transmission alternatives include T-1, T-3, and SONET. Among the network services enabled by these switching and transmission architectures are X.25, frame relay, SMDS, ATM, and broadband ISDN.

It is important to note that there is no single best network service for all applications. Network analysts must carefully match business applications to appropriate network services through careful and thorough analysis of data traffic as well as business objectives.

KEY TERMS

23B+D

2B+D

30B+D

Access line

Asymmetric digital subscriber line (ADSL)

Asynchronous transfer mode

AT&T 5ESS Switch

ATM

ATM access switches

ATM adaptation layer (AAL)

ATM gateway switches

ATM LAN emulation

Automatic number identification

Available bit rate (ABR)

Backward explicit congestion notification (BECN)

Bandwidth on demand interoperability group (BONDING)

Basic rate interface (BRI)

Bearer channels

Bit error rate (BER)

Broadband ISDN (B-ISDN)

Broadband transmission

Call setup packets

Carrierless amplitude and phase (CAP)

Cell relay

Central clock

Circuit-switched network

Circuit switching

Clear request packet

Committed burst size (CBS)

Committed information rate (CIR)

Composite message frame

Connectionless

Connection-oriented

Constant bit rate (CBR)

Customer premises equipment (CPE)

Cyclical redundancy check (CRC)

D-4

Data over voice

Datagrams

D channel

Digital service hierarchy

Discard eligibility (DE)

Discrete multitone (DMT)

Distributed queue dual bus (DQDB)

DS

DS-1

DSE

E-1

Error correction

Error detection

Extended superframe (ESF)

EZ-ISDN

FCS

FDM

Flow control

Forward explicit congestion notification (FECN)

Fractional T-1

Fractional T-1 multiplexers

FAD

Frame check sequence

Frame relay

Frame relay access device (FRAD)

Frame relay switch

Frames

Framing

Framing bit

Frequency division multiplexing
FT-1
Global address
Guardbands
High-level data link control
    (HDLC)
IEEE 802.14
IEEE 802.6
In-band signaling
Interface specification
Inverse multiplexing
IOC
ISDN
ISDN ordering codes
ISDN switch
ISDN terminal adapters
Link access procedure–balanced
    (LAP-B)
Link access procedure–D channel
    (LAP-D)
Local loop transmission
Logical channel
Logical channel number
Multiplexing
Multirate ISDN
Narrowband ISDN
National ISDN-1
Network architecture
Network-to-network interface
Network service
Network termination unit—1
    (NTU-1)
NISDN-1
NNI

Northern Telecom DMS100 Switch
NT-1
OC-1
Octet
Optical carrier (OC)
Out-of-band signaling
Packet assembler/disassembler
    (PAD)
Packetizing
Packet layer protocol (PLP)
Packet-switched network
Packet switches
Packet switching
Payload
Periodic framing
Permanent virtual circuit (PVC)
Polling
POTS
PSE
Public data network (PDN)
Rate-adaptive DSL (RADSL)
Reliable
RJ48c
SDSL
Service profile identifier numbers
Sinks
SMDS
SONET
SONET superframe
SPE
SPID
Statistical time division
    multiplexing (STDM)
Store-and-forward

STS-1
Superframe
SVC
Switched multimegabit data service
Switched virtual circuit
Switching
Switching architecture
Symmetric DSL
Synchronous optical network
Synchronous payload envelope
Synchronous TDM
T-1
T-1 channel bank
T-1 CSU/DSU
T-1 inverse multiplexer (T-1 IMUX)
T-1 multiplexers
T-1 switches
Time division multiplexing (TDM)
Time slot
Transmission architecture
Unreliable
User demands
User network interface (UNI)
Variable bit rate (VBR)
Very high speed DSL (VDSL)
Virtual circuits
Virtual circuit table
Virtual tributary (VT)
VT1.5
Wavelength division multiplexing
    (WDM)
X.25

REVIEW QUESTIONS

1. Differentiate the following multiplexing techniques in terms of mechanics, technology, and application:
    a. Frequency division multiplexing
    b. Time division multiplexing
    c. Statistical time division multiplexing
2. Are multiplexers from different manufacturers interoperable? If not, why not?
3. What limitations in network design or operation would a lack of interoperability cause?
4. What are some of the technological differences between an X.25 network and a frame relay network?
5. What are some of the performance or architectural differences between an X.25 network and a frame relay network?

6. What are frame relay's underlying assumptions regarding transmission media and bit error rates?
7. What types of information are included in packets other than the actual data message itself?
8. How is it possible with a DOV unit that the voice and data don't necessarily have to share the same destination?
9. What are the key shortcomings of TDM, and how does STDM seek to overcome these?
10. What is polling, and what does it have to do with multiplexer efficiency?
11. What is the difference between switching and transmission, and how do the two architectures complement each other?
12. What is the difference between circuit switching and packet switching?

13. What is the difference between a packet assembler/disassembler and a packet switch?

14. What are the positive and negative aspects of a datagram delivery service?

15. What is the difference between connectionless and connection-oriented packet services in terms of overhead, physical transmission path, and reliability?

16. What do connection-oriented services use in place of global addressing?

17. What overhead is involved with the establishment and maintenance of logical channel numbers?

18. What are the differences between PVCs and SVCs in terms of establishment, maintenance, and termination?

19. Which part of the packet-switched network does X.25 actually define?

20. What is meant by the term "bursty data," and what unique transmission challenge does it pose?

21. What is the most common source of intermittent bursts of data?

22. Name the major components of the wide area network architecture and the significance of each.

23. Give examples of switching and transmission architectures in today's network architectures.

24. Differentiate X.25 and frame relay in terms of error control.

25. How is flow control handled in a frame relay network?

26. What is the significance of frame relay's variable-length frames in terms of types of payloads that can be effectively delivered?

27. Why is dynamic allocation of bandwidth an important feature of frame relay?

28. Why is multiple PVCs per access line an important feature of frame relay?

29. What are the primary differences between frame relay and cell relay in terms of architecture and network performance?

30. What is the relationship between cell relay and ATM?

31. Differentiate CBR, VBR, and ABR in terms of architecture and applications.

32. What is the purpose of the AAL protocols?

33. What are the differences between ISDN and B-ISDN?

34. What are the differences between POTS and ISDN?

35. What have been the traditional stumbling blocks to widespread ISDN deployment, and what progress has been made in overcoming these?

36. What is SONET, and where does it fit in the wide area network architecture?

37. What unique performance characteristics does SONET offer, and what type of application might require such characteristics?

38. What is the difference between a T-1 and an E-1?

39. Differentiate the following: time slot, frame, superframe, ESF.

40. What is the significance of NISDN-1?

41. What is the difference between DS-1 and T-1?

42. What is fractional T-1, and what is the business motivation behind such a service?

43. What is ADSL, and what performance characteristics does it offer subscribers?

44. Why might carriers be especially interested in deploying ADSL services?

45. What are some other potential DSL services, and how do they differ from ADSL?

46. What are some of the limitations facing the widespread use of cable modems?

47. What are the roles of the virtual tributaries in SONET?

48. What is B-ISDN, and what switching and transmission architectures does it require?

49. What are some of the services that may be supported by B-ISDN?

50. What is the purpose of the D channel in ISDN?

51. What is the difference between BRI and PRI ISDN?

52. What is inverse multiplexing, and what applications are well suited to it?

53. What is SMDS, and why has it not been adopted as widely as frame relay?

ACTIVITIES

1. Contact your local phone carrier. Is ISDN available in your area? What are the nonrecurring and monthly charges for service? What are the performance guarantees? What special equipment is required? What is the cost of such equipment, and must it be purchased from the carrier? Are both PRI and BRI services available? What intelligent services are available via ISDN? Can all 128 Kbps be used?

2. Contact your local phone carrier. Is ADSL available in your area? What are the nonrecurring and monthly charges for service? What are the performance guarantees? What special equipment is required? What is the cost of such equipment,

and must it be purchased from the carrier? Is Internet access available? For an additional cost?

3. Contact your local cable television provider. Is cable modem service available in your area? What are the nonrecurring and monthly charges for service? What are the performance guarantees? What special equipment is required? What is the cost of such equipment, and must it be purchased from the carrier? Is Internet access available? For an additional cost?

4. Gather articles on ATM from trade journals. Create a bulletin board or prepare a research topic summarizing the current issues facing ATM, focusing particularly on obstacles to widespread deployment, such as the pace of the standards development process.

5. Contact the ATM Forum and request literature concerning current standards development activities.

6. Investigate the installation and on-going costs of an X.25 packet-switched service. What are the performance limitations?

7. Investigate the installation and ongoing costs of a frame relay packet-switched service. What are the performance limitations?

8. How are frame relay services tariffed in your local area? How are committed information rates and committed burst size negotiated? Is zero CIR available? What happens if you exceed your CIR?

How do frame relay CIRs compare with X.25 transmission speeds?

9. Choose two cities within your LATA (local access transport area). Contact your local carrier for a quote on the cost of a leased line between these two cities. Compare pricing for both analog and digital lines of various sizes. Are switched digital services available? What are the installation and recurring costs?

10. Now choose another city just outside your local LATA. Contact several long-distance carriers for the information you requested in question 9. How do the quotes from the various long-distance companies compare? How do the long-distance carrier quotes compare to the local carrier quotes? What was the impact on cost of leaving your LATA? Did recurring or nonrecurring costs increase more? Explain your results.

11. Can your local carrier now offer inter-LATA data services thanks to the Telecommunications Act of 1996?

12. Research the wavelength division multiplexing technology market. How large is the market currently? What are the expected growth rates over the next five years? Who are the major vendors? Who are the major customers? How exactly does WDM work? Report on the results of your research.

CHAPTER 10

CASE STUDY

WESTCORP BRACING FOR RAPID UPGRADE

Three-Person Staff to Handle Six-Month WAN Project

Dan Erfurt isn't a man to back down from a challenge. His latest directive? Upgrade his company's nationwide, 210-site WAN with a new service provider and new routers in six months, with a staff of three network technicians to help him.

"If you can imagine managing 210 sites with three guys, the integration issues are pretty over-

whelming," says Erfurt, vice president of network services at West-Corp Financial Services, a $33 million company in Irvine, Calif. "When you come up against a major migration where you have to change every site in a short period of time, you come to grips with reality pretty quickly."

Erfurt should know. He's had a lot of reality checks to deal with lately. In addition to the WAN, he and his staff oversee a LAN at the company's headquarters that supports another 600 users and 1,100 PCs. Erfurt and crew just carried out a major upgrade to the LAN

that included a migration from 10Base-T precursor SynOptics Communications Inc. LattisNet to fast Ethernet spread across two buildings.

The WAN project, which is now under way, is no minor challenge either. A big bottom-line push to improve efficiency has created a real sense of urgency behind West-Corp's rapid WAN upgrade. The company's contract with its current frame-relay service provider is expiring, and while shopping around, the company found a better deal with MCI Communications Corp. By combining voice and data traffic on MCI lines, WestCorp stands to save $500,000 a year.

Meanwhile, Cisco Systems Inc. PC-based router cards that sit in remote sites are being discontinued. A trade-in allowance on the router cards as well as the better management capabilities of Cisco's rack-mounted routers convinced West-Corp to upgrade its remote sites. "Our current routers are not made to scale to large networks," says Erfurt. Given the speed and scope of the WAN upgrade at hand, neither is his team.

Because of this realization, Erfurt has opted for third-party help: Unisys Global Customer Services, the systems-integration division of Unisys Corp. in Blue Bell, Penn. The $2 billion integrator brings to the upgrade "feet on the street and one throat to choke," says Erfurt, referring to its global network of field representatives who can be dispatched to WestCorp's remote sites at a moment's notice.

Although WestCorp needed a systems-integration partner and a new wide-area service provider, it decided to stay with its wide-area service. Frame relay fits the company's nationwide network perfectly. The company runs 56Kbps to 256Kbps fractional T-1 links at its remote sites, which can have between 10 and 100 users. Host circuits at the company's Irvine headquarters are full T-1 1.5Mbps. The traffic running over the lines includes telnet and remote-control sessions for remote users running mission-critical automobile-financing applications at the Irvine office.

"We analyze the bandwidth utilization routinely," says Erfurt. "It is very acceptable, if not overkill. When users complain about response time from a remote location, it's usually due to distance-related latency." He adds that the wide-area response time of IPX traffic generated by his roughly 2,600 Novell Inc. NetWare clients cannot be improved by increasing bandwidth.

The decision to stay with frame relay was also made on the merits of the technology itself. Private-line networks require one router port for each remote site; more if West-Corp wants redundancy. With the frame-relay network the company averages one host router port for every 33 branch offices. Redundancy is built into the frame-relay cloud, so if a circuit between any two points has a problem, the traffic is automatically routed to an alternate path.

Finally, WestCorp says there is a strategic advantage in continuing to use T-1 frame-relay links. Going forward, the company envisions carrying voice, data, and video over the circuits. Video applications might include video-based training and other internal applications as well as external consumer applications. The company's mortgage banking group, for instance, is investigating video teleconferencing for home-loan services at remote offices. "Video is a glimmer in our eye," admits Erfurt, "but things come at us in a really rapid speed here."

Rapid Rollout   Today WestCorp is in the middle of its rollout. At the end of February [1997] the first six remote sites had been brought online. The rest should be up by the end of June [1997], coming online at the rate of five a week. The key to the rollout is handing over as much of the tactical deployment to Unisys as possible, enabling it to act as the central point of contact and control for the upgrade effort. This frees Erfurt and his staff to concentrate on core business concerns, including how to make best use of the new WAN infrastructure once it's in place. It also gives Erfurt the opportunity to oversee the plethora of other network deployments and upgrades in progress at WestCorp.

For its part, Unisys has taken on much of the project manager's role that Erfurt previously had, overseeing configuration, staging, and asset

tagging for the WAN upgrade. Unisys is also responsible for staffing the project from the ranks of its 200 onsite technicians.

This level of precision is possible because all technicians on the job are Unisys employees. Consequently, a high level of communication has been established among all involved in the WestCorp rollout. A Lotus Notes database holds the configuration information for every site, escalation procedures, contact information for WestCorp and Unisys, and nationwide alert policies. The intention is to let any authorized Unisys representative access the Notes database on the fly and fix a problem. The ultimate goal, says Dave Dragonetti, regional director at Unisys in Costa Mesa, Calif., is to have every level of the network upgrade scheduled down to the hour, technology, and technician. "We can't have someone sitting onsite waiting for a circuit to come up," he explains.

For instance, a key component of the upgrade methodology is the configuration and staging of the Cisco routers. Instead of deploying unconfigured routers and sending out Unisys technicians to configure these at each remote site, Unisys builds the designs and configurations on a server and downloads that information, along with multiple IP addresses from a central site, to each router. "That way, we can roll out a live router that can do 95 percent of the job. Then we go in remotely and update the configurations based on what we see as we start scaling the network," explains Dragonetti.

Another key to the upgrade is Unisys' approach to the frame relay-circuit switch-over—moving from the old frame-relay provider to MCI. To minimize the cost of running two circuits simultaneously at a site, Dragonetti cancels the old circuit well before the MCI circuit is installed.

"[The old service provider] has a 30-day cancellation policy. So we start cancelling them about 25 days before the MCI turn-up date," says Dragonetti. "That can save them close to a month's worth of billing at 200-plus sites."

But it gives MCI only five days to bring up the circuit. What happens if MCI can't deliver on time? "I can always reinstate the old circuit about five days before cancellation," he says. "I just cancel the cancel order."

Worth noting is that Unisys not only shoulders the burden for most of the WAN infrastructure upgrade, but the systems integrator also interfaces with MCI. That means the work MCI does to help WestCorp size and optimize its network is filtered through Unisys. This includes ongoing optimization and load bal-

ancing. In effect, Unisys becomes the customer.

The telco side of the upgrade is the only area Dragonetti readily admits is basically out of the integrator's hands. Although MCI can control the frame-relay portion of the WAN, the other services are more volatile. Analog lines are needed for remote T-1 management, and ISDN service will be necessary for disaster-recovery backup. To deal with this, Unisys is having to contact every local regional Bell operating company (RBOC) or Postal, Telephone, and Telegraph (PTT) company to get service, and the quality of that service—especially installation—can fluctuate wildly with the expertise of local technicians. As a result, Dragonetti is expecting that

about 15 percent of WestCorp's remote sites will encounter a problem, such as incorrect information on an ISDN line or an uninstalled modem line, by the time the project is finished.

With the deployment methodology in place, the trickiest part of WestCorp's WAN upgrade is behind the company. The key to completing the nationwide job successfully and on time will depend on Unisys' actual implementation of its planning, methodologies, and project management. At this point, Erfurt and his staff are ready to concentrate on other network issues. "The objective is to turn as much of this over to Unisys as possible," says Erfurt. "That frees us to handle the things that fall through the cracks."

Source: Brent Dorshkind, "WestCorp Bracing for Rapid Upgrade," *LAN Times* (March 31, 1997), Copyright March 31, 1997, The McGraw-Hill Companies, Inc.

BUSINESS CASE STUDY QUESTIONS ⋯⋯⋯⋯⋯⋯⋯⋯⋯⋯⋯⋯⋯⋯⋯⋯⋯⋯⋯⋯⋯⋯⋯⋯⋯⋯

Activities

1. Complete a top-down model for this case by gleaning facts from the case and placing them in the proper layer of the top-down model. After having completed the top-down model, analyze and detail those instances where requirements were clearly passed down from upper layers to lower layers of the model and where solutions to those requirements were passed up from lower layers to upper layers of the model.
2. Detail any questions about the case that may occur to you for which answers are not clearly stated in the article.

Business

1. What business activities were carried out by this organization?
2. What were the business layer requirements or constraints that were dictated regarding the network upgrade?
3. What was the solution that met these business layer requirements?
4. What was the potential savings by combining both voice and data over frame relay?
5. What types of future business services could have a significant impact on the future network demands?

Application

1. What type of applications are run at remote sites and at headquarters?

Data

1. What network operating system and network and transport layer protocols are used in this network?
2. What types of traffic does the company envision carrying over the WAN in the future?

Network

1. How many sites were on the WestCorp WAN?
2. How many users and nodes are on the WestCorp LAN?
3. What is the LAN network architecture (data link layer protocol)?
4. Which WAN service is currently employed?
5. What was the bandwidth of the various circuits at remote sites and at headquarters?

Technology

1. How did the current router technology affect the upgrade plan?
2. How is redundancy ensured in a private line versus frame relay network?
3. How are analog (POTS) and ISDN lines used in the network?
4. Is there a problem with ordering these services?

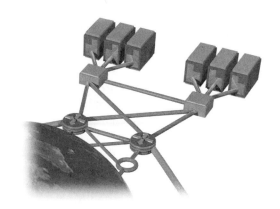

CHAPTER 11

REMOTE ACCESS AND WIRELESS NETWORKING

Concepts Reinforced

OSI Model
Top-Down Model
Internetwork Design
Network Operating Systems

Internet Suite of Protocols Model
Protocols and Compatibility
Internetworking Technology

Concepts Introduced

Remote Access
Remote Node
Remote Access Security
Wireless WAN services
Remote Access Network Design

Remote Control
Mobile Computing
Wireless LANs
Remote Access Technology

OBJECTIVES

After mastering the material in this chapter, you should understand the following:

1. The difference between and proper application of remote node versus remote control computing

2. The business motivation behind the need for remote access network design

3. The importance of and networking implication of mobile computing

4. How to successfully design logical and physical topologies for remote access networks, including wireless LAN and WAN services

5. How to evaluate remote access technology including hardware, software, and WAN services

6. The unique security issues introduced by remote access and mobile computing

▨ INTRODUCTION

In order to understand the importance of remote access and wireless technology, it is first important to appreciate the business forces that have created the increased demand for such technology.

One of the most important things to understand about LAN remote access is the relatively limited bandwidth of the wide area network links that individuals will use to connect to corporate information resources. Although the goal of LAN remote access may be to offer transparent remote LAN connectivity, decreases in bandwidth by a factor of 100 on WAN links as compared to LAN links cannot be ignored.

The overall goal of this chapter is to outline a methodology for the proper design of remote access solutions based on a thorough understanding of user needs, network architecture alternatives, available technology, and available WAN services.

Managerial Perspective

BUSINESS ISSUES OF REMOTE ACCESS

As information has come to be seen as a corporate asset to be leveraged to competitive advantage, the delivery of that information to users working at remote locations has become a key internetworking challenge. Corporate downsizing has not only increased remaining employees' responsibilities, but pushed those responsibilities ever closer to the corporation's customers. As a result, the voice mail message, "I'll be virtual all day today," is becoming more and more common. The business-oriented motivations for remote access to local LAN resources fall into three general categories: telecommuting, mobile computing, and technical support.

The first category of remote LAN access is **telecommuting,** or more simply, working from home with all the information resources of the office LAN at one's fingertips. This category of connectivity and computing is often referred to as **SOHO,** or **small office home office.**

Studies have indicated that the following are some of the ways in which telecommuting can increase overall worker productivity:

- Better, quicker, more effective customer service

- Increased on-time project completion and quicker product development

- Increased job satisfaction among highly mobile employees, which can lead to both greater productivity and employee retention

- Decreased worker turnover, leading to decreased training and recruiting budgets

- Increased sales

A variation of telecommuting, **mobile computing,** addresses the need for field representatives to be able to access corporate information resources in order to offer superior customer service while working on the road. These field representatives may or may not have a corporate office PC into which to dial.

Although some of the positive results of enabling remote access to corporate data for mobile workers are similar to those of telecommuters, the increased customer focus of the mobile worker is evident in the following benefits:

- Faster responses to customer inquiries

- Improved communications with coworkers and support staff at corporate offices

- Better, more effective customer support

- Increased personal productivity by the mobile workers, such as being able to complete more sales calls

- Increased ability to be "on the road" in front of customers

- Ability for service personnel to operate more efficiently

The third major usage of remote computing is use for **technical support** organizations, which must be able to dial in to client systems and appear as a local workstation or take control of those workstations, in order to diagnose and correct problems remotely. Being able to diagnose and solve problems remotely can have significant impacts:

- Quicker response to customer problems

- Increased ability to handle problems without sending service personnel for on-site visits

- More-efficient use of subject matter experts and service personnel

- Increased ability to avoid revisits to customer sites owing to a lack of proper parts

- Greater customer satisfaction

The worldwide market for remote access technology in 1998 was expected to reach $3.7 billion, growing at a rate of 27 percent per year.

THE HIDDEN COSTS OF TELECOMMUTING

Managerial Perspective

To fully understand the total costs involved in supporting telecommuters, one must first understand which employees are doing the telecommuting. Telecommuting employees generally fall into one of the following categories:

- Full-time, day shift, at-home workers

- After-hours workers who have a corporate office but choose to extend the workday by working remotely from home during evenings and weekends

Most studies indicate that more than 75 percent of telecommuters are the occasional, after-hours variety. However, corporate costs to set up and support these occasional users are nearly equal to the costs for setting up and supporting full-time at-home users—over $4000 per year. Among the hidden costs to be considered when evaluating the cost/benefit of telecommuting are the following:

- Workers may not be within local calling area of corporate resources, thereby incurring long distance charges.

- Workers may need to add wiring from street to home or within home to support additional phone lines.

- If existing phone lines are used, personnel time is used to sort personal calls from business calls.

- In order to provide sufficient bandwidth, more expensive ISDN lines are often installed, if they are available.

- Some applications, especially those not optimized for remote access, run very slowly over dial-up lines, leading to decreased productivity.

◾ ARCHITECTURAL ISSUES OF REMOTE ACCESS

There are basically only four steps to designing a dial-in/dial-out capability for a local LAN:

- Needs analysis

- Logical topology choice

- Physical topology choice

- Current technology review and implementation

These steps are explained in the following sections.

Logical Design Issues

Needs Analysis   As dictated by the top-down model, before designing network topologies and choosing technology, determine what is to be accomplished in terms of LAN-based applications and use of other LAN-attached resources. Among the most likely possibilities for the information sharing needs of remote users are the following:

- Exchange e-mail

- Upload and download files

- Run interactive application programs remotely

- Utilize LAN-attached resources

The purpose in examining information sharing needs in this manner is to validate the need for the remote PC user to establish a connection to the local LAN, which offers all of the capabilities of locally attached PCs.

In other words, if the ability to upload and download files is the extent of the remote PC user's information sharing needs, then file transfer software, often included in asynchronous communications software packages, would suffice at a very reasonable cost. A network-based bulletin-board service (BBS) package is another way in which information can be shared by remote users easily. Likewise, if e-mail exchange is the total information-sharing requirement, then e-mail gateway software loaded on the LAN would meet that requirement.

However, in order to run LAN-based interactive application programs or to use LAN-attached resources such as high-speed printers, CD-ROMs, mainframe connections, or fax servers, a full-powered remote connection to the local LAN must be established. From the remote user's standpoint, this connection must offer transparency. In other words, the remote PC should behave as if it were connected locally to the LAN. From the LAN's perspective, the remote user's PC should behave as if it were locally attached.

Logical Topology Choice: Remote Node versus Remote Control   In terms of logical topology choices, two different logical methods for connection of remote PCs to LANs are possible. Each method has advantages, disadvantages, and proper usage situations. The two major remote PC operation mode possibilities are as follows:

- **Remote node**

- **Remote control**

The term *remote access* is most often used to describe the process of linking remote PCs to local LANs without implying the particular functionality of that link (remote node versus remote control). Unfortunately, the term is also sometimes more specifically used as a synonym for remote node.

Figure 11-1 outlines some of the details, features, and requirements of these two remote PC modes of operation. Figure 11-2 highlights the differences between remote node and remote control installations.

Remote node, or remote client, computing implies that the remote client PC should be able to operate as if it were locally attached to network resources. In other words, the geographic separation between the remote client and the local LAN resources should be transparent. That's a good theory, but in practice, the comparative bandwidth of a typical dial-up link (33.6 Kbps for a V.34+ modem), as compared with the Mbps bandwidth of the LAN, is anything but transparent. Whereas a NIC would normally plug directly into an expansion slot in a computer, a remote node connection merely extends that link via a relatively low speed dial-up link. Client applications run on the remote client rather than a local LAN-attached client.

Client/server applications that require large transfers of data between client and server will not run well in remote node mode. Most successful remote node

Functional Characteristic	Remote Node	Remote Control
Also Called	Remote client Remote LAN node	Modem remote control
Redirector hardware/software required?	Yes	No
Traffic Characteristics	All client/server traffic	Keystrokes and screen images
Application Processing	On the remote PC	On the LAN-attached local PC
Relative Speed	Slower	Faster
Logical Role of WAN Link	Extends connection to NIC	Extends keyboard and monitor cables
Best Use	With specially written remote client applications optimized for execution over limited bandwidth WAN links	DOS applications because graphics on Windows applications can make response time unacceptable

Figure 11-1   Remote Node versus Remote Control Functional Characteristics

Remote Access

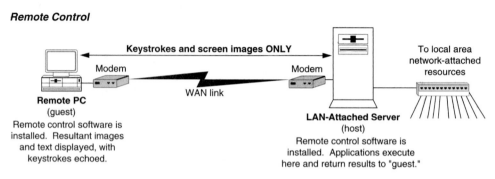

Figure 11-2 Remote Node versus Remote Control Installations

applications are rewritten to minimize large data transfers. For example, modified remote node e-mail client software allows just the headers of received messages—which include sender, subject, and date/time—to be transferred from the local e-mail server to the remote client. The remote client selects which e-mail messages should have the actual e-mail message body and attachments transferred. Local e-mail client software, which assumes plenty of LAN bandwidth, does not bother with such bandwidth conserving modifications. Other client/server applications must be similarly modified if they are to execute acceptably in remote node mode.

Although transparent interoperability was discussed as one of the goals of remote access, that does not necessarily mean that a worker's mobile computer programs must be identical to those running on one's desktop at the price of terrible performance. One of the most commonly overlooked aspects in deploying remote access solutions is the need to customize applications for optimal performance in a remote access environment.

Remote node mode requires a full client network operating system protocol stack to be installed on the remote client. In addition, wide area network communication software must be incorporated with the remote client NOS protocol stack. Remote node software often also includes optional support of remote control functionality.

Remote control differs from remote node mode both in the technology involved and in the degree to which existing LAN applications must be modified. In remote control mode, the remote PC is merely supplying input and output devices for the local client, which interacts as normal with the local server and other locally attached LAN resources. Client applications still run on the local client, which is able to communicate with the local server at native LAN speeds, thereby precluding the need to rewrite client applications for remote client optimization.

Remote control mode requires only remote control software to be installed at the remote PC rather than a full NOS client protocol stack compatible with the NOS installed at the local LAN. The purpose of the remote control software is only to extend the input/output capabilities of the local client out to the keyboard and monitor attached to the remote PC. The host version of the same remote control package must be installed at the host or local PC. There are no interoperability standards for remote control software.

One of the most-significant difficulties with remote control software is confusion by end users as to logical disk assignments. Recalling that the remote PC supplies only the keyboard and monitor functionality, remote users fail to realize that a C: prompt refers to the C: drive on the local LAN-attached PC and not the C: drive of the remote PC they are using. This can be particularly confusing with file transfer applications.

Protocols and Compatibility   At least some of the shortcomings of both remote node and remote control modes are caused by the underlying transport protocols responsible for delivering data across the WAN link.

In the case of remote control, the fact that proprietary protocols are used between the guest and host remote control software is the reason that remote control software from various vendors is not interoperable.

In the case of remote node, redirector software in the protocol stack must take LAN-based messages from the NDIS or ODI protocols and convert them into proper format for transmission over asynchronous serial WAN links.

Some remote node software uses TCP/IP as its protocol stack and PPP (point-to-point protocol) as its data link layer WAN protocol. In this manner, remote node sessions can be easily established via TCP/IP, even using the Internet as the connecting WAN service should that connection satisfy the security needs of the company in question. Once the TCP/IP link is established, the remote control mode of this software can be executed over TCP/IP as well, overcoming the proprietary protocols typically associated with remote control programs. In addition, with PPP's ability to transport upper layer protocols other than TCP/IP, these remote node clients can support communications with a variety of different servers.

Figure 11-3 illustrates the protocol-related issue of typical remote control and remote node links as well as TCP/IP based links.

Security   Although security from an enterprisewide perspective will be dealt with in Chapter 13, security issues specifically related to remote access of corporate information resources are introduced here. Security-related procedures can be logically grouped into the following categories:

- Password assignment and management: Change passwords frequently; consider single-use passwords. Passwords should not be actual words found in a dictionary, but should ideally be a random or meaningless combination of letters and numbers.

- Intrusion responses: User accounts should be locked after a preset number of unsuccessful logins. These accounts should only be able to be unlocked by a system administrator.

- Logical/physical partitioning of data: Separate public, private, and confidential data onto separate physical servers to avoid giving users with minimum security clearances unauthorized access to sensitive or confidential data.

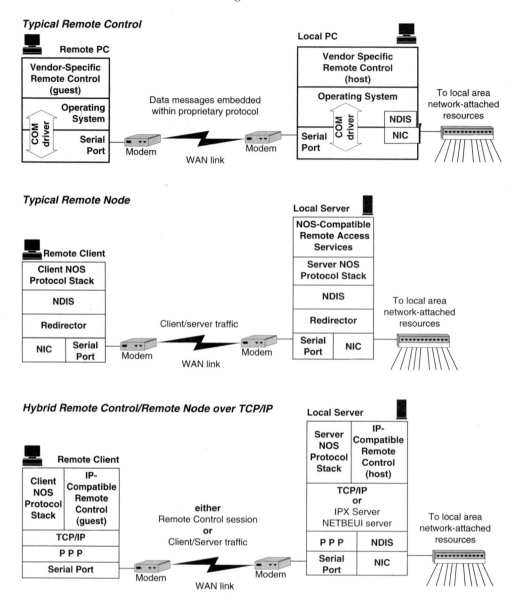

Figure 11-3 Protocol Issues of Remote Control and Remote Node Links

- Encryption: Although it is important for any sensitive or proprietary corporate data to be encrypted, it is especially important that passwords be encrypted to avoid interception and unauthorized reuse.

- Dial-back systems: After remote users enter proper UserID and passwords, these systems terminate the call and dial the authorized user back at preprogrammed phone numbers.

- Remote client software authentication protocols: Remote client protocol stacks often include software-based authentication protocols such as PAP (password authentication protocol) or CHAP (challenge handshake authentication protocol).

One remote access security category that deserves further explanation is hardware-based **token authentication.** Although exact implementation details may vary from one vendor to the next, all token authentication systems include server components linked to the communications server, and client components used with the remote access clients. Physically, the token authentication device employed at the remote client location may be a hand-held device resembling a calculator or a floppy disk, or it may be an in-line device linked to the remote client's serial or parallel port. Figure 11-4 illustrates the physical topology of a typical hardware-based token authentication remote access security arrangement.

TOKEN AUTHENTICATION

In Sharper Focus

Logically, token authentication schemes work in either of two different ways:

- **Token response** authentication schemes work as follows:
    1. Remote user dials in and enters private identification number (PIN).
    2. Authentication server responds with a challenge number.
    3. Remote user enters that number into hand-held client authentication unit, or it is received automatically by in-line client authentication unit.
    4. Client authentication unit generates challenge response number, which is either automatically transmitted back to the authentication server or entered manually by the remote user.
    5. Transmitted challenge response is received by the authentication server and compared with the expected challenge response number generated at the server. If they match, the user is authenticated and allowed access to network-attached resources.

- **Time-synchronous** authentication schemes work as follows:
    1. Random authentication numbers are generated in time-synchronous fashion at both the authentication server and client.
    2. Remote user enters PIN and the current random authentication number displayed on the client authentication unit.

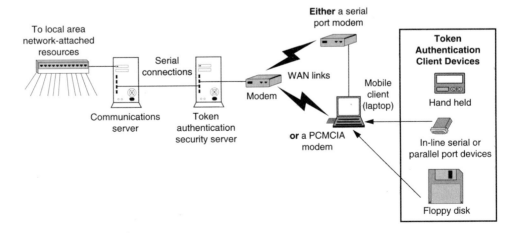

Figure 11-4   Token Authentication Physical Topology

3. With time synchronization, the server authentication unit should have the same current random authentication number, which is compared with the one transmitted from the remote client.

4. If the two authentication numbers match, the authentication server authenticates the user and allows access to the network-attached resources.

A few other important operational issues concerning token authentication security systems for remote access are as follows:

- Most authentication servers have a management console that provides supervisory access to the authentication security system. Transmission between the management console and the authentication server should be encrypted.

- Valid passwords and UserIDs may be stored either on the management console or on the authentication server. In either case, security-related data such as userIDs and passwords should be stored in encrypted form.

- The authentication server's response to failed attempts at remote login should include both account disabling and the ability to generate an alarm, preferably both audible and as a data message to the management console. Ideally, the authentication server should pass alarms seamlessly to enterprise management systems via SNMP to avoid having separate management consoles for every management function.

- Although this functionality is also supplied by such remote access server products as Windows NT RAS, the authentication server should also be able to limit access from remote users to certain times of day or days of the week.

- As can be seen in Figure 11-4, the authentication server must be able to transparently interoperate with the communications or remote access server. This fact should not be assumed, but demonstrated or guaranteed by the authentication server vendor.

Physical Design Issues

Physical Topology: Alternative Access Points   As Figure 11-5 illustrates, there are three basic ways in which a remote PC user can gain access to the local LAN resources.

- Serial port of a LAN-attached PC: Perhaps the simplest physical topology or remote access arrangement is to establish a communications link to a user PC located in the corporate office. However, many field representative or mobile computing users no longer have permanent offices and workstations at a corporate building and must depend on remote access to shared computing resources.

- Communications server: As an alternative to having a dedicated PC at the corporate office for each remote user to dial into, remote users could attach to a dedicated multiuser server, known as an **access server** or **communications server,** through one or more modems. Depending on the software loaded on the communications server, it may deliver remote node functionality, remote control functionality, or both.

Access Point 1: Serial Port of LAN-Attached PC

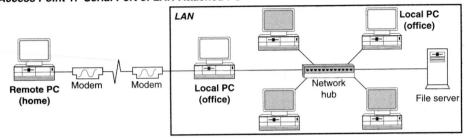

Access Point 2: Communications Server

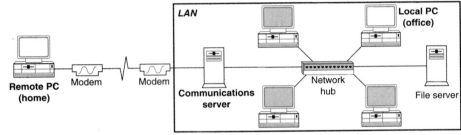

Access Point 3: LAN Modems

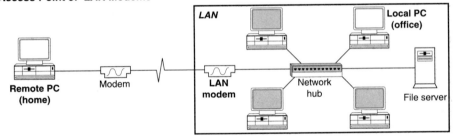

Figure 11-5   Physical Topology: Alternative Access Points

- LAN modem: Another alternative is to install a specialized device known as a **LAN modem,** also known as a **dial-in server,** to offer shared remote access to LAN resources. LAN modems come with all necessary software preinstalled and therefore do not require additional remote control or remote node software. LAN modems are often limited to a single network architecture such as ethernet or token ring, or to a single network operating system protocol such as IP, IPX (NetWare), NetBIOS, NetBEUI, or Appletalk.

The physical topology using the communications server (Figure 11-5, middle diagram) actually depicts two different possible remote LAN connections. Most communications servers answer the modem, validate the UserID and password, and log the remote user onto the network. Some communications servers go beyond this to allow a remote user to access or remotely control a particular networked workstation. This scenario offers the same access capabilities as if the networked workstation had its own modem and software, but it also offers the centralized management, security, and possible financial advantage of a network attached communications server.

The three access arrangements illustrated are examples of possible physical topologies and do not imply a given logical topology such as remote node, remote control, or both. It is important to understand that the actual implementation of each of these LAN access arrangements may require additional hardware, software, or both. They may also be limited in their ability to utilize all LAN-attached resources, or to dial out of the LAN through the same access point.

■ REMOTE ACCESS TECHNOLOGY

Hardware

Communications Servers and Remote Access Servers   As is often the case in the wonderful but confusing world of data communications, communications servers are also known by many other names. In some cases these names may imply, but don't guarantee, variations in configuration, operation, or application. Among these varied labels for the communications server are the following:

- Access servers

- Remote access servers

- Remote node servers

- Telecommuting servers

- Network resource servers

- Modem servers (usually reserved for dial-out only)

- Asynchronous communications servers

A communications server offers both management advantages and financial payback when large numbers of users wish to gain remote access to or from a LAN. Besides the cost savings of a reduced number of modems, phone lines, and software licenses, perhaps more important are the gains in control over the remote access to the LAN and its attached resources. By monitoring the use of the phone lines connected to the communications server, it is easier to determine exactly how many phone lines are required to service those users requiring remote LAN access.

Multiple remote users can dial into a communications server simultaneously. Exactly how many users can gain simultaneous access will vary with the sophistication and cost of the communications server and the installed software. Most communications servers serve at least four simultaneous users.

Figure 11-6 provides an I-P-O (Input-Processing-Output) diagram illustrating options for the key functional components of a communications server.

As can be seen from Figure 11-6, there are three key hardware components of the communications server:

- Serial Ports

- CPU(s)

- Network Interface Card(s)

The relative number of each of these three components included in a particular communications server is a key differentiating factor in communications server ar-

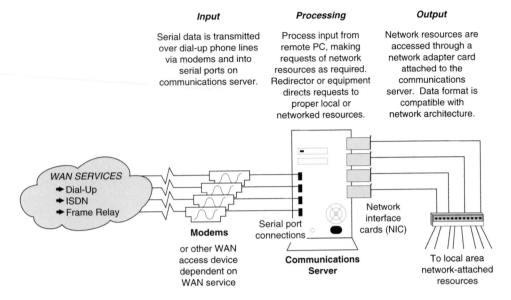

Input	Processing	Output
Serial data is transmitted over dial-up phone lines via modems and into serial ports on communications server.	Process input from remote PC, making requests of network resources as required. Redirector or equipment directs requests to proper local or networked resources.	Network resources are accessed through a network adapter card attached to the communications server. Data format is compatible with network architecture.

WAN SERVICES
→ Dial-Up
→ ISDN
→ Frame Relay

Modems
or other WAN access device dependent on WAN service

Serial port connections

Communications Server

Network interface cards (NIC)

To local area network-attached resources

Figure 11-6   Communications Server Components

chitectures or configurations. Although not guaranteed, the differentiation between communications servers and remote node servers is generally considered the following:

- Communications servers include several CPU boards inside a single enclosure. These servers combine both applications server functionality and remote node server functionality. Applications are physically loaded and executed on the communications server. Communications servers are often used for remote control functionality as an alternative to having several separate desktop PCs available for remote control. Consolidating the CPUs into a single enclosure provides additional fault tolerance and management capabilities over the separate PCs model. Examples of communications servers and vendors are as follows:

Communications Server	Vendor
J&L Chatterbox	J&L Information Systems
CubixConnect Server	Cubix Corp.
CAPServer	Evergreen Systems

- **Remote node servers** are strictly concerned with controlling remote access to LAN-attached resources and acting as a gateway to those resources. Applications services are supplied by the same LAN-attached applications servers that are accessed by locally attached clients.

The functional differences between communications servers and remote node servers are illustrated in Figure 11-7. Currently, remote node server solutions fall into three major categories:

- **Software-only solutions** in which the user supplies a sufficiently powerful server and adds a remote node server software package such as Windows

Communications Server

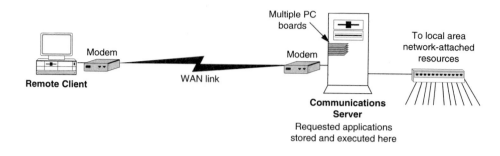

Remote Node Server

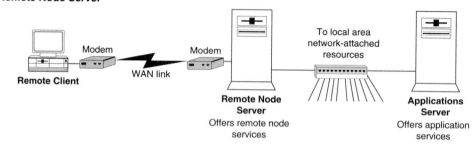

Figure 11-7 Communications Servers versus Remote Node Servers

NT RAS or NetWare Connect or other third-party remote node software package. In some cases, a multiport serial board may be included with the software in order to add sufficient serial ports to the user's server. More information about software-only solutions is offered in the section on remote node software.

- **Turnkey or hardware/software solutions** in which fully configured remote node servers are compatible with existing network architectures and operating systems. Integrated modems may or may not be included. The remote node server software included on these turnkey systems must be compatible with the installed network operating system. Among the more popular remote node servers are the following:

Remote Node Server	Vendor
LANexpress 4000	Microcom
RLN Turnkey Server	Attachmate
LAN Rover Access Switch	Shiva
NetBlazer	Telebit
Total Control Hiper Access System	3Com
Remote Annex 2000	Xylogics
MAX TNT	Ascend Communications
AS5300 Universal Access Server	Cisco
Bay Networks	System 5000

Hawk 2290 Remote Access Server	Access Beyond
RASCAL RS1000	Ariel
CommPlete Communications Server	Multi-Tech
RAServer 2500	RAScom

- **LAN modems,** also occasionally known as dial-up servers, which may be thought of as a remote node server with one or more integrated modems. Included security and management software are also installed on the LAN modem. Given the rapid increase in modem transmission speeds owing to evolving modem transmission standards, integrating a modem that cannot be upgraded within a remote node server may be less beneficial than using external modems, which can be more easily upgraded. Perhaps in response to this need for convenient modem upgrades, some remote node servers now come with four or eight PC card (PCMCIA) slots into which the latest modem technology can be easily inserted. LAN modems are generally included in reviews of remote node servers rather than being looked upon as a distinct product category.

When employing a self-contained remote node server including both hardware and software, take into account compatibility with existing network resources on a number of different levels. These compatibility issues as well as key functional issues of remote node servers are outlined in Figure 11-8.

Remote Node Server Compatibility/Functional Issue	Importance/Implication
Network Architecture Compatibility	• Because the remote node server includes network interface cards, these must be compatible with the network architecture (Ethernet, Token Ring) of the network in which it is to be installed. • Most all remote node servers have Ethernet models; fewer offer Token Ring models. • Media compatibility must also be ensured. For example, Ethernet may use AUI, BNC, or RJ-45 interfaces.
Network Operating System Compatibility	• The remote node server software installed in the server must be compatible with the network operating system installed in the network-attached applications servers. • These are third-party hardware/software turnkey systems, so the remote node server software is not the same as the native software-only solutions such as Windows NT RAS or NetWare Connect, which imply guaranteed compatibility with their respective network operating systems. • The remote node server must also be compatible with the underlying transport protocols used by the installed network operating system. • Can the remote node server access the network operating system's user authorization files to avoid having to build and maintain a second repository of UserIDs and passwords? • In the case of NetWare LANs, integration with NetWare Bindery (3.12) or NDS (4.1) should be provided.

Remote Client Software Compatibility	• The remote node server software must be compatible with the remote node software executed on the remote clients. • This remote client software must be compatible with the native operating system on the remote client. • If compatible remote client software is not supplied with the remote node server, is compatibility with third-party PPP client or remote client software guaranteed? • Cost of remote client software may be included in remote node server purchase cost or may be an additional $50/client.
Physical Configuration	• Number of serial ports: Most models start at 8, and some are expandable up to 128. • Serial port speed: Most support serial port speeds of 110.2 Kbps. Some support speeds of 230.4 Kbps.

Transmission Optimization	• Use of the limited bandwidth WAN link can be optimized in a variety of ways:
	  • Compression: Are both headers and data compressed?
	  • Spoofing: Are chatty protocols restricted from the WAN link?
	  • Are users warned before launching remote applications that may bog down the WAN link and offer poor performance?

Routing Functionality	• Routing functionality would allow LAN-to-LAN or remote server–to–local server connectivity rather than connectivity from a single remote client to the local server. • Routing functionality allows the remote node server to also act as a dial-up router. Dial-up routers must be used in pairs.
WAN Services Supported	• Is connectivity to ISDN, X.25, frame relay as well as dial-up lines supported? • Some remote node servers have high-speed serial ports for connection to higher-speed WAN services such as T-1 (1.544 Mbps).
Call Management	• Are dropped calls automatically redialed? • Can connect-time limits be enforced? • Can status of all remote access calls be viewed and controlled from a single location? • Are event logs and reports generated? • Are status and alarm messages output via SNMP agents? • Is fixed and variable callback supported? • Is encryption supported?

Figure 11-8 Compatibility and Functional Issues of Remote Node Servers

DIALING-OUT FROM THE LAN

Normally, when a modem is connected directly to a PC, the communications software expects to direct information to the local serial port to which the modem is attached. However, in the case of a pool of modems attached to a remote node server, the communications software on the local clients must redirect all information for modems through the locally attached network interface card, across the local LAN, to the remote node server, and ultimately to an attached modem. This ability to redirect information for **dial-out** modem applications from LAN-attached PCs is a cooperative task accomplished by the software of the remote node server and its corresponding remote client software. Not all remote node servers support dial-out functionality.

The required redirection is accomplished through the use of industry standard software redirection interrupts. The interrupts supported or enabled on particular remote node servers can vary:

- **Int14,** or Interrupt 14, is one of the supported dial-out software redirectors and is most often employed by Microsoft network operating systems. Int14 is actually an IBM BIOS serial port interrupt used for the purpose of redirecting output from the local serial port. A TSR (terminate-and-stay-resident) program running on the client intercepts all of the calls and information passed to Int14 and redirects that information across the network to the modem pool.

- **NASI,** or NetWare Asynchronous Services Interface, is a software interrupt that links to the NetWare shell on NetWare clients. As with the Int14 implementation, a TSR intercepts all of the information passed to the NASI interrupt and forwards it across the network to the dial-out modem pool.

Figure 11-9 illustrates some of the issues involved in dialing out from the LAN.

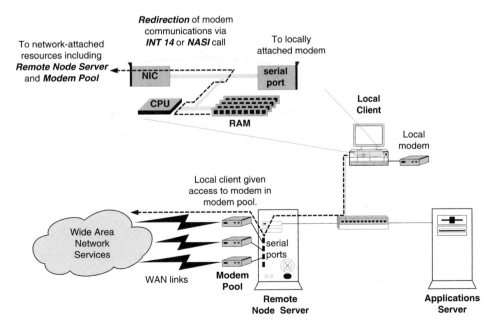

Figure 11-9   Dialing Out from the LAN

Wireless LANs   Wireless LANs play a role in the overall objective of "untethering" workers in order to increase productivity and customer satisfaction. Although wireless LANs may have been initially marketed as a means of replacing wire-bound LANs, that marketing strategy has not been reflected in their applied uses to date.

Mobile computing can be performed within the confines of a corporate or campus environment as well as over longer distances with the assistance of wireless bridges or WAN services. Portable or notebook PCs equipped with their own wireless LAN adapters can create an instant LAN connection merely by getting within range of a server-based wireless LAN adapter or wireless hub. In this way, a student or employee can sit down anywhere and log into a LAN as long as he or she is within range of the wireless hub and has the proper wireless adapter installed in a portable PC. These implementations are especially helpful in large warehouse or inventory settings.

Meeting rooms could be equipped with wireless hubs to allow spontaneous workgroups to log into network resources without running cables all over the meeting room. Similarly, by quickly installing wireless hubs and portable PCs with wireless adapters, temporary expansion needs or emergency/disaster recovery situations can be handled quickly and with relative ease. No rerunning of wires or finding the proper cross-connects in the wiring closet would be required.

Finally, wireless LAN technology allows entire LANs to be preconfigured at a central site and shipped "ready to run" to remote sites. The nontechnical users at the remote site literally just have to plug the power cords into the electrical outlets and they have an instant LAN. For companies with a great number of remote sites and limited technical staff, such a technology is ideal. No preinstallation site visits are necessary. Also avoided are costs and supervision of building wiring jobs and troubleshooting building wiring problems during and after installation.

Wireless LANs are a relatively new technological phenomena. Although they have been called a technology looking for a market or, perhaps more aptly, a solution looking for a problem, they do offer significant flexibility and spontaneity not possible with traditional wire-bound LANs. It is important to note that in general, wireless LANs cannot match the speed of their wired equivalent network architectures. For example, most Ethernet wireless LANs are limited to around 2 Mbps in comparison with Ethernet's 10 Mbps wire-based capacity.

There are currently two popular wireless transmission technologies in the local area network technology area:

- **Spread spectrum transmission**

- **Infrared transmission**

Each of these wireless transmission technologies are explained further in the following paragraphs.

In Sharper Focus

FREQUENCY HOPPING VS. DIRECT SEQUENCE SPREAD SPECTRUM TRANSMISSION

Spread spectrum transmission, as its name implies, spreads a data message across a wide range or spectrum of frequencies. This technique was originally employed as a security measure because a receiver would need to know exactly how the message was spread across the frequency spectrum in order to intercept the message in meaningful form. Spread spectrum transmission for wireless LANs is most often limited to two frequency ranges:

- 902–928 MHz

- 2.4–2.4835 GHz

- 5.72–5.85 GHz

In addition, only two spread spectrum techniques are allowed by the FCC for wireless LANs:

- **Frequency-hopping spread spectrum**

- **Direct sequence spread spectrum**

As can be seen in Figure 11-10, direct sequence spread spectrum is more commonly employed in wireless LAN technology and is generally capable of delivering higher data throughput rates than frequency-hopping spread spectrum (FHSS). Di-

Wireless LAN	Manufacturer	Network Architecture	Wireless Transmission Technology	Data Throughput	Maximum Distance
AirLAN	Solectek Corp.	Ethernet	Direct sequence Spread spectrum 902–928 MHz	2 Mbps	800 ft
ArLAN	Aironet Wireless Communications Inc.	Ethernet or Token Ring	Direct sequence Spread spectrum 902–928 MHz	860 Kbps	1000 ft
			Direct sequence Spread spectrum 2.4–2.4835 GHz	2 Mbps	500 ft
Collaborative	Photonics Corp.	Ethernet	Diffuse infrared	1 Mbps	30 ft radius
FreePort	Windata	Ethernet	Direct sequence Spread spectrum 902–928 MHz	5.7 Mbps	260 ft
Infranet	JVC	Ethernet	360 degree infrared	10 Mbps	16.5 ft radius
InfraLAN	InfraLAN Wireless	Ethernet	Line-of-sight infrared	10 Mbps	90 ft
NetWave	Xircom Inc.	Ethernet	Frequency hopping Spread spectrum 2.4–2.4835 GHz	1.6 Mbps	750 ft
RangeLAN2	Proxim Inc.	Ethernet	Frequency hopping Spread spectrum 2.4–2.4835 GHz	1.6 Mbps	1000 ft
Roamabout	Digital Equipment Corp.	Ethernet	Direct sequence Spread spectrum 2.4–2.4835 GHz	2 Mbps	800 ft
WaveLAN	AT&T G.I.S.	Ethernet	Direct sequence Spread spectrum 902–928 MHz	2 Mbps	800 ft

Figure 11-10 Wireless LAN Functional and Technical Analysis

rect sequence spread spectrum (DSSS) transmits at a particular frequency within the allowable range. In order to distinguish between transmissions from multiple wireless workstations, DSSS adds at least 10 bits to the data message in order to uniquely identify a particular transmission. DSSS receivers must be able to differentiate between these bits, known as chips, in order to properly distinguish transmissions. For security purposes, decoy data is transmitted on other frequencies making it more difficult to identify frequencies carrying true data. The addition, removal, and interpretation of chips in DSSS adds complexity, cost, and processing overhead. Nonetheless, DSSS generally delivers superior throughput to FHSS, generally 2–6 Mbps.

Frequency-hopping spread spectrum (FHSS) hops from one frequency to another throughout the allowable frequency range. The pattern of frequency hopping must be known by the wireless receiver so that the message can be reconstructed correctly. A given wireless transceiver's signal is on a given frequency for less than 1 second. Another desirable effect of all of the hopping from one frequency to another is that the transmission tends to be less affected by interference, an especially desirable characteristic for mobile computing applications. Transmission range for FHSS is two miles outdoors and 400 feet indoors with throughput from 250 Kbps to 2 Mbps.

Practical Advice and Information

Interference with wireless LANs using the 2.4 GHz to 2.4835 GHz frequency range can be generated by microwave ovens. Other electronic devices such as cordless phones and wireless scanners are also licensed to use the 902 MHz to 928 MHz frequency range.

Infrared transmission has become a part of nearly everyone's daily lives with the proliferation of remote control electronic devices. Infrared transmission typically supports distances of 100 feet and throughput of up to 10 Mbps dependent on the type of infrared transmission employed. The four major methods for infrared transmission are:

- Line of sight—transmitter and receiver must be optically aligned, solid objects can interfere with transmission

- Reflective—requires a central reflector unit that reflects infrared signals to end nodes

- Scatter—rather than being reflected off of a central reflector unit, infrared signals are reflected off floors, walls, and ceilings

Although spread spectrum and infrared are the primary wireless transmission methods today, Motorola produced a wireless LAN product known as Altair until 1995 using microwave transmission on frequencies it had licensed with the FCC. A new wireless Ethernet offering from RadioLAN, Inc., operates in the 5.8 GHZ microwave frequency and claims to offer 10 Mbps performance at distances of 120 feet to 300 feet, depending on obstacles.

Some of the technical and functional differences between these wireless LAN technologies are summarized in Figure 11-10. Some functional issues of wireless LANs not addressed in Figure 11-10 are as follows:

- Network Interface Cards: Because wireless LAN technology seems to be shifting toward an emphasis on mobile computing via laptops and portables, it should come as no surprise that most wireless LAN network interface cards are available as PC cards (PCMCIA). In such a case, card and socket service compatibility should be verified. Parallel port adapters that can be attached to portable computers are also available on some wireless LANs, as are ISA adapters.

- Encryption: Data is being sent through the air, so it is especially important to consider security with wireless LANs. Some wireless LANs support DES (data encryption standard) encryption directly on the network interface card, usually through the installation of an optional encryption chip.

WIRELESS LAN STANDARDS: IEEE 802.11 AND MOBILE IP

In Sharper Focus

One of the key shortcomings to date of wireless LANs has been a lack of interoperability among the wireless LAN offerings of different vendors. In an effort to address this shortcoming, a proposal for a new wireless LAN standard known as **IEEE 802.11** has been proposed. Key points included in the standard are as follows:

- Physical Layer: The standard defined physical layer protocols for each of the following transmission methods:
  - Frequency-hopping spread spectrum
  - Direct-sequence spread spectrum
  - Pulse position modulation infrared (diffuse infrared rather than line of sight)

- Media Access Control Layer: The standard defined **CSMA/CA (carrier sense multiple access with collision avoidance)** as the MAC layer protocol. The standard is similar to CSMA/CD except that collisions cannot be detected in wireless environments as they can in wire-based environments. CSMA/CA avoids collisions by listening to the network prior to transmission and not transmitting if other workstations on the same network are transmitting. Before transmitting, workstations wait a predetermined amount of time in order to avoid collisions, and they set up a point-to-point wireless circuit to the destination workstation. Data link layer header and information fields such as Ethernet or Token Ring are sent to the destination workstation. It is the responsibility of the wireless LAN access device to convert IEEE 802.3 or 802.5 frames into IEEE 802.11 frames. The wireless point-to-point circuit remains in place until the sending workstation receives an acknowledgment that the message was received errorfree.

- Data Rate: Either 1 or 2 Mbps selectable either by the user or by the system, depending on transmissions conditions.

One important issue not included in the IEEE 802.11 standard is **roaming** capability, which allows a user to transparently move between the transmission ranges of wireless LANs without interruption. Proprietary roaming capabilities are currently offered by many wireless LAN vendors. **Mobile IP**, under consideration by the IETF, may be the roaming standard wireless LANs require. Mobile IP, limited to TCP/IP networks, employs two pieces of software in order to support roaming:

- A mobile IP client is installed on the roaming wireless client workstation.

- A mobile IP home agent is installed on a server or router on the roaming user's home network.

The mobile IP client keeps the mobile IP home agent informed of its changing location as it travels from network to network. The mobile IP home agent forwards any transmissions it receives for the roaming client to its last reported location.

Practical Advice and Information

In January 1997 the Federal Communications Commission set aside an additional 300 MHz of bandwidth for a new class of wireless LANs and other wireless devices. The frequencies, from 5150 MHz to 5350 MHz and from 5725 MHz to 5825 MHz, are collectively known as the unlicensed national information infrastructure (U-NII). Compliant devices could include PCs and laptops with built-in or external radio receivers.

Software

Remote Control Software   **Remote control software,** especially designed to allow remote PCs to "take-over" control of local PCs, should not be confused with the asynchronous communications software used for dial-up connections to asynchronous hosts via modems. Modem operation, file transfer, scripting languages, and terminal emulation are the primary features of asynchronous communications software.

Taking over remote control of the local PC is generally available only by remote control software. Remote control software allows the keyboard of the remote PC to control the actions of the local PC, with screen output being reflected on the remote PC's screen. The terms *remote* and *local* are often replaced by **guest** (remote) and **host** (local), when referring to remote control software.

Operating remote control software requires installation of software programs on both the guest and host PCs. Various remote control software packages do not interoperate. The same brand of remote control software must be installed on both guest and host PCs. Guest and host pieces of the remote control software may or may not be included in the software package price. Remote control software must have modem operation, file transfer, scripting language, and terminal emulation capabilities similar to those of asynchronous communications software. However, in addition, remote control software should possess features to address the following situations unique to its role:

- Avoid lockups of host PCs

- Allow the guest PC to disable the keyboard and monitor of the host PC

- Additional security precautions to prevent unauthorized access

- Virus detection software

Additionally, Windows-based applications pose a substantial challenge for remote control software. The busy screens of this graphical user interface can really bog down transmission even with V.32bis or V.34 modems. Some remote control software vendors have implemented proprietary Windows screen transfer utilities that allow Windows-based applications to run on the guest PC as if they were sitting in front of the host PC. Others do not support Windows applications remotely at all.

Figure 11-11 summarizes the important features of remote control software as well as their potential implications. The following are among the more popular remote control software packages:

Software	Vendor
COSession Remote 7.0	Artisoft
PCAnywhere32 v.7.5	Symantec
Close Up LAN Pro 6.1	Norton/Lambert
Carbon Copy32	Microcom
LapLink for Windows 95 v.7.5	Traveling Software
Reach Out 7.0	Stac Electronics

Prices range from $79 to $199, with most in the $149 range.

Feature Category	Feature	Importance/Implication
Protocol Compatibility	Windows support	• How are Windows applications supported? Are full bit-mapped screens transmitted, or only the changes? • Does it include proprietary coded transmission of Windows screens?
	Windows 95 support	• Are Windows 95 applications supported?
	Network operating system protocols	• Which network operating system protocols are supported? IP, IPX, NetBIOS?
LAN Compatibility	LAN versions	• Are specific multiuser LAN server versions available or required?
	Host/guest	• Are both host and guest (local and remote) versions included?
	Operating system	• Does the remote control package require the same operating system at host and guest PCs?
Operational Capabilities	Printing	• Can remote PC print on local network-attached printers?
	File transfer	• Which file transfer protocols are supported? Kermit, XModem, YModem, ZModem, proprietary? • Is **Delta file transfer,** which allows only changes to files to be transferred, supported? • Is automated file and directory synchronization available? (This is important to mobile workers who also have desktop computers at home or at the office.)
	Drive mapping	• Can guest (remote) PC drives be mapped for host access? • Can local (host) PC drives be mapped for guest access?
	Scripting language	• Can repetitive call setups and connections be automated?
	On-line help system	• Is it context sensitive, giving help based on where the user is in the program?

	Color/resolution limitations	• What color and resolution settings are available? Different packages vary from 16 colors to 16 million colors and 800×600 to 2048×1280 pixels resolution.
	Terminal emulation	• How many different terminals are emulated? Most common are VT100, VT102, VT320, TTY.
	Simultaneous connections	• Does the package allow more than one connection or more than one session per connection, such as simultaneous file transfer and remote control?
Security	Password access	• Is password access available? This should be the minimum required security for remote logon.
	Password encryption	• Is encryption available? Since passwords must be transmitted over WAN links it would be more secure if they were encrypted.
	Keyboard disabling	• Is keyboard disabling available? Since the local PC is active but controlled remotely, it is important that the local keyboard be disabled to prevent unauthorized access.
	Monitor blanking	• Is monitor blanking available? Similar to rationale for keyboard disabling, since output is being transmitted to the remote PC, it is important to blank the local monitor so that processing cannot be viewed without authorization.
	Call-back system	• Is there a call-back system? This added security, although not hacker-proof, hangs up on dial in and calls back at preprogrammed or entered phone number.
	Access restriction	• Are remote users able to be restricted to certain servers, directories, files, or drives? Can the same user be given different restrictions when logging in locally or remotely?
	Remote access notification	• Can system managers or enterprise network management systems be notified when remote access or password failures have occurred?
	Call logging	• Can information about all calls be logged, sorted, and reported?
	Remote host reboot	• Can the remote PC (guest) reboot the local host if it becomes locked up?
	Limited logon attempts	• Are users locked out after a set number of failed logon attempts?

Virus protection	• Is virus protection available? This feature is especially important given file transfer capabilities from remote users. • Can remote users be restricted to read-only access?
Logoff after inactivity time-out	• In order to save on long-distance charges, can users be logged off (and calls dropped) after a set length of time?

Figure 11-11   Remote Control Software Technology Analysis

The remote control software loaded onto a communications server for use by multiple simultaneous users is not the same as the remote control software loaded onto single remote (guest) and local (host) PCs. Communications servers' remote control software has the ability to handle multiple users, and in some cases, multiple protocols. Because of this, it is considerably more expensive than the single PC variety. Prices range from $399 for two users to $6850 for 16 users. The following are examples of LAN remote control software:

Software	Vendor
RLN Remote Plus	Attachmate
Close Up/LAN Pro 6.5 Host and Remote	Norton/Lambert
WinFrame 1.6	Citrix Systems
RemoteWare 3.1 for Windows NT	XcelleNet

Remote Node Software   Traditionally remote node client and server software were supplied by the vendor of the network operating system on the server to be remotely accessed. **Windows NT RAS** (remote access service) and **NetWare Connect** are two examples of such NOS-specific **remote node server** software. Third-party software vendors have also offered remote node server products that vary as to operating system or network operating system compatibility. These are software-only solutions, installed on industry standard Intel 486 or higher application servers as opposed to the proprietary hardware of specialized remote access or communications servers. Representative remote node server software, required operating system or network operating system, and vendors are listed in Figure 11-12.

Some of the important functional characteristics of remote node server software other than operating system/network operating system compatibility are listed in Figure 11-13.

Remote Node Server Software	Required Operating System or Network Operating System	Vendor
Windows NT RAS	Windows NT 3.5 or 4.0	Microsoft
NetWare Connect	NetWare 3.12 or 4.1	Novell
IBM LAN Distance	OS/2	IBM
Remote Office Communications Server	DOS	Access Beyond
Wanderlink	NetWare 3.1x or 4.1	Funk Software

Figure 11-12   Remote Node Server Software Operating System Compatibility

Remote Node Server Software Functional Characteristic	Importance/Implication
NOS protocols supported	• Most remote node server software supports IP and IPX, but support of NetBIOS, NetBEUI, Appletalk, VINES, LANtastic, and SNA is more limited. • If IP is supported, is the full IP protocol stack including applications and utilities supplied?
WAN data link layer protocol	• Most remote node server software now supports PPP; others support proprietary protocols. Proprietary protocols are fine in single-vendor environments.
Modem support	• How many serial ports can be supported simultaneously? Numbers vary from 32 to 256. • How many modem setup strings are included? If the setup string for a particular type of modem is not included, configuration could be considerably more difficult. Numbers vary from 75 to over 400. • Does the remote node server software support modem pools or does there have to be a modem dedicated to every user? • Does the remote node server software support dial-out functionality over the attached modems?
Management	• How is the remote node server managed? Via a specialized console or any attached workstation with proper software? • Does the remote node server software output management information in SNMP format? • Can remote users be limited as to connect time or by inactivity time-out?
Security	• Is forced passed renewal (password aging) supported? • Are passwords encrypted? • Is the remote node server software compatible with third-party security servers such as token authentication servers? • Does the remote node server support call-back (dial-back) capabilities?
Client support	• Which types of client platforms are supported? DOS, Macintosh, Windows, Windows for Workgroups, Windows 95, Windows NT, OS/2? • Are both NDIS and ODI driver specifications supported?

Figure 11-13   Remote Node Server Software Functional Characteristics

Most of the remote node server software packages also include compatible **remote node client** software. A problem arises, however, when a single remote node client needs to logon to a variety of different servers running a variety of different network operating systems or remote node server packages. What is required is some sort of universal remote access client. In fact, such remote node clients are available. These standardized remote clients with the ability to link to servers running a variety of different network operating systems are sometimes referred to as **PPP clients.** In general, they can link to network operating systems which support IP, IPX, NetBEUI, or XNS as transport protocols. Those that support IPX are generally installable as either NetWare VLMs (virtual loadable modules) or NLMs (NetWare loadable modules). In addition, these PPP client packages include sophisticated authentication procedures to ensure secure communications, compression to ensure optimal use of the WAN link, and most of the important features of remote control software. The inclusion of remote control software allows users to choose between remote node and remote control for optimal performance.

Among the specialized compression and authentication algorithms included with a majority of these PPP clients are the following:

- **CIPX** for compression of IPX headers

- **VJ** for compression of IP headers

- **CHAP MD 5** for PPP encrypted authentication

- **CHAP MD80** authentication for Windows NT RAS

- **SPAP,** Shiva's proprietary authentication protocol, which includes password encryption and call-back capability

Some of the available PPP clients and their vendors are as follows, although not all include both fully functional remote control software and full TCP/IP stacks and utilities:

Software	Vendor
Remotely Possible /32	Avalan Technology
Timbuktu Pro	Farallon Computing
WanderLink PPP Client	Funk Software
PPP	Klos Technologies
LAN Express PPP Client	Microcom
TCP Pro	Network TeleSystems
ShivaPPP	Shiva
Remote Office Gold	Access Beyond

Mobile-Aware Operating Systems   The mobile computer user requires flexible computing functionality in order to easily support at least three possible distinct computing scenarios:

- Stand-alone computing on the laptop or notebook computer

- Remote node or remote control computing to corporate headquarters

- Synchronization of files and directories with desktop workstations at home or in the corporate office

Operating systems that are able to easily adapt to these different computing modes with a variety of included supporting accessory programs and utilities are sometimes referred to as **mobile-aware operating systems.** Windows 95 is perhaps the best current example of such an operating system. Among the key functions offered by such mobile-aware operating systems are the following:

- Auto-detection of multiple configurations: If external monitors or full-size keyboards are used at home or in the corporate office, the operating system should automatically detect these and load the proper device drivers.

- Built-in multiprotocol remote node client: Remote node software should be included that can automatically and transparently dial into a variety of different network operating system servers, including Windows NT RAS or NetWare Connect. The remote node client should support a variety of network protocols including IP, IPX, and NetBEUI as well as open data-link WAN protocols such as SLIP and PPP.

- Direct Cable Connection: When returning from the road, users should be able to be link portables easily to desktop workstations via direct connection through existing serial or parallel connections. The software utilities to initiate and manage such connections should be included.

- File transfer and file/directory synchronizations: Once physical connections are in place, software utilities should be able to synchronize files and directories between either the laptop and the desktop or the laptop and the corporate LAN server.

- Deferred printing: This feature allows printed files to be spooled to the laptop disk drive and saved until the mobile user is next connected to corporate printing resources. At that point, instead of having to remember all of the individual files requiring printing, the deferred printing utility is able to automatically print all of the spooled files.

- Power management: Since most mobile computing users depend on battery-powered computers, anything the operating system can do to extend battery life is beneficial. The demand for higher-resolution screens has meant increased power consumption in many cases. Power management features offered by operating systems have been standardized as the **advanced power management (APM)** specification.

- Infrared connection: To avoid the potential hassle of physical cable connections, mobile-aware operating systems are including support for infrared wireless connections between laptops and desktops. In order to ensure multivendor interoperability, the infrared transmission should conform to the **IrDA (Infrared Data Association)** standards. The IrDA standard defines line-of-sight infrared transmission parameters rather than diffuse infrared transmission as defined by IEEE 802.11 IR. IrDA is currently limited to point-to-point distances of only 3 feet.

Mobile-Aware Applications Beyond the shortcomings of remote node applications already delineated, mobile applications that depend on inherently unreliable wireless transmission services must be uniquely developed or modified in order to optimize performance under these circumstances.

Oracle Mobile Agents, formerly known as Oracle-in-Motion, is perhaps the best example of the overall architecture and components required to produce **mobile-aware applications.** As illustrated in Figure 11-14, the Oracle Mobile Agents architecture adheres to an overall **client/agent/server** architecture, as opposed to the

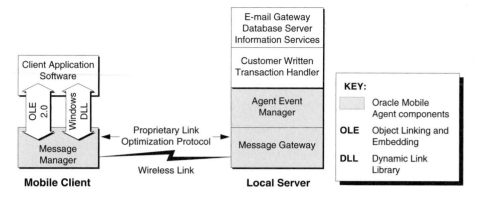

Figure 11-14   Client/Agent/Server Architecture Support Mobile-Aware Applications

more common LAN-based client/server architecture. The overall objective of such an architecture is to reduce the amount of client to server network traffic by building as much intelligence as possible into the server-based agent, so that it can act on behalf of the client application. Oracle's testing of applications developed and deployed in this wireless architecture have produced performance improvements of up to 50:1.

The agent portion of the client/agent/server architecture consists of three cooperating components:

- The **message manager** executes on the mobile client and acts as an interface between client applications requesting services and the wireless link over which the requests must be forwarded. It keeps track of requests pending on various servers that are being handled by intelligent agents. Oracle Mobile Agents also operates over LAN links or PPP based dial-up links.

- The **message gateway** can execute on the local server or on a dedicated UNIX or Windows workstation. It acts as an interface between the client's message manager and the intelligent agent on the local server. The gateway also acts as a holding station for messages to and from temporarily unreachable mobile clients. The client-based message manager and the message gateway communicate with each other via a communications protocol developed by Oracle, which provides reliable message delivery over wireless transmission services while minimizing acknowledgment overhead.

- The **agent event manager** is combined with a customer-written transaction handler to form an entity known as the **intelligent agent** that resides on the local server. Once the agent event manager receives a request from a mobile client, it acts on behalf of that client in all communications with the local server until the original client request is totally fulfilled. During this processing time in which the intelligent agent is representing the mobile client, the wireless connection can be dropped. Once the original client request has been fulfilled, the entire response is sent from the intelligent agent to the client-based message manager in a single packet, thereby conserving bandwidth and transmission time. Having received the response to a pending request, the client-based message manager deletes the original request from its pending request queue.

Mobile Middleware   An emerging category of software that seeks to offer maximum flexibility to mobile computing users while optimizing performance is known as **mobile middleware.** Although specific products within this software category can vary significantly, the ultimate goal of mobile middleware is to offer mobile users transparent client/server access independent of the following variables:

- Client or server platform (operating system, network operating system)
- Applications (client/server or client/agent/server)
- Wireless transmission services

Figure 11-15 illustrates the basic components and interactions of mobile middleware.

As shown in Figure 11-15, the primary purpose of mobile middleware is to consolidate client/server traffic from multiple applications for transmission over a variety of potential wireless (or wire-based) transmission services. By consolidating client requests from multiple applications into a single transmission, overall transmission time and expense can be reduced. In some cases, the mobile middleware has sufficient intelligence to inform clients or servers if the intended destination is currently reachable or not, thereby saving time and transmission expense. Some mobile middleware also has the ability to evaluate among available wireless services between the mobile client and the local server and to choose an optimal wireless transmission service based on performance, expense, or both.

Mobile middleware is an emerging category of software characterized by proprietary APIs and a resultant lack of interoperability. As a result, applications writ-

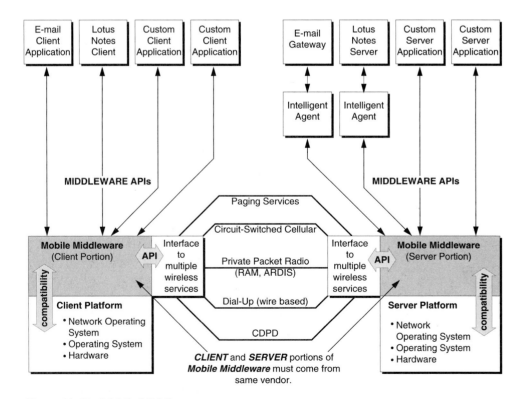

Figure 11-15   Mobile Middleware

ten to interact with one vendor's mobile middleware probably won't interact with another vendor's mobile middleware. As can be seen in Figure 11-15, mobile middleware interacts with two sets of APIs: one between the mobile middleware and the applications, and one between the middleware and the wireless transmission services. In an effort to standardize wireless APIs for mobile middleware, two standardization efforts are currently underway:

- The Winsock 2 Forum is developing standardized Winsock 2 APIs for linking mobile middleware with Windows-based applications. This API would be able to deliver transmission-related information such as signal strength and transmission characteristics to the applications themselves. Such information could make the applications more intelligent and responsive to changing transmission quality.

- The PCCA (Portable Computer and Communications Association) is developing the standardized API for linking mobile middleware to a variety of wireless transmission services. This API will provide extensions to existing multiprotocol data link layer device specifications such as NDIS and ODI.

Among the currently available mobile middleware packages and their vendors are the following:

Software	Vendor
Instant RF Workbench	NetTech Systems
Advanced Radio communication on Tour (ARTour)	IBM
Ericsson Virtual Office	Ericsson
MobileSync	Adaptive Strategies
MobileWare	MobileWare
WorldLink	Technology Development Systems
RemoteWare	XcelleNet
Transnet II	Teknique
Mobilera	Business Partners Solutions
Via	Moda Systems

Management and Configuration of Remote Access Technology

OPTIMIZING REMOTE NODE AND REMOTE CONTROL SOFTWARE PERFORMANCE

Practical Advice and Information

As previously described in the section on the remote node logical topology, suitable performance of remote client applications is severely hampered by the limited transmission speed of the WAN links combined with the high-band width demands of client/server applications. Besides rewriting the client/server application to minimize the amount of remote client to local server traffic, several other opportunities to improve over remote access performance are available. These optimization techniques will also improve performance of remote control applications:

- Use V.34 modems. This new modem specification can support transmission speeds of up to 28.8 Kbps over dial-up lines.

- Use ISDN (Integrated Services Digital Network) services, if available, as an alternative to asynchronous dial-up with the V.34 modem. ISDN BRI (basic rate interface) delivers up to 144 Kbps of switched digital bandwidth. Using ISDN requires ISDN terminal adapters, the equivalent of an ISDN modem, and compatible communications software.

- Use 16550 UARTs and matching serial port drivers The UART (universal asynchronous receiver transmitter) transmits and receives data to and from a PC's serial port, which interfaces to the modem. The 16550 UART includes increased buffering capacity in order to match the performance of faster modems such as the V.34.   Transmission via serial ports and UARTs is controlled by operating system software known as serial or COM drivers. Some of these COM drivers have limitations of 19.2 Kbps. More recent operating systems, such as Windows 95, and many asynchronous communications packages support serial transmission rates of at least 110.2 Kbps.

- Use data compression software/hardware and set communications software transmission speed to/from the modem to the PC (DTE rate) high enough to take full advantage of the compression software's capabilities. V.34 modems include V.42bis built-in data compression capabilities, which can yield compression ratios of up to 4:1 depending on file content. Because V.34 modems have a maximum transmission speed of 28.8 Kbps and V.42bis supplies 4:1 data compression, maximum serial transmission rates of 110.2 Kbps (28.8 x4) should be supported by PC hardware and software.

- Make sure that the remote control or remote node software being used supports **screen caching,** which allows only changes to screens, rather than entire screens, to be transmitted over the limited bandwidth WAN links. Screen caching will reduce the amount of actual traffic transmitted over the WAN link.

- Not to be confused with screen caching software, **network caching** or **LAN caching** software is able to improve overall remote node performance up to five times by caching repetitive applications commands and systems calls. These add-on packages are composed of both client and server pieces, which work cooperatively to cache application commands and reduce network traffic over relatively low-speed WAN links. Network caching software is network operating system and protocol dependent, requiring that compatibility be ensured prior to purchase. Two network caching software packages and their vendors are good examples:

Software	Vendor
Powerburst	AirSoft, Inc.
Shared LAN Cache	Measurement Techniques, Inc.

Mobile MIB To integrate the management of mobile computing users into an overall enterprise network management system such as HP Openview or IBM Systemview, a specialized MIB was required in order to store configuration and location information specific to remote users. The Mobile Management Task Force (MMTF) has proposed a **mobile MIB** capable of feeding configuration and location information to enterprise network management systems via SNMP. A key to the design of the mobile MIB was to balance the amount of information required in order to effectively manage remote clients while taking into account the limited bandwidth and expense of the remote links over which the management data must be transmitted. From the enterprise network management system's side, controls will need to be installed as to how often remote clients are to be polled via dial-up or wireless transmission for the purpose of gathering up-to-date management information. Among the fields of information included in the proposed mobile MIB are the following:

- Current user location
- Type and speed of connection device
- Type of remote client or remote control software installed on remote device
- Battery power
- Memory

■ NETWORK SERVICES

Wireless WAN Services

Although wireless LANs offer mobility to users across a local scope of coverage, a variety of wireless services is available for use across wider geographic spans. These **wireless WAN services** vary in many ways, including availability, applications, transmission speed, and cost. Among the available wireless WAN services that will be explained further are the following:

- Circuit-switched analog cellular
- CDPD (cellular digital packet data)
- Private packet radio
- Enhanced paging and two-way messaging
- ESMR (enhanced specialized mobile radio)
- Microcellular spread spectrum
- PCS (personal communications services)

Applied Problem Solving

A TOP-DOWN APPROACH TO WIRELESS WAN SERVICES ANALYSIS

With the many variable factors concerning these wireless WAN services, it is important to take a top-down approach when considering their incorporation into an organization's information systems solution. Questions and issues to be considered on each layer of the top down model for wireless WAN services are summarized in Figure 11-16.

Top-Down Layer	Issues/Implications
Business	• What is the business activity that requires wireless transmission? • How will payback be calculated? Has the value of this business activity been substantiated? • What are the anticipated expenses for the six-month, one-year, and two-year horizons? • What is the geographic scope of this business activity? Localized? National? International?
Application	• Have applications been developed especially for wireless transmission? • Have existing applications been modified to account for wireless transmission characteristics? • Have training and help-desk support systems been developed?
Data	• What is the nature of the data to be delivered via the wireless WAN service? Short "bursty" transactions, large two-way messages, faxes, file transfers? • Is the data time-sensitive, or could transmissions be batched during off-peak hours for discounted rates? • What is the geographic scope of coverage required for wireless data delivery?
Network	• Must the WAN service provide error correction? • Do you wish the WAN service also to provide and maintain the access devices?
Technology	• Which wireless WAN service should be employed? • What type of access device must be employed with the chosen WAN service? • Are access devices proprietary or standards-based?

Figure 11-16   Top-Down Analysis for Wireless WAN Services

To use the top-down model for wireless WAN services analysis, start with the business situation that requires wireless support and examine the applications and data characteristics supporting the business activity in question. For example, which of the following best describes the data to be transmitted by wireless means?

- Fax

- File transfer

- E-mail

- Paging

- Transaction processing

- Database queries

The content, geographic scope, amount, and urgency of the data to be transmitted will have a direct bearing on the particular wireless WAN service employed. Unfortunately, no single wireless WAN service fits all application and data needs. Once a wireless WAN service is chosen, compatibility with existing local area network architectures and technology must be established. Typical uses of the currently most widely available wireless WAN services are as follows:

- Transaction processing and database queries: CDPD
    - Advantages: Fast call setup; inexpensive for short messages
    - Disadvantages: Limited availability but growing; expensive for large file transfers

- Large file transfers and faxes: Circuit-switched cellular
    - Advantages: Widely available; call duration pricing is more reasonable for longer transmissions than per kilopacket pricing
    - Disadvantages: Longer call setup time than CDPD (up to 30 seconds versus less than 5 seconds); expensive for short messages

- Short bursts of messages and e-mail: Private packet radio
    - Advantages: Wide coverage area; links to commercial e-mail systems
    - Disadvantage: Proprietary networks; expensive for larger file transfers

The key characteristics of these and other wireless WAN services are summarized in Figure 11-17.

Two-Way Messaging

Two-way messaging, sometimes referred to as enhanced paging, allows short text messages to be transmitted between relatively inexpensive transmission devices such as PDAs (personal digital assistants) and alphanumeric pagers. Two distinct architectures and associated protocols have the potential to deliver these services.

One such architecture is based on **CDPD (cellular digital packet data)** and is being proposed and supported by AT&T Wireless Services, formerly known as Mc-Caw Cellular. CDPD uses idle capacity in the circuit-switched cellular network to transmit IP-based data packets. The fact that CDPD is IP-based allows it to easily interface to IP-based private networks as well as to the Internet and other e-mail services.

By adding a protocol known as **LSM (limited size messaging),** CDPD will be able to transport two-way messaging, which will offer the following key services beyond simple paging:

- Guaranteed delivery to destination mobile users, even if those devices are unreachable at the time the message was originally sent

- Return receipt acknowledgments to the party that originated the message

An alternative two-way messaging architecture is proposed by the PCIA (Personal Communicator Industry Association). Rather than building on existing IP-based networks as the CDPD/LSM architecture did, the **TDP (telocator data protocol)** architecture is actually a suite of protocols defining an end-to-end system for two-way messaging to and from paging devices. Figure 11-18 illustrates the differences between the LSM and TDP two-way messaging protocols.

Analog Cellular

The current circuit-switched analog cellular network is more properly known by the transmission standard to which it adheres, known as **advanced mobile phone**

Wireless WAN Service	Geographic Scope	Directionality	Data Characteristics	Billing	Access Device	Standards and Compatibility
Circuit Switched Analog Cellular	National	Full-duplex Circuit switched	14 Kbps maximum	Call duration	Modems with specialized error correction for cellular circuits	MNP-10 (adverse channel enhancements) and ETC (enhanced throughput cellular)
CDPD	Limited to large metropolitan areas	Full-duplex Packet-switched digital data	19.2 Kbps maximum	Flat monthly charge plus usage charge per kilopacket	CDPD modem	Compatible with TCP/IP for easier internetwork integration
Private Packet Radio	Nearly national. More cities than CDPD; fewer than circuit-switched cellular	Full-duplex Packet-switched digital data	4.8 Kbps	Per character	Proprietary modem compatible with particular private packet radio service	Proprietary. Two major services: RAM Mobile Data and Ardis
Enhanced Paging	National	One- or two-way Relatively short messages	100 characters or fewer	Flat monthly charges increasing with coverage area	Pagers	
ESMR	Currently limited	One- or two-way, voice, paging, or messaging	4.8 Kbps	Unknown; service is under development	Proprietary integrated voice/data devices	
Mircocell Spread Spectrum	Limited to those areas serviced by microcells; good for college and corporate campuses	Full-duplex	11–45 Mbps	Flat monthly fee	Proprietary modem	Most provide access to Internet, e-mail services.
PCS	Under development; should be national	Full-duplex, all-digital voice and data services	Up to 25 Mbps		Two-way pagers, personal digital assistants, PCS devices	Standards-based; should ensure device/service interoperability

Figure 11-17 Wireless WAN Services Technology Analysis

LSM: Limited Size Messaging

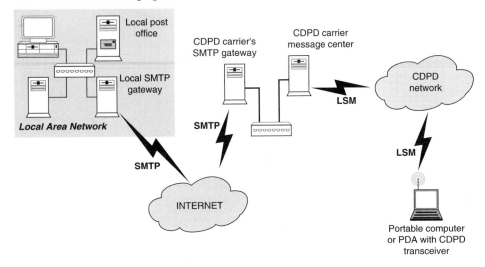

TDP: Telocator Data Protocol

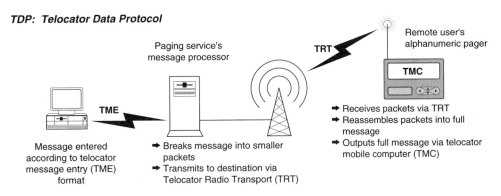

Figure 11-18   Two-Way Messaging Protocols: LSM and TDP

service (AMPS). AMPS operates in the 800 MHz frequency range. Transmitting data over analog cellular networks requires modems that support specialized cellular transmission protocols on both ends of the cellular transmission in order to maximize throughput. Examples of such protocols are **MNP-10 adverse channel enhancements** and **enhanced throughput cellular (ETC).** In some cases, cellular service providers are deploying modem pools of cellular-enhanced modems at the **mobile telephone switching office (MTSO),** where all cellular traffic is converted for transmission over the wireline public switched telephone network (PSTN). Figure 11-19 illustrates data transmission over the circuit-switched analog cellular network.

Digital Cellular/Personal Communications Services

PCS, or **personal communications services,** is a visionary concept of an evolving all-digital network architecture that could deliver a variety of telecommunications services transparently to users at any time, regardless of their geographic location. PCS is not a totally new "from the bottom up" telecommunications architecture. In

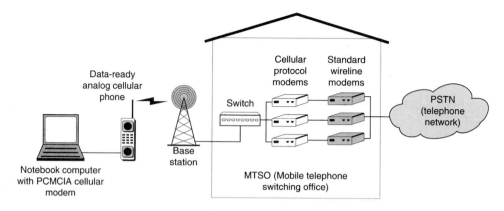

Figure 11-19   Data Transmission over the Circuit-Switched Analog Cellular Network

fact, it is the integration of a number of existing telecommunications environments. PCS seeks to combine the capabilities of the PSTN, otherwise known as the **landline telephone network,** with a new all-digital cellular network, along with paging networks and satellite communications networks.

The need for seamless delivery of a combination of all of these services is easily illustrated by the plight of today's mobile professional. One person has a phone number for the home phone, a voice and fax number for the office, a cellular phone number for the automobile, a pager phone number for the pager, and perhaps even another phone number for the satellite service phone for use outside of cellular phone areas. The premise of PCS is rather straightforward: one person, one phone number.

This **personal phone number** or **PPN** would become the user's interface to PCS and the vast array of transparently available telecommunications services. This personal phone number is a key concept to PCS. It changes the entire focus of the interface to the telecommunications environment from the current orientation of a number associated with a particular location regardless of the individual to a number associated with particular individual regardless of the location, even globally, of the accessed facility. Figure 11-20 illustrates the basic elements of PCS.

Digital Cellular Standards   Given the limited bandwidth allocated to PCS (only about 140 MHz from 1.85 GHz to 1.99 GHz, referred to as the 2 GHz band) and the potentially large number of subscribers needing to share that limited bandwidth, a key challenge for PCS is the ability to maximize the number of simultaneous conversations over a finite amount of bandwidth. Just as multiplexing was originally introduced in the study of wide area networks as a means of maximizing the use of wire-based circuits, two variations of multiplexing are being field tested as a means of maximizing the use of the allocated bandwidth of these air-based circuits.

TDMA (time division multiple access) and **CDMA (code division multiple access)** are the two methodologies currently being researched in PCS field trials. TDMA-based digital cellular may be able to support three times (some tests indicate six or seven times) the transmission capacity of analog cellular; CDMA could offer as much as a 10-fold increase. Note that the names of each of these techniques end in the words *multiple access* rather than *multiplexing*. The multiple access refers to multiple phone conversations having access to the same bandwidth and yet not interfering with each other.

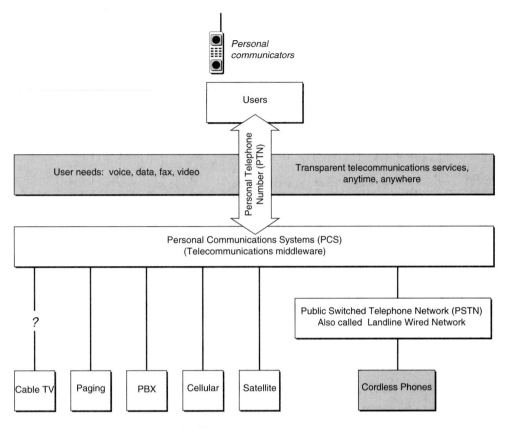

Figure 11-20   Basic Elements of PCS

TDMA achieves more than one conversation per frequency by assigning time-slots to individual conversations. Ten timeslots per frequency are often assigned, with a given cellular device transmitting its digitized voice only during its assigned timeslot. Receiving devices must be in synch with the timeslots of the sending device in order to receive the digitized voice packets and reassemble them into a natural-sounding analog signal. TDMA should be able to transmit data at 9.6 Kbps. TDMA digital standards to handle call setup, maintenance, and termination have been defined by the Telecommunications Industry Association (TIA) as follows:

- IS-130: TDMA radio interface and radio link protocol 1

- IS-135: TDMA services, asynchronous data, and fax

CDMA is the newest and most advanced technique for maximizing the number of calls transmitted within a limited bandwidth by using a spread spectrum transmission technique. Rather than allocate specific frequency channels within the allocated bandwidth to specific conversations, as is the case with TDMA, CDMA transmits digitized voice packets from numerous calls at different frequencies spread all over the entire allocated bandwidth spectrum.

The *code* part of CDMA lies in the fact that in order to keep track of these various digitized voice packets from various conversations spread over the entire spectrum of allocated bandwidth, a code is appended to each packet, indicating which voice conversation it belongs to. This technique is not unlike the datagram connectionless service used by packet-switched networks to send packetized data over numerous switched virtual circuits within the packet-switched network. By identifying the source and sequence of each packet, CDMA maintains the original message integrity while maximizing the overall performance of the network. CDMA should be able to transmit data at up to 14.4 Kbps. The CDMA standard defined by the TIA is IS-99: data services option for wideband spread spectrum digital cellular systems. Figure 11-21 illustrates both TDMA and CDMA.

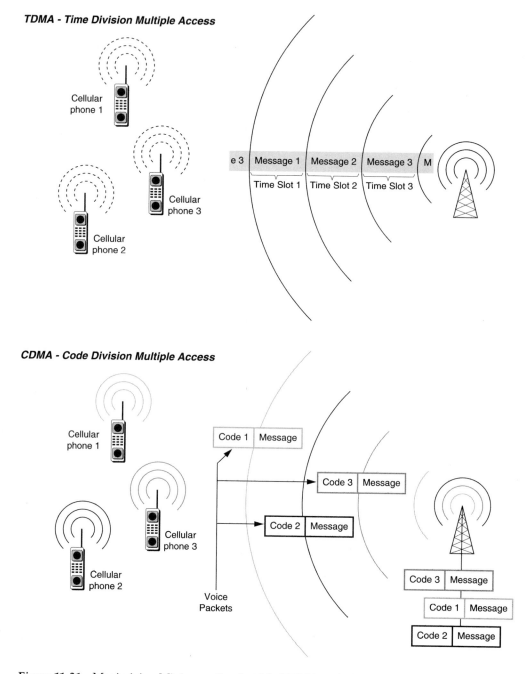

Figure 11-21 Maximizing Minimum Bandwidth: TDMA and CDMA

TDMA and CDMA are being pursued and implemented primarily by cellular carriers in North America. In Europe and much of the rest of the world, **Global System for Mobile Communication (GSM)** is either currently deployed or planned for implementation. **Personal Handyphone System (PHS)** is the digital cellular standard being implemented in Japan. These various digital cellular transmission standards are presently not interoperable, thereby precluding the possibility of transparent global access to digital cellular services.

Digital cellular systems will be deployed as needed in the most congested metropolitan areas. As a result, existing analog cellular networks will be required to co-exist and interoperate with newer digital cellular networks. Transmission protocols such as TDMA and CDMA must be compatible with analog transmission protocols, and next-generation cellular phones must be able to support both analog and digital transmission.

Transmitting digital data from a notebook computer over digital cellular networks will not require modulation as was required with analog cellular networks. As a result, notebook computers should be able to interface directly to TDMA- or CDMA-based digital cellular phones via serial ports. Figure 11-22 illustrates data transmission over a digital cellular network.

THE FUTURE OF PCS

Managerial Perspective

PCS faces significant challenges on its way to worldwide deployment. Required changes in thinking and behavior on the part of PCS users should not be overlooked. For instance, if a person can be called regardless of location thanks to the PPN (personal phone number), who should pay for that call—the called party or the calling party? Caller ID services will now display the calling party's name or personal number rather than the number of the phone from which that person is calling. Remember, with PCS, numbers are associated with people, not with equipment and phone lines.

If the caller is to be responsible for payment, he or she would probably like to know where the call is going before placing the call. However, as a potentially called party, would you want just anybody knowing your location? Vandals or your supervisor could pinpoint your location without even placing a call. Advanced call-screening services could allow only certain calls to be received on a person's

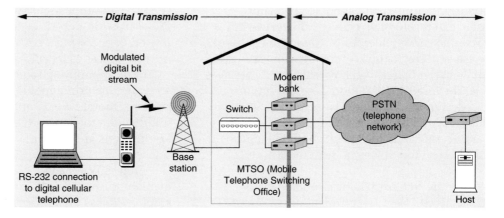

Figure 11-22   Data Transmission over a Digital Cellular Network

personal communicator, while forwarding others to voice mail. With any dramatically new technology, societal impact and changes will result. PCS should be no exception.

Perhaps the most significant hurdles are the individual and, at times, conflicting business missions of the various industries that must somehow evolve to produce a comprehensive, seamless, global, transparent personal communications service for subscribers. Another industry with its own distinct mission and on a possible collision course with the telecommunications industry is the cable television industry. PCS spread spectrum communicators have been successfully demonstrated on CATV networks.

PCS vendors bid $7.7 billion for auctioned spectrum in 1995 and 1996. Somewhere between an additional $10 billion and $50 billion will need to be spent on PCS infrastructure before services can be deployed. However, PCS vendors must price their services attractively enough to gain market share while maintaining enough cash flow to surrender a tremendous amount of debt.

Finally, future PCS deployment levels may be determined by simple market demand. There is always the possibility that a seamless, comprehensive, location-independent communications system such as PCS is of more interest to the companies who stand to profit from it than to the buying public who is supposedly demanding it.

SUMMARY

Remote access to LANs has taken on increased importance in response to major changes in business conditions. As indicated by the top-down model, network functionality must respond to changing business conditions. Expectations of LAN remote access are significant. Remote users expect the same level of data accessibility, application services, and performances on the road as they receive at the office. Delivering this equivalent functionality is the challenge faced by networking professionals today. The major obstacle to this lofty objective is the bandwidth, availability, and quality of the wide area network service expected to deliver remote connectivity to mobile users. Increasingly, wireless WAN services are at the forefront of remote access solutions.

In designing remote access solutions, start with a thorough understanding of the needs of remote users. These needs will dictate both the logical and physical topologies of the remote access network.

There are two basic logical topologies for remote access. Remote control allows a remote PC to take over or control a local PC. Processing occurs on the local PC, and only keyboard strokes and screen images are transported over the WAN link. Remote node allows the remote PC to act as a full-fledged LAN client to the local LAN server. In this case, full client/server traffic travels over the WAN link as the application executes on the remote client PC. One of these logical topologies is not preferable in all cases. Each situation must be analyzed on an individual basis.

Physical topologies include accessing a local LAN-attached PC directly via modem, accessing a shared communications server that might include PC boards for embedded shared computing power, or accessing a LAN modem that would provide access to local LAN computing resources.

Mobile computing requires specialized software, including mobile-aware operating systems, mobile-aware applications, and mobile middleware to interface between multiple applications and multiple possible wireless WAN services.

Wireless WAN services vary widely in terms of availability, bandwidth, reliability, and cost. No single wireless WAN service is appropriate for all mobile computing applications. It is important to understand the application needs and data characteristics of mobile applications before choosing a wireless WAN service. Digital cellular and personal communications services may hold the promise of higher-bandwidth reliable wireless transmission. However, substantial infrastructure development remains before such services will be universally available.

KEY TERMS

Access server	IEEE 802.11	PPP clients
Advanced mobile phone service (AMPS)	Infrared data association	Private packet radio
Advanced power management (APM)	Infrared transmission	Remote access
	Int14	Remote control
Adverse channel enhancements	Intelligent agent	Remote control software
Agent event manager	IrDA	Remote node
Carrier sense multiple access with collision avoidance	LAN caching	Remote node client software
	Landline telephone network	Remote node servers
Cellular digital packet data (CDPD)	LAN modem	Remote node server software
CHAP MD5	Limited size messaging (LSM)	Remote node software
CHAP MD80	Message gateway	Roaming
CIPX	Message manager	Screen caching
Circuit-switched cellular	Microcell spread spectrum	Small office home office (SOHO)
Client/agent/server	MNP-10	SPAP
Code division multiple access (CDMA)	Mobile-aware applications	Spread spectrum transmission
	Mobile-aware operating systems	Technical support
Communications server	Mobile computing	Telecommuting
CSMA/CA	Mobile IP	Telocator data protocol (TDP)
Delta file transfer	Mobile MIB	Time division multiple access (TDMA)
Dial-in server	Mobile middleware	
Direct sequence spread spectrum	Mobile telephone switching office (MTSO)	Time synchronous authentication
Enhanced paging	NASI	Token authentication
Enhanced throughput cellular	NetWare Connect	Token response authentication
ESMR	Network caching	Two-way messaging
ETC	Oracle Mobile Agents	VJ
Frequency-hopping spread spectrum	Personal communications services (PCS)	Windows NT RAS
		Wireless WAN services
Global system for mobile communication (GSM)	Personal handyphone system (PHS)	
	Personal phone number (PPN)	

REVIEW QUESTIONS

1. What key business trends have led to an increased interest in LAN remote access?
2. What is the importance of needs analysis to LAN remote access design?
3. Differentiate remote node and remote control in terms of functionality and network impact.
4. What is the major limitation in terms of delivering transparent access to remote LAN users?
5. Describe how it is possible to run remote control software via a remote node connection. What are the advantages of such a setup?
6. What are some of the security issues unique to remote access situations?
7. What added security capability can token authentication systems offer?
8. What advantages does a communications server offer over separate remote access links to multiple PCs? Disadvantages?
9. What is the common differentiation between communications servers and remote node servers?
10. Differentiate the three major categories of remote node servers.

11. Why are dial-out solutions for remote node servers different from dial-in solutions?
12. How can dial-out solutions be implemented on LANs equipped with remote node servers?
13. Differentiate the two spread spectrum transmission techniques approved by the FCC in terms of functionality and application.
14. Why are wireless LAN NICs most often PCMCIA?
15. Differentiate between CSMA/CD and CSMA/CA.
16. What is roaming, and why is it important to remote access users?
17. How does mobile IP work?
18. What is the relationship between the guest and host remote control software?
19. Why is remote control software not interoperable?
20. Differentiate between remote control and remote node software in terms of transport protocols and client protocol stacks.
21. Differentiate between LAN (multiuser) remote control software and point-to-point remote control software.
22. What are some of the unique functional requirements of remote control software beyond being able to control local (host) PCs?
23. What are some of the unique functional requirements of remote node server software?
24. What advantage do PPP clients offer?
25. What are some of the unique functional requirements of mobile-aware operating systems?
26. Differentiate the client/agent/server architecture and the client/server architecture.
27. How do mobile-aware applications need to adjust to or compensate for wireless transmission services?
28. Describe the interaction between the components of Oracle Mobile Agents.
29. What two distinct interfaces do mobile middleware products transcend?
30. What are the functional objectives of mobile middleware?
31. How can the proprietary nature of mobile middleware products be overcome?
32. Describe standards development efforts that may effect mobile middleware.
33. What are some of the ways in which remote node or remote control applications can be optimized?
34. What is the difference between screen caching and network caching?
35. What unique information is required in a mobile MIB and why?
36. What are the conflicting objectives or limitations of mobile management software and the mobile MIB?
37. Why is CDPD of such interest to circuit-switched cellular vendors?
38. What standards are important to a person wishing to purchase a "cellular-ready" modem?
39. Match each of the following to the most appropriate wireless WAN service and justify your answer: transaction processing, short messages, large file transfers.
40. What are the advantages of two-way messaging systems for data transfer?
41. Differentiate between analog and digital cellular transmission systems in terms of data transfer capabilities and equipment requirements.
42. How is the notion of a personal phone number central to PCS, and what changes in thinking about phone systems does it require?
43. Differentiate TDMA and CDMA.
44. What are some of the obstacles to the vision of universal PCS?

ACTIVITIES

1. Gather articles regarding business trends that have contributed to the rise in LAN remote access. Relate these business trends to market trends for remote access technology and wireless WAN services. Use graphical presentation wherever possible.
2. Find an organization currently supporting LAN remote access. Analyze the situation from a business perspective. Which business activities are being supported? Was cost/benefit or payback period analysis performed or considered?
3. In the organization being studied, what is the physical topology employed? Links to multiple PCs? Communications server? LAN modems? Prepare a diagram of the physical topology, including all software components such as network operating systems and transport protocols.
4. In the organization being studied, is remote node functionality supported? If so, which remote client software is installed? Are remote users able to access servers with multiple different network operating systems? Are PPP clients installed?
5. In the organization being studied, are dial-out capabilities supplied? If so, how?
6. In the organization being studied, have any efforts been made to optimize the performance of remote node or remote control applications? If so, what

were those adjustments, and what impact did they have?

7. What types of additional security precautions, if any, are instituted for remote users?

8. Investigate infrared wireless LANs. What is the difference between line-of-sight and diffuse infrared? Where are infrared wireless LANs being deployed? What is the percentage market share of infrared wireless LANs versus spread spectrum wireless LANs?

9. Why did the FCC choose the frequency bands it did for spread spectrum transmission?

10. What devices other than wireless LANs use the 902 MHz to 928 MHz frequency range? Could this be a problem?

11. What is the difference between the CSMA/CA employed in IEEE 802.11 and that employed in Appletalk networks?

12. What is the current status of IEEE 802.11? What are the perceived shortcomings of the standard?

13. Research current PCS or digital cellular pilot tests. Compare how many use TDMA and how many use CDMA. What have been the results of these pilot tests?

CHAPTER 11

CASE STUDY

BRAZILIAN BREWER DRAFTS SATELLITE NETWORK

Grupo Antarctica Overcomes Infrastructure Limits

What you notice first as you enter the grounds of Grupo Antarctica's compound in São Paulo is the unmistakable fragrance. It's not the flora decorating the outdoor spaces. It's beer—barley and hops, heated and fermenting.

This is natural because Antarctica is Brazil's second-largest beer maker and the fifth-largest in the world. Although it's the beer you smell on the premises, the company is also proud of its leadership in the Brazilian soft-drinks market. This position was achieved primarily by its concoction based on an extract of the Amazon guaraná tree fruit, Guaraná Antarctica, which is purported to be uniquely invigorating and restorative—not to mention its reputation as an aphrodisiac.

The company, which generated $3.6 billion in revenue during 1995 and employs 17,000 workers, is also expanding. Last year, for example, Antarctica inked a deal with St. Louis–based Anheuser-Busch Companies, Inc. to bring Budweiser to South America and to export Antarc-

tica's Rio Cristal beer to the United States.

The company's success and expansion help explain the next thing you notice while touring the brewery's property: the imposing and somewhat incongruous satellite earth station next to one of the buildings.

Last month [April 1997] Antarctica, which has 27 plants sprinkled throughout Brazil—threw the switch on its first-ever WAN, using satellite data-communications technology to move the information.

IS managers in the United States and Europe might find it hard to believe that a company of such size could function without a WAN. What on earth did the giant company do to communicate between sites before the satellite system was installed?

"Fax," shrugs a grinning Sérgio Barbieri, Antarctica's IS support manager.

In fact, according to both network managers and vendors, Antarctica's previous data-communications plight is not uncommon in Brazil. Reliance on the state-owned telecommunications monopoly, Empresa Brasileira de Telecomunicações S.A., has hindered infrastruc-

ture development and kept costs extremely high for the limited X.25-based data-communications services that were available. The current government is committed to telecommunications reform, promising to open the market to competition over the next five years, but the anticipated boon to wide-area networking is still in the future.

For now, Antarctica's Barbieri says that satellite networking, getting approximately 2.5 Mbps of aggregate bandwidth from a cell-relay network provided by GSI, the Brazilian equivalent of IBM's Global Network organization, is cheaper than a comparable land-based solution.

To make the connection, each site was outfitted with a digital satellite modem from ComStream (a Spar Company) and a multiplexer/router from Motorola Inc.

Antarctica's deployment of a satellite WAN is the latest in a series of technology initiatives to overhaul its IS architecture. Despite being a Big Blue shop, Antarctica is moving away from mainframe systems to client/server applications. Most notably, the company is using the one-two punch of the SAP AG R/3 decision-support system and Lotus

Notes groupware to modernize and "rightsize" the organization's business processes.

"The most important thing is that we will speed the interchange of information between the plants," Barbieri says of the IT overhaul's objectives.

Despite its strategy to unplug the mainframe, Antarctica remains loyal to IBM. The IS department is building the new applications infrastructure with a range of IBM products in addition to the satellite service it is leasing from GSI and the deployment of Lotus Notes. Over 1200 desktop and 100 notebook PCs connect to LANs anchored by 150 servers running IBM OS/2 Warp Server. It's also a token-ring network, built using IBM 82xx-series hubs and switches at 50 percent of the sites (the others use hubs and switches from RAD Data Communications).

Finally, the core applications are based on AIX running on IBM RISC processors. "We'd like to use Intel [Corp. CPU] technology, but we had to use RS/6000s because of the size of the applications," says Marcelo Giugliano, software coordinator at Antarctica. He says Microsoft Windows NT is under evaluation but has too many compatibility problems.

A predisposition toward, if not utter dependence on, IBM is also not uncommon in Brazil. Until recently, severe PC technology import restrictions imposed by the government limited product availability to what could be developed within the country's borders. IBM's advantage over many competitors in the country was twofold: It has had a presence in Brazil for 80 years, which made it a native entity, albeit adoptive, and mainframes were not subject to the same rigorous tariffs as PCs and other consumer-electronics goods.

The Mistakes of Others Now, according to technologists in the region, somewhat more enlightened trade policies combined with an economy finally stabilized after 15 years of runaway inflation is spurring the kind of corporate IT investment exhibited by Antarctica. As a result, the PC and networking technology landscape, populated with all the familiar names, closely resembles that in the United States and Europe.

The company's IS team does not think it has fallen behind the times with its delayed switch to distributed computing and networked applications. In fact, according to Barbieri, Antarctica has learned valuable lessons from the hardships encountered by those, such as its U.S. partner Anheuser-Busch, who went before it into the wilds of client/server architectures.

Antarctica's move to contemporary IT strategies, which likely will soon include intranet approaches to collaboration based on Lotus Domino, extends beyond the satellite WAN and distributed-applications architecture to the IS team itself. The company employs 90 staffers, banking heavily on partnerships and outsourcing, especially in the areas of applications development and infrastructure.

The in-house staff analyzes problems and then outsources tasks. "We don't employ people to pull cable," says Barbieri.

Enabling the technical staff to focus on business-related issues is at the heart of Antarctica's IT agenda. With the first step completed—moving applications and enabling basic intersite data communications—they can begin to focus their energy on other benefits of a connected enterprise, including distributed services and remote-user support.

Barbieri says the company also wants to connect all of its distributors over the next two years as a way of generating direct competitive advantage from its new network.

Progress, of course, will yield some casualties along with benefits for Antarctic beer drinkers. Before exiting the IT command center to try a free sample of the famous Guaraná Antarctica soft drink, a visitor pointed to an IBM 3090 series machine standing forlornly in a corner and asked about its future. Would it at least find a role as an applications server or a storage subsystem?

"No," said Barbieri laughing and thrusting his thumb over his shoulder. "It's gone. Do you want to take it with you?"

Source: Jeremiah Caron, "Brazilian Brewer Drafts Satellite Network," *LAN Times* (May 12, 1997), Copyright May 12, 1997, The McGraw-Hill Companies, Inc.

BUSINESS CASE STUDY QUESTIONS ·······················

Activities

1. Complete a top-down model for this case by gleaning facts from the case and placing them in the proper layer of the top-down model. After having completed the top-down model, analyze and detail those instances where requirements were clearly passed down from upper layers to lower layers of the model and where solutions to those requirements were passed up from lower layers to upper layers of the model.

2. Detail any questions about the case that may occur to you for which answers are not clearly stated in the article.

Business

1. What are the primary business activities of this organization?
2. How did the company communicate prior to the WAN installation?
3. How does government reform affect network design in this case?
4. What efforts are being made to rightsize the organization's business processes?
5. What is seen as the most important benefit of the WAN?
6. What economic issues have had an impact on investment in IT and availability of IT technology alternatives?

Application

1. What types of applications is the company running?

2. Is the information system centralized (mainframe-based) or distributed (client/server)?
3. What are some future possibilities for applications?

Data

1. What types of computers were used to run the core applications at headquarters? Why?

Network

1. Describe the current WAN installation.
2. What network services were available from the local carrier?
3. What was the problem with the network services available from the local carrier?
4. How much bandwidth does the WAN provide?
5. What network operating system and network architecture (data link layer protocol) are employed?

Technology

1. What technology is required at each site to connect to the WAN?

CLIENT/SERVER INFORMATION SYSTEMS ADMINISTRATION

INTRODUCTION

Now that Parts 1, 2, and 3 have demonstrated how hardware and software technology components can be integrated to produce an effective client/server information system, Part 4 discusses how such information systems can be effectively managed and secured.

Chapter 12, Client/Server Information Systems Management, stresses that the successful implementation of a network management strategy requires a combination of policy, process, people, and technology. Merely throwing network management technology in a vacuum at a network management opportunity will not produce the desired results. This chapter introduces the reader to the business issues as well as the technology and underlying concepts concerning the effective management of client/server information systems.

In Chapter 13, Client/Server Information Systems Security, the various processes, concepts, protocols, standards, and technology associated with information systems security are reviewed. Maintaining a realistic approach, this chapter emphasizes the importance of people and their basic honesty and integrity as the underlying foundation for any successful information system security implementation.

CHAPTER 12

CLIENT/SERVER INFORMATION SYSTEMS MANAGEMENT

Concepts Reinforced
....

OSI Model
Enterprise Network Architectures
Distributed Information Systems

Top-Down Model
Network Development Life Cycle
Protocols and Interoperability

Concepts Introduced
....

Enterprise Network Management
Server Management
Desktop Management
Distributed Applications Management
Internetwork Device Management
Distributed Network Management

Systems Administration
Help Desk Management
Consolidated Services Desk
LAN Management
Internet/WWW Management
Network Management Technology

OBJECTIVES

After mastering the material in this chapter you should understand the following:

1. The business motivations and forces at work in the current systems administration and network management arena

2. The relationship between network management processes, personnel, and technology in order to produce a successful network management system

3. The differences between systems administration processes and network management processes

4. The protocols and technology associated with each area of system administration and network management

5. How systems administration and network management technology can be most effectively implemented

■ INTRODUCTION

At this point in the text, it should be clear to all readers that a client/server information system is a complex combination of hardware and software technologies linked by networking technologies. Once these various categories of technologies are successfully integrated, they must be properly managed. The purpose of this chapter is to expose the reader to how each of the elements of a client/server information system can be managed. Although entire texts are written on network and information systems management, this chapter will provide an overview of the key issues surrounding the management of each major aspect of client/server information systems, including standards and protocols, interoperability issues, currently available technology, key vendors, and market trends. Figure 12-1 highlights some of the elements of a client/server information system that must be managed.

■ APPLICATION AND DATABASE MANAGEMENT

Distributed Application Management

Although distributed applications can be developed for client/server information systems that possess the power equivalent to those deployed on mainframes, client/server–based applications have not yet matched mainframe applications in terms of reliability and manageability. This is primarily due to a lack of effective application management tools and underlying application management protocols that can expose an application's dependencies and measure numerous aspects of performance. This lack of application management tools can make it impossible to diag-

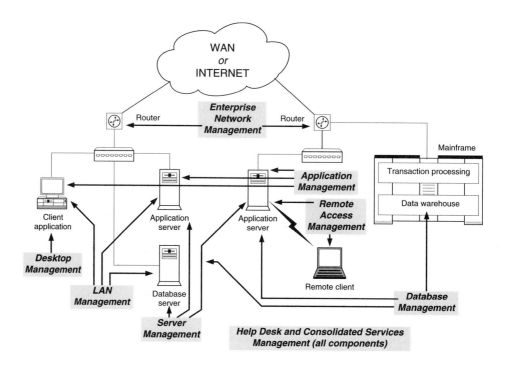

Figure 12-1 Elements of a Client/Server Information System That Must Be Managed

nose and correct application problems ranging from poor performance to system crashes.

Fortunately, an effort is underway to build self-diagnosing intelligence into applications during the development stage. By having these predefined events and **performance metrics** included within the application, management consoles will be able to detect problems with application performance and take corrective action. These embedded performance metrics are sometimes referred to as **instrumentation.** Two such development environments are Unify VISION and Forte Application Environment. In between the intelligent application, reporting on event conditions and performance metrics, and the management console is an autonomous piece of software known as an **agent,** which collects these performance statistics and properly formats them for transmission to the application management console. In turn, these agents are able to communicate with a variety of application management consoles or any SNMP-based administrative program. Examples of agents include AgentWorks from Computer Associates and AppMan from Unify. Eventually, such application management information will hopefully be consolidated into enterprise management frameworks such as CA-Unicenter and Tivoli Management Environment.

An alternative to developing your own applications with embedded management intelligence is to purchase a prewritten **event management tool** that has been written to monitor specific commercially available applications such as Lotus Notes, SAP R2/R3, Oracle Financials, or a variety of databases including IBM DB2, Oracle, Informix, and Sybase. PATROL from BMC Software, Inc., is an example of such an event management tool. Although effective, PATROL supports only proprietary protocols for application management data.

One of the key stumbling blocks to widespread deployment and support of distributed application management is the lack of a standard for what application performance information should be gathered and how that information should be reported. One proposal for standardizing how instrumentation should be developed within applications is known as the **applications management specification (AMS).** AMS outlines a set of management objects that define distribution, dependencies, relationships, monitoring and management criteria, and performance metrics that can subsequently be processed by agents and forwarded to management consoles. These AMS agents are placed into applications through the use of the ARM software developers kit, which is an API that can be used by applications developers. ARM, **application response measurement,** can measure several key application statistics. Agents are able to forward application performance statistics to ARM-compatible application management consoles. ARM 2.0 added the capability to track applications to multiple servers, to track business-specific transaction information, and to more effectively explain application performance problems. Vendors such as Hewlett Packard, Tivoli, Oracle, and Compuware have committed to supporting the ARM specification. Figure 12-2 illustrates some of the key concepts involved in a distributed application management architecture.

Another possible standard for distributed application management is a proposed IETF standard known as **web-based enterprise management (WBEM)** that integrates SNMP, HTTP, and DMI (desktop management interface) into an application management architecture that can use common web browser software as its user interface. Another IETF initiative is developing a two-part applications MIB. The first part is known as the SysAppl MIB, dealing with collection of applications performance data without the use of instrumentation, and the second part deals with the collection of performance data that requires instrumentation (performance

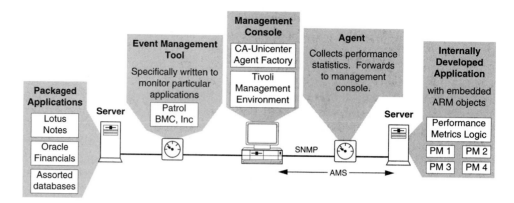

Figure 12-2 Distributed Application Management Architecture

metrics). The RMON Application MIB is explained in more detail later in this chapter. As can be seen from the previous paragraph, when it comes to application management, the standards arena is anything but decided.

Enterprise Database Management

Distributed database management is also important to overall enterprise information system management. Although most distributed data management platforms provide their own management system for reporting performance statistics, there is currently no way to consolidate these separate management systems into a single enterprisewide view. Because of corporate mergers and the need to consolidate once-isolated departmental databases, corporations commonly have data stored in a wide variety of incompatible database systems. The IETF has been working on a **database MIB** specification that would allow any enterprise data management system to report performance statistics back to any SNMP-compliant enterprise network management system.

Enterprise database management tools that are able to manage a variety of different databases should include the following important major functional areas:

- Global user administration: User and group authorization and security management across a variety of different databases are important characteristics for an enterprisewide database management system.

- Heterogeneous data schema and content manipulation: In other words, from one console, an administrator can change the database record layout or the contents of those records, regardless of the particular database management system. In some cases, these changes can be automated across an entire enterprise's databases, scheduled to be run at a later time, or saved for future reuse. Such systems should be able to add columns to or otherwise modify database tables automatically across a variety of different databases. In some cases, databases may need to be replicated from one platform to another, or one database's schema, or a portion thereof, may need to be copied to a different database platform.

- Effective troubleshooting: Enterprise database management systems must be able to monitor a variety of different databases for such critical events as inadequate free space, runaway processes, high CPU utilization, or low swap space. Events and alarms should be able to trigger e-mail, pagers, or on-screen events. In some cases, the enterprise database management system can take corrective action as defined by user-supplied script files.

- The databases such an enterprise database management system support should include Oracle, Informix, SQL Server, Adaptive Server, and DB2. In addition, it could run on the following computing platforms: Windows NT, OS/2, Windows 95, Windows 3.1, and UNIX on such platforms as SPARC, RS/6000, Irix, Digital Alpha, and HP-UX.

Among the enterprise data management tools currently available are the following:

Enterprise Data Management Tool	Vendor
Platinum Enterprise DBA 2.2	Platinum Technology
Patrol DB Series	BMC
Tivoli Management Enterprise 10	Tivoli Systems

CLIENT AND DESKTOP MANAGEMENT

Desktop Management

Desktop management is primarily concerned with the configuration and support of desktop workstations or client computers. In most cases, this management is more concerned with the assorted hardware and operating systems software of the desktop machines than with the applications or database software discussed in the previous section.

Desktop Management Architecture and Protocols   Desktop management systems rely on an architecture and associated protocols proposed by the **Desktop Management Task Force (DMTF),** which is composed of more than 50 companies including Intel, Microsoft, IBM, Digital, Hewlett Packard, Apple, Compaq, Dell, and Sun. The overall desktop management architecture is known as the **DMI,** or **desktop management interface,** and is illustrated in Figure 12-3.

Although differing in both strategic intent and governing standards-making organizations, desktop management and enterprise management systems must still be able to transparently interoperate. DMI-compliant desktop management systems store performance and configuration statistics in a **MIF (Management Information Format),** and enterprise management systems employ a MIB, so a MIF-to-MIB mapper is required in order to link desktop and enterprise management systems. The DMI architecture is composed of four primary components:

- **DMI services layer** is the DMI application that resides on each desktop device to be managed. The DMI services layer does the actual processing of desktop management information on the client platform and serves as an interface to two APIs.

- The **management interface API** is designed to interface to the desktop system management program, which will consolidate the information from this client with all other desktop information.

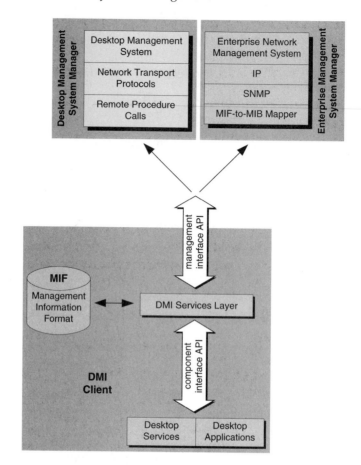

Figure 12-3 Desktop Management Interface Architecture

- The **component interface API** is designed to interface to the individual application programs or desktop components that are to be managed and monitored on the local client.

- Information about the local desktop components is stored locally in a MIF.

Desktop Management Technology Desktop management technology offerings from different vendors are best characterized as suites of associated desktop management applications. Current offerings differ in the variety of management modules included within a given suite as well as in the extent of integration between suite modules. Modules that some, but not necessarily all, desktop management suites include are the following:

- Hardware and software inventory

- Asset management

- Software distribution

- License metering

- Server monitoring

- Virus protection

- Help desk support

The following are examples of desktop management suites and their vendors:

Desktop Management Suites	Vendor
LANDesk Management Suite	Intel
Saber LAN Workstation	McAfee
Norton Administrator Suite	Symantec
Desktop Management Suite	Seagate

Key functional characteristics of desktop management systems are listed in Figure 12-4. Many of the functional areas described briefly in Figure 12-4 will be explained in further detail later in the chapter.

Mobile Desktop Management Extending desktop management functionality such as software distribution, change analysis, job scheduling, asset monitoring, and backup to mobile laptop computers linked only occasionally to corporate headquarters over relatively low bandwidth network links presents some unique challenges. The need for such management software is indeed important when one considers that laptop usage is supposed to more than double between 1998 and 2002 from 50 to 108 million users. Mobile users have a need to not only receive updates to their application software, but also to incorporate data such as product and pricing information. It is equally important for support personnel at corporate headquarters to know exactly what hardware and software technology is installed on each laptop computer.

XcelleNet, Inc., produces a series of remote management modules known collectively as RemoteWare that are able to manage software distribution, virus protection, backup, and inventory management for laptop computers. RemoteWare differs from traditional desktop management software packages primarily in the fact that all files transmitted between the management software and the remote laptop computers are in a compressed format. If the transmission is interrupted midstream, the transmission is able to restart where it left off, rather than having to start over at the beginning. Once it is received at the remote laptop computer after disconnection from the transmission line, the installation application is executed locally on the laptop. Backup management software saves time and bandwidth by transmitting only changes to files rather than the entire file in a process known as delta file synchronization.

Callisto markets similar remote laptop management software known as Orbiter. A key difference between Orbiter and RemoteWare is the fact that the Orbiter software uses a mobile agent architecture that works in conjunction with the management server at headquarters. In such a scenario, the client-based agent software executes applications and updates on a timed basis in an off-line manner as programmed by the management software. The next time that the laptop and management server are connected, the client agent updates the management server with the status of all of the jobs that it was scheduled to execute in the interim.

Functional Category	Importance/Implication
Integration	• Are all desktop management applications tied together through a single interface to a single console? • Do all desktop management applications share information with one another via a single database? • Can software modules be added individually as needed? Suites may be either modular or tightly integrated in design. • Does the system support the DMI architecture? Output data in MIF format?
Network Operating System Compatibility	• Which network operating system must the desktop management console or server run over? • Which network operating systems is the desktop management system able to monitor? Some desktop management systems can monitor only a single NOS. For example, Novell Manage-Wise is able to monitor only NetWare networks, and Microsoft's System Management Server is able to manage only Microsoft networks, although this may not always be the case. • Examples of supported network operating systems include NetWare, Windows NT, IBM LAN Server, Banyan VINES, Airsoft LANtastic, DEC Pathworks, and AppleTalk.
Desktop Compatibility	• The primary objective of this software category is to manage desktops, so as many desktop platforms as possible should be supported. • Examples of supported client platforms include DOS, Macintosh, OS/2, Windows 95, Windows NT Workstation, Windows for Workgroups, and Windows 3.11.
Hardware and Software Inventory (Asset Management)	• Can the inventory software autodetect client hardware and software? • Can changes in files or configuration be tracked? • Can versions of software be detected and tracked? • How many applications can be identified? Libraries of 6,000 are not uncommon. • Can CPU types and speeds be correctly identified? • Is a query utility included to identify workstations with given characteristics?
Server Monitoring	• Does the software support the setting of threshold limits for CPU activity, remaining disk space, and so on? • What server attributes can be tracked? CPU activity, memory usage, free disk space, number of concurrent logins or sessions?
Network Monitoring	• Can data link layer traffic be monitored and reported on? • Can network layer protocol traffic activity be monitored and reported on? • Can MAC layer addresses be sensed and monitored? • Can activity thresholds be established for particular data link or network layer protocols?
Software Distribution	• Can software be distributed to local client drives as well as network servers? • Can updates be automatically installed? • Can the system track which software needs to be updated through ties with the software inventory system? • Can updates be uninstalled automatically? • Can progress and error reports be produced during and after software distribution?

License Metering	• Where can software licenses be tracked?
	  • Clients
	  • Server
	  • Across multiple servers
	• Can license limit thresholds be set?
	• Will the manager be notified before the license limit is reached?
	• Will users be notified if license limit has been reached?
	• Will users be put into a queue for next available license after license limit has been reached?

Virus Protection	• Can virus protection be provided for both clients and servers? • Can diskette drives as well as hard drives be protected? • Can viruses embedded within application programs be detected?
Help Desk Support	• Are trouble-ticketing and call-tracking utilities included? • Are query capabilities included to search for similar problems and solutions? • Are reports available to spot trends and track help desk effectiveness and productivity?
Alarms	• Can managers be notified of changes to files or configuration? • Can violations of preset thresholds be reported? • Can alarms be sent by e-mail, pager, fax, cellular phone?
Remote Control Management	• Can managers take over remote client workstations for monitoring or troubleshooting purposes? • Can this be done via modem as well as over the local LAN? • Can files be transferred to and from the remote client? • Can files on remote client be viewed without taking over complete control of the remote client? • Can remote reboots be initiated?
Reporting Capabilities	• How many predefined reports are available? • Can users define their own reports? • Can information be exported to documents, spreadsheets, or databases? • Which export file formats are supported?

Figure 12-4   Functional Categories of Desktop Management Systems

In terms of standardized protocols for mobile desktop management, the Desktop Management Task Force has created a **mobile MIF** as an extension to the Desktop Management Interface (DMI) 2.0. Among the types of information that management software supporting the mobile MIF will be able to gather from compliant laptops are the following:

- Battery levels
- AC lines
- Docking status
- Infrared ports
- Video display types
- Pointing devices
- Device bays

Configuration Management

Single Sign-On Providing single sign-on services for distributed applications deployed across multiple servers is a benefit to users as well as systems administrators. By establishing a distributed security directory housed on a central security server, single sign-on software is able to provide a single login location for multiple types of computing platforms. This precludes users from having to remember multiple passwords and allows systems administrators to maintain user accounts and privileges for an entire enterprise from a single location. Single sign-on software is ideally deployed as part of the consolidated service desk. Among multiplatform single sign-on technology and vendors are the following:

Single Sign-On Software	Vendor
OmniGuard/Enterprise SignOn	Axent Technologies
CKS MyNet	CKS North America
AccessManager	ICL, Inc.
Connection	Open Horizon

Configuration or Policy-Based Management Tools Once hardware and software desktop configuration standards have been established and enforced, ongoing maintenance and monitoring of those standards can be ensured by configuration management tools such as electronic software distribution tools, license metering tools, and automated inventory tools. In order to more easily integrate configuration management tools with corporate policy and standards regarding desktop configurations, a new breed of **policy-based management tools** has emerged.

Policy-based management tools in their simplest form are able to automate certain tasks by using job-scheduling utilities to schedule background and after-hours jobs. Another key point about these tools is that they are able to administer multiple types of client platforms such as DOS, Windows 3.x, Windows 95, Windows NT, OS/2, HP-UX, AIX, SunOS, and Solaris to name but a few. More-advanced tools not only automate administrative tasks but also provide an interface for managing the corporate desktop configuration policies themselves. Administrators are able to set policies for an entire global enterprise, for specified domains, or for individual workstations. For example, some policy-based management software can store policies in a knowledge base that arranges the policies hierarchically in order to identify policy conflicts. However, once again, merely throwing technology at a problem will not provide an adequate solution. First, internal policies must be developed within the corporate environment before they can be entered into the policy-based management system. This policy development may involve a tremendous amount of work before the software can ever be implemented. The types of policies that might be enforced by policy-based management tools could be any of the following:

- User access rights to files, directories, servers, and executables

- Desktop start-up applications and background colors, or corporate office–approved screen savers

- User network access denial if desktop virus checking or metering has been disabled

- Facilitation of changes when applications move or devices are added to the network

- Denial of users' ability to install and run programs their desktops can't support

A few examples of policy-based management tools and their vendors are as follows:

Policy-Based Management Tool	Vendor
Saber Tools	McAfee
Norton Desktop Administrator	Symantec
AdminCenter	Hewlett Packard
Tivoli/Admin	IBM/Tivoli

Help Desks

As processing power has moved from the centralized mainframe room to the user's desktop, the support organization required to support that processing power has undergone significant changes as well. When mission-critical business applications are shifted to client/server architectures, effective help desk operations must be in place and ready to go.

Although some help desk management technology is aimed at setting up small help desks on a single PC or workstation to provide simple trouble ticketing and tracking, the higher end of help desk technology supports additional processes:

- Asset management

- Change management

- Integration with event management systems

- Support of business-specific processes and procedures

The basic objective of this higher-end technology is to proactively manage system and network resources to prevent problems rather than merely to react to system or network problems.

Because the help desk is held accountable for its level of service to end users, help desk management technology must be able to gather the statistics necessary to measure the impact of its efforts. Because a significant amount of the interaction with a help desk occurs over the phone, help desk management software should be able to interact with call center management technology such as **automatic call distributors (ACD)** and **interactive voice response units (IVRU).** The overall integration of computer-based software and telephony equipment in known as **computer telephony integration (CTI).**

The heart of any help desk management software package is the **knowledge base,** which contains not just the resolutions or answers to problems, but the logic structure or decision tree that takes a given problem and leads the help desk staff person through a series of questions to the appropriate solution. Interestingly, the knowledge bases supplied with help desk management software may be supplied by third parties under license to the help desk management software vendor. Obviously, the knowledge base is added to by help desk personnel with corporate-specific problems and solutions, but the amount of information supplied initially by a given knowledge base can vary. The portion of the software that sifts through the knowledge base to the proper answer is sometimes referred to as the **search engine.**

Figure 12-5 summarizes some of the other key functional areas for help desk management software.

Help Desk Management Software Functionality	Explanation/Importance
Administration, Security, and Utilities	• What types of adds, deletes, and changes can be made with the system up and running, and what types require a system shutdown? • Must all help desk personnel be logged out of the system in order to perform administrative functions? • Can major changes be done on a separate version off-line, followed by a brief system restart with the new version? • Can changes be tested off-line before committing to live installation? • Is security primarily group level or individual? Can agents belong to more than one group? • Can priorities and response times be flexibly assigned? • Can information be imported and exported in a variety of formats?
Call Logging	• How easy is it to log calls? • Can call logging link to existing databases to minimize the amount of data that must be entered? • Can the number of steps and keystrokes required to add a user or log a call be controlled? • Can multiple calls be logged at once? • Can one call be suspended (put on hold) while another one is logged? • Can special customers or users be flagged as such?
Call Tracking and Escalation	• How flexible are the call escalation options? • Call escalation options should be able to support internally defined problem resolution and escalation policies and processes. • Can the system support both manual and automatic escalation? • Can automatic escalation paths, priorities, and criteria be flexibly defined? • Can calls be timed as part of service level reporting? • How flexibly can calls be assigned to individual or groups of agents? • Is escalation system tied to work schedule system? • Can subject area or problem experts be identified and used as part of the escalation process?
Customizability	• Customizability is an issue at both the database level and the screen design level. • How easy is it to add knowledge and new problems/solutions to the knowledge base? • Does the software offer customizability for multinational companies? • Can entire new screens or views be designed? • Do existing screens contain undefined fields?

Integration with Other Products	• Is computer telephony integration with automatic call distributors and interactive voice response units available? • Which other integrated modules are included: asset management, change management, scheduling, training, workstation auditing? • Does the software link to enterprise network management software such as HP OpenView or IBM SystemView?
Performance	• Variables to consider when evaluating performance are number of simultaneous users on-line, number of calls per hour, required platform for database/knowledge base and search engine, and required platform for agents. • Which SQL-compliant databases are supported? • Can searches be limited to improve performance?
Problem Resolution	• Products can differ significantly in how they search knowledge bases. This can have a major impact on performance. Decision trees, case-based retrieval, troubleshooting tools, and embedded expert systems or artificial intelligence are the most-intelligent, most-complicated, and most-expensive options for problem resolution methodologies. • Many products provide more than one search engine or problem resolution method. • Some problem resolution products learn about your environment as more problems are entered. • Some problem resolution methods can use numerous different knowledge sources or problem databases.
Reporting	• How many standard reports are included? • How easily can customized reports be created? • How easily can data (especially agent performance data) be exported to spreadsheet or database programs for further analysis?

Figure 12-5   Help Desk Management Software

Asset Management

Asset management is a broad category of management software that has traditionally been divided into three subcategories:

- Electronic software distribution

- License metering software

- LAN inventory management software

Electronic Software Distribution   As the client/server architecture has taken hold as the dominant information systems paradigm, the increased processing power possessed by client workstations had been matched by increasing amounts of sophisticated software installed on these client workstations. The distribution of client software to multiple locally and remotely attached client workstations could be a very personnel-intensive and expensive task were it not for a new category of LAN-enabled software known as **ESD,** or **Electronic Software Distribution.** ESD software can vary widely in the types of services and features offered as well as in the costs for the convenience offered. For example, in addition to simply delivering software to LAN-attached clients, ESD software may also provide other services:

- Update configuration files

- Edit other files

- Capture commands entered during a manual software installation and convert the captured text into an automated script to control subsequent electronic software distribution.

Figure 12-6 summarizes some of the key functional characteristics of ESD software.

License-Metering Software   Although **license-metering software** was originally intended to monitor the number of executing copies of a particular software package versus the number of licenses purchased for that package, an interesting and beneficial side effect of license metering software has occurred. In recognition of this beneficial side effect, this category of software is now sometimes referred to as **license management software.** The previously mentioned beneficial side effect stems from the realization that at any time, fewer than 100 percent of the workstations possess-

ESD Software Functional Category	Description/Implication
NOS Support	• ESD software distributes software via the LAN, so it is important to know which network operating systems are supported. Options are NetWare, LANManager, VINES, LANServer, Windows NT, Windows for Workgroups, PathWorks, LANtastic.
Update Control	• Can updates be scheduled? • Can updates be selectively done based on hardware configuration? • Can updates be done only on selected machines? • Can only certain files be searched for and replaced? • Can files be edited or updated? Examples: CONFIG.SYS, AUTOEXEC.BAT, WIN.INI, SYSTEM.INI • Can files in use be replaced? • Can files be moved and renamed? • Can the update be done in the background on client workstations? • How secure is the update control? • Can updates be scripted? • Can update keystrokes be captured and converted to an automated update control file? • Can users perform their own selected updates from a distribution server? • Are unattended updates possible? • Are in-progress status screens available? • Can outside distribution lists be imported? • Can remote workstations be shut down and rebooted? • How extensive are the update reporting and logging capabilities?
Interoperability	• Is the ESD software integrated with license meeting or LAN hardware/software inventory software? • Are other software packages required in order to execute the ESD software?
Licensing	• Are licensing fees based on numbers of clients or numbers of distribution servers?

Figure 12-6   Electronic Software Distribution Functionality

ing legitimate licenses for a given software product are actually executing that software product.

As a result, with the aid of license management software, fewer licenses can service an equal or greater number of users, thereby reducing the numbers of software licenses purchased and the associated cost of software ownership. License management software is able to dynamically allocate licenses to those users wishing to execute a particular software package in a process known as **license optimization.** Three of the more popular license optimization techniques are as follows:

1. **Dynamic allocation** gives out either single user or suite licenses based on the number of suite applications used. As an example, if a user starts a word-processing package within an application suite, he or she would be issued a single user license for the word-processing package. However, if the user were subsequently to execute a spreadsheet package within the same suite, he or she would be issued a suite license rather than a second single user license.

2. **Load balancing** shifts licenses between servers to meet demands for licenses put on those servers by locally attached users. Licenses are loaned between servers as needed. In this way, every server does not need to have a full complement of licenses to meet all anticipated user demands. This technique is also known as **license pooling.**

3. **Global license sharing** recognizes the opportunity for license sharing presented by the widely distributed nature of today's global enterprise networks. While users on one side of the globe are sleeping, users on the other side of the globe are sharing the same pool of licenses.

License metering and management software has traditionally been supplied as add-on products written by third-party software developers. However, this trend may change abruptly. Novell and Microsoft have cooperated (an unusual circumstance in itself) on a **licensing server API (LSAPI).** This API would build license-metering capability into Microsoft's and Novell's network operating systems and would eliminate the need for third-party license metering software.

LSAPI-compliant applications would communicate with a specialized **license server,** which would issue **access tokens,** more formally known as **digital license certificates,** based on the license information stored in the license server database. Applications wishing to take advantage of the NOS-based license metering service would need only to include the proper commands as specified in the LSAPI.

LAN Inventory Management Software   **LAN inventory management software** is often included or integrated with electronic software distribution or license-metering software. However, it has a unique and important mission of its own in a widely distributed client/server architecture in which hardware and software assets are located throughout an enterprise network. A quality LAN inventory management software system is especially important when it comes to the planning efforts for network hardware and software upgrades. An enormous amount of human energy, and associated expense, can be wasted going from workstation to workstation figuring out the hardware and software characteristics of each workstation when LAN inventory management software can do the job automatically and can report gathered data in useful and flexible formats. Figure 12-7 highlights some of the key functional capabilities of LAN inventory management software.

LAN Inventory Management Functional Category	Description/Functionality
Platforms	• Client platforms supported are DOS, Macintosh, Windows, and OS/2. • Server platforms supported are NetWare, LANManager, LANServer, PathWorks, VINES, NetBIOS (DOS-Based), Windows NT.
Data Collection	• How flexibly can inventory scans be scheduled? • Can inventory scans of client workstations be completed incrementally during successive logins? • Does the inventory software flag the unknown software it finds on client workstations? • How large a catalog of known software titles does the inventory software have? A 6000-title catalog is among the best. • Can software titles be added to the known software list? • Are fields for data collection user-definable? • Can the inventory management software audit servers as well as client workstations? • Are hardware and software inventory information stored in the same database? • What is the database format? • Can the inventory management software differentiate between and track the assets of multiple laptop computers that share a single docking bay?
Reporting	• How many predefined reports are available? • Are customized reports available? • How easy is it to produce a customized report? • Can reports be exported in numerous formats, such as popular word-processing, spreadsheet, and presentation graphics formats?
Query	• How user-friendly and powerful are the query tools? • Can queries be generated on unique hardware and software combinations? • Can inventory information be gathered and displayed on demand?

Figure 12-7   LAN Inventory Management Software Functionality

■ CLIENT/SERVER INFRASTRUCTURE ARCHITECTURE

Having covered the issues involved in the management of client workstations, whether mobile or desktop oriented, we now must look at what is involved with the management of the remainder of the client/server infrastructure. In order to delineate the processes and technology involved with the management of the infrastructure that underlies an enterprisewide client/server information system, one must first define those components that compose the infrastructure to be managed. Traditionally, a client/server infrastructure is composed of a wide variety of servers and the various networks that connect those servers to one another and to the clients that they serve. There is no single right way to divide the processes or responsibility for the management of these various components. For the purposes of this chapter, client/server infrastructure management is segmented into the following components:

- **Systems administration** focuses on the management of client and server computers and the operating systems and network operating systems that allow the client and server computers to communicate. This could also be considered local area network administration.

- **Enterprise network management** focuses on the hardware, software, media, and network services required to seamlessly link and effectively manage distributed client and server computers across an enterprise. This could also be considered internetwork (between LANs) administration.

Both systems administration and enterprise network management are composed of several subprocesses, as illustrated in Figure 12-8.

As local area networks, internetworks, and wide area networks have combined to form enterprise networks, the management of all of these elements of the enterprise has been a key concern. LANs, internetworks, and WANs have traditionally each had their own set of management tools and protocols. Once integrated into a single enterprise, these disparate tools and protocols do not necessarily meld into an integrated cohesive system.

Figure 12-9 summarizes the key functional differences between enterprise network management and systems administration and lists some representative technologies of each category.

The Network Management Forum associated with the OSI reference model has divided the field of network management into five major categories in a document

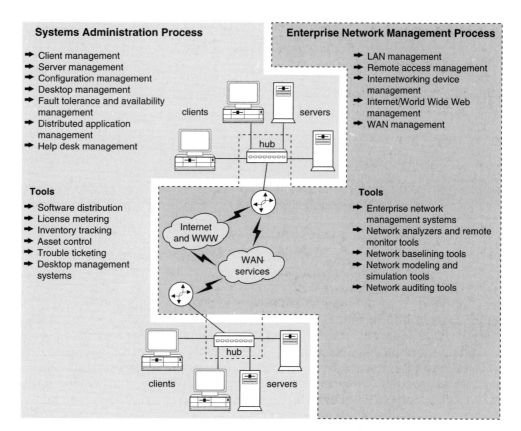

Figure 12-8   Client/Server Infrastructure Architecture Systems Administration and Enterprise Network Management

	Functionality	Technology
Enterprise Network Management	• Monitor and manage internetwork technology—switches, routers, bridges, hubs • Monitor and manage WAN links	• HP Openview • Tivoli TME • Sun Solstice Enterprise Manager • CA Unicenter
Systems Administration (Also Known as Desktop Management)	• Track hardware and software inventory • Perform license metering • Monitor LAN and server activity • Perform software distribution • Perform asset management • Do server monitoring	• SaberLAN Workstation—McAfee • Brightworks—McAfee • LANDesk Suite—Intel • Norton Administrator for Networks—Symantec • Frye Utilities for Desktops—Seagate • System Management Server—Microsoft • ManageWise—Novell

Figure 12-9   Systems Administration versus Enterprise Network Management

known as the *ISO Management Framework* (ISO 7498-4). This categorization is somewhat arbitrary because standards and network management technology apply to multiple categories, and even the categories themselves are interdependent. However, it is important for the network analyst to be aware of this categorization because it is often referred to when discussing network management architectures and technology. Figure 12-10 lists and explains the five OSI categories of network management.

Consolidated Service Desk

Although the division of client/server infrastructure management processes into systems administration and enterprise network management is helpful in terms of distinguishing between associated function, protocols, and technology, how are these various processes actually supported or implemented in an enterprise? Reflective of the evolution of information systems in general, client/server infrastructure management has undergone an evolution of its own. The current trend in client/server infrastructure management is to offer a **consolidated service desk (CSD)** approach to end-user and infrastructure support. Such an approach offers a number of benefits:

- As a single point of contact for all network and application problem resolution, appropriate personnel processes can be matched with associated network management technologies. This match of standardized processes with technology yields more-predictable service levels and accountability. CSD software should include features to support problem escalation, trouble ticketing and tracking, and productivity management reporting. Users should be able to easily check on the status of the resolution of reported problems.

- The consolidation of all problem data at a single location allows correlation between problem reports to be made, thereby enabling a more proactive

OSI Category of Network Management	Explanation/Importance
Fault Management	• Monitor the network or system state. • Receive and process alarms. • Diagnose the causes of faults. • Determine the propagation of errors. • Initiate and check error recovery measures. • Introduce trouble ticket system. • Provide a user help desk.
Configuration Management	• Compile accurate description of all network components. • Control updating of configuration. • Control remote configuration. • Support network version control. • Initiate jobs and trace their execution.
Performance Management	• Determine quality of service parameters. • Monitor network for performance bottlenecks. • Measure system and network performance. • Process measurement data and produce reports. • Perform capacity planning and proactive performance planning.
Security Management	• Monitor the system for intrusions. • Provide authentication of users. • Provide encryption in order to ensure message privacy. • Implement associated security policy.
Accounting Management	• Record system and network usage statistics. • Maintain usage accounting system for chargeback purposes. • Allocate monitor system or network usage quotas. • Maintain and report usage statistics.

Figure 12-10   OSI Categories of Network Management

than reactive management style. Incorporated remote control software will allow CSD personnel to take over users' computers and fix problems remotely in a swift manner.

• Resolutions to known user inquiries can be incorporated into intelligent help desk support systems in order to expedite problem resolution and make the most effective use of support personnel. On-line knowledge bases allow users to solve their own problems in many cases.

• The consolidated services desk can also handle other processes not directly related to problem resolution such as inventory and asset tracking and asset optimization through the use of such technology as license-metering software. It can also coordinate hardware and software upgrades. Software upgrades could be centrally handled by electronic software distribution technology. The management of these systems changes is referred to as change management.

- Network security policies, procedures, and technology can also be consolidated at the CSD.

- It can eliminate or reduce "console clutter" in which every monitored system has its own console. In large multinational corporations, this can lead to well over 100 consoles. Because all of these consoles must be monitored by people, console consolidation can obviously lead to cost containment.

Figure 12-11 conceptually illustrates how policy, procedures, personnel, and technology all merge at the consolidated service desk. It is important to note the inclusion of policy and procedures in the illustration. The formation of a CSD provides a marvelous opportunity to define or redesign processes to meet specific business and management objectives. Any technology incorporated in the CSD should be chosen based on its ability to support the previously defined corporate policies and procedures in its area of influence. It is important not to first choose a CSD tool and then let that tool dictate the corporate processes and procedures in that particular area of management.

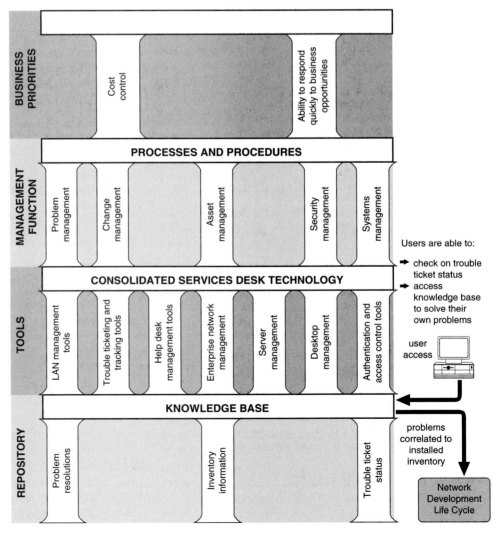

Figure 12-11   Consolidated Service Desk

■ SERVER MANAGEMENT AND SYSTEMS ADMINISTRATION

Server Management

At the heart of systems administration is the administration of the servers that are the workhorses and providers of basic system functionality. As servers continue to take on increasingly important roles to the entire enterprise, such as electronic messaging servers and enterprise directory servers, it is becoming more important to be able to effectively manage, troubleshoot, and remotely configure these critical elements of the enterprise infrastructure. Server management software seeks to ease systems administrators' chores by effectively monitoring, reporting, troubleshooting, and diagnosing server performance. Some server management software is particular to a certain brand of server; other server management software can manage multiple brands of servers. Ultimately, to be especially useful in meeting overall goals of systems reliability and end-user satisfaction, server management software must provide **server capacity planning** capabilities by monitoring server performance trends and proactively recommending server component upgrades.

An important point to remember about server management software is that it most often requires a software or hardware module to be installed on all servers to be monitored and managed. This module will require varying amounts of system resources (CPU cycles, memory) and will have varying degrees of impact on system performance. Some server management systems perform most of the processing on the managed servers, but others perform most of the processing on the server management console or workstation. Likewise, some server management systems require a dedicated management workstation, and others will operate on a multifunction management workstation. Figure 12-12 summarizes some of the key potential

Server Management System Function	Importance/Explanation
Server hardware problem diagnosis	• Can alarm thresholds and status be flexibly defined? • How many alarm levels are possible? • Can RAID drive arrays be monitored and diagnosed? • Is predictive hardware failure analysis offered? • Is a diagnostic hardware module required? • Can server temperature and voltage be monitored? • Can bus configuration and utilization be reported?
Server software problem diagnosis	• Does the server management software track version control and correlate with currently available versions? • Can version control indicate potential impacts of version upgrades? • What diagnostics or routines are supplied to diagnose server software problems?
Server capacity planning and performance enhancement	• Are performance enhancement and capacity-planning capabilities included? • Are trend identification routines included? • Are inventory, asset management, and optimization modules included?

Sharing of data with other management platforms	• Can data be passed to frameworks and integrated suites such as HP OpenView or Tivoli TME? • Can alerts and alarms trigger pagers, e-mail, dial-up? • Can data be exported to an ODBC-compliant database?
Remote configuration capability	• Can servers be remotely configured from a single console? • Is out-of-band (dial-up) management supported? • Is remote power cycling supported? • Is screen redirection/remote console control supported?
Report generation	• Are alert logs automatically generated? • Can reports be flexibly and easily defined by users?
Protocol issues	• Is TCP/IP required for the transport protocol? • Is IPX supported? • Is SNMP the management protocol? • Are any proprietary protocols required?
Server platforms management	• Possibilities include Windows NT, NetWare 3.x, NetWare 4.x, SCO UNIX and other UNIX varieties, OS2, VINES.
Console requirements	• Is a Web browser interface supported? • Is a dedicated workstation required for the console? • Are there operating system requirements for the console? • Are there hardware requirements for the console?
Statistics tracking and reporting	• Logged in users • Applications running • CPU utilization • I/O bus utilization • Memory utilization • Network interface card utilization • Disk performance and utilization • Security management • System usage by application and by user
Mapping capabilities	• Can the administrator map or group servers flexibly? • Can statistics be viewed across multiple server groups defined by a variety of characteristics? • How effective is the server topology map? • Can screen displays be easily printed?

Figure 12-12   Server Management Software Functionality

functional areas of server management software. Figure 12-13 illustrates the implemented architecture of a server management system.

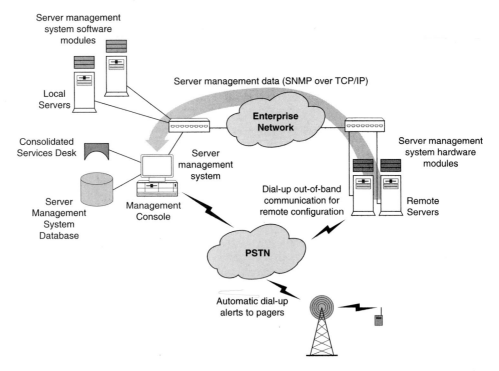

Figure 12-13   Server Management System Architecture

■ ENTERPRISE NETWORK MANAGEMENT

Enterprise Network Management Architecture and Protocols

As illustrated in Figure 12-14, today's enterprise network management architectures are composed of relatively few elements.

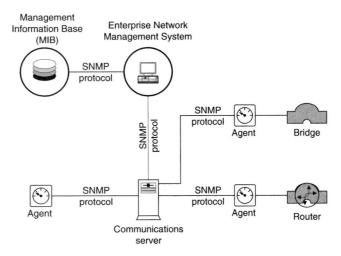

Figure 12-14   Enterprise Network Management Architecture

Agents are software programs that run on networking devices such as servers, bridges, and routers to monitor and report the status of those devices. Agent software must be compatible with the device that it is reporting management statistics for, as well as with the protocols supported by the enterprise network management system to which those statistics are fed. Agents from the numerous individual networking devices forward this network management information to **enterprise network management systems,** which compile and report network operation statistics to the end user, most often in some type of graphical format. Enterprise network management systems are really management application programs running on a management server.

The network management information gathered must be stored in some type of database with an index and standardized field definitions so that network management workstations can easily access this data. A **MIB,** or **management information base,** as these databases are known, can differ in the fields defined for different vendors' networking devices. These fields within the MIBs are known as **objects.** One fairly standard MIB is known as the **RMON MIB,** which stands for remote network monitoring MIB. Finally, a protocol is required to encapsulate the management data for delivery by network and transport layer protocols. Partly due to the dominance of TCP/IP as the internetworking protocol of choice, **SNMP (simple network management protocol)** is the de facto standard for delivering enterprise management data. Numerous variations of SNMP, MIB, and RMON standards are explained in further detail later in the chapter.

As originally conceived, the enterprise management console would collect the performance data from all of the devices, or elements, comprising an enterprise network in a single, centralized location. However, as networks grew in both complexity and size and as the numbers of devices to be managed exploded, the amount of management traffic flowing over the enterprise network has begun to reach unacceptable levels. In some cases, management traffic alone can account for 30 percent of network bandwidth usage, thereby reporting on the problems that it is itself creating.

An alternative to the centralized enterprise management console approach known as the **distributed device manager (DDM)** has begun to emerge. DDM takes an end-to-end full network view of the enterprise network as opposed to the centralized enterprise management console architecture, which takes an individual device or element focus. A DDM architecture relies on **distributed network probes** that are able to gather information from a variety of network devices manufactured by multiple vendors and relay that information to numerous distributed device manager consoles. Probes are strategically placed throughout the enterprise network, especially at junctions of LAN and WAN segments in order to isolate the source of network traffic problems. Management traffic is minimized and remains localized rather than monopolizing enterprise network bandwidth supplying the centralized enterprise management console. Figure 12-15 provides a conceptual view of a distributed device manager architecture.

Web-Based Management   Another possible evolutionary stage in enterprise network management architectures is web-based enterprise management, first mentioned in the section on distributed application management. The WBEM logical architecture is illustrated in Figure 12-16. The overall intention of the architecture is that the network manager could manage any networked device or application from any location on the network, via any **HMMP (hypermedia management protocol)**-compliant browser. Existing network and desktop management protocols such as SNMP

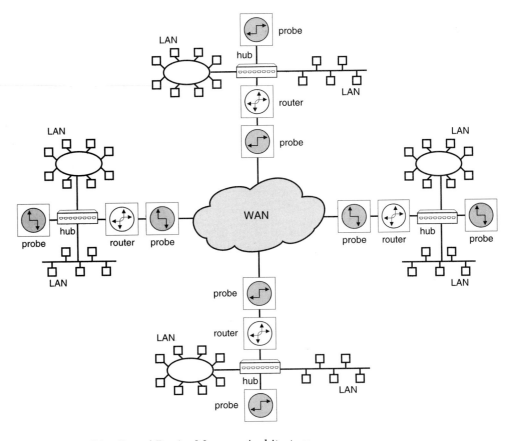

Figure 12-15   Distributed Device Manager Architecture

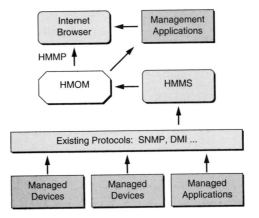

Figure 12-16   Web-Based Enterprise Management Logical Architecture

and DMI may either interoperate or be replaced by HMMP. Current plans call for HMMP to communicate either by Microsoft's DCOM (Distributed Component Object Model) or by CORBA (Common Object Request Broker Architecture). (For more information on DCOM and CORBA, see Chapter 6, Middleware.) Management data from a variety of software agents would be incorporated into the web-based enterprise management architecture via the **HMMS (hypermedia management schema).** All web-based management information would be stored and retrieved by the request broker formerly known as **HMOM (hypermedia object manager),** now known simply as the object manager.

A proposed protocol currently under development by the DMTF (Desktop Management Task Force) that would support HMMS is known as **CIM,** or **common information model.** CIM would permit management data gathered from a variety of enterprise and desktop voice and data technology all to be transported, processed, displayed, and stored by a single CIM-compliant web browser. Management data to be used by CIM would be stored in **MOF (modified object format),** as opposed to DMI's MIF format or SNMP's MIB format. Figure 12-17 illustrates the interaction of the various types of management data.

Managerial Perspective

Some would argue that CIM is finally the answer to the challenge of achieving transparency of enterprise management technology. Others would argue that CIM is nothing more than an added layer of complexity on top of an enterprise management system that is already overly complex. An alternative would be to make existing management protocols such as SNMP, DMI, and CMIP more interoperable, to eliminate the need for additional layers of protocols. However, owing to political issues and turf wars, achieving such interoperability is easier said than done, thereby creating opportunities for new all-encompassing protocols such as CIM.

From a practical standpoint, web-based management could benefit both vendors and users:

- Users would have to deal with only one common interface regardless of the enterprise network device that was to be managed.

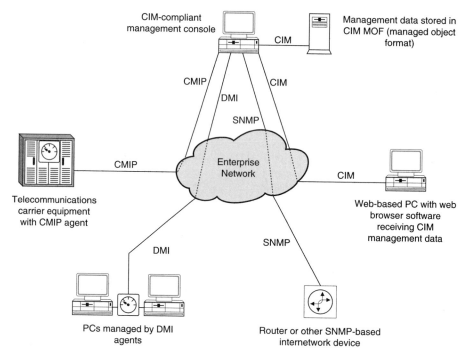

Figure 12-17   Management Data: CIM, CMIP, DMI, and SNMP

- Vendors could save a tremendous amount of development costs by developing management applications for only a single platform.

However, the fact that a management tool is web-based is not enough. It must deliver all of the functionality of the proprietary management software packages written for specific devices. Some of the most important functions for such software are listed in Figure 12-18.

Web-based network management technology is relatively new, and the market is still being defined. Current technology in this category provides a web browser interface to the user in one of two ways:

- A web server application is embedded with the enterprise network management platform, and the user accesses that embedded web server via a web browser. Communication between the actual network devices being managed and the enterprise network management platform is still by SNMP, as illustrated in Figure 12-14.

- A web server application is embedded within a given network device, thereby giving a user direct access to the management data of that device through any client-based web browser. Communication between the user and the network device is via HTTP.

Among the early vendors and their products in the web-based management market are the following:

Web-Based Management Application	Vendor
NovaWeb	Acacia Networks
IntraSpection	Asante Technologies
Cyber Sentry	NetBrowser Communications
Netscape Administration Server	Netscape Communications
NetDirector@Web	Newbridge Networks

Functional Category	Importance/Explanation
Configuration	• Ability to remotely configure network attached devices • Ability to detect changes to remote device configurations
Polling	• Ability to poll network-attached devices for performance and traffic statistics
Analysis	• Ability to consolidate and analyze statistics from multiple devices across the network • Ability to discern initial errors from cascading errors • Ability to detect trends • Ability to proactively predict potential trouble spots
Response	• Ability to respond in an appropriate manner to alarms and preset thresholds • Ability to detect false alarms • Ability to escalate problems as appropriate • Ability to notify proper personnel by a variety of means

Figure 12-18 Web-Based Management Tool Functionality

Which SNMP Is the Real SNMP?   The original SNMP protocol required internetworking device–specific agents to be polled for SNMP encapsulated management data. Alarm conditions or exceptions to preset thresholds could not be directly reported as needed from the agents to the enterprise network management software. Agents' inability to initiate communications with enterprise network management systems causes constant polling of agents. As a result of the constant polling, considerable network bandwidth is consumed.

Also, the original SNMP protocol did not provide for any means of manager-to-manager communication. As a result, only one enterprise network manager could be installed on a given network, forcing all internetworked devices to report directly to the single enterprise network manager. Hierarchical arrangements in which regional managers are able to filter raw management data and pass only exceptional information to enterprise managers is not possible with the original SNMP.

Another major shortcoming of the original SNMP is that it was limited to using TCP/IP as its transport protocol. It was therefore unusable on NetWare (IPX/SPX), Macintosh (Appletalk), or other networks. Finally, SNMP does not offer any security features that would authenticate valid polling managers or encrypt traffic between agents and managers.

The need to reduce network traffic caused by the SNMP protocol and to deal with other aforementioned SNMP shortcomings led to a proposal for a new version of SNMP known as **SNMP2,** or **SMP (simple management protocol).** SNMP2's major objectives can be summarized as follows:

- Reduce network traffic

- Segment large networks

- Support multiple transport protocols

- Increase security

- Allow multiple agents per device

Through a new SNMP2 procedure known as the **bulk retrieval mechanism,** managers can retrieve several pieces of network information at a time from a given agent. This precludes the need for a constant request and reply mechanism for each piece of network management information desired. Agents have also been given increased intelligence, which enables them to send error or exception conditions to managers when requests for information cannot be met. With SNMP, agents simply sent empty datagrams back to managers when requests could not be fulfilled. The receipt of the empty packet merely caused the manager to repeat the request for information, thus increasing network traffic.

SNMP2 allows the establishment of multiple manager entities within a single network. As a result, large networks that were managed by a single manager under SNMP can now be managed by multiple managers in a hierarchical arrangement in SNMP2. Overall network traffic is reduced as network management information is confined to the management domains of the individual network segment managers. Information is passed from the segment managers to the centralized network management system via manager-to-manager communication only on request of the central manager or if certain predefined error conditions occur on a subnet or local area network. Figure 12-19 illustrates the impact of SNMP2 manager-to-manager communications.

Before: Manager-to-Agent Communications

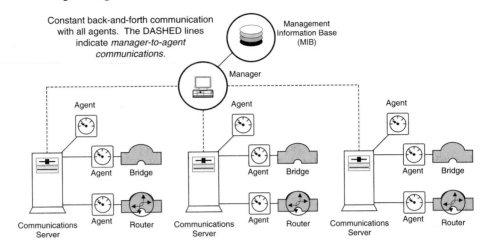

After: Manager-to-Manager Communications

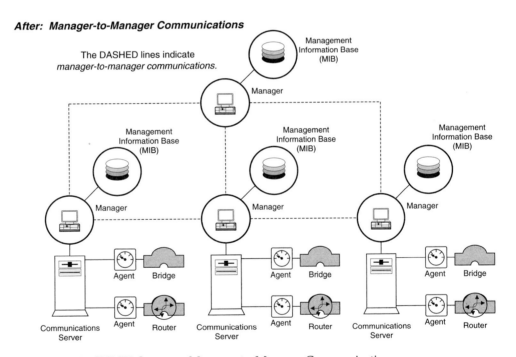

Figure 12-19 SNMP2 Supports Manager-to-Manager Communications

SNMP was initially part of the Internet suite of protocols and therefore was deployed only on those networks equipped with the TCP/IP protocols. SNMP2 works transparently with Appletalk, IPX, and OSI transport protocols.

Increased security in SNMP2 allows not just monitoring and management of remote network devices, but also actual **remote configuration** of those devices. Furthermore, SNMP2 or a variation of SNMP known as **Secure SNMP** will allow users to access carriers' network management information and incorporate it into the wide area component of an enterprise network management system. This ability to actually access data from within the carrier's central office has powerful implications for users and enables many advanced user services such as SDN, or software-defined network.

Perhaps the most significant SNMP2 development in terms of implication for distributed client/server management is the ability to deploy multiple agents per device. As a practical example, on a distributed server, one agent could monitor the processing activity, a second agent could monitor the database activity, and a third could monitor the networking activity, with each reporting back to its own manager. In this way, rather than having merely *distributed* enterprise network management, the entire distributed information system could be *managed*, with each major element of the client/server architecture managed by its own management infrastructure.

Unfortunately, considerable debate over portions of the SNMP2 protocol have delayed its deployment for years. Some people believe that features of SNMP2, especially the security aspects, are too difficult to implement and use. Others blame the delay on concerns over marketing position and competitive advantage from technology vendors. In the interim, alternative upgrades to SNMP have been proposed by both officially sanctioned organizations such as the IETF and ad hoc forums. Figure 12-20 summarizes key points of the various SNMP2 alternatives.

SNMP Standard	Also known as	Advantages	Disadvantages
SNMP		• Part of TCP/IP suite • Open standard • Works with defined MIBs	• Execessive polling • No manager-to-manager communication • Supports only TCP/IP • No security
SNMP2	SMP Secure SNMP	• Supports bulk retrieval • Supports manager-to-manager communication • Supports multiple protocols • Provides security • Remote configuration	• Never implemented due to squabbling among standards bodies
Updated SNMP2	SNMP2t SNMP2C SNMP1.5	• Supposedly easier to implement owing to removal of security features	• No security features • No manager-to-manager communications • No remote configuration
Interim SNMPV2	SNMP2u SNMP2*	• Adds back some of features taken out of updated SNMP2	• SNMP2u and SNMP2* are incompatible
SNMP3	SNMP2	• Adds security features back into SNMP2 • Merges concepts and technical elements of SNMP2u and SNMP2*	• Lack of support from official standards-making organization • Vendor-specific solutions are being offered as alternatives

Figure 12-20 Alternative SNMP2 Proposals

MIBs   Management information bases (MIBs) serve as repositories for enterprise network performance information to be displayed in meaningful format by enterprise network management systems. The original RMON MIB standard, which was developed in 1991, has been updated as **RMON2**. Although the original RMON MIB required compatible technology to be able to collect and analyze statistics only on the physical and data link layers, RMON2 requires collection and analysis of network layer protocols as well. In addition, RMON2 requires compatible technology to be able to identify from which application a given packet was generated. RMON2 compatible agent software, which resides within internetworking devices and reports performance statistics to enterprise network management systems, is referred to as an **RMON probe.** Overall, RMON2 should enable network analysts to more effectively pinpoint the exact sources and percentages of the traffic that flows through their enterprise networks. Figure 12-21 summarizes some of the key functional areas of the RMON2 specification.

To implement RMON2-based monitoring, a network manager would purchase RMON2 probes and associated RMON2 management software. Among the major vendors and RMON2 technology are the following:

RMON2 Management Software and Probes	Vendor
Traffix Manager, LAN-Sentry Manager, Enterprise Monitor	3Com
MeterWare	Technically Elite
Ethernet LANProbe	Hewlett Packard
Optivity Analysis	Bay Networks
LANMaster RMON Utilities	SolCom Systems

RMON2 Function	Explanation/Importance
Protocol Distribution	• Tracks and reports data link layer protocols by percentage • Tracks and reports network layer protocols by percentage • Tracks and reports application source by percentage
Address Mapping	• Maps network layer addresses to MAC layer addresses • Maps MAC layer addresses to hub or switch port
Network Layer Host Table	• Tracks and stores in table format network layer protocols and associated traffic statistics according to source host
Network Layer Matrix Table	• Tracks and stores in a matrix table format network layer protocols and associated traffic statistics according to sessions established between two given hosts
Application Host Table	• Tracks and stores in table format application-specific traffic statistics according to source host
Application Matrix Table	• Tracks and stores in a matrix table format application-specific traffic statistics according to sessions established between two given hosts
Probe Configuration	• Defines standards for remotely configuring probes that are responsible for gathering and reporting network activity statistics
History	• Tracks and stores historical traffic information according to parameters determined by the user

Figure 12-21   RMON2 Specifications

Besides differing in the number of RMON2 options and groups implemented, probes and RMON2 management software also differ significantly in their ability to integrate transparently with enterprise network management systems such as HP Openview, Tivoli TME 10, Sunnet Manager, Solstice, and IBM Netview.

One shortcoming of RMON2 is its inability to collect and provide data regarding wide area network (WAN) performance. **RMON3** is expected to provide much-needed standards for the WAN monitoring and management technology category. RMON3 would provide a way for many of the current proprietary WAN management tools to interoperate and share data. In addition, RMON3 is supposed to offer management and statistics-gathering support for switched networks and virtual LANs, as well as the ability to measure application program response times in order to monitor the performance of distributed applications.

Another effort to monitor distributed applications is known as the **application MIB**. Proposals for such an application MIB identify three key groups of variables for proper application tracking and management:

- **Definition variables** would store background information concerning applications such as application name, manufacturer, version, release, installation date, license number, and number of consecutive users.

- **State variables** would report on the current status of a given application. Three possible states are up, down, or degraded.

- **Relationship variables** would define all other network-attached resources on which a given distributed application depends. This would include databases, associated client applications, and other network resources.

One of the major difficulties with developing and implementing an application MIB is the vast differences that exist among distributed applications.

Enterprise Network Management Technology

Technology Architectures   All of the systems administration and network management processes reviewed in this chapter can be enabled by associated technology. In most cases, network management products offer functionality across more than one category of network or systems management. One way to distinguish between network management technology is to focus on the architecture of that technology. In general, network management technology can be categorized into three possible architectures:

- **Point products**—also known as **element managers**—are specifically written to address a particular systems administration or network management issue. Point products are narrow in scope, provide the sought-after solution, and are usually relatively easy to install and understand. However, they do not necessarily integrate with other systems administration and network management tools. Any necessary correlation between point products must be done by network management personnel. Backup and restoral tools, license optimization tools, or management tools specifically written for a particular vendor's equipment are examples of point solutions.

- **Frameworks**—offer an overall systems administration or network management platform with integration between modules and a shared database into which all alerts, messages, alarms, and warnings can be stored and correlated. Perhaps more importantly, most frameworks also offer open APIs or an entire application development environment so that third-party application developers can create additional systems administration or network management modules that will be able to plug into the existing framework and share management information with other modules. A well-integrated framework can offer the network administrator a single, correlated view of all systems and network resources. However, the development or integration of modules within the framework can be difficult and time consuming. In addition, not all management modules may be compatible with a given framework.

- **Integrated suites** could perhaps be looked upon as a subset of frameworks, although the two terms are often used interchangably. The difference between integrated suites and frameworks is the fact that integrated suites are filled with their own network management and systems administration applications rather than offering the user an open framework into which to place a variety of chosen applications. With integrated suites the applications are more tightly integrated and linked by a set of common services, which tend to offer the user a more consolidated view of network resources. However, they usually do not offer the open pick-and-choose architecture of the framework. Some products in this category offer an integrated suite of applications but also support open APIs in order to accommodate third-party systems administration and network management applications.

Desired Functionality Beyond the choices of architecture, systems administration and network management technology packages also differ in the level of functionality offered. For example, although most network management software can report on network activity and detect abnormal activities and report alarms, fewer packages are able to diagnose or fix problems. Among the commonly noted functions that network administrators would like to see delivered by systems administration and network management technology are the following:

- The ability to track the operational status of distributed applications

- The ability to automate reporting of system status information

- The ability to automate repetitive system management tasks

- The ability to integrate application management and systems administration information with network management information

- The ability to improve application performance by properly responding to system status messages

Currently Available Technology Enterprise network management systems must be able to gather information from a variety of sources throughout the enterprise network and display that information in a clear and meaningful format. Furthermore, enterprise network management systems are being called on to monitor and manage additional distributed resources:

- Workstations and servers
- Distributed applications
- Distributed data management systems

One of the current difficulties with actually implementing enterprise network management systems is a lack of interoperability between different enterprise network management systems and third-party or vendor-specific network management systems. The following are popular enterprise network management systems that could be considered frameworks or integrated suites:

- HP Openview
- Sun Soft Solstice Enterprise Manager
- Computer Associates' CA-Unicenter TNG (The Next Generation)
- TME 10 by IBM/Tivoli Systems (includes IBM SystemView)
- PatrolView by BMC Software
- Spectrum Enterprise Manager by Cabletron

Examples of third-party or vendor-specific network management systems, sometimes known as element managers or point products, include these systems:

- 3Com Transcend Enterprise Manager
- Cisco CiscoWorks
- Bay Networks Optivity Enterprise
- Legato Networker
- Cabletron Spectrum Element Manager
- American Power Conversion PowerNet

The lack of interoperability between third-party applications and enterprise network management systems has various manifestations:

- Separate databases are maintained by each third-party application and enterprise network management system.
- Redundant polling of agent software occurs in order to gather performance statistics.
- Multiple agents are installed and executed on networked devices in order to report to multiple management platforms.

The lack of interoperability between different enterprise network management systems makes some tasks difficult if not impossible:

- Exchanging of network topology information and maps
- Exchanging of threshold performance parameter and alarm information

The major cause of all of this lack of interoperability is the lack of common APIs, both between different enterprise network management systems and between an enterprise network management system and third-party network management systems. Figure 12-22 illustrates an architectural view of how enterprise network management systems interface to other enterprise network components. Interoperability APIs included in Figure 12-22 are either proposed or under development.

In addition to the interoperability issues previously discussed, key functional areas of enterprise network management software are listed in Figure 12-23.

Analysis — Network Analyzers

The only real effective way to diagnose problems with network performance is to be able to unobtrusively peer into the network transmission media and actually see the characteristics of the packets of data that are causing performance problems. LAN and WAN **network analyzers** are able to capture network traffic in real time without interrupting normal network transmission. In addition to capturing packets of data from the network, most network analyzers are able to decode those packets, monitor packet traffic statistics, and simulate network traffic through traffic generators. Filtering provided by network analyzers can isolate certain types of protocols or traffic from only particular workstations or servers. Given the multitude of protocols and the tidal wave of packets on a given network, effective filtering capabilities are enormously important to network analyzer usefulness.

Network analyzers may be software based (user supplies the PC), hardware-based (fully installed in their own dedicated PC), or hybrid, in which an add-on hardware device with installed software is linked to the notebook PC via the

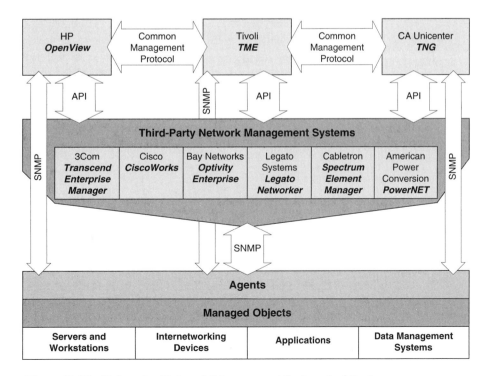

Figure 12-22   Enterprise Network Management System Architecture

Functional Category	Importance/Implication
Operating System Compatibility	• Which operating systems does the enterprise network management system run over? • HP UX • Sun OS • Solaris SPARC • IBM AIX • Windows NT • How many simultaneous operators of the enterprise network management system are supported? • Can multiple operators be distributed across the enterprise network?
Database Compatibility	• Which databases can the enterprise network management system interoperate with? • Oracle • Ingres • SyBase • Informix • Proprietary • DB2 • Flat file
Network Size and Architecture	• Is there a limit to the number of notes supported? • Can the software map all network architectures? (Ethernet, Token Ring, FDDI, switched LANs, WANs, ATM) • Can mainframes be integrated into the enterprise network management system? • Can IPX as well as IP devices be managed?
Third-Party Application Support	• How many third-party applications are guaranteed to incorporate with this enterprise network management system?
MIB and Management Protocol Support	• How many different MIBs are supported? MIBs can be both IETF sanctioned or vendor specific. Enterprise network management systems can easily support more than 200 different MIBs. • Are management protocols other than SNMP supported, such as CMIP (common management information protocol), proprietary protocols, SNMP2?
Self-Configuration	• To what extent is the enterprise network management software able to self-configure or autodiscover the enterprise network topology? • Can the self-configuration process by customized or controlled?
Cascading or Effect Alarms	• Is the system able to identify and report alarms triggered by other alarms in order to more easily pinpoint the cause of problems? This capability may be known as event correlation.

Figure 12-23 Functional Categories of Enterprise Network Management Systems

parallel port. Still other analyzers, such as the Network General Sniffer, are shipped with a PCMCIA (PC card) ethernet adapter and software for installation on a limited number of supported notebook computers. Preconfigured Sniffers are also available. Network analyzers can also differ in the number of LAN and WAN protocols that can be analyzed, the number of nodes from which traffic can be captured, and the ease of use, understanding, and flexibility of the user interface. Some network analyzers include expert systems that are able to predict oncoming problems based on observed traffic trends.

Network analyzer capabilities are most easily compared and categorized according to the seven-layer OSI model, as outlined in Figure12-24. In some cases, devices are specific to particular layers. For example, layer 1 testers are commonly known as **cable scanners** or cable testers. Devices that test layers 2 through 7 are often called **protocol analyzers.** Other devices combine both functionalities into a single device. Names of some popular network analyzers and their vendors are included in the following list:

Network Analyzer	Vendor
Sniffer Internetwork Analyzer	Network Associates
Fluke LANMeter	Fluke
Internet Advisor	Hewlett Packard
Domino Internetwork Analyzer	Wandel and Goltermann
COMPAS	Microtest
WAN/LAN 900 Expert Protocol Analyzer	Digitech Industries

Monitoring — Network Baselining Tools

By combining the ability to monitor and capture SNMP, RMON, and RMON2 data from multivendor networking technology with the abilities to analyze the captured data and report on trends and exceptions, **network baselining tools** are able to track network performance over extended periods of time and report on anomalies

OSI Model Layer	Network Analyzer Functionality
Layer 7 — Application	• Some analyzers can display actual text and numbers being transmitted across a medium. Because passwords and credit card numbers can be displayed by such a device, it is understandable why network analyzers are sometimes considered a security threat. The ability to display protocols from layers 4 through 7 is referred to as embedded protocol decoding.
Layer 6 — Presentation	• Embedded protocol decodes
Layer 5 — Session	• Embedded protocol decodes
Layer 4 — Transport	• Embedded protocol decodes
Layer 3 — Network	• Network layer protocols: X.25, ISDN Q.931, IP, IPX, Appletalk
Layer 2 — DataLink	• Hardware interface modules (LAN): Ethernet, Token Ring, switched Ethernet, fast Ethernet, FDDI • Hardware interface modules (WAN): ISDN BRI, DDS, ATM • DataLink WAN Protocols: BiSync, HDLC, SDLC, PPP, LAPB, LAPD, SLIP, frame relay, SNA

Layer 1—Physical

- Also known as cable scanners or cable testers
- Cable scanners can pinpoint cable problems including locations of breaks, short circuits, miswiring, and polarity problems.
- Although a variety of different media types might be tested, the two most popular are Category 5 unshielded twisted pair and fiber optic cable.
- Layer 1 protocols V.35, RS-232, RS-449, 423, 422, 530, T-1 (variety of interfaces)
- Among the key features and measurements of cable testers are the following:
  - Ambient noise: level of external noise (from fluorescent lights, motors) where a cable is installed
  - Attenuation: loss of signal strength over the distance traveled through media
  - Attenuation-to-crosstalk: extent to which a medium resists crosstalk
  - BERT (bit error rate tester): able to determine percent of received bits received in error
  - Capacitance: capacity of the medium to store an electrical charge
  - Continuity: an uninterrupted electrical path along the medium
  - Impedance: opposition to flow of a signal within a medium, measured in ohms; the lower the impedance, the better the conductor
  - Loopback device: cable tester function that sends transmitted signal out through medium and back into device for test and measurement
  - Loop resistance: resistance encountered in completing a full electrical circuit
  - Injector device: part of cable tester that creates signal, verifies transmission, and manages testing
  - NeXT (near-end crosstalk): signals being transmitted on one end overcoming and interfering with the weaker signals being received on the same end
  - NVP (nominal velocity of propagation): the speed of the data transmission through the tested media compared to speed of light transmission through a vacuum
  - OTDR (optical time division reflectometer): device that measures the time it takes for light to be reflected through a medium in order to detect breaks or crimps
  - SNR (signal to noise ratio): comparison of signal strength to background noise, measured in decibels
  - Split pair: when a wire of one pair gets spliced to the wire of an adjacent pair
  - TDR (time domain reflectometer): able to measure cable lengths and distance to breaks by reflected electrical signals through a medium
  - Two way NeXT: measures near-end crosstalk as well as far-end crosstalk, which is crosstalk in same direction as signal
  - Wire map: verifies and graphically displays pin-to-pin continuity and checks for polarity reversal, short circuits, and open circuits

Figure 12-24 Network Analyzer Functional Capabilities by OSI Model Layer

or deviations from the accumulated baseline data. Also known as **proactive network management tools** or **network trending products,** such tools usually need several weeks of SNMP data in order to establish realistic baseline network performance averages. Network baselining tools may possess autodiscovery capabilities that allow them to build graphical representations of networks by monitoring network management traffic. Such tools also exhibit characteristics such as flexible polling and event correlation that allow them to proactively seek information from network-attached devices and assimilate that information with previously collected data in order to form conclusions and make recommendations. Most network baselining tools share the results of their efforts through predefined and user-defined reports.

Typical reports would offer statistics:

- Current network volume by day, week, and month as compared with historical averages

- Network traffic volume leaders by node, with actual versus expected utilization, errors, or collisions

- Nodes that are in violation of user-defined thresholds

- Predicted number of days before a node will cross a user threshold

- Nodes whose performance is degrading

The following are examples of network baselining tools and vendors:

Network Baselining Tool	Vendor
Network Health	Concord Communications
Kaspia Network Audit	Kaspia Systems
TREND, TRENDweb	DeskTalk Systems

Simulation — Network Modeling and Simulation Tools

Simulation software tools are also sometimes known as **performance engineering** software tools. All simulation systems share a similar trait in that the overall network performance they are able to model is a result of the net effect of a series of mathematical formulas. These mathematical formulas represent and are derived from the actual performance of the circuits and networking equipment comprising the final network design.

The value of a simulation system is its ability to predict the performance of various networking scenarios, otherwise known as **what-if analysis.** Simulation software uses the current network configuration as a starting point and applies what-if scenarios. The benefits of a good network simulation package include the following:

- Ability to spot network bottlenecks such as overworked servers, network failures, or disk capacity problems

- Ability to test new applications and network configurations before actual deployment (New applications may run well in a controlled test environment but may perform quite differently on the shared enterprise network.)

- Ability to recreate circumstances in order to reproduce intermittent or occasional network problems.

- Ability to replicate traffic volume as well as traffic transaction type and protocol mix.

The key characteristics that distinguish simulation software are listed in Figure 12-25.

Among network simulation packages and vendors are the following:

Network Simulation Package	Vendor
ComNet Predictor	CACI Products
ComNet III	CACI Products
CANE-RAD	ImageNet
CANE	ImageNet
NetMaker XA	Make Systems
BONES	Systems and Networks
AutoNet	Network Design and Analysis Group

Auditing — Network Auditing Tools

Network auditing tools have not enjoyed the popularity to date of other previously described network management technology. This trend is slowly changing as network managers realize the value that network auditing tools can provide in such areas as consolidated service desks, inventory management, network management, and security. What network auditing tools all seem to have in common is the ability to provide records of which network files have been accessed by which users. The value provided by network auditing tools is sometimes provided at a performance cost. Auditing software must be installed and constantly executed on every client and server PC to be audited. The audit statistics gathered can consume significant amounts of disk space and may or may not warn of impending disk storage problems. Among the other services that some, but not necessarily all, network auditing tools offer are the following:

- Keep time logs of file accesses

- Determine which users are deleting files that seem to just disappear

- Audit when users copy files to diskettes

- Audit which software programs (authorized and unauthorized) are installed or running on any computer

- Audit only specified files or specified users

- Integrate with security, systems management, or help desk products

- Report output in text-based or graphical format, and export to spreadsheet, word-processing, or database products

- Track and report on configuration changes

- Track logins and logouts

Network Simulation Software Characteristic	Importance/Explanation
Network Types	• Which different types of networks can be simulated? (Circuit switched, packet switched, store-and-forward, packet-radio, VSAT, microwave)
Network Scope	• How many of the following—modems and multiplexers, LANs, netware, Internetworks, WANs, MANs—can the simulation software model, either individually or in combination with one another?
Network Services	• How many of the following advanced services can be modeled? (frame relay, ISDN (BRI & PRI), SMDS, X.25, ATM)
Network Devices	• Some simulation systems have developed performance profiles of individual networking devices to the point where they can model particular networking devices (bridges, routers, muxes) made by particular manufacturers.
Network Protocols	• In addition to the network transport protocols listed in the analysis and design section, different router-to-router or WAN protocls can have a dramatic impact on network performance. Examples are RIP, OSPF, and PPP.
Different Data Traffic Attributes	• As studied in previous chapters, all data traffic does not have identical transmission needs or characteristics. Can the software simulate data with different traits? For example, can it model bursty LAN data, streaming digitized voice or video, real-time transaction-oriented data, batch-oriented file transfer data?
Traffic Data Entry	• Any simulation needs traffic statistics in order to run. How these traffic statistics may be entered can make a major difference in the ease of use of the simulation system. Possibilities include manual entry by users of traffic data collected elsewhere, traffic data entered "live" through a direct interface to a protocol analyzer, a traffic generator that generates simulated traffic according to the user's parameters, or auto discovery from SNMP and RMON data generated by enterprise network management systems.
User Interface	• Many simulation software tools now offer easy-to-use graphical user interfaces with point-and-click network design capability for flexible "what-if" analysis. Some, but not all, produce graphical maps that can be output to printers or plotters. Others require users to learn a procedure-oriented programming language.
Simulation Presentation	• Some simulation tools have the ability to animate the performance of the simulated network in real time; others perform all mathematical calculations and then play back the simulation when those calculations are complete.

Figure 12-25   Network Simulation Software Functionality

Among network auditing packages and vendors are the following:

Network Auditing Package	Vendor
Site Inventory (Part of DP Umbrella Suite)	McAfee Associates
LT Auditor+	Blue Lance
AuditTrack	E. G. Software
LANAuditor	Horizons Technology
CentaMeter	Tally Systems
Advanced Professional Design and Audit	NetSuite Development

■ BUSINESS ISSUES

The successful implementation of a client/server information system management strategy requires a combination of policy, process, people, and technology. Merely throwing management technology at a management opportunity will not produce the desired results. What these desired results are may be a matter of perspective.

From the top-down or business-first perspective, senior management may look to the proper management of information resources to enable a competitive advantage and to be able to deploy new network services quickly and as needed at a reasonable cost. Meanwhile, the desired result of business unit management might be that end users can successfully execute those applications that have been implemented to enable business processes and achieve business objectives. Successful execution of applications can be quantified in terms such as transactions per second, mean time between failures, average response time to database queries, and so on. Such guarantees of proper execution and delivery of end-user applications are sometimes quantified in terms of **quality of service (QOS)** guarantees. Network management personnel tend to take a more infrastructure-centric approach by concentrating on those elements of the network infrastructure that support the enterprise applications. Examples of such infrastructure components could be server performance, network traffic analysis, internetwork device performance, and WAN analysis.

How can network managers simultaneously deploy new services, control costs, provide competitive advantage and provide guaranteed quality of service in an increasingly complicated, multivendor, multiplatform, multiprotocol environment? To a great extent, the answer is to combine the processes embedded in the top-down model and the network development life cycle. The top-down model forces the network manager to constantly evaluate business objectives, the nature of the applications that will meet those business objectives, the nature of the data that will support those applications, the functional requirements of the network that will deliver that data, and finally, the configuration of the technology that will provide the required network functionality. The network development life cycle forces the network manager to engage in an ongoing process of network monitoring, planning, analysis, design, modeling, and implementation based on network performance.

Network infrastructures must be flexible as well as reliable. The ability to have networks change in response to changing business conditions and opportunities is of critical importance to the successful network manager.

Cost Containment

Before network managers can contain or reduce costs, they must first have an accurate representation of the source of those costs. Although this may sound like common sense, it is easier said than done, and it is sometimes not done at all. Figure 12-26 lists some practical suggestions for systems administration and network management cost containment.

Outsourcing

In terms of cost control, one of the key weapons in the arsenal of network managers is **outsourcing,** or the selective hiring of outside contractors to perform specific network management duties. Outsourcing is also becoming increasingly necessary for global corporations in order to cost-effectively secure required systems and network support personnel throughout the world. There are several keys to outsourcing success:

- The successful identification of those processes which can be most appropriately outsourced is the first key issue. Which processes does the company really need to manage itself, and which could be more cost-effectively managed by a third party? Which skills are worth investing in for the strategic needs of the corporation itself, and which skills are better hired on as needed? Which tasks can an outsourcer do more cheaply than internal personnel? For which tasks can outsourcers supply new or on-demand expertise? Which tasks can be outsourced in order to free corporate personnel for more strategically important issues? Are there tasks that could be more effectively managed by outside experts?

- The successful management of the outsourcing process is required once network management activities have been outsourced as appropriate. It is a good idea to establish communication and evaluation mechanisms as part of the contract negotiation. Issues to be discussed include performance reporting requirements, problem resolution mechanisms, change negotiation mechanisms, performance criteria to be used for outsourcer evaluations, and penalties or bonuses based on outsourcer performance.

- Choosing the right outsourcing provider for the job is critical. For example, any of the following areas may be outsourced, although it is unlikely that any one outsourcer could be considered an expert in all areas: application development, application maintenance, client/server systems migration, data center operation, server management, help desk operations, LAN management, end-user support, PC and workstation management, network monitoring, off-site backup and recovery, remote network access, user training and support, and WAN management. The two most common outsourcing areas are application development and data center operation. Among the key evaluation criteria that could be used to narrow the choices of outsourcing vendors are financial stability, networking skill set, geographic coverage, customer references, and pricing structure.

Cost Containment Issue	Importance/Explanation
Take inventory.	• Gather accurate statistics and information on every device, including hardware and software configuration information, that is currently requiring support. • This initial inventory will produce an overall accounting of how many different platforms and standards must be supported.
Determine support costs.	• Perform task analysis on network support personnel to determine how costly personnel are spending their time. • Are there too many crises to allow ongoing maintenance? • Are networking personnel being managed effectively? • What is the cost of supporting multiple platforms and standards? • Are networking personnel required at all corporate sites? • Are more networking personnel required as networks become more complex?
Consolidate and centralize.	• Consolidate support personnel and deliver one-stop support for end users. • Centralize purchasing authority. • Pool network support personnel to optimize use of costly personnel. • Implement centralized license metering and software distribution to help standardize software platforms deployed throughout the enterprise. • How can network management functions and technology be centralized in order to cap or reduce the number of network personnel required to support enterprise networks? • Centralize standardized applications on a server rather than allowing desktops to install a wide variety of applications.
Support process redesign.	• Once task analysis has been performed on network support personnel, redesign network support processes to optimize end-user support while minimizing support costs. • Use consolidated help desk and trouble ticketing systems to organize user support efforts while minimizing the "firefighting" mentality.
Standardize.	• Standardize on hardware and software platforms, network architectures, network protocols, and network management platforms in order to simplify management tasks and reduce costs. • Standardized desktop platforms will lead to reduced support and maintenance costs. • Implement a software version control program so that network support people don't have to deal with multiple versions of multiple software packages.

Figure 12-26 Systems Administration and Network Management Cost Containment

Flexibility

Delivering network flexibility at a reasonable cost in order to respond quickly to pending business opportunities has become a priority for many network managers. Most network managers who have achieved success in this area cite a few key underlying philosophies:

- Remove dependencies on customized or proprietary hardware and software.

- Move toward adoption of open protocols and off-the-shelf hardware and software technologies. Examples of open protocols include TCP/IP for network transport and SNMP for management information.

- Adopt network management and systems administration packages that support open APIs and can easily accommodate add-in modules.

How can such a flexible strategic technology planning process be managed? Again the top-down model provides the framework to build the technology analysis grid, in which technologies to be considered are measured against requirements dictated by the upper layers of the top-down model.

SUMMARY

Network management, like other network-related technology-based solutions, can be effectively implemented only when combined with the proper processes, people, and procedures. As information technology departments have had to become more business-oriented, network management has become more focused on cost containment. Outsourcing is one way in which costs may be contained. However, outsourcing opportunities must be properly analyzed and managed in order to ensure the delivery of quality network management.

The overall field of network management can be logically segmented into systems administration and enterprise network management. Systems administation is most concerned with the management of clients, servers, and their installed network operating systems, whereas enterprise network management is concerned with the elements of the enterprise network that connect these distributed systems. One solution to providing comprehensive systems administration and enterprise management services is known as the consolidated service desk.

Server management, help desk management, configuration management, desktop management, LAN management, and distributed application management are all segments of systems administration. Although each of these segments may contain unique functionality and require unique technology, there is a great deal of integration of functionality and overlap of technology.

Enterprise network management architectures and protocols can vary from one installation to the next. New architectures and protocols are under development in order to bring some order to the multiplatform, multivendor, multiprotocol mix of today's enterprise networks.

A variety of enterprise network management technology is available to allow network managers to be proactive rather than reactive. Besides a wide variety of enterprise network management integrated suites and element managers, other enterprise network management tools include network analyzers, network baselining tools, network modeling and simulation tools, and network auditing tools.

KEY TERMS

Agent
Application MIB
Application response measurement
  (ARM)
Applications management
  specification (AMS)
Automatic call distributors (ALDs)
Bulk retrieval mechanism
Cable scanners
Common information model (CIM)
Component interface API
Computer telephony integration
  (CTI)
Consolidated service desk
Database MIB
Definition variables
Desktop management interface
  (DMI)
Desktop management task force
  (DMTF)
Distributed device manager (DDM)
Distributed network probes
DMI services layer
Element managers
Enterprise network management
Enterprise network management
  system
Event management tool

Frameworks
Hypermedia management protocol
  (HMMP)
Hypermedia management schema
  (HMMS)
Hypermedia object manager
  (HMOM)
Instrumentation
Integrated suites
Interactive voice response unit
ISO Management Framework
IVRU
Knowledge base
Management information base
  (MIB)
Management information format
  (MIF)
Management interface API
Modified object format (MOF)
Network analyzers
Network auditing tools
Network baselining tools
Network modeling and simulation
  tools
Network trending tool
Objects
Outsourcing
Performance engineering

Performance metrics
Point products
Policy-based management tools
Proactive network management
  tool
Protocol analyzers
Quality of service (QOS)
Relationship variables
Remote configuration
RMON MIB
RMON probe
RMON2
RMON3
Search engine
Secure SNMP
Server capacity planning
Simple management protocol
  (SMP)
Simple network management pro-
  tocol (SNMP)
SNMP2
State variables
Systems administration
Web-based enterprise management
  (WBEM)
What-if analysis

REVIEW QUESTIONS

1. Describe some of the business-oriented pressures faced by network managers as well as some of the responses to those pressures.
2. What are some of the advantages and disadvantages to outsourcing?
3. Differentiate systems administration and enterprise network management.
4. Differentiate the various layers of management defined by the OSI management framework.
5. What is a consolidated service desk, and what unique functionality or advantages does it offer? How does it differ from previous network management technologies?
6. What are some of the important advantages and disadvantages of server management software?
7. Why is it important for help desk software to be able to integrate with call center technology?

8. What is the difference between a knowledge base and a search engine, and why are both important?
9. What are the unique features of policy-based management tools, and what is the significance of such features?
10. What is the purpose and structure of the DMI?
11. How does desktop management software functionality differ from enterprise network management software functionality?
12. What are the key limitations of distributed application management, and how are these limitations overcome?
13. What is the difference between distributed device management and centralized enterprise network management?
14. What disadvantage of centralized network management does distributed network management attempt to overcome?

15. Differentiate the following terms: agent, MIB, RMON, object, SNMP.
16. What is a distributed network probe, and how does it differ from an SNMP agent or an RMON probe?
17. What is CIM, and what interoperability issues does it hope to overcome?
18. Describe the relationships between the various components of WBEM.
19. What are some of the shortcomings of SNMP, and how are they overcome in SNMP2?
20. Why has SNMP2 not been widely accepted and implemented?
21. Differentiate RMON and RMON2.
22. Differentiate point products, frameworks, and integrated suites as alternate enterprise network management technology architectures.

23. What are some of the most important functional characteristics of enterprise network management systems?
24. What are some of the important functional characteristics of network analyzers?
25. What is the difference between a cable scanner and a protocol analyzer?
26. What is the overall purpose or value of a network baselining tool?
27. What is the overall purpose or value of a network modeling and simulation tool?
28. What are some of the ways in which current network configuration information can be loaded into a network modeling and simulation package?
29. What is the overall purpose of network auditing tools?
30. Why are network auditing tools becoming more popular than they once were?

ACTIVITIES

1. Investigate the current status of SNMP2. Is the IETF still working on the standard? What are businesses doing in the meantime? What key issues are the cause of debate?
2. Survey businesses or organizations that have implemented enterprise network management systems. Which enterprise network management system was chosen? Why? Which third-party network management systems (if any) does the enterprise system interface with? What functionality of the enterprise network management system has actually been implemented? What do the organizations feel has been the benefit of these systems? What has been the level of effort to implement and support these systems?
3. Investigate the current state of the desktop management systems market. What percentage of products support the DMI architecture? What percentage of products interface directly to enterprise network management systems? Does one product have a dominant market share? Analyze and report on your results.
4. Research the outsourcing phenomenon. Is outsourcing still increasing in popularity? What has been learned about the advantages and disadvantages of outsourcing? Which types of activities are most often outsourced? Find and interview an organization that has hired an outsourcer. Find and interview a company that provides outsourcing services. Do you think

outsourcing is a passing phenomenon?
5. Review currently available help desk technology and report on your findings. Find a corporation using help desk software and determine how well the software fits the corporation's business processes and policies. Investigate the technology selection process to determine whether evaluation criteria were established before the purchase.
6. Review currently available policy-based management technology, and report on your findings. Find a corporation using policy-based management software, and determine how well the software fits the corporation's business processes and policies. Investigate the technology selection process to determine whether evaluation criteria were established before the purchase.
7. Investigate the field of distributed application management. Has the percentage of applications managed via embedded instrumentation increased? Are application developers including more embedded instrumentation within their applications? Survey corporations in your area to determine how many are using or planning to use distributed application management.
8. Investigate the current status and availability of products supporting the WBEM architecture.
9. Investigate the extent to which network simulation, network baselining, and network auditing tools are being used by corporations in your area. What common characteristics do the corporations using these tools share?

CHAPTER 12

CASE STUDY

PLOTTING PAIN-FREE WINDOWS MOVE

Furniture Maker Relies on Inventory, Remote Control to Upgrade Desktops Automatically

Herman Miller Inc., a Midwestern furniture manufacturer, plans to use its enterprisewide network to furnish 2,500 desktops nationwide with new OSes.

By performing the migration electronically, the company expects to save about $100,000 in employee time and travel expenses while ensuring uniform installation and configuration.

Central to the migration plan is proper planning. And here again Herman Miller will rely on network connections to save time—the company has been able to plan the software migration using information gathered through the network.

Paul Babcock, the senior systems analyst who is heading the desktop OS migration project at Herman Miller, said the company "has a complete picture" of its hardware and software. "We were able to create a list of what we needed to do to prepare each workstation for [Microsoft] Windows 95 or Windows NT" with this information, he said.

To gather this asset information, Herman Miller is using Symantec Corp. Norton Administrator Suite. The product's hardware and software inventories provided Babcock and his group with a database that let them form a detailed picture of what was needed to prepare each workstation for the new OS and new 32-bit applications.

In addition, Norton Administrator Suite provides the electronic software-distribution function that will deliver the new OSes and ap-

plications packages. "There are no disks; no one will be dispatched to do an update," said Babcock, who expects that the 35-person department responsible for the task will temporarily contract an additional 10 employees until the software change is complete. In addition to saving on travel and labor costs, Babcock says, the electronic distribution of the new software will ensure it is installed uniformly. "In the past, if we had five people doing software installation, we would have five different ways of installing the package," he said. "Now we will have one way."

Reaching Out About 80 percent of Herman Miller's PCs are at sites in a 15-mile radius around Zeeland, Mich., where the company's headquarters and a major manufacturing facility are located. The Zeeland-area facilities are connected by a fiber-optic Ethernet-backbone network.

The world's second-largest office-furniture maker, Herman Miller has 40 sites throughout North America, most of which are connected by the company's WAN. About 25 percent of Herman Miller's PC users are designers, engineers, and factory-floor users. The remainder of the 2,500 machines are used for financial, administrative, and marketing tasks. In addition to the desktop PCs and 40 servers, Babcock's group supports 400 portable computers used in large part by the company's sales staff.

About 80 percent of the client machines will be outfitted with Windows 95, and the remainder will run Windows NT Workstation. Babcock said he hopes to expand the proportion of users running NT Workstation as his group becomes

more familiar with Windows NT and can support it as efficiently as it supports Windows 95. With an eye toward Windows NT Workstation, Herman Miller now requires that new PCs be powered by 133 MHz Intel Corp. Pentium chips and be equipped with 32MB of RAM and a 1GB hard disk.

Whenever They May Roam Babcock is looking to Windows NT in the long term because he believes NT Workstation provides "valuable multitasking functions" and the capability of supporting "roaming users." This is an important consideration at Herman Miller, where users can log on to the company network from any portable computer or company desktop and access their own customized GUI and local files as if they were sitting at their own desks. They can also easily print to any of the company's 200 printers.

Babcock said he plans to distribute much of the new software in the evening to minimize the disruption to end users. Once software has been downloaded to users' machines, Babcock and his staff will use remote-control software to perform any additional installation or configuration tasks that may be required.

To complete this part of the installation, Herman Miller staffers will use Symantec Norton pcANYWHERE for Windows. The product supports Microsoft WinSock (Windows Socket)-compliant TCP/IP protocols for remote control across the company's LANs and WAN.

"We have customized and added to the Microsoft setup program so that we can install pcANYWHERE with Windows 95 and NT," Babcock said. "If there is a problem with the installation, I am able to take over the process and complete it."

For example, Babcock said he could use pcANYWHERE to view the screen of one of the company's computers in Los Angeles. "That way, I see what the user sees and can then assess and fix the problem myself." Previously, the Herman Miller support staff had to guide users through computer problems over the phone without being able to see the user's computer screen.

Thus far, "50 technically sophisticated" users have had their OSes upgraded with Windows 95 and NT software.

Completing computer inventory and installing software over the network have worked for Herman Miller. Using this strategy, systems analysts can ensure computers are capable of running the new OS and new 32-bit applications.

"We have been very successful," said Babcock. The next step for the company is to convert an additional 150 machines to the new software before embarking on a general roll-out encompassing all of Herman Miller's PCs.

"Our approach is 90 percent planning and 10 percent implementation," said Babcock. "We want to work out any show stoppers before performing the bulk of the upgrade."

Source: Michael Fahey, "Plotting Pain-Free Windows Move," *LAN Times* (January 10, 1997), Copyright January 10, 1997, The McGraw-Hill Companies, Inc.

BUSINESS CASE STUDY QUESTIONS

Activities

1. Complete a top-down model for this case by gleaning facts from the case and placing them in the proper layer of the top-down model. After having completed the top-down model, analyze and detail those instances where requirements were clearly passed down from upper layers to lower layers of the model and where solutions to those requirements were passed up from lower layers to upper layers of the model.
2. Detail any questions about the case that may occur to you for which answers are not clearly stated in the article.

Business

1. What business activities did this organization engage in?
2. How was the company planning to save money on the OS migration?
3. How much money did the company think it could save?
4. What are benefits of electronic software distribution other than cost savings?

Application

1. What applications were required to achieve the planned electronic migration?
2. How was asset information gathered?

Data

1. How was information gathered from the network used to plan the migration?

Network

1. How many desktops nationwide were part of the OS upgrade?
2. How are the facilities near corporate headquarters networked with one another?
3. How many PCs are in Herman Miller's network?
4. How will the remote control portion of the software installation be achieved?

Technology

1. What operating systems will be installed on the PCs?
2. What are the hardware requirements for PCs?
3. Why is NT preferred in the long run?
4. What benefits and functionality does pcANYWHERE provide?

13

CLIENT/SERVER INFORMATION SYSTEMS SECURITY

Concepts Reinforced

OSI Model   Internet Suite of Protocols Model
Top-Down Model   Standards and Protocols

Concepts Introduced

Security Policy Development   Virus Protection
Firewalls   Authentication
Encryption   Applied Security Technology

OBJECTIVES

After mastering the material in this chapter, you should understand the following:

1. The many processes involved with the development of a comprehensive security policy

2. The importance of a well-developed and implemented security policy and associated people processes to effective security technology implementation

3. The concepts, protocols, standards, and technology related to virus protection

4. The concepts, protocols, standards, and technology related to firewalls

5. The concepts, protocols, standards, and technology related to authentication

6. The concepts, protocols, standards, and technology related to encryption

■ INTRODUCTION

As Internet interest and activity has mushroomed, and as telecommuters and remote users increasingly need access to corporate data, network security has become a dominant topic in data communications. As the various processes, concepts, protocols, standards, and technology associated with network security are reviewed in this chapter, remember the importance of people and their basic honesty and integrity as the underlying foundation for any successful network security implementation. Merely throwing network security technology at a problem without establishing a comprehensive, vigorously enforced network security policy including sound business processes will surely not produce desired results. As the saying goes, such action "is like putting a steel door on a grass hut."

BUSINESS IMPACT

What is the impact on business when network security is violated by on-line thieves? Consider these facts provided by the National Computer Security Association (NCSA):

- According to federal law enforcement estimates, more than $10 billion worth of data is stolen annually in the United States.

- In a single incident, 60,000 credit and calling card numbers were stolen.

- Approximately 50 percent of computer crimes are committed by a company's current or former employees.

- In a survey of 1320 companies in 1996, 78 percent said they had lost money from security breaches, 63 percent had suffered losses from viruses, and at least 20 respondents admitted to losing over $1 million.

One of the problems with gauging the true business impact of security breaches is many companies' understandable reluctance to publicly admit that they have suffered significant losses owing to failed network security. Network security is a business problem. It is not merely a network problem or an information technology problem. The development and implementation of a sound network security policy must start with strategic business assessment followed by strong management support throughout the policy development and implementation stages.

However, this management support for network security policy development and implementation cannot be assumed. For example, according to the NCSA, 71 percent of executives surveyed stated that they lacked confidence in the ability of their company's network security to fend off attacks from within or without. This stated lack of confidence has not translated into an infusion of support for network security efforts. From the same survey previously referenced, 73 percent of responding companies had three or fewer employees dedicated to network security, and 55 percent of respondents said that less than 5 percent of their information technology budgets went to network security. In another survey, although 82 percent of surveyed companies had a security policy in place in 1992, only 54 percent of respondents had a security policy in place in 1996.

Enterprise network security goals must be set by the corporate president or board of directors. The real leadership of the corporation must define the vision and allocate sufficient resources to send a clear message that corporate information and network resources are valuable corporate assets that must be properly protected.

SECURITY POLICY DEVELOPMENT

The Security Policy Development Life Cycle

One methodology for the development of a comprehensive network security policy is known as the **security policy development life cycle (SPDLC).** As illustrated in

Figure 13-1, the SPDLC is aptly depicted as a cycle because evaluation processes validate the effectiveness of original analysis stages. Feedback from evaluation stages causes renewed analysis, with possible ripple effects of changes in architecture or implemented technology. The feedback provided by such a cycle is ongoing but will work only with proper training and commitment from the people responsible for the various processes depicted in the SPDLC.

Each of the processes identified in the SPDLC is explained further in Figure 13-2.

A successful network security implementation requires a marriage of technology and process. Roles and responsibilities and corporate standards for business processes and acceptable network-related behavior must be clearly defined, effectively shared, universally understood, and vigorously enforced in order for implemented network security technology to be effective. Process definition and setting of corporate security standards must precede technology evaluation and implementation.

Security Requirements Assessment

Proper security requirements assessment implies that appropriate security processes and technology have been applied for any given user group's access to any potential corporate information resource. The proper development and application of these security processes and technology requires a structured approach in order to ensure that all potential user group/information resource combinations have been considered.

To begin to define security requirements and the potential solutions to those requirements, a network analyst can create a matrix grid mapping all potential user groups against all potential corporate information resources. An example of such a security requirements assessment grid is illustrated in Figure 13-3. User groups and corporate information resources form the row and column headings of the grid, and the intersections of these rows and columns will be the suggested security processes and policies required for each unique user group/information resource combination. These security processes refer not just to restrictions to information access im-

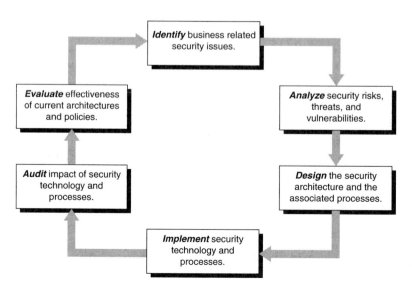

Figure 13-1 The Security Policy Development Life Cycle

SPDLC Process	Explanation/Importance
Identification of business-related security issues	• What do we have to lose? • What do we have worth stealing? • Where are the security holes in our business processes? • How much can we afford to lose? • How much can we afford to spend on network security?
Analysis of security risks, threats, vulnerabilities	• Information asset evaluation: what do you have that's worth protecting? • Network architecture documentation: What is the current state of your network? • How many unauthorized modems are dialing in? • Identify all assets, threats, and vulnerabilities. • Determine risks and create protective measures.
Architecture and process design	• What is the logical design of security architecture and associated processes? • What must be the required functionality of the implemented technology? • What business processes implemented and monitored by people must complement this security architecture?
Security technology and process implementation	• Choose security technology based on logical design requirements. • Implement all security technology with complementary people processes. • Increase the overall awareness of network security, and implement training. • Design an ongoing education process for all employees, including senior management.
Audit of impact of security technology and processes	• Ensure that implemented policy and technology are meeting initial goals. • Institute a method to identify exceptions to security policy standards and deal with these exceptions swiftly.
Evaluation of effectiveness of current architecture and processes	• Based on results of ongoing audits, evaluate the effectiveness of current policy and architecture toward meeting high-level goals. • Adjust policy and architecture as required, and renew the cycle.

Figure 13-2   Processes of the Security Policy Development Life Cycle

posed upon each user group, but also to the responsibilities of each user group for security policy implementation and enforcement. Another category of information for each intersection would be the security technology to be applied to each unique user group/information resource combination in order to implement the documented security processes.

The security requirements assessment grid is meant to provide an example of potential user groups and information resource categories. The grid should be modified to provide an accurate reflection of each different corporate security environment. Furthermore, the grid should be used as a dynamic strategic planning tool. It

User Group	Legacy Data Access	Intranet Access	Internet— Inbound Access	Internet— Outbound Access	Global E-Mail Access
Corporate HQ Employees					
Executives					
I.S. Development Staff Members					
Network Managers					
Network Technicians					
Department Managers					
End Users					
Remote Branch Employees					
Telecommuters					
Trading Partners					
Customers					
Vendors					
Browsers					
Casual Browsers					
Prospective Customers					
Consultants and Outsourcers					

Figure 13-3   Security Requirements Assessment Grid

should be reviewed periodically and should be modified to reflect changes in either user groups or information resources. Only through ongoing auditing, monitoring, evaluation, and analysis can a security requirements assessment plan remain accurate and reflect a changing corporate network environment.

Scope Definition and Feasibility Studies

Before proceeding blindly with a security policy development project, properly define the scope or limitations of the project. In some cases, this scope may be defined in advance owing to a management edict to develop a corporate security policy, perhaps in response to an incident of breached security. In other cases, feasibility studies may be performed in advance of the decision that determines the scope of the full security policy development effort.

The pilot project or feasibility study provides an opportunity to gain vital information on the difficulty of the security policy development process as well as the assets (human and financial) required to maintain such a process. In addition, vital information concerning corporate culture, especially management attitudes, and the company's readiness for the development and implementation of corporate network security can be gathered. Only after the feasibility study has been completed can one truly assess the magnitude of the effort and assets required to complete a wider-scope policy development effort.

One of the key issues addressed during scope definition or feasibility studies is deciding on the balance between security and productivity. Security measures that are too stringent can be just as damaging to user productivity as can a total lack of enforced security measures. The optimal balance point is the proper amount of implemented security process and technology that will adequately protect corporate information resources while optimizing user productivity. Figure 13-4 attempts to graphically depict this balance.

Another issue commonly dealt with during the scope definition stage is the identification of those key values that a corporation expects an implemented security policy and associated technology to deliver. By defining these key values during scope definition, the company can develop policy and associated architecture to ensure that each of these values is maintained. These key values represent the objectives or intended outcomes of the security policy development effort. Figure 13-5 lists and briefly explains the five most typical fundamental values of network security policy development.

Yet another way to organize an approach to security policy and architecture development is to use a model or framework such as **ISO 7498-2,** the **OSI security architecture.** This framework maps 14 different security services to specific layers of the OSI seven-layer reference model. The OSI model security architecture can be used as an open framework in which to categorize security technology and protocols, just as the OSI seven-layer model can be used to categorize internetworking technology and protocols. Although it is more specific and varies slightly in terminology from the five fundamental values listed in Figure 13-5, the OSI security architecture includes all of these fundamental values. As illustrated in Figure 13-6, the ISO 7498-2 security architecture could be used as a checklist to assess whether the listed security service has been provided for each associated OSI model layer

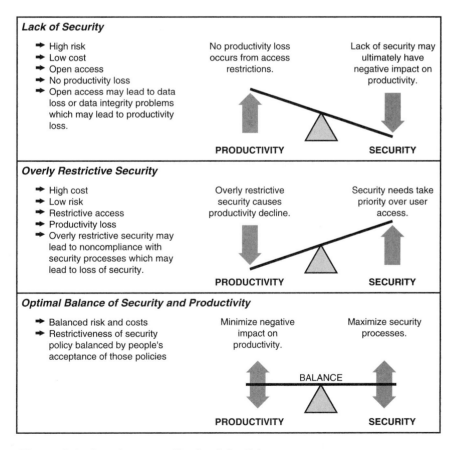

Figure 13-4   Security versus Productivity Balance

Value of Network Security Policy Development	Explanation/Implication
Identification/Authorization	Want to be assured that users can be accurately identified and that only authorized users are allowed access to corporate resources
Access Control	Want to be assured that even authorized users are allowed access to only authorized information and network resources
Privacy	Want to be assured that network based communication is private and not subject to eavesdropping
Data Integrity	Want to be assured that data is genuine and cannot be changed without proper controls
Non-Repudiation	Want to be assured that users cannot deny the occurrence of given events or transactions

Figure 13-5 Fundamental Values of Network Security Poilcy Development

protocols and by what technologies each service is to be provided. Not all services will necessarily be provided to all suggested layers in all corporate settings. However, this does not diminish the value of the OSI security architecture as a planning framework.

Assets, Threats, Vulnerabilities, and Risks

Although Figure 13-4 graphically illustrates the theoretical goal of the security policy development process—balance between productivity and security—how can such a balance actually be delineated within the context of a structured methodology such as the security requirements assessment grid? Most security policy development methodologies boil down to the following five major steps:

1. **Identify assets.**
2. **Identify threats.**
3. **Identify vulnerabilities.**
4. **Consider the risks.**
5. **Take protective measures.**

The terms used within these five major steps are related in a process-oriented manner.

Assets are corporate property of some value that require varying degrees of protection. In the case of network security, assets most often include corporate data and the network hardware, software, and media used to transport and store that data.

Threats are processes or people that pose a potential danger to identified assets. A given asset can potentially be endangered by numerous threats. Threats can be intentional or unintentional, natural or created. Network-related threats include hackers, line outages, fires, floods, power failures, equipment failures, dishonest employees, or incompetent employees.

ISO 7498-2 Security Architecture	Associated OSI Model Layers
Peer Entity Authentication: Verifies that a peer entity in an association is the one claimed; provides verification to the next layer	Application, Transport, Network
Data Origin Authentication: Verifies that the source of the data is as claimed; provides verification to the next layer	Application, Transport, Network
Access Control Service: Protects against unauthorized access of network resources, including by authenticated users	Application, Transport, Network
Connection Confidentiality: Provides for the confidentiality of all data at a given layer for its connection to a peer layer elsewhere, provided primarily by encryption technology	Application, Transport, Network, Data Link
Connectionless Confidentiality: Same security as above applied to a connectionless communication environment	Application, Transport, Network, Data Link
Selective Field Confidentiality: Provides for the confidentiality of selected fields of application level information on a connection, such as a customer's PIN (personal ID number) on a ATM transaction	Application, Transport, Network, Data Link
Traffic Flow Confidentiality: Protects against unauthorized traffic analysis such as capture of source and destination addresses	Application, Network, Physical
Connection Integrity with Recovery: Provides for data integrity for data on a connection at a given time and detects any modifications with recovery attempted	Application, Transport
Connection Integrity without Recovery: Same as above except no recovery attempted	Application, Transport, Network
Selective Field Connection Integrity: Provides for the integrity of selected fields transferred over a connection and determines whether the fields have been modified in any manner	Application
Connectionless Integrity: Provides integrity assurances to the layer above it and may also determine if any modifications have been performed	Application, Transport, Network
Selective Field Connectionless Integrity: Provides for the integrity of selected fields and may also determine if any modifications have been performed	Application
Nonrepudiation, Origin: Gives the recipient of the data proof of the origin of the data; provides protection against the sender's denying the transmission of the data	Application
Nonrepudiation, Delivery: Gives the sender proof that the data was delivered; protects against attempts by the recipient to falsify the data or deny receipt of the data	Application

Figure 13-6   OSI 7498-2 Security Architecture

Vulnerabilities are the paths by which threats are able to attack assets. Vulnerabilities can be thought of as weak links in the overall security architecture and should be identified for every potential threat/asset combination. Vulnerabilities that have been identified can be blocked.

Once vulnerabilities have been identified, how should a network analyst develop defenses to these vulnerabilities? Which vulnerabilities should be dealt with first? How can a network analyst determine an objective way to prioritize vulnerabilities? By considering the **risk,** or probability that a particular threat will successfully attack a particular asset in a given amount of time via a particular vulnerability, network analysts are able to quantify the relative importance of threats and vulnerabilities. A word of caution, however: Risk analysis is a specialized field of study, and quantification of risks should not be viewed as exact. In identifying the proper prioritization of threats and vulnerabilities to be dealt with, network analysts should combine subjective instincts and judgment with objective risk analysis data.

Once the order in which threats and vulnerabilities will be attacked has been determined, network analysts can design and take **protective measures** that effectively block the vulnerability in order to prevent threats from attacking assets. Because multiple vulnerabilities (paths) may exist between a given asset and a given threat, multiple protective measures may need to be established between threat/asset combinations. The following are major categories of potential protective measures:

- Virus protection

- Firewalls

- Authentication

- Encryption

An explanation of each of these categories of protective measures, as well as examples and applications of each category, is supplied in the remainder of this chapter. Figure 13-7 illustrates the relationships between assets, threats, vulnerabilities, risks, and protective measures.

Attack Strategies

Attack strategies often concentrate on vulnerabilities of specific network operating systems. For example, attack strategies for NetWare servers differ from those intended for Windows NT or UNIX servers. Often such attack strategies are shared openly on the Internet. To understand how to properly protect servers, network analysts should use all possible means to discover the servers' vulnerabilities. Paying attention to hackers' forums on the Internet is one way to stay on top of these issues.

Most attack strategies specific to NetWare center around gaining access to the SUPERVISOR account. Among the more common attacks on NetWare servers are the following:

- Remove the NetWare bindery from the server so that it thinks it was just installed.

- Load NLMs at the server console to change passwords.

- Grab SUPERVISOR connection to gain supervisory privileges.

- Enter debugger and disable password checking.

- Collect passwords with a trojan horse login program.

- Replace the logout program with a program that appears to logout normally but leaves users logged in (tailgating).

- Place personal login scripts through mail directories.

- Use a dictionary attack of passwords in which all words in the dictionary are attempted as passwords.

Many of these attack strategies were devised for NetWare servers running versions of NetWare prior to version 4.11. However, new attack strategies have been developed for the NDS (Novell Directory Services) that replaced the bindery in the new versions of NetWare. A hacker utility known as Pandora allows passwords to be extracted and deciphered from NDS databases. In a similar manner, hacker utilities known as NTPASS are able to perform similar operations on Windows NT servers. In each case, hackers must have physical access to the server console. This point brings up the need to pay careful attention to physical security. It is extremely

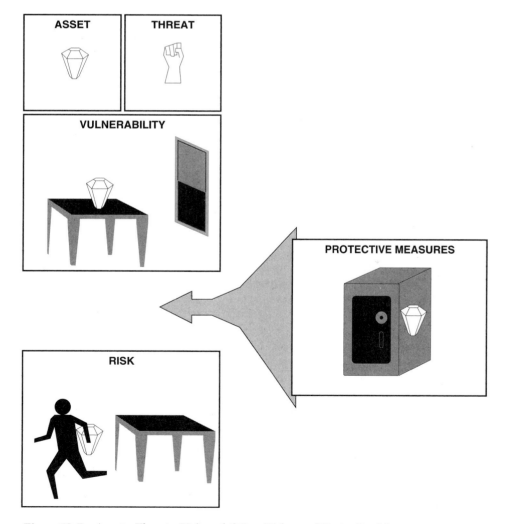

Figure 13-7   Assets, Threats, Vulnerabilities, Risks, and Protective Measures

important to prevent physical access to server consoles. These consoles should not remain logged in if authorized personnel are not present.

Figure 13-8 lists some common attack strategies and potential protective measures.

Rather than attack a specific network operating system, some hackers choose to attack the underlying transport protocols that are used to communicate between servers. The most common transport protocol is **TCP**, or **transmission control protocol.** When two servers that are communicating via TCP wish to set up a connection with each other, they engage in a three-step exchange of addresses and confirmations known as a **three-way handshake.** Although the result is the same, legitimate users are unable to gain access to the network. The following two attack strategies take advantage of this three-way handshake in slightly different ways:

- **Denial of service attack:** In the denial of service attack, the hacker floods the server with requests to connect to other servers that do not exist. The server tries to establish connections with the nonexistent servers and waits for a response while being flooded with thousands of other bogus connection requests. This causes the server to deny service to legitimate users because it is overwhelmed trying to handle the bogus requests.

- **Land attack:** The land attack is a variation of the denial of service attack in which the hacker substitutes the targeted server's own address as the address of the server requesting a connection. This causes the attacked server to continuously try to establish connections to itself, thereby often crashing the server.

Network/Information System Attack Strategies	Explanation	Protective Measure
Masquerading	Posing as a valid user	Authentication
Eavesdropping	Intercepting transmission	Encryption
Man-in-the-middle Attack	Tampering with or altering transmission	Digital certificates, digital signatures
Address Spoofing	Providing false source addresses	Firewalls
Data Diddling	Altering stored data	Encrypted message digest
Dictionary Attack	Method for cracking or guessing passwords	Strong passwords, intruder detection
Replay Attack	Intercept and re-use transmitted information	Time stamping or sequence numbering
Virus Attack	Destructive code infestation	Virus management policy
Trojan Horse Attack	Hide malicous programs or viruses within innocent looking programs	Firewalls
Denial of Service Attack	Overwhelm server with bogus connection requests	Authentication, service filtering

Figure 13-8   Network/Information System Vulnerabilities and Protective Measures

Web Specific Attack Strategies All web servers employ some type of operating or network operating system and are subject to any of the previously mentioned attack strategies. In addition, there are other web-specific vulnerabilities and associated attack strategies. In order to minimize the possibility of attack, the following techniques should be considered:

- Eliminate all unused user accounts, especially default accounts such as GUEST.

- Remove or disable all unused services such as FTP, Telnet, and Gopher. If such services must be enabled, consider installing a proxy server or application layer firewall.

- Remove unused UNIX command shells and interpreters so that hackers can't access the web server's operating system directly.

- Be sure that permission levels on files and directories are properly set. Default permissions often grant access to too many user groups or individual user accounts.

- Consult WWW Security Frequently Asked Questions (FAQ) sites regularly to stay up to date with current attack strategies and defenses.

- Common gateway interface (CGI) programs are capable of extracting a UNIX-based web server's password file.

- Server Side Includes (SSIs) can be embedded in web pages such as guest books and can instruct a web server to remove an entire directory's contents.

Management Role and Responsibilities

Once the scope of the security policy development effort has been determined and assets, threats, vulnerabilities, risks, and protective measures have been identified, it is time to secure management buy-in for the security policy development process. Results of the feasibility study will form the basis of the presentation for management.

Be certain that this presentation for management is objective and that any estimates of financial losses owing to security threats can be substantiated. You will be asking for financial and moral support from management. Your success at securing this support will be a simple matter of management's perception of the cost/benefit analysis of your threat/asset/protective measure scenarios. In other words, have you clearly proven that the costs involved to provide protective measures for corporate assets are outweighed by the benefits of ensuring proper protection of those assets?

Having substantiated the existence of security threats and vulnerabilities, propose your plan of action to develop and implement a solution. It is important not to underestimate the labor resources and time requirements necessary to scale up your security analysis from a limited scope feasibility study to a full-fledged enterprisewide security policy development and implementation process.

But what are the responsibilities of executives and managers beyond merely approving budgets and providing policy enforcement? Figure 13-9 provides a brief list of key executive responsibilities, and Figure 13-10 provides a brief list of depart-

Executives' Responsibilities for Protection of Information Resources

1. Set the security policy (acceptable use policy) of the entire organization.

2. Allocate sufficient staff, funding, and positive incentives to successfully implement policy.

3. State the value of information as a corporate resource to your organization.

4. Demonstrate your organization's commitment to the protection of its information resources.

5. Make it clear that the protection of the corporate information resources is everyone's responsibility.

6. Assign ultimate responsibility for information and network security to specific individuals.

7. Require computer and network security and awareness training.

8. Hold employees personally responsible for the resources in their care, including network access and corporate information.

9. Monitor and assess security through external and internal audits (overt and covert).

10. State and follow through on penalties for non-adherence to network security policies.

11. Lead by example.

Source: Data exerpted from National Institute of Standards and Technology Special Publication SP 500-169: *Executive Guide to the Protection of Information Resources*.

Figure 13-9   Executives' Responsibilties for Protection of Information Resources

Department Managers' Responsibilities for Protection of Information Resources

1. Assess the consequences of a security breach in the area for which you are responsible. Risks include inability or impairment to perform necessary duties; waste, misuse, or theft of funds or resources; and internal or external loss of credibility.

2. Find the optimal balance between security needs and productivity needs.

3. Assess vulnerabilities. How long can each information resource be unavailable before business processes become threatened?

4. Ensure data integrity within the systems for which you are responsible.

5. Maintain required confidentiality and data privacy.

6. Ensure that nonrepudiation and auditing are present in the systems for which you are responsible.

7. Adhere by and enforce corporate acceptable use policies.

Source: Data exerpted from National Institute of Standards and Technology Special Publication SP 500-170: *Management Guide to the Protection of Information Resources*.

Figure 13-10   Managers' Responsibilties for Protection of Information Resources

ment managers' responsibilities. Each list was summarized from publications available from the National Institute of Standards and Technology. The NIST publishes a series of Federal Information Processing Standards (FIPS) as well as a series of special publications on a variety of computer and network security–related topics.

Policy Development Process

It is important to reiterate that although technology may well be implemented as part of the protective measures to eliminate vulnerabilities and protect assets from their associated threats, it is the processes and policies associated with each of those protective measures that really determine the success or failure of a network security policy implementation.

Be sure that all affected user groups are represented on the policy development task force. Start from a business perspective with a positive philosophy and a universally supportable goal. An example is, "The purpose of this policy is to protect our vital corporate resources in order to ensure that we can all keep our jobs. This is in our collective best interests." The emphasis should be on corporatewide awareness and shared values of the importance of protecting corporate resources such as information and network access. The policy should not be portrayed as administrative edicts to be obeyed under consequence of termination.

Areas that may be considered for development of acceptable use policies are listed in Figure 13-11.

The list of suggested areas for policy development in Figure 13-11 is not meant to be exhaustive or all-inclusive. Each corporation should amend such a list to include areas of policy development most appropriate to their corporation. Once policies have been developed for those agreed-upon areas, those policies should be measured against the user group/information resource matrix produced in the security requirements assessment grid (Figure 13-3) to be sure that all potential needs for acceptable use policies have been met.

Potential Areas for Development of Acceptable Use Policies

1. Password protection and management (e.g., it is against corporate policy to write your password on a sticky note and paste it to your monitor; it is against corporate policy to allow anyone else to use your user ID or password)

---

2. Software license policy (policies on using illegal or pirated software on corporate machines, policy on use of shareware on corporate machines, policy regarding who is allowed to install any type of software on corporate machines)

---

3. Virus protection policy (policies regarding use of diskettes on network-attached PCs, use of corporate computing resources by consultants and outsourcing company personnel, and use of the Internet)

---

4. Internet access policy (policies on acceptable use of Internet for corporate business)

---

5. Remote access policy (policies regarding use of single use passwords, Smart Cards, secure transfer of corporate data)

---

6. E-mail policy (policies on enrollment in e-mail news groups and personal use of e-mail systems)

---

7. Policies regarding penalties, warnings, and enforcements for violation of corporate acceptable use policies

---

8. Physical access policies (policies about access to locked areas, offices, computer, and telecommunications rooms; combinations for limited access areas; visitors; and logging out or locking keyboard when leaving office)

Figure 13-11 Potential Areas for Development of Acceptable Use Policies

Policy Implementation Process

Once policies have been developed, it is up to all employees to support those policies in their own way. The required types of support of executives and department managers were listed in Figures 13-9 and 13-10, respectively. Having been included in the policy development process, users should also actively support the implemented acceptable use policies. Users' responsibilities for the protection of information resources are included in Figure 13-12.

At this point, an effective security policy, including associated technology and processes, should have been developed and be ready for implementation. If user involvement was substantial during the policy development stage and if buy-in was ensured at each stage of the policy development, then implementation stands a better chance of succeeding. However, policy implementation will inevitably force changes in people's behaviors, which can cause resistance. Resistance to change is both natural and predictable. Handled properly, resistance to change can be just a temporary implementation hurdle. Handled improperly, it can spell disaster for an otherwise effective network security policy. Figure 13-13 summarizes some of the

Users' Responsibilities for Protection of Information Resources

1. You are ultimately responsible for protecting the data to which you have access.

2. Know which information is especially sensitive or confidential. When in doubt, ask.

3. Information is a valuable, shared corporate asset—as valuable as buildings, stock price, sales, or financial reserves.

4. The computing resources that the company provides for you are the property of the company and should be used only for purposes that benefit the company directly.

5. Familiarize yourself with the acceptable use policies of your company and abide by them.

6. Understand that you will be held accountable for whatever actions you take with corporate computing or networking resources.

7. If you ever observe anything or anyone unusual or suspicious, inform your supervisor immediately.

8. Never share your password or user ID with anyone.

9. If you are allowed to choose a password, choose one that could not be easily guessed.

10. Log off before leaving your computer or terminal.

11. Keep sensitive information, whether on diskettes or on paper, under lock and key.

12. Don't allow others to look over your shoulder if you are working on something confidential.

13. Don't smoke, eat, or drink near computer equipment.

14. Know the location of the nearest fire extinguisher.

15. Back up your data onto diskettes early and often.

Source: Data exerpted from National Institute of Standards and Technology Special Publication SP 500-171: *Computer Users' Guide to the Protection of Information Resources.*

Figure 13-12 Users' Responsibilities for the Protection of Information Resources

Critical Success Factors for Network Security Policy Implementation

1. The policy must have been developed in a team effort with all affected users feeling that they had input to the process. Policy development must be a bottom-up, grass roots effort rather than a top-down, administration-imposed effort.

2. The security policy must be coordinated and compliant with other corporate policies regarding disaster recovery, employee rights, and personnel policies.

3. It is important to ensure that no part of the security policy is illegal. This is particularly important for corporations that do business in multiple states or countries. For example, in some localities it is illegal to monitor phone conversations of employees.

4. Technology must not be promoted as a security solution. Having dedicated people consistently implementing well-designed processes, combined with the effective use of technology, is the only means to a true security solution.

5. The network security policy must not be put on a shelf and forgotten. Security awareness must be a priority, and ongoing auditing and monitoring should ensure that security remains at the forefront of people's thoughts.

6. An attitude must be fostered that security threats are indeed real and that they can and will happen in your company if people do not follow corporate security procedures.

7. Management must be ready to impose set penalties on employees who fail to follow corporate security policy. To do otherwise will quickly send the message that the security policy is a farce.

8. Corporate culture may indeed need to change. This is especially true for growing companies that started out as very open, entrepreneurial cultures. Such companies often have difficulty adjusting to structure and controlled access to corporate resources imposed by corporate security policies.

Figure 13-13   Critical Success Factors for Network Security Policy Implementation

key behaviors and attitudes that can help ensure a successful network security policy implementation.

Auditing

Manual Audits   To judge whether a corporate security policy is successful, the policy must be audited and monitored continuously. Auditing as it relates to network security policy may be either automated or manual. Manual audits can be done by either internal or external personnel. Manual audits verify the effectiveness of policy development and implementation, especially the extent to which people understand and effectively execute their assigned processes in the overall corporate security policy. Manual audits are also referred to as **policy audits** or **off-line** audits. Consulting firms that specialize in network security have generated some rather startling results during security audits. In one instance a firm gained entry to a corporate president's office, accessed his e-mail account, and sent e-mail to the chief information officer informing him he was fired for his lack of effective security policy. As it turns out, the CIO was not really fired. However, it was poorly designed and poorly executed people-oriented processes that allowed this incident to occur. A receptionist was solely responsible for physical access to the executive offices, and the president had left his PC logged in.

Automated Audits Automated audits, otherwise known as **event detection** or **real-time audits,** depend on software that is able to assess the weaknesses of your network security and security standards. Most audit software depends on capturing large amounts of event data and then filtering that data for exceptional or unusual events. Captured events can be telephone calls, login attempts, network server directory access attempts, access to Internet news groups or web sites, or remote access attempts via dial-up lines. In order to generate meaningful exception reports, audit software allows users to create filters that will allow only those events deemed exceptional by the users to appear on reports.

Some automated audit tools are able to analyze the network for potential vulnerabilities and make recommendations for corrective action. Others merely capture events so that you can figure out who did what and when after a security breach has occurred. Other automated tools are able to benchmark or compare events and security-related parameters against a set of government-issued security standards known as C2 or Orange Book standards (officially known as the *Trusted Computer System Evaluation Criteria* or *TCSEC*) and issue a report card or "top 10 risks" list showing how well a given network measures up. The C2 standards and other security standards will be explained later in the chapter. Some audit tools are able to save previous audit data as baseline information so that network analysts and security specialists can measure improvement in network security, including the impact of any security improvements that may have been implemented. The following are currently available security auditing tools:

Security Auditing Tool	Vendor
BindView EMS	Bindview Development
LT Auditor+	Blue Lance
AuditTrack	e.g., Software
Kane Security Analyst	Intrusion Detection
Network Flight Recorder	Network Flight Recorder

Security Probes and Intrusion Detection Systems Unlike audit tools that passively gather network statistics, security probes actively test various aspects of enterprise network security and report results and suggest improvements. **Intrusion detection systems** test the perimeter of the enterprise network through dial-up modems, remote access servers, web servers, or Internet access. In addition to merely detecting intrusions, such as unsuccessful login attempts over a preset limit, some tools are also able to provide automated responses to these intrusion attempts. Also, some of the more-sophisticated intrusion detection systems are dynamic or self-learning and are able to become better at detecting intrusions or to adjust exception parameters as they gain experience in a given enterprise network environment.

Another security probe known as **Security Analyzer Tool for Analyzing Networks (SATAN)** is able to probe networks for security weak spots. The SATAN probe was written especially to analyze UNIX and TCP/IP based systems, and once it has found a way to get inside an enterprise network, it continues to probe all TCP/IP machines within that enterprise network. Once all vulnerabilities have been found, SATAN generates a report that not only details the vulnerabilities found, but also suggests methods for eliminating the vulnerabilities. SATAN tries to start TCP/IP sessions with target computers by launching applications such as Telnet, FTP, DNS, NFS, and TFTP. It is able to target specific computers because all TCP/IP based machines use the same 16-bit address or port number for each of these previously mentioned applications. This application-specific–port address plus the 32-bit IP address is known as a socket. Although SATAN was developed as a tool for network managers to detect weaknesses in their own networks, it is widely available on the Internet and can easily be employed by hackers seeking to attack weaknesses in target networks of their choice. Because of the potential for unscrupulous use of SATAN, tools such as Courtney from the Department of Energy's Computer Incident Advisory Capability and Gabriel from Los Altos Technologies are able to detect the use of SATAN against a network and are able to trigger alarms.

Internet Security Systems has developed a security probe known as RealSecure that looks for 130 known security weaknesses on firewalls, routers, UNIX machines, Windows machines, Windows NT machines, or any other device that uses TCP/IP as its transport protocol stack. RealSecure combines network analyzer, attack signature recognition, and attack response in a single unit. If an attack is detected, RealSecure is able to terminate the connection by spoofing both hosts involved in the communication.

En Garde Systems has developed two products that could be used legitimately for network monitoring and management but that have also been used by hackers. Hackers can hijack network connections after gaining access to the root directory of a computer, to masquerade as legitimate users and to watch and capture FTP, Telnet, and HTTP sessions. TTY-Watcher allows users to take over one machine, and IP Watcher allows users to monitor all sessions on an IP-based network.

▧ VIRUS PROTECTION

Virus protection is often the first area of network security addressed by individuals or corporations. A comprehensive virus protection plan must combine policy, people, processes, and technology in order to be effective. Too often virus protection is thought to be a technology-based quick fix. Nothing could be further from the truth. A survey conducted by the National Computer Security Association in 1996 revealed the following:

- Computer viruses are the most common microcomputer security breach.

- Of the organizations surveyed with 500 or more PCs, 90 percent experience at least one virus incident per month.

- Complete recovery from a virus infection costs an average of $8300 and 44 hours over a period of 22 working days.

- In June 1996 there were over 6000 known viruses, with as many as 200 new viruses appearing per month.

- Virus infection is escalating. In January 1997 over 99 percent of IS managers at 300 companies admitted to a recent virus encounter, meaning that more virus encounters happened in one month than in the previous six. And 73 percent of those infected sites were running antivirus software.

Virus Categories

Although definitions and parameters may vary, the term *computer virus* is generally used to describe any computer program or group of programs that gains access to a computer system or network with the potential to disrupt the normal activity of that system or network. Virus symptoms, methods of infection, and outbreak mechanisms can vary widely, but all viruses do share a few common characteristics or behaviors:

- Most viruses work by infecting other legitimate programs and causing them to become destructive or disrupt the system in some other manner.

- Most viruses use some type of replication method in order to get the virus to spread and infect other programs, systems, or networks.

- Most viruses need some sort of trigger or activation mechanism to set them off. Viruses may remain dormant and undetected for long periods of time.

Viruses that are triggered by the passing of a certain date or time are referred to as **time bombs.** Viruses that require a certain event to transpire are known as **logic bombs.** Logic bombs in event-driven or visual programs may appear as a button supposedly providing a search or some other function. However, when the button is pushed, the virus is executed, causing a wide range of possibilities from capturing passwords to wiping out the disk drive. One of the ways in which viruses are able to infect systems in the first place is a mechanism known as a **trojan horse.** In such a scenario, the actual virus is hidden inside an otherwise benign program and delivered to the target system or network to be infected. The Microsoft Word macro (or concept) virus is an example of a trojan horse virus because the virus itself is innocently embedded within otherwise legitimate Word documents and templates. **Macro viruses** can infect Macintosh as well as Windows-based computers. They are not limited to Word, but can also infect files through such programs as Corel Word-Perfect, Lotus WordPro, and Microsoft Excel.

Although new types of viruses will continue to appear, Figure 13-14 lists the major virus categories and gives a brief explanation of each.

AntiVirus Strategies

An effective antivirus strategy must include policy, procedures, and technology. Policy and procedures must be tied to those vulnerabilities that are specific to virus infection. Viruses can attack systems at the client PC, the server PC, or the network's connection to the Internet. By far the most common physical transport mechanism for the spread of viruses is the diskette. Effective antivirus policies and procedures must first focus on the use and checking of all diskettes before pursuing technology-based solutions. In fact, 61 percent of all viral infections are caused by infected diskettes. However, the macro viruses that infect Word documents and Excel spreadsheets are becoming a predominant owing to the frequency with which such documents are shared between coworkers and across networks as e-mail attachments.

Figure 13-15 lists some examples of antivirus strategies, although this list should be tailored for each situation and reviewed and updated regularly.

As collaborative applications such as groupware have become more commonplace in corporations, a new method of virus infection and virus reinfection has emerged. Because groupware messages and data are stored in a shared database, and because documents can be distributed throughout the network for document conferencing or workflow automation, the virus is spread throughout the network. Moreover, groupware servers usually replicate their databases in order to ensure

Virus Category	Explanation/Implication

File Infectors	• File infectors attach themselves to a variety of types of executable files.
	• Subcategories of file infectors:
	  • Direction action file infectors infect a program each time it is executed.
	  • Resident infectors use the infected program to become resident in memory, where they attack other programs as they are loaded into memory.
	  • Slow infectors infect files as they are changed or created, thus ensuring that the infection is saved.
	  • Sparse infectors seek to avoid detection by striking only certain programs on an occasional basis.
	  • Companion viruses create new infected programs that are identical to the original uninfected programs.
	  • Armored viruses are equipped with defense mechanisms to avoid detection and antivirus technology. **Polymorphic viruses** change their appearance each time an infected program is run in order to avoid detection.

System/Boot Infectors	• These attack the files of the operating system or boot sector rather than application programs. • System/boot sector viruses are memory resident.
Multipartite Viruses	• Also known as boot-and-file viruses, these viruses attack both application files and system and boot sectors.
Hostile Applets	• Although specific to web technology and Java-embedded programs, hostile applets could still be considered viruses. **Attack applets** are intent on serious security breaches, whereas **malicious applets** tend to be annoying rather than destructive. Hostile applets are unknowingly downloaded while web surfing. Hostile ActiveX components present a similar threat. Some people would argue that such malicious code is not technically a virus. However, there is little doubt as to the potential destructiveness of the code.
E-Mail Viruses	• Some sites report that 98 percent of viruses are introduced through e-mail attachments. • Antivirus software must be version specific to the e-mail messaging system (e.g., Exchange Server 5.5). Such software scans files after decryption before releasing the files to the users, while quarantining questionable files.
Cluster/File System Viruses	• These viruses attack the file systems, directories, or file allocation tables so that viruses can be loaded into memory before requested files.

Figure 13-14   Virus Categories

that all servers on the network are providing consistent information, so the virus will continue to spread. Even if the virus is eliminated from the originating server, responses from still-infected replicated servers will reinfect the original server as the infection/reinfection cycle continues. Virus scanning software specially designed for groupware databases has been designed to combat this problem. Norton

Antivirus Strategies
1. Identify virus infection vulnerabilities and design protective measures.
2. Install virus-scanning software at all points of attack. Ensure that network-attached client PCs with detected viruses can be quarantined in order to prevent the spread of the virus over the network.
3. All diskettes must be scanned at a stand-alone scanning PC before being loaded onto network attached clients or servers.
4. All consultants and third-party contractors should be prohibited from attaching notebook computers to the corporate network until the computer has been scanned in accordance with security policy.
5. All vendors must run demonstrations on their own equipment.
6. Shareware or downloaded software should be prohibited or controlled and scanned.
7. All diagnostic and reference diskettes must be scanned before use.
8. Write-protect all diskettes with .exe and .com files.
9. Create a master boot record that disables writes to the hard drive when booting from a floppy or disable booting from a floppy, depending on the operating system.

Figure 13-15   Antivirus Strategies

AntiVirus for Lotus Notes is an example of such a specialized antivirus tool. Figure 13-16 illustrates the collaboration software infection/reinfection cycle.

Managerial Perspective

Virus awareness and a mechanism for quickly sharing information regarding new virus outbreaks must accompany the deployment of any antivirus technology. These virus awareness and communications mechanisms must be enterprisewide rather than confined to a relatively few virus-aware departments. Procedures and policies on how and when antivirus technology is to be employed must be universally understood and implemented.

Antivirus Technology

Viruses can attack locally attached client platforms, remotely attached client platforms, server platforms, or the entrance to the corporate network via the Internet, so all four points of attack must be protected. Viruses must be detected and removed at each point of attack. **Virus scanning** is the primary method for successful detection and removal. However, virus-scanning software most often works from a library of known viruses, or more specifically the unique digital signatures of these viruses, while new viruses appear at the rate of nearly 200 per month. Because of this fact, it is important to buy virus-scanning software whose vendor supplies updates of virus signatures at least once per month. As virus introduction accelerates, virus signature updates to virus scanning software will likely become more frequent as well. Vendors are currently updating virus signatures files every four hours, with hourly updates expected in the near future. Also, some virus scanners can remove a virus from an infected file while others merely destroy the infected file as a remedy. Because virus scanners are really scanning for known digital signatures of viruses, they are sometimes referred to as **signature scanners.**

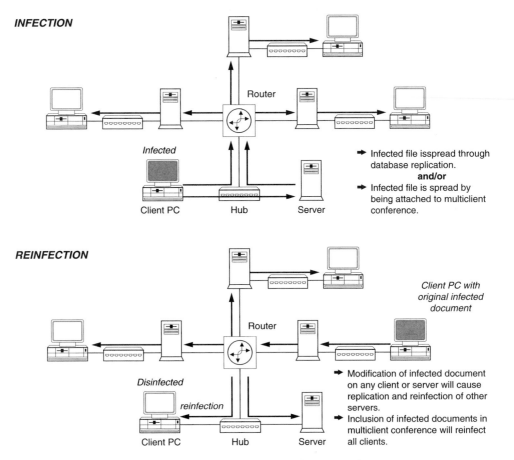

Figure 13-16   Collaborative Software Infection/Reinfection Cycle

In an effort to be more proactive than reactive, **emulation technology** attempts to detect as-yet unknown viruses by running programs with a software emulation program known as a **virtual PC.** In so doing, the executing program can be examined in a safe environment for any unusual behavior or other tell-tale symptoms of resident viruses. Such programs can identify potentially unknown viruses based on their behavior rather than relying on identifiable signatures of known viruses. Because of their ability to monitor behavior of programs, this category of antivirus technology is also sometimes known as **activity monitors** or **heuristic analysis.** Such programs can also trap encrypted or polymorphic viruses that are capable of constantly changing their identities or signatures. In addition, some of these programs are self-learning, thereby increasing their knowledge of viruslike activity with experience. Obviously, the key operational advantage is that potentially infected programs are run in the safe, emulated test environment before they are run on actual PCs and corporate networks.

A third category of antivirus technology, known as **CRC checkers** or **hashing checkers,** creates and saves a unique cyclical redundancy check (CRC) character or hashing number for each file to be monitored. Each time that file is subsequently saved, the new CRC is checked against the reference CRC. If the CRCs do not match, then the file has been changed. These changes are then evaluated by the program in order to determine the likelihood that the change was caused by a viral infection. The shortcoming of such technology is that it is only able to detect viruses after infection, which may already be too late. As a possible solution to this problem, **decoys** are files that are allowed to become infected in order to detect and report on virus activity.

Antivirus software is now available for clients, servers, e-mail gateways, web browsers, firewalls, and groupware. It is even being installed in the firmware on network interface cards. Antivirus products are now certified by the **National Computer Security Association (NCSA),** which also maintains a list of known or sighted viruses. Among currently available antivirus technology and vendors are the following:

Antivirus Technology	Vendor
InocuLAN	Cheyenne/Computer Associates
Dr. Solomon's Toolkit	Dr. Solomon's Software
NetShield	McAfee
Norton AntiVirus	Symantec
ServerProtect/PC-cillin	Trend Micro
IBM Antivirus Enterprise Edition	IBM

Figure 13-17 illustrates the typical points of attack for virus infection as well as potential protective measures to the combat those attacks.

▣ FIREWALLS

When a company links to the Internet, a two-way access point out of, as well as *into,* that company's confidential information systems is created. In order to prevent unauthorized access from the Internet into a company's confidential data, specialized software known as a **firewall** is often deployed. Firewall software usually runs on a dedicated server that is connected to, but outside of, the corporate network. All network packets entering the firewall are filtered, or examined, to determine whether those users have authority to access requested files or services and whether the information contained within the message meets corporate criteria for forwarding over the internal network. Firewalls provide a layer of isolation between the inside network and the outside network. The underlying assumption in such a design scenario is that all of the threats come from the outside network. As evidenced by the statistic cited earlier, this is often not the case. In addition, outside threats may be able to circumvent the firewall entirely if dial-up modem access remains uncontrolled or unmonitored. In addition, incorrectly implemented firewalls can actually exacerbate the situation by creating new and sometimes undetected security holes.

Firewall Architectures

Another difficulty with firewalls is that there are no standards for firewall functionality, architectures, or interoperability. As a result users must be especially aware of how firewalls work in order to evaluate potential firewall technology purchases. Firewall functionality and architectures are explained in the next few sections.

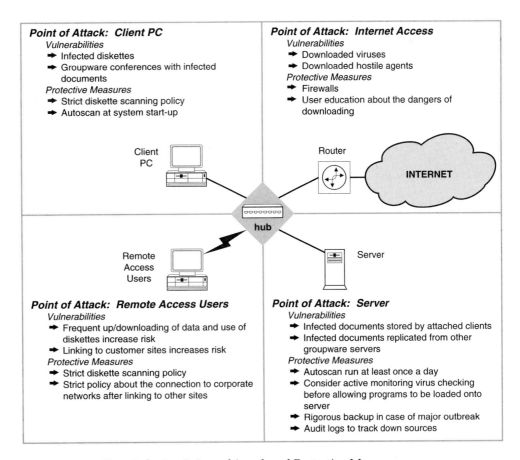

Point of Attack: Client PC
Vulnerabilities
➡ Infected diskettes
➡ Groupware conferences with infected documents
Protective Measures
➡ Strict diskette scanning policy
➡ Autoscan at system start-up

Point of Attack: Internet Access
Vulnerabilities
➡ Downloaded viruses
➡ Downloaded hostile agents
Protective Measures
➡ Firewalls
➡ User education about the dangers of downloading

Point of Attack: Remote Access Users
Vulnerabilities
➡ Frequent up/downloading of data and use of diskettes increase risk
➡ Linking to customer sites increases risk
Protective Measures
➡ Strict diskette scanning policy
➡ Strict policy about the connection to corporate networks after linking to other sites

Point of Attack: Server
Vulnerabilities
➡ Infected documents stored by attached clients
➡ Infected documents replicated from other groupware servers
Protective Measures
➡ Autoscan run at least once a day
➡ Consider active monitoring virus checking before allowing programs to be loaded onto server
➡ Rigorous backup in case of major outbreak
➡ Audit logs to track down sources

Figure 13-17   Virus Infection Points of Attack and Protective Measures

Packet Filtering   Every packet of data on the Internet is uniquely identified by the source address of the computer that issued the message and the destination address of the Internet server to which the message is bound. These addresses are included in a portion of the packet called the header.

A **filter** is a program that examines the source address and destination address of every incoming packet to the firewall server. Network access devices known as routers are also capable of filtering data packets. **Filter tables** are lists of addresses whose data packets and embedded messages are either allowed or prohibited from proceeding through the firewall server and into the corporate network. Filter tables can also limit the access of certain IP addresses to certain directories. This is how anonymous FTP users are restricted to only certain information resources. It obviously takes time for a firewall server to examine the addresses of each packet and compare those addresses to filter table entries. This filtering time introduces **latency** to the overall transmission time. A filtering program that examines only source and destination addresses and determines access based on the entries in a filter table is known as a **port-level filter, network-level filter,** or **packet filter.**

Packet filter gateways can be implemented on routers. This means that an existing piece of technology can be used for dual purposes. However, maintaining filter tables and access rules on multiple routers is not a simple task, and packet filtering does have its limitations in terms of the level of security it is able to provide. Dedicated packet-filtering firewalls are usually easier to configure and require less in-depth knowledge of protocols to be filtered or examined. Packet filters can be breached by hackers in a technique known as **IP spoofing.** Because packet filters make all filtering decisions based on IP source and destination addresses, if a hacker can make a packet appear to come from an authorized or trusted IP address, then it can pass through the firewall.

Application Gateways Application-level filters, otherwise known as **assured pipelines, application gateways,** or **proxies,** go beyond port-level filters in their attempts to prevent unauthorized access to corporate data. Although port-level filters determine the legitimacy of the party asking for information, application-level filters ensure the validity of what users are asking for. Application-level filters examine the entire request for data rather than just the source and destination addresses. Secure files can be marked as such, and application-level filters will not allow those files to be transferred, even to users authorized by port-level filters.

Certain application-level protocol commands that are typically used for probing or hacking into systems can be identified, trapped, and removed. For example, SMTP (simple mail transfer protocol) is an e-mail interoperability protocol that is a member of the TCP/IP family and used widely over the Internet. It is often used to mask attacks or intrusions. MIME (multipurpose Internet mail extension) is also often used to hide or encapsulate malicious code such as hostile Java applets or ActiveX components. Other application protocols that may require monitoring include World Wide Web protocols such as HTTP, as well as Telnet, FTP, Gopher, and Real Audio. Each of these application protocols requires its own proxy, and each application-specific proxy must be intimately familiar with the commands within each application that will need to be trapped and examined. For example, an SMTP proxy, should be able to filter SMTP packets according to e-mail content, message length, and type of attachments. A given application gateway may not include proxies for all potential application-layer protocols.

Circuit-level proxies provide proxy services for transport layer protocols such as TCP. **Socks** creates a proxy data channel to the application server on behalf of the application client. Because all data goes through Socks, it can audit, screen, and filter all traffic in between the application client and server. Socks can control traffic by disabling or enabling communication according to TCP port numbers. Socks4 allowed outgoing firewall applications, and Socks5 supports both incoming and outgoing firewall applications. In Socks5 authentication is also supported. The key negative characteristic is that applications must be "socksified" in order to communicate with the Socks protocol and server. In the case of Socks4 this meant that local applications literally had to be recompiled. However, with Socks5, a launcher is employed that avoids "socksification" and recompilation of client programs that don't natively support Socks in most cases. Socks5 uses a private routing table and hides internal network addresses from outside networks.

Application gateways are concerned with what services or applications a message is requesting in addition to who is making that request. Connections between requesting clients and service-providing servers are created only after the application gateway is satisfied with the legitimacy of the request. Even once the legitimacy of the request has been established, only proxy clients and servers actually communicate with each other. A gateway firewall does not allow actual internal IP addresses or names to be transported to the external nonsecure network. To the external network, the proxy application on the firewall appears to be the actual source or destination, as the case may be.

An architectural variation of an application gateway that offers increased security is known as a **dual-homed gateway.** In this scenario, the application gateway is physically connected to the private secure network, and the packet-filtering router is connected to the nonsecure network or the Internet. Between the application gateway and the packet filter router is an area known as the screened subnet. Also attached to this screened subnet are information servers, WWW servers, or other servers that the company may wish to make available to outside users. However, all outside traffic still goes through the application gateway first, and then to the information servers. TCP/IP forwarding is disabled, and access to the private network is available only through one of the installed proxies. Remote logins are allowed only to the gateway host.

An alternative to the dual-homed gateway that seeks to relieve all the reliance on the application gateway for all communication, both inbound and outbound, is known as a **trusted gateway** or trusted application gateway. In a trusted gateway, certain applications are identified as trusted and are able to bypass the application gateway entirely and establish connections directly rather than be executed by proxy. In this way, outside users can access information servers and WWW servers without tying up the proxy applications on the application gateway. Figure 13-18 differentiates between packet filters, application gateways, proxies, trusted gateways, and dual-homed gateways.

Proxies are also capable of approving or denying connections based on directionality. Users may be allowed to upload files but not download. Some application-level gateways have the ability to encrypt communications over these established connections. The level of difficulty associated with configuring application-level gateways versus router-based packet filters is debatable. Router-based gateways tend to require a more intimate knowledge of protocol behavior, whereas application-level gateways deal with more upper level application-layer protocols. Proxies introduce increased latency as compared with port-level filtering. The key weakness of an application-level gateway is its inability to detect embedded malicious code such as trojan horse programs or macro viruses.

Internal Firewalls   Not all threats to a corporation's network are perpetrated from the Internet by anonymous hackers, and firewalls are not a stand-alone, technology-based quick fix for network security as evidenced by the following facts provided by the NCSA:

- 60% of network attacks are made by internal users, people inside the firewall

- 568 out of 600 incidents of network hacking were conducted by disgruntled employees, former employees, or friends of employees

- 30% of Internet sites that reported breaches had firewalls in place

In response to the reality that most episodes of computer crime are inside jobs, a new category of software known as **internal firewalls** has begun to emerge. Internal firewalls include filters that work on the datalink, network, and application layers to examine communications that occur only on a corporation's internal network, inside the reach of traditional firewalls. Internal firewalls also act as access control mechanisms, denying access to any application for which a user does not have specific access approval. In order to ensure the security of confidential or private files, encryption may also be used, even during internal communication of such files.

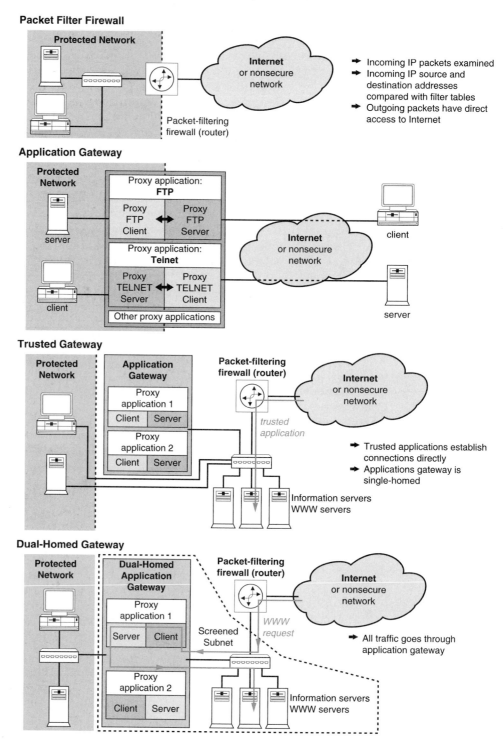

Figure 13-18 Packet Filters, Application Gateways, Proxies, Trusted Gateways, and Dual-Homed Gateways

Firewall Plus from Network-1 Software and Technology is an example of an internal firewall product.

Firewall Functionality and Technology Analysis

Commercially available firewalls usually employ either packet filtering or proxies as a firewall architecture and add an easy-to-use graphical user interface in order to ease the configuration and implementation tasks. Some firewalls even use industry standard web browsers as their GUIs. Firewall technology is now certified by the **National Computer Security Association.** The NCSA certifies the following:

- That firewalls meet the minimum requirements for reliable protection

- That firewalls perform as advertised

- That Internet applications perform as expected through the firewall

Figure 13-19 summarizes some of the key functional characteristics of firewall technology. Figure 13-20 lists some of the leading firewalls, their vendors, and some key characteristics.

Small Office Home Office (SOHO) Firewalls   As telecommuting has boomed and independent consultants have set up shop in home offices, the need for firewalls for the small office home office (SOHO) market has grown as well. These devices are most often integrated with ISDN-based multiprotocol routers that supply bandwidth on demand capabilities for Internet access. Some of these SOHO firewalls offer sophisticated features such as support for virtual private networks and NCSA certification at a reasonable price, less than $3000. Among the technology and vendors in the SOHO firewall market are the following:

SOHO Firewall Technology	Vendor
Ascend Pipeline 75 Secure Access Firewall	Ascend Communications
3COM OfficeConnect NETBuilder	3COM
Portmaster ISDN Router	Livingston Enterprises
WebRamp IP	Ramp Networks

■ AUTHENTICATION AND ACCESS CONTROL

The overall purpose of **authentication** is to ensure that users attempting to gain access to networks are really who they claim to be. Password protection was the traditional means to ensure authentication. However, password protection by itself is no longer sufficient. As a result, a wide variety of technology has been developed. Authentication products break down into three overall categories:

- *What you know:* Authentication technology can deliver **single sign-on (SSO)** access to multiple network-attached servers and resources via passwords.

- *What you have:* Authentication technology can use one-time or session passwords or other techniques to authenticate users and validate the authenticity

Firewall Functional Characteristic	Explanation/Importance
Encryption	• This allows secure communication through firewall. • It supports DES encryption schemes. • Encryption key length supported is 40, 56, 128 bits.
Virtual Private Network Support	• This allows secure communication over the Internet in a virtual private network topology. • VPN security protocols support IPsec.
Support of Application Proxies	• How many different application proxies are supported? Internet application protocols (HTTP, SMTP, FTP, Telnet, NNTP, WAIS, SNMP, rlogin, ping traceroute)? Real Audio? • How many controls or commands are supported for each application?
Proxy Isolation	• In some cases, proxies are executed in their own protected domains in order to prevent penetration of other proxies or the firewall operating system should a given proxy be breached.
Support of Operating Systems	• UNIX and varieties, Windows NT, UnixWare may be supported.
Virus Scanning	• Because many viruses enter through Internet connections, the firewall would be a logical place to scan for viruses.
Web Tracking	• In order to ensure compliance with corporate policy regarding use of the World Wide Web, some firewalls provide web tracking software. The placement of the web tracking software in the firewall makes sense because all web access must pass through the firewall. Access to certain URLs can be filtered.
Violation Notification	• How does the firewall react when access violations are detected? Options include SNMP traps, e-mail, pop-up windows, pagers, reports.
Support of Authentication	• As a major network access point, the firewall must support popular authentication protocols and technology. Options include SecureID, Cryptocard, Enigma Logic, DES Gold, DES Silver, Safeword, Radius, ASSUREnet, FW-1, Digital Pathways, S/Key, OS Login.
Support of Network Interfaces	• Which network interfaces and associated data link layer protocols are supported? Options include Ethernet, fast Ethernet, FDDI, Token Ring, high-speed serial for CSU/DSUs, ATM, ISDN, T-1, T-3, HDLC, PPP.
System Monitoring	• Are graphical systems monitoring utilities available to display such statistics as disk usage or network activity by interface?
Auditing and Logging	• Is auditing and logging supporting? • How many different types of events can be logged? • Are user-defined events supported? • Can logged events be sent to SNMP managers?

Attack Protection	• Following is just a sample of the types of attacks that a firewall should be able to guard against: TCP denial of service attack, TCP sequence number prediction, source routing and routing information protocol (RIP) attacks, exterior gateway protocol infiltration and Internet control message protocol (ICMP) attacks, authentication server attacks, finger access, PCMAIL access, domain name server (DNS) access, FTP authentication attacks, anonymous FTP access, SNMP access, remote access, remote booting from outside networks, IP, media access control (MAC) and address resolution protocol (ARP) spoofing and broadcast storms, trivial FTP and filter to/from the firewall, reserved port attacks, TCP wrappers, Gopher spoofing, and MIME spoofing.
Administration Interface	• Is the administration interface graphical in nature? Forms-based?
	• Is a mastery of UNIX required to administer the firewall?

Figure 13-19   Functional Characteristics of Firewall Technology

Firewall Technology	Vendor
Firewall-1	Checkpoint Software Technologies
Cyberguard Firewall 3	CyberGuard
Sidewinder Security Server	Secure Computing
AltaVista Firewall	AltaVista Internet Software
Black Hole 3.0	Milky Way Networks
Eagle Firewall 4.0	Raptor Systems
Gauntlet Internet Firewall 3.2	Trusted Information Systems

Figure 13-20   Firewall Technology (NCSA Certified)

of messages or files. This category of technology requires the user to possess some type of smart card or other token authentication device in order to generate these single-use passwords.

- *What you are:* Authentication technology can validate users based on some physical characteristic such as fingerprints, hand geometry, or retinal scans.

Token Authentication — Smart Cards

Token authentication technology provides one-time-use session passwords that are authenticated by associated server software. This token authentication technology may take multiple forms:

- Hardware-based **smart cards** or smart IDs that are about the size of a credit card with a numeric keypad

- In-line token authentication devices that connect to the serial port of a computer for dial-in authentication through a modem

- Software tokens that are installed on the client PC and authenticate with the server portion of the token authentication product transparently to the end user, only requiring the user to enter a personal ID number (PIN) to activate the authentication process

Token authentication technology is really a system of interacting components that could include any or all of the following:

- A smart card to generate the session password

- Client software to enter session passwords and communicate with the token authentication server software

- Server software to validate entries for session passwords and keep track of which smart cards are issued to which users

- Application development software to integrate the token authentication technology with existing information systems

There are two overall approaches to the token authentication process.

- **Challenge-response token authentication**

- **Time-synchronous token authentication**

Challenge-response token authentication involves the following steps:

1. The user enters an assigned user ID and password at the client workstation.

2. The token authentication server software returns a numeric string known as a challenge.

3. The challenge number and a PIN are entered on the hand-held smart card.

4. The smart card displays a response number on the LCD screen.

5. This response number is entered on the client workstation and transmitted back to the token authentication server.

6. The token authentication server validates the response against the expected response from this particular user and this particular smart card. If the two match, the user is deemed authentic, and the login session is enabled.

Time-synchronous token authentication uses slightly more sophisticated technology in order to simplify the challenge-response procedure somewhat. The result is that in time-synchronous token authentication, there is no server-to-client challenge step. SecurID tokens from Security Dynamics are examples of time-synchronous token authentication using a protocol known as SecurID ACE (access control encryption).

1. Every 60 seconds, the time-synchronous smart card and the server-based software generate a new access code.

2. The user enters a user ID, PIN, and the access code currently displayed on the smart card.

3. The server receives the access code and authenticates the user by comparing the received access code to the expected access code unique to that smart card, which was generated at the server in time-synchronous fashion.

Figure 13-21 differentiates challenge-response token authentication and time-synchronous token authentication.

Biometric Authentication

If the security offered by token authentication is insufficient, **biometric authentication** can authenticate users based on fingerprints, palm prints, retinal patterns, voice recognition, or other physical characteristics. Passwords can be stolen and smart cards can be stolen, but fingerprints and retinal patterns cannot. All biometric authentication devices require that valid users first register by storing copies of their fingerprints, voice, or retinal patterns in a validation database. This gives the biometric device something to reference each time an intended user logs in.

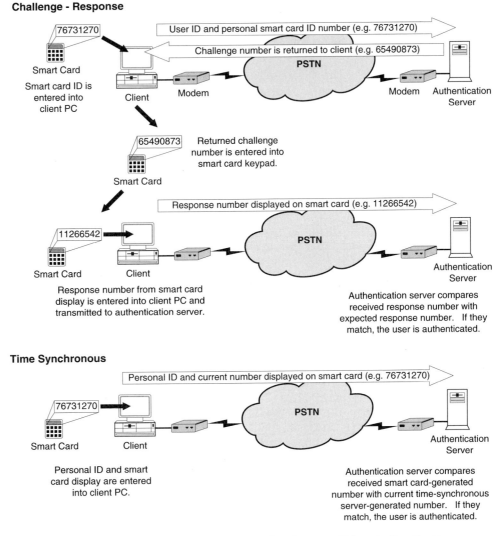

Figure 13-21 Challenge-Response versus Time-Synchronous Token Authentication

Biometric authentication devices are not yet perfect or foolproof. Most biometric authentication devices must be calibrated for sensitivity. If the biometric device comparison algorithm is set too sensitively, then **false rejects** will occur when valid users are denied access because of slight variations detected between the reference biometric characteristic and the current one. If the biometric device comparison algorithm is not set sensitively enough, then **false accepts** will occur when impostors are allowed access because the comparison was not detailed enough. Users of biometric authentication equipment must calibrate the sensitivity of the equipment in order to produce acceptable levels of false rejects and false accepts.

Authorization

Sometimes perceived as a subset of authentication, authorization is concerned with ensuring that only properly authorized users are able to access particular network resources or corporate information resources. In other words, while authentication ensures that only legitimate users are able to log into the network, authorization ensures that these properly authenticated users access only the network resources for which they are properly authorized. This assurance that users are able to log into a network, rather than each individual server and application, and only be able to access resources for which they are properly authorized is known as **secure single login.**

The authorization security software can be either server-based, also known as **brokered authorization,** or workstation-based, also referred to as **trusted node.**

Kerberos

Perhaps the most well known combination authentication/authorization software is **Kerberos,** developed originally at Massachusetts Institute of Technology and marketed commercially by a variety of firms. The Kerberos architecture is illustrated in Figure 13-22.

As illustrated in Figure 13-22, a Kerberos architecture consists of three key components:

- Kerberos client software

- Kerberos authentication server software

- Kerberos application server software

To ensure that only authorized users are able to access a particular application, Kerberos must be able to communicate directly with that application. As a result, the source code of the application must be "Kerberized," or modified to be compatible with Kerberos. If source code is not available, perhaps the software vendor sells Kerberized versions of their software. Kerberos is not able to offer authorization protection to applications with which it cannot communicate. Kerberos enforces authentication and authorization through the use of a ticket-based system. An encrypted **ticket** is issued for each server-to-client session and is valid only for a preset amount of time. The ticket is valid only for connections between a designated client and server, thus precluding users from accessing servers or applications for which they are not properly authorized.

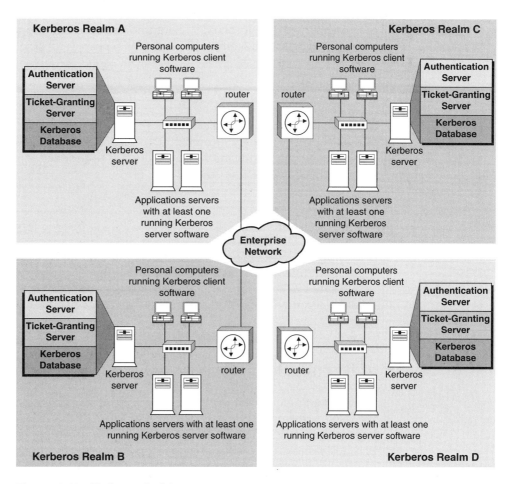

Figure 13-22 Kerberos Architecture

Logically, Kerberos works as follows:

1. Users are first authenticated by the Kerberos authentication server, which consults its database and grants a ticket for the valid user to communicate with the ticket-granting server (TGS). This ticket is known as a **ticket-granting ticket.**

2. Using this ticket, the user sends an encrypted request to the TGS requesting a ticket for access to a particular applications server.

3. If the TGS determines that the request is valid, it issues a ticket that will allow the user to access the requested server. This ticket is known as a **service-granting ticket.**

4. The user presents the validated ticket to the application server, which evaluates the ticket's validity. If the application determines that the ticket is valid, a client/server session is established. This session can optionally be encrypted.

Enterprise networks implementing Kerberos are divided into Kerberos **realms,** each served by its own Kerberos server. If a client wishes to access a server in another realm, it requests an **interrealm** ticket-granting ticket from its local ticket-granting server. The local TGS can authorize access to the remote TGS, which can authorize access to the remote applications server.

Managerial Perspective

From a network analyst's perspective, concern should be centered on the amount of overhead or network bandwidth consumed by the addition of Kerberos security. Research has indicated that, in fact, the network impact is minimal. However, the additional administrative responsibility of maintaining the Kerberos databases—which indicate which users are authorized to access which network resources—should not be ignored.

ENCRYPTION

Encryption involves the changing of data into an indecipherable form prior to transmission. In this way, even if the transmitted data is somehow intercepted, it cannot be interpreted. The changed, unmeaningful data is known as **ciphertext.** Encryption must be accompanied by decryption, a way to change the unreadable text back into its original form.

DES — Private Key Encryption

The decrypting device must use the same algorithm or method to decode or decrypt the data as the encrypting device used to encrypt the data. For this reason **private key encryption** is sometimes also known as symmetric encryption. Although proprietary standards do exist, a standard known as **DES (data encryption standard)** originally approved by the National Institute of Standards and Technology (NIST) in 1977 is often used, allowing encryption devices manufactured by different manufacturers to interoperate successfully. The DES encryption standard actually has two parts, which offer greater overall security. In addition to the standard algorithm or method of encrypting data 64 bits at a time, the DES standard also uses a 64-bit key.

The encryption key customizes the commonly known algorithm to prevent anyone without this private key from possibly decrypting the document. This private key must be known by both the sending and the receiving encryption devices and allows so many unique combinations (nearly 2 to the 64th power), that unauthorized decryption is nearly impossible. The safe and reliable distribution of these private keys among numerous encryption devices can be difficult. If this private key is somehow intercepted, the integrity of the encryption system is compromised.

RSA — Public Key Encryption

As an alternative to the DES private key standard, **public key encryption** can be utilized. The current standard for public key encryption is known as **RSA,** named after the three founders of the protocol (Rivest, Shamir, and Adelman). Public key encryption could perhaps more accurately be named public/private key encryption because the process actually combines usage of both public and private keys. In public key encryption, the sending encryption device encrypts a document using the intended recipient's public key and the originating party's private key.

This public key is readily available in a public directory or is sent by the intended recipient to the message sender. However, in order to decrypt the document, the receiving encryption/decryption device must be programmed with its own private key and the sending party's public key. In this method, the need for transmission of private keys between sending and receiving parties is eliminated.

Digital Signature Encryption

As an added security measure, **digital signature encryption** uses this public key encryption methodology in reverse as an electronic means of guaranteeing authenticity of the sending party and guaranteeing that encrypted documents have not been altered during transmission.

With digital signature encryption, a document's digital signature is created by the sender using a private key and the original document. The original document is processed by a hashing program such as Secure Hash Algorithm, Message Digest 2, or Message Digest 5 to produce a mathematical string that is unique to the exact content of the original document. This unique mathematical string is then encrypted using the originator's private key. The encrypted digital signature is then appended to and transmitted with the encrypted original document.

To validate the authenticity of the received document, the recipient uses a public key associated with the apparent sender to regenerate a digital signature from the received encrypted document. The transmitted digital signature is then compared by the recipient to the regenerated digital signature produced by using the public key and the received document. If the two digital signatures match, the document is authentic (truly produced by the alleged originator) and has not been altered. Figure 13-23 illustrates the differences between private key encryption, public key encryption, and digital signature encryption, and Figure 13-24 summarizes some key facts about currently popular encryption standards.

Key Management Alternatives

Before two computers can communicate in a secure manner, they must be able to agree upon encryption and authentication algorithms and establish keys in a process known as key management. There are two standards for key management:

- **ISAKMP (Internet Security Association and Key Management Protocol)** from the IETF

- **SKIP (Simple Key Management for IP)** from Sun

Public key dissemination must be managed such that users can be assured that public keys received are actually the public keys of the companies or organizations that they are alleged to be. This added level of assurance is provided by **public key certificates.** The organization required to manage digital keys is generally described as the public key infrastructure (PKI). **PKIX (Public Key Infrastructure X.509)** is an international ISO standard for public key certificates. The IETF has been working on an alternative public key infrastructure standard that is oriented toward varying authorization levels rather than personal identities, by using what are known as privilege-based certificates. This draft standard, known as **SPKI/SDSI (simple public key infrastructure/simple distributed security infrastructure),** specifies a

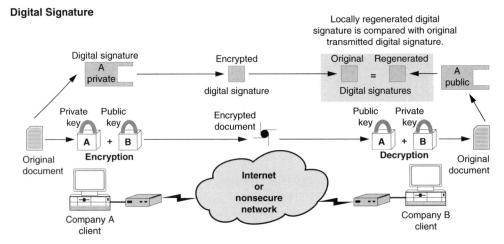

Figure 13-23   Private Key Encryption, Public Key Encryption, and Digital Signature Encryption

distributed client/server model in which humanly readable certificates and the authorization levels they represent can be delegated and processed according to user-defined rules.

Public key infrastructures that link a particular user to a particular public key are implemented through the use of server-based software known as **certificate servers.** Certificate server software also supports encryption and digital signatures while flexibly supporting directory integration, multiple certificate types, and a va-

Standard	Type	Key Size	Explanation
3DES	Private	40, 56 bits	Triple DES. Uses 2 or 3 keys and multiple passes
DES	Private	40, 56 bits	Digital encryption standard. Widely used for private key encryption
DSA	Digital Signature	1024	Digital signature algorithm. Generates appended digital signatures based on original document to ensure document has not been altered
ECC	Public	160	Elliptical curve cryptography. Claims to produce equivalent security of 1024-bit RSA key in only 160 bits
IDEA	Private	128 bit	International data encryption algorithm. Generates one-time-use session keys; used in PGP (pretty good privacy)
MD5	Digest		Produces 128-bit hash number based on original document. Can then be incorporated into digital signature. Replaced MD4 and MD2
RSA	Public	512–2048 bits	Rivest-Shamir-Adelman. Popular public key encryption standard; minimum key length of 1024 recommended
Skipjack	Private	80	Used for Clipper and Capstone encryption chips and Defense Messaging System (DMS)

Figure 13-24   Encryption Standards

riety of request fulfillment options. Among the certificate server software currently available are the following:

Certificate Server Software	Vendor
Entrust/WebCA 1.02	Entrust Technologies
Netscape Certificate Server 1.02	Netscape Communications
Sentry CA 1.41	Xcert Software

Third-party key certification services, or **certificate authorities (CAs),** issue the public keys along with a certificate ensuring the authenticity of the key. Such certification authorities issue public keys of other organizations, along with certificates of authenticity, guaranteed by their own digital signature. VeriSign is one example of a trusted third-party issuer of X.509 public-key certificates. The U.S. Postal Service has also announced plans to begin issuing public key certificates.

Digital certificates or **Digital IDs** issued from CAs such as VeriSign contain an organization's encrypted public key along with a minimal amount of information about the organization such as e-mail address, department, company, state or province, and country. Once a certificate has been issued by a CA, an organization can post its digital ID on a web page and be assured that the CA will stand behind the Digital ID's authenticity.

Digital IDs may one day replace passwords for Internet-based communications. Recognizing the potential for electronic commerce vendors to quickly gather demographic data about their customers, VeriSign has enhanced its Class 1 Digital ID format to include additional fields in which to store demographic data such as gender, age, address, zip code, or other personal data. Information stored in the encrypted Class 2 Digital ID could allow customized web pages to be built based on the information contained therein. The Digital ID service from VeriSign costs $6.00 per year for a Class 1 Digital ID and $12.00 per year for a Class 2 Digital ID.

APPLIED SECURITY SCENARIOS

Overall Design Strategies

Although it is impossible to prescribe a network security design that would be appropriate for any given situation, some general guidelines that would apply to most situations are as follows:

- Install only software and hardware that you really need on your network. Every time that hardware or software is installed on a network, potential security vulnerabilities due to misconfiguration or design flaws are introduced.

- Allow only essential traffic into and out of the corporate network and eliminate all other types by blocking with routers or firewalls. E-mail and domain name service (DNS) queries are a good place to start.

- Investigate the business case for outsourcing web-hosting services so that the corporate web server is not physically on the same network as the rest of the corporate information assets.

- Use routers to filter traffic by IP address. Allow only known authorized users to have access through the router and into the corporate information network.

- Make sure that router operating system software has been patched to prevent denial of service and land attacks by exploiting TCP vulnerabilities, or better still, block all incoming TCP traffic.

- Identify those information assets that are most critical to the corporation, and protect those servers first. It is better to have the most important assets well protected than to have all of the information assets somewhat protected.

- Implement physical security constraints to hinder physical access to critical resources such as servers.

- Monitor system activity logs carefully, paying close attention to failed login attempts and file transfers.

- Develop a simple, effective, and enforceable security policy, and monitor its implementation and effectiveness.

- Consider installing a proxy server or applications layer firewall.

- Block incoming DNS queries and requests for zone transfers. This is how hackers are able to map a corporation's internal network resources.

- Don't publish the corporation's complete DNS map on DNS servers that are outside the corporate firewall. Publish only those few servers that the Internet needs to know: e-mail gateway, DNS server, web site.

- Disable all TCP ports and services that are not essential so that hackers are not able to exploit and use these services.

Integration with Information Systems and Application Development

Authentication products must be integrated with existing information systems and applications development efforts. APIs (application program interfaces) are the means by which authentication products are able to integrate with client/server applications. Beyond APIs are application development environments or software development kits that combine an application development language with the supported APIs. APIs or application development environments must be compatible with the programming language in which applications are to be developed.

AT&T provides a software development kit that includes a library of C language security APIs and software modules for integrating digital signature and other security functionality into Windows NT and Windows 95 applications.

Security Dynamics, which markets SecurID time-synchronous token authentication products, also provides software development kits known as BSAFE 3.0 and Toolkit for Interoperable Privacy Enhanced Messaging.

Microsoft's CryptoAPI (CAPI) allows security services such as authentication, encryption, certificate management services, and digital signatures to be integrated with applications. Obviously, these applications must then be executed over Microsoft platforms.

Intel, IBM, and Netscape have collaborated on a multi-API security framework for encryption and authentication known as common data security architecture (CDSA) that can be integrated with Java-based objects. Other security APIs may be forthcoming from Sun and Novell also.

An open API that would allow applications to communicate with a variety of security authorization programs is known as **GSS-API (generic security service–applications program interface)** and is documented in RFCs (request for comments) 1508 and 1509. Security products companies such as Nortel, producers of the Entrust file signing and encryption package, and Cybersafe Corporation support the GSS-API. GSS-API is described as open because it interfaces between user applications and a variety of security services such as Kerberos, secure FTP, or encryption services. The applications developer does not need to understand the intricacies of these security services and is able to flexibly choose those security services that best meet the needs of the application under development. The GSS-API can also be integrated with Intel's CDSA.

Remote Access Security

The biggest challenge facing remote access security is how to manage the activity of all of the remote access users that have logged in through a variety of multivend or equipment and authentication technology. A protocol and associated architecture known as **remote authentication dial-in user service (RADIUS)** (RFC 2058) is supported by a wide variety of remote access technology and offers the potential to enable centralized management of remote access users and technology. The RADIUS architecture is illustrated in Figure 13-25. This architecture is referred to as three-tiered because it enables communication across the following three tiers of technology:

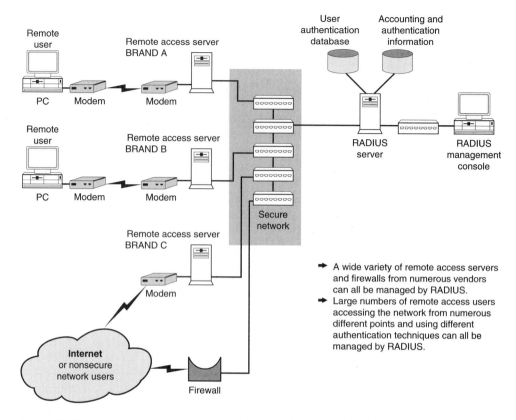

Figure 13-25   Remote Authentication Dial-In User Services (RADIUS) Architecture

- Remote access devices such as remote access servers and token authentication technology from a variety of vendors, otherwise known as network access servers (NAS)

- Enterprise database that contains authentication and access control information

- RADIUS authentication server

In this architecture, users request connections and provide user IDs and passwords to the network access servers, which, in turn, pass the information along to the RADIUS authentication server for authentication or denial.

RADIUS allows network managers to centrally manage remote access users, access methods, and logon restrictions. It allows centralized auditing capabilities such as keeping track of volume of traffic sent and amount of time on-line. RADIUS also enforces remote access limitations such as server access restrictions or on-line time limitations. For authentication, it supports **password authentication protocol (PAP), challenge handshake authentication protocol (CHAP),** and SecurID token authentication. RADIUS transmits passwords in encrypted format only. Some RADIUS-based centralized management products may require that a new centralized database of remote access user information be built, but others, such as Funk Software's Steel Belted RADIUS, are able to use an existing network operating system's directory services, such as NetWare's NDS, as the management database.

RADIUS is not the only open protocol for communication between centralized remote access management technology and multivendor remote access technology.

Extended terminal access controller access–control system (XTACACS), also known as TACACS or the updated version TACACS+ (RFC 1492), is another example of remote access management protocol that supports three-tiered remote access management architectures. The most widely known implementation of TACACS is as Cisco System's server-based security protocol. TACACS transmits authentication information in clear text format, whereas TACACS+ employs MD hashing and encrypts the entire packet. TACACS+ can also handle multiprotocol logins (IP and IPX) and incorporate PAP/CHAP as well.

PAP/CHAP   PAP and CHAP, incorporated within RADIUS as previously described, are two other protocols that can be used on a stand-alone basis for remote access authentication. **Password authentication protocol** (RFC 1334) is the simpler of the two authentication protocols designed for dial-in communication. PAP repeatedly sends the user ID and password to the authenticating system in clear text pairs until either it is acknowledged or the connection is dropped. Otherwise known as a two-way handshaking protocol, there is no encryption performed with PAP.

   Challenge handshake authentication protocol (RFC 1994) provides a more secure means for establishing dial-in communication. It uses a three-way challenge or handshake that includes the user ID, password, and a key that encrypts the ID and password. The process of sending the pair to the authentication system is the same as with PAP, but the encryption reduces the chance that someone will be able to pick up the ID and password and use it to access a system. CHAP is initiated by the server by issuing a challenge to the client that wishes to log in. The client must calculate a value using a one-time key and the challenge that it just received from the server. The server would then verify the calculated value based on the challenge it had initially sent the client. The problem with this, and any single key system for that matter, is that some mechanism must be in place for both the receiver and sender to know and have access to the key. To address this problem, a public key technique may be used to encrypt the single private key for transmission. In addition, CHAP repeats the authentication procedure after the link is initially established to ensure that the session or link has not been compromised or taken over by an unauthorized party.

E-Mail, Web, and Internet/Intranet Security

Two primary standards exist for encrypting traffic on the World Wide Web:

- **S-HTTP: secure hypertext transport protocol**
- **SSL: secure sockets layer**

S-HTTP   Secure HTTP is a secure version of HTTP that requires both client and server S-HTTP versions to be installed for secure end-to-end encrypted transmission. S-HTTP, based on public key encryption, is described as providing security at the document or application level because it works with the actual HTTP applications to secure documents and messages. S-HTTP uses digital signature encryption to ensure that the document possesses both authenticity and message integrity. The use of S-HTTP has diminished with the growing popularity of Netscape's secure browser and server as well as other alternatives for secure web-based transmissions.

SSL   SSL is described as wrapping an encrypted envelope around HTTP transmissions. Whereas S-HTTP encrypts only web documents, SSL can be wrapped around other Internet service transmissions such as FTP, Telnet, and Gopher as well as HTTP. SSL is a connection level encryption method providing security to the network link itself. SSL Version 3 (SSL3) added support for more key exchange and encryption algorithms as well as separate keys for authentication and encryption.

SSL and S-HTTP are not competing or conflicting standards, although they are sometimes viewed that way. In an analogy to the postal service, SSL provides the locked postal delivery vehicle and S-HTTP provides the sealed, tamper-evident envelope that allows only the intended recipient to view the confidential document contained within.

Another Internet security protocol directed specifically toward securing and authenticating commercial financial transactions is known as **Secure Courier** and is offered by Netscape. Secure Courier is based on SSL and allows users to create a secure digital envelope for transmission of financial transactions over the Internet. Secure Courier also provides consumer authentication for the cybermerchants inhabiting the commercial Internet.

PCT   Microsoft's version of SSL is known as **PCT,** or **Private Communications Technology.** The key difference between SSL and PCT is the fact that PCT supports secure transmissions across unreliable (UDP rather TCP based) connections by allowing transmitted records to be decrypted independently from one another, as transmitted in the individual datagrams. PCT is targeted primarily toward on-line commerce and financial transactions, whereas SSL is more flexibly targeted toward web and internet applications in general.

PEM   **Privacy enhanced mail** was the application standard encryption technique for e-mail use on the Internet and was used with SMTP, simple mail transport protocol. It was designed to use both DES and RSA encryption techniques, but it would work with other encryption algorithms as well. PEM did not receive much support, however, and it has been placed in "historical status" by the IETF, meaning that it is no longer being implemented. PEM did not gain support from either the vendor or user populations. The vendors supported their own products and the user population preferred using other e-mail programs and protocols, such as PGP and S/MIME.

PGP   An Internet e-mail specific encryption standard that also uses digital signature encryption to guarantee the authenticity, security, and message integrity of received e-mail is known as **PGP,** which stands for **pretty good privacy** (RFC 1991). PGP overcomes inherent security loopholes with public/private key security schemes by implementing a web of trust, in which e-mail users electronically sign one another's public keys to create an interconnected group of public key users. Digital signature encryption is provided using a combination of RSA and **MD5** (Message Direct Version 5) encryption techniques. Combined documents and digital signatures are then encrypted using **IDEA (International Data Encryption Algorithm),** which makes use of one-time 128-bit keys known as **session keys.** PGP is also able to compress data transmissions as well. PGP/MIME overcomes PGP's inability to encrypt multimedia (MIME) objects.

SET   **Secure electronic transactions (SETs)** are a series of standards to ensure the confidentiality of electronic commerce transactions. These standards are being largely promoted by credit card giants VISA and MasterCard. SET standards are specifically aimed at defining how bank-card transactions can be conducted securely over the Internet. However, the assurance of e-commerce confidentiality is not without costs in terms of processing overhead. A single SET-compliant electronic transaction could require as many as six cryptographic functions, taking from one-third to one-half a second on a high-powered UNIX workstation. The impact of thousands or millions of transactions per second could be enormous.

A large part of guaranteeing the authenticity of e-commerce will depend on trusting that e-customers and e-vendors are really who they say they are. An important aspect of the SET standards is the incorporation of digital certificates or digital IDs, more specifically known as SET digital IDs, that are issued by such companies as VeriSign.

S/MIME   Secure multipurpose Internet mail extension secures e-mail traffic in e-mail applications that have been S/MIME enabled. S/MIME encrypts and authenticates e-mail messages for transmission over SMTP-based e-mail networks. S/MIME will enable different e-mail systems to exchange encrypted messages and is able to encrypt multimedia as well as text-based e-mail.

Virtual Private Network Security

In order to provide virtual private networking capabilities using the Internet as an enterprise network backbone, specialized **tunneling protocols** needed to be developed that could establish private, secure channels between connected systems. Two rival standards are examples of such tunneling protocols:

- Microsoft's **Point-to-Point Tunneling Protocol (PPTP)**

- Cisco's **Layer Two Forwarding (L2F)**

An effort is underway to have the Internet Engineering Task Force (IETF) propose a unification of the two rival standards known as **Layer Two Tunneling Protocol (L2TP).** One shortcoming of the proposed specification is the fact that it does not deal with security issues such as encryption and authentication. Figure 13-26 illustrates the use of tunneling protocols to build virtual private networks using the Internet as an enterprise network backbone.

Two rival specifications currently exist for establishing security over VPN tunnels.

- **IPsec** is largely supported by the firewall vendor community and is intended to provide interoperability between VPN firewalls from different vendors.

- PPTP is Microsoft's tunneling protocol that is specific to Windows NT servers and remote access servers. It has the backing of several remote access server vendors.

IPSec — Secure IP   IPsec is a protocol that ensures encrypted (56-bit key DES) communications across the Internet via virtual private networks through the use of manual key exchange. IPsec supports only IP-based communications. IPsec is a standard that, in theory at least, should enable interoperability between firewalls supporting the protocol. Although firewalls of the same brand seem to interoperate sufficiently via IPsec, that does not seem to be the case between different brands of firewall technology.

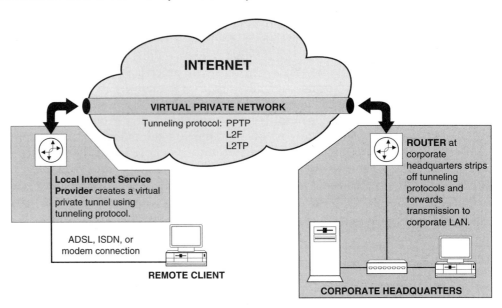

Figure 13-26 Tunneling Protocols Enable Virtual Private Networks

IPsec is also proposed to be able to support both authentication and encryption. These capabilities are optional for IPv4 and mandatory for **IPv6** and are outlined in IETF RFCs 1825 through 1829. In addition to encryption and authentication, IPsec also includes the ISAKMP (Internet Security Association key management protocol). In order to deliver these functions, two new headers enhance the existing IP header:

- **The authentication header** (RFC 1826) provides data integrity and allows for the authentication of IP packets. It can specify the security association to provide authentication between the source and destination parties, and it can also supply data to be used by the agreed-upon authentication algorithm.

- The **encapsulating security payload header (ESP)** (RFC 1827) ensures the privacy of the transmission. The ESP header can be used in two different modes depending on the user's privacy needs:

  - **Transport mode ESP** is used to encrypt the data carried by the IP packet. The contents of the data field of an IP (network layer) packet are the upper layer or transport layer protocols, TCP (connection-oriented) or UDP (connectionless). These transport layer envelopes encapsulate upper layer data.

  - **Tunnel mode ESP** encrypts the entire IP packet, including its own header. This mode is effective at countering network analyzers or sniffers from capturing IP address information. Tunnel mode is most often used in a network topology that includes a firewall separating a protected network from an external nonsecure network.

Mere inclusion of fields in a protocol does not ensure implementation. Applications, authentication products, and trusted security associations would all have to modify hardware or software technology to avail themselves of the protocol's new functionality. Figure 13-27 illustrates an IPsec packet with authentication and encryption headers added.

PPTP—Point-to-Point Tunneling Protocol   PPTP is essentially just a tunneling protocol that allows managers to choose whatever encryption or authentication technology they wish to hang off one end of the established tunnel. PPTP supports multiple network protocols including IPX, NetBEUI, and IP. PPTP is primarily concerned with secure remote access in that PPTP-enabled clients would be able to dial in to a corporate network via the Internet.

Enterprise Network Security

In order to maintain proper security over a widely distributed enterprise network, it is essential to be able to conduct certain security-related processes from a single, centralized security management location. Among these processes or functions are the following:

- **Single point of registration (SPR)** allows a network security manager to enter a new user's information (or delete a terminated user's data) from a single centralized location. The manager can assign all associated rights, privileges, and access control to enterprise resources from this single point rather than having to enter this new user's information on multiple resources distributed throughout the enterprise.

- **Single sign-on (SSO),** also sometimes known as secure single sign-on (SSSO), allows users to login to the enterprise network and to be authenticated from a client PC location. It is not necessary for users to remember a

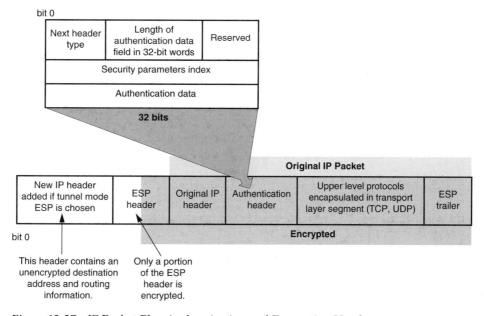

Figure 13-27   IP Packet Plus Authentication and Encryption Headers

variety of user IDs and passwords to the numerous different enterprise servers from which they may request services. Because this is users' single entry point onto the enterprise network, auditing software can be used to provide non-repudiation of all activities and transactions. Any of the variety of authentication technologies discussed earlier can be used in support of single sign-on.

- **Single access control view** allows users' access from the client workstation to display only those resources for which the users actually have authorization. Any differences between server platforms should be shielded from users. Users should not need to memorize different commands or control interfaces for the variety of enterprise servers that they may need to access.

- **Security auditing and intrusion detection** is able to track and identify suspicious behaviors from both internal employees and potential intruders. In addition to detection and reporting of these instances, it is essential to be able to respond in an appropriate and automated fashion to these events. Although the intrusions may take place anywhere on the widely distributed network, the detection and response to such events must be controlled from a centralized security management location.

GOVERNMENT IMPACT

Government agencies play a major role in the area of network security. These various government agencies have two primary functions:

- Standards-making organizations set standards for the design, implementation, and certification of security technology and systems.

- Regulatory agencies control the export of security technology to a company's international locations.

Standards-Making Organizations

Although many standards-making organizations are involved to varying degrees in the field of network security, following are some of the most significant ones.

ANSI   The American National Standards Institute, or ANSI, is the U.S. representative to the International Standards Organization, or ISO. Any submissions to the ISO from other U.S. standards organizations must first be submitted to ANSI.

NIST   The National Institute of Standards and Technology, or the NIST, was formed in 1987. Prior to 1987, it was known as the National Bureau of Standards. This organization issues publications called the Federal Information Processing Standards, or FIPS publications. Category 5 FIPS publications deal with computer security standards and guidelines and include subcategories of access control, cryptography, general computer security, risk analysis and contingency planning, and security labels. The NIST also publishes a series of special publications related to computer security included in the SP 500 and SP 800 series. The NIST also operates a very useful computer security resource clearinghouse on the World Wide Web at http://csrc.ncsl.nist.gov/.

IAB   The Internet Architecture Board is the policy setting and decision review board for the Internet. The IETF, or Internet Engineering Task Force, is a subgroup of the IAB that is responsible for setting the technical standards that run the Internet. This is the group responsible for issuing and gathering the responses to RFCs (requests for comments).

ISO   The International Standards Organization is a voluntary organization sanctioned by the United Nations. It is responsible for international standards in a variety of fields, not just data communications. Besides the OSI seven-layer reference model, the ISO is also responsible for the security-related addendum to the OSI model known as ISO 7498/2 , the OSI security architecture.

NSA   The National Security Agency is a secretive governmental organization that works closely with the NIST and is responsible for the design and use of nonmilitary encryption technology. The NSA also runs the NCSC, or the National Computer Security Center.

NCSC   The purpose of this organization is to work with members of the computer industry to provide guidelines to help them develop trusted systems and computer products. This organization is also known for a security certification program called the Trusted Computer System Evaluation Criteria (TCSEC). It is commonly known as the Orange Book because of the color of the jacket. There is also a Red Book from the NCSC, which was developed in 1987 as a supplement to the Orange Book. These "colored book" security guidelines have been criticized for focusing primarily on computer security rather than network security.

Orange Book Certification
The primary focus of the Orange Book is to provide confidential protection of sensitive information based on six fundamental requirements:

- Security policy: An explicit and well-defined security policy must be enforced by the system.

- Marking: Access control labels must be associated with all objects.

- Identification: Individual users must be identified.

- Accountability: Audit information must be kept and protected so that actions affecting security can be traced to the responsible party.

- Assurance: The system must contain hardware or software components that can be evaluated independently to provide sufficient assurance that the security policy and accountability criteria can be enforced.

- Continuous protection: The preceding components that enforce these basic requirements must be continuously protected against tampering and unauthorized changes.

The Orange Book is broken into two primary parts. The first is illustrated in Figure 13-28. This part specifies the criteria that must be met in order to achieve a spe-

Divison	Protection	Class	Protection	Description
D	Minimal	D	Minimal	Was evaluated but does not meet any higher class requirements
C	Discretionary	C1	Discretionary security	Has achieved confidence in hardware and software controls; isolates and authenticates users and data
		C2	Controlled access	Encapsulates resources; contains login and explicit auditing
B	Mandatory	B1	Labeled security	Explicit protection model; requires execution domains, file labels, system security officer, and documentation
		B2	Structured	Formal security model; requires kernelized, covert channel ID and mandatory controls including communication lines
		B3	Security domains	Must include central encapsulation, reference monitor, recovery procedures, be tamper proof, and be protected against authentication attacks
A	Verified	A1	Verified design	Contains extensive security considerations during all developmental phases. Requires math tools, formal models with explicit math theorems, formal top-level specifications, and trusted software distribution
		Beyond A1		Developmental; requires source verification

Figure 13-28 Orange Book Certification Criteria

cific rating. The criteria are defined in hierarchical fashion, with four different ratings possible. The *A* rating signifies the most security possible, and the *D* rating corresponds to the lowest security possible.

The second portion of the Orange Book contains information about the basic objectives, rationale, and government policy behind the development of each criterion. It is also intended to provide guidelines for product developers, to help them achieve a specific criterion.

The Orange Book certification process is both costly and lengthy. Typically the certification process is projected to take two years to complete, at a cost of $17 million. To date, both NetWare and NT Server have achieved the C2 certification. Many products advertise a *compliance* with an Orange Book certification level; however, compliance and certification are two very different terms. Any vendor can claim compliance, but only vendors that have spent the time and money to pursue the certification process can claim that their products are C2 *certified*.

Encryption Export Policy and Key Recovery

Many corporations and organizations depend on the ability to have private and confidential communication on an international basis. However, in the United States, export of encryption software is tightly controlled. The traditional limit on exportable encryption technology was a 40-bit key. However, 40-bit keys can be cracked in a matter of minutes and do not offer much protection. Businesses conducting operations internationally obviously want to be able to use stronger encryption technology. The government, on the other hand, wishes to gain greater control over international encrypted communication, as evidenced by its **clipper chip** initiative.

The clipper chip initiative proposed that every phone and data communications device in the United States would be equipped with a clipper chip to support encryption. The part of the proposal that had businesses and individuals concerned was the stipulation that the government would hold a spare set of keys that could decrypt any message encrypted by a clipper chip device. The notion of trusting the government with a spare set of keys caused quite an uproar, and the proposal was not pursued. However, the initiative clearly showed the government's intent to seek greater control of international encrypted communications.

The current regulation, which some might consider a compromise, holds that U.S. companies with international subsidiaries may export 56-bit key-based encryption technology provided that they establish within two years a **key recovery mechanism** that will offer a back door into encrypted data for the government. Once the key recovery mechanism is in place, the companies are allowed to export keys of any length. All banks, whether U.S. based or not, are also allowed to export 56-bit encryption technology. However, even 56-bit keys can be cracked. Experts estimate that 56-bit keys can be cracked in 19 days at a cost of $500,000. The new regulation also moved responsibility for encryption product export from the U.S. State Department to the U.S. Commerce Department. This means that encryption technology is no longer classified as munitions, which speeds the export permit approval process.

Key recovery schemes basically ensure that a spare set of encryption keys are always available. With key recovery, the actual information used to reconstruct a key travels with the message header. However, someone with the key decryption codes (the spare set of keys) must combine the decryption codes with the key information in the message header in order to decrypt the message. The big question seems to be, "Who will hold the keys?" Key escrow agencies, otherwise known as trusted third parties, are the most commonly proposed solution. Other proposals say that large multinational corporations should be able to act as their own key escrow agents. At the moment there are about 13 different key recovery mechanisms. No single standard has been proposed, although an IBM-led key-recovery alliance with 40 corporate members has been formed. If key recovery were to be extended to a domestic basis, the implications could be phenomenal. Everyone who uses the Internet for communication would need a key and a key escrow agent. This could mean tens of millions of keys unless some type of key sharing was initiated.

SUMMARY

Without question, the overriding theme in this chapter has been that the implementation of security technology in the absence of a comprehensive security policy including senior management support is a waste of time and money. Security policy must be developed as part of an overall increase in security awareness on the part of all users. It must be accompanied by a clear understanding of business processes and personal responsibilities as they relate to security policy implementation. Only in the context of a dynamic, constantly audited security policy can security technology implementation be successful.

The first security process that is generally addressed is virus protection, most often in response to a virus incident. Virus-scanning technology is of little use without comprehensive, enforced policies regarding use and handling of diskettes and downloaded files. Activity monitors and signature scanners are two major types of virus-scanning software.

The next security process that is generally addressed is authentication—ensuring that users attempting to log into network resources are really who they claim to be. Authentication technology includes challenge-response and time-synchronous token authentication systems.

Authorization and access control ensures that authenticated users are able to access only those files, directories, and applications to which they

are entitled. Kerberos is the best example of a comprehensive authentication/authorization system.

Firewalls are an effective means of shielding private, secure, internal networks from nonsecure external networks. Like other security technology, they must be implemented correctly and in accordance with the overall security policy. Two major categories of firewalls are packet filters, which discriminate between traffic based on source and destination addresses, and application gateways of proxies, which examine individual commands within applications.

Privacy of network communications is guaranteed by encryption. Private key encryption, public key encryption, and digital signature encryption are the major categories of encryption technology. Encryption sessions are customized through the use of keys. The longer the key, in bits, the more secure the transmission.

Encryption technology is regulated as to the key length that can be exported from the United States. Key recovery mechanisms are plans through which the government would be able to decipher encrypted communications. In order for organizations to be able to encrypt communication internationally, they must be willing to submit a key recovery mechanism to the U.S. government.

KEY TERMS

Activity monitors
Application gateways
Application-level filters
Assets
Assured pipelines
Attack applets
Authentication
Authentication header
Biometric authentication
Brokered authorization
C2 certification
Certificate authorities (CA)
Certificate servers
Challenge handshake
  authentication protocol (CHAP)

Challenge response token
  authentication
Ciphertext
Circuit-level proxy
Clipper chip
CRC checkers
Data encryption standard (DES)
Denial of service attack
Digital IDs
Digital signature encryption
Dual-homed gateway
Emulation technology
Encapsulating security payload
  header (ESP)
Event detection

Extended terminal access control
  access system
False accepts
False rejects
Filter
Filter tables
Firewall
Generic security service-
  applications program interface
  (GSS-API)
Hashing checkers
Heuristic analysis
Internal firewalls
International data encryption
  algorithm (IDEA)

Internet Security Association and
   key management protocol
Interrealm
Intrusion detection systems
IPsec
IP spoofing
IPv6
ISAKMP
ISO 7498/2
Kerberos
Key escrow agencies
Key recovery mechanism
Land attack
Latency
Layer Two Forwarding (L2F)
Layer 2 Tunneling Protocol (L2TP)
Logic bombs
Malicious applets
MD5
National Computer Security Associ-
   ation (NCSA)
Network level filter
OSI security architecture
Packet filter
Password authentication protocol
   (PAP)
PKIX
Point-to-point tunneling protocol
   (PPTP)
Policy audits
Polymorphic viruses

Port-level filter
Pretty good privacy (PGP)
Privacy enhanced mail (PEM)
Private communications technology
   (PCT)
Private key encryption
Protective measures
Proxies
Public key certificates
Public key encryption
Realms
Real-time audits
Remote Authentication Dial-In User
   Service (RADIUS)
Risks
RSA
Secure Electronic Transactions
Secure hypertext transport protocol
   (S-HTTP)
Secure multipurpose Internet mail
   extension (S/MIME)
Secure single login
Secure sockets layer (SSL)
Security analyzer tool for analyzing
   networks (SATAN)
Security auditing and intrusion
   detection
Security policy development life
   cycle (SPDLC)
Security probes
Service-granting ticket

Session keys
SET
Signature scanners
Simple key management for IP
Single access control view
Single point of registration (SPR)
Single sign-on (SSO)
SKIP
Smart cards
Socks
Threats
Three-way handshake
Ticket
Ticket-granting ticket
Time bombs
Time-synchronous token authenti-
   cation
Token authentication
Transmission control protocol (TCP)
Transport mode ESP
Trojan horse
Trusted gateway
Trusted node
Tunneling protocols
Tunnel mode ESP
Virtual PC
Virus scanning
Vulnerabilities
X.509
XTACACS

REVIEW QUESTIONS

1. What are some recent changes in the business and networking worlds that have brought network security to the forefront?
2. What is the importance of the cyclical nature of the security policy development life cycle?
3. What is the purpose of the security requirements assessment grid?
4. What is the dilemma involved with the security/productivity balance?
5. How do the critical success factors introduced with the network development life cycle apply to security policy development?
6. What is the purpose of the OSI security architecture, and how does it relate to the OSI seven- layer reference model?
7. Differentiate the following and give an example of each in a network security context: asset, threat, vulnerability, risk, protective measures.

8. Are all of the entities listed in the previous question related by one-to-one relationships? Give an example to defend your answer.
9. Briefly summarize the roles of executives, department managers, and users in the successful development and implementation of security policy.
10. What is the difference between off-line audits and real-time audits?
11. What is the difference between event detection technology and intrusion detection technology?
12. What is the difference between security audit tools and security probes?
13. What is a virus?
14. What is the difference between a logic bomb and a time bomb?
15. What is a trojan horse?
16. What is a polymorphic virus?

17. What are hostile applets, and in which environment do they exist?
18. Why are collaborative applications such as groupware an especially friendly environment for viruses?
19. Differentiate virus scanning and activity monitors as antivirus technology.
20. What is the shortcoming of CRC and hashing checkers as antivirus solutions?
21. What is a firewall?
22. Differentiate packet filtering firewalls and application gateway firewalls.
23. Describe the advantages and disadvantages of proxies.
24. What is a dual-homed gateway?
25. What is a trusted gateway?
26. How does a trusted gateway differ from a dual-homed gateway?
27. What is an internal firewall, and what is the motivation for such a device?
28. What is authentication?
29. Differentiate challenge-response authentication and time-synchronous authentication.
30. What is biometric authentication? Give some examples of biometric authentication technology.
31. What is Kerberos?
32. How does Kerberos ensure both authentication and authorization?
33. Differentiate private key encryption, public key encryption, and digital signature encryption.
34. Why are public key certificates and certificate authorities necessary?

35. Why are APIs and application development environments required in order to integrate security services with information systems? What would be the alternative?
36. What is RADIUS, and what added functionality does it offer over an environment without a three-tiered approach?
37. Differentiate S-HTTP and SSL.
38. Differentiate PAP and CHAP.
39. What is PGP? What are its advantages and disadvantages?
40. What is SET, and what industry is it targeted toward?
41. What is a tunneling protocol, and why is it necessary?
42. What is Secure IP (IPv6), and what services can it offer?
43. What is the difference between transport mode ESP and tunnel mode ESP?
44. What is the difference between single sign-on, single point of registration, and single access control view? What do they all have in common?
45. What is Orange Book or C2 certification?
46. What is the clipper chip?
47. What is the purpose of a key recovery mechanism, and how does it work?
48. What is the role of key escrow agencies in enabling a key recovery mechanism?
49. What are the potential implications if all Internet users were required to use key recovery mechanisms?

ACTIVITIES

1. Research topics such as network security losses or computer crime and report on your results. What is the trend of the statistics over the last five years? How accurately do statistics reflect the extent of the problem?
2. Find an organization or business that will let you prepare a security policy document. Run the entire process as a well-organized plan, using project management software if possible. Start with a small feasibility study and report your results before defining the full project scope. Use the planning tools supplied in the chapter, adapting them to your own situation as needed.
3. Choose any network security–related topic of interest and research it using only Internet resources. Two good sites to start with are http://www.ncsa.com and http://csrc.ncsl.nist.gov/.
4. Consider this statement: "The implementation of security technology in the absence of a comprehensive security policy is like putting a steel door on a grass hut." Find actual examples of network security implementations to either support or refute the statement.
5. Download a copy of Security Analyzer Tool for Analyzing Networks from ftp://ftp.win.tue.nl/pub/security/index.html. After obtaining proper permissions, run the analysis tool, and report on your results.
6. Log into the Internet Security Systems web site at www.iss.net and review information regarding its RealSecure network-based attack analyzer. Compare its features with those of SATAN. What would be the most appropriate use for each technology?
7. Create a virus clearinghouse and information center for your school, business, or organization if

one does not already exist. Does your organization have a published antivirus strategy? If not, create one. Report on your results.

8. Research the problem of hostile applets and components. What are the potential solutions to the problem? Is this a problem with the development languages?

9. What is Word Macro Concept virus? Find out exactly how it works, and figure out how it can be eradicated and kept from spreading. How much of the solution is technology? How much involves procedures?

10. Design and prepare a budget for a safe remote access network including remote access server, firewall, authentication technology, and modems. Prepare alternative budget proposals for challenge-response versus time synchronous token authentication technology. Was the price difference significant? If so, how could the price difference be justified?

11. Research the field of biometric authentication technology. What are the most stable and dependable products? What are the latest products? Can you find data on false accept and false reject rates of biometric authentication technology?

12. What is the current rate of acceptance and implementation of Kerberos in industry? What are the strengths and limitations of the architecture?

13. Research the issue of privacy in the age of electronic commerce. What impact might digital IDs and key recovery schemes have on an individual's right to privacy? Consider debating the issue in class. What are the conflicting motivations or goals behind the issue?

14. Research virtual private networks. What is the extent of actual implementation of virtual private networks, as opposed to the amount of press coverage and technology development? Explain your results.

15. Research and prepare a presentation, timeline, or bulletin board on the government's role in encryption technology control, especially in terms of export control. Begin with the clipper chip initiative and follow it through to the present day.

CHAPTER 13

CASE STUDY

WRONG ARM OF THE LAW

Historic Boston Law Firm Needs Security Guarantee before It Moves Apps from Notes to the Web

You think your legacy applications are tough to leave behind? Consider the plight of Boston-based law firm Fish & Richardson.

Founded in 1878, the firm counts Alexander Graham Bell among its earliest clients. Fish & Richardson helped Bell acquire his first U.S. patent, and the firm's founding president, Frederick Fish, later went on to become president of Bell's first telephone company.

That long history of innovation, however, gave the company no advantage when Fish & Richardson's IS managers had to get their 400 employees off the phone and onto groupware. It was a tough job.

But they succeeded. And now Fish & Richardson has a tougher challenge: telling eager users that the latest World Wide Web–based groupware technologies aren't ready for prime time.

That's a tall order, especially considering the substantial investment the firm has made in groupware. Fish & Richardson's network, which links a fast-Ethernet backbone with ISDN and frame-relay links to its seven U.S. offices, has become a pipeline for collaborative-messaging and -database technologies. These branch offices use the network to share case information among 140 attorneys who specialize in patent law and technology. The employees also regularly participate in discussion databases created on Lotus Notes.

"We're so spread out that we needed a special architecture to make people feel like they're together," says Ian Steward, IS director at Fish & Richardson.

"We have hundreds of Notes collaborative and case-management databases in which people discuss everything going on," explains Steward.

Although Notes has been a success for Fish & Richardson, the recent boom in intranet applications has led Steward to reconsider the company's large investment in Lotus' technology, which is duplicated on three Microsoft Windows NT servers in Boston; Menlo Park, Calif.; and Houston. He will soon be deciding between the numerous Web-based systems and proprietary technologies.

"There's really going to be a battle between the Web and Notes, but we're excited to bring in [Lotus] Domino to see what we can do with that. People find the Notes interface interesting, and it doesn't involve much training."

No Web Yet But a large-scale move to Web-based applications is being put off for the time being. "With Web products, the security just isn't there yet," he explains. He's been looking into virtual private networking software from companies such as Raptor Systems Inc. and is interested in what Netscape Communications Corp. will do with encrypted tunneling in its forthcoming Netscape Communicator groupware package. But he'll wait until these products are shipping and the technologies mature before he buys them.

Because of the security issue, Steward has made a decision to stick with Notes for the time being and to move the company's Lotus cc:Mail system to Notes Mail rather than a Web-based mail client. Another factor in this decision is that the company uses Notes and third-party add-on software to route forms, images, photographs, and diagrams between its offices and users.

But Steward is planning the next move for messaging applications, which he sees happening next year. "We'll either stick with Notes and add Domino or go to the Web," he says.

For security reasons, Steward isolates the Web applications from the nuts-and-bolts network, which consists of 26 Novell Inc. NetWare 3.12 servers and seven Windows NT servers that are used to access legal databases, CD-ROM drives, and Notes. One NT server functions as the intranet server, but it is only used to point employees to helpful research links on the Web and is not used to store proprietary case data.

Internet connectivity—as well as the company's Web site—is com-pletely outsourced to BBN Planet Corp. Employees surf the Internet by means of a private T-1 link to BBN. The intranet consists of a single Microsoft Internet Information Server running on one of the company's seven NT servers.

Steward insists that separating the architectures of the internal network and Internet connectivity lets people get out to the Internet but allows no one to get in. "I see employees eventually sharing information on the Web, but the security is not there yet," says Steward.

Fish & Richardson uses numerous WAN technologies to link the Boston headquarters to the other offices in Houston; Menlo Park; La Jolla, Calif.; Minneapolis; New York; and Washington. In addition to frame-relay links that connect the Boston LAN to the remote offices, the company maintains a full T-1 ISDN Primary Rate Interface connection that links the remote offices through a PictureTel Inc. videoconferencing system. There is also a dial-up backup system as well as Citrix Systems Inc. WinFrame servers to provide remote access to employees.

To link to the remote offices, Fish & Richardson uses 3Com Corp. NETBuilder routers. To link to the Internet, the company uses a Cisco Systems Inc. 2500 router.

The T-1 lines enable a committed information rate of 256Kbps, but the service lets the company bump up to full T-1 rates when bandwidth is needed.

Stopgap Solution In addition to requiring access to Notes databases, the company's attorneys need constant access to databases residing on the NetWare servers and the two dozen CD-ROM drives used to access large image files.

"Eighty percent of our employees are on the network at any given time, and none can afford to wait for information," says Steward.

This heavy demand for bandwidth led the company to migrate from token ring to fast Ethernet. According to Steward, ATM was deemed too expensive. He saw a fast-Ethernet backbone with Ethernet to the desktop as an affordable stopgap solution that would supply adequate bandwidth through next year.

"By using Ethernet only to the desktop, we were able to save money on adapter cards, but we will still benefit from fast Ethernet on the backbone," says Steward.

In Boston, where 320 of the firm's 500 users work, the IS department installed 11 3Com LinkSwitch 1000 SuperStack workgroup switches, which deliver 10Mbps Ethernet workstations and provide 100Mbps divided among the 3Com LinkBuilder FMS 100 hubs.

The infrastructure upgrade now makes it possible for Steward to plan changes for the database and Web applications. In addition to testing Domino technology for collaborative messaging, he also plans to move the company's many databases to Microsoft SQL Server running on Windows NT. This will lead to a gradual migration of some of the NetWare servers but not all of them. "We won't completely do away with NetWare," adds Steward. "In fact, we'll probably upgrade some of them to NetWare 4.x."

Steward also likes SQL Server because he believes it should integrate easily with the Web.

"We have plans to use [Microsoft] ActiveX technology to access SQL databases," Steward says. However, he once again stresses that Web technology has not necessarily caught up with the hype. "It's fashionable to talk about Web-database integration right now, but it's not yet where people think it is."

Source: R. Scott Raynovich, "Wrong Arm of the Law," *LAN Times* (February 1, 1997), Copyright February 1, 1997, The McGraw-Hill Companies, Inc.

BUSINESS CASE STUDY QUESTIONS

Activities

1. Complete a top-down model for this case by gleaning facts from the case and placing them in the proper layer of the top-down model. After having completed the top-down model, analyze and detail those instances where requirements were clearly passed down from upper layers to lower layers of the model and where solutions to those requirements were passed up from lower layers to upper layers of the model.
2. Detail any questions about the case that may occur to you for which answers are not clearly stated in the article.

Business

1. What was the primary business activity at this organization?
2. What was the business problem or opportunity that the case presented?
3. What is the perceived problem with web-based products?
4. What are the issues regarding information availability and response time?

Application

1. What was the problem with the web-based groupware technologies?
2. How is Lotus Notes used at the law firm?
3. What is the difference between Domino and Notes?

Data

1. What types of information are shared over the law firm's network?

2. How and where is the Notes data duplicated?
3. To which types of data must the attorneys have constant access?
4. What database migration is planned? Why?
5. How might web-database integration be achieved?

Network

1. Describe the local and wide area network architecture.
2. What is virtual private networking and encrypted tunneling?
3. How are web technologies isolated from the production network?
4. How is Internet connectivity handled?
5. Is Internet connectivity two-way (incoming and outgoing)?
6. How is the corporate intranet supported?
7. What are some of the WAN services and technologies used to link the various law firm offices?
8. Is bandwidth on demand supported? If so, how?
9. What is the local area network architecture (data link layer protocol)? Explain.

Technology

1. What groupware technologies are used at the law firm?
2. Which technologies may solve the law firm's security requirements?
3. How is remote access supported?

GLOSSARY

2B+D 2 64 KBps B channels plus one 16 K D channel; configuration of BRI ISDN

3D Memory Module 3D memory modules, not to be confused with 3DRAM, stack memory chips on top of each other

3DRAM 3-dimensional RAM

4 mm DAT DDS 1 Digital audio tape backup device with 2 GB capacity and 21–23 MB/min throughput

4 mm DAT DDS 2 Digital audio tape backup device with 4 GB capacity and 23–30 MB/min throughput

8 mm 8 mm digital magnetic tape backup device with 5 GB capacity and 15–29 MB/min throughput

16-bit subsystem A shared memory address space, sometimes referred to as a 16-bit subsystem, allows 16-bit applications to execute in a 32-bit operating environment.

23B+D 23 bearer channels (64 KBps ea.) plus one 64 K D channel; configuration of PRI ISDN

30B+D 30 64 KBps bearer channels plus one 64 K D channel; European PRI which maps to an E-1

AAL ATM adaptation layer protocols convert user input payloads into ATM cells

ABR Available bit rate; ATM bandwidth management scheme that takes a fixed minimum amount of bandwidth plus whatever VBR (variable bit rate) is not using

Absolute path names In UNIX, absolute path names start at the root directory in the listing of the path to the destination directory, while relative path names start at the current directory.

Accelerated graphics port *See* AGP

Access control list Authorization screens users according to user IDs and passwords and determines by examining access control lists whether a given user is authorized to access requested files or system resources

Access line Local loop from customer premises to network service entry point

Access server *See* Communications server

ACE MNP-10 protocol designed to optimize data transmission over cellular links

Acid test A set of rules that describe the capabilities of a transaction process monitoring system

ACL *See* Access control list

Active assistance subsystems Active assistance subsystems allow users to describe what they wish to accomplish, such as purchasing an airline ticket or receiving inventory at a loading dock, and the system will lead them step by step through the desired transaction.

Active data objects *See* ADO

Active directory service *See* ADS

Active matrix Active matrix displays employ transistors at each point on the display grid to actively control color and intensity of each "dot" in the display. This technology enables brighter colors, sharper images, and faster response to changing images.

ActiveX ActiveX is an object-based technology from Microsoft used to build and distribute software components. The term *ActiveX* can refer to the entire DCOM architecture, but it is most commonly used to refer to specific software components.

Activity monitors Antivirus technology that can monitor behavior of programs

Actor A term specific to the Chorus microkernel; the functional equivalent of a task in a Mach microkernel or a process in a UNIX environment

Adaptive segmented lookahead cache Adaptive segmented lookahead buffers are able to dynamically adjust the number and size of buffers, dependent on the situation.

Address bus The width of the address bus is the controlling factor as to how much memory a given computer system can access.

Ad hoc workflow A type of workflow can be considered ad hoc if it is generally short lived and is usually only a one-time process.

ADO Active data objects are part of the OLE DB API. Active data objects replace the RDO and DAO interfaces from the initial ODBC standard.

ADS NT 5.0's enterprise-oriented directory service

ADSL Asymmetric digital subscriber line; local loop data service able to offer 6 MBps download and 640

KBps upload over existing copper pairs without interfering with existing POTS service

Advanced Mobile Phone Service *See* AMPS

Advanced Peer-to-Peer Networking *See* APPN

Advanced Power Management *See* APM

Adverse Channel Enhancements *See* ACE

Agent An autonomous piece of software in between the intelligent application, reporting on event conditions and performance metrics, and the management console; collects these performance statistics and properly formats them for transmission to the application management console

Agent event manager One of three cooperating components of the agent portion of the client/agent/server architecture; the agent event manager is combined with a customer written transaction handler to form an entity known as the intelligent agent, which resides on the local server; once the agent event manager receives a request from a mobile client, it acts on behalf of that client in all communications with the local server until the original client request is totally fulfilled

AGP Accelerated graphics ports move graphics traffic from the PCI bus that is shared with other system traffic to a dedicated channel that links directly to the system chip set and subsequently to the system memory.

AMP Asymmetric multiprocessing characterized by entire applications processes, rather than threads, being assigned to a particular processor; processor loads can become unbalanced; in AMP systems, each CPU is generally assigned its own memory and other subsystems

AMPS The current circuit-switched analog cellular network's transmission standard, advanced mobile phone service; operates in the 800 MHz frequency range

AMS The applications management specification; a proposal for standardizing how instrumentation should be developed within applications

API Application program interfaces allow a single application to work with multiple database management systems. APIs prevent programmers from having to write specific versions of programs for each unique database management system, network operating system, operating system combination possible for all servers to which the front-end tool may ever wish to speak.

API A type of software specification known as a network applications program interface; allows requests for services from application programs to be passed along to the network-attached servers that provide these services

API wrapping The process of converting a main-frame application to a support client/server computing; the clients access data on the server via a specialized piece of middleware that communicates with the server application via the server application's APIs

APM Power management features offered by operating systems have been standardized as the advanced power management specification.

Applet An application that runs inside of another application; most commonly used to describe Java applications that run inside of a web browser

Application gateways Concerned with what services or applications a message is requesting in addition to who is making that request; connections between requesting clients and service-providing servers are created only after the application gateway is satisfied as to the legitimacy of the request; even once the legitimacy of the request has been established, only proxy clients and servers actually communicate with each other

Application-level filter Application-level filters, or assured pipelines, go beyond port-level filters in their attempts to prevent unauthorized access to corporate data.

Application MIB Identifies three key groups of variables for proper application tracking and management

Application response measurement *See* ARM

Application rightsizing Implies that applications are designed for and deployed on the platform, or type and size of computer, which makes the most sense: the "right" size computer; the right computer or platform implies that the choice is based on maximizing the efficiency with which the application runs

Application services The server network operating system is responsible for application services, which include not only executing the back-end engine portion of the application, but also supplying the messaging and communications services to enable interoperability between distributed clients and servers.

Applications management specification *See* AMS

Applications software Divided into client front ends and server back ends or engines; is concerned with accomplishment of a specific type of task or transaction; LAN applications software can be divided into two major subcategories: LAN productivity software and LAN resource management software

APPN Advanced Peer-to-Peer Networking; an IBM multiprotocol solution that allows computers to talk directly on an SNA network

ARM An API that can be used by applications developers, and can measure several key application statistics

ASMP   *See* AMP

Assembly language   A low-level programming language that uses pneumonic instructions rather than numeric machine instructions; also known as assembler

Assets   Corporate property of some value that requires varying degrees of protection

Assured pipeline   Application-level filters that go beyond port-level filters in their attempts to prevent unauthorized access to corporate data

Assured pipelines   *See* Application gateways

Asymmetric digital subscriber line   *See* ADSL

Asymmetric multiprocessing   *See* AMP

Asynchronous   Interprocess dialogue in which a distributed application could generate a message for another distributed application, forward it to the message queue, and resume its own processing activity

Asynchronous application communications   A communications model where an application does not have to wait for a reply before continuing processing; the opposite of synchronous communications

Asynchronous conferencing   Non–real-time conferencing

Asynchronous transfer mode   *See* ATM

ATA   Integrated drive electronics disk drives are distinguished from earlier offerings by the inclusion of the drive controller with the disk drive in a single integrated unit and the use of a bus interface known as ATA (AT Attachment). The key limitation of IDE drives was their capacity limitation of 528 MB and ATA's 2–3 MBps data transfer rate.

ATA-2   *See* E-IDE

ATM   Asynchronous transfer mode; cell relay standard for 53 octet cells

ATM access switches   Interface between ATM switches and legacy LANs

ATM adaptation layer   *See* AAL

ATM gateway switches   *See* ATM access switches

ATM LAN emulation   ATM service that allows Ethernet or Token Ring traffic to travel across higher speed ATM networks without requiring changes to LAN workstations

AT&T 5ESS SWITCH   One of the switches that supports ISDN

Attack applets   Java applets, downloaded from the web, intent on serious security breaches

AT&T SVR4   One of the two popular versions of UNIX; AT&T System V Release 4, was originally developed by AT&T and later reorganized as USL (UNIX Systems Laboratory), which AT&T subsequently sold to Novell

Audio conferencing   Real-time conferencing

Auditing system   In NetWare 4.1, an extensive auditing system monitors and reports on what valid users are doing. The auditor acts independently of the supervisor and separately monitors activity on both the file system and the NetWare Directory Services database.

Authentication   Ensures that messages between clients and servers in the distributed processing environment are genuine and have actually been sent from the processor claiming to be the source node on the network; authentication is usually provided by a dedicated authentication server running specialized software developed specifically for distributed environments, uses digital signatures attached to transmitted documents in order to ensure both the authenticity of the author and the document's message integrity, which verifies that the document has not been tampered with

Authentication Header   In Secure IP, the authentication header provides data integrity and allows for the authentication of IP packets.

Authorization   Authorization is the familiar user ID/password process, which ensures that a certain user is authorized to access a particular enterprise resource. Enhancements to authorization for remote users include callback security. It determines by examining access control lists whether a given user is authorized to access requested files or system resources.

Autodetection and configuration   Autodetection and configuration of installed controllers, interface cards, and peripherals by network operating systems is dependent on the network operating system's possessing a compatible driver for that device.

Automatic failover   Implies that a clustered server will automatically and transparently take over for another failed server in the same cluster

Automatic number identification   Service available via either ISDN or in-band signaling

Auto-server shutdown   Some UPSs also have the ability to link directly to servers, advising them of a loss of power, thereby triggering user notification and an orderly shutdown. This feature must be compatible with the particular server operating system installed.

Available bit rate   *See* ABR

Back end   The server portion of the program

Backside bus   In a P6 CPU, the second cavity is occupied by a 256KB SRAM L2, or secondary cache, linked directly to the neighboring Pentium Pro chip through a dedicated 64-bit bus known as the backside bus.

Backward compatibility   Legacy application support;

determines whether current applications will run without modification on the new network operating system

Backward explicit congestion notification *See* BECN

Bandwidth on demand interoperability group *See* BONDING

BASIC An English-like programming language that is easy for beginning programmers to learn; however, it is a powerful programming language that is often used to develop client applications in the Microsoft Windows environment

Basic rate interface *See* BRI

Bearer channels ISDN channels that actually bear, or carry, data and voice

BECN Backward explicit congestion notification; a frame relay flow control mechanism

BER Bit error rate; measurement of errors on a given transmission line

Bindery Network operating systems have always depended on some sort of naming service or directory in which to store information about users as well as systems resources such as disks, servers, and printers. NetWare 3.x servers stored this type of information in a bindery.

Biometric authentication Can authenticate users based on fingerprints, palm prints, retinal patterns, voice recognition, or other physical characteristics

B-ISDN Broadband ISDN; ATM switching plus SONET transmission

Bit error rate *See* BER

Blocking The process of forcing an application to wait on a response from another application before it can continue; directly associated with synchronous application communication

BONDING Bandwidth on demand interoperability group; inverse multiplexing standard

Branch prediction An intelligent instruction handling technique employed in many CPU chips in which the CPU predicts which condition of the branch statement will be true, and automatically loads the associated conditional branch statement

Branch target buffer Branch target cache that holds the results of as many as the last 256 branches executed in a given program

BRI Basic rate interface; 2B+D ISDN

Broadband ISDN *See* B-ISDN

Broadband transmission In general, any transmission service at the T-1 level or greater

Broadcast filtering The process of removing SNA broadcast messages at a router to prevent them from proliferating across an internetwork

Brokered authorization Authorization security software can be either server-based, also known as brokered authorization, or workstation-based, also referred to as trusted node.

BSD UNIX One of the two popular versions of UNIX; BSD (Berkeley Software Distribution) UNIX from the University of California at Berkeley

Bulk retrieval mechanism A new SNMP2 procedure in which managers can retrieve several pieces of network information at a time from a given agent

Bulletin board system A computer system that serves as an information center and message-passing center for users who have a connection to the system

Bus A connection between components within a CPU chip, between a CPU chip and system components, or between system components

Business communications services Videoconferencing, simultaneous document sharing, electronic data interchange, global fax service, electronic document distribution, paging, e-mail, news and information services

Business process reengineering An analysis methodology that provides an opportunity to critically reexamine business processes

Bus width Measured in bits, refers to the number of bits that can travel in parallel down a bus; common bus widths are 8, 16, 32, 64 and 128 bits

Bytecode An intermediate file format that is supported on multiple operating platforms; Java applications are compiled into bytecode, which can then be executed by a Java virtual machine regardless of the base hardware and operating system

C A high-level programming language commonly used to develop operating systems and application programs

C++ A version of the C programming language that supports object-oriented programming

C2 certification The Orange Book certification process; this is both costly and lengthy; typically, the certification process is projected to take two years to complete at a cost of $17 million; to date, both NetWare and NT Server have achieved the C2 certification

C2-level security Server operating systems often claim to implement C2-level security. C2-level security is actually part of a specification known as "Trusted Computer System Evaluation Criteria," which is specified in a Department of Defense document commonly known as "The Orange Book." The book concentrates on seven levels of data confidentiality from D (low) to A1 (high).

CA Certificate authority; third-party key certification services that issue public keys along with a certificate ensuring the authenticity of the key

Cable scanners   Layer 1 testers

Cache bus   Responsible for quickly delivering data and instructions to/from L2 cache to/from the CPU

Calendar access protocol   Allows users to mix and match different calendaring and scheduling clients and servers

Calendar exchange format   Defines a standard representation for calendaring and scheduling information

Calendaring   The placement and manipulation of data onto a calendar

Calendar interoperability protocols   Protocols required for different calendaring and scheduling products to communicate with each other; will allow communication over Internet e-mail and other transports such as hypertext transport protocol

Call set-up packets   Used to establish virtual circuits in frame relay networks

CAP   A de facto standard, deployed in many trial ADSL units, developed by AT&T Paradyne

Carrierless amplitude & phase   *See* CAP

Carrier Sense Multiple Access with Collision Avoidance   *See* CSMA/CA

CASE   *See* Computer assisted systems engineering

CBR   Constant bit rate; an ATM bandwidth management scheme that provides a guaranteed amount of bandwidth to a given virtual path, thereby producing the equivalent of leased T-1 or T-3 line

CBS   Commited burst size; defines the extent to which a user can exceed CIR over a period of time in a frame relay network

CDE   A cross-platform windowing environment for UNIX named the Common Desktop Environment, jointly produced by UNIX hardware and software vendors Hewlett Packard, Sun, IBM and Novell (UNIX Systems Laboratory)

CDMA   Code division multiple access; a bandwidth-sharing methodology for digital cellular that transmits digitized voice packets from numerous calls at different frequencies spread all over the entire allocated bandwidth spectrum

CDPD   Cellular digital packet data; a service that uses idle capacity in the circuit-switched cellular network to transmit IP-based data packets; the fact that CDPD is IP-based allows it to easily interface to IP-based private networks as well as to the Internet and other e-mail services

CDRAM   Cached DRAM

Cell relay   Fast packet-switching technology employing fixed length cells

Cellular digital packet data   *See* CDPD

Central clock   A central clock or timing device in the TDM gives each input device its allotted time to empty its buffer into an area of the TDM where the combined data from all of the polled input devices is conglomerated into a single message frame for transmission over the composite circuit.

Central Processing Unit   *See* CPU

Certificate authorities   *See* CA

CGI   A method of developing scripts that run on a web server; through the use of common gateway interface scripts, a web browser can access server-based data

Challenge handshake authentication protocol   *See* CHAP

Challenge response token authentication   A token authentication protocol in which a user uses a smart card to generate a one-time session key response to a server initiated challenge

CHAP   Challenge handshake authentication protocol; provides a more secure means for establishing dial-in communication; it uses a three-way challenge that includes the user ID, password, and also a key that encrypts the ID and password

CHAP MD5   A protocol for PPP-encrypted authentication included with most PPP clients

CHAP MD80   A protocol for authentication for Windows NT RAS included with most PPP clients

Chorus microkernel   A microkernel developed by Chorus Systems (France) that has been used as the nucleus for numerous operating systems

CIM   Common information model; a proposed protocol currently under development by the DMTF (Desktop Management Task Force) that would support HMMS; CIM would permit management data gathered from a variety of enterprise and desktop voice and data technology to be transported, processed, displayed, and stored by a single CIM-compliant web browser

Ciphertext   In encryption, the changed, unmeaningful data

CIPX   A protocol for compression of IPX headers included with most PPP clients

CIR   Committed information rate; the minimum bandwidth guaranteed to users for "normal" transmission in a frame relay network

Circuit-switched cellular   Analog cellular service capable of supporting 14.4 KBps

Circuit-switched network   A network based on circuit-switched services in which users are able to use the entire bandwidth of physical circuits created solely for their transmissions

Circuit switching A switching process in which physical circuits are created, maintained, and terminated for individual point-to-point or multipoint connections

CISC In CISC architecture, instructions are interpreted into executable code by microcode, which is itself a small computer software program running on the CPU chip. In effect, CISC requires one software program to translate another software program.

CISC-to-RISC decoder In a process which Intel refers to as dynamic execution, the P6 breaks complex CISC instructions down into simpler RISC-like, but not true RISC, instructions known as micro-ops.

Clear request packet In frame relay networks, the special packet that terminates virtual circuits

Client/agent/server The overall objective of a client/agent/server architecture, as opposed to the more common LAN-based client/server architecture, is to reduce the amount of mobile client to server network traffic by building as much intelligence as possible into the server-based agent so that it can act on behalf of the mobile client application.

Client front ends The portion of a distributed client/server application program that runs on the client PC

Client network operating systems Integrate traditional operating system functionality with advanced network operating system features to enable communication with a variety of different types of network operating system servers

Client/server information system A system that takes advantage of the processing power now available on desktop computers by splitting the job of delivering quality information to end users among multiple computers

Client/server network operating systems Offer the ability to support hundreds of users and the ability to interact with other network operating systems via gateways; these systems are both considerably more expensive and considerably more complicated to install and administer than peer-to-peer network operating systems

Client software architecture The overall organization of software categories within a typical client workstation, including presentation, application, data management, network operating system, and operating system categories

Clipper Chip The Clipper Chip initiative proposed that every phone and data communications device in the United States would be equipped with a Clipper Chip to support encryption.

Clock-divided frequency The clock speed of a bus may be the full clock speed of the CPU, measured in

MHz, or may be one-half, one-third, or one-fourth of the CPU clock speed, which is known as clock-divided frequency.

Clock multiplying When clock speeds on a given CPU chip are doubled or tripled, the CPU chip works at the higher rate internally only as instructions are processed in the pipelines at the new, higher rate

Clock speed Specialized clock circuitry within the CPU chip is used to keep precise timing of CPU operations. Clock speed is measured in megahertz, which means millions of cycles per second.

Clustering Using the CPU power of multiple CPUs located in separate computing platforms to produce a single, more powerful, virtual computer; clusters are also sometimes referred to as virtual parallel machines

COBOL A high-level programming language traditionally used to develop applications that run in a mainframe environment

Code division multiple access *See* CDMA

Color depth The number of displayed colors; another performance criterion that differentiates monitors; common color depths are 16 colors, 256 colors; 65,000 colors, 16.7 million colors

COM A method of developing object-oriented systems developed by Microsoft; commonly distributed across multiple computers as part of DCOM

Committed burst size *See* CBS

Committed information rate *See* CIR

Common Desktop Environment *See* CDE

Common gateway interface *See* CGI

Common information model *See* CIM

Common mail calls A cross-platform messaging API released by the X.400 API association (XAPIA); provides a basic set of services, such as send, receive, and address lookups, through the 12 API calls it supports

Common object model *See* COM

Common object request broker *See* CORBA

Communications server A dedicated multiuser server, also known as an access server, to which remote users can attach through one or more modems; depending on the software loaded on the communications server, it may deliver remote node functionality, remote control functionality, or both

Compatibility Successfully bridging the gap or communicating between two or more technology components, whether hardware or software

Compiler A software tool that converts high-level programs into machine language–executable programs

Component interface API   Interfaces to the individual application programs or desktop components that are to be managed and monitored on the local client

Composite message frame   The frame that is built by combining the contents of individual channel buffers in a multiplexer

Computer-assisted systems engineering   Any software tool that aids in the development of application programs; components vary from planning and project management tools through code generation tools

Computer system   A system made up of a processor or CPU, memory subsystem, storage subsystem, and video or input/output subsystem

Connectionless service   A packet-switched service that supports globally addressed unreliable datagram service

Connection-oriented service   A packet-switched service that supports virtual circuits

Consolidated service desk   A single point of contact for all network and application problem resolution; appropriate personnel processes can be matched with associated network management technologies

Constant bit rate   *See* CBR

Continuous operations   Avoids planned downtimes such as scheduled maintenance and/or component (disk drive, CPU) replacement

Cooperative multitasking   Multitasking implies that an operating system can be running more than one program simultaneously. Cooperative multitasking implies that a given application has access to all required system resources until that program relinquishes that control.

Coprocessors   Math coprocessors are separate CPU chips that include floating-point logic and can be purchased separately at the discretion of the computer owner.

CORBA   A set of object-oriented middleware specifications published by the Object Management Group; the CORBA specifications define the way objects are defined, created, dispatched, and invoked and how they communicate with one another

Corporate downsizing   Elimination of positions within a corporation through attrition, early retirement, closed operations, or forced lay-offs

CPE   Customer premises equipment, Telecomm equipment located at a customer site

CPU   The processor chip or central processing unit in which software instructions are actually executed

CRC   Cyclical redundancy check; a type of frame check or error check sequence

CRC Checkers   Category of antivirus technology also known as hashing checkers; creates and saves a unique cyclical redundancy check character or hashing number for each file to be monitored

CSMA/CA   Carrier sense multiple access with collision avoidance; part of the IEEE 802.11 standard; similar to CSMA/CD except that collisions cannot be detected in wireless environments as they can in wire-based environments; before transmitting, workstations wait a predetermined amount of time in order to avoid collisions, and set up a point-to-point wireless circuit to the destination workstation

Customer premises equipment   *See* CPE

CVRAM   Cached VRAM (video RAM)

Cybermalls   The experience offered by at least some of these providers enables the production of professional quality presentations that can then be incorporated into cybermalls with other professional quality web pages adhering to the standards established by the cybermall management; a collection of electronic commerce web pages

Cyclical redundancy check   *See* CRC

D channel   Delta channel; in ISDN, used for transport of management and control information

D-4   A type of T-1 framing in which 24 8-bit time slots are combined with a framing bit to form 193-bit frames

DAO   A high-level API for Microsoft ODBC programming environments; commonly used to address data in the Microsoft Jet database engine

DARPA   Defense Advanced Research Projects Agency

Data   The final element of a workflow application

Data access objects   *See* DAO

Database connectivity software   Software concerned with connecting a variety of front-end tools with a variety of distributed DBMS engines

Database MIB   A specification that would allow any enterprise data management system to report performance statistics back to any SNMP-compliant enterprise network management system

Database wrapping   The process of developing a new client application that integrates with the legacy system directly through the legacy application's data store

Data bus   Delivers data to/from the L1 cache and processing pipelines

Data bus width   The number of bits of data the CPU can read from and write to the L2 cache for each tick of the memory bus clock; most often 32 or 64 bits

Data cache   A special area in the write-back stage where the results of the executed instruction are written out to a memory location or register

Data conferencing Allows people to share data in real time and combines various collaborative technologies, such as electronic whiteboards and chatting, into one comprehensive product

Data display channel *See* DDC

Data encryption standard *See* DES

Datagrams Globally addressed message packets found in connectionless frame relay networks

Data Link Switching IBM's version of encapsulating SNA traffic in TCP/IP

Data migration Data migration utilities manage the migration of data among different types of storage devices as part of a comprehensive hierarchical storage management program.

Data transparency In order to qualify as a true Distributed Database Management System, the product in question must offer data transparency to the end user without regard for front-end tool or distributed application, type of server computer (Intel-based, minicomputer, mainframe, etc.), physical location of the server, physical details, and protocols of the network path to the server.

Data over voice unit A type of frequency division multiplexer

DCE *See* Distributed computing environment

DCOM Distributed Common Object Model; a Microsoft proprietary solution for building distributed object-oriented applications; DCOM allows objects to be defined, created, dispatched and invoked and to communicate with one another

DDC Data display channel with which PnP compliant monitors will be controlled and configured

DDM Distributed device manager; a DDM architecture relies on distributed network probes that are able to gather information from a variety of network devices manufactured by multiple vendors and relay that information to numerous distributed device manager consoles

DE Discard eligibility; flag in frame relay frame indicating those frames that can be discarded in the event of network congestion

Decode stage Converts the fetched instruction into low-level code understood by the CPU

Definition variables In application MIB, definition variables would store background information concerning applications such as application name, manufacturer, version, release, installation date, license number, number of consecutive users, and so on.

Delphi An event-driven programming environment developed by Borland that uses the Pascal structured programming language

Delta file synchronization Perhaps the most significant file synchronization option in terms of its potential impact on reducing required bandwidth and file transfer time to accomplish the synchronization; rather than sending entire files across the dial-up or LAN link, delta file synchronization transfers only the changes to those files

Delta file transfer Delta file transfer allows only changes to files to be transferred.

DES Although proprietary standards do exist, a standard known as DES (Data Encryption Standard), originally approved by the National Institute of Standards and Technology (NIST) in 1977, is often used, allowing encryption devices manufactured by different manufacturers to interoperate successfully. The DES encryption standard actually has two parts, which serve to offer greater overall security.

Desktop management interface *See* DMI

Desktop management task force *See* DMTF

Device drivers Small software programs specifically written to be compatible with a particular operating system and a particular type of hardware device, which interface the kernel to the various hardware components and their controllers

Dial-in server *See* LAN modem

Dial-out modem applications This ability to re-direct information for dial-out modem applications from LAN-attached PCs is a cooperative task accomplished by the software of the remote node server and its corresponding remote client software; not all remote node servers support dial-out functionality

Dial-up server *See* Remote node server

Digital Encryption Standard *See* DES

Digital IDs Digital certificates issued from CAs such as VeriSign, containing an organization's encrypted public key along with a minimal amount of information about the organization such as e-mail address, department, company, state or province, and country

Digital service hierarchy Series of standards defining high speed digital services (DS-1 = 1.544 Mbps)

Digital signature Signatures attached to transmitted documents in order to ensure both the authenticity of the author and the document's message integrity, which verifies that the document has not been tampered with

Digital signature encryption Encryption using public key encryption methodology in reverse as an electronic means of guaranteeing authenticity of the sending party and as an assurance that encrypted documents have not been tampered with during transmission

DII A CORBA object interface that allows for dynamic binding between CORBA-compliant objects

DIMM Dual in-line memory module; memory module in which the DRAMs are mounted on both sides of the small circuit board

DIP Dual in-line pin chips; originally attached to circuit boards as a means of packaging and selling RAM

Direct Memory Access *See* DMA

Directory services Network operating systems have always depended on some sort of directory or naming service in which to store information about users as well as systems resources such as disks, servers, and printers.

Directory synchronization software *See* File synchronization software

Direct sequence spread spectrum Transmits at a particular frequency within the allowable range; in order to distinguish between transmissions from multiple wireless workstations, DSSS adds at least 10 bits to the data message in order to uniquely identify a particular transmission; DSSS receivers must be able to differentiate between these bits, known as chips, in order to properly distinguish transmissions

Discard eligibility *See* DE

Discrete multitone *See* DMT

Disk duplexing Seeks to overcome the single point of failure inherent in disk mirroring by linking a separate disk controller to each mirrored disk drive

Disk mirroring Two disks attached to the same controller act as mirror images of one another. Everything written to one disk is identically written to the other. In the event that one disk fails, the other disk immediately takes over.

Distributed applications An application that has been divided to execute cooperatively across two or more computers

Distributed architecture Information systems constructed according to the distributed architecture paradigm are often referred to as client/server information systems because the overall information system's duties are shared between client and server computers.

Distributed component object model *See* DCOM

Distributed computing Also known as distributed processing; dividing an application program into two or more pieces, and subsequently distributing and processing those distributed applications onto two or more computers, either clients or servers

Distributed computing environment An open standard middleware architecture; the distributed computing environment is represented by a single source

code currently owned and maintained by The Open Group (formerly the Open Software Foundation)

Distributed database management systems Allow a user to access data without regard for front-end tool or distributed application, type of server computer (Intel-based, minicomputer, mainframe, etc.), physical location of the server, physical details and protocols of the network path to the server

Distributed device manager *See* DDM

Distributed network probes Probes in the DDM architecture that are able to gather information from a variety of network devices manufactured by multiple vendors and relay that information to numerous distributed device manager consoles

Distributed object technology Enables distributed applications to be more easily developed thanks to the reusability and encapsulation quality of the objects themselves

Distributed parallel processing *See* DPP

Distributed queue dual bus *See* DQDB

Distributed transaction processing *See* DTP

Distributed transaction processing monitor *See* DTPM

DLT Digital linear tape backup device with 10 GB capacity and 90–150 MB/min throughput

DLUR/S The protocol that implements SNA integration into the IBM APPN architecture

DMA Direct memory access data transfer that allows data to be transferred between the disk drive and system memory without intervention from the CPU; this allows for both faster data transfer and fewer CPU interruptions

DMI Desktop management interface; the overall desktop management architecture; desktop management systems rely upon an architecture and associated protocols proposed by the Desktop Management Task Force (DMTF), which is composed of more than 50 companies including Intel, Microsoft, IBM, Digital, Hewlett Packard, Apple, Compaq, Dell, and Sun

DMI services layer The DMI application that resides on each desktop device to be managed

DMT Discrete multitone; has been approved as an ADSL standard (ANSI Standard T1.413) by the ANSI T1E1.4 working group

DMTF The Desktop Management Task Force (DMTF), composed of more than 50 companies including Intel, Microsoft, IBM, Digital, Hewlett Packard, Apple, Compaq, Dell, and Sun

Document management Document management products organize and manage electronic files for a company.

Domain directory services Network operating systems have always depended on some sort of naming service or directory in which to store information about users as well as systems resources such as disks, servers, and printers. Windows NT uses a domain directory service.

Domains Domain directory services see the network as a series of linked subdivisions known as domains.

Double speed CD-ROM speed specification yielding sustained average data throughput of 300 KBps

Downsizing When a mainframe-based application has been redeployed to run on a smaller computer platform; that smaller platform may or may not be a distributed client/server information system

DPP Distributed parallel processing; future versions of NetWare will support clustering through this systems architecture

DQDB Distributed queue dual bus; SMDS network architecture

DRAM Dynamic RAM; memory that requires refresh cycles every few milliseconds to preserve its data

DS Digital service; *See* digital service hierarchy

DS-1 1.544 MBps

DSE Data switching exchanges, otherwise known as packet switched networks

DTP Distributed transaction processing; with the advent of client/server information systems, multiple geographically dispersed computers are linked, allowing transactions to be posted across multiple distributed computers; requires a distributed TP monitor; DTP is sometimes also known as Enterprise Transaction Processing, or ETP

DTP API protocol The distributed transaction processing monitor is able to interface to the local transaction processing monitor thanks to a distributed transaction processing application program interface protocol supported by both TP monitors.

DTPM Distributed transaction process monitoring; actually requires two levels of TP monitoring; first, the local TP monitor must ensure the integrity of local postings; however, these local postings are just part of a single distributed transaction posting that must be coordinated overall by the distributed transaction processing monitor (DTPM)

Dual-homed gateway A gateway computer or server with two NICs; the application gateway is physically connected to the private secure network and the packet filtering router is connected to the nonsecure network or the Internet; between the application gateway and the packet filter router is an area known as the screened subnet

Dual-issue processor A CPU that has two pipelines and can issue two instructions simultaneously

Dual-ported VRAM The primary modification made by VRAM is that a portion of memory is reserved for servicing the screen refresh function in order to optimize performance for high resolution graphics. RAM segmented in this manner is sometimes referred to as dual-ported VRAM.

DVD Digital versatile disk or digital video disk; widely believed to be the next-generation successor to CD-ROM for high-capacity storage and distribution; one of the major hurdles standing in the way of widespread adoption of DVD as the medium of choice for PC-based storage is the current array of conflicting standards

DX Implies a built-in math coprocessor (1989)

DX2 Implies that the clock speed has been doubled above DX clock speeds (1992)

DX4 Implies that the clock speed has been tripled above DX clock speeds (1994)

Dynamic execution A process in which the P6 breaks complex CISC instructions down into simpler RISC-like, but not true RISC, instructions known as micro-ops

Dynamic invocation interface *See* DII

Dynamic RAM *See* DRAM

Dynamic reconfiguration Enables such things as PCMCIA cards being inserted into and removed from computers without a need to reboot and hot docking (powered up) of laptop computers into docking bays or stations; dynamic reconfiguration-aware applications software could automatically respond to changes in system configuration

Dynamic scalability Clustering, or using the CPU power of multiple CPUs located in separate computing platforms to produce a single more powerful virtual computer

E-1 European standard for high-speed digital transmission 2.048 MBps

ECC memory Error checking and correcting (ECC) memory, also known as error correction code memory; has the ability to detect and correct errors in data stored in and retrieved from RAM memory; it is more expensive than conventional RAM but is worth the added cost in the case of servers

E-commerce *See* Electronic commerce

EDAP The RAID Advisory Board (RAB) has issued detailed specifications for the following classifications of Extended data availability and protection (EDAP): failure resistant, failure tolerant, disaster tolerant.

EDI *See* Electronic data interchange

EDORAM Extended data out RAM; extended data output chips minimize or eliminate the time the CPU has to wait (zero-wait-state) for output from memory by reading the next stored data bit at the same time it's transferring the first requested bit to the CPU

EDOSRAM Extended data out SRAM

EDOVRAM Extended data out VRAM

EDRAM Enhanced DRAM

E-IDE Extended IDE disk drive standard to be known as ATA-2 once adopted by ANSI; features up to 8.4 GB capacity, 4 daisy-chained devices, and 11.1 MBps performance

EISA Extended industry standard architecture bus specification features 32-bit bus width with 33 MBps throughput

Electronic commerce Conducting business on-line, which includes buying and selling products with digital cash

Electronic data interchange The transfer of business documents by electronic means rather than traditional means; EDI is generally text-based, whereas electronic commerce can be text-based and can also contain other data types

Electronic mail By far the most popular and most widely used component of groupware

Electronic meeting When people meet and exchange ideas and information using technology that allows for the transmission of information

Electronic whiteboards Tools that allow meeting participants to share, edit, and save meeting notes; electronic whiteboards have the capability to transmit the written image or words to remote locations

Element managers Point products specifically written to address a particular systems administration or network management issue

E-mail *See* Electronic mail

Emulation technology Attempts to detect as-yet-unknown viruses by running programs with a software emulation program known as a virtual PC

Encapsulating Security Payload Header *See* ESP

Encapsulation The process of placing one protocol into another protocol for processing

Encryption Renders data indecipherable to any unauthorized users that might be able to examine packets of data traffic

End nodes End-user processing nodes, either clients or servers without any information on the overall network, available internetwork links, or routing tables

Engine The server portion of the program, often called the back end

Engine *See* Server back-end

Enhanced paging A pager-based wireless service capable of delivering one or two way messages of 100 characters or less

Enhanced Throughput Cellular *See* ETC

Enterprise network The enterprise network is the transportation system of the client-server architecture; together with middleware, it is responsible for the transparent cooperation of distributed processors and databases

Enterprise network management Focuses on the hardware, software, media, and network services required to seamlessly link and effectively manage distributed client and server computers across an enterprise

Enterprise network management system Enterprise Network Management Systems that compile and report network operation statistics to the end user, most often in some type of graphical format; enterprise Network Management Systems are really management application programs running on a management server; systems that are able to manage multivendor, multiplatform enterprise networks; examples include HP Open View, IBM System View and Sun SunNet Manager

Enterprise transaction processing *See* DTP

Error correction Request for retransmission upon error detection

Error detection Comparison of CRCs in order to detect transmission errors

ESF 24 D-4 frames

ESMR Enhanced specialized mobile radio; currently under development, this wireless WAN service offers one- or two-way voice, paging, or messaging at speeds up to 4.8 KBps over proprietary integrated voice/data devices

ESP In Secure IP, the encapsulating security payload header (ESP) ensures the privacy of the transmission.

ETC Enhanced throughput cellular; proprietary protocol from AT&T Paradyne for optimization of data transmission over cellular networks

ETP *See* DTP

Event A circumstance that causes processing to be performed in an event-driven programming environment; examples include mouse clicks, key presses, or incoming data

Event detection Most audit software depends on capturing large amounts of event data and then filtering that data for exceptional or unusual events

Event handler The procedure that executes as the result of an event's occurrence

Event management tool   An alternative to developing your own applications with embedded management intelligence is to purchase a prewritten event management tool that has been written to monitor specific commercially available applications.

Exceptions   Error conditions or unexpected events that the operating system must be prepared to handle appropriately; these exceptions are generally related to the operating system's responsibility to effectively manage system resources

Execute stage   The stage in which the instruction is executed

Execution units   Pipeline execution stages can be especially written to be optimized for certain operations such as handling only floating point operations, integer operations, or branch logic (if-then-else) operations. These operation-specific options are called execution units.

Expansion bus   Connects add-in cards and peripheral devices such as modems, fax boards, sound cards, additional serial ports, and additional input devices

Extended data availability and protection   *See* EDAP

Extended superframe   *See* ESF

Extended Terminal Access Control Access System   *See* XTACACS

External bus   A bus located outside of a CPU chip

Extranet   A network that uses Internet technology to link businesses with their partners, customers, suppliers, and other businesses that share common goals

E-zines   Specifically targeted electronic magazines

EZ-ISDN   An alternative ordering code scheme proposed by the National ISDN Users Forum to try to further simplify the ISDN ordering process

FAD   *See* FRAD

False accepts   When impostors are allowed access because the comparison was not detailed enough

False rejects   When valid users are denied access because of slight variations detected between the reference biometric characteristic and the current one

FAQ groups   Frequently asked questions groups; similar to ListServe groups that users can subscribe to via e-mail

Fast SCSI-2   An expansion bus specification: 8-bit bus width, 10 MHz clock speed, 10 MBps throughput

Fast and wide SCSI-2   An expansion bus specification: 16-bit bus width, 10 MHz clock speed, 20 MBps throughput

Fat client   When the business logic is distributed on the client in a two-tiered architecture, that architecture is known as fat client.

Fat server   When the business logic is distributed on the server in a two-tiered architecture, that architecture is known as fat server.

Fault tolerance   Usually provided by hardware solutions with supporting software; provides 100 percent availability, zero unexpected downtime, with no data loss; detects, avoids, and corrects faults in order to avoid downtime

FCS   Frame check sequence; an error detection technique

FDM   Frequency division multiplexing; each channel gets a portion of the bandwidth for 100 percent of the time

FECN   Forward explicit congestion notification; a flow control mechanism in frame relay networks

Fetch stage   The stage that brings an instruction into the pipeline from a holding area in the CPU known as the instruction cache

File synchronization software   Software that is able to synchronize versions of files on laptops and desktop workstations; it is now often included as a standard or optional feature in client network operating systems; also known as version control software or directory synchronization software

Filter   A program that examines the source address and destination address of every incoming packet to the firewall server

Filter tables   Lists of addresses whose data packets and embedded messages are either allowed or prohibited from proceeding through the firewall server and into the corporate network

Firewall   In order to prevent unauthorized access from the Internet into a company's confidential data, specialized software known as a firewall is often deployed. All network packets entering the firewall are filtered, or examined, to determine whether or not those users have authority to access requested files or services and whether or not the information contained within the message meets corporate criteria for forwarding over the internal network.

Flash RAM   Flash memory; remembers its data contents until it is flashed by a larger voltage and is used widely as main memory for portable computers

Flow control   Ability to have FRADs throttle back transmission in a frame relay network in order to avoid network congestion

Forms processing   Many applications today allow for the user to fill in the form and then the form is routed based on the information contained within it. Forms processing is one area within workflow that is very popular and can save a company a lot of money.

Forward explicit congestion notification   *See* FECN

FPM   Fast page mode

Fractional T-1   *See* FT-1

Fractional T-1 multiplexers   A T-1 multiplexer that is able to use less than a full T-1 as its composite output channel

FRAD   Frame relay access device; access device for frame relay network that transforms raw data into frame relay–compliant frames

FRAM   Ferroelectric RAM

Frame check sequence   *See* FCS

Frame relay   A type of fast packet-switching process that switches variable length frames; primarily intended for data payloads

Frame relay access device   *See* FRAD

Frame relay switch   Network switch capable of switching frame relay frames

Frames   Header and trailer layout that surrounds user data in variable length frames in accordance with the frame relay interface specification

Frameworks   Offer an overall systems administration or network management platform with integration between modules and a shared database into which all alerts, messages, alarms, and warnings can be stored and correlated

Framing   An adaptation of the TDM; T-1 framing differentiates between channels

Framing bit   The 193rd bit added to the 24 8-bit time slots to indicate the end of one D-4 frame

Frequency division multiplexing   *See* FDM

Frequency hopping spread spectrum   Hops from one frequency to another throughout the allowable frequency range; the pattern of frequency hopping must be known by the wireless receiver so that the message can be reconstructed correctly

Front end   The client portion of the program is often called the front end

Front-end tools   Front-end tools for database management systems fall into two major categories: database query and reporting tools and multiplatform client/server application development tools.

FT-1   Fractional T-1, broadband service that allows customer to access less than the full 24 DS-0s in a T-1

FTP   File transfer protocol; a TCP/IP protocol required for users to download, or transfer, information back to their client PCs

FTP servers   Servers that support FTP activity

Functions   Software modules that return a single result based on the parameters passed to them

Gateway   A hardware/software solution that allows for the translation between different physical signals and/or protocols

Generic Security Service-Applications Program Interface   *See* GSS-API

Global address   Address attached to a datagram in a frame relay network that allows it to be properly delivered

Global directory services   *See* NDS

Global e-mail   Millions of users are connected worldwide to the Internet via the global e-mail subsystem.

Global system for mobile communications   *See* GSM

Gopher   A menu-based client/server system that features search engines that comb through all of the information in all of these information servers

Gopher server   Gopher client software is most often installed on a client PC and interacts with software running on a particular Gopher server, which transparently searches multiple FTP sites for requested information and delivers that information to the Gopher client.

Granularity   How finely access can be controlled (by disk, directory, or file level)

Graphical user interfaces   *See* GUI

Graphics accelerator chip   Key component of a graphics accelerator card commonly differentiated by data path width, either 32 bit or 64 bit

Group document editing   Group document editing can be very useful for teams that are collaboratively developing documents. It can also be very useful for teams that are geographically dispersed by allowing them to develop, edit, and revise documents remotely.

Groupware   Technologies that allow people to work together electronically to become more productive and increase communication regardless of physical location or time

GSM   In Europe and much of the rest of the world, global system for mobile communication is either currently deployed or planned for implementation as the digital cellular standard.

GSS-API   An open API that would allow applications to communicate with a variety of security authorization programs

Guardbands   Used in FDM to prevent cross-channel interference

Guest   A synonym for the term *remote* when referring to remote control software

GUI   Graphical user interfaces such as Windows, OS/2 Presentation Manager, X Windows-based systems such as Motif and OpenLook, or the Macintosh Desktop; the monitor-based image with which the user interacts, as contrasted to a character-based interface or a social user interface

HAL Hardware abstraction layer; windows NT is a microkernel-based operating system with a minimum of hardware-specific code confined to this portion of the microkernel

Hardware abstraction layer *See* HAL

Hardware-based RAID More expensive than software-based RAID, but is also more reliable and is able to support more operating systems

Hardware cache A disk cache made up of memory chips placed directly on the disk controller

Hardware emulation In order to improve Windows application performance, Apple has introduced the DOS card for the PowerMacintosh. This add-on card contains a 486DX2 66 MHz processor and is an example of hardware emulation.

Hardware independent operating systems Because all of the hardware-specific code is restricted to the microkernel, modular operating systems can be ported to any processor that can communicate with the microkernel on which that modular operating system is based.

Hashing Checkers Category of antivirus technology, also known as CRC checkers; creates and saves a unique cyclical redundancy check character or hashing number for each file to be monitored

HDLC High-level data link control; data link layer protocol for X.25

Hierarchical storage management *See* HSM

High-level data link control *See* HDLC

High-level languages Text-based programming languages that resemble standard language; the high-level language code is then compiled into machine language for execution by the processor

HMMP The overall intention of the WBEM architecture is that the network manager could manage any networked device or application from any location on the network, via any HMMP (hypermedia management protocol)-compliant browser.

HMMS Management data from a variety of software agents would be incorporated into the web-based enterprise management architecture via the HMMS (Hypermedia Management Schema).

HMOM All web-based management information is stored and retrieved by the request broker known as HMOM (Hypermedia Object Manager).

Horizontal integration The integration between middleware layers on two different computers; for horizontal integration to occur, both computers must be running compatible middleware solutions

Horizontal software compatibility Transparency between similar software layers between different clients and servers

Host A synonym for the term *local* when referring to remote control software

Host-controller RAID The controller board that contains the RAID intelligence is installed in an available expansion slot; this requires bus interface compatibility

HSM Hierarchical storage management; a technology seeking to make optimal use of available storage media while minimizing the need for human intervention

HTML The presentation language used to format data for World Wide Web browsers; HTML provides a means of both entering content and formatting the content for presentation

HTML Web pages are programmed using text formatted with HTML (hypertext markup language).

HTTP These web servers run specialized web server software that supports HTTP (hypertext transport protocol) in order to handle the organization of servicing the multiple web client requests for web pages.

Hypermedia management protocol *See* HMMP

Hypermedia management schema *See* HMMS

Hypermedia object manager *See* HMOM

Hypertext link A link within a given web page that uses URLs to allow hypertext links to other related web pages, documents, or services such as e-mail

Hypertext markup language *See* HTML

Hypertext transport protocol *See* HTTP

IAP Internet access providers; are primarily concerned with getting a subscriber company physically hooked up to the Internet

IBM 3270 A screen-at-a-time terminal solution associated with IBM mainframe computers; the first terminal that implemented this functionality was the model 3270

IDE Integrated drive electronics disk drives are distinguished from earlier offerings by the inclusion of the drive controller with the disk drive in a single integrated unit and the use of a bus interface known as ATA (AT Attachment). The key limitation of IDE drives was their capacity limitation of 528 MB and ATA's 2-3 MBps data transfer rate.

IDEA International Data Encryption Algorithm; makes use of one-time 128-bit keys known as session keys

IDL A high-level universal notation language used to define the interfaces of an RPC interface; IDL derivatives are also used to define interfaces for dynamic binding in CORBA and DCOM solutions

IEEE 802.11 A lack of interoperability among the

wireless LAN offerings of different vendors is a shortcoming being addressed by a proposal for a new wireless LAN standard known as IEEE 802.11

IEEE 802.14   The access methodologies for sharing cable bandwidth via cable modems are being standardized as IEEE 802.14 cable network specifications

IEEE 802.6   IEEE specification for DQDB, the SMDS network architecture

IIOP   Internet interorb protocol; a standard protocol implemented in all CORBA-based ORBs that provides for interorb communications via TCP/IP

IMAP   Internet mail access protocol; a more recent standard; possesses features added in response to increased remote connectivity and mobile computing including selective downloading, server side folder hierarchies, shared mail, and mailbox synchronization

In-band signaling   When signal bandwidth is robbed to transport managerial or control information

Indexed sequential access method   *See* ISAM

Information consumers   Users of information; when it comes to Internet access, companies can be information consumers, information providers, or a combination of the two functions

Information providers   Providers of information; when it comes to Internet access, companies can be either information consumers or information providers or a combination of the two functions

Information systems downsizing   Downsizing implies that a mainframe-based application has been redeployed to run on a smaller computer platform. That smaller platform may or may not be a distributed client/server information system.

Infrared Data Association   An organization whose IrDA standard ensures that conformed infrared transmission provides multivendor interoperability between laptops and mobile-aware operating systems

Infrared transmission   A wireless LAN transmission methodology limited by its line-of-sight requirement

Inheritance interface   An interface on a class object that allows instances of the class to gain information about changes in the class structure

Instances   An object in an object-oriented programming environment that is based on a class model; an instance can be thought of as an entity created from a class mold

Instantiation   The process of creating instances from classes in an object-oriented environment

Instruction cache   A holding area for instructions pending execution in the CPU

Instrumentation   Embedded performance metrics

Int14   Interrupt 14; one of the supported dial-out software redirectors; most often employed by Microsoft network operating systems; Int14 is actually an IBM BIOS serial port interrupt used for the purpose of redirecting output from the local serial port

Integrated client/server management system   Manages a multivendor enterprise network and supplies the following management capabilities: enterprise database management, enterprise desktop management, enterprise transaction processing management, enterprise distributed processing management

Integrated suites   Platforms filled with their own network management and systems administration applications; *See* Frameworks

Integration   The transitionary period of time in the migration process when both network operating systems must be running simultaneously and interacting to some degree

Integration/migration services   Integration refers to that transitionary period of time in the migration process when both network operating systems must be running simultaneously and interacting to some degree. Migration features are aimed at easing the transition from NetWare 3.12 to either NetWare 4.1 or Windows NT.

Intelligent agent   *See* Agent event manager

Interdomain trust   When the remote or foreign server receives the user authentication from the user's primary domain controller (local server) in the case of a domain directory service such as Windows NT 3.51

Interface   The logical gap between hardware or software components

Interface definition language   *See* IDL

Interface specification   Bit-by-bit layout of frames that user data must be transformed into before entering network switches

Interleaving   A technique that allows the graphics accelerator controller chip to perform two different operations to adjacent rows of video memory with each tick of the clock

Internal bus   A bus located strictly within a CPU chip

Internal firewalls   Include filters that work on the datalink, network, and application layers to examine communications that occur only on a corporation's internal network, inside the reach of traditional firewalls

International data encryption algorithm   *See* IDEA

Internet   A wide area network linking millions of host computers

Internet access providers   *See* IAP

Internet e-mail gateway Acts as a translator, speaking a LAN-specific e-mail software protocol on one side and speaking the Internet's SMTP (Simple Mail-Transport Protocol) on the other

Internet Explorer A front-end software tool or web browser

Internet gateway Offers a LAN-attached link for client PCs to access a multitude of Internet-attached resources including e-mail, FTP/Telnet, newsgroups, Gopher, and the World Wide Web

Internet interorb protocol *See* IIOP

Internet mail access protocol *See* IMAP

Internet presence providers Are primarily concerned with designing, developing, implementing, managing, and maintaining a subscriber company's presence on the Internet

Internet relay chat A very popular Internet service; enables people connected anywhere on the Internet to join in live discussions

Internet server Runs a server application and offers e-mail services, Gopher services, newsgroup services, or World Wide Web services to all Internet-attached users

Internet suite of protocols TCP/IP (transmission control protocol/Internet protocol) is the term generally used to refer to an entire suite of protocols used to provide communication on a variety of layers between widely distributed different types of computers. Strictly speaking, TCP and IP are just two of the protocols contained within the family of protocols more properly known as the Internet suite of protocols.

Interpreter Converts a high-level language to machine language for execution in real time

Interprocess communication *See* IPC

Interrealm In Kerberos, if a client wishes to access a server in another realm, it requests an interrealm ticket-granting ticket from its local ticket-granting server to authorize access to the remote ticket-granting server, which can authorize access to the remote applications server.

Interrupts When the CPU is interrupted to stop doing one thing in order to do something else; key hardware components such as the system bus, the keyboard, the video controller, and serial ports are all assigned interrupt numbers; higher priority subsystems such as the system bus, keyboard, and video receive lower interrupt numbers than serial port devices such as modems

Intranet A private network based on TCP/IP protocols belonging to an organization accessible only by the organization's members, employees, or others with authorization

Intrusion detection systems Test the perimeter of the enterprise network through dial modems, remote access servers, web servers, or Internet access

Inverse multiplexing Process of conglomerating multiple high-speed WAN links to support a single high-bandwidth-demand application

IOC Depending on what combinations of voice, video, or data traffic a user wishes to transmit over ISDN, up to 20 or more ISDN Ordering Codes (IOC) are possible

IPC Interprocess communication; a mechanism that will allow the multiple pieces of the application to communicate with one another

I-P-O Model The I-P-O model provides a framework in which to focus on the difference between the data that came into a particular networked device (I) and the data that came out of that same device (O). By defining this difference, the processing (P) performed by the device is documented.

IPP *See* Internet presence provider

IPsec For establishing security over VPN tunnels; IPsec is largely supported by the firewall vendor community and is intended to provide interoperability between VPN firewalls from different vendors

IP spoofing Packet filters can be breached by hackers in a technique known as IP spoofing. Since packet filters make all filtering decisions based on IP source and destination addresses, if a hacker can make a packet appear to come from an authorized or trusted IP address, then it can pass through the firewall.

IRC *See* Internet relay chat

IrDA *See* Infrared Data Association

ISA Industry standard architecture bus specification with 16-bit bus width and 8 MBps throughput

ISAM Indexed sequential access method; a method for managing how a computer accesses records and files stored on a hard disk

ISDN Integrated services digital network; a switched digital local loop alternative

ISDN ordering codes *See* IOC

ISDN switch Switch that supports circuit switching for ISDN services

ISDN terminal adapters Allows analog devices (phones, fax machines) to hook to ISDN services

ISO 7498/2 This framework maps 14 different security services to specific layers of the OSI seven-layer reference model

ISO Management Framework The Network Management Forum associated with the OSI reference model has divided the field of network management into five major categories in a document known as the ISO Management Framework (ISO 7498-4).

IT *See* Interdomain trust

Java A programming environment originally developed by Sun Microsystems that allows a programmer to write a single program that can execute on any platform that contains a Java virtual machine

Kerberos A three-stage client/server security system; perhaps the most well known combination authentication/authorization software, developed originally at Massachusetts Institute of Technology and marketed commercially by a variety of firms

Kernel The operating system program itself

Key Escrow agencies Trusted third parties; will hold the keys necessary to decrypt key recovery documents

Key recovery mechanism A back door into encrypted data for the government; U.S. companies with international subsidiaries may now export 56-bit key-based encryption technology provided that they establish within two years a key recovery mechanism

Knowledge base A set of resolutions or answers to problems, but also the logic structure or decision tree that takes a given problem and leads the help desk staff person through a series of questions to the appropriate solution

L1 cache High-speed memory placed directly on the processor chip as a buffer between the slower system memory (RAM) and the fast pipelines; also known as on-board cache, on-chip cache, primary cache, or Level 1 cache

L2 cache A high-speed memory cache not directly on but closely connected to the CPU chip; also known as off-chip cache, secondary cache, or Level 2 cache; the L2 cache is connected to the CPU chip through a memory bus whose speed is also measured in MHz

L2F Cisco's Layer Two Forwarding (L2F) tunneling protocol for virtual private networks

L2TP An effort is underway to have the Internet Engineering Task Force (IETF) propose a unification of the two rival virtual private network tunneling standards known as Layer 2 Tunneling Protocol.

LAN caching *See* Network caching

Landline Telephone Network Otherwise known as the PSTN, or wireline public switched telephone network

LAN modem Also known as a dial-in server; offers shared remote access to LAN resources; LAN modems come with all necessary software preinstalled and therefore do not require additional remote control or remote node software; LAN modems are often limited to a single network architecture such as Ethernet or Token Ring, and/or to a single network operating system protocol such as IP, IPX (NetWare), NetBIOS, NetBEUI, or Appletalk

LAN productivity software Application software that contributes directly to the productivity of its users; in other words, this is the software that people use not only to get their work done, but more importantly, to get their work done more quickly, effectively, accurately, or at a lower cost than if they did not have the benefit of this software

LAN resource management software Software concerned with providing access to shared network resources and services; examples of such shared network-attached resources include printers, fax machines, CD-ROMs, modems, and a variety of other devices and services

LAN software architecture In order to organize and illustrate the interrelationships between the various categories of LAN software, a LAN software architecture can be constructed divided into two major categories: network operating systems and applications software. Also included are security software and management software.

LAP-B Link access procedure-balanced; data link layer protocol for X.25

LAP-D Link access procedure-D Channel, where the D channel refers to the 16 KBps delta channel in BRI (Basic Rate Interface) ISDN (Integrated Services Digital Network)

Latency It obviously takes time for a firewall server to examine the addresses of each packet and compare those addresses to filter table entries. This filtering time introduces latency, or delay due to processing, to the overall transmission time.

Layer 2 Tunneling Protocol *See* L2TP

Layer Two Forwarding *See* L2F

LCD Liquid crystal display; LCD technology employs a fluorescent backlight that shines through a "multilayer sandwich" of polarizers, liquid crystals, color filters, and an electrode grid to produce the image on the screen

LDAP Lightweight Directory Access Protocol; LDAP is basically a simplification of X.500's directory access protocol that allows computers executing LDAP client software to manage a hierarchical directory database using TCP/IP as a transport protocol; this protocol is currently the favorite of directory access protocols; it can be used to consolidate personnel information profiles, application and device, and security management; it provides for a single point of administration across multiple directory systems

Legacy applications Existing non-client/server applications, commonly implemented on mainframe computers, that contain important data and information; *See* Backward compatibility

Lightweight directory access protocol *See* LDAP

Limited size messaging   *See* LSM

Line conditioner   Protects computer equipment from "dirty" power conditions such as surges, brownouts, and static spikes

Link access procedure-balanced   *See* LAP-B

Link access procedure-D channel   *See* LAP-D

Links   A unique aspect of the UNIX file system that allows a given file to be known by and accessed by more than one name; a link is nothing more than an entry in a directory that points to a file stored in another directory or another whole directory

Load balancing   When multiple CPU's are controlled by the SMP operating system and individual threads of application processes are assigned to particular CPUs on a first-available basis, all CPUs are kept equally busy in a process known as load balancing.

Local bus   Any bus that interfaces directly to the system bus

Local loop transmission   Narrowband Transmission services from customer premises to central office

Local security authority   In Windows NT, the platform-specific login process interacts with the local security authority, which actually provides the user authentication services.

Logical channel   Virtual circuit in frame relay network

Logical channel number   Identifier assigned to virtual circuit in frame relay network

Logical network design   The network performance criteria that could be referred to as what the implemented network must do in order to meet the business objectives outlined at the outset of the top-down analysis

Logic bombs   Viruses that require a certain event to transpire

Logon process   The process responsible for the interaction with users on whatever computer platform they may wish to login on

Lookahead cache   Lookahead buffer is the simplest or most generic buffer, implying only that a sequence of data blocks beyond that requested by the CPU is stored in anticipation of the next data request

Loosely coupled systems architectures   Systems architectures characterized by each CPU's interacting with its own pool of system memory and devices; coordination among the loosely coupled CPUs is achieved by some type of messaging mechanism such as interprocess communication between the separate CPUs and their individual copies of the operating system; most AMP system architectures would be considered loosely coupled

Low-level languages   Programming languages that represent the actual processor instructions; the two classes of low-level languages are machine language and assembly language

LSM   Limited size messaging; by adding this protocol, CDPD will be able to transport two-way messaging, which will offer the following key services beyond simple paging: guaranteed delivery to destination mobile users even if those devices are unreachable at the time the message was originally sent and return receipt acknowledgments to the party that originated the message

Machine language   The actual series of instructions executed by the computer processor; machine language consists entirely of binary numbers; high-level language programs are converted to machine language through the use of interpreters and compilers

Mach microkernel   A microkernel developed at Carnegie-Mellon University that is one example of a microkernel used as the nucleus for numerous operating systems; because microkernel-based operating systems can be built in a modular fashion, limited only by the requirement to interface to the microkernel through the minimal number of microkernel system calls, it is possible for different operating systems to be developed from the same microkernel

MacOS   The release of MacOS Version 8.0 achieves at least three important goals for Apple: It creates a powerful new microkernel-based operating system, runs legacy applications well, and removes hard-coded hardware-to-operating system links to enable Mac clone hardware vendors and third-party Mac software vendors to fully participate in the Power-Mac market.

Magneto-Optical   Disk technology backup device with 13 GB capacity and 48–96 MB/min throughput

Mail filtering   Companies are using mail-based rules and filtering as a way to deal with the amount of e-mail received and to deal with information overload. Most mail systems allow for sequential routing and event-based rules.

Mainframe   A large multiuser, multiprocessing computer; a mainframe can support thousands of users concurrently and was the main technology used for data processing prior to the advent of client/server computing

Malicious applets   Java applets downloaded from the web, which tend to be annoying rather than destructive

Management information base   *See* MIB

Management information format   *See* MIF

Management interface API   Designed to interface to the desktop system management program, which will consolidate the information from this client with all other desktop information

Management software   Software that must be incorporated in order to provide a single, consolidated view of all networked resources, both hardware and software

Massively parallel processing   *See* MPP

Maximum video bandwidth   A performance criterion that is a direct result of desired resolution and refresh rate; maximum video bandwidth can be computed with the following formula: required video bandwidth = resolution × height × resolution width × refresh rate × 1.5

MCA   Microchannel architecture bus specification featuring 32-bit bus width with 20 MBps throughput

MD5   Produces 128-bit hash number based on original document; can then be incorporated into digital signature; replaced MD4 and MD2

MDAC   Microsoft data access components; collectively, the latest versions of ODBC, OLE DB, and ADO

Megahertz   Millions of cycles per second

Memory bus   Connects the L2 cache to the CPU chip; memory bus speed is also measured in MHz

Message gateway   One of three cooperating components of the agent portion of the client/agent/server architecture; the message gateway can execute on the local server or on a dedicated UNIX or Windows workstation, and it acts as an interface between the client's message manager and the intelligent agent on the local server; the gateway also acts as a holding station for messages to and from mobile clients that are temporarily unreachable

Message integrity   When the document has not been tampered with; authentication uses digital signatures attached to transmitted documents in order to ensure both the authenticity of the author and the message integrity of the document

Message manager   One of three cooperating components of the agent portion of the client/agent/server architecture; the message manager executes on the mobile client and acts as an interface between client applications requesting services and the wireless link over which the requests must be forwarded

Message passing   Also known as message delivery, message queuing, and distributed messaging; differs significantly from other middleware subcategories in its ability to establish various types of interprocess communications modes other than the send-and-wait mode

Message passing interface   *See* MPI

Message queuing   A middleware communication so-

lution through which applications exchange messages through buffered queues; message queuing middleware is asynchronous in nature, allowing each application continue to process data rather than waiting for a response from other application

Messaging   The "back end" or "server" upon which e-mail operates; messaging provides the infrastructure upon which e-mail can reside

Messaging application programming interface   This is the most popular of the messaging APIs; it was developed by Microsoft and is supported by almost every vendor; MAPI provides a way for applications to access different types of messaging systems

Messaging middleware   A category of middleware that operates through the passing of independent messages between applications

Messaging services   Software resFponsible for receiving, sorting, and delivering e-mail from one computer to another

Methods   The defined set of commands for a software object; other objects can invoke an object's methods

MIB   The network management information gathered must be stored in some type of database with an index and standardized field definitions so that network management workstations can easily access this data. A MIB, or Management Information Base as these databases are known, can differ in the fields defined for different vendor's networking devices.

Microcell spread spectrum   Limited to those areas such as college and corporate campuses that are served by microcells, this wireless WAN service offers full-duplex transmission at rates up to 104.5 MBps via proprietary modems

Microkernel   A subset of the overall operating system; it contains a minimum of hardware-specific instructions written to interact with a particular CPU chip

Microsoft data access components   *See* MDAC

Middleware   An enabling software layer that provides a transparent means of accessing information between clients and servers

MIF   Management information format; DMI-compliant desktop management systems store performance and configuration statistics in a MIF

Migration   Migration features are aimed at easing the transition from NetWare 3.12 to either NetWare 4.1 or Windows NT

MIME   A protocol known as Multipurpose Internet mail extension that allows documents to be attached to e-mail regardless of the source application program, operating system, or network operating system

MIP Processing power is often measured in MIPs (millions of instructions/second)

Mirrored server link In NetWare 4.1 SFT III, the synchronization of the servers is accomplished through this dedicated link

MMX Multimedia extensions; series of 57 additional instructions added to the x86 CISC instruction set implemented on Pentium CPUs to allow multiple mathematical operations to be simultaneously performed on multiple data sets

MNP-10 Microcom Networking Protocol Class 10, which includes protocols designed for optimizing data transmission over cellular networks

Mobile-aware applications The overall objective of mobile-aware applications is to reduce the amount of mobile client to server network traffic by building as much intelligence as possible into the server-based agent so that it can act on behalf of the mobile client application.

Mobile-aware operating systems Operating systems that are able to easily adapt to different computing modes with a variety of included supporting accessory programs and utilities

Mobile computing Addresses the need for field representatives to be able to access corporate information resources in order to offer superior customer service while working on the road; these field reps may or may not have a corporate office PC into which to dial

Mobile IP Under consideration by the IETF; may be the roaming standard that wireless LANs require; mobile IP, limited to TCP/IP networks, employs two pieces of software in order to support roaming: A mobile IP client is installed on the roaming wireless client workstation, and a mobile IP home agent is installed on a server or router on the roaming user's home network

Mobile MIB The Mobile Management Task Force has proposed a mobile management information base capable of feeding configuration and location information to enterprise network management systems via SNMP. A key to the design of the mobile MIB was to balance the amount of information required in order to effectively manage remote clients while taking into account the limited bandwidth and expense of the remote links over which the management data must be transmitted.

Mobile middleware The ultimate goal of mobile middleware is to offer mobile users transparent client/server access independent of the following variables: client or server platform (operating system, network operating system), applications (client/server or client/agent/server), wireless transmission services.

Mobile Telephone Switching Office *See* MTSO

Modified object format *See* MOF

MOF Management data to be used by CIM would be stored in MOF (modified object format) as opposed to DMI's MIF format or SNMP's MIB format

Monolithic architecture A monolithic architecture exists if required operating system components such as the file management system or the input/output and disk storage subsystems are arranged in a layered architecture with each layer only communicating directly with the layers immediately above and below it.

Motif Motif from the Open Software Foundation is X Window Manager that communicates with X server software and serves as a GUI for UNIX environments.

MPC level 1 CD-ROM standard proposed by the Multimedia PC Marketing Council (MPC); 150 KBps sustained transfer rate, 1 second maximum average seek time, and 40% maximum CPU usage

MPC level 2 CD-ROM standard proposed by the Multimedia PC Marketing Council (MPC); 300 KBps sustained transfer rate, 400 msec maximum average seek time, and 60% maximum CPU usage

MPI Message-passing interface; messages need to be passed between the multiple computers that comprise the cluster according to a standard protocol; among the current message passing protocols for clusters are parallel virtual machine, MPI and MPI2, and virtual interface architecture

MPP Massively parallel processing; MPP systems architectures employ thousands of CPUs, each with their own system memory; these MPP system architectures may be installed in a single machine or may span several machines

MPS In order to allow greater freedom of choice in matching SMP server hardware with SMP server operating systems, an SMP specification for the hardware/software interface known as multiprocessing specification 1.1 (MPS) has been proposed by Intel and is widely supported by SMP hardware and software vendors.

MS-DOS An acronym for Microsoft Disk Operating System; originally designed to work on stand-alone, single user PCs; DOS introduced multiuser networking capabilities such as record and file locking with the release of Version 3.1; network operating systems are able to call these DOS commands transparently to the networking operating system users

MTSO Mobile Telephone Switching Office; telecommunications facility where cellular network interfaces to PSTN landline (wired) network

Multiple personality operating system Multiple personality subsystems are just further examples of the extendibility or customizability of a microkernel-based operating system. As a specific example, Windows NT includes OS/2, 32-bit Windows, 16-bit Windows, and POSIX subsystems, which allow applications written for any of those environments to be run on a Windows NT platform.

Multiple workplace environments *See* Multiple personality operating systems

Multiplexing Process that combines outputs of several channels into a single composite output

Multiprocessing An operating system that supports multiprocessing is able to split the processing demands of applications programs across more than one processor or CPU

Multiprocessing specification 1.1 *See* MPS

Multiprocessor server Although two or four supported processors is a common number for most multiprocessor servers, some supercomputer-type multiprocessor servers can employ 64 or more CPUs and cost well over $1 million. Although Intel's Pentium chip at various clock speeds is perhaps the most commonly used CPU chip in multiprocessor servers, several other chips are also employed.

Multiprotocol routing Provides the functionality necessary to actually process and understand multiple network protocols as well as translate between them; without multiprotocol routing software, clients speaking different network protocols cannot be supported

Multipurpose Internet Main Extension *See* MIME

Multirate ISDN Multirate ISDN uses a technique known as inverse multiplexing in which a collection of 64 KBps B channels are dialed up and combined together into a single logical channel of sufficient bandwidth to meet application needs such as videoconferencing.

Multisync Refers to the monitor's ability to automatically adjust to the installed video card's specifications and display the desired resolution at the accompanying refresh rate

Multithreaded A multithreaded operating system allows multiple threads per task to operate simultaneously. Each thread from a single task is free to communicate individually with other threads throughout the distributed environment.

Multiuser Multiuser operating systems allow more than one user to login simultaneously. In addition, multiuser operating systems are able to run the multiple application programs of those multiple users simultaneously.

Narrowband ISDN A switched digital network service offering both voice and nonvoice connectivity to other ISDN end users

NASI NetWare asynchronous services interface; a software interrupt that links to the NetWare shell on NetWare clients; as with the Int14 implementation, a TSR intercepts all of the information passed to the NASI interrupt and forwards it across the network to the dial-out modem pool

National Computer Security Association Certifies firewall technology

National ISDN-1 *See* NISDN-1

NC Client computer platforms that have minimal memory, no disk storage, and an operating system specifically designed to run software downloaded at application run time; most NCs are designed to run Java applications

NCB Network control block; requests for network-attached resources are formatted in this agreed-upon NetBIOS API format

NCP NetWare core protocol, NetWare's network API; equivalent in functionality to NETBIOS in most other network operating systems

NDS NetWare Directory Services, a global directory service; network operating systems have always depended on some sort of naming service or directory in which to store information about users as well as systems resources such as disks, servers, and printers

Near-line In HSM, information that is less frequently accessed is stored on near-line or near-on-line devices such as optical jukeboxes

NetBEUI A Microsoft-enhanced version of NetBIOS known as NetBIOS Extended User Interface

NetBIOS Network basic input/output fsystem, an API that has become the de facto standard of network APIs for PC-based networks

NetBIOS application program Application programs that interface with the NETBIOS API that have been developed to perform specialized tasks on client and server PCs in order to enable this client/server communication; two of the most famous of these NETBIOS application programs or protocols are the NetBIOS redirector, on the client, and the server message block (SMB) server, on the server

Net PC Low-end personal computers optimized to run applications from a network file server; similar in concept to diskless workstations, these platforms are designed to run existing Windows applications directly on the distributed platform

Netscape Internet information consumers wishing to access the World Wide Web will require a client PC configured with a front-end software tool or web browser such as Netscape Communicator.

NetWare 4.1 SFT III   Offers an automatic fail-over version known as server duplexing

NetWare 4.1 SMP   SMP version of NetWare that loads a second operating system kernel, known as the SMP kernel, which works cooperatively with the first or native operating system kernel

NetWare Connect   NetWare remote access server software

NetWare Core Protocol   *See* NCP

NetWare Directory Services   *See* NDS

Network access device   Clients, servers, and local area networks are connected to the Internet via a network access device such as a modem, an ISDN network access device, or a router.

Network analyzers   LAN and WAN network analyzers are able to capture network traffic in real time without interrupting normal network transmission. In addition to capturing packets of data from the network, most network analyzers are able to decode those packets, monitor packet traffic statistics, and simulate network traffic through traffic generators.

Network architecture   Switching architecture plus transmission architecture

Network auditing tools   Tools that have the ability to provide records of which network files have been accessed by which users

Network baselining tools   By combining the ability to monitor and capture SNMP and RMON data with the abilities to analyze the captured data and report on trends and exceptions, network baselining tools are able to track network performance over extended periods of time and report on anomalies or deviations from the accumulated baseline data.

Network caching   Network caching or LAN caching software is able to improve overall remote node performance up to five times by caching repetitive applications commands and systems calls. These add-on packages are comprised of both client and server pieces which work cooperatively to cache application commands and reduce network traffic over relatively low-speed WAN links. Network caching software is network operating system and protocol dependent, requiring that compatibility be ensured prior to purchase.

Network computer   A client computer including a Java based operating system designed to run Java applications; all configuration information and applications are kept on servers and sent across the network as required

Network computing   Client/server based systems that use low-powered clients connected to high-powered servers to deliver distributed applications; net-

work computing solutions can be categorized as NCs, Net PCs, or Windows terminals

Network control block   *See* NCB

Network File System   *See* NFS

Network-level filter   A filtering program that examines only source and destination addresses and determines access based on the entries in a filter table; also known as a port-level filter or packet filter

Network message concentration   The process of combining multiple messages into a single session between clients and servers rather than maintaining multiple sessions

Network modeling and simulation tools   Simulation software uses the current network configuration as a starting point and applies what-if scenarios

Network-to-network interface   *See* NNI

Network news transfer protocol   UseNet servers transfer news items among one another using this specialized transfer protocol, also known as NNTP servers. Users wishing to access NNTP servers and their newsgroups must have NNTP client software loaded on their client PCs.

Network nodes   Any device that connects to a data network

Network objects   In some cases, directory services may view all users and network resources as network objects with information concerning them stored in a single database, arranged by object type; object attributes can be modified, and new network objects can be defined.

Network operating system   A layer of software installed on both clients and servers that is responsible for the successful transport of messages across the network; a NOS is responsible for network-based resource sharing

Network operating systems   Network operating systems are concerned with providing an interface between LAN hardware, such as network interface cards, and the application software installed on a particular client or server. The network operating system's job is to provide transparent interoperability between client and server portions of a given application program.

Network service   Network services are offered to customers by carriers dependent on the capabilities of their network architecture

Network termination unit-1   *See* NTU-1

Network user interface   *See* NUI

NFS   Network File System; originally developed by Sun Microsystems as part of the Open Network Computing environment; NFS allows different computing platforms to share files

NISDN-1 National ISDN-1 defines a national standard for ISDN switches as well as interswitch communication

NNI Network-to-network interface; standards that govern interswitch communication

NNTP *See* Network news transfer protocol

Nonpersistent queues A message queue that does not maintain its contents when restarted

Non–real-time conferencing When people work together collaboratively using various technologies not in real time; also called asynchronous conferencing

Nonuniform memory access *See* NUMA

Northern Telecom DMS100 Switch One of the switches that is able to support ISDN services

NOS *See* Network operating system

Novell DOS Originally known as DR (Digital Research)-DOS, Novell DOS Version 7 (ND7) is intended as an alternative to MS-DOS 6.22. ND7 is really three products in one: DOS, universal NetWare client, personal NetWare.

NT-1 *See* NTU-1

NTU-1 A network termination unit-1; required to physically connect the ISDN line to a user's ISDN CPE; most integrated ISDN equipment includes built-in NT-1s, although stand-alone models are available

NUI Network user interface; provide a single browserlike interface for communicating transparently with all resources, whether local or remote

NUMA The most popular current clustering architecture, non-uniform memory access; characterized by multiple SMP computers connected via some sort of intelligent interconnect that allows the entire cluster to appear as a single SMP machine to application programs

Object An object can be thought of as data and the logic and rules to process that data, which is treated as a single, encapsulated entity that can subsequently interoperate with or be included in (encapsulate) other objects. Fields within MIBs are also known as objects.

Object layering and embedding *See* OLE

Object layering and embedding custom controls *See* OCX

Object management layer Objects and inter-object communication can be distributed transparently across an enterprise network without application development programmers being required to know the physical location of required objects. This object management layer would reside between the network operating system layer and the distributed application layer in a client/server technology architecture.

Object-oriented design A programming paradigm designed around the concept of self-contained, reusable software components known as objects

Object-oriented user interface With these interfaces users will no longer work by executing a particular application program, but will choose to accomplish a particular task; the combination of application programs required to complete that task will execute without direct actions from the user

Object-oriented user interfaces Interfaces that the user with a graphical desktop on which objects such as files, directories, folders, disk drives, programs, or devices can be arranged according to the user's whim

Object request broker *See* ORB

OC Optical carrier, standards for optical transmission

OC-1 Optical transmission standard, 51.84 MBps

Octet 8 bits of user payload (data, voice, or video)

OCX A software object that conforms to Microsoft's Object Layering and embedding specification

ODBC Open database connectivity; a Microsoft solution that allows a client to seamlessly communicate with any relational database server as long as the data structures are consistent

OLE A compound document standard from Microsoft; OLE allows an object from one application to be embedded into another application

OLTP On-line transaction processing systems; in order to keep information real-time, business transactions must be posted immediately, rather than in nightly batches, using these systems

On-board cache High-speed memory placed directly on the processor chip as a buffer between the slower system memory (RAM) and the fast pipelines; also known as on-chip cache, primary cache, or L1 (Level 1) cache

On-line transaction processing *See* OLTP

OOUI *See* Object-oriented user interface

Open database connectivity *See* ODBC

Open Look OpenLook from Sun Microsystems is an X Window Manager that communicates with X server software and serves as a GUI for UNIX environments

Operands stage Any additional data or numbers, the operands, required to complete the instruction are fetched in the operands stage

Operating system architecture The manner in which the various components of an operating system interact; the two major categories of operating system architectures are monolithic architectures and microkernel architectures

Optical carrier *See* OC

Oracle Mobile Agents Formerly known as Oracle-in-Motion; perhaps the best example of the overall architecture and components required to produce mobile-aware applications; the Oracle Mobile Agents architecture adheres to an overall client/agent/server architecture, as opposed to the more common LAN-based client/server architecture

ORB Object request broker; a distributed software component that provides an interface through which objects make requests and receive responses

OS/2 Warp Connect From an architectural standpoint, OS/2 Warp Connect is similar to Windows NT in that separate virtual machines are implemented for 16-bit and 32-bit applications. OS/2 Warp Connect can run 16-bit Windows and DOS applications as well as native OS/2 applications.

OSI model Open systems interconnection model; a framework for organizing networking technology and protocol solutions developed by the International Standards Organization

OSI security architecture This framework maps 14 different security services to specific layers of the OSI seven-layer reference model

Out-of-band signaling Management and controlling signaling using a channel other than that used for data or voice transmission

Out-of-order execution Allows other pipelines to continue processing if one stalls

Outsourcing The selective hiring of outside contractors to perform specific network management duties

Overdrive chips Replacement CPU chips, manufactured by Intel, that offer clock multiplying capabilities

P6 The P6 or Pentium Pro CPU chip itself is just one of two chips mounted in separate cavities in a single die or chip container, sometimes referred to as a package. This second cavity is occupied by a 256 KB SRAM L2, or secondary cache, linked directly to the neighboring Pentium Pro chip through a dedicated 64-bit bus known as the backside bus.

P7 Next-generation Intel chip featuring 4–6 superscalar pipelined architecture, larger primary caches, integrated secondary caches, more execution units, larger buffers to support deeper paths of speculative execution, speculative execution down both branches of conditional branch statements, 20+ million transistors

Packaged L2 cache In a P6 CPU, the second cavity is occupied by a 256 KB SRAM L2, or secondary cache, linked directly to the neighboring Pentium Pro chip through a dedicated 64-bit bus known as the backside bus. This directly linked L2 cache is also known as packaged L2 cache.

Packet assembler/disassembler *See* PAD

Packet filter A filtering program that examines only source and destination addresses and determines access based on the entries in a filter table; also known as a port-level filter or network-level filter

Packetizing Process of adding overhead or management data to raw user data in order to ensure proper delivery

Packet layer protocol *See* PLP

Packet signing In NetWare 4.1, every packet transmitted from a particular client workstation can have a unique, encrypted digital signature attached to it which can only be authenticated by the server in a process known as packet signing. However, a performance price of 5–7% is paid for the increased security as valuable CPU cycles are spent encrypting and decrypting digital signatures.

Packet-switched network As opposed to circuit switched networks, physical circuits are shared by numerous users transmitting their own packets of data between switches

Packet switches Used to route user's data from source to destination

Packet switching As opposed to circuit switching, user's data shares physical circuits with data from numerous other users

PAD Device that transforms raw data into properly formatted packets

P-A-D architecture The delivery of quality information to end users depends on the interaction of three fundamental processes: presentation (also known as user interface), application (also known as application logic or processing), data (also known as data management or data manipulation)

PAP Password authentication protocol; repeatedly sends the user ID and password to the authenticating system in clear text pairs until it is either acknowledged or the connection is dropped; there is no encryption performed with PAP

Paradigms Unique combinations of systems architectures and people architectures

Paradigm shift The period of time when information systems professionals are madly scrambling to gain competitive advantage for their companies by implementing the "new" paradigm

Parallel processing Systems that support multiple CPUs in which multiple program instructions can be executed in parallel simultaneously; the two primary alternative system architectures or subcategories of parallel processing are symmetric multiprocessing and asymmetric multiprocessing

Parallel virtual machine *See* PVM

Pascal A high-level procedural programming language named after Blaise Pascal; used in Borland's Delphi event-driven programming environment

Passive matrix Passive matrix displays do not employ transistors and therefore do not have individual control over each point in the display grid. As a result, screens are painted and repainted a line at a time in a serial fashion.

Password Authentication Protocol *See* PAP

Path names Path names are used in UNIX to identify the specific path through the hierarchical file structure to a particular destination file

Payload Generic term referring to data, voice, or video that may be transmitted over WANs

PCI The PCI (peripheral component interconnect) bus provides its own clocking signal at 33 MHz and has a bus width of either 32 bits or 64 bits.

PCI hot plug specification A supplement to the PCI specification that will allow PCI cards to be added or replaced without powering down the computer into which they are being installed

PCMCIA Personal Computer Memory Card International Association; a series of specifications that represent the physical and functional/electrical standards for technology adhering to these specifications

PCS Personal communications services; provide national full duplex digital voice and data at up to 25 MBps via two-way pagers, PDAs, and PCS devices

PCS Personal communications services; a visionary concept of an evolving all-digital network architecture that could deliver a variety of telecommunications services transparently to users at any time regardless of their geographic location

PCT Microsoft's version of SSL, known as private communications technology; the key difference between SSL and PCT is that PCT supports secure transmissions across unreliable (UDP- rather TCP-based) connections by allowing decryption of transmitted records independently from each other, as transmitted in the individual datagrams

PDA Personal digital assistant; an electronic device that looks like a palm-top computer; PDAs have specific functions such as electronic diary, memo taker, alarm clock, and calculator

PDC Domain directory services associate network users and resources with a primary server known as a primary domain controller

PDN Public data network, another name for packet-switched network

Peer-to-peer network operating systems LANs that offer easy to install and use file and print services for workgroup and departmental networking needs; also known as DOS-based LANs or low-cost LANs

PEM Privacy enhanced mail; the application standard encryption technique for e-mail use on the Internet, used with SMTP; it was designed to use both DES and RSA encryption techniques, but it works with other encryption algorithms as well

Pentium Includes a 64-bit on-chip data path that allows twice as much information to be fetched with each tick of the CPU clock as a 486 chip; the Pentium chip is superscalar, containing two processing pipelines with three execution units to choose from: two integer and one floating point; it contains the equivalent of 3.3 million transistors and implements branch prediction using a branch target buffer

Pentium II The Pentium II CPU runs at 233, 266, and 300 MHz and adds support for other system improvements such as synchronous DRAM memory, accelerated graphics port (AGP) for enhanced video performance, faster disk drive access at 33 MBps, and support for the MMX multimedia extensions to the x86 instruction set. It runs at 2.8 volts rather than the more common 3.3 volts and is physically mounted on a single-edge connect cartridge that plugs into slot 1 on the motherboard rather than the dual-cavity pin grid array used by the Pentium Pro.

Pentium Pro *See* P6

Performance engineering Simulation software tools are also sometimes known as performance engineering software tools

Performance metrics By having predefined events and performance metrics included within the application, management consoles will be able to detect problems with application performance and take corrective action.

Performance monitoring Performance monitoring software should offer the ability to set thresholds for multiple system performance parameters. If these thresholds are exceeded, alerts or alarms should notify network management personnel of the problem and offer advice as to possible diagnoses or solutions. Event logging and audit trails are often included as part of the performance monitoring package.

Periodic framing Framing used in T-1 services to combine 24 DS-0s into a D-4 frame

PERL language The Practical Extraction and Reporting Language; adds the following functionality to that offered by the Korn and Bourne shells: list processing, associative arrays, modern subroutines and functions, more control statements, better I/O, full function library

Permanent virtual circuit   *See* PVC

Persistent queues   A message queue that maintains its contents when restarted

Personal communications services   *See* PCS

Personal handyphone system   *See* PHS

Personal phone number   *See* PPN

PGP   Pretty good privacy; an Internet e-mail specific encryption standard that also uses digital signature encryption to guarantee this authenticity, security, and message integrity of received e-mail

Photo CD   Also known as Kodak Photo CD, this is a standard for displaying photographs proposed by Kodak

PHS   Personal handyphone system; digital cellular standard as deployed in Japan

Physical network design   The technology layer analysis will determine how various hardware and software components will be combined to build a functional network that will meet predetermined business objectives. The delineation of required technology is often referred to as the physical network design.

PIM   Personal information manager; a product targeted at one person's productivity, not a department's or an enterprise's, which allows for a lot more than just calendaring and scheduling

PIO   *See* Processor I/O

Pipelines   Analogous to an assembly line in a manufacturing plant; typically divides the overall process of completing a computer instruction into the following five stages or subprocesses: fetch, decode, operands, execute, write back

Pixels   Picture elements; resolution refers to the number of pixels contained in the viewable area of the monitor screen and is reported as resolution height $\times$ resolution width; in simple terms, a greater number of pixels on the screen will produce a sharper image

PLP   Packet layer protocol; network layer protocol for X.25

Plug-n-play   *See* PnP

PnP   Plug-n-play; the goal of plug-n-play is to free users from having to understand and worry about such things as interrupt requests, direct memory access channels, memory addresses, COM ports, and CONFIG.SYS editing whenever they want to add a device to their computer

PnP BIOS   A PnP basic input output system is required to interface directly to both PnP and non-PnP compliant hardware

Point-to-point protocol   A transport protocol belonging to the TCP/IP family of protocols, more properly known as the Internet suite of protocols, that supports communication over serial or dial-up lines; more recently released and more functional than serial line Internet protocol

Point-to-Point Tunneling Protocol   *See* PPTP

Point products   Products specifically written to address a particular systems administration or network management issue; also known as element managers

Policy audits   Manual audits serve to verify the effectiveness of policy development and implementation, especially the extent to which people understand and effectively execute their assigned processes in the overall corporate security policy.

Policy-based management tools   In order to more easily integrate configuration management tools with corporate policy and standards regarding desktop configurations, a new breed of policy-based management tools has emerged.

Polling   In TDM multiplexing, the process of emptying each channels buffer in order to build the composite frame

Polymorphic viruses   Viruses that change their appearance each time an infected program is run in order to avoid detection

POP   Post office protocol; a mail server management protocol

POP-3   A client-side mail protocol that facilities offline operations; messages are downloaded and manipulated on the client

Port   A port can be thought of as a queue, or communications pipe, through which computer resources can be assigned to a task.

Portability   The ability for client/server applications to be developed in one computing environment and deployed in others

Port-level filter   A filtering program that examines only source and destination addresses and determines access based on the entries in a filter table; also known as a network-level filter or packet filter

Post office protocol   *See* POP

POTS   Plain old telephone service; dial-up analog

PowerPC   The PowerPC is a true RISC chip whose features include 64-bit internal data paths, 64 KB of on-chip L1 cache, superscalar architecture with six execution units, branch prediction, speculative execution, and out-of-order execution

PPN   Personal phone number; changes the entire focus of the interface to the telecommunications environment from the current orientation of a number being associated with a particular location regardless of the individual using the facility to a number being associated with a particular individual regardless of the location, even globally, of the accessed facility

PPP *See* Point-to-point protocol

PPP clients Standardized remote clients with the ability to link to servers running a variety of different network operating systems; in general, they can link to network operating systems that support IP, IPX, NetBEUI, or XNS as transport protocols

PPTP Point-to-point tunneling protocol; PPTP is Microsoft's tunneling protocol that is specific to Windows NT Servers and remote access servers; it has the backing of several remote access server vendors

Preemptive multitasking Preemptive multitasking operating systems prevent misbehaving applications from monopolizing system resources by allocating system resources to applications according to priority or timing.

Presentation-application-data *See* P-A-D architecture

Pretty Good Privacy *See* PGP

Primary cache High-speed memory placed directly on the processor chip as a buffer between the slower system memory (RAM) and the fast pipelines; also known as on-chip cache, on-board cache, or L1 (Level 1) cache

Primary data cache Primary caches specialized for storing data in order to increase overall efficiency

Primary domain controller *See* PDC

Primary instruction cache Primary caches specialized for storing instructions in order to increase overall efficiency

Principle of shifting bottlenecks As one aspect of a system that had been identified as a bottleneck is optimized, the bottleneck shifts to some other interacting component of the system.

Privacy enhanced mail *See* PEM

Private communications technology *See* PCT

Private key encryption The decrypting device must use the same algorithm or method to decode or decrypt the data as the encrypting device used to encrypt the data. For this reason private key encryption is sometimes also known as symmetric encryption.

Private packet radio Proprietary wireless WAN service offered by RAM and Ardis in most major U.S. cities; offers full duplex packet-switched data at speeds of up to 4.8 KBps via proprietary modems

Privileged mode The microkernel runs in what is known as privileged mode, which implies that it is never swapped out of memory and has highest priority for allocation of CPU cycles

Procedural language Languages were the first application development environments to be developed.

These languages allow the programmer to maintain total control over the execution of the code. As the name would imply, procedural languages follow a specific set of instructions exactly in order; also known as imperative languages.

Process-oriented workflow The processes in this area are easy to define and are well-understood business policies and procedures; they can be thought of as the mission-critical business processes

Processor I/O Processor Input/Output; also known as programmed I/O or PIO; this data transfer method relies on a shared memory location in system memory as a transfer point for data between the disk drive and the system or main memory; the CPU is involved with every data transfer between the disk drive and system memory

Productivity paradox In the past decade, over $1 trillion has been invested by business in information technology. Despite this massive investment, carefully conducted research indicates that there has been little if any increase in productivity as a direct result of this investment. This dilemma is known as the productivity paradox.

Protected memory mode Client network operating systems may execute 32-bit applications in their own address space, otherwise known as protected memory mode.

Protective measures Measures are designed and taken that effectively block vulnerability in order to prevent threats from attacking assets

Protocol analyzers Devices that test OSI layers 2 through 7

Protocol conversion Translation between protocols, which may be necessary in order to get any two network nodes to communicate successfully

Protocols Rules for how communicating hardware and software components bridge interfaces or talk to one another

Protocol stack The sum of all of the protocols employed in a particular computer

Proxies *See* Application gateways

Proxy server Some web server software supports proxy servers, which act as holding bins or repositories for previously requested web pages from distant Internet servers.

PSE Packet-switched exchange, another name for packet-switched network

Public data network *See* PDN

Public key certificates A certificate ensuring the authenticity of the public encryption key

Public key encryption Public key encryption could perhaps more accurately be named public/private key encryption because the process actually combines usage of both public and private keys. The sending encryption device encrypts a document using the intended recipient's public key.

PVC Permanent virtual circuit; packet-switched equivalent of a leased line

PVM Parallel virtual machine; messages need to be passed between the multiple computers that comprise the cluster according to a standard protocol. PVM is among the current message passing protocols for clusters

QIC Quarter-inch cartridge magnetic tape with 40 MB–25 GB capacity and 4–96 MB/min throughput

QOS Quality of service guarantees of proper execution and delivery of end-user applications

Quad-issue A CPU with four pipelines; also known as a four-way processor

Quad speed CD-ROM speed specification yielding sustained average data throughput of 600 KBps

Quality of service The acceptable level of network latency for a particular message; quality of service can be thought of as a message prioritization scheme whereby time-critical messages are processed prior to non-time-critical messages

Queue manager A special process that manages message queues and handles delivery of messages in message queuing middleware solutions

RAB Raid Advisory Board; RAID standards are maintained by the RAB, which has issued detailed specifications for the following classifications of extended data availability and protection (EDAP): failure resistant, failure tolerant, disaster tolerant

RADIUS Remote authentication dial-in user service; a protocol and associated architecture supported by a wide variety of remote access technology that offers the potential to enable centralized management of remote access users and technology

RADSL Rate-adaptive digital subscriber line; able to adapt its data rate to the level of noise and interference on a given line; currently, it is not able to support this adaptive rate on a dynamic basis

RAID In an effort to provide large amounts of data storage combined with fault tolerance and redundancy, numerous small disk drives were joined together in arrays and controlled by software that could make these numerous disk appear as one gigantic disk to server operating systems according to a series of standards known as RAID. RAID originally stood for redundant array of inexpensive disks.

RAID Advisory Board *See* RAB

RAID level 0 Disk striping; stripes data across multiple disks without redundancy

RAID level 1 Disk mirroring; also known as shadowing

RAID level 2 Striped array plus hamming code; writes data across multiple disks, adding hamming code for error detection and correction

RAID level 3 Striped array plus parity disk; stripes data a byte at a time; parity is calculated on a byte-by-byte basis and stored on a dedicated parity drive

RAID level 4 Independent striped array plus parity drive; stripes data in sectors; parity stored on parity drive; disks can work independently

RAID level 5 Independent striped array plus striped parity; stripes data in sectors; parity is interleaved and striped across multiple disks

RAID level 6 Independent striped array plus striped double parity; striped data and parity with two parity drives

Rapid recovery Not quite fault tolerance; clustering software solutions provide auto-failover capabilities in less than one second; much more affordable than fault tolerant solutions and good enough for most businesses; minimizes downtime from unexpected interruptions

RAS Windows NT's remote access server software

Rate adaptive DSL *See* RADSL

RDO A high-level API used in Microsoft Windows programming languages such as Visual BASIC and Delphi to access relational database data via ODBC

RDRAM Rambus DRAM

Read-through cache Allows data stored in the cache to be forwarded directly to the CPU without performing a physical disk read

Real-mode device drivers Programs or subroutines that write directly to computer hardware

Realms Enterprise networks implementing Kerberos are divided into Kerberos realms, each served by its own Kerberos server

Real-time audits Most audit software depends on capturing large amounts of event data and then filtering that data for exceptional or unusual events.

Real-time conferencing When people work together collaboratively using various technologies in real time

Real-time systems Information systems that give up-to-the-minute information

Redirector For every request for services coming from a client application program, a software module known as the redirector determines whether those requested resources are locally attached or network attached.

Redundant processor architecture A redundant processor architecture goes beyond traditional symmetrical multiprocessing design. In a redundant processor architecture, each primary CPU is shadowed by a secondary identical tandem processor that executes the same instructions.

Refresh rate   Refresh rate refers to the number of times per second a screen image is redrawn or refreshed. Refresh rate is measured in Hz, with 72 Hz being the current recommended minimum refresh rate.

Relationship variables   In application MIB relationship variables define all other network-attached resources on which a given distributed application depends. This includes databases, associated client applications, or other network resources.

Relative path names   In UNIX relative path names start at the current directory.

Reliable services   Refers to connection-oriented packet switched services which offer guaranteed delivery

Remote access   This term is most often used to generally describe the process of linking remote PCs to local LANs without implying the particular functionality of that link (remote node versus remote control). Unfortunately, the term *remote access* is also sometimes more specifically used as a synonym for remote node.

Remote authentication dial-in user service   *See* RADIUS

Remote configuration   Increased security in SNMP2 allows not just monitoring and management of remote network devices, but also actual remote configuration of those devices.

Remote control   In remote control mode, the remote PC is merely supplying input and output devices for the local client, which interacts as normal with the local server and other locally attached LAN resources.

Remote control software   Remote control software, especially designed to allow remote PCs to take over control of local PCs, should not be confused with the asynchronous communications software used for dial-up connections to asynchronous hosts via modems.

Remote node   Remote node or remote client computing implies that, in theory, the remote client PC should be able to operate as if it were locally attached to network resources. In other words, the geographic separation between the remote client and the local LAN resources should be transparent.

Remote node client software   Most of the remote node server software packages also include compatible remote node client software. A problem arises, however, when a single remote node client needs to

login to a variety of different servers running a variety of different network operating systems or remote node server packages.

Remote node servers   Remote node servers are strictly concerned with controlling remote access to LAN-attached resources and acting as a gateway to those resources. Applications services are supplied by the same LAN-attached applications servers that are accessed by locally attached clients.

Remote node server software   Traditionally remote node client and server software were supplied by the vendor of the network operating system on the server to be remotely accessed. Windows NT RAS and NetWare Connect are two examples of such NOS-specific remote node server software.

Remote node software   Remote node software requires both remote node server and compatible remote node client software in order to successfully initiate remote node sessions.

Remote procedure call   *See* RPC

Resolution   Resolution refers to the number of pixels contained in the viewable area of the monitor screen and is reported as resolution height × resolution width. In simple terms, a greater number of pixels on the screen will produce a sharper image.

Rexx   The Rexx scripting language offers an easier to learn and use alternative to PERL, which supports structured programming techniques such as modularity while still offering access to shell commands.

Rightsizing   Rightsizing implies that applications are designed for and deployed on the platform, or type and size of computer, that makes the most sense: the "right" size computer. The right computer or platform implies that the choice is based on maximizing the efficiency with which the application runs.

RISC   RISC (Reduced Instruction Set Computing) architectures interpret instructions directly in the CPU chip itself without the added overhead of the executing microcode. As a result of this hardware-based decoding, the speed of processing is increased.

Risk   Probability of a particular threat's successfully attacking a particular asset in a given amount of time via a particular vulnerability

RJ48c   Jack in which T-1 services are typically terminated

RMON2   While the original RMON MIB only required compatible technology to be able to collect and analyze statistics on the physical and data link layers, RMON2 requires collection and analysis of network layer protocols as well.

RMON MIB   Remote network monitoring MIB

RMON probe   RMON2-compatible agent software

that resides within internetworking devices and reports performance statistics to enterprise network management systems

Roaming   Roaming capability allows a user to transparently move between the transmission ranges of wireless LANs without interruption. Proprietary roaming capabilities are currently offered by many wireless LAN vendors. Roaming is not included in the IEEE 802.11 standard.

Role   A role defines the job functions independently of the people who do that job.

Routing   Routing is the defined path in which an object travels. An object could be a document, form, or message. Objects should be able to be routed sequentially, one after another, in parallel, or in any form the user would need.

RPC   Remote procedure call; RPCs can be thought of as remote subroutines; the application programmer calls a link to a subroutine or procedure located on a remote server; the local link to the remote procedure is known as a stub function; the stub function transfers the calling parameters to the RPC-based middleware on the server and waits until the server responds

RPC middleware   Remote procedure call middleware works in a manner similar to a locally run application program which activates, or calls, a subroutine stored outside of the application program itself, but usually in a subroutine library on the same computer. The major difference with the remote procedure call is that the call for the execution of a subroutine is made to a remote procedure located on a remote distributed processor via the enterprise network.

RSA   The current standard for public key encryption is known as RSA (Rivest Shamir Adelman).

Rules   Rules can be established when routing objects so that a company can define what information to route and who should get the information. Rules are sometimes referred to as exception handling or conditional routing.

SAMBA   By installing SAMBA on the UNIX host, interoperability is achieved with all SMB-compliant computers without any modifications to the SMB-compliant computers.

Sandbox   A security mechanism used with Java applets; a limited environment called the sandbox is created for the exclusive use of the applet; the applet cannot access any resources beyond the sandbox

SATAN   The SATAN probe is especially written to analyze UNIX and TCP/IP based systems, and once it has found a way to get inside an enterprise network, it continues to probe all TCP/IP machines within that enterprise network.

Scalability   The ability of distributed processing systems to add clients without degrading the overall performance of the system

Scalar processor   A CPU chip with a single pipeline

SCAM   PnP-compliant SCSI controllers will be configured according to a PnP standard known as SCAM, or SCSI configured automatically.

Scheduling   Scheduling can be defined as the communication and negotiation between calendars for the placement of calendar information.

Screen caching   Screen caching allows only changes to screens, rather than entire screens, to be transmitted over the limited bandwidth WAN links. Screen caching will reduce the amount of actual traffic transmitted over the WAN link.

Screen scraper   A screen scraper is a piece of software used to provide interaction between a legacy application and a client through the terminal screen interface originally designed for human use of the legacy system. The screen scraper presents an API to the application programmer and emulates a user terminal session to the business application. From the perspective of the mainframe application, the screen scraper appears as a human operator.

Script wrapper   A script wrapper is used to integrate legacy applications that support command line switches rather than an API. The script wrapper executes the legacy application for each potential command line flag.

SCSI   Small computer system interface; a specification for an expansion bus that is unique in its ability to daisy-chain up to seven SCSI devices together; 8-bit bus width, 5 MHz clock speed, 5 MBps throughput

SCSI-2   An expansion bus specification: 8-bit bus width, 10 MHz clock speed, 10 MBps throughput

SCSI configured automatically   *See* SCAM

SCSI-to-SCSI RAID   SCSI-to-SCSI RAID keeps all the RAID intelligence in the disk array cabinet. The controller card is installed with the RAID subsystem cabinet and connects to the host server via a standard SCSI controller.

SDRAM   Synchronous DRAM; adding clock synchronization to RAM allows memory chips to work at the same clock speed as the CPU

SDSL   Symmetric digital subscriber line differs from ADSL in that it offers upstream and downstream channels of equal bandwidth.

Search engine   The portion of the software that sifts through the knowledge base to the proper answer

Secondary cache   A high-speed memory cache not directly on but closely connected to the CPU chip; this memory is also known as off-chip L2 (Level 2) cache;

the cache is connected to the CPU chip through a memory bus whose speed is also measured in MHz

Sectors Data is stored on disks that are broken up into concentric rings, known as tracks, and portions of those tracks, known as sectors.

Secure Courier Secure Courier is based on SSL and allows users to create a secure digital envelope for transmission of financial transactions over the Internet. Secure Courier also provides consumer authentication for the cybermerchants inhabiting the commercial Internet.

Secure electronic transactions *See* SET

Secure HyperText Transport Protocol *See* S-HTTP

Secure multipurpose Internet mail extension *See* S/MIME

Secure single login Assurance that users are able to log into a network, rather than into each individual server and application, and be only able to access resources for which they are properly authorized

Secure SNMP A variation of SNMP; will allow users to access carriers' network management information and incorporate it into the wide area component of an enterprise network management system

Secure sockets layer SSL is described as wrapping an encrypted envelope around HTTP transmissions. Whereas S-HTTP can only be used to encrypt web documents, SSL can be wrapped around other Internet service transmissions such as FTP and Gopher as well as HTTP. SSL is a connection-level encryption method providing security to the network link itself.

Security account manager In Windows NT, all of the user and user group ID and permission-level information is stored in and maintained by the security account manager, which interacts with the local security authority to verify user IDs and permission levels.

Security analyzer tool for analyzing networks *See* SATAN

Security auditing and intrusion detection Tracks and identifies suspicious behaviors from both internal employees and potential intruders

Security ID *See* SID

Security policy development life cycle *See* SPDLC

Security probes Actively test various aspects of enterprise network security and report results and suggest improvements

Security reference monitor *See* SRM

Segmented lookahead cache Segmented lookahead buffers create multiple smaller buffers in which the next sequential data blocks from several reads can be stored

Send-and-wait When an application program branches to a subroutine, whether a local or a remote procedure, that application program waits for the local or remote procedure to complete execution and return either data or some type of status message before continuing with its own program execution. This style of interprocess communication could be categorized as send-and-wait, also known as synchronous communication.

Serial line Internet protocol A transport protocol belonging to the TCP/IP family of protocols, more properly known as the Internet Suite of Protocols, that supports communication over serial or dial-up lines; *See* Point-to-point protocol

Server back-end Portion of a distributed client/server application that runs on the server PC

Server capacity planning Server management software must provide server capacity planning capabilities by monitoring server performance trends and making recommendations for server component upgrades in a proactive manner.

Server duplexing In server duplexing, not only are the contents of the disks synchronized, but the contents of the servers' memory and CPUs are also synchronized. In case of the failure of the primary server, the duplexed server takes over transparently.

Server message block *See* SMB

Server network operating systems Server network operating systems are able to be chosen and installed based on their performance characteristics for a given required functionality. For example, NetWare servers are often employed as file and print servers, whereas Windows NT, OS/2, and UNIX servers are more likely to be employed as application servers.

Service-granting ticket In Kerberos, if the ticket-granting server determines that the request is valid, a ticket is issued which will allow the user to access the requested server. This ticket is known as a service-granting ticket.

Service profile identifier numbers *See* SPID

Session keys Unique, one-time use keys used for encryption

SET Secure electronic transactions are a series of standards to ensure the confidentiality of electronic commerce transactions. These standards are being largely promoted by credit card giants VISA and Master-Card.

Shared memory In shared-memory clusters, all nodes share the same memory space, thereby precluding the need to rewrite applications.

Shared nothing clusters Clusters in which each node has its own memory space and communicates via message passing; such architectures require that applications would need to be rewritten or segmented so that portions of the application can be executed independently on multiple servers comprising the cluster, with each node being able to keep track of which portions of the program are executing on which node

Shell In UNIX, the command interpreter that is the user's interface to the system is a specialized user process known as a shell.

S-HTTP Secure HTTP is a secure version of HTTP that requires both client and server S-HTTP versions to be installed for secure end-to-end encrypted transmission. S-HTTP is described as providing security at the document level since it works with the actual HTTP applications to secure documents and messages.

SID Security ID; in Windows NT, the local security authority generates a security access token for authorized users which contains security IDs for this user and all of the user groups to which this user belongs

SIDF Storage independent data format; allows portability between tape media and SIDF-compliant backup devices

Signature scanners Because virus scanners are really scanning for known digital signatures or viruses, they are sometimes referred to as signature scanners.

SII An interface used by CORBA objects to interface in a static manner; static interfacing implies that the object's interfaces do not change over time; the interface characteristics for an object are defined using IDL

SIMM Single in-line memory module; the more common method of RAM packaging; SIMMs are small printed circuit boards with attached DRAMs and come in basically two varieties: 30-pin SIMMs comprised of 8-bit DRAMs, and 72-pin SIMMs comprised of 16-bit or 32-bit DRAMs

Simple mail transfer protocol *See* SMTP

Simple management protocol *See* SMP

Simple network management protocol *See* SNMP

Single access control view Allows the user's access from a client workstation to display only those resources that the user actually has access to

Single Point of Registration *See* SPR

Single sign-on *See* SSO

Single solution gateway Single solution gateways can actually offer improved performance due to optimally written code translating between a specific front-end tool and a specific distributed database management system or between two different database engines.

Single speed CD-ROM speed specification yielding sustained average data throughput of 150 KBps

Sinks Packet destinations

Site In a Chorus microkernel-based operating system, a given hardware platform or CPU is considered a site, with one nucleus executing at each site.

SLIP *See* Serial line Internet protocol

Small business network operating systems Small business network operating systems have had to differentiate themselves from client network operating systems and peer-to-peer network operating systems by offering more advanced features such as dedicated 32-bit server software, bundled workgroup software, and an easy migration path to server-based network operating systems.

Small Office Home Office SOHO. *See* Telecommuting

Smalltalk The first object-oriented programming language; developed by Xerox in the late 1960s; Smalltalk provides the most-complete object implementation of any object-oriented programming language

Smart cards Used in token authentication systems, hardware-based smart cards or smart IDs are about the size of a credit card with or without a numeric keypad

Smartsizing Smartsizing implies another level of questioning or reengineering beyond that of rightsizing. Rather than merely reevaluating the application program, smartsizing goes a step further and reevaluates and reengineers the business process that motivated the application in the first place.

SMB Server message block. NETBIOS application programs, otherwise known as NETBIOS protocols, which interface with the NETBIOS API have been developed to perform specialized tasks on client and server PCs in order to enable this client/server communication; two of the most famous of these NETBIOS application programs or protocols are the NetBIOS redirector on the client and the server message block (SMB) server on the server; server message block provides a platform-independent command language offering such services as file and printer sharing, user authentication, and interprocess communications

SMDS Switched multimegabit data service; a connectionless high-speed data service

S/MIME Secure multipurpose Internet mail extension secures e-mail traffic in e-mail applications that have been S/MIME enabled; S/MIME encrypts and authenticates e-mail messages for transmission over SMTP-based e-mail networks

S/MIME standard S/MIME is a proposed standard for encrypting and digitally signing electronic mail messages

SMP Symmetrical multiprocessing is a system architecture in which multiple CPUs are controlled by the SMP operating system and individual threads of application processes are assigned to particular CPUs on a first-available basis.

SMP The need to reduce network traffic caused by the SNMP protocol, as well as to deal with other aforementioned SNMP shortcomings, led to a proposal for a new version of SNMP known as SNMP2, or SMP (simple management protocol).

SMP kernel In the SMP version of NetWare, a second operating system kernel, known as the SMP kernel, is loaded, which works cooperatively with the first or native operating system kernel.

SMP scalability Refers to the percentage of increased performance achieved for each additional CPU

SMS Storage management system; defines an API for third-party backup software to interoperate transparently with NetWare servers

SMTP *See* Simple mail transfer protocol

SMTP This messaging protocol is used in TCP/IP networks to exchange e-mail messages; in conjunction with TCP/IP, it is able to establish connections, provide reliable transport of messages, and terminate connections

SNA Systems Network Architecture, IBM's proprietary network architecture; originally designed to link mainframes

SNMP Partly due to the dominance of TCP/IP as the internetworking protocol of choice, SNMP (Simple Network Management Protocol) is the defacto standard for delivering enterprise management data.

SNMP2 The need to reduce network traffic caused by the SNMP protocol, as well as to deal with other aforementioned SNMP shortcomings, led to a proposal for a new version of SNMP known as SNMP2, or SMP (simple management protocol).

Software-based RAID Uses the CPU of the server to execute the RAID software, which controls the multiple disk drives contained in the redundant array of independent disks

Software cache The use of system memory in the computer reserved for a disk cache

Software emulation An additional layer of software that allowed both Macintosh and Windows programs to execute on PowerPC chips

SOHO *See* Telecommuting

SONET Synchronous optical network, dual ring, high-speed fiber-based transmission architecture

SONET superframe Rather than fitting 24 channels per frame delineated by a single framing bit, a single SONET frame or row is delineated by 3 octets of overhead for control information followed by 87 octets of payload. Nine of these 90 octet rows are grouped together to form a SONET superframe.

Spam mail Unsolicited e-mail usually advertising some products; Spam mail is sent to many mailing lists and newsgroups as well as companies

SPAP Shiva's proprietary authentication protocol, which includes password encryption and callback capability

SPDLC Security policy development life cycle; one methodology for the development of a comprehensive network security policy

SPE The 87 octets of payload per row in each of the time rows of the superframe is known as the synchronous payload envelope.

Speculative execution Begins to execute and store results of predicted branches chosen by branch prediction algorithms

SPID In order to properly interface an end-user's ISDN equipment to a carrier's ISDN services, desired ISDN features must be specified. In some cases, end user equipment such as remote access servers must be programmed with service profile identifier numbers in order to properly identify the carrier's equipment with which the user equipment must interface.

SPR Single point of registration; allows a network security manager to enter a new user (or delete a terminated user) from a single centralized location and assign all associated rights, privileges, and access control to enterprise resources from this single point rather than having to enter this new user's information on multiple resources distributed throughout the enterprise

Spread spectrum transmission Spreads a data message across a wide range or spectrum of frequencies; this technique was originally employed as a security measure since a receiver would need to know exactly how the message was spread across the frequency spectrum in order to intercept the message in meaningful form

SQL Structured query language; a standardized database command language developed to facilitate querying relational database servers; SQL is a comprehensive relational database language providing a means of performing common database operations such as record additions, updates, and database design modifications in addition to query capabilities; the American National Standards Institute (ANSI) has standardized the SQL language

SRAM Static RAM; does not require a refresh cycle between accesses and therefore can be accessed much faster than DRAM; SRAM is more expensive than DRAM

SRM The security reference monitor is primarily concerned with authorization or authentication for processes that wish to access objects and users that wish to access the system via the logon process. It is the only kernel-mode portion of the NT security system.

SSL *See* Secure Sockets Layer

SSL3 SSL is a connection level encryption method providing security to the network link itself. SSL Version 3 (SSL3) added support for more key exchange and encryption algorithms as well as separate keys for authentication and encryption.

SSO Single sign-on; authentication technology that delivers SSO access to multiple network-attached servers and resources via passwords

State variables In application MIB, state variables report on the current status of a given application. Three possible states are up, down, or degraded.

Static RAM *See* SRAM

Statistical time division multiplexing *See* STDM

STDL Standard transaction definition language; a vendor-independent transaction definition language used in transaction processing; a client accesses the transaction processing monitor via STDL

STDM Advanced form of TDM multiplexing that seeks to overcome TDM inefficiencies by dynamically adapting polling of channels

Storage independent data format *See* SIDF

Storage management system *See* SMS

Stored procedures Rather than have the transaction posting application program trigger the integrity check, the database definition itself can be written in such a way that if any particular field in the distributed database is updated, then the SQL database initiates a stored procedure, which would proceed to perform all necessary integrity checking on the distributed databases involved.

Store-and-forward Message passing process employed by X.25 in which messages are kept by packet switch until ACK is received from destination switch

Storing messages This is where the e-mail messages are stored; the messages are usually stored on the hard drive of the messaging server

Structured programming Structured programming is a method of organizing a computer program as a series of hierarchical modules, each having a single entry and exit point. Processing within a module takes place in a step-by-step manner without unconditional branches (such as GOTO statements) to higher levels within the module.

Structured query language *See* SQL

STS-1 The electrical equivalent of the OC-1; the optical SONET superframe standard is known as the STS-1, or synchronous transport signal

Stub function The local link to the remote procedure in a remote procedure call environment

Subroutines Code modules that perform general processing; subroutines can be nested so that one subroutine calls another subroutine; by dividing frequently used code segments into subroutines, a programmer can greatly reduce code repetition within a structured program

Subsystems In microkernel-based operating systems, all additional functionality is written to operate externally to the microkernel in software modules known as servers. Groups of servers are known as subsystems.

Superframe 12 D-4 frames

Superpipelines Some pipelines employ more than five stages to complete a given instruction and are called superpipelined architectures.

Superscalar CPU chips may employ more than one pipeline and are known as superscalar.

SVC Switched virtual circuit; packet-switched equivalent of a circuit switched dial up line

SVRAM Synchronous VRAM; adding clock synchronization to RAM allows memory chips to work at the same clock speed as the CPU

Switched multimegabit data service *See* SMDS

Switched virtual circuit *See* SVC

Switching Process by which messages are routed from switch to switch en route to their final destination

Switching architecture Major component of network architecture along with transmission architecture

SX SX implies no built-in math coprocessor.

Symmetric DSL *See* SDSL

Symmetric multiprocessing *See* SMP

Synchronous *See* Send-and-wait

Synchronous communications Synchronous communication is the most common approach taken in middleware solutions. In this scenario, the client application issues a request to the server application. While waiting for a reply to the request, the client is prevented from performing other application tasks.

Synchronous conferencing Real-time conferencing

Synchronous optical network *See* SONET

Synchronous payload envelope *See* SPE

Synchronous TDM In a technique used in T-1 transmission service known as periodic framing or synchronous TDM, 24 channels of eight bits each (192 bits total) are arranged in a frame.

System bus The superhighway of the buses that leave the computer system's CPU as other buses such as the local, I/O, and peripheral buses interface directly to the system bus.

System calls Application programs request computer resources by interfacing to the operating system through mutually supported system calls.

Systems administration Focuses on the management of client and server computers and the operating systems and network operating systems that allow the client and server computers to communicate

Systems Network Architecture *See* SNA

T-1 1.544 MBps digital WAN service adhering to the DS-1 standard

T-1 channel bank Device that can take a variety of voice and data inputs, digitize them, and multiplex them onto a T-1 circuit

T-1 CSU/DSU Device that interfaces between a T-1 circuit and another device such as a multiplexer, bridge, or router

T-1 IMUX Inverse multiplexer that can combine four or more T-1s for bandwidth on demand applications

T-1 inverse multiplexer *See* T-1 IMUX

T-1 multiplexers Multiplexers that combine several digitized voice or data inputs into a T-1 output

T-1 switches Switches that are able to redirect T-1s or the DS-0s contained therein

Task The basic addressable unit of program execution; it is sometimes referred to as an execution environment to which resources such as CPU cycles or virtual memory space can be assigned

TCP/IP Transmission control protocol/Internet protocol; refers to an entire suite of protocols used to provide communication on a variety of layers between widely distributed different types of computers; strictly speaking, TCP and IP are just two of the protocols contained within the family of protocols more properly known as the Internet suite of protocols

TCP/IP Model Although not identical to the OSI seven-layer model, the four-layer TCP/IP model is no less effective at organizing protocols required to establish and maintain communications between different computers.

TDM Time division multiplexing; with TDM, from a connected terminal's point of view, 100% of the bandwidth is available for a portion of the time

TDMA Time division multiple access; a bandwidth-sharing methodology for digital cellular that achieves more than one conversation per frequency by assigning timeslots to individual conversations

TDP Telocator data protocol; an alternative two-way messaging architecture is proposed by the PCIA (Personal Communicator Industry Association); rather than building on existing IP-based networks as the CDPD/LSM architecture did, the TDP architecture is actually a suite of protocols defining an end-to-end system for two-way messaging to and from paging devices

Teamware A category of software that enables colleagues, especially geographically dispersed colleagues, to collaborate on projects; typically, teamware uses the Internet and the World Wide Web to facilitate communication among the team members

Telecommuting Working from home with all the information resources of the office LAN at one's fingertips; often referred to as SOHO, or small office home office

Telnet Text-based information stored in Internet-connected servers can be accessed by remote users logging into these servers via a TCP/IP protocol known as Telnet.

Telocator data protocol *See* TDP

Thread A task can be accomplished or executed through the work accomplished by one or more threads. Threads are the basic unit of execution and are assigned resources only through a given task. Tasks spawn threads in order to accomplish their instructions.

Threats Processes or people who pose a potential danger to identified assets

Three-tiered C/S architecture Three-tiered client/server architectures deliver the presentation logic on the client, the business logic on a dedicated server of its own, and the database logic on a superserver or mainframe.

Ticket In Kerberos, an encrypted ticket is issued for each server to client session and is valid only for a preset amount of time.

Ticket-granting ticket Users are first authenticated by the Kerberos authentication server, which consults its database and grants a ticket for the valid user to communicate with the ticket-granting server (TGS). This ticket is known as a ticket-granting ticket.

Tightly coupled Tightly coupled systems architectures are characterized by CPUs that share a common pool of system memory as well as other devices and subsystems; coordination among the multiple CPUs is achieved by system calls to/from the controlling operating system; most SMP system architectures would be considered tightly coupled

Time bombs   Viruses that are triggered by the passing of a certain date or time

Time division multiple access   *See* TDMA

Time division multiplexing   *See* TDM

Time slot   8 bits of digitized information collected in one sample and assigned to one of 24 channels in a T-1 D-4 frame

Time synchronous authentication   With time synchronous authentication, due to the time synchronization, the server authentication unit should have the same current random authentication number which is compared to the one transmitted from the remote client.

Time synchronous token authentication   A token authentication process in which no challenge is sent since both the SecureID card and the server are time synchronized, so only the displayed one-time session key is transmitted

Token authentication   All token authentication systems include server components linked to the communications server and client components used with the remote access clients. Physically, the token authentication device employed at the remote client location may be a hand-held device resembling a calculator or a floppy disk, or it may be an in-line device linked to either the remote client's serial port or a parallel port.

Token authentication   Token authentication technology provides one-time-use session passwords that are authenticated by associated server software.

Token response authentication   Token response authentication schemes begin when the transmitted challenge response is received by the authentication server and compared to the expected challenge response number which was generated at the server. If they match, the user is authenticated and allowed access to network attached resources.

Top-down model   The top-down model is a graphical representation of the top-down approach. Insisting that a top-down approach to network analysis and design is undertaken should ensure that the network design implemented will meet the business needs and objectives that motivated the design in the first place.

Total cost of ownership   There are three major expense categories associated with the deployment of distributed client applications platforms: initial implementation costs, user training costs, and administration and maintenance costs. Collectively these costs equal total cost of ownership.

TP monitors   Transaction-posting monitors; transaction processing requires careful monitoring in order to ensure that all, and not just some, postings related

to a particular business transaction are successfully completed; this monitoring of transaction posting is done by a specialized type of software known as TP monitors

Tracks   Data is stored on disks which are broken up into concentric rings, known as tracks, and portions of those tracks, known as sectors.

Transaction   The sequence or series of predefined steps or actions, taken within an application program, in order to properly record that business transaction

Transaction applications   Many workflow applications today allow for transaction workflow. By storing the rules and information on the server, transactions can be routed to various places based on the programmed rules.

Transaction process monitor   *See* TP monitors

Transition costs   Costs associated with the transition from mainframe-based systems to client/server systems such as application redevelopment, management tool development, and expenses to run both systems simultaneously

Transmission architecture   Key component of network architecture along with switching architecture

Transmission control protocol/Internet protocol   *See* TCP/IP

Transparency   The ability of distributed processing systems to combine clients and servers of different operating systems, network operating systems, and protocols into a cohesive system processing distributed applications without regard to the aforementioned differences

Transport mode ESP   In Secure IP, transport mode ESP is used to encrypt the data carried by the IP packet.

Triggers   Signals an "integrity-assurance subroutine" to run that would check all of the necessary distributed database fields involved and verify that their current contents are correct based on the latest transaction

Triple speed   CD-ROM speed specification yielding sustained average data throughput of 450 KBps

Trojan horse   The actual virus is hidden inside an otherwise benign program and delivered to the target system or network to be infected

Trusted gateway   In a trusted gateway, certain applications are identified as trusted and are able to bypass the application gateway entirely and establish connections directly rather than be executed by proxy.

Trusted node   Authorization security software can be either server-based, also known as brokered authorization, or workstation-based, also referred to as trusted node.

TSR   Programs stored in this extended memory are often stored as TSRs, or terminate and stay resident, programs. Terminate and stay resident programs do not utilize any CPU processing time until they are reactivated.

Tunneling protocols   In order to provide virtual private networking capabilities using the Internet as an enterprise network backbone, specialized tunneling protocols needed to be developed that could establish private, secure channels between connected systems.

Tunnel mode ESP   In Secure IFP, tunnel mode ESP encrypts the entire IP packet including its own header. This mode is effective at countering network analyzers or sniffers from capturing IP address information.

Two-tiered C/S architecture   Two-tiered client/server architectures deliver the presentation logic on the client and the database logic on the server.

Two-way messaging   Two-way messaging, sometimes referred to as enhanced paging, allows short text messages to be transmitted between relatively inexpensive transmission devices such as PDAs (Personal Digital Assistants) and alphanumeric pagers.

Ultra SCSI   An expansion bus specification: 32-bit bus width, 10 MHz clock speed, 40 MBps throughput

UNI   User network interface; in ATM, cell format that carries information between the user and the ATM network

Uniform resource locator   Indexed Web pages which may be located throughout the Internet are accessible through LYCOS via these hot-clickable links known as URLs.

Uninterruptable power supply   *See* UPS

Universal client capability   A client workstation's ability to interoperate transparently with a number of different network operating system servers without the need for additional products or configurations

Universal data access   An umbrella term covering object layering and embedding database services (OLE DB) and active data objects (ADO)

Universal data access system   A universal data access system, such as EDA/SQL, acts as a middleware layer, trapping SQL requests from clients and reformatting them as necessary before transporting them to the appropriate server.

Universal inbox   Universal inbox implies that users can get all of their e-mails, faxes, and voice messages in a single interface. From the universal inbox the users can read, respond, file and delete all of their messages.

UNIX   UNIX as a client workstation operating system is limited primarily to implementations in high-powered scientific or engineering workstations. UNIX itself is actually not just a single operating system, but many, largely incompatible, variations of a single operating system.

UNIX system kernel   Fulfills requests for services from UNIX systems programs by interacting with the hardware layer and returning requested functionality to the systems programs and utilities

UNIX systems programs   UNIX systems programs and utilities deliver requested functionality to users by issuing system calls to the UNIX system kernel.

Unreliable networks   Connectionless networks with globally addressed datagrams that cannot guarantee delivery

UPS   Uninterruptable power supplies for server PCs serve two distinct purposes: They provide sufficient backup power in the event of a power failure to allow for a normal system shutdown and they function as a line conditioner during normal operation by protecting computer equipment from "dirty" power conditions such as surges, brownouts, and static spikes.

Upsizing   Upsizing might be considered as a subset of rightsizing. When applications lack processing power on their existing computing platform, they may be redesigned and redeployed on larger, more powerful platforms.

URL   *See* Uniform resource locator

USB   Universal Serial Bus; able to support daisy-chained USB compliant devices; frequently, two USB interfaces are supplied on a given PC; one would be used to daisy-chain a keyboard and mouse, eliminating the need for a variety of proprietary keyboard and mouse interfaces and connectors; the other USB connector could actually support up to 127 daisy-chained peripheral USB devices through the use of cascaded 7-port USB hubs; USB-compliant devices will register with the host system automatically, thereby making them truly plug-n-play, and will be able to be attached and detached without powering down and rebooting the host system

UseNet Servers   UseNet Servers or NewsGroup servers share text-based news items over the Internet.

User accounts database   In Windows NT, the user accounts database is physically stored on the primary domain controller except in those cases when an individual workstation may have a need to verify specific User IDs for remote access to that workstation.

User demands   The top layer of the wide area network architecture

User mode   As opposed to privileged mode, user mode applications run in a nonprivileged processor mode with a limited set of interfaces available and limited access to system data.

User network interface *See* UNI

Variable bit rate *See* VBR

VBR Variable bit rate; provides a guaranteed minimum threshold amount of constant bandwidth below which the available bandwidth will not drop; however, as bursty traffic requires more bandwidth than this constant minimum, that required bandwidth will be provided

VDSL Very high speed DSL; provides 52 MBps downstream and between 1.6 and 2.3 MBps upstream over distances of up to only 1,000 ft; it is being explored primarily as a means to bring video on demand services to the home

Vendor independent messaging VIM is an API that is supported by Lotus, Borland, IBM, Apple, Oracle, MCI, Novell, and many other messaging vendors. VIM is a cross-platform interface that allows developers to create mail-enabled applications that work on various platforms.

Version control software *See* File synchronization software

Vertical integration Integration of components within a single computer; the interface to the network operating system and the interface with the business application represent vertical integration

Vertical software compatibility Vertical software compatibility is concerned with making sure that all necessary compatible protocols are in place in order for all of the software and hardware within a single client or server to operate harmoniously and transparently.

Very high speed DSL *See* VDSL

VIA Virtual interface architecture; messages need to be passed between the multiple computers that comprise the cluster according to a standard protocol; VIA is among the current message passing protocols for clusters, along with PVM, MPI, and MPI2

Video BIOS The Video BIOS (Basic Input Output System) is contained on a chip on the graphics accelerator card. Its main function is to identify itself and its operating specifications to the computer's operating system during system startup. The Video BIOS provides the interface between the graphics accelerator card (hardware) and the computer system's operating system (software).

Video conferencing Video and audio conferencing systems are becoming more common today thanks to the many advances made both in the hardware and software areas. Industry research is predicting that the number of people using videoconferencing will be around 3.2 million by 2001.

Video memory Video memory is usually either VRAM or DRAM. VRAM is definitely more expensive than DRAM and is faster on high-end applications requiring high resolutions, high color depth, and high refresh rates such as 3-D imaging. The amount of VRAM required on a graphics accelerator is dependent to some extent on the color depth desired.

VIM *See* Vendor independent messaging

Virtual circuits Paths set up in connection-oriented packet-switched networks

Virtual circuit table The details that relate the LCN to a physical circuit consisting of an actual series of specific packet switches within the packet-switched network are stored in a virtual circuit table.

Virtual corporation What coworkers in the same building can accomplish ought to be able to be accomplished by remote users via the business communications services network; the deliverance of this capability is sometimes referred to as a virtual corporation

Virtual device drivers *See* VxDs

Virtual interface architecture *See* VIA

Virtual machine A Java interpreter that allows Java bytecode to run on the system

Virtual machines Windows NT is able to run applications from other platforms such as OS/2 and 16-bit Windows through specially written multiple personality subsystems. These subsystems in which different types of applications are able to execute are sometimes referred to as virtual machines.

Virtual parallel machines *See* VPM

Virtual PC Emulation technology attempts to detect as yet unknown viruses by running programs with a software emulation program known as a virtual PC.

Virtual tributary *See* VT

Virus scanning The primary method for successful virus detection and removal

Visual BASIC One of the most popular event-driven languages for the development of business applications; designed for the Microsoft Windows family of operating environments, Visual BASIC provides a powerful development platform, yet it is easy to program; as the name would suggest, Visual BASIC uses the BASIC language for the development of event handlers

VJ A protocol for compression of IP headers included with most PPP clients

VPM Virtual parallel machines; clustering implies using the CPU power of multiple CPUs located in separate computing platforms to produce a single, more powerful, virtual computer; also known as clusters

VSAM A file management system used on IBM mainframes; VSAM (Virtual Storage Access Method) speeds up address to data in files through the use of an inverted index known as a B+tree

VTs Virtual tributaries; flexibly defined channels within the SONET payload area

VT1.5 SONET virtual tributary equivalent to a mapped T-1

Vulnerabilities The manner or path by which threats are able to attack assets

VxDs Virtual device drivers; more-secure 32-bit operating systems control access to hardware and certain system services via VxDs

WAIS Wide area information services; a type of information server that offers a text-searching service; WAIS indexers generate multiple indexes for all types of files which organizations or individuals wish to offer access to via the Internet

WAIS servers Wide area information services servers; offer these multiple indexes to other Internet-attached WAIS servers; WAIS servers also serve as search engines which have the ability to search for particular words or text strings in the indexes located across multiple Internet-attached information servers of various types

Wavelength division multiplexing *See* WDM

WBEM Web-based enterprise management; a possible standard for distributed application management; WBEM integrates SNMP, HTTP, and desktop management interface into an application management architecture that can use common web browser software as its user interface

WDM Wavelength division multiplexing; a technique in fiber optic transmission in which multiple bits of data can be transmitted simultaneously over a single fiber by being represented by different light wavelengths

Web-based enterprise management *See* WBEM

Web browsers A client-based category of software that is undergoing tremendous development due to the vast interest in the World Wide Web

Web conferencing Web conferencing software supports data, document, audio, and video conferencing over the World Wide Web. Web conferencing is quickly evolving to meet the needs of businesses.

Web server Web servers run specialized web server software which supports HTTP in order to handle the organization of servicing the multiple web client requests for web pages.

Web site Companies wishing to use the World Wide Web as a marketing tool establish a web site on the Internet and publicize the address of that web site.

What-if analysis The value of a simulation system is its ability to predict the performance of various networking scenarios, otherwise known as what-if analysis.

Wide area information services *See* WAIS

Wide SCSI-2 An expansion bus specification: 16-bit bus width, 5 MHz clock speed, 20 MBps throughput

Win32 API This is the full-blown 32-bit API created for Windows NT

Win32c API The *c* stands for *compatible*; this is the API included with Windows 95, and it contains nearly all of the functionality offered by NT's Win32 API while still remaining backward compatible with 16-bit Windows 3.1 applications

Win32s API The *s* stands for *subset*; this API was created for applications which need the processing power of 32-bit applications but must still be able to execute under 16-bit Windows 3.1

Window manager The window manager, part of the GUI operating system, monitors the application for events. When an event occurs, the event manager starts a process to complete the code associated with the event handler for the triggered event.

Windows 95 Windows 95 could be considered an all-in-one client software product as it includes graphical user interface, network operating system, and operating system functionality all in a single package. Among the key operating system related features incorporated within Windows 95 are new graphical user interface, 32-bit API in a preemptive multitasking environment, and plug-n-play capability.

Windows 98 Among the key features introduced in Windows 98 are overall compatibility with Windows 95, offering increased performance and reliability, and inclusion of Microsoft Internet Explorer 4.0 for tighter integration of the web browser and desktop.

Windows CE Windows CE is a 32-bit, multitasking, multithreaded operating system designed to run on hand-held PCs, the smaller palm PCs, and even the newer speech-enabled automobile PCs.

Windows NT RAS Microsoft's remote node server software for Windows NT

Windows NT Workstation A top-to-bottom client software product; Windows NT is a true 32-bit, pre-emptive multitasking operating system; all 32-bit applications execute in protected memory space

Windows terminal Windows terminals act as a graphical terminal for Windows applications running on a remote host. This approach is conceptually very similar to mainframe style processing. Terminals display the output of client applications running on a remote host and serve as input devices to the remote client application.

Wireless WAN services A variety of wireless services are available for use across wider geographic spans; these wireless WAN services vary in many ways including availability, applications, transmission speed, and cost

Wizards Context-sensitive help programs or "walk-you-through-it" help characters are commonly referred to as wizards. In other operating environments wizards are known as experts or agents.

Workflow automation Many companies looked at ways to automate routine business processes by implementing technology capable of workflow automation.

World Wide Web The World Wide Web (WWW) is a collection of servers accessed via the Internet that offer graphical or multimedia (audio, video, image) presentations about a company's products, personnel, or services.

WRAM Windows RAM

Wrapping The process of taking a legacy application and making its functionality and data accessible in a client/server; a new software envelope that hides the actual implementation details from the end user is developed to surround the legacy application; wrapping can be considered the process of developing new user interfaces for existing legacy applications

Write back cache Cache that services the write back stage is logically known as write back cache. Write-back cache allows disk writes to be stored in the cache right away so that processing can continue rather than waiting for the disk to be idle before doing a physical write to the disk. The danger in using write-back caches is that if power is lost before physical writes are done to the disk, then that data is lost.

Write-back stage The results of the executed instruction are written out to a memory location or register, usually in a special area called a data cache in the write-back stage.

Write through cache Cache that services only the fetch stage is known as write through cache

WWW *See* World Wide Web

X Windows X Windows itself is not a GUI and should not be confused with Microsoft Windows. X Windows is a standardized system that defines the underlying communication between X server and X client software modules, which combine to present a multiwindowed graphical user interface on a specially designed X terminal or a client workstation running some type of X terminal emulation.

X.25 Packet-switching standard that defines interface specification for packet switched networks

X.400 This standard was defined by the Consultative Committee for International Telephony & Telegraphy (CCITT); this standard was used mainly by large companies that have geographic locations around the globe; the X.400 standard covers the exchange of electronic messages between computer systems

X.500 As enterprise networks become more heterogeneous, composed of network operating systems from a variety of different vendors, the need will arise for different network operating systems to share one another's directory services information. A directory services specification known as X.500 offers the potential for this directory services interoperability.

X.500 A CCITT standard designed to provide directory information in a global setting; many people feel as though the X.500 standard is too complex to use

X.509 An international standard for public key certificates

XA Extended Architecture for CD-ROM is Microsoft's Level 2 CD-ROM specification that supports simultaneous playback of voice, video, image and text

XDR XDR (External Data Representation) is a presentation layer protocol responsible for formatting data in a consistent manner so that all NFS clients and servers can process it, regardless of the computing platform or operating system on which the NFS suite may be executing.

XML An advanced markup language that may replace HTML as the standard for document formatting on the World Wide Web

XTACACS Extended Terminal Access Control Access System; a remote access management protocol that supports three-tiered remote access management architectures

Index